Frederic William Farrar

The gospel according to St. Luke

With maps, notes and introduction by F.W. Farrar

Frederic William Farrar

The gospel according to St. Luke
With maps, notes and introduction by F.W. Farrar

ISBN/EAN: 9783742858894

Manufactured in Europe, USA, Canada, Australia, Japa

Cover: Foto ©ninafisch / pixelio.de

Manufactured and distributed by brebook publishing software (www.brebook.com)

Frederic William Farrar

The gospel according to St. Luke

The Cambridge Bible for Schools and Colleges.

GENERAL EDITOR:—J. J. S. PEROWNE, D.D.,
BISHOP OF WORCESTER.

THE GOSPEL ACCORDING TO ST LUKE,

WITH MAPS, NOTES AND INTRODUCTION

BY

THE VEN. F. W. FARRAR, D.D.
ARCHDEACON OF WESTMINSTER.

EDITED FOR THE SYNDICS OF THE UNIVERSITY PRESS.

Cambridge:
AT THE UNIVERSITY PRESS.

London: C. J. CLAY AND SONS,
CAMBRIDGE UNIVERSITY PRESS WAREHOUSE,
AVE MARIA LANE.

1891

PREFACE
BY THE GENERAL EDITOR.

THE General Editor of *The Cambridge Bible for Schools* thinks it right to say that he does not hold himself responsible either for the interpretation of particular passages which the Editors of the several Books have adopted, or for any opinion on points of doctrine that they may have expressed. In the New Testament more especially questions arise of the deepest theological import, on which the ablest and most conscientious interpreters have differed and always will differ. His aim has been in all such cases to leave each Contributor to the unfettered exercise of his own judgment, only taking care that mere controversy should as far as possible be avoided. He has contented himself chiefly with a careful revision of the notes, with pointing out omissions, with suggesting occasionally a reconsideration of some question, or a fuller treatment of difficult passages, and the like.

Beyond this he has not attempted to interfere, feeling it better that each Commentary should have its own individual character, and being convinced that freshness and variety of treatment are more than a compensation for any lack of uniformity in the Series.

DEANERY, PETERBOROUGH,
14th Feb. 1880.

CONTENTS.

		PAGES
I.	INTRODUCTION.	
	Chapter I. The Gospels	7—17
	Chapter II. Life of St Luke	18—22
	Chapter III. Authenticity of the Gospel	22—23
	Chapter IV. Characteristics of the Gospel	23—30
	Chapter V. Analysis of the Gospel	30—36
	Chief Uncial MSS. of the Gospels	37—38
	The Herods	39
II.	TEXT AND NOTES	41—367
III.	EXCURSUS I—VII	368—385
IV.	INDEX	386

Map	I.	Environs of Jerusalem	*Frontispiece*
	II.	Palestine	*to face p.* 65
,,	III.	Galilee	,, 101
,,	IV.	Sea of Galilee	,, 112

✱✱✱ The Text adopted in this Edition is that of Dr Scrivener's *Cambridge Paragraph Bible.* A few variations from the ordinary Text, chiefly in the spelling of certain words, and in the use of italics, will be noticed. For the principles adopted by Dr Scrivener as regards the printing of the Text see his Introduction to the *Paragraph Bible,* published by the Cambridge University Press.

> "Luke the beloved, the sick soul's guide."
>
> KEBLE.

Almighty God who calledst Luke the Physician, whose praise is in the Gospel, to be an Evangelist and Physician of the soul: May it please Thee that by the wholesome medicines of the doctrine delivered by him, all the diseases of our souls may be healed; through the merits of Thy Son Jesus Christ our Lord. Amen.

Collect for St Luke's Day.

INTRODUCTION.

CHAPTER I.

THE GOSPELS.

THE word Gospel[1] is the Saxon translation of the Greek *Euangelion*. In early Greek (e.g. in Homer) this word meant *the reward* given to one who brought good tidings. In Attic Greek it also meant a *sacrifice* for good tidings but was always used in the plural *euangelia*. In later Greek, as in Plutarch and Lucian, *euangelion* meant the good news actually delivered. Among all Greek-speaking Christians the word was naturally adopted to describe the best and gladdest tidings ever delivered to the human race, the good news of the Kingdom of God. In the address of the Angel to the shepherds we find the words "*I bring you good tidings* of great joy," where the verb used is *euangelizomai*. From this Greek word are derived the French *Évangile*, the Italian *Evangelio*, the Portuguese *Evangelho*, &c. Naturally the word which signified "good news" soon came to be used as the title of the books which contained the history of that good news.

The existence of four separate, and mainly if not absolutely, independent Gospels, is a great blessing to the Church of Christ. It furnishes us with such a weight of contemporaneous testimony as is wanting to the vast majority of events in Ancient History. A fourfold cord is not easily broken.

---

[1] By euphony for *godspel*, as gossip for godsib, and gossamer for god-summer. The word seems to have acquired its currency from Wyclif's translation. On the title "New Testament" see note on xxii. 10.

Of these four Gospels the first three are often called the Synoptic Gospels. The Greek word *Synopsis* has the same meaning as the Latin *Conspectus*, and the first three Evangelists are called "Synoptists" because their Gospels can be arranged and harmonised, section by section, in a tabular form, since they are mainly based on a common outline. The term appears to be quite modern, but has been rapidly brought into general use, probably by Griesbach. It is intended to indicate the difference of plan which marks these Gospels as compared with that of St John[1].

In the Synoptic Gospels we find much that is common to all, and something which is peculiar to each. It has been ascertained by Stroud that "if the total contents of the several Gospels be represented by 100, the following table is obtained[2]:

St Mark	has	7	*peculiarities*,	and	93	*coincidences.*	
St Matthew	,,	42	,,	,,	58	,,	
St Luke	,,	59	,,	,,	41	,,	
St John	,,	92	,,	,,	8	,,	"

Reuss has further calculated that the total number of verses *common* to all the Synoptists is about 350; that St Matthew has 350 verses peculiar to himself, St Mark 68, and St Luke 541. The coincidences are usually in the record of sayings: the peculiarities in the narrative portion. In St Matthew, the narrative occupies about one fourth; in St Mark one half; and in St Luke one third.

Another important fact is that when St Matthew and St Luke verbally agree, St Mark always agrees with them; that the resemblances between St Luke and St Mark are much closer than those between St Luke and St Matthew[3]; that where St Mark has additional touches St Luke usually has them also,

---

[1] See Holtzmann in Schenkel, *Bibel-Lexicon*, s. v. Evangelien; and Ebrard in Herzog, s. v. Harmonie. I am not aware of any earlier use of the *word* "Synopsis," as applied to a tabular view of the first three Gospels, than Georgii Sigelii *Synopsis historiae Jes. Christi quemadmodum Matthaeus, Marcus, Lucas descripsere in forma tabulae proposita*. Noribergae. 1585. Folio.

[2] Westcott, *Introd. to the Study of the Gospels*, p. 179.

[3] Bp. Marsh, *On Michaelis*, V. 317.

but not when these additions are found only in St Matthew; and that where St Mark is silent, St Luke often differs from St Matthew[1].

The dates at which the four Gospels were published cannot be ascertained with certainty; but there are some reasons to believe that St Matthew's was written first, possibly in Aramaic, and about A.D. 64; that St Mark's and St Luke's were published within a few years of this date[2], and certainly before the destruction of Jerusalem in A.D. 70; and that St John's was written in old age at Ephesus before the year A.D. 85. It is probable that most, if not all, of St Paul's Epistles had been written before the earliest Gospel was published in its present form. To what extent the Synoptists were influenced by written records of previous oral teaching is a difficult and complicated question about which there have been multitudes of theories, as also respecting the question whether any of the three used the Gospel of either of the others. That previous attempts to narrate the Life of Christ were in existence when St Luke wrote we know from his own testimony; but it may be regarded as certain that among these "attempts" he did *not* class the Gospels of St Matthew and St Mark. The inference that he was either unaware of the existence of those Gospels, or made no direct use of them, suggests itself with the utmost force when we place side by side any of the events which they narrate in common, and mark the minute and inexplicable differences which incessantly occur even amid general similarity.

The language employed by the Evangelists is that dialect

---

[1] Reuss. To give the passages and details would occupy too much space. They are adduced in several critical editions, and are sometimes noticed in the notes. St Luke and St Matthew *both* give but few passages omitted by St Mark (e.g. the Lost Sheep, Matt. xviii. 12—14; Lk. xv. 4—7, and compare Matt. viii. 5 sq., xxii. 1 sq. with Lk. vii. 1 sq., xiv. 15 sq.).

[2] Some writers think that the Gospel of St Luke was written as early as A.D. 60, during St Paul's imprisonment at Caesarea. The subject is not one on which positive certainty can be attained; but the absence of any direct reference to this Gospel in the Epistles of the Captivity and the Pastoral Epistles, and the comparatively late date at which it is authoritatively recognised by name as canonical, make it more probable that it was not published till after the death of St Paul.

of Greek which was in their day generally current—the Macedonian or Hellenistic Greek. It was a stage of the Greek language less perfect than that of the classical period, but admirably plastic and forcible.

ST MATTHEW and ST JOHN were Apostles and eyewitnesses of the ministry of our Lord from the baptism of John until the Ascension. The other two Evangelists were as St Jerome says not Apostles but "Apostolic men." ST MARK may have been a partial eyewitness of some of the later scenes of the life of Christ, and it is the unanimous tradition of the Early Church that his Gospel reflects for us the direct testimony of St Peter. ST LUKE expressly implies that he was not an eyewitness, but he made diligent use of all the records which he found in existence, and he derived his testimony from the most authentic sources. It may be regarded as certain that he sets before us that conception of the Life and Work of Christ which was the basis of the teaching of St Paul[1]. Thus we have the Gospel "according to" the view and teaching of four great Apostles, St Matthew, St Peter, St Paul, and St John.

The differences between the SYNOPTISTS and ST JOHN have been noticed from the earliest ages of the Church. They are mainly these. The Synoptists dwell almost exclusively on Christ's Ministry in Galilee; St John on His Ministry in Judaea. The Synoptists dwell chiefly on the Miracles, Parables, and

---

[1] Irenaeus, *adv. Haer.* III. 1 and III. 14. Tertullian, *adv. Marc.* IV. 2, 5. Origen apud Euseb. *H. E.* VI. 25, and *id.* III. 4. Jerome, *De Virr. Illustr.* 7. A long list of words and phrases are common to St Luke and St Paul, which may be seen in Davidson's *Introd. to the New Test.* II. 12—19. The student may compare the following:

St Luke, iv. 22.	St Paul, Col. iv. 6.
iv. 32.	1 Cor. ii. 4.
vi. 36.	2 Cor. i. 3.
vi. 39.	Rom. ii. 19.
ix. 56.	2 Cor. x. 8.
x. 8.	1 Cor. x. 27.
xi. 41.	Tit. i. 15.
xviii. 1.	2 Thess. i. 11.
xxi. 36.	Eph. vi. 18.
xxii. 19, 20.	1 Cor. xi. 23—29.
xxiv. 46.	Acts xvii. 3.
xxiv. 34.	1 Cor. xv. 5.

external incidents of His work; in St John the prominent feature is the high discourse and inmost spiritual meaning of His life. The Synoptists portrayed Him to the world; St John more specially for the Church. To use a common term they present a more objective, and St John a more subjective view of the Work of Christ. The complete portraiture of the Saviour "comprised the fulness of an outward presence, as well as the depth of a secret life. In this respect the records correspond to the subjects. The first record [that of the Synoptists] is manifold; the second is one: the first is based on the experience of a society, the second on the intuition of a loved disciple." "The Synoptic Gospels contain the Gospel of the infant Church; that of St John the Gospel of its maturity. The first combine to give the wide experience of the many, the last embraces the deep mysteries treasured up by the one." "The threefold portrait of Charles I. which Vandyke prepared for the sculptor is an emblem of the work of the first three Evangelists: the complete outward shape is fashioned, and then at last another kindles the figure with a spiritual life[1]." But the object of each and all of the Gospels is that expressed by St John "that ye might believe that Jesus is the Christ the Son of God, and that believing ye might have life through His name[2]."

Elaborate and repeated attempts have been made to settle the interrelation of the Synoptists with each other. All such attempts have hitherto failed. Each Gospel in turn has been assumed to be the earliest of the three; and the supposition that the other two worked on the existing narrative of a third has required for its support as many subordinate hypotheses of fresh recension, translation, &c., as the Ptolemaic system of Astronomy required epicycles to account for its theory of the motions of the heavenly bodies. The general conclusion to which all these enquiries seem to point is (1) That there existed in the Early Church a cycle of authoritative oral teaching, which being committed to memory[3] tended to assume a fixed

---

[1] Westcott, *Introd.* pp. 197, 234, 231. [2] John xx. 31.
[3] The Mishna was similarly transmitted *by memory* for at least two centuries, and the Jewish scribes of this age were on that account

peculiarity of diction; (2) That this authoritative tradition would gradually be committed to writing by some of the disciples; (3) That these written memorials would naturally be utilized by those who "attempted" to set forth a continuous sketch of the ministry of Christ; and (4) that the most authentic and valuable of them would be to a considerable extent incorporated into the narratives of the Evangelists themselves. If some such theory as this be not adequate to account (α) for resemblances which extend even to the use of peculiar verbal forms (ἀφέωνται, Lk. v. 20), diminutives (ὠτίον, Matt. xxvi. 51), and the use of a double augment (Matt. xii. 13);—and (β) for differences which extend to the transposition of whole sections, and the omission of entire discourses,—at least no more reasonable theory has yet been proposed[1].

Early Christian writers compared the four Gospels to that river, which, flowing out of Eden to water the garden of God, was parted into four heads compassing lands like that of Havilah of which "the gold is good" and where is "bdellium and the onyx stone."

> "Paradisi hic fluenta
> Nova fluunt sacramenta
>   Quae descendunt coelitus:
> His quadrigis deportatur
> Mundo Deus, sublimatur
>   Istis arca vectibus."
>
> ADAM DE S. VICTORE.

A still more common symbol of the four Evangelists was derived from "the Chariot" as the chapter was called which describes the vision of Ezekiel by the river Chebar[2]. Each one of

---

called *Tanaim* or "repeaters" (from *tanah* the Chaldee form of the Hebrew *shanah*). They were succeeded about A.D. 220, by the *Amoraim*, or Recorders.

[1] The force of these particular resemblances (which are noted by Archbishop Thomson in the *Speaker's Commentary*, I. p. ix), is a little weakened by the fact that in Mk. ii. 9; Matt. ix. 2, ℵ, B, &c., read ἀφίενται. It may be doubted whether the other forms were not those generally current in the Hellenistic Greek of Palestine.

[2] Ezek. i. 5—26.

the living creatures combined in "the fourfold-visaged four" was taken as the emblem of one of the Evangelists. The applications differed, but the one which has been almost universally adopted, and of which there are traces in Christian Art as far back as the fifth century, assigns the Man or Angel to St Matthew, the Lion to St Mark, the Ox to St Luke, and the Eagle to St John[1]. The reasons offered for the adoption of these emblems also differed; but it was usually said that the Man is assigned to St Matthew because he brings out Christ's human and Messianic character; the Lion to St Mark because he sets forth the awfulness (x. 24, 32), energy, power and royal dignity (i. 22, 27, ii. 10, v. 30, vi. 2, 5, &c.) of Christ; the Ox, the sacrificial victim, to St Luke, because he illustrates the Priestly office of Christ; and the Eagle to St John, because, as St Augustine says, "he soars to heaven as an eagle above the clouds of human infirmity, and reveals to us the mysteries of Christ's Godhead, and of the Trinity in Unity, and the felicities of Life Eternal; and gazes on the light of Immutable Truth with a keen and steady ken[2]." Thus, to quote the eloquent language of Bishop Wordsworth, "The Christian Church, looking at the origin of the Four Gospels, and the attributes which God has in rich measure been pleased to bestow upon them by His Holy Spirit, found a Prophetic picture of them in the Four living Cherubim, named from heavenly knowledge, seen by the Prophet Ezekiel at the river of Chebar. Like them the Gospels are Four in number; like them they are the Chariot of God Who sitteth between the Cherubim; like them, they bear Him on a winged throne into all lands; like them they move wherever the Spirit guides them: like them they are marvellously joined together, intertwined with coincidences and differences; wing interwoven with wing, and wheel interwoven with wheel: like them they are full of eyes, and sparkle with heavenly light: like them they sweep from heaven to earth, and from earth to heaven, and fly with lightning speed and with the noise of

---

[1] See Mrs Jameson's *Sacred and Legendary Art*, I. 132—172.
[2] Aug. *De Consens. Evang.* I.

many waters. *Their sound is gone out into all lands, and their words to the end of the world*[1]."

But whatever may be the archaeological and artistic interest of these universal symbols, it must be admitted that they are fanciful and arbitrary; and this is rendered more obvious from the varying manner in which they used to be employed and justified. It is much more important to get some clear and unimaginative conception of the distinctive peculiarities of each Evangelist. And at this it is not difficult to arrive.

Combining the data furnished by early and unanimous tradition with the data furnished by the Gospels themselves we see generally that,

i. ST MATTHEW wrote in Judaea, and wrote for Jews, possibly even in Aramaic, as was the general belief of the early Church. If so, however, the Aramaic original is hopelessly lost, and there is at least a possibility that there may have been a confusion between a supposed Hebrew Gospel of St Matthew and the "Gospel of the Hebrews," which may have been chiefly based on it and which was in use among the Nazarenes and Ebionites. However that may be, the object which St Matthew had in view goes far to illustrate the specialities of his Gospel. It is the Gospel of the Hebrew nation; the Gospel of the Past, the Gospel of *Jesus as the Messiah*[2]. Thus it opens with the words "The book of the generation of Jesus Christ *the son of David, the son of Abraham:*"—the son of David and therefore the heir of the Jewish kingdom: the son of Abraham and therefore the heir of the Jewish promise. That it is the Gospel which connects Christianity with Judaism and with

---

[1] *Greek Test.*, The Four Gospels, p. xli.

[2] It should be carefully borne in mind that these characteristics are merely *general* and *relative*. It is not meant that the Evangelists represent our Blessed Lord *exclusively*, but only *predominantly*, under the aspects here mentioned. It must not be supposed that any one of the Evangelists wrote with a deliberate subjective bias. They dealt with facts not theories, and in no way modified those facts in the interests of any special view. It is only from the *grouping* of those facts, and from the prominence given to particular incidents or expressions throughout the several Gospels, that we deduce the predominant conceptions of the inspired writers.

the Past appears in the constantly recurrent formula "*that it might be fulfilled.*" So completely is the work of Christ regarded as the accomplishment of Prophecy that in no less than five incidents narrated in the first two chapters, the Evangelist points to the verification of ancient predictions. Another marked peculiarity of the Gospel is its *didactic* character. It records with fulness five great discourses—The sermon on the Mount[1]; the address to the Apostles[2]; the parables on the Kingdom of Heaven[3]; the discourse on Offences and on Forgiveness[4]; and the discourses and parables of Judgment[5]. These discourses,—which all bear on the triple offices of our Lord as Lawgiver, King, and Judge of the New Kingdom,—make the Gospel of St Matthew "as it were the *ultimatum* of Jehovah to His ancient people;—Recognise Jesus as your Messiah, or accept Him as your Judge[6]."

ii. ST MARK wrote in Rome for the Roman world, during the imprisonment and before the death of his teacher and spiritual father, St Peter (1 Pet. v. 13). His Gospel is emphatically the Gospel of the Present; the Gospel of Jesus apart from retrospect or prophecy; of *Jesus as the Lord of the World.* The speech of St Peter to Cornelius has been called "the Gospel of St Mark in brief." St Mark's Gospel consists of "*Apostolic Memoirs*" marked by the graphic vividness which is due to the reminiscences of an eyewitness; it is the Gospel of which it was the one aim to describe our Lord as He lived and moved among men. The notion that St Mark was a mere compiler of St Matthew (*tamquam pedissequus et breviator ejus,* Aug.) has long been exploded. He *abounds* in independent notices which have led many Germans to regard his Gospel, or

---

[1] v. vi. vii.   [2] x.   [3] xiii.   [4] xviii.
[5] xxiii. xxiv. xxv. This predominance of discourses has however no bearing on the term *logia* ('oracles') applied by Papias to the Gospel of St Matthew.
[6] Godet, *Bibl. Studies,* E. Tr. p. 23. But it must be remembered that St Matthew's point of view is so little exclusive that he can admit passages which point to the evanescence of the Law (Matt. ix. 16, xii. 7, 8, &c.) and the spread of the Gospel (xiii. 31 sq., xxvii. 19); and he alone narrates the recognition of Christ by the heathen Magi (ii. 1 sq.).

some form of it, as the original Gospel (*Proto-Marcus, Ur-Marcus*); but this theory is now more or less abandoned.

iii. ST LUKE wrote in Greece for the Hellenic world[1]. In style this Gospel is the purest; in order the most artistic and historical. It forms the first half of a great narrative which traced the advance of Christianity from Jerusalem to Antioch, to Macedonia, to Achaia, to Ephesus, to Rome. Hence it neither leans to the yearnings of the past[2], nor is absorbed in the glories of the present, but is written with special reference to the aspirations of the future. It sets forth Jesus to us neither as the Messiah of the Jews only, nor as the Universal Ruler, but as *the Saviour of sinners*. It is a Gospel not national, but cosmopolitan; not regal, but human. It is the Gospel for the world; it connects Christianity with man. Hence the genealogy of Jesus is traced not only to David and to Abraham, but to Adam and to God[3].

iv. One more great sphere of existence remained—Eternity. Beyond these records of dawning and expanding Christianity, there was needed some record of Christianity in its inmost life; something which should meet the wants of the spirit and of the reason: and St John dropped the great keystone into the soaring arch of Christian revelation, when, inspired by the Holy Ghost, he drew the picture of Christ, neither as Messiah only nor as King only, nor even only as the Saviour of mankind, but as *the Incarnate Word;*—not only as the Son of Man who ascended into heaven, but as the Son of God who came down

---

[1] Hence he omits particulars (e.g. in the Sermon on the Mount) which would have been less intelligible to Greek readers, and substitutes *Epistates* or *Didaskalos* ('Master' or 'Teacher') for Rabbi; 'lawyer' for 'scribe;' 'yea' or 'verily' for Amen; the Greek *phoros* for the Latin *census;* the *Lake* for the Sea of Galilee, &c.

[2] Thus St Luke has only 24 Old Test. quotations as against 65 of St Matthew, and (except iv. 18, 19) none which are peculiar to himself, except in the first two (i. 17—25, ii. 23, 24) and the 22nd and 23rd chapters (xxii. 37, xxiii. 31, 46).

[3] Yet St Luke never excludes passages which speak of the spiritual perpetuity of the Law (xvi. 17) and obedience to it (ii. 22 sq., v. 14, &c.). See too i. 32, ii. 49, xix. 46, xxii. 30. This is of course due to the fact that the Evangelists were primarily faithful recorders, and were in no way actuated by party bias.

from heaven; not only as the Divine Man but as the Incarnate God. The circle of Gospel revelation was, as it were, finally rounded into a perfect symbol of eternity when St John was inspired to write that "In the beginning was the Word, and the Word was with God, and the Word was God....And the Word was made flesh, and dwelt among us, and we beheld His glory, the glory as of the only begotten of the Father, full of grace and truth."

To sum up these large generalizations in a form which has been recognised by all thoughtful students as giving us a true though not an exclusive or exhaustive aspect of the differences of the Four Gospels, we may say that

ST MATTHEW'S is the Gospel for the Jews; the Gospel of the Past; the Gospel which sees in Christianity a *fulfilment* of Judaism; the Gospel of Discourses; the Didactic Gospel; the Gospel which represents Christ as the Messiah of the Jew.

ST MARK'S is the Gospel for the Romans; the Gospel of the Present; the Gospel of incident; the anecdotical Gospel; the Gospel which represents Christ as the Son of God and Lord of the world.

ST LUKE'S is the Gospel for the Greeks; the Gospel of the Future; the Gospel of Progressive Christianity, of the Universality and Gratuitousness of the Gospel; the Historic Gospel; the Gospel of Jesus as the Good Physician and the Saviour of Mankind.

ST JOHN'S is pre-eminently the Gospel for the Church; the Gospel of Eternity; the Spiritual Gospel; the Gospel of Christ as the Eternal Son, and the Incarnate Word.

If we were to choose special mottoes as expressive of main characteristics of the Gospels, they might be as follows:—

St Matthew: "*I am not come to destroy but to fulfil,*" v. 17.

St Mark: "*Jesus came.... preaching the Gospel of the Kingdom of God,*" i. 14.

St Luke: "*Who went about doing good, and healing all that were oppressed of the devil,*" Acts x. 38 (comp. Lk. iv. 18).

St John: "*The Word was made flesh,*" i. 14.

CHAPTER II.

LIFE OF ST LUKE.

"Utilis ille labor, per quem vixere tot aegri;
Utilior, per quem tot didicere mori."

"He was a physician: and so too all his words are medicines of the drooping soul." S. JER. *Ep. ad Paulin.*

If we sift what we know about St Luke from mere guesses and tradition, we shall find that our information respecting him is exceedingly scanty.

He does not once mention himself by name in the Gospel or in the Acts of the Apostles, though the absolutely unanimous voice of ancient tradition, coinciding as it does with many conspiring probabilities derived from other sources, can leave no shadow of doubt that he was the author of those books.

There are but three places in Scripture in which his name is mentioned. These are Col. iv. 14, "Luke, the beloved physician, and Demas, greet you;" 2 Tim. iv. 11, "Only Luke is with me;" and Philem. 24, where he is mentioned as one of Paul's "fellow-labourers." From these we see that St Luke was the faithful companion of St Paul, both in his first Roman imprisonment, when he still had friends about him, and in his second Roman imprisonment, when friend after friend deserted him, and was 'ashamed of his chain.' From the context of the first allusion we also learn that he was not "of the circumcision," and indeed tradition has always declared that he was a Gentile, and a 'proselyte of the gate[1].'

The attempt to identify him with "Lucius of Cyrene" in Acts xiii. 1 is a mere error, since his name Lucas is an abbreviation not of Lucius but of Lucanus, as Annas for Ananus, Zenas for Zenodorus, Apollos for Apollonius, &c. The guess that he was one of the Seventy disciples is refuted by his own words, nor is

---

[1] This also appears from Acts i. 19. (See my *Life of St Paul*, 1. 480.)

there any probability that he was one of the Greeks who desired to see Jesus (John xii. 20) or one of the two disciples at Emmaus (Luke xxiv. 13). Eusebius and Jerome say that he was a Syrian of Antioch, and this agrees with the intimate knowledge which he shews about the condition and the teachers of that Church. If in Acts xi. 28 we could accept the isolated reading of the Codex Bezae (a reading known also to St Augustine), which there adds συνεστραμμένων δὲ ἡμῶν, 'but while *we* were assembled together,' it would prove that St Luke had been acquainted with the Apostle shortly after his arrival from Tarsus to assist the work of Barnabas. In that case he may well have been one of the earliest Gentile converts whom St Paul admitted into the full rights of Christian brotherhood, and with whom St Peter was afterwards, for one weak moment, ashamed to eat. We cannot however trace his connexion with St Paul with any certainty till the sudden appearance of the first personal pronoun in the plural in Acts xvi. 10, from which we infer that he joined the Apostle at Troas, and accompanied him to Macedonia, becoming thereby one of the earliest Evangelists in Europe. It is no unreasonable conjecture that his companionship was the more necessary because St Paul had been recently suffering from an acute visitation of the malady which he calls "the stake, or cross, in the flesh." Since the "*we*" is replaced by "*they*" after the departure of Paul and Silas from Philippi (Acts xvii. 1), we infer that St Luke was left at that town in charge of the infant Macedonian Church. A physician could find means of livelihood anywhere, and he seems to have stayed at Philippi for some seven years, for we find him in that Roman colony when the Apostle spent an Easter there on his last visit to Jerusalem (Acts xx. 5). There is however every reason to believe that during this period he was not idle, for if he were "the brother, whose praise is in the Gospel" (i.e. in preaching the good tidings) "throughout all the churches" (2 Cor. viii. 18), we find him acting with Titus as one of the delegates for the collection and custody of the contributions for the poor saints at Jerusalem. The identification of St Luke with this brother no doubt originated in a mistaken notion that "the Gospel" here means the written Gospel[1]; but it is probable on other grounds, and is supported by the tradition embodied in the superscription, which tells us that the Second Epistle to the Corinthians was conveyed from Philippi by Titus and Luke.

From Philippi St Luke accompanied his friend and teacher to Jerusalem (Acts xxi. 18), and there we again lose all record of his movements. Since, however, he was with St Paul at Caesarea when he was sent as a prisoner to Rome, it is probable that he was the constant companion of his imprisonment in that town. If the great design of writing the Gospel was already in his mind, the long and otherwise unoccupied stay of two years in Caesarea would not only give him ample leisure, but would also furnish him with easy access to those sources of information which he tells us he so diligently used. It would also enable him to glean some particulars of the ministry of Jesus from survivors amid the actual scenes where He had lived. From Caesarea he accompanied St Paul in the disastrous voyage which ended in shipwreck at Malta, and proceeding with him to Rome he remained by his side until his liberation, and probably never left him until the great Apostle received his martyr's crown. To him—to his allegiance, his ability, and his accurate preservation of facts—we are alone indebted for the greater part of what we know of the Apostle of the Gentiles.

We finally lose sight of St Luke at the abrupt close of the Acts of the Apostles. Although we know from the Pastoral Epistles[2] that he must have lived with St Paul for some two years beyond the point which his narrative has there reached, he may not have arranged his book until after Paul was dead, and the course of the narrative may have been suddenly cut short either by accident or even by his own death. Irenaeus (*adv. Haer.* III. 1) expressly tells us that even his Gospel was written after the death of Peter and Paul. The most trustworthy tradition says that he died in Greece; and it was believed that Constantine transferred his remains to the Church of the Apostles in Constantinople from Patrae in Achaia. Gregory of Nazianzus tells us in a vague way that he was martyred, but it is idle to repeat

---

[1] Jer. *De Virr. Ill.* 7.   [2] 2 Tim. iv. 11.

such worthless legends as that he was crucified on an olive-tree at Elaea in the Peloponnesus, &c., which rest on the sole authority of Nicephorus, a writer who died after the middle of the 15th century. The fancy that he was a painter, often as it has been embodied in art, owes its origin to the same source, and seems only to have arisen from the discovery of a rude painting of the Virgin in the Catacombs with an inscription stating that it was "one of seven painted by Luca." It is not impossible that there may have been a confusion between the name of the Evangelist and that of a Greek painter in one of the monasteries of Mount Athos.

But leaving 'the shifting quagmire of baseless traditions' we see from St Luke's own writings, and from authentic notices of him, that he was master of a good Greek style;—an accomplished writer, a close observer, an unassuming historian, a well-instructed physician, and a most faithful friend[1]. If the Theophilus to whom he dedicates both his works was the Theophilus mentioned in the Clementines as a wealthy Antiochene, who gave up his house to the preaching of St Peter, then St Luke may have been his freedman. Physicians frequently held no higher rank than that of slaves, and Lobeck, one of the most erudite of modern Greek scholars, has noticed that contractions in *as* like Lucas from Lucanus, were peculiarly common in the names of slaves. One more conjecture may be mentioned. St Luke's allusions to nautical matters, especially in Acts xxvii., are at once remarkably *accurate* and yet *unprofessional* in tone. Now the ships of the ancients were huge constructions, holding sometimes upwards of 300 people, and in the uncertain length of the voyages of those days, we may assume that the presence of a physician amid such multitudes was a matter of necessity. Mr Smith of Jordanhill, in his admirable monograph on the voyage of St Paul, has hence been led to the inference that St Luke must have sometimes exercised his

---

[1] Dr Plumptre, in the *Expositor* (No. xx. 1876), has collected many traces of St Luke's medical knowledge (cf. Acts iii. 7, ix. 18, x. 9, 10, xii. 23, xx. 31, xxvi. 7, xxviii. 8; Lk. iv. 23, xxii. 44, &c.), and even of its possible influence on the language of St Paul.

art in the crowded merchantmen which were incessantly coasting from point to point of the Mediterranean. However this may be, the naval experience of St Luke as well as his medical knowledge would have rendered him a most valuable companion to the suffering Apostle in his constant voyages.

CHAPTER III.

AUTHENTICITY OF THE GOSPEL.

Supposed allusions to St Luke's Gospel may be adduced from Polycarp († A.D. 167), Papias, and Clement of Rome (A.D. 95); but passing over these as not absolutely decisive, it is certain that the Gospel was known to Justin Martyr († A.D. 168), who, though he does not name the authors of the Gospels, makes distinct reference to them, and has frequent allusions to, and citations from, the Gospel of St Luke. Thus he refers to the Annunciation and the Enrolment in the days of Quirinius; the sending of Jesus bound to Herod, the last words on the cross, &c.; and uses in various instances language only found in this Gospel.

Hegesippus has at least two passages which appear to be verbal quotations from Luke xx. 21, xxiii. 24.

The Gospel is mentioned as the work of St Luke in the Muratorian Fragment on the Canon, of which the date is not later than A.D. 170.

Among heretics it was known to, and used by, the Ophites; by the Gnostics, Basilides and Valentinus; by Heracleon (about A.D. 180), who wrote a comment on it; by the author of the *Pistis Sophia;* and by Marcion (about A.D. 140), who not only knew the Gospel, but adopted it as the basis of his own Gospel with such mutilations as suited his peculiar heresies. This fact is not only asserted by Irenaeus, Tertullian, Epiphanius, &c., but may now be regarded as conclusively proved by Volkmar, and accepted by modern criticism. Marcion omitted chapters i. ii. and joined iii. 1 with iv. 31.

It is alluded to in the Clementine Homilies (about A.D. 175) and Recognitions; and in the Epistle of the Churches of Vienne and Lyons, A.D. 177.

Celsus refers to the genealogy of Christ as traced upwards to Adam.

Theophilus of Antioch (A.D. 170) makes direct allusions to it.

Irenaeus (about A.D. 180) expressly attributes it to St Luke; Tertullian († A.D. 220) and Clemens of Alexandria († about A.D. 216) also quoted it as St Luke's. Origen († A.D. 254) speaks of the 'Four Gospels admitted by all the Churches under heaven;' and Eusebius ranks it among the *homologoumena*, i.e. those works of whose genuineness and authenticity there was no doubt in the Church.

It is found in the Peshito Syriac (3rd or 4th century), and the Vetus Itala.

CHAPTER IV.

CHARACTERISTICS OF THE GOSPEL.

"God sending His own Son in the likeness of sinful flesh."
Rom. viii. 3.

"The Son of Man is come to seek and to save that which was lost."
Luke xix. 10.

"Whose joy is, to the wandering sheep
To tell of the great shepherd's love;
To learn of mourners while they weep
The music that makes mirth above;
Who makes the Gospel all his theme,
The Gospel all his pride and praise."
KEBLE, *St Luke's Day.*

This rich and precious Gospel is marked, as are the others, by special characteristics.

Thus:

(i) St Luke must be ranked as the *first Christian hymnologist*. It is to his inspired care that we owe the preservation of three sacred hymns, besides the Ave Maria (i. 28—33) and the Gloria in Excelsis (ii. 14), which have been used for ages in the worship of the Church:—the BENEDICTUS, or Song of Zacharias (i. 68—79), used in our Morning Service; the MAGNIFICAT, or Song of the Blessed Virgin (i. 46—55); and the NUNC DIMITTIS, or Song of Symeon (ii. 29—32), used in our Evening Service[1]. In these Canticles the New Aeon is represented not merely as the fulfilment of the Old, but also as a kingdom of the Spirit; as a spring of life and joy opened to the world; as a mystery, prophesied of indeed because it is eternal, but now in the appointed time revealed to men[2].

(ii) In this Gospel *thanksgiving* is also prominent. "The Gospel of the Saviour begins with hymns, and ends with praises; and as the thanksgivings of the meek are recorded in the first chapter, so in the last we listen to the gratitude of the faithful[3]." Mention is made no less than seven times of 'glorifying God' by the utterance of gratitude and praise (ii. 20, v. 25, vii. 16, xiii. 13, xvii. 15, xviii. 43, xxiii. 47).

(iii) It also gives special prominence to *Prayer*. It not only records (as Matt. vi.) the Lord's Prayer, but alone preserves to us the fact that our Lord prayed on six distinct and memorable occasions. (1) At His baptism. (2) After cleansing the leper. (3) Before calling the Twelve Apostles. (4) At His Transfiguration. (5) On the Cross for His murderers, and (6) with His last breath[4]. St Luke too, like St Paul, insists on the duty of unceasing Prayer as taught by Christ (xviii. 1, xi. 8, xxi. 36, Rom. xii. 12, &c.); and emphasizes this instruction by alone recording the two Parables which encourage us to a persistent energy, a holy importunity, a storming of the kingdom of Heaven by violence in our prayers—the parables of the Friend at Midnight (xi. 5—13) and of the Unjust Judge (xviii. 1—8).

---

[1] "Thou hast an ear for angel songs,
A breath the Gospel trump to fill,
And taught by thee the Church prolongs
Her hymns of high thanksgiving still."—KEBLE.

[2] See Maurice, *Unity of the New Testament*, p. 236.

[3] Westcott, *Introd. to Gospels*, p. 354. [4] See p. 92.

(iv) But the Gospel is marked mainly by its presentation of *the Good Tidings in their universality and gratuitousness.* It is pre-eminently the Gospel of pardon and of pity. "By grace ye are saved through faith[1]," and "the second man is the Lord from heaven" (1 Cor. xv. 47)[2], might stand as the motto of St Luke as of St Paul. Thus the word 'grace' (*charis*, eight times), 'saviour' and 'salvation' (only once each in St John), and 'tell glad tidings of' (ten times), occur in it far more frequently than in the other Gospels; and these are applied neither to Jews mainly, nor to Gentiles mainly, but *universally*[3]. It is the Gospel of "a Saviour" and of "good will *towards men;*" the Gospel of Jesus, not only as the heir of David's throne, and of Abraham's promise, but as the Federal Head and Representative of Humanity—"the son of Adam, which was the Son of God." And what a picture does this great *ideal* painter set forth to us of Christ! He comes with angel carols; He departs with priestly benediction. We catch our first glimpse of Him in the manger-cradle at Bethlehem, our last as from the slopes of Olivet He vanishes "into the cloud" with pierced hands upraised to bless! The Jewish religion of that day had degenerated into a religion of hatreds. The then 'religious world,' clothing its own egotism under the guise of zeal for God, had for the most part lost itself in a frenzy of detestations. The typical Pharisee hated the Gentiles; hated the Samaritans; hated the tax-gatherers. He despised poverty and despised womanhood. In St Luke, towards every age, towards either sex, towards all nations, towards all professions, towards men of every opinion and every shade of character, our Blessed Lord appears as CHRISTUS CONSOLATOR; the good Physician of bodies and of souls; the Gospeller of the poor; the Brother

---

[1] xv. 11, xvii. 10, xviii. 11, &c.

[2] Κύριος, 'Lord,' as a substitute for 'Jesus,' occurs 14 times in St Luke, and elsewhere only in Mk. xvi. 19, 20 of the Synoptists. The combination "the Lord Jesus" (if genuine) occurs only in Lk. xxiv. 3, though common in the Epistles. See note on that verse.

[3] Sections of St Luke which are in peculiar accordance with those views which marked the Gospel of St Paul (Rom. ii. 16) are iv. 16—30, vii. 36—50, xviii. 14, xix. 1—10, xxiii. 39—43. See Van Oosterzee in Lange's *Commentary,* Introd. p. 3, and above, p. 10.

who loves all His brethren in the great family of man; the unwearied healer and ennobler of sick and suffering humanity; the Desire of all nations; the Saviour of the world, who "went about doing good" (Acts x. 38). In accordance with this conception,

(v) St Luke reveals especially the sacredness of *infancy*. He alone tells us of the birth and infancy of the Baptist; the Annunciation; the meeting of Mary and Elizabeth; the songs of the herald Angels; the Circumcision; the Presentation in the Temple; the growth in universal favour and sweet submission. And he alone preserves the one anecdote of the Confirmation of Jesus at twelve years old which is the solitary flower gathered from the silence of thirty years. Hence this Gospel is preeminently *anti-docetic*[1]. St Luke alludes to the human existence of our Lord before birth (i. 42); as a babe (ii. 16); as a little child (ii. 27); as a boy (ii. 40); and as a man (iii. 22).

(vi) He dwells especially on Christ's ministry *to the world;* that He was to be a Light to lighten the Gentiles, as well as the glory of His people Israel. He alone adds to the quotation from Isaiah respecting the mission of the Baptist the words "And ALL FLESH shall see the salvation of God." He alone introduces the parallels of Elijah sent to the heathen Sarepta, and Elisha healing the heathen Naaman; as well as full details of that mission of the Seventy who by their number typified a mission to the supposed number of the nations of the world. St Luke's Gospel might stand as a comment on the words of St Paul at Athens, that God "hath made of one blood all nations of men...that they should seek the Lord, if haply they might feel after Him, and find Him, though He be not far from every one of us" (Acts xvii. 27).

(vii) St Luke's is specially the Gospel of *Womanhood*, and he prominently records the graciousness and tenderness of Christ towards many women. He tells us how Jesus raised the dead boy at Nain, being touched with compassion because "he was

---

[1] See Van Oosterzee, *Introd.* p. 4. The Docetae were an ancient heretical sect who denied the *true* humanity of Christ.

the only son of his mother, and she was a widow." He alone tells us the remarkable fact that Jesus in his earlier mission journeys was accompanied not by warriors like David, not by elders like Moses, not by nobles and kings like the Herods, but by a most humble band of ministering women (viii. 1—3). His narrative in the first two chapters must have been derived from the Virgin Mary, and has been thought to shew in every line the pure and tender colouring of a woman's thoughts. He alone mentions the widow Anna (ii. 36), and tells us about eager Martha cumbered with serving, and Mary choosing the better part (x. 38—42); he alone how our Lord once addressed to a poor, crushed, trembling, humiliated woman the tender name of "daughter" (viii. 48), and how He spoke of another as a daughter of Abraham (xiii. 16); he alone how He at once consoled and warned the "daughters of Jerusalem" who followed Him weeping to Calvary (xxiii. 28). The Scribes and Pharisees gathered up their robes in the streets and synagogues lest they should touch a woman, and held it a crime to look on an unveiled woman in public; our Lord suffered a woman to minister to Him out of whom He had cast seven devils

(viii) He seems to delight in all the records which told of the mercy of the Saviour towards *the poor, the humble, the despised* (ii. 24, vi. 20—25, 30, viii. 2, 3, xii. 16—21, 33, xvi. 13, 19—25, xiv. 12—15, &c.). Hence his Gospel has even been called (though very erroneously) the Gospel of the Ebionites. He narrates the Angel Visit to the humble maiden of Nazareth; the Angel Vision to the humble shepherds; the recognition of Jesus in the Temple by the unknown worshipper, and the aged widow. He records the beatitudes to the poor and the hungry, the parables of Dives and Lazarus and of the Rich Fool; the invitation of "the poor, the maimed, the halt, the blind" to the Great Supper; the exaltation of the humble who choose the lowest seats; the counsel to the disciples to "sell what they have," and to the Pharisees to "give alms." He does not denounce riches, but only the wealth that is not "rich towards God;" nor does he pronounce a beatitude upon poverty in the abstract, but only on the poverty which is patient and submissive. He had learnt from his Lord to 'measure wisdom by simplicity, strength by suffering, dignity by lowliness.'

(ix) Further, it is specially the Gospel of *the outcast*,—of the Samaritan (ix. 52—56, xvii. 11—19), the Publican, the harlot, and the Prodigal. Jesus came to seek and to save that which was lost (xix. 10). See instances in Zacchæus (xix. 1—10); the Prodigal Son; Mary of Magdala (vii. 36—50); the woman with the issue of blood (viii. 43—48); the dying robber (xxiii. 39—43). This peculiarity is doubtless due to that intense spirit of sympathy which led St Luke alone of the Evangelists to record that the boy of Nain was the *only* son of his mother (vii. 12); and the 'little maid' of Jairus his only daughter (viii. 42); and the lunatic boy his father's only son (ix. 38).

(x) Lastly, it is the Gospel of *tolerance*. There was a deadly blood-feud between the Jews and the Samaritans, and St Luke is careful to record how Jesus praised the one grateful Samaritan leper, and chose the good Samaritan rather than the indifferent Priest and icy-hearted Levite as the type of love to our neighbour. He also records two special and pointed rebukes of the Saviour against the spirit of intolerance:—one when the Sons of Thunder wanted to call down fire from heaven on the churlish Samaritan village—*Ye know not what manner of spirit ye are of. For the Son of Man is not come to destroy men's lives, but to save them:* the other when he rebuked the narrowness which said "We forbad him, because he followeth not us," with the words *Forbid him not; for he that is not against us is for us*[1].

We may notice lastly that St Luke's Gospel is characterised by
(xi)   Its careful chronological order (i. 3);
(xii) Its very important preface; and
(xiii) Its command of the Greek language[2].

---

[1] Lk. ix. 49—56.

[2] "Lucam tradunt veteres...magis Graecas literas scisse quam Hebraeas. Unde et sermo ejus...comptior est, et saecularem redolet eloquentiam." Jer. *ad Damas. Ep.* 20. Where the style is less pure, and abounds in Hebraisms, we find internal evidence that St Luke is closely following some Aramaic document in which the oral tradition had been reduced to writing.

Although there is an Hebraic tinge in the hymns and speeches which St Luke merely records, his own style abounds in isolated phrases and words chiefly classical, and his style is more flowing than that of St Matthew and St Mark. His peculiar skill as a writer lies rather in 'psychologic comments[1],' and the reproduction of conversations with their incidents, than in such graphic and vivid touches as those of St Mark. He is also a great master of light and shade, i.e. he shews remarkable skill in the presentation of profoundly instructive contrasts—e.g. Zacharias and Mary; Simon and the Sinful Woman; Martha and Mary; the Pharisee and the Publican; the Good Samaritan, Priest, and Levite; Dives and Lazarus; beatitudes and woes; tears and Hosannas; and the penitent and impenitent robber.

It is the presence of these characteristics that has earned for this Gospel the praise of being "the most beautiful book that has ever been written[2]."

The Miracles peculiar to St Luke are

1. The miraculous draught of fishes. v. 4—11.
2. The raising of the widow's son at Nain. vii. 11—18.
3. The woman with the spirit of infirmity. xiii. 11—17.
4. The man with the dropsy. xiv. 1—6.
5. The ten lepers. xvii. 11—19.
6. The healing of Malchus. xxii. 50, 51.

The Parables peculiar to St Luke are

1. The two debtors. vii. 41—43.
2. The good Samaritan. x. 25—37.
3. The importunate friend. xi. 5—8.
4. The rich fool. xii. 16—21.
5. The barren fig-tree. xiii. 6—9.

---

[1] iii. 15, vi. 11, vii. 29, 30, 39, xvi. 14, &c. Bp Ellicott, *Hist. Lect.* p. 28.

[2] This praise is the more striking because of the source from which it comes. The writer adds that it shews "un admirable sentiment populaire, une fine et touchante poésie, le son clair et pur d'une âme tout argentine." "C'est surtout dans les récits de l'Enfance et de la Passion que l'on trouve un art divin.... Le parti qu'il a tiré de Marthe et de Marie sa sœur est chose merveilleuse; aucune plume n'a laissé tomber dix lignes plus charmantes. L'épisode des disciples d'Emmaus est un des récits les plus fins, les plus nuancés qu'il y ait dans aucune langue."

6. The lost piece of silver. xv. 8—10.
7. The prodigal son. xv. 11—32.
8. The unjust steward. xvi. 1—13.
9. Dives and Lazarus. xvi. 19—31.
10. The unjust judge. xviii. 1—8.
11. The Pharisee and the publican. xviii. 10—14.

The two first chapters and the great section, ix. 51—xviii. 14, are mainly peculiar to St Luke.

And in addition to those already noted above, other remarkable incidents or utterances peculiar to him are John the Baptist's answers to the people (iii. 10—14); the weeping over Jerusalem (xix. 41—44); the conversation with Moses and Elias (ix. 28—36); the bloody sweat (xxii. 44); the sending of Jesus to Herod (xxiii. 7—12); the address to the Daughters of Jerusalem (27—31); the prayer, "Father, forgive them" (xxiii. 34); the penitent robber (40—43); the disciples at Emmaus (xxiv. 13—31); particulars of the Ascension (xxiv. 50—53). Additional touches which are sometimes of great importance may be found in iii. 22 ("in a bodily shape"), iv. 13 ("for a season"), iv. 1—6, v. 17, 29, 39, vi. 11, vii. 21, &c.

CHAPTER V.

ANALYSIS OF THE GOSPEL.

Many writers have endeavoured to arrange the contents of this and the other Gospels in schemes illustrative of the dogmatic connexions in accordance with which the various sections are supposed to be woven together and subordinated to each other. Without here giving any opinion about the other Gospels, I must state my conviction that, as far as St Luke is concerned, such hypothetic arrangements have not been successful. No two writers have agreed in their special schemes, and the fact that each writer who has attempted such an analysis has seized on very different points of connexion, shews that all such attempts have been more or less arbitrary, however ingenious. It seems to me that if the Gospels had been arranged on these purely subjective methods the clue to such arrangement would have been more obvious, and also that we should, in that case, lose something of that transparent and childlike simplicity of motive which adds such immense weight to the testimony of the Evangelists as the narrators of simple facts. Nor is it probable that the existence of this subjective symmetry of composition would have escaped the notice of so many centuries of Christian students and Fathers. When St Luke tells Theophilus that he had decided to set forth *in order* the accepted facts of the Christian faith, I believe that the order he had in view was *mainly chronological*, and that the actual sequence of events, so far as it was recoverable from the narratives (διηγήσεις) or the oral sources which he consulted, was his chief guide in the arrangement of his Gospel[1]. Various lessons may be observed or imagined in the order in which one event is placed after another, but these lessons lie deep in the chronological facts themselves, not in the method of the writer. The sort of analysis attempted by modern writers has hitherto only furnished each subsequent analyst with an opportunity for commenting on the supposed failures of his predecessors. For those however who disagree with these views, able and thoughtful endeavours to set forth the narrative in accordance with such a predetermined plan may be found in Van Oosterzee's *Introduction*, § 5, in Westcott's *Introduction to the Gospels*, pp. 364—366, and McClellan's *New Testament*, 427—438.

The Gospel falls quite simply and naturally into the following sections:—

I. INTRODUCTION. i. 1—4.

II. THE PREPARATION FOR THE NATIVITY. i. 5—80.
    i. Announcement of the Forerunner. i. 5—25.
    ii. Announcement of the Saviour. 26—38.
    iii. Hymns of thanksgiving of Mary and Elizabeth. 39—56.

---

[1] The subordinate notes of time in the great section, ix. 51—xviii. 14, are vague.

  iv. Birth and Circumcision of the Forerunner. 57—66.
    The Benedictus. 67—79.
  v. Growth of the Forerunner. 80.

 III. NATIVITY OF THE SAVIOUR. ii. 1—20.
  i. The Birth in the Manger. ii. 1—7.
    Songs and thanksgivings of the Angels and the Shepherds. 8—20.

 IV. THE INFANCY OF THE SAVIOUR. ii. 21—38.
  i. The Circumcision. ii. 21.
  ii. The Presentation in the Temple. 22—24.
    Songs and thanksgivings of Simeon and Anna. 25—38.

 V. THE BOYHOOD OF THE SAVIOUR. ii. 39—52.
  i. His growth. 39, 40.
  ii. His first visit to Jerusalem. 41—48.
  iii. His first recorded words. 49, 50.
  iv. His development from boyhood to manhood. 51, 52.

 VI. THE MANIFESTATION OF THE SAVIOUR (iii. 1—iv. 13), by
  i. The preaching of John the Baptist. iii. 1—14, and
    His prophecy of the coming Messiah. 16—18.
    (Parenthetic anticipation of John's imprisonment. 19, 20.)
  ii. By the descent of the Spirit and the Voice at the Baptism. 21, 22.
    The Son of Adam and the Son of God. 23—38.
  iii. By victory over the Tempter. iv. 1—13.

 VII. LIFE AND EARLY MINISTRY OF THE SAVIOUR. iv. 14—vii. 50.
  i. His teaching in Galilee. iv. 14, 15.
  ii. His first recorded Sermon, and rejection by the Nazarenes. 16—30.
  iii. His Work in Capernaum and the Plain of Gennesareth. iv. 31—vii. 50.
  iv. A great Sabbath at Capernaum. iv. 31—44.
    α. Healing of a Demoniac. 33—37.
    β. Healing of Peter's wife's mother. 38, 39.
    γ. Healing of a multitude of the sick. 40—44.
  v. The miraculous draught of fishes. v. 1—11.

INTRODUCTION. 33

 vi. Work amid the sick, suffering, and sinful. v. 12—32.
  α. Healing of a leper and other works of mercy. 12—17.
  β. Healing the paralytic. 18—26.
  γ. The Call and feast of Matthew. 27—32.

 vii. The Saviour teaching and doing good. v. 33—vii. 50.
  α. The new and the old. v. 33—39.
  β. The Sabbath. vi. 1—12.
  γ. Choosing of the Apostles. 13—16.
  δ. The Sermon on the Mount. 17—49.
  ε. The centurion's servant. vii. 1—10.
  ζ. The widow's son raised from the dead. 11—17.
  η. His witness to John the Baptist. 18—30.
  θ. His complaint against that generation. 31—35.
  ι. The woman that was a sinner. 36—50.

VIII. LATER MINISTRY IN GALILEE AND ITS NEIGHBOURHOOD. viii.
 i. The first Christian sisterhood. viii. 1—3.
 ii. Incidents of two great days. 4—56.
  α. The first Parable. 4—15.
  β. The similitude of the lamp. 16—18.
  γ. Who are His mother and His brethren. 19—21.
  δ. Stilling the storm. 22—25.
  ε. The Gadarene demoniac. 26—40.
  ζ. The daughter of Jairus and the woman with the issue of blood. 41—56.

IX. LATEST PHASES OF THE GALILEAN MINISTRY, AND JOURNEY NORTHWARDS. ix. 1—50.
 i. Mission of the Twelve. ix. 1—6.
 ii. Alarm of Herod. 7—9.
 iii. Feeding the five thousand at Bethsaida Julias. 10—17.
 iv. Culmination of the training of the Apostles. 18—50.
  α. The Confession of St Peter. 18—22.
  β. Warning of the coming end. 23—27.
  γ. The Transfiguration on Mount Hermon. 28—36.
  δ. The Lunatic Boy. 37—42.
  ε. Nearer warnings of the coming end. 43—45.
  ζ. Lesson of Humility. 46—48.
  η. Lesson of Tolerance. 49, 50.

X. INCIDENTS OF THE GREAT FINAL PHASE OF THE SAVIOUR'S MINISTRY AFTER LEAVING GALILEE. ix. 51—xix. 27[1].

    i. Tolerance to the Samaritans. The spirit of Elijah and the spirit of the Saviour. 51—56.
    ii. The sacrifices of true discipleship. 57—62.
    iii. The Mission of the Seventy. x. 1—20.
    iv. The Saviour's joy at its success and blessedness. 21—24.
    v. Love to our neighbour. The Good Samaritan. 25—37.
    vi. The one thing needful. Martha and Mary. 38—42.
    vii. Lessons of Prayer. xi. 1—13.
    viii. Open rupture with the Pharisees, and connected incidents and warnings. xi. 14—xii. 59.
    ix. Teachings, Warnings, Parables, and Miracles, of the Journey in preparation for the coming end. xiii. 1—xviii. 30.

        a. Parables:

            The Great Supper. xiv. 15—24.
            Shorter similitudes:
              The Unfinished Tower. 25—30.
              The Prudent King. 31—33.
              Savourless Salt. 34, 35.
            The Lost Sheep. xv. 1—7.
            The Lost piece of Silver. 8—10.
            The Prodigal Son. 11—32.
            The Unjust Steward. xvi. 1—12.
            Warnings against avarice; Rich Man and Lazarus. 13—31.

        β. Shorter sayings:

            Offences, xvii. 1, 2. Forgiveness, 3, 4. Faith, 5, 6. Service, 7—10. Gratitude (the Ten Lepers), 11—19. Coming of the kingdom of God, 20—37. Prayer (the Importunate Widow), xviii. 1—8. The Pharisee and the Publican, 9—14. Children, 15—17. Sacrifice for Christ's sake. The Great Refusal, 18—30.

---

[1] The whole section is sometimes, but inadequately, called the *Gnomology*, or "collection of moral teaching."

XI. LAST STAGE OF THE JOURNEY FROM JERICHO TO JERUSALEM. xviii. 31—xix. 46.
    i. Prediction of the approaching end. xviii. 31—34.
    ii. The healing of Blind Bartimaeus. xviii. 35—43.
    iii. The Repentant Publican, Zacchaeus. xix. 1—10.
    iv. The Parable of the Pounds. 10—27.
    v. The Triumphal Entry into Jerusalem. 28—40.
    vi. The Saviour weeping over Jerusalem. 41—44.
    vii. The Cleansing of the Temple. 45, 46.

XII. THE LAST DAYS OF THE SAVIOUR'S LIFE. xix. 47—xxi. 38.
    i. The day of Questions. xx.
        α. Question of the Priests and Elders. 1—8. Parable of the Vineyard. 9—18.
        β. Question about the tribute-money. 19—26.
        γ. Question of the Sadducees. 27—39.
        δ. Question of Christ. 39—44. Last denunciation of the Scribes. 45—47.
    ii. Farewell to the Temple, and last warnings. xxi.
        α. The widow's mite. 1—4.
        β. Prophecy against the Temple. 5, 6.
        γ. Signs and warnings of the last times. 7—38.

XIII. LAST HOURS OF THE SAVIOUR ON EARTH. xxii. 1—xxiii. 49.
    i. The plots of enemies. xxii. 1—6.
    ii. The Last Supper. Warnings and farewells. 7—38.
    iii. The Agony in the Garden. 39—46.
    iv. The Betrayal. 47—49.
    v. The Arrest. 50—53.
    vi. Trial before the Priests, and Peter's denials. 54—62. First derision. 63—65.
    vii. Trial before the Sanhedrim. 66—71.
    viii. Trial before Pilate, and first acquittal. xxiii. 1—4.
    ix. Trial before Herod. Second derision, and acquittal. 5—12.
    x. Pilate's endeavours to release Him. The Jews choose Barabbas. Condemnation to Death. 13—26.
    xi. The Daughters of Jerusalem. 27—31.
    xii. The Crucifixion. 32—38.
    xiii. The Penitent Robber. 39—45.
    xiv. The Saviour's Death. 46—49.

XIV. THE BURIAL, RESURRECTION, AND ASCENSION. xxiii. 50—xxiv. 53.

    i. The Entombment. xxiii. 50—56.
    ii. The Resurrection. xxiv. 1—12.
    iii. The Disciples at Emmaus. 13—32.
    iv. Appearance to the Twelve, and last teachings of the Risen Saviour. 33—49.

XV. THE ASCENSION. 50—53.

CHIEF UNCIAL MANUSCRIPTS OF THE GOSPELS.

Sign.	Name. Codex	Date.	Remarks.
ℵ	Sinaiticus.	4th century.	Found by Tischendorf at the monastery of St Catharine, 1859. Now at St Petersburg.
A	Alexandrinus.	5th century.	Now in British Museum. Presented to Charles I. by Cyril Lucar, Patriarch of Constantinople in 1628.
B	Vaticanus.	4th century.	Now in the Vatican Library at Rome.
C	Ephraemi.	5th century.	Now in Paris. A palimpsest traceable under copy of the works of Ephraem the Syrian.
D	Bezae.	6th century.	Greek and Latin. Contains remarkable interpolations. Given by Beza to the University Library at Cambridge in 1581.
E	Basiliensis.	8th century.	An Evangelistarium or Service book. Now at Basle.
F	Boreeli.	9th century.	Now at Utrecht.
G	Wolfii A.	10th century.	At British Museum, and fragment at Trinity Coll., Cambridge.
L	Regius.	8th or 9th.	Now at Tours.
M	Campianus.	9th century.	At Paris.

The most important Ancient Versions are—

- The Peshito Syriac (made in the 3rd century).
- The Curetonian Syriac, possibly representing an older form of the Peshito (2nd century). A 5th century MS. of this version was found by Canon Cureton in the British Museum.
- The Philoxenian Syriac (made in the 6th century).
- The Jerusalem Syriac (5th or 6th century).
- The Vetus Itala is the oldest existing form of a Latin Version made in the 2nd century.
- The Vulgate is mainly St Jerome's revision of the Vetus Itala, A.D. 383—5.
- The Sahidic or Thebaic and the Memphitic (2nd or 3rd century).
- The Gothic Version of Bp Ulfilas (4th century).

INTRODUCTION. 39

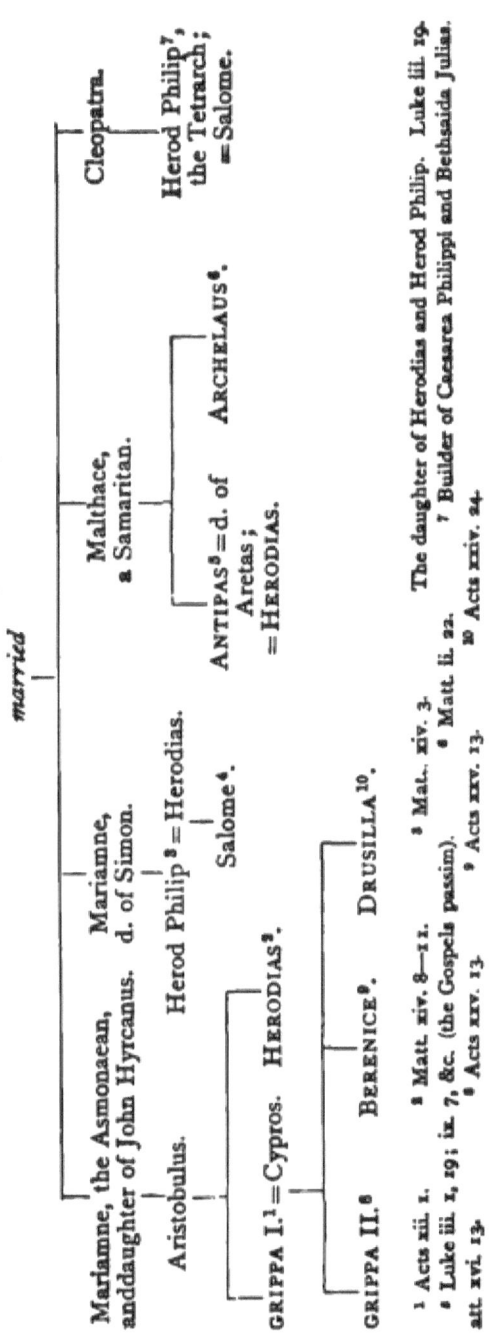

THE HERODS (*as mentioned in the Gospels and the Acts*).

HEROD THE GREAT (Matt. ii. 1), married

Mariamne, the Asmonaean, anddaughter of John Hyrcanus. — Mariamne, d. of Simon. — Malthace, a Samaritan. — Cleopatra.

Aristobulus. — Herod Philip³ = Herodias. | Salome⁴. — ANTIPAS⁵ = d. of Aretas; = HERODIAS. — ARCHELAUS⁶. — Herod Philip⁷, the Tetrarch; = Salome.

GRIPPA I.¹ = Cypros. HERODIAS².

GRIPPA II.⁸ BERENICE⁹. DRUSILLA¹⁰.

1 Acts xii. 1. ² Luke iii 1, 19; ix. 7, &c. (the Gospels passim). ³ Mat. xiv. 3. ⁴ Matt. xiv. 8—11. ⁵ Matt. xiv. 3. ⁶ Matt. ii. 22. ⁷ Builder of Caesarea Philippi and Bethsaida Julias. The daughter of Herodias and Herod Philip. Luke iii. 19. att. xvi. 13. ⁹ Acts xxv. 13. ⁹ Acts xxv 13 ¹⁰ Acts xxiv. 24.

THE GOSPEL ACCORDING TO ST LUKE.

Ch I. 1—4. *Introduction.*

1 FORASMUCH as many have taken in hand to set forth in order a declaration of those things which are most

Ch. I. 1—4. Introduction.

Forasmuch as] This brief preface is in several respects most interesting and important.

i. It is the only personal introduction to any historic book in the Bible except the Acts. It is specially valuable here as authenticating the first two chapters and shewing that Marcion's excision of them was only due to his desire to suppress the true humanity of Christ, as his other mutilations of the Gospel—(which made it "like a garment eaten by moths," Epiphan.)—were due to hostility to the Old Testament. See Mill's *Mythical Interpretation*, p. 103.

ii. The style in which it is written is purer and more polished than that of the rest of the Gospel, though it is "the most literary of the Gospels." It was the custom of antiquity to give special elaboration to the opening clauses of a great work, as we see in the Histories of Thucydides, Livy, &c. In the rest of the Gospel the style of the Evangelist is often largely modified by the documents of which he made such diligent use.

iii. It shews us in the simplest and most striking manner that the Divine Inspiration was in no way intended to supersede the exercise of human diligence and judgment.

iv. It proves how "*many*" early attempts to narrate the Life of Christ have perished. We may well suppose that they have only perished because the Four Evangelists were guided by "a grace of superintendency" to select and to record all that was most needful for us to know, and to preserve everything which was accurate and essential in the narratives (διηγήσεις) which had previously been published.

v. It furnishes us on the very threshold with a key to the aims of the Evangelist in the more systematic and comprehensive history which he is now led to write. With a modesty, which is also evinced by his self-suppression in the Acts of the Apostles, he here lays claim to nothing beyond methodical order and diligent research.

surely believed among us, even as they delivered *them* unto us, which from the beginning were eyewitnesses, and minis-

vi. We see at once from this preface the association of thought and expression between St Luke and his great Teacher. Several of the most marked words, 'attempted,' 'most surely believed,' 'orally instructed,' 'certainty,' are only found elsewhere in the letters and speeches of St Paul.

1. *many*] Whether the Gospels of St Matthew and St Mark had been written when St Luke's appeared is a question which cannot be answered with certainty; but it *is* certain that he does not here allude to those Gospels, and that he did not make any use of them (see Introd. p. 9).

These many attempts to narrate the earthly life of the Saviour were probably those collections of traditional memorials, parables and miracles (*logia, diegēseis*), of which all that was most valuable was incorporated in our four Gospels. Setting aside the Apocryphal Gospels, which are for the most part worthless and even pernicious forgeries, Christian tradition has not preserved for us one trustworthy event of the Life of Christ, and barely a dozen sayings (*agrapha dogmata* like that preserved by St Paul in Acts xx. 35) which are not found in the Gospels.

have taken in hand to set forth in order a declaration] Literally, **attempted to draw up a narrative.** A remarkable parallel to this passage is found in Josephus (*Contra Ap.* I. 10); but no *censure* is here expressed. The word 'attempted' shews indeed that these endeavours were not wholly successful, and the use of the aorist implies that they had already failed. (Acts xix. 13.) "*Conati sunt* qui *implere* nequiverunt," Aug. The works to which St Luke alludes were fragmentary and ill-arranged but not necessarily misleading. Origen (*Hom. in Luc.*) is hardly justified in supposing that the authors are rebuked for temerity, and Dr McClellan goes much too far in calling them "false Evangelists."

of those things which are most surely believed among us] Others render it '*which have been fulfilled,*' '*have found their accomplishment;*' but the analogous uses of the same Greek verb in Rom. iv. 21, xiv. 5, and 2 Tim. iv. 17, and especially of the substantive *plerophoria* in 1 Thess. i. 5, Heb. vi. 11, support the English version. The expression is most important as shewing that whatever might be the defects of the *narratives* there was no hesitation about the *facts*. (Bp Marsh, p. 364.) "The work of these unknown first Evangelists was new only in form and not in substance." Westcott, *Introd.* p. 174.

2. *even as they delivered them unto us, which*] The English version is here ambiguous; and the way in which it is often read shews how completely it is misunderstood. It does not mean 'that the writers of these narratives delivered them to St Luke and others who were eyewitnesses, &c.,' but that 'since many undertook to rearrange the facts which have been delivered (1 Cor. xi. 23, xv. 3; 2 Thess. ii. 15) as a sacred treasure or tradition (1 Tim. vi. 20; 2 Tim. i. 14) to us Christians

ters of the word; it seemed good to me also, having had ³ perfect understanding of all *things* from the very first, to write unto thee in order, most excellent Theophilus, that ⁴ thou mightest know the certainty of *those* things, wherein thou hast been instructed.

by those who became eyewitnesses' (which St Luke does not claim to be) 'and ministers of the word, I too determined, &c.' The words imply that the narratives to which St Luke alludes were *secondhand*—that they were *rearrangements of an oral tradition* received from apostles and original disciples. Clearly therefore there can be no allusion to the Gospel of St Matthew, who wrote *his own* narrative and would have had no need to use one which had been 'delivered' and 'handed down' to him.

eyewitnesses, and ministers] Those who delivered to the Church the facts of the Saviour's life had 'personal knowledge and practical experience,' which these narrators had not. (See Acts i. 21, 22.)

3. *having had perfect understanding*] Rather, **having accurately traced out** or **followed up**. See the same word in 1 Tim. iv. 6; 2 Tim. iii. 10. St Luke modestly puts himself exactly on the same footing as these narrators in not having the primary apostolic qualification, but claims continuous and complete knowledge and careful research.

from the very first] St Luke's Gospel differed from these narratives in beginning from the birth of John the Baptist, and the Annunciation, whereas they began at the manhood and Public Ministry of Christ, as do St Mark and St John. See Acts i. 22; Lk. xvi. 16, "the Law and the Prophets were *until John:* since that time the Kingdom of God is preached."

in order] A favourite word of St Luke only, viii. 1; Acts xi. 4, iii. 24, xviii. 23. St Luke's order is mainly objective, i.e. chronological; St Matthew's, on the other hand, is much guided by subjective considerations, i.e. by moral sequence and unity of topics.

most excellent] This is the title of official personages of high position, e.g. Felix, Acts xxiii. 26, and Festus, xxvi. 25. Whether it is here used in this technical, or in a more general sense, like the Latin 'optime,' it is impossible to say.

Theophilus] A very common name. It means 'Dear to God,' but it is unlikely that it is here an ideal name. Absolutely nothing is known of him. Some from the *title* "most excellent" have conjectured that Sergius Paulus (Acts xiii. 7—12) is meant, to whom they think that the Acts might have naturally been dedicated. But the *name* seems to shew that *a Greek* is intended, and St Luke is writing mainly for Greeks (see Introduction, p. 16). A Theophilus, who held some high distinction at Antioch, is mentioned in the Clementine Recognitions; and as St Luke was, not improbably, a proselyte of Antioch, this may be the person for whom he wrote. Others make him a Bishop of Caesarea Philippi.

4. *mightest know*] Rather, **mayest fully know**.

5—25. *The Announcement of the Birth of the Forerunner.*

5 There was in the days of Herod, the king of Judea, a certain priest named Zacharias, of the course of Abia: and

of those things, wherein thou hast been instructed] Rather, of those accounts in which thou wast orally instructed. Gal. vi. 6. From the word κατηχεῖν 'to teach orally' comes our '*catechise*,' &c. Oral instruction (*katechesis*) flourished especially at Alexandria, which was famous for its catechetical school. This may possibly have favoured the notion that Theophilus was an Alexandrian.

5—25. THE ANNOUNCEMENT OF THE BIRTH OF THE FORERUNNER.

5. *There was in the days*] The elaborate style of the Preface is at once replaced by one of extreme directness and simplicity, full of Hebraic expressions; shewing that here St Luke begins to use, and probably to translate, some Aramaic document which had come into his hands. The remainder of this chapter is known as the *Protevangelium*—the Gospel History before the Birth of Christ. The sweetness and delicate reserve of the narrative, together with the incidents on which it dwells, have led to the not unreasonable conjecture that the Virgin Mary had written down some of those things which she long 'kept in her heart.'

of Herod, the king] Towards the close of the reign of Herod the Great. The true sceptre had departed from Judah. Herod was a mere Idumaean usurper imposed on the nation by the Romans. "Regnum *ab Antonio* Herodi datum, victor Augustus auxit." Tac. *Hist.* v. 9.

of Judea] Besides Judaea, Samaria, and Galilee, his kingdom included the most important regions of Peraea (Jos. *Antt.* XV. 5, § 6, 7; B. *J.* I. 20, § 3, 4).

Zacharias] The common Jewish name Zachariah (2 Kings xiv. 29; Ezra viii. 3, 11; Zech. i. 1; 1 Macc. v. 18, &c.) means 'remembered by Jehovah.' The Jews highly valued the distinction of priestly birth (Jos. *Vit.* 1). The notion that Zacharias was a High Priest and that his vision occurred on the great Day of Atonement is refuted by the single word ἔλαχε "his *lot* was," vs. 9.

of the course] The word *ephemeria* means first 'a daily ministry' (Heb. *Mishmereth*) and then a class of the priesthood which exercised its functions for a week. Aaron had four sons, but the two elder Nadab and Abihu were struck dead for using strange fire in the sanctuary (Lev. x.). From the two remaining sons Eleazar and Ithamar had sprung in the days of David twenty-four families, sixteen from the descendants of Eleazar, and eight from those of Ithamar. To these David distributes by lot the order of their service from week to week, each for eight days inclusively from sabbath to sabbath (1 Chr. xxiv. 1—19; 2 Chr. xxxi. 2). After the Babylonish exile only four of the twenty-four courses returned —a striking indication of the truth of the Jewish saying that those who returned from the exile were but like the chaff in comparison of the

his wife *was* of the daughters of Aaron, and her name *was* Elisabeth. And they were both righteous before God, walk- 6 ing in all the commandments and ordinances of the Lord blameless. And they had no child, because that Elisabeth 7

wheat. The four families of which the representatives returned were those of Jedaiah, Immer, Pashur, and Harim (Ezra ii. 36—39). But the Jews concealed the heavy loss by subdividing these four families into twenty-four courses to which they gave the original names, and this is alluded to in Nehem. xiii. 30 ("I...appointed the *wards* of the priests and the Levites, every one in his business"). This arrangement continued till the fall of Jerusalem A.D. 70 at which time, on the ninth of the month Ab (Aug. 5), we are told that the course in waiting was that of Jehoiarib (Jos. *Bell. Jud.* VI. 5), *Taanith*, IV. 6: Derenbourg, *Palest.* p. 291. Reckoning back from this we find that the course of Abijah went out of office on Oct. 9, B.C. 6, A.U.C. 748 (but see Lewin, *Fasti Sacri*, p. 191). The reader should bear in mind that our received era for the Birth of Christ (A.U.C. 753) was only fixed by the Abbot Dionysius Exiguus in the 6th century, and is probably four years wrong.

of Abia] 1 Chr. xxiv. 10, "the eighth [lot came forth] to Abijah." This was not one of the four families which had returned, but the name was soon revived (Neh. xii. 4). Josephus tells us that he enjoyed the high distinction of belonging by birth to the first of the twenty-four courses (*Vit.* 1).

Elisabeth] The same name as Elisheba ('one whose oath is by God,' comp. Jehoshebah, 2 Kings xi. 2), the wife of Aaron, Ex. vi. 23; mentioned by name according to Ibn Ezra as 'the mother of the priesthood.'

6. *righteous*] One of the oldest terms of high praise among the Jews (Gen. vi. 9, vii. 1, xviii. 23—28. See Ps. xxxvii. 37; Ezek. xviii. 5—19, &c.). It is used also of Joseph, Matt. i. 19; and is defined in the following words in the almost technical sense of strict legal observance which it had acquired since the days of the Maccabees. The true Jashar (upright man) was the ideal Jew. Thus Rashi calls the Book of Genesis 'the book of the *upright*, Abraham, Isaac, and Jacob.'

in all the commandments and ordinances] The two words occur in the LXX. version of Gen. xxvi. 5 (of Abraham) and 2 Chron. xvii. 4 (of Jehoshaphat). '*Commandments*' means the moral precepts of natural and revealed religion (Rom. vii. 8—13). '*Ordinances*' had come to be technically used of the *ceremonial* Law (Heb. ix. 1). The distinctions were not accurately kept, but the two words together would, to a pious Jew of that day, have included all the positive and negative precepts which later Rabbis said were 613 in number, namely 248 positive, and 365 negative.

7. *And they had no child*] This was regarded as a heavy misfortune because it cut off all hope of the birth of the Messiah in that family. It was also regarded as often involving a moral reproach, and as being a punishment for sin. See Gen. xi. 30, xviii. 11, xxx. 1—23; Ex. xxiii. 26; Deut. vii. 14; Judg. xiii. 2, 3; 1 Sam. i. 6, 27; Is. xlvii. 9.

was barren, and they both were *now* well stricken in years. ⁸ And it came to pass, *that* while he executed the priest's ⁹ office before God in the order of his course, according to the custom of the priest's office, his lot was to burn incense ¹⁰ when he went into the temple of the Lord. And the whole multitude of the people were praying without at the time of ¹¹ incense. And there appeared unto him an angel of the

well stricken in years] A priest apparently might minister until any age, but Levites were *partially* superannuated at 50 (Num. iii. 1—39, iv., viii. 25).

8. *executed the priest's office*] The priest who had the highest functions allotted to him was called 'the chief of the course.' There are said to have been some 20,000 priests in the days of Christ, and it could therefore never fall to the lot of the same priest *twice* to offer incense. Hence this would have been, apart from the vision, the most memorable day in the life of Zacharias.

9. *his lot was to burn incense*] Rather, **he obtained by lot the duty of entering and burning incense.** This was the loftiest and most coveted of priestly functions, Ex. xxx. 1—10; Num. xvi. 1—40. King Uzziah was smitten with leprosy for trying to usurp it (2 Chr. xxvi. 18). Incense was a symbol of prayer (Ps. cxli. 2; Heb. ix. 4; Rev. viii. 3, 4), and Philo tells us that it was offered twice a day,—before the morning and after the evening sacrifice of a lamb.

into the temple] Rather, **shrine** or **Holy Place.** The golden altar of incense stood before the veil which separated the Holy Place from the Holy of Holies (Ex. xxx. 6). The priest entered in white robes and with unsandalled feet with two attendants who retired when they had made everything ready. The people waited outside in the Court of Israel praying in deep silence till the priest who was sacrificing the evening lamb at the great altar of Burnt Offering in the Court gave a signal to his colleague in the shrine, perhaps by the tinkling of a bell (Ex. xxx. 1—10; Ps. cxli. 2; Mal. i. 11). He then threw the incense on the fire of the golden altar, and its fragrant smoke rose with the prayers of the people. It was while performing this solemn function that John Hyrcanus also had received a divine intimation (Jos. *Antt.* XIII. 103).

10. *the whole multitude*] This seems to shew that the vision took place either on a sabbath, or some great feast-day.

praying] The Temple was mainly used for sacrifice. Prayer in the Tabernacle is only once mentioned in the Pentateuch (Deut. xxvi. 12—15). But the Temple had naturally become a 'House of Prayer' (Is. lvi. 7; Neh. xi. 17; Matt. xxi. 13). One of the Rabbis went so far as to argue that prayer was a Rabbinic not a Mosaic institution! See Cohen, *Jud. Gottesdienst*, p. 186.

11. *an angel*] St Luke dwells more than any of the Evangelists on the ministry of angels, i. 26, ii. 9, 13, 21, xii. 8, xv. 10, xvi. 22, xxii. 43, xxiv. 4, 23, and frequently in the Acts. Compare the births of Isaac, Samson, and Samuel.

Lord standing on the right side of the altar of incense. And when Zacharias saw *him*, he was troubled, and fear fell upon him. But the angel said unto him, Fear not, Zacharias: for thy prayer is heard; and thy wife Elisabeth shall bear thee a son, and thou shalt call his name John. And thou shalt have joy and gladness; and many shall rejoice at his birth. For he shall be great in the sight of the Lord, and shall drink neither wine nor strong drink; and he shall

the right side] i.e. the South. It was the propitious side so to speak, Mk. xvi. 5; Matt. xxv. 33; and ib. Schöttgen, *Hor. Hebr.*

the altar of incense] A small movable table of acacia wood overlaid with gold. See Ex. xxx. 1—38, xxxvii. 25; 1 Kings vii. 48. In Heb. ix. 4 the word may possibly mean 'censer.'

12. *he was troubled*] Such is the effect always recorded of these supernatural appearances. See Judg. xiii. 22; Dan. x. 7—9; Ezek. i. 28; Mark xvi. 8; Rev. i. 17.

13. *Fear not*] The first utterance of the Dawn of the Gospel. St Luke begins with this angelic encouragement, and ends with the Apostles 'blessing and praising God;' see the beautiful remarks of Bengel ad loc.

thy prayer is heard] Rather, **thy supplication was heard.** Δέησις implies a special prayer, and with the aorist verb shews that Zacharias had been just praying either to have a son, or at least that the days of the Messiah might come.

John] Jehochanan, 'the favour of Jehovah' (comp. Gen. xvii. 19). It is interchanged with Jona in Matt. xvi. 17 (comp. John i. 42), and in various forms was not uncommon, 1 Chron. iii. 24, xxviii. 12, &c.

14. *gladness*] Rather, **exultation**, vs. 44; Acts ii. 46; Heb. i. 9.
many] The Pharisees and leading Jews did not accept John's baptism (vii. 30; Matt. xxi. 27), and his influence, except among a few, seems to have been shortlived.

> "There burst he forth: 'All ye whose hopes rely
> On God, with me amid these deserts mourn,
> Repent, repent, and from old errors turn!'
> Who listened to his voice, obeyed his cry?—
> Only the echoes which he made relent
> Rang from their flinty caves Repent! repent!"
> DRUMMOND.

15. *great in the sight of the Lord*] See vii. 24—30; Matt. xi. 11.
shall drink neither wine nor strong drink] He shall be a Nazarite (vii. 33; Num. vi. 1—4); like Samson (Judg. xiii. 2—7); and the Rechabites (Jer. xxxv. 6). 'Strong drink' (*Sikera* from Heb. *Shakar* 'he is intoxicated') was also forbidden to ministering priests, Lev. x. 8. The term seems to have been specially applied to *palm* wine (Plin. *Hist. Nat.* XIV. 19), and all intoxicants (e.g. beer, &c.) which are not made of the juice of the grape. '*Ne Syder*,' Wyclif.

be filled with the Holy Ghost, even from his mother's womb.
16 And many of the children of Israel shall he turn to the
17 Lord their God. And he shall go before him in the spirit and power of Elias, to turn the hearts of the fathers to the children, and the disobedient to the wisdom of the
18 just; to make ready a people prepared for the Lord. And Zacharias said unto the angel, Whereby shall I know this? for I am an old man, and my wife well stricken in years.
19 And the angel answering said unto him, I am Gabriel, that

shall be filled with the Holy Ghost] The contrast between the false and hateful excitement of drunkenness and the divine exaltation of spiritual fervour is also found in Eph. v. 18, "Be not drunk with wine...but be filled with the Spirit." Comp. Acts ii. 13.

even from his mother's womb] Compare 1 Sam. i. 11; Jer. i. 5.

16. *many...shall he turn*] Ezek. iii. 19; Is. xl. 3; Matt. iii. 3—6. The word for '*turn*' is sometimes rendered '*convert*' as in xxii. 32, 'when thou art converted.' These words resume the thread of prophecy which had been broken for three centuries (Mal. iv. 6).

17. *And he shall go before him*] Shall go before the Messiah. The English version should have added, "in His (God's) presence" (ἐνώπιον αὐτοῦ).

in the spirit and power of Elias] From the last words of Malachi (iv. 4—6, iii. 1), the Jews universally believed (as they do to this day) that Elijah would visibly return to earth as a herald of the Messiah. It required the explanation of our Lord to open the eyes of the Apostles on this subject. "This is Elias which was for to come," Matt. xi. 14. "Elias truly shall first come and restore all things...Then the disciples understood that He spake unto them of John the Baptist," Matt. xvii. 10—14. The resemblance was partly in external aspect (2 Kings i. 8; Matt. iii. 4); and partly in his mission of stern rebuke and invitation to repentance (1 Kings xviii. 21, xxi. 20).

to turn the hearts of the fathers to the children] Rather, **of fathers to children**; i.e. as in the original meaning of Malachi, to remedy disunion and restore family life.

to the wisdom] Rather, **in** or **by** the wisdom.

18. *for I am an old man*] So "Abraham fell upon his face, and laughed, and said in his heart, Shall a child be born unto him that is a hundred years old?" Gen. xvii. 17. But he had believed the original promise (Gen. xv. 6) though he asked for a confirmation of it (vs. 8). "He believed...God who quickeneth the dead," Rom. iv. 17.

19. *Gabriel*] The name means 'Hero of God.' He is also mentioned in vs. 26, and in Dan. viii. 16, ix. 21—23 ('idem Angelus, idem negotium,' Bengel). The only other Angel or Archangel (1 Thess. iv. 16; Jude 9) named in Scripture is Michael ('Who is like God?' Dan. x. 21). In the Book of Enoch we read of 'the *four* great

stand in the presence of God; and am sent to speak unto thee, and to shew thee these glad tidings. And behold, 20 thou shalt be dumb, and not able to speak, until the day that these *things* shall be performed, because thou believest not my words, which shall be fulfilled in their season. And 21 the people waited for Zacharias, and marvelled that he tarried *so* long in the temple. And when he came out, he 22

Archangels Michael, Uriel, Raphael, Gabriel,' and so too in *Pirke Rabbi Eliezer*, IV. In Tobit xii. 15, "I am Raphael (Healer of God), one of the seven holy Angels which present the prayers of the saints, and which go in and out before the glory of the Holy One." Since Michael was despatched on messages of wrath and Gabriel on messages of mercy, the Jews had the beautiful saying that "Gabriel flew with two wings, but Michael with only one."

that stand in the presence of God; and am sent to speak unto thee] He was thus one of the "Angels of the Presence" (Is. lxiii. 9; cf. Matt. xviii. 10),

"One of the Seven
Who in God's presence, nearest to His throne,
Stand ready at command, and are His eyes
That run through all the heavens, and down to the earth
Bear His swift errands over moist and dry,
O'er sea and land."
MILTON, *Paradise Lost*, III. 650.

See Rev. viii. 2; Dan. vii. 10; 1 Kings xxii. 19. The supposed resemblance to the Amshaspands in the Zendavesta is shewn by Dr Mill to be purely superficial. *Mythical Interpretation*, p. 127.

to shew thee these glad tidings] The word *euangelisasthai* 'to preach the Gospel' is common in St Luke and St Paul, but elsewhere is only found in 1 Pet. i. 12; Matt. xi. 5. It comes from the LXX. (Is. xl. 9, lxi. 1).

20. *thou shalt be dumb, and not able to speak*] He receives the sign for which he had unfaithfully asked (Matt. xii. 38), but it comes in the form of a punishment. This positive and negative way of expressing the same thing is common, especially in Hebrew literature, 2 Sam. xiv. 5; Exod. xxi. 11; Is. xxxviii. 1; Lam. iii. 2, &c.

in their season] "I will certainly return unto thee according to the time of life," Gen. xviii. 10, i.e. after the usual nine months.

21. *he tarried so long*] Priests never tarried in the awful precincts of the shrine longer than was absolutely necessary for the fulfilment of their duties, from feelings of holy fear, Lev. xvi. 13, "that he die not." (T. B. *Yoma* f. 52. 2.) See Excursus VII.

22. *And when he came out*] The moment of the priest's reappearance from before the ever-burning golden candlestick, and the veil which hid the Holiest Place, was one which powerfully affected the Jewish imagination, Ecclus. l. 5—21.

could not speak unto them: and they perceived that he had seen a vision in the temple: for he beckoned unto them, and remained speechless. And it came to pass *that*, as soon as the days of his ministration were accomplished, he departed to his own house. And after those days his wife Elisabeth conceived, and hid herself five months, saying, Thus hath the Lord dealt with me in the days wherein he looked on *me*, to take away my reproach among men.

26—38. *The Annunciation.*

And in the sixth month the angel Gabriel was sent from

he could not speak unto them] They were waiting in the Court to be dismissed with the usual blessing, which is said to have been usually pronounced by the *other* priest. Numb. vi. 23—26. "Then he" (the High Priest Simon) "went down and lifted up his hands over the whole congregation of the children of Israel, to give the blessing of the Lord with his lips, and to rejoice in His name. And they bowed themselves down to worship the second time, that they might receive a blessing from the Most High." Ecclus. l. 20.

a vision] *Optasian.* Used especially of the most vivid and 'objective' appearances, xxiv. 23; Acts xxvi. 19; 2 Cor. xii. 1; Dan. ix. 23.

he beckoned unto them] Rather, **he was himself making signs to them.**

remained speechless] "Credat Judaeus ut *loqui* possit" (let the Jew believe that he may be able to speak) says St Augustine. Origen, Ambrose, and Isidore, see in the speechless priest vainly endeavouring to bless the people, a fine image of the Law reduced to silence before the first announcement of the Gospel. The scene might stand for an allegorical representation of the thesis so powerfully worked out in the Epistle to the Hebrews (see Heb. viii. 13). Zacharias became dumb, and Saul of Tarsus blind, for a time. "Praeludium legis ceremonialis finiendae Christo veniente." Bengel.

23. *the days of his ministration*] They lasted from the evening of one Sabbath to the morning of the next. 2 Kings xi. 5.

24. *hid herself*] We can only conjecture her motive. It may have been devotional; or precautionary; or she may merely have wished out of deep modesty to avoid as long as possible the idle comments and surmises of her neighbours.

25. *to take away my reproach*] So Rachel, when she bare a son, said, "God hath taken away my reproach," Gen. xxx. 23. See Is. iv. 1; Hos. ix. 11; 1 Sam. i. 6—10. Yet the days were coming when to be childless would be regarded by Jewish mothers as a blessing. See xxiii. 29.

26—38. THE ANNUNCIATION.

26. *in the sixth month*] i.e. after the vision of Zachariah. This is

God unto a city of Galilee, named Nazareth, to a virgin 27
espoused to a man whose name was Joseph, of the house
of David; and the virgin's name *was* Mary. And the angel 28
came in unto her, and said, Hail, *thou that art* highly favoured, the Lord *is* with thee: blessed *art* thou among women.
And when she saw *him*, she was troubled at his saying, and 29
cast in her mind what manner of salutation this should be.

the only passage which indicates the age of John the Baptist, as half
a year older than our Lord.

Galilee] Thus began to be fulfilled the prophecy of Is. ix. 1, 2.
Galilee of the Gentiles (*Gelîl haggoyîm*), one of the four great Roman
divisions of Palestine, was north of Judaea and Samaria, west of
Peraea, and comprised the territories of Zebulun, Naphthali, Issachar
and Asher (Matt. iv. 13). Josephus describes it as rich in trees and
pastures, strong, populous, containing 204 towns, of which the least
had 15000 inhabitants, and occupied by a hardy and warlike race,
Bell. Jud. III. 3; *Vit.* 45, 52. See Map, and note on iii. 2.

named Nazareth] The expression shews that St Luke is writing
for those who were unfamiliar with Palestine. See on ii. 51.

a virgin] Is. vii. 14; Jer. xxxi. 22. The many miraculous and
glorifying legends which soon began to gather round her name in the
Apocryphal Gospels are utterly unknown to Scripture.

27. *espoused*] Rather, **betrothed**. The betrothal, which is in the
East a ceremony of the deepest importance, usually took place a year
before the marriage.

Joseph, of the house of David] We are nowhere told that Mary
was of the house of David, for both the genealogies of the Gospels
are genealogies of Joseph. See Excursus II. The fact that it seems
always to be assumed that Mary also was of the lineage of David
(vs. 32), makes it probable that the genealogy of Mary is involved
in that of Joseph, and that they were first cousins.

Mary] The same name as Miriam and Marah, Exod. xv. 20; Ruth
i. 20. Her early residence at Nazareth, before the birth of Christ
at Bethlehem, is narrated by St Luke alone. It does not however
follow that St Matthew was unaware of it (Matt. xiii. 55, 56). After
the narrative of the Nativity she is very rarely mentioned. The *Ave
Maria* of the Roman Catholics did not assume its present form till the
16th century.

28. *highly favoured*] marg. "graciously accepted" or "much
graced." Literally, **having been graced** (by God). Eph. i. 6,
"accepted." Not as in the Vulgate "Gratiâ *plena*" but "gratiâ *cumu-
lata.*" "Not a mother of grace, but a daughter." Bengel.

blessed art thou among women] These words are of dubious authenticity, being omitted by B and various versions. They may have been
added from vs. 42. With this address comp. Judg. vi. 12.

29. *And when she saw him, she was troubled*] Rather, **But she
was greatly troubled.**

30 And the angel said unto her, Fear not, Mary: for thou hast
31 found favour with God. And behold, thou shalt conceive
in *thy* womb, and bring forth a son, and shalt call his name
32 JESUS. He shall be great, and shall be called the Son of
the Highest: and the Lord God shall give unto him the
33 throne of his father David: and he shall reign over the
house of Jacob for ever; and of his kingdom there shall be
34 no end. Then said Mary unto the angel, How shall this
35 be, seeing I know not a man? And the angel answered and
said unto her, The Holy Ghost shall come upon thee, and
the power of the Highest shall overshadow thee: therefore
also *that* holy thing which shall be born of thee shall be

31. *Jesus*] The Greek form of the Hebrew name Jehoshua (Num. xiii. 8), Joshua, Jeshua (Zech. iii. 1), which means 'The salvation of Jehovah' (Philo, I. 597). It was one of the commonest Jewish names. Jesus is used for Joshua (to the great confusion of English readers) in Acts vii. 45; Heb. iv. 8. St Matthew (i. 21) explains the reason of the name—"for He Himself shall *save* His people *from their sins*." On Joshua as a type of Christ see Pearson *On the Creed*, Art. ii.
He shall save His people from their sins, "Summa Evangelii." Bengel.

32. *shall be called*] i. e. shall be. The best comment on this verse is furnished by the passages of Scripture in which we find the same prophecy (Mic. v. 4; 2 Sam. vii. 12; Is. ix. 6, 7, xi. 1, 10, xvi. 5; Jer. xxiii. 5, xxx. 9; Ezek. xxxiv. 24; Hos. iii. 5; Ps. cxxxii. 11) and its fulfilment (Phil. ii. 9—11; Rev. xxii. 16).
the throne of his father David] according to Ps. cxxxii. 11.

33. *reign...for ever*] Dan. ii. 44, "a kingdom which shall never be destroyed...it shall stand for ever." (Comp. Dan. vii. 13, 14, 27; Mic. iv. 7.) "Thy throne, O God, is for ever and ever" (Ps. xlv. 6; Heb. i. 8). "He shall reign for ever and ever," Rev. xi. 15. In 1 Cor. xv. 24—28 the allusion is only to Christ's *mediatorial* kingdom,—His *earthly* kingdom till the end of conflict.

34. *How shall this be?*] Mary does not doubt the fact as Zacharias had done; she only enquires as to *the mode* of accomplishment. The village maiden amid her humble daily duties shews a more ready faith in a far more startling message than the aged priest in the Holy Place amid the Incense.

35. *shall overshadow thee*] as with the Shechinah and Cloud of Glory (see on ii. 9, ix. 34). See the treatise on the Shechinah in Meuschen, pp. 701—739. On the high theological mystery see Pearson *On the Creed*, Art. iii. See on ii. 9.
that holy thing] "Holy, harmless, undefiled, separate from sinners," Heb. vii. 26. "Who did no sin," 1 Pet. ii. 22.
which shall be born of thee] Rather, **which is in thy womb**. Gal. iv. 4, "born of a woman."

called the Son of God. And behold, thy cousin Elisabeth, 36
she hath also conceived a son in her old age: and this is
the sixth month with her, who was called barren. For with 37
God nothing shall be unpossible. And Mary said, Behold 38
the handmaid of the Lord; be it unto me according to thy
word. And the angel departed from her.

39—45. *The Visit of Mary to Elisabeth.*

And Mary arose in those days, and went into the hill 39

the Son of God] This title is given to our Lord by almost every one of the sacred writers in the N.T. and in a multitude of passages.

36. *thy cousin*] Rather, "*thy kinswoman.*" What the actual relationship was we do not know. It is a mistake to infer from this, as Ewald does, that Mary too was of the tribe of Levi, for except in the case of heiresses there was free intermarriage between the tribes (Ex. vi. 23; Judg. xvii. 7; Philo *De Monach.* II. 11; Jos. *Vit.* 1).

37. *nothing*] Rather, no word. For the thought see Gen. xviii. 14; Matth. xix. 26. "There is nothing too hard for thee," Jer. xxxii. 17.

38. *be it unto me according to thy word*] The thoughts of the Virgin Mary seem to have found their most natural utterance in the phrases of Scripture. 1 Sam. iii. 18, "If it be the Lord let Him do what seemeth Him good." For Mary too was aware that her high destiny must be mingled with anguish.

And the angel departed from her] We can best appreciate the noble simplicity of truthfulness by comparing this narrative of the Annunciation with the diffuse inflation of the Apocryphal Gospels. Take for instance such passages as these from one of the least extravagant of them, 'The Gospel of the Nativity of Mary.' "The Angel Gabriel was sent to her...to explain to her the method or order of the Conception. At length having entered unto her, he filled the chamber where she abode with an immense light, and saluting her most courteously said, 'Hail Mary! most acceptable Virgin of the Lord! Virgin full of grace...blessed art thou before all women; blessed art thou before all men hitherto born.' But the Virgin who already knew the countenance of angels, and was not unused to heavenly light, was neither terrified by the angelic vision nor stupefied by the greatness of the light, but was troubled at his word alone; and began to think what that salutation so unwonted could be, or what it portended, or what end it could have. But the Angel, divinely inspired and counteracting this thought, said, Fear not, Mary, as though I meant something contrary to thy chastity by this salutation; for &c., &c." The reader will observe at once the artificiality, the tasteless amplifications, the want of reticence;—all the marks which separate truthful narrative from elaborate fiction. (See B. H. Cowper, *The Apocryphal Gospels*, p. 93.)

39—45. THE VISIT OF MARY TO ELIZABETH.

39. *in those days*] Rather, these. Probably within a month of the Annunciation.

⁴⁰ country with haste, into a city of Juda; and entered into
⁴¹ the house of Zacharias, and saluted Elisabeth. And it came
to pass *that*, when Elisabeth heard the salutation of Mary,
the babe leaped in her womb; and Elisabeth was filled with
⁴² the Holy Ghost: and she spake out with a loud voice, and

went into the hill country] Palestine west of the Jordan lies in *four* parallel lines of very different formation. 1. The coast. 2. The *Shephēlah*, or maritime plain, broken only by the spur of Carmel. 3. The *Har* or Hill country,—the mass of low rounded hills which formed the main part of the Roman provinces of Judaea and Samaria south of the intervening plain of Esdraelon, and of Galilee north of it; and 4. The *Ghôr* or deep dint of the Jordan Valley. See Deut. i. 7, "in the plain (*Arabah*), in the hills (*Har*), in the vale (*Shephēlah*), and in the south (*Negeb*), and by the sea side (*Chooph hayyâm*)." (Josh. ix. 1; Judg. v. 17.) The *specific* meaning of 'hill country' is the elevated district of Judah, Benjamin and Ephraim. (Gen. xiv. 10; Num. xiii. 29; Josh. ix. 1, x. 40, xi. 16.)

with haste] The same notion of haste is involved in the aorist participle '*anastasa*' rising up. As a betrothed virgin she would live without seeing her future husband. When however a few weeks sufficed to shew her condition, the female friends about her would be sure to make it known to Joseph. Then would occur the enquiries and suspicions, so agonising to a pure maiden, which are alluded to by St Matthew (i. 18—25). After the dream which vindicated her innocence we can understand the "haste" with which she would fly to the sympathy of her holy and aged kinswoman and seek for peace in the seclusion of the priestly home. Nothing but the peculiarity of her condition could have permitted the violation of Jewish custom involved in the journey of a betrothed virgin. But for the incidents recorded by St Matthew we should be wholly unable to account for this expression. Its naturalness under the circumstances is an undesigned coincidence.

into a city of Juda] Similarly, Nazareth is described as "a city of Galilee." The name of the city is not given. Had the home of Zacharias been at Hebron it would probably have been mentioned. Reland (*Palest.* p. 870) ingeniously conjectures that we should read *Jutta*, which was in the hill country (Josh. xv. 55) and was one of the cities of Judah which were assigned to the priests (ib. xxi. 9, 16). We can hardly venture to alter the reading, but as Juttah was only a large village (Euseb. *Onomast.* s. v.) and is not mentioned in 1 Chr. vi. 57—59 it may have been the home of Zacharias, and the actual name may easily have been omitted as obscure. Tradition names *Ain Karim*. 'Judah' is here used for Judaea (Matt. ii. 6).

41. *leaped*] The same word is applied to unborn babes in Gen. xxv. 22, LXX.

42. *with a loud voice*] For '*phonē*,' voice, B has the stronger word '*kraugē*,' cry.

said, Blessed *art* thou among women, and blessed *is* the fruit of thy womb. And whence *is* this to me, that the mother of my Lord should come to me? For lo, as soon as the voice of thy salutation sounded in mine ears, the babe leaped in my womb for joy. And blessed *is* she that believed: for there shall be a performance of those *things* which were told her from the Lord.

46—56. *The Magnificat.*

And Mary said,
My soul doth magnify the Lord,

Blessed art thou among women] i.e. preeminently blessed, as "fairest among women," Cant. i. 8. Similar expressions are used of Ruth (Ruth iii. 10), and, on a far lower level of meaning, of Jael (Judg. v. 24), and of Judith. "All the women of Israel blessed her," Jud. xv. 12. In the latter instances the blessing is *pronounced by* women, but here the word means 'blessed by God.'

43. *the mother of my Lord*] The words shew a remarkable degree of divine illumination in the mind of Elizabeth. See John xx. 28, xiii. 13. Yet she does not address Mary as *Domina*, but as 'mater Domini' (Bengel); and such expressions as *Theotokos* and 'Mother of God' are unknown to Scripture.

44. *for joy*] Rather, **in exultation**.

45. *blessed is she that believed*] Perhaps Elizabeth had in mind the affliction which had followed her husband's doubt. Comp. John xx. 29.

for there shall be a performance] The words may also mean 'she that believed *that* there shall be,' &c.

46—56. THE MAGNIFICAT.

46. *And Mary said*] This chapter is remarkable for preserving a record of two inspired hymns—the *Magnificat* and the *Benedictus*—which have been used for more than a thousand years in the public services of Christendom. The Magnificat first appears in the office of Lauds in the rule of St Caesarius of Arles, A.D. 507. (Blunt, *Annotated Prayer Book*, p. 33.) It is so full of Hebraisms as almost to form a mosaic of quotations from the Old Testament, and it is closely analogous to the Song of Hannah (1 Sam. ii. 1—10). It may also be compared with the Hymn of Judith (Jud. xvi. 1—17). But it is animated by a new and more exalted spirit, and is specially precious as forming a link of continuity between the eucharistic poetry of the Old and New Dispensation. (See Bp Wordsworth, ad loc.)

My soul doth magnify the Lord] 1 Sam. ii. 1; Ps. xxxiv. 2, 3. The soul ($\psi\upsilon\chi\dot{\eta}$) is the natural life with all its affections and emotions; the spirit ($\pi\nu\epsilon\tilde{\upsilon}\mu\alpha$) is the diviner and loftier region of our being, 1 Thess. v. 23; 1 Cor. ii. 10.

47 And my spirit hath rejoiced in God my Saviour.
48 For he hath regarded the low estate of his handmaiden:
For behold, from henceforth all generations shall call me blessed.
49 For he *that is* mighty hath done to me great things;
And holy *is* his name.
50 And his mercy *is* on them that fear him
From generation to generation.
51 He hath shewed strength with his arm;
He hath scattered the proud in the imagination of their hearts.
52 He hath put down the mighty from *their* seats,
And exalted them of low degree.

47. *hath rejoiced*] Rather, **exults**. In the original it is the *general*, or *gnomic* aorist.

in God my Saviour] Is. xlv. 21, "a just God and a Saviour." Comp. Is. xii. 2, xxv. 9. The expression is also found in the later Epistles of St Paul, "God our Saviour," 1 Tim. i. 1; Tit. iii. 4.

48. *he hath regarded*] Rather, **He looked upon**.

the low estate] So Hagar (Gen. xvi. 11) and Hannah (1 Sam. i. 11; cf. Ps. cxxxviii. 6, cii. 17). The word may be rendered **humiliation**, Acts viii. 33; Is. i. 9, 10. The reader will notice in this hymn more than one anticipation of the Beatitudes.

all generations shall call me blessed] "Blessed is the womb that bare Thee," Lk. xi. 27. "Leah said, The daughters will call me blessed," Gen. xxx. 13; Ps. lxxii. 17. We cannot but wonder at the vast faith of the despised and persecuted Virgin of Nazareth, whose inspired anticipations have been so amply fulfilled.

49. *he that is mighty*] *El Shaddai*, Job viii. 3; also *Gibbôr*, Ps. xxiv. 8. See Pearson *On the Creed*, Art. i.

great things] *Gedolôth*, Ps. lxxi. 21, cxxvi. 3.

holy is his name] Ps. cxi. 9; "Thou only art holy," Rev. xv. 4. *Shem*, 'name,' is often a reverent periphrasis in Hebrew for God Himself. Ps. xci. 14; 2 Chr. vi. 20, &c.

50. *his mercy*] Ps. lxxxix. 2, 3 and passim.

From generation to generation] Rather, **Unto generations and generations**; *ledôr vadôr*, Gen. xvii. 9, &c. See Deut. vii. 9.

51. *with his arm*] "Thou hast a mighty arm," Ps. lxxxix. 13. The nearest parallel to the remainder of the verse is Job v. 12.

52. *He hath put down the mighty from their seats*] Rather, **He puts down potentates from thrones**. The aorists throughout are *gnomic*, i.e. they do not express single but *normal* acts. The thought is common throughout the Bible, e.g. Lk. xviii. 14; Dan. iv. 30; 1 Sam. ii. 6—10; Ps. cxiii. 6—8; 1 Cor. i. 26—29. The ancients noticed the fact (κύκλος

He hath filled the hungry with good *things*; 53
And the rich he hath sent empty away.
He hath holpen his servant Israel, 54
In remembrance of *his* mercy,
(As he spake to our fathers), 55
To Abraham, and to his seed for ever.
And Mary abode with her about three months, and returned 56 to her own house.

57—80. *The Birth of John the Baptist.*

Now Elisabeth's full time came that she should be delivered; and she brought forth a son. And *her* neighbours 58 and her cousins heard how the Lord had shewed great mercy upon her; and they rejoiced with her. And it came to pass, 59 *that* on the eighth day they came to circumcise the child; 57

τῶν ἀνθρωπηΐων ἐστὶ πρηγμάτων, Hdt. I. 207; "Irus et est subito qui modo Croesus erat," Ov. *Trist.* III. vii. 41) but did not draw the true lessons from it.

53. *filled the hungry with good things*] "My servants shall eat but ye shall be hungry, &c.," Is. lxv. 13, xxv. 6; Ps. xxxiv. 10, and the Beatitude Matt. v. 6. (See Lk. xviii. 14, the Publican and the Pharisee.)

54. *hath holpen*] Literally, "took by the hand." Is. xli. 8, 9, LXX. The proper punctuation of the following words is **to remember His mercy—(even as He spake to** (πρὸς) **our fathers)—to** (τῷ) **Abraham and his seed for ever.** Mic. vii. 20, "Thou wilt perform...the mercy to Abraham, which thou hast sworn unto our fathers from the days of old." Gal. iii. 16, "Now to Abraham and his seed were the promises made."

56. *about three months*] As this would complete the nine months of Elisabeth's 'full time,' it might seem probable that the Virgin Mary at least remained until the birth of the Baptist.

returned] The word used—*hupestrepsen*—is a favourite word of St Luke, and almost (Gal. i. 17; Heb. vii. 1) peculiar to him. It occurs twenty-one times in this Gospel.

57—80. THE BIRTH OF JOHN THE BAPTIST.

58. *her cousins*] Rather, **her kinsfolk**, which was the original meaning of the word *cousins* (*con-sobrini*). See vs. 36.

59. *on the eighth day*] According to the ordinance of Gen. xvii. 12; Lev. xii. 3;—Phil. iii. 5. The name was then given, because at the

and they called him Zacharias, after the name of his father.
60 And his mother answered and said, Not *so;* but he shall be
61 called John. And they said unto her, There is none of thy
62 kindred that is called by this name. And they made signs
63 to his father, how he would have him called. And he asked
for a writing table, and wrote, saying, His name is John.
64 And they marvelled all. And his mouth was opened immediately, and his tongue *loosed*, and he spake, and praised
65 God. And fear came on all that dwelt round about them:
and all these sayings were noised abroad throughout all the
66 hill country of Judea. And all they that heard *them* laid
them up in their hearts, saying, What *manner of* child shall
67 this be! And the hand of the Lord was with him. And his

institution of circumcision the names of Abram and Sarai had been changed, Gen. xvii. 15. The rite was invested with extreme solemnity, and in later times a chair was always put for the prophet Elijah.

they called] Rather, **they wished to call**. Literally, 'they were calling,' but the imperfect by an idiomatic use often expresses an unfulfilled attempt. So in Matt. iii. 14, 'he tried to prevent Him' (*diekōluen*).

61. *none of thy kindred*] We find a John among hierarchs in Acts iv. 6, v. 17. Those priests however who passed the High Priesthood from one to another—a clique of Herodian Sadducees—the Boethusim, Kamhiths, Benî Hanan, &c.—were partly of Babylonian and Egyptian origin, and had been introduced by Herod to support his purposes. They would not be of the kin of Zacharias.

62. *made signs*] The discussion whether Zacharias was deaf as well as mute is a very unimportant one, but the narrative certainly seems to imply that he was.

63. *table*] Rather, **tablet**. A small wooden tablet (*abacus*) either smeared with wax, or with sand sprinkled over it, on which words were written with an iron *stylus*. Thus 'John,' 'the grace of Jehovah,' is the first word *written* under the Gospel; the aeon of the written Law had ended with *Cherem*, 'curse,' in Mal. iii. 24 (Bengel).

64. *he spake*] Rather, **he began to speak** (imperfect), the previous verb 'was opened' being an aorist.

65. *fear*] The minds of men at this period were full of dread and agitated expectancy, which had spread even to the heathen. Virg. *Ecl.* IV.; *Orac. Sibyl.* III.; Suet. *Vesp.* 4; Tac. *Hist.* V. 13; Jos. *Bell. Jud.* VI. 5, § 4.

66. *What manner of child*] Rather, **What then will this child be?**
And] Rather, **For indeed**, with ℵ, B, C, D, L, which read καὶ γάρ.
the hand of the Lord was with him] The turn of expression is Hebraistic, as throughout the chapter. Comp. xiii. 11; Acts xi. 21. "Let thy hand be upon the man of thy right hand," Ps. lxxx. 17.

father Zacharias was filled with the Holy Ghost, and prophesied, saying,

  Blessed *be* the Lord God of Israel;
  For he hath visited and redeemed his people,
  And hath raised up a horn of salvation for us
  In the house of his servant David;
  (As he spake by the mouth of his holy prophets,
  Which have been since the world began:)
  That *we* should be saved from our enemies,

68. *Blessed*] This hymn of praise is hence called the BENEDICTUS. It has been in use in Christian worship perhaps as far back as the days of St Benedict in the sixth century, and it was early recognised that it is the last Prophecy of the Old Dispensation, and the first of the New, and furnishes a kind of key to the evangelical interpretation of all prophecies. It is also a continual acknowledgment of the Communion of Saints under the two dispensations; for it praises God for the salvation which has been raised up for all ages out of the house of His servant David, and according to the ancient covenant which He made with Abraham (see Rom. iv. 11; Gal. iii. 29). Blunt, *Annotated Prayer Book*, p. 16.

the Lord God] Rather, **the Lord, the God.**

redeemed] Literally, "*made a ransom for.*" Tit. ii. 14.

69. *a horn of salvation*] A natural and frequent metaphor. Ezek. xxix. 21, "In that day will I cause the horn of the house of Israel to bud forth." Lam. ii. 3, "He hath cut off...all the horn of Israel." Ps. cxxxii. 17; 1 Sam. ii. 10, "He shall exalt the horn of His anointed." A Rabbinic writer says that there are ten horns—those of Abraham, Isaac, Joseph, Moses, the horn of the Law, of the Priesthood, of the Temple, and of Israel; and some add of the Messiah. They were all placed on the heads of the Israelites till they sinned, and then they were cut off and given to the Gentiles. Schöttgen, *Hor. Hebr.* ad loc. We find the same metaphor in classic writers. "Tunc pauper *cornua* sumit," Ov. *Art. Am.* I. 239; "addis *cornua* pauperi," Hor. *Od.* III. xxi. 18.

his servant] The word does not here mean 'son' in the original, being the rendering of the Hebrew *ebed*, Ps. cxxxii. 10.

70. *by the mouth of his holy prophets*] namely "in the Law of Moses, and in the Prophets, and in the Psalms," see on xxiv. 44.

since the world began] Rather, **of old** ($\dot{\alpha}\pi'$ $\alpha\dot{\iota}\hat{\omega}\nu os$). "At sundry times and in divers manners" (Heb. i. 1) but even "in old time" (2 Pet. i. 21) and dating back even to the promises to Eve and to Abraham (Gen. iii. 15, xxii. 18, xlix. 10) and the sceptre and the star of Balaam (Numb. xxiv. 17).

71. *That we should be saved*] Rather, **Salvation**—referring back to "a horn of salvation," to which it is in apposition. The previous verse is a parenthesis.

And from the hand of all that hate us;
72 To perform the mercy *promised* to our fathers,
And to remember his holy covenant;
73 The oath which he sware to our father Abraham,
74 That *he* would grant unto us, that *we* being delivered out of the hand of our enemies
Might serve him without fear,
75 In holiness and righteousness before him,
All the days of our life.
76 And thou, child, shalt be called the prophet of the Highest:
For thou shalt go before the face of the Lord
To prepare his ways;
77 To give knowledge of salvation unto his people
By the remission of their sins,

from our enemies] No doubt in the first instance the "enemies" from which the prophets had promised deliverance were literal enemies (Deut. xxxiii. 29; Is. xiv. 2, li. 22, 23, &c.), but every pious Jew would understand these words as applying also to spiritual enemies.

72, 73. *mercy...remember...oath*] These three words have been thought by some to be an allusion to the three names John ('Jehovah's *mercy*'); Zacharias ('*remembered* by Jehovah'), and Elizabeth (see p. 45). Such *paronomasiae*, or plays on words, are exceedingly common in the Bible. For similar possible instances of *latent* paronomasiae see the author's *Life of Christ*, I. 65; II. 200, 240.

72. *To perform the mercy promised to our fathers*] It is simply to do mercy towards our fathers. The "promised" is a needless addition of the E.V.

73. *The oath which he sware*] Gen. xii. 3, xvii. 4, xxii. 16, 17; comp. Heb. vii. 13, 14, 17.

75. *In holiness*] towards God,

and righteousness] towards men. We have the same words contrasted in 1 Thess. ii. 10, "how holily and righteously;" Eph. iv. 24, "in righteousness and holiness of the truth." Ὅσιος, 'holy,' is the Hebrew *Chásíd*, whence the 'Chasidim' (Pharisees); and δίκαιος the Hebrew *Tsaddík*, whence 'Sadducees.'

76. *child*] Rather, **little child** (*paidion*)—"quantillus nunc es," Bengel.

To prepare his ways] An allusion to the prophecies of the Forerunner in Is. xl. 3; Mal. iii. 1.

77. *knowledge of salvation*] A clear proof that these prophecies had not the local and limited sense of national prosperity which some have supposed.

By the remission] Rather, **In remission**. Comp. Acts v. 31, "to be a Prince and a Saviour, for to give repentance to Israel, and forgiveness of sins."

Through the tender mercy of our God; 78
Whereby the dayspring from on high hath visited us,
To give light to them that sit in darkness and *in* the 79
shadow of death,
To guide our feet into the way of peace.

And the child grew, and waxed strong in spirit, and was in 80 the deserts till the day of his shewing unto Israel.

78. *Through the tender mercy of our God*] Literally, "*Because of the heart of mercy.*" Σπλάγχνα (literally 'bowels') is a favourite word with St Paul to express emotion (2 Cor. vii. 15; Phil. i. 8, ii. 1; Philem. 7, 12, 20, &c.). The expression is common to Jewish (Prov. xii. 10, &c.) and classical writers.

the dayspring] The word *Anatole* is used by the LXX. to translate both *Motsah* 'the Dawn' (Jer. xxxi. 40) and *Tsemach* 'branch' (Zech. iii. 8, vi. 12. See on Matt. ii. 23). Here the context shews that the Dawn is intended. Mal. iv. 2, "Unto you that fear my name shall the Sun of Righteousness arise with healing in His wings." See Is. ix. 2; Matt. iv. 16; John i. 4, 5.

hath visited] or **shall visit**, in some MSS.

79. *in the shadow of death*] The Hebrew *Tsalmaveth*. Job x. 21, xxxviii. 17; Ps. xxiii. 4, cvii. 10; Is. ix. 2; Matt. iv. 16, &c.

80. *the child grew, and waxed strong in spirit*] The description resembles that of the childhood of Samuel (1 Sam. ii. 26) and of our Lord (Lk. ii. 40—52). Nothing however is said of 'favour with men.' In the case of the Baptist, as of others, 'the boy was father to the man,' and he probably shewed from the first that rugged sternness which is wholly unlike the winning grace of the child Christ. "The Baptist was no Lamb of God. He was a wrestler with life, one to whom peace does not come easily, but only after a long struggle. His restlessness had driven him into the desert, where he had contended for years with thoughts he could not master, and from whence he uttered his startling alarms to the nation. He was among the dogs rather than among the lambs of the Shepherd." (*Ecce Homo.*)

was in the deserts] Not in sandy deserts like those of Arabia, but in the wild waste region south of Jericho and the fords of Jordan to the shores of the Dead Sea. This was known as *Araboth* or *ha-Arabah*, 2 Kings xxv. 4, 5 (Heb.); Jer. xxxix. 5, lii. 8. See on vs. 39. This region, especially where it approached the Ghôr and the Dead Sea, was lonely and forbidding in its physical features, and would suit the stern spirit on which it also reacted. In 1 Sam. xxiii. 19 it is called Jeshimon or 'the Horror.' John was by no means the only hermit. The political unsettlement, the shamelessness of crime, the sense of secular exhaustion, the wide-spread Messianic expectation, marked 'the fulness of time.' Banus the Pharisee also lived a life of ascetic hardness in the Arabah, and Josephus tells us that he lived with him for three years in his mountain-cave on fruits and water. (Jos. *Vit.* 2.) But there is not in the Gospels the faintest trace of any intercourse be-

Ch. II. 1—7. *The Birth of Jesus Christ.*

2 And it came to pass in those days, *that* there went out a decree from Cesar Augustus, that all the world should be

tween John, or our Lord and His disciples, with the Essenes. The great Italian painters follow a right conception when they paint even the boy John as emaciated with early asceticism. In 2 Esdras ix. 24 the seer is directed to go into a field where no house is and to "taste no flesh, drink no wine, and eat only the flowers of the field," as a preparation for 'talking with the Most High.' It is doubtful whether Christian Art is historically correct in representing the infant Jesus and John as constant friends and playmates. Zacharias and Elizabeth, being aged, must have early left John an orphan, and his desert life began with his boyish years. Further, the habits of Orientals are exceedingly stationary, and when once settled it is only on the rarest occasions that they leave their homes. The training of the priestly boy and the 'Son of the Carpenter' (Matt. xiii. 55) of Nazareth had been widely different, nor is it certain that they had ever met each other until the Baptism of Jesus (John i. 31).

his shewing] his public ministry, literally, "appointment" or *manifestation*. The verb (*anedeixen*) occurs in x. 1; Acts i. 24. Thus St John's life, like that of our Lord, was spent first in hallowed seclusion, then in public ministry.

At this point ends the first very interesting document of which St Luke made use. The second chapter, though in some respects analogous to it, is less imbued with the Hebraic spirit and phraseology.

Ch. II. 1—7. The Birth of Jesus Christ.

1. *there went out a decree from Cesar Augustus, that all the world should be taxed*] Rather, **that there should be an enrolment of the habitable world.** The verb *apographesthai* is here probably passive, though we have the aorist middle *apograpsasthai* 'to enroll himself' in vs. 5. The registration (*apographē*) did not necessarily involve a taxing (*apotimēsis*), though it was frequently the first step in that direction. Two objections have been made to the historic credibility of the decree, and both have been fully met.

i. It is said 'that there is no trace of such a decree in secular history.' The answer is that (α) the *argumentum e silentio* is here specially invalid because there happens to be a singular deficiency of minute records respecting this epoch in the 'profane' historians. The history of Nicolaus of Damascus, the flatterer of Herod, is not extant. Tacitus barely touches on this period (*Ann.* I. 1, "*pauca* de Augusto"). There is a hiatus in Dion Cassius from A.U.C. 748—752. Josephus does not enter upon the history of these years. (β) There *are* distinct *traces* that such a census took place. Augustus with his own hand drew up a *Rationarium* of the Empire (a sort of Roman Doomsday Book, afterwards epitomised into a *Breviarium*), which included the allied

taxed. (*And* this taxing was first made when Cyrenius was
kingdoms (Tac. *Ann.* I. 11; Suet. *Aug.* 28), and appointed twenty Commissioners to draw up the necessary lists (Suidas s.v. ἀπογραφή).

2. It is said 'that in any case Herod, being a *rex socius* (for Judaea was not annexed to the Province of Syria till the death of Archelaus, A.D. 6), would have been exempt from such a registration.' The answer is that (α) the Clitae were obliged to furnish such a census though they were under an independent prince, Archelaus (Tac. *Ann.* VI. 41; cf. I. 11, *regna*). (β) That Herod, a mere creature of the Emperor, would have been the last person to resist his wishes (Jos. *Antt.* XIV. 14. 4; XV. 6. 7; XVI. 9. 3). (γ) That this Census, enforced by Herod, was so distasteful to the Jews that it probably caused the unexplained tumults which occurred at this very period (Jos. *Antt.* XVII. 2. 4; *B. J.* I. 33, § 2). This is rendered more probable by the Targum of Jonathan on Hab. iii. 17, which has, "the Romans shall be rooted out; they shall collect no more tribute (*Kesooma* = census) from Jerusalem" (Gfrörer, *Jahrh. d. Heils*, I. 42). That the Emperor could issue such a decree for Palestine shews that the fulfilment of the old Messianic promises was near at hand. The sceptre had departed from Judah; the Lawgiver from between his feet.

As regards both objections, we may say (i) that St Luke, a writer of proved carefulness and accuracy, writing for Gentiles who could at once have detected and exposed an error of this kind, is very unlikely (taking the lowest grounds) to have been guilty of such carelessness. (ii) That Justin Martyr, a native of Palestine, writing in the middle of the second century, three times appeals to the census-lists (ἀπογραφαί) made by Quirinus when he was first Procurator, bidding the Romans search their own archives as to the fact (*Apol.* I. 34. 46; *Dial. c. Tryph.* 78), as also does Tertullian (*Adv. Marc.* IV. 7. 19). (iii) If St Luke had made a mistake it would certainly have been challenged by such able critics as Celsus and Porphyry;—but they never impugn his statement. On every ground therefore we have reason to trust the statement of St Luke, and in this as in many other instances (see my *Life of St Paul*, I. 113) what have been treated as his 'manifest errors' have turned out to be interesting historic facts which he alone preserves for us.

all the world] Rather, **the habitable world**, i.e. the Roman Empire, the *orbis terrarum* (Acts xi. 28, &c.; Polyb. VI. 50).

2. *this taxing was first made when Cyrenius was governor of Syria*] Rather, **this first enrolment took place** (literally 'took place as the *first*') **when Quirinus was governor of Syria**. We are here met by an apparent error on which whole volumes have been written. Quirinus (or Quirinius, for the form of his name is not absolutely certain) was governor (Praeses, Legatus) of Syria in A.D. 6, *ten years after this time*, and he *then* carried out a census which led to the revolt of Judas of Galilee, as St Luke himself was aware (Acts v. 37). Hence it is asserted that St Luke made an error of ten years in the governorship of Quirinus, and the date of the census, which vitiates his historic authority. Two ways of obviating this difficulty may finally be rejected.

³ governor of Syria.) And all went to be taxed, every one
⁴ into his own city. And Joseph also went up from Galilee,

(α) One is to render the words 'took place *before* (*protē*) Quirinus was governor.' The translation is entirely untenable, and is not supported by *protos mou* 'before me' in John i. 30. And if this were the meaning the remark would be most unnecessary.

(β) Others would render the verb *egeneto* by 'took effect:'—this enrolment was begun at this period (B.C. 4 of our vulgar era) by P. Sentius Saturninus, but not completed till the Procuratorship of Quirinus A.D. 6. But this is to give a strained meaning to the verb, as well as to take the ordinal (*protē*) as though it were an adverb (*proton*).

(γ) A third, and more tenable, view is to extend the meaning of *hegemoneuontos* 'was governor' to imply that Quirinus, though not actually *Governor* of Syria, yet might be called *hegemon*, either (i) as one of the twenty taxers or commissioners of Augustus, or (ii) as holding some procuratorial office (as *Epitropos* or joint *Epitropos* with Herod; comp. Jos. *Antt.* XV. 10. 3; *B. J.* I. 10. 4). It is, however, a strong objection to solution (i) that the commissioners were ἄριστοι, *optimates* or nobles, whereas Quirinus was a *novus homo*: and to (ii) that St Luke is remarkably accurate in his use of titles.

(δ) A fourth view, and one which I still hold to be the right solution, is that first developed by A. W. Zumpt (*Das Geburtsjahr Christi*, 1870), and never seriously refuted though often sneered at. It is that Quirinus was *twice* Governor of Syria, once in B.C. 4 when he began the census (which may have been *ordered*, as Tertullian says, by Varus, or by P. Sentius Saturninus); and once in A.D. 6 when he carried it to completion. It is certain that in A.U.C. 753 Quirinus conquered the Homonadenses in Cilicia, and was *rector* to Gaius Caesar. Now it is highly probable that these Homonadenses were at that time under the jurisdiction of the propraetor of the Imperial Province of Syria, an office which must in that case have been held by Quirinus between B.C. 4—B.C. 1. The indolence of Varus and his friendship with Archelaus may have furnished strong reasons for superseding him, and putting the diligent and trustworthy Quirinus in his place. Whichever of these latter views be accepted, one thing is certain, that no error is *demonstrable*, and that on independent historical grounds, as well as by his own proved accuracy in other instances, we have the strongest reason to admit the probability of St Luke's reference.

Cyrenius] This is the Greek form of the name Quirinus, Orelli ad Tac. *Ann.* II. 30. All that we know of him is that he was of obscure and provincial origin, and rose to the consulship by activity and military skill, afterwards earning a triumph for his successes in Cilicia. He was harsh, and avaricious, but a loyal soldier; and he was honoured with a public funeral in A.D. 21 (Tac. *Ann.* II. 30, III. 22, 48; Suet. *Tib.* 49, &c.).

3. *every one into his own city*] This method of enrolment was a

PALESTINE
IN THE TIME OF OUR SAVIOUR

out of the city of Nazareth, into Judea, unto the city of David, which is called Bethlehem; (because he was of the house and lineage of David:) to be taxed with Mary his espoused wife, being great with child. And so it was *that*, while they were there, the days were accomplished that she

concession to Jewish prejudices. The Roman method was to enrol each person at his own place of residence. Incidentally this unexplained notice proves that St Luke is dealing with an historical enrolment.

4. *the city of David*] 1 Sam. xvii. 12, "David was the son of that Ephrathite of Bethlehem-Judah whose name was Jesse."

Bethlehem] Thus was fulfilled the prophecy of Mic. v. 2, "Thou, Bethlehem-Ephratah...out of thee shall he come forth unto me that is to be ruler in Israel." Cf. iv. 8, "And thou, O tower of the flock" (*Migdol Eder*, Gen. xxxv. 21), "unto thee shall it come, even the first dominion."

Bethlehem ('House of Bread,' to which the mystical method of Scriptural interpretation refers such passages as Is. xxxiii. 16, LXX.; John vi. 51, 58) is the very ancient Ephrath ('fruitful') of Gen. xxxv. 16, xlviii. 7; Ps. cxxxii. 6. It is a small town six miles from Jerusalem. It was the scene of the death of Rachel (Gen. xxxv. 19); of the story of Ruth, and of the early years of the life of David (1 Sam. xvi. 1; 2 Sam. xxiii. 15). The name is now corrupted into *Beitlahm*, 'house of flesh.'

of the house and lineage (rather, **family**) *of David*] The humble condition of Joseph as a provincial carpenter in no way militates against this. Hillel, the great contemporary Rabbi, who also claimed to be a descendant of David, began life as a half-starved porter; and numbers of beggars in the East wear the green turban which shews them to be undisputed descendants of Mohammed.

5. *to be taxed*] Rather, **to enrol himself**.

with Mary] It is uncertain whether her presence was obligatory (Dion. Hal. IV. 5; Lact. *De Mort. Persec.* 23) or voluntary; but it is obvious that at so trying a time, and after what she had suffered (Matt. i. 19), she would cling to the presence and protection of her husband. Nor is it wholly impossible that she saw in the providential circumstances a fulfilment of prophecy.

his espoused wife] Or, *who was betrothed to him*; 'wife' is omitted in B, D, L.

6. *the days were accomplished*] There is a reasonable certainty that our Lord was born B.C. 4 of our era, and it is *probable* that He was born (according to the unanimous tradition of the Christian Church) in winter. There is nothing to guide us as to the actual *day* of His birth. It was unknown to the ancient Christians (Clem. Alex. *Strom.* I. 21). Some thought that it took place on May 20 or April 20. There is no trace of the date Dec. 25 earlier than the fourth century, but it is accepted by Athanasius, Jerome, Ambrose, &c.

7 should be delivered. And she brought forth her firstborn son, and wrapped him in swaddling clothes, and laid him in a manger; because there was no room for them in the inn.

7. *firstborn*] The word has no bearing on the controversy as to the 'brethren of Jesus,' as it does not necessarily imply that the Virgin had other children. See Heb. i. 6, where first-born=only-begotten.

wrapped him in swaddling clothes] Ezek. xvi. 4. In her poverty she had none to help her, but (in the common fashion of the East) wound the babe round and round with swathes with her own hands.

in a manger] If the Received Text were correct it would be 'in *the* manger,' but the article is omitted by A, B, D, L. *Phatnē* is sometimes rendered 'stall' (as in Luke xiii. 15; 2 Chron. xxxii. 28, LXX.); but 'manger' is probably right here. It is derived from *pateomai*, 'I eat' (Curtius, *Griech. Et.* II. 84), and is used by the LXX. for the Hebrew אֵבוּס, 'crib,' in Prov. xiv. 4. Mangers are very ancient, and are to this day sometimes used as cradles in the East (Thomson, *Land and Book*, II. 533). The ox and the ass which are traditionally represented in pictures are only mentioned in the *apocryphal* Gospel of Matthew, xiv., and were suggested by Is. i. 3, and Hab. iii. 2, which in the LXX. and the ancient Latin Version (Vetus Itala) was mistranslated "Between two animals thou shalt be made known."

there was no room for them in the inn] *Kataluma* may also mean *guest-chamber* as in xxii. 11, but *inn* seems to be here the right rendering. There is another word for inn, *pandocheion* (x. 34), which implies an inn with a host. Bethlehem was a poor place, and its inn was probably a mere *khan* or *caravanserai*, which is an enclosed space surrounded by open recesses of which the paved floor (*leewan*) is raised a little above the ground. There is often no host, and the use of any vacant *leewan* is free, but the traveller pays a trifle for food, water, &c. If the khan be crowded the traveller must be content with a corner of the courtyard or enclosed place among the cattle, or else in the stable. The stable is often a limestone cave or grotto, and there is a very ancient tradition that this was the case in the khan of Bethlehem. (Just. Martyr, *Dial. c. Tryph.* c. 78, and the Apocryphal Gospels, *Protev.* xix., *Evang. Infant.* iii. &c.) If, as is most probable, the *traditional* site of the Nativity is the *real* one, it took place in one of the caves where St Jerome spent so many years (Ep. 24, *ad Marcell.*) as a hermit, and translated the Bible into Latin (the Vulgate). The khan perhaps dated back as far as the days of David under the name of the House or Hotel (*Gĕrooth*) of Chimham (2 Sam. xix. 37, 38; Jer. xli. 17).

The tender grace and perfect simplicity of the narrative is one of the marks of its truthfulness, and is again in striking contrast with the endlessly multiplied miracles of the Apocryphal Gospels. "The unfathomable depths of the divine counsels were moved; the fountains of the great deep were broken up; the healing of the nations was issuing forth; but

8—20. *The Angels to the Shepherds.*

And there were in the same country shepherds abiding in the field, keeping watch over their flock by night. And lo, *the* angel of the Lord came upon them, and the glory of the Lord shone round about them: and they were sore afraid. And the angel said unto them, Fear not: for behold, I bring you good tidings of great joy, which shall be to all people. For unto you is born this day in the city of David a Saviour, 8 9 10 11

nothing was seen on the surface of human society but this slight rippling of the water." Isaac Williams, *The Nativity.*

8—20. THE ANGELS TO THE SHEPHERDS.

8. *in the same country*] Tradition says that they were natives of the little village Beth-zur (Josh. xv. 58; Neh. iii. 16). They were feeding their flocks in the same fields from which David had been summoned to feed Jacob, God's people, and Israel His inheritance.

shepherds] Why these were the first to whom was revealed the birth of Him who was called the Lamb of God, we are not told. The sheep used for the daily sacrifice were pastured in the fields of Bethlehem.

abiding in the field] This does not prove, as some have supposed, that the Nativity took place in spring, for in some pastures of Palestine the shepherds to this day bivouac with their flocks in winter.

9. *And lo*] The phrase often introduces some strange or memorable event.

the angel] Rather, **an Angel**.

came upon them] *Epestê*—a common word in St Luke, who uses it eighteen times, xxiv. 4; Acts xii. 7, &c. It may mean *stood by them.*

the glory of the Lord] The Shechinah, or cloud of brightness which symbolised the Divine Presence, as in Ex. xxiv. 16; 1 Kings viii. 10; Is. vi. 1—3; Acts vii. 55. See on i. 35. The presence of the Shechinah was reckoned as one of the most precious blessings of Israel, Rom. ix. 4.

10. *good tidings*] the rendering of the verb *euangelizomai* (see on i. 19).

of great joy] See Is. lii. 7, lxi. 1; Rom. v. 11; 1 Pet. i. 8. The contrast of the condition of despair and sorrow into which the heathen world had sunk and the joy of Christians even in the deepest adversity —as when we find "*joy*" to be the key-note of the letter written to Philippi by the suffering prisoner St Paul—is a striking comment on this promise. Even the pictures and epitaphs of the gloomy catacombs are full of joy and brightness.

to all people] Rather, **to all the people**, i.e. of Israel.

11. *a Saviour*] It is a curious fact that 'Saviour' and 'Salvation,' so common in St Luke and St Paul (in whose writings they occur forty-four times), are comparatively rare in the rest of the New Testament. 'Saviour' only occurs in John iv. 42; 1 John iv. 14; and six times in

12 which is Christ the Lord. And this *shall be* a sign unto you; Ye shall find *the* babe wrapped in swaddling clothes,
13 lying in a manger. And suddenly there was with the angel a multitude of the heavenly host praising God, and saying,
14 Glory to God in the highest,
  And on earth peace,

2 Pet. and Jude; 'salvation' only in John iv. 22, and thirteen times in the rest of the N. T.

Christ the Lord] "God hath made that same Jesus whom ye crucified both Lord and Christ," Acts ii. 36; Phil. ii. 11. 'Christ' or 'Anointed' is the Greek equivalent of Messiah. In the Gospels it is almost invariably an appellative, 'the Christ.' But as time advanced it was more and more used without the article as a proper name. Our Lord was 'anointed' with the Holy Spirit as Prophet, Priest and King.

the Lord] In the lower sense the word is used as a mere title of distinction; in the higher sense it is (as in the LXX.) the equivalent of the Hebrew 'Jehovah'—the ineffable name. "We preach Christ Jesus the Lord," 2 Cor. iv. 5 (see Phil. ii. 11; Rom. xiv. 9; 1 Cor. viii. 6; "No one can say that Jesus is the Lord but by the Holy Ghost," 1 Cor. xii. 3).

12. *a sign*] Rather, **the sign.**
the babe] Rather, **a babe.**
13. *a multitude of the heavenly host*] The Sabaoth; Rom. ix. 29; Jas. v. 4. "Ten thousand times ten thousand stood before Him," Dan. vii. 10; Rev. v. 11, 12. The word is also used of the stars as objects of heathen worship, Acts vii. 42.

14. *in the highest*] i.e., in highest heaven, Job xvi. 19; Ps. cxlviii. 1; comp. "the heavenlies" in Eph. i. 3, &c.; Ecclus. xliii. 9.
on earth peace]

> "No war or battle's sound
>   Was heard the world around;
>   The idle spear and shield were high uphung:
>   The hookèd chariot stood
>   Unstained with hostile blood,
>   The trumpet spake not to the armèd throng;
>   And kings sat still with awful eye
>   As if they surely knew their sovran Lord was by."
>   MILTON, *Ode on the Nativity*.

This however is only an ideal aspect of affairs, and the closing at this time of the Temple of Janus had little or no meaning. It was not in *this* sense that the birth of Christ brought Peace. If we understood the expression thus we might well say with Coleridge:

> "Strange Prophecy! if all the screams
>   Of all the men that since have died

Good will towards men.

And it came to pass, as the angels were gone away from them into heaven, the shepherds said one to another, Let us now go *even* unto Bethlehem, and see this thing which is come to pass, which the Lord hath made known unto us. And they came with haste, and found Mary, and Joseph, and the babe lying in a manger. And when they had seen *it*, they made known abroad the saying which was told them concerning this child. And all they that heard *it* wondered at those *things* which were told them by the shepherds.

> "To realize war's kingly dreams
>   Had risen at once in one vast tide,
> The choral song of that vast multitude
>   Had been o'erpowered and lost amid the uproar rude."

The Angels sang indeed of such an *ultimate* Peace; but also of "the peace which passeth understanding;" of that peace whereof Christ said, "Peace I leave with you, my peace I give unto you; not as the world giveth give I unto you." See Prov. iii. 17, on which the Book of Zohar remarks that it means peace in heaven and on earth, and in this world and the next. As regards earthly peace He himself said, "Think not that I am come to send peace on earth: I came not to send peace, but a sword," Matt. x. 34; Lk. xii. 51. See this contrast magnificently shadowed forth in Is. ix. 5, 6.

Good will towards men] The reading *eudokia*, 'goodwill,' is found in B, but ℵ, A, D read *eudokias*, and if this be the right reading the meaning is "on earth peace **among men of good will**" (*hominibus bonae voluntatis*, Vulg.), i.e. those with whom God is well pleased. "The Lord taketh pleasure in them that hope in His mercy," Ps. cxlvii. 11; comp. xii. 32, "it is your Father's *good pleasure* to give you the kingdom." The construction "men of good will" would be rare in this sense, but the triple parallelism of the verse,

| Glory | to God | in the highest |
| Peace | to men whom God loves | on earth |

seems to favour it. In either case the verse implies that "being justified by faith we have peace with God through our Lord Jesus Christ," Rom. v. 1. In any case the "*towards*" is wrong, and must be altered into "among" (ἐν).

"Glory to God on high, on earth be peace,
  And love towards men of love—salvation and release."—KEBLE.

15. *Let us now go*] Rather, Come now! let us go.

16. *found*] The word is not merely εὗρον but ἀνεῦρον, *discovered* after search. The lamp hung from the centre of a rope would guide them to the khan, but among a crowd it would not be easy to find the new-born babe of the humble travellers.

17. *made known abroad*] Thus they were the first Christian preachers.

19 But Mary kept all these things, and pondered *them* in her
20 heart. And the shepherds returned, glorifying and praising God for all *the things* that they had heard and seen, as it was told unto them.

21. *The Circumcision.*

21 And when eight days were accomplished for the circumcising of the child, his name was called JESUS, which was *so* named of the angel before he was conceived in the womb.

22—24. *The Presentation in the Temple.*

22 And when the days of her purification according to the

19. *all these things*] or 'words.'

pondered] Literally, "*casting together*," i.e. comparing and considering; like our 'casting in mind.' Comp. Gen. xxxvii. 11, "his father *observed* the saying." She did not at once understand the full significance of all these events.

21. THE CIRCUMCISION.

21. *for the circumcising of the child*] Gen. xvii. 12. Doubtless the rite was performed by Joseph. "Jesus Christ was a minister of the circumcision" (i.e. went to the Jew first) "for the truth of God to confirm the promises made unto the fathers," Rom. xv. 8. Thus it became him 'to be made like unto His brethren, and to fulfil all righteousness,' Matt. iii. 15. Christ suffered pain thus early for our sake to teach us that, though He ordained for us the painless rite of baptism, we must practise the spiritual circumcision—the circumcision of the heart. He came "not to destroy the Law but to *fulfil*," Matt. v. 17—

" He, who with all heaven's heraldry whilere
  Entered the world, now bleeds to give us ease.
  Alas, how soon our sin
    Sore doth begin
      His infancy to seize!"

MILTON, *The Circumcision.*

his name was called JESUS] See on i. 31. The name of the child was bestowed at circumcision, as with us at baptism. Among Greeks and Romans also the *genethlia* and *nominalia* were on the eighth or ninth day. Observe the brief notice of Christ's circumcision compared with the fuller and more elaborate account of John's. "In the person of John the rite of circumcision solemnised its last glories."

22—24. THE PRESENTATION IN THE TEMPLE.

22. *her purification*] Rather, **their purification.** The reading αὐτῆς, 'her,' of the Received Text is almost unsupported. All the Uncials read αὐτῶν, 'their,' except D, which probably by an oversight reads αὐτοῦ,

law of Moses were accomplished, they brought him to Jerusalem, to present *him* to the Lord; (as it is written in 23 the law of the Lord, Every male that openeth the womb shall be called holy to the Lord;) and to offer a sacrifice 24 according to that which is said in the law of the Lord, A pair of turtledoves, or two young pigeons.

25—35. *Simeon and the Nunc Dimittis.*

And behold, there was a man in Jerusalem, whose name 25 *was* Simeon; and the same man *was* just and devout, waiting for the consolation of Israel: and the Holy Ghost

'His.' Strictly speaking, the *child* was never purified, but only the mother. The purification took place on the fortieth day after the Nativity, and till then a mother was not permitted to leave her house. The feast of the Presentation was known in the Eastern Church as the *Hypapanté*.

according to the law of Moses] See this Law in Lev. xii. 2—4. Jesus was "made of a woman, made under the Law, to redeem those that were under the Law, that we might receive the adoption of sons," Gal. iv. 4, 5.

23. *as it is written in the law of the Lord*] The tribe of Levi were sanctified to the Lord in lieu of the firstborn, and originally all the firstborn in excess of the number of the Levites had to be redeemed with five shekels of the sanctuary (about 15 shillings), a rule afterwards extended to *all* the firstborn. Ex. xiii. 2, xxii. 29, xxxiv. 19; Num. iii. 13, xviii. 15, 16.

24. *A pair of turtledoves, or two young pigeons*] The offering appointed was a yearling lamb for a burnt-offering, and a young pigeon or turtledove for a sin-offering, which were to be brought to the door of the tabernacle and with which "the priest made an atonement for her and she shall be clean." But the Law of Moses, with that thoughtful tenderness which characterises many of its provisions, allowed a *poor* mother to bring two turtledoves instead; and since turtledoves (being migratory) are not always procurable, and *old* pigeons are not easily caught, offered the alternative of "two *young* pigeons." Lev. xii. 6—8. (Tristram.)

25—35. SIMEON AND THE NUNC DIMITTIS.

25. *a man...whose name was Simeon*] This cannot be Rabban Shimeon the son of Hillel (whom the Talmud is on this account supposed to pass over almost unnoticed), because he would hardly have been spoken of so slightly as "*anthropos*," 'a person.' The Apocryphal Gospels call him "the great teacher" (*James* xxvi., *Nicod*. xvi.).

waiting for the consolation of Israel] See Gen. xlix. 18. "They shall not be ashamed that wait for me," Is. xlix. 23. "Comfort ye, comfort ye my people, saith your God," Is. xl. 1. Joseph of Arima-

26 was upon him. And it was revealed unto him by the Holy Ghost, that *he* should not see death, before he had seen the
27 Lord's Christ. And he came by the Spirit into the temple: and when the parents brought in the child Jesus, to do for
28 him after the custom of the law, then took he him *up* in his arms, and blessed God, and said,
29   Lord, now lettest thou thy servant depart
     In peace, according to thy word:
30   For mine eyes have seen thy salvation,
31   Which thou hast prepared before the face of all people;
32   A light to lighten the Gentiles, and the glory of thy people Israel.

thea is also described as one who "*waited* for the Kingdom of God," Mk. xv. 43. "May I see the consolation of Israel!" was a common Jewish formula, and a prayer for the Advent of the Messiah was daily used.

26. *it was revealed unto him*] Christian legend says that he had stumbled at Is. vii. 14, "Behold, a virgin shall conceive," and had received a divine intimation that he should not die till he had seen it fulfilled (Nicephorus, A.D. 1450). The notion of his extreme age is not derived from Scripture but from the 'Gospel of the Nativity of Mary,' which says that he was 113.

the Lord's Christ] The Anointed of Jehovah.

27. *by the Spirit*] Rather, **in the Spirit.**

brought in the child] The Arabic Gospel of the Infancy (vi.) says that he saw Him shining like a pillar of light in His mother's arms, which is probably derived from vs. 32.

28. *in his arms*] Hence he is sometimes called *Theodokos*, 'the receiver of God,' as Ignatius is sometimes called *Theophoros*, 'borne of God,' from the fancy that he was one of the children whom Christ took in His arms (see on ix. 47).

29. *Lord, now lettest thou thy servant depart in peace*] Rather, **Now art Thou setting free Thy slave, O Master, according to Thy word, in peace.** This rapturous Psalm—the *Nunc Dimittis*—has formed a part of Christian evening worship certainly since the fifth century. *Despotes* is not often used of God (Acts iv. 24; Rev. vi. 10).

In peace] On leaving a *dying* person the Jews said, 'Go *in peace*' (*B*eshalôm), Gen. xv. 15. Otherwise they said, 'Go *to peace*' (*Le* shalôm) as Jethro did to Moses. See on vii. 50.

30. *thy salvation*] Not τὴν σωτηρίαν but τὸ σωτήριον which seems to have a wider meaning.

32. *to lighten the Gentiles*] Rather, **for revelation to.** A memorable prophecy, considering that even the Apostles found it hard to grasp the full admission of the Gentiles, clearly as it had been indicated in older prophecy, as in Ps. xcviii. 2, 3. "All the ends of the earth have seen

And Joseph and his mother marvelled at those *things* 33 which were spoken of him. And Simeon blessed them, 34 and said unto Mary his mother, Behold, this *child* is set for the fall and rising again of many in Israel; and for a sign which shall be spoken against; (yea, a sword shall pierce 35 through thy own soul also,) that the thoughts of many hearts may be revealed.

the salvation of our God," Is. lii. 10. "I will give thee for a covenant of the people, for a light of the Gentiles," Is. xlii. 6, xlix. 6.

33. *Joseph*] The undoubted reading is "*His father*," א, B, D, L, &c.

of him] Rather, **about Him.**

34. *is set*] Literally, "*lies.*" The metaphor is taken from a stone which may either become 'a stone of stumbling' and 'a rock of offence' (Is. viii. 14; Rom. ix. 32, 33; 1 Cor. i. 23), or 'a precious corner-stone' (1 Pet. ii. 7, 8; Acts iv. 11; 1 Cor. iii. 11).

for the fall and rising again of many in Israel] Rather, **for the falling and rising**. For the fall of many Pharisees, Herodians, Sadducees, Nazarenes, Gadarenes; and for the rising—a savour of life unto life—of all that believed on Him. In some cases—as that of Peter and the dying robber—they who fell afterwards rose.

which shall be spoken against] Rather, **which is spoken against**. "As concerning this sect we know that *everywhere* it is spoken against," Acts xxviii. 22. Jesus was called "this deceiver," "a Samaritan," "a demoniac," and in the Talmud he is only alluded to as 'So and So' (*Peloni*), '*that* man' (*Otho haîsh*), 'Absalom,' 'the hung' (*Thalooi*), 'the son of Pandera,' &c. To this day *Nusrâni*, 'Christian,' is—after 'Jew'—the most stinging term of reproach throughout Palestine. Among Pagans the Christians were charged with cannibalism, incest, and every conceivable atrocity, and Suetonius, Pliny, Tacitus have no gentler words for Christianity than 'an execrable, extravagant, or malefic superstition.' To holy men like Zacharias and Simeon God had revealed that the Glory of the Messiah was to be perfected by suffering (Heb. ii. 10). They, at least, did not expect an earthly conqueror—

> "Armed in flame, all glorious from afar,
> Of hosts the captain, and the Lord of War."

35. *a sword*] The word *rhomphaia*, probably a broad Thracian sword, only occurs elsewhere in the New Testament in Rev., i. 16, &c., but it is used in the LXX., as in Zech. xiii. 7, "Awake, O sword, against my shepherd." Almost from the very birth of Christ the sword began to pierce the soul of the '*Mater Dolorosa;*' and what tongue can describe the weight of mysterious anguish which she felt as she watched the hatred and persecution which followed Jesus and saw Him die in anguish on the cross amid the execrations of all classes of those whom He came to save!

that the thoughts of many hearts may be revealed] Rather, **that the reasonings out of many hearts may be revealed.** The word *dialo-*

36—40. *Anna the Prophetess. The Return to Nazareth.*

36 And there was *one* Anna, a prophetess, the daughter of Phanuel, of the tribe of Aser: she was of a great age, and
37 had lived with a husband seven years from her virginity; and she was a widow of about fourscore and four years, which departed not from the temple, but served *God* with fastings
38 and prayers night and day. And she coming in that instant gave thanks *likewise* unto the Lord, and spake of

gismoi generally has a bad sense as in v. 22; Matt. xv. 19; Rom. i. 21. By way of comment see the reasonings of the Jews in John ix. 16: 1 Cor. xi. 19; 1 John ii. 19.

36—40. ANNA THE PROPHETESS. THE RETURN TO NAZARETH.

36. *Anna*] The same name as Hannah (1 Sam. i. 20), from the root *Chânan*, 'he was gracious.'

a prophetess] like Miriam, Deborah, Huldah (2 Chron. xxxiv. 22).

Phanuel] 'The Face of God;' the same word as Peniel, Gen. xxxii. 30.

Aser] Though the Ten Tribes were lost, individual Jews who belonged to them had preserved their genealogies. Thus Tobit was of the tribe of Naphthali (Tob. i. 1). Comp. "our twelve tribes," Acts xxvi. 7; James i. 1.

from her virginity] I.e. she had been married only seven years, and was now 84 years old. ℵ, A, B, L read ἕως (for ὡς) which is best taken with "of great age," the intervening words being parenthetic, *a widow even unto fourscore years*.

37. *departed not*] She was present (that is) at all the stated hours of prayer; unless we suppose that her position as a Prophetess had secured her the right of living in one of the Temple chambers, and perhaps of doing some work for it like trimming the lamps (as is the Rabbinic notion about Deborah, derived from the word *Lapidoth* 'splendours').

fastings] The Law of Moses had only appointed one yearly fast, on the Great Day of Atonement. But the Pharisees had adopted the practice of 'fasting twice in the week,' viz. on Monday and Thursday, when Moses is supposed to have ascended, and descended from, Sinai (see on xviii. 12), and had otherwise multiplied and extended the simple original injunction (v. 33).

prayers] Rather, *supplications* (a more special word).

night and day] 'Night' is put first by the ordinary Hebrew idiom (as in the Greek word νυχθήμερον) which arose from their notion that 'God made the world in six days and seven nights.' Comp. Acts xxvi. 7, "unto which promise our twelve tribes, instantly serving God night and day (Greek), hope to come." 1 Tim. v. 5, "she that is *a widow indeed, and desolate*, trusteth in God, and continueth in supplications and prayers night and day."

him to all them that looked for redemption in Jerusalem.
And when they had performed all *things* according to the 39
law of the Lord, they returned into Galilee, to their own city
Nazareth. And the child grew, and waxed strong in spirit, 40
filled with wisdom: and the grace of God was upon him.

41—52. The Passover Visit to the Temple.

Now his parents went to Jerusalem every year at the feast 41

38. *that looked for redemption*] See xxiv. 21; Mk. xv. 43; 1 Cor. i. 7; Tit. ii. 13; Heb. ix. 28. See Excursus VII.

in Jerusalem] The readings vary. Perhaps it should be *for the redemption of Jerusalem*.

39. Between this verse and the last come the events narrated by St Matthew only—namely the Visit of the Magi; the Flight into Egypt; and the massacre of the Innocents. It is difficult to believe that either of the Evangelists had seen the narrative of the other, because the primâ facie inference from either singly would be imperfectly correct. They *supplement* each other, because they each narrate the truth, though probably neither of them was aware of *all* that has been delivered to us.

40. *filled*] Rather, **being filled.** The growth of our Lord is here described as a natural human growth. The nature of the 'Hypostatic Union' of His Divine and Human nature—what is called the *Perichoresis* or *Communicatio idiomatum*—is one of the subtlest and least practical of mysteries. The attempt to define and enter into it was only forced upon the Church by the speculations of Oriental heretics who vainly tried "to soar into the secrets of the Deity on the waxen wings of the senses." This verse (and still more vs. 52) is a stronghold against the Apollinarian heresy which held that in Jesus the Divine Logos took the place of the human soul. Against the four conflicting heresies of Arius, Apollinarius, Nestorius and Eutyches, which respectively denied the true Godhead, the perfect manhood, the indivisible union, and the entire distinctness of the Godhead and manhood in Christ, the Church, in the four great Councils of Nice (A.D. 325), Constantinople (A.D. 381), Ephesus (A.D. 431), and Chalcedon (A.D. 451), established the four words which declare her view of the nature of Christ—*alethôs, teleôs, adiairetôs, asunchutôs*—'truly' God; 'perfectly' Man; 'indivisibly' God-Man, 'distinctly' God and Man. See Hooker, *Eccl. Pol.* V. lv. 10.

the grace of God was upon him] Is. xi. 2, 3. "Full of grace and truth," John i. 14. "Take notice here that His doing nothing wonderful was itself a kind of wonder...As there was power in His actions, so is there power in His silence, in His inactivity, in His retirement." Bonaventura. The worthless legends and inventions of many of the Apocryphal Gospels deal almost exclusively with the details of the Virginity of Mary, and the Infancy of Christ, which are passed over in the Gospels in these few words.

41—52. THE PASSOVER VISIT TO THE TEMPLE.

41. *his parents*] The great Rabbi Hillel had *recommended* women to

42 of the passover. And when he was twelve years old, they
43 went up to Jerusalem after the custom of the feast. And
when they had fulfilled the days, as they returned, the child

attend the Passover. It was not enjoined by the Law, but the Jews admired it as a pious practice. (*Mechilta*, f. 17. 2 in Schöttgen.)

at the feast of the passover] Ex. xxiii. 15—17; Deut. xvi. 1—16. The custom of going up *three times* a year seems long to have fallen into abeyance with most Jews. 1 Sam. i. 21, "the yearly sacrifice."

42. *when he was twelve years old*] No single word breaks the silence of the Gospels respecting the childhood of Jesus from the return to Nazareth till this time. We infer indeed from scattered hints in Scripture that He "*began to do*" His work before He "*began to teach*," and being "tempted in all points like as we are" won the victory from His earliest years, alike over positive and negative temptations. (Heb. v. 8. See Ullmann, *Sinlessness of Jesus*, E. Tr. p. 140.) Up to this time He had grown as other children grow, only in a childhood of stainless and sinless beauty—"as the flower of roses in the spring of the year, and as lilies by the waters," Ecclus. xxxix. 13, 14. This incident of His 'confirmation,' as in modern language we might call it, is "the solitary flowret out of the wonderful enclosed garden of the thirty years, plucked precisely there where the swollen bud at a distinctive crisis bursts into flower." Stier, *Words of Jesus*, I. 18.

This silence of the Evangelists is a proof of their simple faithfulness, and is in striking contrast with the blaze of foolish and dishonouring miracles with which the Apocryphal Gospels degrade the Divine Boyhood. See my *Life of Christ*, I. 58—66. Meanwhile we are permitted to see (i) That our Lord never attended the schools of the Rabbis (Mk. vi. 2; John vi. 42, vii. 15), and therefore that His teaching was absolutely original, and that He would therefore be regarded by the Rabbis as a 'man of the people,' or 'unlearned person.' (See Acts iv. 13; T. B. *Berachôth*, f. 47. 2; Ecclus. xxxviii. 24 fg.) (ii) That He had learnt to write (John viii. 6). (iii) That He was acquainted not only with Aramaic, but with Hebrew, Greek, and perhaps Latin (*Life of Christ*, I. 91); and (iv) That he had been deeply impressed by the lessons of nature (id. I. 93).

twelve years old] Up to this age a Jewish boy was called 'little,' afterwards he was called 'grown up,' and became a 'Son of the Law,' or 'Son of the Precepts.' At this age he was presented on the Sabbath called the 'Sabbath of Phylacteries' in the Synagogue, and began to wear the phylacteries with which his father presented him. According to the Jews twelve was the age at which Moses left the house of Pharaoh's daughter, and Samuel was called, and Solomon gave his judgment, and Josiah carried out his reform. (Jos. *Antt.* II. 9. 6, V. 10. 4.)

43. *fulfilled the days*] Ex. xii. 15.

the child Jesus] Rather, "*the boy Jesus*" (ὁ παῖς). St Luke seems purposely to have narrated something about the Saviour at every stage

Jesus tarried behind in Jerusalem; and Joseph and his mother knew not *of it*. But they, supposing him to have 44 been in the company, went a day's journey; and they sought him among *their* kinsfolk and acquaintance. And when they 45 found him not, they turned back again to Jerusalem, seeking him. And it came to pass, *that* after three days they found 46 him in the temple, sitting in the midst of the doctors, both hearing them, and asking them *questions*. And all that heard 47

of His earthly existence as babe (ii. 16), little child (ii. 40), boy, and man.

tarried behind] Among the countless throngs of Jews who flocked to the Passover—nearly three millions according to Josephus (*Antt.* VI. 9. 3)—nothing would be easier than to lose sight of one young boy in the thronged streets, or among the thousands of booths outside the city walls. Indeed it is an incident which to this day often occurs at Jerusalem in similar cases. It should be also remembered that at the age of 12 an Eastern boy is far more mature than is the case with Northern nations, and that at that age a far wider liberty was allowed him.

Joseph and his mother] The true reading is probably **His parents**, ℵ, B, D, L.

knew not of it] The fact is very interesting as shewing the naturalness and unconstraint in which our Lord was trained.

44. *went a day's journey*] Probably to *Beeroth*, six miles north of Jerusalem. In the numerous and rejoicing caravans of kinsmen and fellow-countrymen relations are often separated without feeling any anxiety.

sought him] The word implies *anxious* and *careful* search.

46. *after three days*] This, in the Jewish idiom, probably means 'on the third day.' One day was occupied by the journey to Beeroth; on the second, they sought him in the caravans and at Jerusalem; the next day they found him in the Temple. The unsettled state of the country would add to their alarm.

in the temple] Probably in one of the numerous chambers which ran round the Court, and abutted on the actual building.

sitting] Doubtless at the feet of the Rabbis, as was the custom of Jewish boys when sitting began to be permitted.

in the midst of the doctors] Rather, **teachers**. The most eminent Rabbis of this period—some of whom may have been present—were Hillel, his rival Shammai, and his son Rabban Shimeon, Babha ben Butah, Nicodemus, Jochanan ben Zakkai, &c.

hearing them, and asking them questions] Obviously with all modest humility. The Apocryphal Gospels characteristically degrade this scene, and represent the boy Christ as behaving with a forwardness which most flagrantly contradicts the whole tenor of the narrative, and would have been specially displeasing to Jewish elders (*Pirke Abhôth*, V. 12. 15).

⁴⁸ him were astonished at his understanding and answers. And when they saw him, they were amazed: and his mother said unto him, Son, why hast thou thus dealt with us? behold, ⁴⁹ thy father and I have sought thee sorrowing. And he said unto them, How *is it* that ye sought me? wist ye not that I ⁵⁰ must be about my Father's *business?* And they understood ⁵¹ not the saying which he spake unto them. And he went down with them, and came to Nazareth, and was subject

47. *were astonished*] Similar incidents are narrated of Rabbi Eliezer Ben Azariah; of Rabbi Ashi, the compiler of the Babylonian Talmud; and (by himself) of Josephus (*Vit.* 2). See Excursus VII.

48. *they were amazed*] The "*people of the land,*" such as were the simple peasants of Galilee, held their great teachers in the deepest awe, and hitherto the silent, sweet, obedient childhood of Jesus had not prepared them for such a scene.

Son, why hast thou thus dealt with us?] Rather, **My child, why didst thou treat us thus?**

have sought thee sorrowing] Rather, **were searching for thee with aching hearts.**

49. *about my Father's business*] Rather, **in my Father's house.** See Excursus I. These words are very memorable as being *the first recorded words of Jesus.* They bear with them the stamp of authenticity in their half-vexed astonishment, and perfect mixture of dignity and humility. It is remarkable too, that He does not accept the phrase "Thy father" which Mary had employed. "Did ye not know?" recalls their fading memory of Who He was; and the "I must" lays down the law of devotion to His Father by which He was to walk even to the Cross. Ps. xl. 7—9. "My meat is to do the will of Him that sent Me and to finish His work," John iv. 34. For His *last* recorded words, see Acts i. 7, 8.

my Father's] It is remarkable that Christ always says ὁ πατήρ μου (with the article) but teaches us to say πατὴρ ἡμῶν (without the article): e.g. in John xx. 17 it is, "I ascend unto the Father of me and Father of you." God is His Father in a different way from that in which He is ours. He is our Father only because He is *His* Father. See Pearson *On the Creed*, Art. i.

50. *they understood not*] Words which might stand as the epitome of much of His ministry, ix. 45, xviii. 34; Mk. ix. 32; John x. 6, i. 10, 11. The meaning however is not that they had any doubt as to what the grammatical construction of His words implied; but only as to their bearing and appropriateness to the circumstances of so young a child.

51. *with them*] We may infer from the subsequent omission of Joseph's name, and from the traditional belief of his age, that he died shortly after this event, as the Apocryphal Gospels assert.

to Nazareth] In many respects there was a divine fitness in this spot for the human growth of Jesus—"as a tender plant and a root out of the dry ground." Apart from the obscurity and evil fame of Nazareth

unto them: but his mother kept all these sayings in her heart. And Jesus increased in wisdom and stature, and in 52 favour with God and man.

CH. III. 1—9. *Baptism and Preaching of John the Baptist.*

Now in the fifteenth year of the reign of Tiberius Cesar, 3

which were meant to teach lessons similar to those of which we have just spoken, we may notice (i) its *seclusion*. It lies in a narrow cleft in the limestone hills which form the boundary of Zabulon entirely out of the ordinary roads of commerce, so that none could say that our Lord had learnt either from Gentiles or from Rabbis. (ii) Its beauty and peacefulness. The flowers of Nazareth are famous, and the appearance of its inhabitants shews its healthiness. It was a home of humble peace and plenty. The fields of its green valley are fruitful, and the view from the hill which overshadows it is one of the loveliest and most historically striking in all Palestine.

was subject unto them] "He made Himself of no reputation, and took upon Him the form of a servant," Phil. ii. 7; Is. liii. 2. With the exception of these two verses, the Gospels preserve but one single word to throw light on the Life of our Lord, between His infancy and His baptism. That word is "*the carpenter*" in Mk. vi. 3, altered in some MSS. out of irreverent and mistaken reverence into "*the son of the* carpenter." They shew that (i) our Lord's life was spent in *poverty* but not in pauperism; (ii) that He sanctified labour as a pure and noble thing; (iii) that God looks on the heart, and that the dignity or humility, the fame or obscurity, of the outer lot is of no moment in His eyes. Rom. xiv. 17, 18.

52. *increased*] Rather, **advanced**. The word is derived from pioneers *cutting down* trees in the path of an advancing army. Comp. 1 Sam. ii. 26, and the description of an ideal youth in Prov. iii. 3, 4.

stature] Rather, **age** (as in xii. 25), though the word sometimes means stature (xix. 3).

favour with God and man] Rather, **men**. Prov. iii. 4, "So shalt thou find favour and good success (*marg.*) in the sight of God and man." *Pirke Abhôth*, III. 10, "In whomsoever the mind of men delights, in him also the Spirit of God delights."

CH. III. 1—9. BAPTISM AND PREACHING OF JOHN THE BAPTIST.

1. *in the fifteenth year of the reign of Tiberius Cesar*] If the accession of Tiberius be dated from the death of Augustus, Aug. 19, A.U.C. 767, this would make our Lord *thirty-two* at His baptism. St Luke, however, follows a common practice in dating the reign of Tiberius from the period of his *association with Augustus* as joint Emperor A.U.C. 765. (Tac. *Ann.* I. 3; Suet. *Aug.* 97; Vell. Paterc. 103.) Our Lord's baptism thus took place in A.U.C. 780.

Pontius Pilate being governor of Judea, and Herod being tetrarch of Galilee, and his brother Philip tetrarch of Iturea

Tiberius Cesar] The stepson and successor of Augustus. At this period of his reign he retired to the island of Capreae (Tac. *Ann.* IV. 74), where he plunged into horrible private excesses, while his public administration was most oppressive and sanguinary. The recent attempts to defend his character break down under the accumulated and unanimous weight of ancient testimony.

Pontius Pilate] He was Procurator for ten years, A.D. 25—36. His predecessors had been Coponius (A.D. 6—10), M. Ambivius, Annius Rufus, and Valerius Gratus (A.D. 14—25). He was succeeded by Marcellus, Fadus, Tiberius Alexander, Cumanus, Felix, Festus, Albinus and Florus. For an account of him see on xxiii. 1.

governor] His strict title was *epitropos* or Procurator (Jos. *Antt.* xx. 6, § 2), which does not however occur in the N.T. except in the sense of 'steward' (Lk. viii. 3). *Hegemon* was a more general term. (Matt. x. 18; 1 Pet. ii. 14.) His relation to the Herods was much the same as that of the Viceroy of India to the subject Maharajahs.

Herod] Herod Antipas, the son of Herod the Great and the Samaritan lady Malthace. He retained his kingdom for more than 40 years, at the end of which he was banished (A.D. 39) to Lugdunum (probably St Bertrand de Comminges), chiefly through the machinations of his nephew Herod Agrippa I. (the Herod of Acts xii. 1). See the *Stemma Herodum* on p. 39, and for further particulars of his character see on xiii. 32.

tetrarch] The word properly means a ruler of a *fourth part* of a country, but afterwards was used for any tributary prince or ethnarch. At this time Judaea, Samaria and Galilee were the provinces of Judaea. Antipas, Philip and Lysanias are the only three to whom the term 'tetrarch' is applied in the N.T. Antipas also had the courtesy-title of 'king' (Mk. vi. 14, &c.), and it was in the attempt to get this title officially confirmed to him that he paid the visit to Rome which ended in his banishment. He was tetrarch for more than 40 years, from B.C. 4 to A.D. 39.

of Galilee] This province is about 25 miles from North to South, and 27 from East to West,—about the size of Bedfordshire. Lower Galilee included the district from the plain of Akka to the shores of the Sea of Galilee, and was mainly composed of the rich plain of Esdraelon (or Jezreel). Upper Galilee included the mountain range between the Upper Jordan and Phoenicia. Galilee was thus the main scene of our Lord's ministry. It was surpassingly rich and fertile (Jos. *B. J.* I. 15. 5, III. 10, §§ 7, 8). See on i. 26. Herod's dominions included the larger though less populous district of Peraea; but the flourishing towns of Decapolis (Gerasa, Gadara, Damascus, Hippos, Pella, &c.) were independent.

his brother Philip] Herod Philip, son of Herod the Great and Cleopatra, who afterwards married his niece Salome, daughter of the other Herod Philip (who lived in a private capacity at Rome) and of his half-

and of the region of Trachonitis, and Lysanias the tetrarch of Abilene, Annas and Caiaphas being the high priests, the 2

sister and sister-in-law Herodias. This tetrarch seems to have been the best of the Herods (Jos. *Antt.* XVII. 2. § 4), and the town of Caesarea *Philippi* which he beautified was named from him.

of Ituraea and of the region of Trachonitis] His tetrarchate also included Batanaea (Bashan), Auranitis (the Hauran), Gaulanitis (Golân), and some parts about Jamnia (Jos. *B. J.* II. 6, § 3). Ituraea (now Jedûr) was at the foot of Mount Hermon, and was named from Jetur, son of Ishmael (Gen. xxv. 15, 16). The Ituraeans were marauders, famous for the use of the bow, and protected by their mountain fastnesses. (Strabo, XVI. 2; Lucan, *Phars.* VII. 230.) Trachonitis, also a country of robbers (Jos. *Antt.* XVI. 9 §§ 1, 2), is the Greek rendering of the Aramaic Argob (a region about 22 miles from N. to S. by 14 from W. to E.), and means 'a rough or stony tract.' It is the modern province of el-Lejâh, and the ancient kingdom of Og—"an ocean of basaltic rocks and boulders, tossed about in the wildest confusion, and intermingled with fissures and crevices in every direction." Herod Philip received this tetrarchate by bequest from his father (Jos. *B. J.* II. 6, § 3).

Lysanias the tetrarch of Abilene] The mention of this minute particular is somewhat singular, but shews St Luke's desire for at least one rigid chronological *datum*. It used to be asserted that St Luke had here fallen into another chronological error, but his probable accuracy has, in this point also, been completely vindicated. There was a Lysanias king of Chalcis under Mount Lebanon, and therefore in all probability tetrarch of Abilene, in the days of Antony and Cleopatra, 60 years *before* this period (Jos. *B. J.* I. 13, § 1); and there was *another* Lysanias, probably a grandson of the former, in the reigns of Caligula and Claudius, 20 years *after* this period (Jos. *Antt.* XV. 4, § 1). No intermediate Lysanias is recorded in history, but there is not a shadow of proof that the Lysanias *here* mentioned may not be the second of these two, or more probably some Lysanias who came between them, perhaps the son of the first and the father of the second. Even M. Renan admits that after reading at Baalbek the inscription of Zenodorus (Boeckh, *Corp. Inscr. Graec.* no. 4521) he infers the correctness of the Evangelist (*Vie de Jésus*, p. xiii.; *Les Évangiles*, p. 263). It is indeed, on the lowest grounds, inconceivable that so careful a writer as St Luke should have deliberately gone out of his way to introduce so apparently superfluous an allusion at the risk of falling into a needless error. Lysanias is perhaps mentioned because he had Jewish connexions (Jos. *Antt.* XIV. 7, § 4).

of Abilene] Abila was a town 18 miles from Damascus and 38 from Baalbek. The district of which it was the capital is probably here mentioned because it subsequently formed part of the Jewish territory, having been assigned by Caligula to his favourite Herod Agrippa I. in A.D. 36. The name is derived from *Abel* 'a meadow.'

Annas and Caiaphas being the high priests] Rather, **in the high-priesthood of Annas and of Caiaphas**, for the true reading is undoubt-

word of God came unto John the son of Zacharias in the

edly ἀρχιερέως (א, A, B, C, D, E, &c.), and a similar expression occurs in Acts iv. 6. But here St Luke is charged (on grounds as untenable as in the former instances) with yet another mistake. Annas or Hanan the son of Seth had been High Priest from A.D. 7—14, and had therefore, by this time, been deposed for at least 15 years; and his son-in-law Joseph Caiaphas, the *fourth* High Priest since his deposition, had been appointed in A.D. 24. The order had been as follows:—

    Annas or Ananus (Hanan), A.D. 7.
    Ishmael Ben Phabi, A.D. 15.
    Eleazar son of Annas, A.D. 15.
    Simon son of Kamhith, A.D. 16.
    Joseph Caiaphas, A.D. 17.

How then can Annas be called High Priest in A.D. 27? The answer is (i.) that by the Mosaic Law the High priesthood was held for life (Numb. xxxv. 25), and since Annas had only been deposed by the arbitrary caprice of the Roman Procurator Valerius Gratus he would still be legally and religiously regarded as High Priest by the Jews (Numb. xxxv. 25); (ii.) that he held in all probability the high office of *Sagan haccohanim* 'deputy' or 'chief' of the Priests (2 K. xxv. 18), or of *Nasi* 'President of the Sanhedrin,' and at least of the *Ab Beth Dîn*, who was second in the Sanhedrin; (iii.) that the nominal, official, High Priests of this time were mere puppets of the civil power, which appointed and deposed them at will in rapid succession, so that the title was used in a looser sense than in earlier days. The High Priesthood was in fact at this time in the hands of a clique of some half-dozen Herodian, Sadducaean and alien families, whose ambition it was to bear the title for a time without facing the burden of the necessary duties. Hence any one who was unusually prominent among them would naturally bear the title of 'High Priest' in a popular way, especially in such a case as that of Hanan, who, besides having been High Priest, was a man of vast wealth and influence, so that five also of his sons, as well as his son-in-law, became High Priests after him. The language of St Luke and the Evangelists (Joh. xi. 49) is therefore in strict accordance with the facts of the case in attributing the High Priesthood at this epoch rather to *a caste* than to a person. Josephus (*B. J.* II. 20, § 4) who talks of "*one of* the High Priests" and the Talmud which speaks of "the sons of the High Priests" use the same sort of language. There had been no less than 28 of these phantom High Priests in 107 years (Jos. *Antt.* XX. 10, § 1), and there must have been at least five living High Priests and ex-High Priests at the Council that condemned our Lord. The Jews, even in the days of David, had been familiar with the sort of co-ordinate High Priesthood of Zadok and Abiathar. For the greed, rapacity and luxury of this degenerate hierarchy, see my *Life of Christ*, II. 329, 330, 342.

in the wilderness] Mainly, as appears from the next verse, the Arabah, the sunken valley north of the Dead Sea—el Ghôr—"the deepest and hottest chasm in the world" (Humboldt, *Cosmos*, I. 150), where the

wilderness. And he came into all the country about Jordan, 3
preaching the baptism of repentance for the remission of
sins; as it is written in the book of the words of Esaias the 4
prophet, saying, The voice of one crying in the wilderness, Prepare ye the way of the Lord, make his paths

sirocco blows almost without intermission. "A more frightful desert it had hardly been our lot to behold" (Robinson, *Researches*, II. 121). See it described by Mr Grove in Smith's *Bibl. Dict.* s.v. *Arabah*. The stern aspect and terrible associations of the spot had doubtless exercised their influence on the mind of John. See on ii. 80.

3. *he came*] St Luke alone mentions the mission journeys of John the Baptist; the other Evangelists, whose narratives (Matt. iii. 1—12; Mark i. 1—8; John i. 15, 28) should be carefully compared with that of St Luke, describe how the multitudes "came streaming forth" to him.

all the country about Jordan] The Arabah is some 150 miles in extent; the actual river-valley, specified in the O. T. by the curious words *Kikkar* and *Geliloth* (see Stanley, *Sin. and Pal.* p. 284), is not so extensive.

the baptism of repentance for the remission of sins] Comp. Acts ii. 38, iii. 15, v. 31, xxii. 16; where the two expressions are also united. The baptism of John was "a baptism of repentance," not yet "a laver of regeneration" (Tit. iii. 5). It was intended first as a symbol of purification—"Then will I sprinkle clean water upon you, and ye shall be clean," Ezek. xxxvi. 25; (comp. Is. i. 16; Zech. xiii. 1); and then as an initiation into the kingdom which was at hand. The Jews had been familiar with the symbolism of baptism from the earliest days, as a consecration (Exod. xxix. 4), and a purification (Lev. xiv. 8). It was one of the forms by which proselytes were admitted into Judaism. John's adoption of this rite proved (i) his authority (John i. 25); and (ii) his opinion that even Jews needed to be thus washed from sins.

4. *Esaias the prophet*] Is. xl. 3.

saying] This word should be omitted with ℵ, B, D, L, &c.

The voice] Rather, **A voice**. The Hebrew original may be rendered "Hark one crieth."

of one crying in the wilderness] Hence comes the common expression for hopeless warnings, *vox clamantis in deserto*. Probably, however, the "in the wilderness" should be attached *to the words uttered by the voice*, as is required by the parallelism of Hebrew poetry:

"Prepare ye in the wilderness a way for Jehovah,
    Lay even in the desert a highway for our God."

The wilderness is metaphorically the barren waste of the Jewish life in that day (Is. xxxv. 1).

the way of the Lord] Comp. Is. xxxv. 8—10, "And a highway shall be there, and a way, and it shall be called *the way of holiness:*

5 straight. Every valley shall be filled, and every mountain and hill shall be brought low; and the crooked shall be made straight, and the rough ways 6 *shall be* made smooth; and all flesh shall see the sal- 7 vation of God. Then said he to the multitude that came forth to be baptized of him, O generation of vipers, who hath

the unclean shall not pass over it...And the ransomed of the Lord shall return, and come to Zion."

5. *Every valley*, &c.] The metaphor is derived from pioneers who go before the march of a king. There is a remarkable parallel in Josephus (*B. J.* III. 6, § 2), where he is describing the march of Vespasian, and says that among his vanguard were "such as were to make the road even *and straight, and if it were anywhere rough and hard to be passed over, to plane it*, and to cut down the woods that hindered their march (comp. *prokoptein* = 'to advance' in ii. 52), that the army might not be tired." The Jews fabled that the Pillar of Cloud and Fire in the desert smoothed the mountains and filled the valleys before them. *Tanchuma*, f. 70, 3 on Numb. xx. 22.

Every valley shall be filled, &c.] i.e. the humble and meek shall be exalted, and the mighty put down. Compare Is. ii. 12—15, "The day of the Lord of hosts shall be *upon every one that is proud and lofty*, and upon every one that is lifted up, and he shall be brought low....And *upon all the high mountains*, &c." Zech. iv. 7, "Who art thou, O great mountain? *Before Zerubbabel thou shalt become a plain.*"

the crooked shall be made straight] The words in the original recall the names *Jacob* and *Jeshurun;* as though it were "then the Supplanter shall be turned into Prince with God" or "the beloved" (Is. xliv. 2, xi. 4). The general meaning of the prophecy is that no obstacles, whether they arose from depression, or power, or pride, or cunning perversity, or menacing difficulties, should be able to resist the labours of the Pioneers and Heralds of the Kingdom of God. The feeble instrumentality of Galilaeans should be strengthened; the power of the Romans and Herods should be shattered; the duplicity and plots of Pharisees and worldlings should be defeated; the apparently insuperable opposition of Judaism and Heathenism be swept away.

6. *all flesh shall see the salvation of God*] St Luke alone adds these words to the quotation, and his doing so is characteristic of his object, which was to bring out the blessedness and universality of the Gospel. See ii. 10, xxiv. 47, and Introd. p. 25. "The sal- vation" is τὸ σωτήριον, as in ii. 30. When the mountains of earthly tyranny and spiritual pride are levelled, the view of God's saving power becomes clear to all flesh.

7. *to the multitude*] Rather, **multitudes**. Different crowds came from different directions, Matt. iii. 5; Mark i. 5.

O generation of vipers] Rather, **broods of vipers**. They were like "serpents born of serpents." The comparison was familiar to Hebrew

warned you to flee from the wrath to come? Bring forth **8** therefore fruits worthy of repentance, and begin not to say within yourselves, We have Abraham to *our* father: for I say unto you, That God is able of these stones to raise up

poetry (Ps. lxviii. 4; Is. xiv. 9), and we learn from Matt. iii. 7 that it was *specially* pointed at the Pharisees and Sadducees, to whom it was addressed no less sternly by our Lord (Matt. xxiii. 33). It described the venomous hypocrisy which turned religion itself into a vice, and hid a deadly malice under the glittering semblance of a zeal for orthodoxy. But let it be borne in mind that only teachers of transcendent holiness, and immediately inspired by God with fervency and insight, may dare to use such language. The metaphor was one of those desert symbols which would be suggested to St John both by the scene of his preaching and by the language of Isaiah with which he shews special familiarity.

from the wrath to come] The Jews had been taught by Prophecy that the Advent of their Deliverer should be preceded by a time of anguish which they called "the Woes of the Messiah;" comp. Mal. iii. 2, "Who may abide the day of His coming? and who shall stand when He appeareth? For He is like a refiner's fire, and like fuller's soap." *Id.* iv. 1 "Behold I send you Elijah the Prophet *before the coming of the great and dreadful day of the Lord.*" Such prophecies received their primary fulfilment at the Destruction of Jerusalem (see Matt. xxiv. 28; Mark xiii. 19, 20); and await their final fulfilment hereafter. Rev. vi. 16.

8. *Bring forth*] The verb implies instant effort. "Produce *at once.*" *begin not to say*] He cuts off even all *attempt* at self-excuse.

We have Abraham to our father] Rather, **as our father**. The Jews had so exalted a conception of this privilege (John viii. 39) that they could scarcely believe it possible that any son of Abraham should ever be lost. This is seen in many passages of the Talmud, which maintain that a "single Israelite is of more worth in God's sight than all the nations of the world." "Thou madest the world for our sakes. As for the other people...Thou hast said...that they are nothing but be like unto spittle, and hast likened the abundance of them unto a drop that falleth from a vessel....But we Thy people (whom Thou hast called Thy firstborn, Thy only begotten, and Thy fervent lover), &c." 2 Esdr. vi. 56—58. The Prophets had long ago warned them that privileges without duties were no protection (Jer. vii. 3, 4; Mic. iii. 11; Is. xlviii. 2, &c.). Christ taught them that Abraham's seed had no *exclusive* offer of salvation (Matt. viii. 11, 12), and it was a special part of the mission of St Paul to bring home to them that "they are not all Israel which are of Israel" Rom. ix. 6, 7; Gal. iii. 29, vi. 15.

of these stones] He pointed to the rocky boulders, or the flints on the strand of Jordan, around him. He who had made Adam from the clay could make sons of Abraham from those stones (Bengel). St John's imagery is that of the wilderness,—the rock, the serpent, the barren tree.

9 children unto Abraham. And now also the axe is laid unto the root of the trees: every tree therefore which bringeth not forth good fruit is hewn down, and cast into the fire.

10—14. *Answer of the Baptist to the Multitude.*

10 And the people asked him, saying, What shall we do then?
11 He answereth and saith unto them, He that hath two coats, let him impart to him that hath none; and he that hath

9. *is laid*] Literally, "*lies.*" The notion is that of a woodman touching a tree with the edge of his axe to measure his blow before he lifts his arm for the sweep which fells it.

is hewn down and cast into the fire] Literally, "*is being hewn down, and being cast.*" It is almost impossible to reproduce in English the force of this use of the present. It is called the '*praesens futurascens*,' and is used in cases when the doom has been long uttered, and is, by the evolution of the natural laws of God's dealings, in course of inevitable accomplishment. But we see from prophetic imagery that even when the tree has been felled and burned "the watchers and holy ones" may still have charge to leave the stump of it in the tender grass of the field that it may grow again, Dan. iv. 25: and we see from the express language of St Paul that the olive tree of Jewish life was not to be cut down and burned for ever (Rom. ix. x.). A barren fig tree was also our Lord's symbol of the Jewish nation. Lk. xiii. 6.

10—14. ANSWER OF THE BAPTIST TO THE MULTITUDE.

10. *What shall we do then?*] Rather, **What then are we to do?** Compare the question of the multitude to Peter on the day of Pentecost (Acts ii. 37) and that of the Philippian jailor (xvi. 30).

11. *He that hath two coats*] St Luke alone preserves for us the details in this interesting section. Beyond the single upper garment (*chiton, cetoneth*), and garment (*himation*) and girdle, no other article of dress was necessary. A second 'tunic' or *cetoneth* was a mere luxury, so long as thousands were too poor to own even one.

let him impart to him that hath none] St Paul gave similar advice (2 Cor. viii. 13—15), and St James (ii. 15—17), and St John (1 John iii. 17), because they had learnt this spirit from Christ. A literal fulfilment of it has often been represented by Christian Art in the "Charity of St Martin."

meat] Rather, **food.** The word has now acquired the specific sense of 'flesh,' which it never has in our E. V. For instance the "meat-offering" was generally an offering of flour and oil.

We may notice the following particulars respecting the preaching of the Baptist:

(1) It was *stern*, as was natural to an ascetic whose very aspect and mission were modelled on the example of Elijah. The particulars of his life, and dress, and food—the leathern girdle, the mantle of camel's

meat, let him do likewise. Then came also publicans to 12

hair, the living on locusts and wild honey—are preserved for us by the other Evangelists, and they gave him that power of mastery over others which always springs from perfect self-control, and absolute self-abnegation. Hence "in his manifestation and agency he was like a burning torch; his whole life was a very earthquake; the whole man was a sermon."

(2) It was absolutely *dauntless*. The unlettered Prophet of the Desert has not a particle of respect for the powerful Sadducees and long-robed luxurious Rabbis, and disdains to be flattered by their coming to listen to his teaching. Having nothing to hope from man's favour, he has nothing to fear from man's dislike.

(3) It shews remarkable *insight into human nature*, and into the needs and temptations of every class which came to him,—shewing that his ascetic seclusion did not arise from any contempt of, or aversion to, his fellowmen.

(4) It was *intensely practical*. Not only does it exclude all abstract and theological terms such as 'justification,' &c., but it says nothing directly of even faith, or love. In this respect it recalls the Old Testament, and might be summed up in the words of Balaam preserved in the prophet Micah, "He hath shewed thee, O man, what is good; and what doth the Lord require of thee, but to do justly, and to love mercy, and to walk humbly with thy God?" Mic. vi. 8.

(5) Yet though it still belongs to the dispensation of the shadow it *prophesies of the dawn*. His first message was "Repent;" his second was "The kingdom of heaven is at hand:" and this message culminated in the words " Behold the Lamb of God," which shewed that the *Olam habba* or 'future age' had already begun. These two great utterances "contain the two capital revelations to which all the preparation of the Gospel has been tending." "Law and Prophecy; denunciation of sin and promise of pardon; the flame which consumes and the light which consoles—is not this the whole of the covenant?" Lange.

(6) *It does not claim the credentials of a single miracle*. The glory and greatness of John the Baptist, combined with the fact that not a single wonder is attributed to him, is the strongest argument for the truth of the Gospels against the 'mythical theory' of Strauss, who reduces the Gospel miracles to a circle of imaginative legends devised to glorify the Founder of Christianity. At the same time this acknowledged absence of miraculous powers enhances our conception of the enormous moral force which sufficed, without a sign, to stir to its very depths the heart of a sign-demanding age.

(7) *It had only a partial and temporary popularity*. Rejected by the Pharisees who said that "he had a devil," the Baptist failed to produce a permanent influence on more than a chosen few (John v. 35; Lk. vii. 30; Matt. xi. 18, xxi. 23—27; Acts xviii. 25, xix. 3, 4). After his imprisonment he seems to have fallen into neglect, and he himself felt from the first that his main mission was to prepare the way for another, and to decrease before him. He was "the lamp kindled

be baptized, and said unto him, Master, what shall we do?
13 And he said unto them, Exact no more than that which is
14 appointed you. And *the* soldiers likewise demanded of him, saying, And what shall we do? And he said unto them,

and shining" (John v. 35) which becomes needless and ceases to be noticed when the sun has dawned.

12. *the publicans*] Rather, **tax-gatherers** (without the article). The word is a corruption of the Latin *publicani* 'farmers of the taxes.' The Roman government did not collect its own taxes, but leased them out to speculators of the equestrian order, who were called *publicani*, and who made their own profit out of the transaction. These knights appointed subordinates, who from the unpleasant character of the task could only be secured from the lowest of the people. These officials were not only detested as the agents of an odious system, but also for their notorious malpractices. A strict Jew could hardly force himself even to *pay* taxes, and therefore naturally looked with scorn and hatred on any Jew who could sink so low as to *collect* them. Hence in our Lord's time the word "publican" had become proverbial, as expressive of the worst opprobrium (Matt. xviii. 17). The Jews were not however peculiar in their dislike of publicans. The Greeks too regarded the word as a synonym of 'plunderer,' and an 'innocent publican' was regarded as a marvellous phenomenon (Suet. *Vesp.* 1). Suidas defines the life of a publican as "unrestrained plunder, unblushing greed, unreasonable pettifogging, shameless business." The relation of the publicans to John is referred to in Matt. xxi. 32.

Master] Rather, **Teacher**. The word is not *Epistata* (as in viii. 24) but *Didaskale*. See vii. 29.

what shall we do?] We have the same question, but with the answer which was only possible after the Resurrection, in Acts ii. 37; xvi. 30; xxii. 10.

13. *Exact no more*] This was their habitual sin, and later historians often allude to the *immodestia* (i.e. the extravagant greed) of the publicans and their cruel exactions (Caes. *Bell. Civ.* III. 32). The cheating and meddling for which Zacchaeus promised fourfold restoration (xix. 8) were universal among them.

14. *the soldiers*] Rather, **soldiers on the march**. On what expedition these soldiers were engaged it is impossible to say. They cannot have been Roman soldiers, and were certainly not any detachment of the army of Antipas marching against his injured father-in-law Hareth (Aretas), ethnarch of Arabia, for their quarrel was long subsequent to this.

demanded of him] Rather, **asked him**. The imperfect tense however (as before in vs. 10) implies that such questions were put to him by bodies of soldiers in succession.

Do violence to no man] Rather, **Extort money by threats from no one**. *Diaseio*, like the Latin *concutio*, is a technical word. It implies robbery and violence.

Do violence to no man, neither accuse *any* falsely; and be content with your wages.

15—20. *The Messianic Announcement. Imprisonment of John.*

And as the people were in expectation, and all *men* mused in their hearts of John, whether he were the Christ, or not; John answered, saying unto *them* all, I indeed baptize you with water; but one mightier than I cometh, the latchet of

accuse any falsely] Rather, **cheat by false accusation**. The Greek implies pettifogging charges on trivial grounds, and is the word from which *sycophant* is derived. The temptation of soldiers, strong in their solidarity, was to terrify the poor by violence, and undermine the rich by acting as informers. The best comment on the Baptist's advice to them is the XVIth Satire of Juvenal, which is aimed at their brutality and threats.

be content with your wages] Rather, **pay**. This is a late meaning of the word *opsonia* (Rom. vi. 23), which means in the first instance 'boiled fish eaten as a relish with meat.' It is remarkable that the Baptist does not bid even soldiers to *abandon* their profession, but to serve God in it. This is important as shewing that he did not hold up the life of the hermit or the ascetic as a model or ideal for all. He evidently held, like the good St Hugo of Avalon, that "God meant us to be good men, not monks and hermits." Josephus, when (*Antt.* XVIII. v. 2) he sums up the teaching of the Baptist by saying that "he commanded the Jews to practise virtue both in righteousness to one another and piety to God," rightly estimates the *practical*, but omits the *prophetic* side of his teaching.

15—20. THE MESSIANIC ANNOUNCEMENT. IMPRISONMENT OF JOHN.

15. *were in expectation*] The Messianic expectations of the day had even reached the Gentiles, many of whom even at Rome and in high society were proselytes, or half proselytes, to Judaism.

mused] Rather, **reasoned**.

whether he were the Christ] Rather, **whether haply he were himself the Christ.**

16. *John answered*] The answer, as we find from John i. 19—28, was given in its most definite form to a Pharisaic deputation of Priests and Levites, who were despatched by the Sanhedrin expressly to ask him to define his claims.

one mightier] Rather, **the stronger than I.**

the latchet] i.e. the thong. The word, now obsolete in this sense, is from the same root perhaps as the Latin *laqueus* (Ital. *laccio*, Portug. *lasso*, old French *lacs*, Fr. *lacet*, Engl. *lace*).

shoes] Rather, **sandals**.

whose shoes I am not worthy to unloose: he shall baptize
17 you with the Holy Ghost and *with* fire: whose fan *is* in his
hand, and he will throughly purge his floor, and will gather
the wheat into his garner; but the chaff he will burn with
18 fire unquenchable. And many other *things* in his exhortation
19 preached he unto the people. But Herod the tetrarch, being

to unloose] In Matt. iii. 11 it is 'to carry his sandals;' i.e. I am not adequate to be his humblest slave.

baptize you with the Holy Ghost and with fire] Rather, **in the Holy Ghost and fire**. The preposition *en* distinguishes between the mere *instrumentality* of the water, and the *spiritual element* whereby and wherein the child of the kingdom is baptized. This baptism by the Spirit had been foretold in Is. xliv. 3; Joel ii. 28. Its first obvious fulfilment was at Pentecost (Acts i. 5, ii. 3) and subsequent outpourings after baptism (Acts xi. 15, 16). But it is fulfilled without visible supernatural signs to all Christians (1 Cor. vi. 11; "by one Spirit are we all baptized into one body," 1 Cor. xii. 13).

and with fire] In its first and most literal sense the allusion is to the fiery tongues of Pentecost (Acts ii. 3); but the secondary and metaphoric allusion is to the burning zeal and illuminating light of the Spirit. St Jerome sees a further allusion to fiery trials (xii. 49; Mark ix. 49; 1 Pet. iv. 12) and to the fire of judgment (1 Cor. iii. 13); but these allusions cannot be regarded as certain.

17. *fan*] Rather, **winnowing-fan**. The Latin *vannus*, a great shovel with which corn was thrown up against the wind to separate it from the chaff.

his floor] Rather, **threshing-floor**. The word is the same as that from which our *halo* is derived, since the threshing-floors of the ancients were circular.

the chaff] The word includes straw and stubble. We find similar metaphors in Ps. i. 4, "the ungodly...are like the chaff;" Mal. iv. 1, "all that do wickedly shall be stubble;" Jer. xv. 7, "I will fan them with a fan in the gates of the land." So far as the allusion is to the separation of good from evil elements in the Church we find similar passages in Matt. xiii. 30; 1 Joh. ii. 19, &c. But it may refer also to the destruction of *the evil elements in a mixed character*, as in xxii. 31, "Simon...Satan hath desired to have you, *that he may sift you as wheat.*"

into his garner] Comp. Matt. xiii. 30, "gather the wheat into my barn."

burn] Rather, **burn up**.

18. *many other things*] Of which some are recorded by St John alone (i. 29, 34, iii. 27—36).

preached he] εὐηγγελίζετο, literally, "*he was preaching the Good Tidings.*"

19. *But Herod the tetrarch*] The incident which follows is here introduced by anticipation, that the subsequent narrative may not be

reproved by him for Herodias his brother Philip's wife, and for all the evils which Herod had done, added yet this above all, that he shut up John in prison. 20

21—38. *The Baptism of Jesus. The Genealogy.*

Now when all the people were baptized, it came to pass, 21

disturbed. It should be compared with the fuller notice in Mark vi. 17—20; Matt. xiv. 3—5. From these passages we learn that John had reproved Antipas for many crimes, and that Antipas was so convinced of his holiness and justice as habitually to listen to him with pleasure (ἡδέως αὐτοῦ ἤκουεν), and after paying earnest heed to him was greatly at a loss about him. We learn further that he resisted the constant urgency of Herodias to put him to death.

being reproved] The reproof was of course based on Lev. xviii. 16, xx. 21, and was perfectly uncompromising (Matt. xiv. 4). In this respect the dauntless courage of John, under circumstances of far greater peril, contrasts most favourably with the timid and disgraceful concessions of the Reformers in the matter of the marriage of Philip of Hesse.

his brother Philip's] The two first words are omitted by some of the best uncials, and "Philip's" by nearly all of them. On *this* Herod Philip—who was not the tetrarch of that name—see on iii. 1.

20. *added yet this above all*] The Jews as well as St Luke regarded the treatment of the Baptist by Antipas as the worst of his crimes, and the cause of his subsequent defeat and disgrace (Jos. *Antt.* XVIII. 5. 1—4).

in prison] This prison, as we learn from Josephus (*Antt.* XVIII. 5, § 2), was the stern and gloomy fortress of Makor or Machaerus, on the borders of Arabia to the north of the Dead Sea. It is situated among black basaltic rocks and was believed to be haunted by evil demons. Its ruins have been visited in recent years by Canon Tristram (*Land of Moab*, p. 259) and other travellers, and dungeons are still visible of which one may have witnessed the great Prophet's tragic end.

21—38. THE BAPTISM OF JESUS. THE GENEALOGY.

21. *Now when all the people were baptized*] The expression (which is peculiar to St Luke) seems to imply that on this day Jesus was baptized *last;* and from the absence of any allusion to the multitude in this and the other narratives we are almost forced to conjecture that His baptism was in a measure private. St Luke's narrative must be supplemented by particulars derived from St Matthew (iii. 13—17), who alone narrates the unwillingness of the Baptist, and the memorable conversation between him and Jesus; and St Mark (i. 9—11) mentions that Jesus went into the river, and that it was He who first saw the cleaving heavens, and the Spirit descending.

that Jesus also being baptized, and praying, the heaven
22 was opened, and the Holy Ghost descended in a bodily
shape like a dove upon him, and a voice came from heaven,

Jesus also being baptized] Our Lord Himself, in reply to the objection of the Baptist, stated it as a reason for His Baptism that "thus it becometh us to fulfil all righteousness;" i.e. that it was His will to observe all the requirements of the Mosaic law, which He came "not to destroy but to fulfil." Other reasons have also been suggested, as (i) that He baptized (as it were) the water—"to sanctify water to the mystical washing away of sin" (Ignat. *ad Eph.* 18; Maxim. Serm. 7, *de Epiphan.*; Ps.-Aug. *Serm.* 135. 4); or (ii) that He was baptized as it were *vicariously*, as Head of His body, the Church (Just. Mart. *c. Tryph.* 88); or (iii) as a consecration of *Himself* to His work, followed by the special consecration from the Father; or (iv) as a great act of humility (St Bernard, *Serm.* 47, *in Cant.*). See my *Life of Christ*, I. 117 n.

and praying] This deeply interesting touch is peculiar to St Luke, who similarly on eight other occasions calls attention to the Prayers of Jesus—after severe labours (v. 16); before the choosing of the Apostles (vi. 12); before Peter's great Confession (ix. 18); at His transfiguration (ix. 28, 29); for Peter (xxii. 32); in Gethsemane (xxii. 41); for His murderers (xxiii. 34); and at the moment of death (xxiii. 46). He also represents the duty and blessing of urgent prayer in two peculiar parables—the Importunate Friend (xi. 5—13) and the Unjust Judge (xviii. 2). See Introd. p. 24.

22. *in a bodily shape*] This addition is peculiar to St Luke, and is probably added to shew the distinctness and reality of what Theodoret calls the 'spiritual vision' (πνευματικὴ θεωρία).

like a dove] The expression ὡς or ὡσεί used by each of the Evangelists, and St John's "and it abode upon Him" (John i. 32), sufficiently prove that no *actual* dove is intended. The Holy Spirit is symbolised by a dove from early times. The Talmudic comment on Gen. i. 2 is that "the Spirit of God moved on the face of the waters *like a dove*"—

"And with mighty wings outspread
Dovelike sat'st brooding on the vast abyss."
MILTON (*Par. Lost*, I. 20).

Comp. 2 Esdr. v. 26, "of all the fowls that are created thou hast named thee one dove." Matt. x. 16. A mystical reason was assigned for this in some fathers, because the numerical value of the letters of the Greek word *peristera*, 'a dove,' amounts to 801, which is also the value of Alpha Omega. We are probably intended to understand a dovelike, hovering, lambent flame descending on the head of Jesus; and this may account for the unanimous early legend that a fire or light was kindled in Jordan (Just. Mart. *c. Tryph.* 88, and the Apocryphal Gospels).

a voice came from heaven, which said] Rather, **out of heaven**. The last words should be omitted with the best MSS. This *Bath Kôl* or Voice from heaven also occurred at the Transfiguration (Matt. xvii. 5)

which said, Thou art my beloved Son; in thee I am well pleased.

And Jesus himself began *to be* about thirty years of age, 23 being (as was supposed) the son of Joseph, which was *the son* of Heli, which was *the son* of Matthat, which was *the son* 24 of Levi, which was *the son* of Melchi, which was *the son* of Janna, which was *the son* of Joseph, which was *the son* of 25 Mattathias, which was *the son* of Amos, which was *the son* of Naum, which was *the son* of Esli, which was *the son* of Nagge, which was *the son* of Maath, which was *the son* of Mattathias, 26 which was *the son* of Semei, which was *the son* of Joseph, which was *the son* of Juda, which was *the son* of Joanna, 27 which was *the son* of Rhesa, which was *the son* of Zorobabel, which was *the son* of Salathiel, which was *the son* of Neri, which was *the son* of Melchi, which was *the son* of Addi, 28 which was *the son* of Cosam, which was *the son* of Elmodam, which was *the son* of Er, which was *the son* of Jose, which 29 was *the son* of Eliezer, which was *the son* of Jorim, which was *the son* of Matthat, which was *the son* of Levi, which was 30 *the son* of Simeon, which was *the son* of Juda, which was *the*

and in the closing week of Christ's life (John xii. 28—30). This is one of the passages which so distinctly imply the doctrine of the Blessed Trinity.

I am well pleased] Rather, **I was well pleased.**

23. *began to be about thirty years of age*] Rather, **was about thirty years of age on beginning (His work).** So it was understood by Tyndale, but the E. V. followed Cranmer, and the Geneva. The translation of our E. V. is, however, ungrammatical, and a strange expression to which no parallel can be adduced. The word *archomenos*, standing absolutely for 'when he began his ministry,' is explained by the extreme prominency of this *beginning* in the thought of St Luke (see Acts i. 1, 22), and his desire to fix it with accuracy. The age of 30 was that at which a Levite might enter on his full services (Numb. iv. 3, 47), and the age at which Joseph had stood before Pharaoh (Gen. xli. 46), and at which David had begun to reign (2 Sam. v. 4), and at which scribes were allowed to teach.

as was supposed] "Is not this the carpenter's son?" Matt. xiii. 55; John vi. 42.

On the genealogy which follows, and its relations to that in the Gospel of St Matthew, many volumes have been written, but in the Excursus I have endeavoured to condense all that is most important on the subject, and to give those conclusions which are now being accepted by the most careful scholars. See Excursus II., The genealogies of Jesus in St Matthew and St Luke.

son of Joseph, which was *the son* of Jonan, which was *the*
31 son of Eliakim, which was *the son* of Melea, which was *the*
son of Menan, which was *the son* of Mattatha, which was *the*
32 son of Nathan, which was *the son* of David, which was *the*
son of Jesse, which was *the son* of Obed, which was *the son*
of Booz, which was *the son* of Salmon, which was *the son* of
33 Naasson, which was *the son* of Aminadab, which was *the son*
of Aram, which was *the son* of Esrom, which was *the son* of
34 Phares, which was *the son* of Juda, which was *the son* of
Jacob, which was *the son* of Isaac, which was *the son* of
Abraham, which was *the son* of Thara, which was *the son* of
35 Nachor, which was *the son* of Saruch, which was *the son* of
Ragau, which was *the son* of Phalec, which was *the son* of
36 Heber, which was *the son* of Sala, which was *the son* of
Cainan, which was *the son* of Arphaxad, which was *the son* of
Sem, which was *the son* of Noe, which was *the son* of Lamech,
37 which was *the son* of Mathusala, which was *the son* of Enoch,
which was *the son* of Jared, which was *the son* of Maleleel,
38 which was *the son* of Cainan, which was *the son* of Enos,
which was *the son* of Seth, which was *the son* of Adam, which
was *the son* of God.

CH. IV. 1—13. *The Temptation.*

4 And Jesus being full of the Holy Ghost returned from
2 Jordan, and was led by the Spirit into the wilderness, being

CH. IV. 1—13. THE TEMPTATION.

1. *being full of the Holy Ghost*] Omit '*being*.' St Luke often calls special attention to the work of the Spirit, iii. 22, iv. 14; Acts vi. 3, vii. 55, xi. 24. The expression alludes to the outpouring of the Spirit upon Jesus at His baptism, John iii. 34. The narrative should be compared with Matt. iv. 1—11; Mk. i. 12, 13. St John, who narrates mainly what he had himself *seen*, omits the temptation.

returned] Rather, **went away**.

was led] A divine impulse led him to face the hour of peril alone. St Mark uses the more intense expression, "immediately the Spirit *driveth Him forth*." He only devotes two verses (Mk. i. 12, 13) to the Temptation, but adds the graphic touch that "He was with the wild beasts" (comp. Ps. xci. 13), and implies the *continuous* ministration of angels (*diekonoun*) to Him.

by the Spirit] Rather, **in the Spirit**, comp. ii. 27. The phrase

forty days tempted of the devil. And in those days he did

emphasizes the "full of the Holy Ghost," and has the same meaning as "in the power of the Spirit," vs. 14.

> "Thou Spirit, who ledd'st this glorious eremite
> Into the desert, his victorious field
> Against the spiritual foe, and brought'st Him thence
> By proof the undoubted Son of God."
>
> MILTON, *Par. Reg.* I.

into the wilderness] Rather, **in**. He was 'in the Spirit' during the whole period. The scene of the temptation is supposed to be the mountain near Jericho, thence called Quarantania. The tradition is not ancient, but the site is very probable, being rocky, bleak, and repellent—

> "A pathless desert, dusk with horrid shades."
>
> MILTON.

Scripture everywhere recognises the need of solitude and meditation on the eve of great work for God (Ex. xxiv. 2; 1 K. xix. 4; Gal. i. 17), and this would be necessary to the human nature of our Lord also.

2. *forty days*] The number was connected in the Jewish mind with notions of seclusion, and revelation, and peril;—Moses on Sinai, Ex. xxxiv. 18; Elijah, 1 K. xix. 8; the wanderings of the Israelites, Num. xiv. 34; Judg. xiii. 1.

tempted] The present participle implies that the temptation was continuous throughout the forty days, though it reached its most awful climax at their close.

of the devil] The Jews placed in the wilderness one of the mouths of Gehenna, and there evil spirits were supposed to have most power (Num. xvi. 33; Matt. xii. 43). St Mark uses the Hebrew form of the word—'Satan.' Both words mean 'the Accuser,' but the Greek *Diabolos* is far more definite than the Hebrew *Satan*, which is loosely applied to any opponent, or opposition, or evil influence in which the evil spirit may be supposed to work (1 Chr. xxi. 1; 2 Cor. xii. 7; 1 Thess. ii. 18). This usage is far more apparent in the original, where the word rendered 'adversary' is often *Satan*, Num. xxii. 22; 1 Sam. xxix. 4; 1 Kings xi. 14, &c. On the other hand, the Greek word *Diabolos* is comparatively rare in the N.T. (The word rendered 'devils' for the '*evil spirits*' of demoniac possession is *daimonia*.) St Matthew also calls Satan "the tempter." Few suppose that the Devil came incarnate in any visible hideous guise. The narrative of the Temptation could only have been communicated to the Apostles by our Lord Himself. Of its intense and absolute reality we cannot doubt; nor yet that it was so narrated as to bring home to us the clearest possible conception of its significance. The best and wisest commentators in all ages have accepted it as the symbolic description of a mysterious inward struggle. Further speculation into the special *modes* in which the temptations were effected is idle, and we have no data for it. Of this only can we be sure, that our Lord's temptations were in every respect *akin* to ours

eat nothing: and when they were ended, he afterward hun-
3 gered. And the devil said unto him, If thou be the Son of
4 God, command this stone that it be made bread. And

(Heb. iv. 15, ii. 10, 18); that there was "a direct operation of the evil spirit upon His mind and sensibility;" that, as St Augustine says, "Christ conquered the tempter, that the Christian may not be conquered by the tempter." All enquiries as to whether Christ's sinlessness arose from a '*possibility* of *not* sinning' (*posse non peccare*) or an 'impossibility of sinning' (*non posse peccare*), are rash intrusions into the unrevealed. The Christian is content with the certainty that He "was in all points tempted like as we are, yet without sin" (see Heb. v. 8).

he did eat nothing] St Matthew says more generally that 'He fasted,' and St Luke's phrase probably implies no more than this (see Matt. xi. 18). The Arabah at any rate supplied enough for the bare maintenance of life (Jos. *Vit.* 2), and at times of intense spiritual exaltation the ordinary needs of the body are almost suspended. But this can only be for a time, and when the reaction has begun hunger asserts its claims with a force so terrible that (as has been shewn again and again in human experience) such moments are fraught with the extremest peril to the soul. This was the moment which the Tempter chose. We rob the narrative of the Temptation of all its spiritual meaning unless in reading it we are on our guard against the Apollinarian heresy which denied the perfect Humanity of Christ. The Christian must keep in view two thoughts: 1. Intensely real temptation. 2. Absolute sinlessness. It is man's trial 'to feel temptation' (*sentire tentationem*); Christ has put it into our power to *resist* it (*non consentire tentationi*). Temptation only merges into *sin* when man consents to it.

> "'Tis one thing to be tempted, Escalus,
> Another thing to fall."—SHAKESPEARE.

The temptation must be *felt* or it is no temptation; but we do not sin until temptation really sways the bias of the heart, and until delight and consent follow suggestion. The student will find the best examination of this subject in Ullmann's treatise *On the Sinlessness of Jesus* (Engl. Transl.).

3. *If thou be the Son of God*] Doubtless an allusion to the divine Voice at His baptism (iii. 22). The same words were tauntingly addressed to our Lord on the Cross (Matt. xxvii. 40). The Greek *strictly* means "*Assuming that Thou art*," but in Hellenistic Greek words and phrases are not always used with their earlier delicate accuracy.

command this stone] The Greek implies that the suggestion called direct attention to a particular stone. In this desert there are loaf-shaped fossils known to early travellers as *lapides judaici*, and to geologists as *septaria*. Some of these siliceous accretions assume the shape of fruit, and are known as 'Elijah's melons' (Stanley, *Sin. and Pal.* 154). They were popularly regarded as petrified fruits of the Cities of the Plain. Such deceptive semblances would intensify the pangs of hunger,

Jesus answered him, saying, It is written, That man shall not live by bread alone, but by every word of God. And the devil, taking him up into a high mountain, shewed 5

and add to the temptation the additional torture of an excited imagination. (See a sketch of such a *septarium* in the Illustrated Edition of my *Life of Christ*, p. 99.)

that it be made bread] Rather, **that it may become a loaf**. The subtle malignity of the temptation is indescribable. It was a temptation to "the lust" (i.e. the desire) "of the flesh;" a temptation to gratify a natural and blameless appetite; an appeal to free-will and self-will, closely analogous to the devil's first temptation of the race. 'You may; you can; it will be pleasant: why not?' (Gen. iii. 1—15). But it did not come in an undisguisedly sensuous form, but with the suggestive semblance of Scriptural sanctions (1 Kings xix. 8; Deut. viii. 16; Ps. lxxviii. 19).

4. *It is written*] The perfect *gegraptai* means 'it has been written,' it standeth written as an eternal lesson. Jesus foils the tempter *as* man *for* man. He will not say 'I am the Son of God,' and 'does not consider equality with God a prize at which to grasp' (Phil. ii. 6), but seizes "the sword of the Spirit, which is the Word of God" (Eph. vi. 17).

man shall not live by bread alone] The quotation is from Deut. viii. 3, where Moses tells the people that God has suffered them to hunger, and fed them with manna, to shew them the dependence of man on God, and the fact that life is something more than the mere living, and can only be sustained by diviner gifts than those which are sufficient for man's lower nature. Bread sustains the body; but, that we may *live*, the soul also, and the spirit must be kept alive. Exod. xvi. 4, 15. "They did all eat the same *spiritual* meat." 1 Cor. x. 3.

but by every word of God] These words, though *implied*, are probably added in this place from Matt. iv. 4, since they are omitted by א, B, D, L, and various versions. "*Word*" is not in the original Hebrew. The verse conveys a most deep truth, and by referring to it our Lord meant to say 'God will support my needs in His own way, and the lower life is as nothing in comparison with the higher.' There are many most valuable and instructive parallels; see John iv. 32—34, "I have meat to eat that ye know not of...My meat is to do the will of Him that sent me, and to finish His work." Job xxiii. 12, "I have esteemed *the words of His mouth more than my necessary food*." Jer. xv. 16, "Thy words were found, *and I did eat them;* and thy word was unto me the joy and rejoicing of my heart." Wisd. xvi. 6, "God's word nourisheth man." The Jewish Rabbis had the remarkable expression, "The just *eat* of the glory of the Shechinah." Comp. John vi. 27—63.

5. *And the devil, taking him up into a high mountain*] Probably "the devil" and "into a high mountain" are added from St Matthew. How the devil took Him up we are not told. Scripture, to turn away our thoughts from the secondary to the essential, knows nothing of those journeys through the air which we find in Apocrypha and in the 'Gospel of the Hebrews.'

unto him all the kingdoms of the world in a moment of
6 time. And the devil said unto him, All this power will I
give thee, and the glory of them: for *that* is delivered unto
7 me; and to whomsoever I will I give it. If thou therefore
8 wilt worship me, all shall be thine. And Jesus answered

It is remarkable that St Luke (whom Milton follows in the *Par. Regained*) here adopts a different *order* of the temptations from St Matthew, perhaps because he thought that the temptation to spiritual pride (which he places third) was keener and subtler than that to temporal ambition; perhaps, too, because he believed that the ministering angels only appeared to save Christ from the pinnacle of the Temple. That the *actual* order is that of St Matthew is probable, because (1) he alone uses notes of sequence, "*then*," "*again;*" (2) Christ closes the temptation by "Get thee behind me, Satan" (see on vs. 8); (3) as an actual Apostle he is more likely to have heard the narrative from the lips of Christ Himself. But in the chronology of spiritual crises there is little room for the accurate sequence of 'before' and 'after.' They crowd eternity into an hour, and stretch an hour into eternity.

of the world] See above on ii. 1.

in a moment] Rather, **in a second**; comp. 1 Cor. xv. 52, "in the twinkling of an eye"—in the sudden flash of an instantaneous vision. The splendour of the temptation, and the fact that it appealed to

"the spur which the clear spirit doth raise,
The last infirmity of noble minds,"

might seem to Satan to make up for its impudent, undisguised character. He was offering to One who had lived as the Village Carpenter the throne of the world.

6. *All this power will I give thee*] Rather, in the emphatic order of the original, **To Thee will I give this power, all of it, and the glory of them.**

for that is delivered unto me] The original is even stronger, **has been entrusted to me.** Hence the expressions, "the prince of this world," John xii. 31, xiv. 30; "the prince of the power of the air," Eph. ii. 2. Satan is in one sense "a world-ruler (*kosmokratōr*) of this darkness" (Eph. vi. 12). The Rabbis went even further, and called him 'Lord of this age' (*sar hâolâm*), and even "another God" (*ēl achēr*), which is Manicheeism; whereas in this verse, by the very admission of Satan, all Manicheeism is excluded.

to whomsoever I will I give it] Comp. Rev. xiii. 2, "the dragon gave him his power, and his seat, and great authority." Here however we note the exaggeration of the father of lies. How different was the language of our Lord to His ambitious disciples (Matt. xx. 23).

7. *wilt worship me*] Rather, **wilt do homage before me.** Comp. Ps. xxii. 27.

all shall be thine] Rather, **it (the habitable world) shall all be thine**, for the true reading is *pâsa* (all the uncials) not *panta*. There

and said unto him, Get thee behind me, Satan: for it is written, Thou shalt worship the Lord thy God, and him only shalt thou serve. And he brought him to Jerusalem, and set him on a pinnacle of the temple, and said unto him, If thou be the Son of God, cast thyself down from hence: for it is written, He shall give his angels

was then living, one to whom in as high an ambitious sense as has ever been realised, it *did* all belong—the Emperor Tiberius. But so far from enjoying it he was at this very time the most miserable and most degraded of men (Tac. *Ann.* VI. 6, IV. 61, 62, 67; Plin. *H. N.* XXVIII. 5).

8. *Get thee behind me, Satan*] These words should here be omitted with ℵ, B, D, L, &c., as having been added from Matt. iv. 10. Similar words were used to Peter (Matt. xvi. 23).

Thou shalt worship...and him only] The quotation is slightly altered from Deut. vi. 13, "Thou shalt *fear* the Lord thy God, and serve Him." St Matthew has the same variation, this being one of his *cyclic* quotations (i. e. those common to him with other Evangelists). Since Satan had now revealed himself in his true character, there was no need for Jesus to tell him of another and a divine Kingdom over which he had no power. It was sufficient to reprove his impious blasphemy.

9. *a pinnacle*] Rather, **the pinnacle, or battlement.** Some well-known pinnacle of the Temple, either that of the Royal Portico, which looked down from a dizzy height into the Valley of the Kidron (Jos. *Antt.* XV. 11 § 5); or the Eastern Portico, from which tradition says that St James was afterwards hurled (Euseb. *H. E.* II. 23). 'Battlement' is used for the corresponding Hebrew word *Canaph* (lit. 'wing') in Dan. ix. 27.

cast thyself down from hence] The first temptation had been to natural appetite and impulse: the second was to unhallowed ambition; the third is to rash confidence and spiritual pride. It was based, with profound ingenuity, on the expression of absolute trust with which the first temptation had been rejected. It asked as it were for a splendid proof of that trust, and appealed to perverted spiritual instincts. It had none of the vulgar and sensuous elements of the other temptations. It was at the same time a confession of impotence. "Cast *thyself* down." The devil may place the soul in peril and temptation, but can never *make* it sin. "It is," as St Augustine says, "the devil's part to suggest, it is ours not to consent."

10. *For it is written*]

> "The devil can cite Scripture for his purpose.
> An evil soul producing holy witness
> Is like a villain with a smiling cheek,
> A deadly apple rotten at the heart."
>
> SHAKESPEARE.

11 charge over thee, to keep thee: and in *their* hands they shall bear thee up, lest at any time thou dash
12 thy foot against a stone. And Jesus answering said unto him, It is said, Thou shalt not tempt the Lord
13 thy God. And when the devil had ended all the temptation, he departed from him for a season.

> "In religion
> What damned error but some sober brow
> Will bless it and approve it with a text,
> Hiding the grossness with fair ornament?"
> *Id.*

to keep thee] The quotation is from Ps. xci. 11, but the tempter omits "*in all thy ways*," which would have defeated his object, since the "ways" referred to are only the ways of him "who dwelleth under the defence of the Most High." But, as the *next* verse prophesies, Christ 'trod upon the lion and adder' of Satanic temptation.

12. *Thou shalt not tempt*] Rather, **Thou shalt not utterly tempt, or tempt to the extreme.** It is impious folly to *put God to the test* by thrusting ourselves into uncalled-for danger. The angels will only guard our perilous footsteps when we are walking in the path of duty. We cannot claim miracles when we *court* temptations. The quotation is from Deut. vi. 16, and it is remarkable that the *three* quotations with which our Lord met the tempter are all taken from the 6th and 8th chapters of this book.

13. *had ended all the temptation*] Rather, **every temptation**. "He had," as Bengel says, "shot his last dart." The temptations had been addressed (1) to the desire of the flesh—trying to make the test of Sonship to God consist not in obedience but in the absence of pain; (2) to the pride of life—as though earthly greatness were a sign of God's approval, and as though greatness consisted in power and success; (3) to spiritual pride—as though the elect of God might do as they will, and be secure against consequences.

he departed] "Resist the devil, and he will flee from you," James iv. 7.

for a season] Rather, **until an opportunity**, though the meaning comes to be the same (Acts xiii. 11). St Matthew adds "And lo! angels came and began to minister unto Him." We do not again meet with angels in a visible form till the Agony in Gethsemane. It must not be imagined that our Lord was only tempted at this crisis. He shared temptation with us, as the common lot of our humanity. "Many other were the occasions on which he endured temptation," Bonaventura, *Vit. Christi.* See xxii. 28; Heb. iv. 15. We may however infer from the Gospels that henceforth His temptations were rather the *negative* ones caused by *suffering*, than the *positive* ones caused by allurement. Ullmann, p. 30. See Matt. xxvii. 40 (like the first temptation); John vii. 3, 4 (analogous to the second in St Matthew's order); John vii. 15 (like the third); Van Oosterzee. See too xxii. 3, 53; Matt. xvi. 22; John xiv. 30, viii. 44.

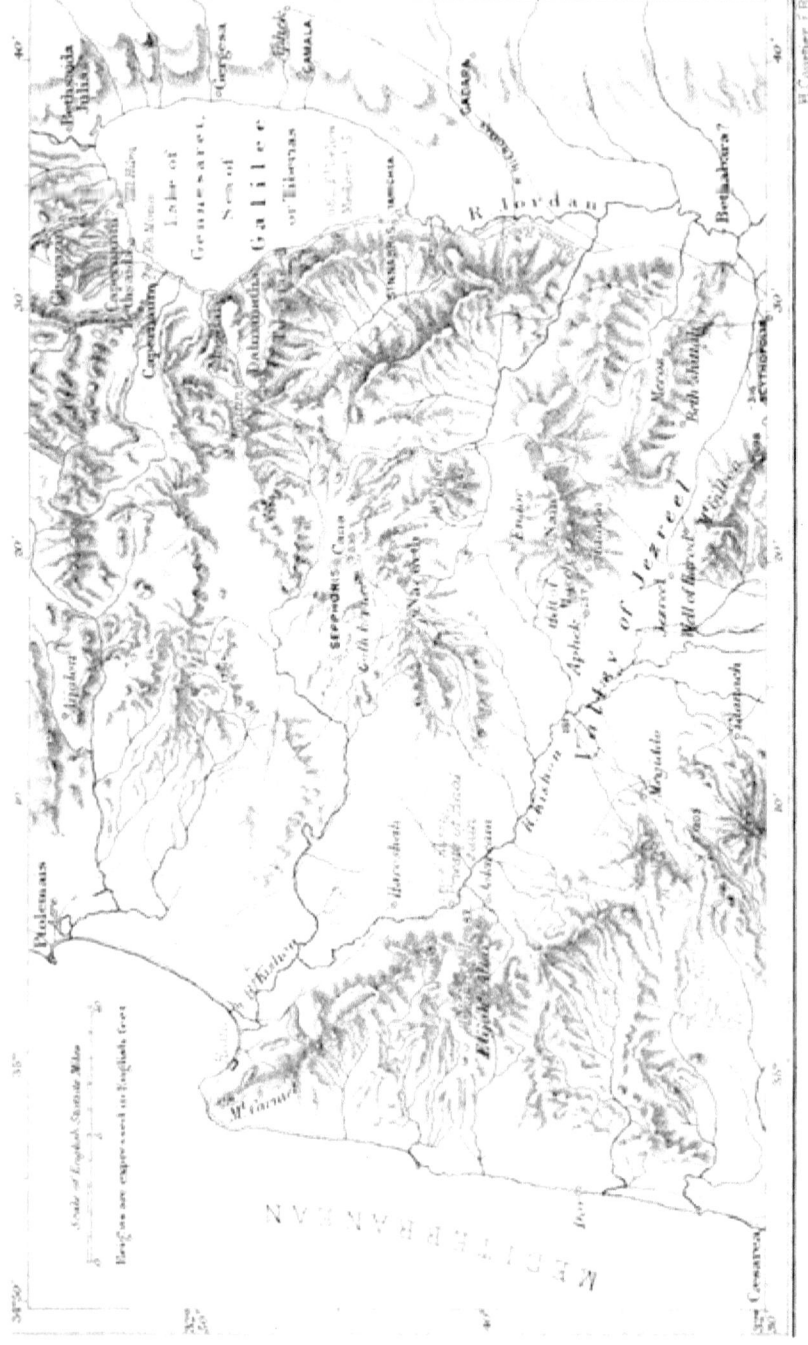

14—23. *Jesus returns to Nazareth and preaches there.*

14 And Jesus returned in the power of the Spirit into Galilee: and there went out a fame of him through all the region round about. 15 And he taught in their synagogues, being glorified of all. 16 And he came to Nazareth, where he had been brought up: and, as his custom was, he went into the synagogue on the sabbath day, and stood up for to read.

14—23. JESUS RETURNS TO NAZARETH AND PREACHES THERE.

14. *And Jesus returned*] St Luke here omits that series of occurrences which is mainly preserved for us by the Apostle who recorded the Judaean ministry—St John; namely the deputation of the Sanhedrin to the Baptist (i. 19—28), and his testimony about the baptism of Jesus (29—34); the call of Andrew and Simon (35—43); of Philip and Nathanael (44—51); the First Miracle, at Cana, and visit to Capernaum (ii. 1—12); the Passover at Jerusalem and first cleansing of the Temple (ii. 13—25); the secret visit of Nicodemus (iii. 1—21); the baptism of the disciples of Jesus, and the Baptist's remarks to his disciples (iii. 22—36). St Luke has already mentioned by anticipation the imprisonment of John the Baptist (iii. 19, 20), which probably hastened the return of Jesus to Galilee; but St John alone preserves the deeply interesting revelation to the Woman of Samaria, and the preaching among the Samaritans (John iv. 4—42). This must have occurred during the journey from Judaea to Galilee mentioned in this verse.

into Galilee] This district was the starting-point and main centre of our Lord's ministry, Acts x. 37, "which was published throughout all Judaea, and began from Galilee." Lk. xxiii. 5, "He stirreth up the people, *beginning from Galilee.*"

15. *he taught in their synagogues, being glorified of all*] The word 'He' is emphatic. 'He Himself,' in contrast with the *rumour* about Him. The word *autos* in this Gospel comes to mean "the Master," as a sort of title of honour, as in the "*Autos epha*"—"the Master said it" of the Pythagoreans. The verse shews that the journey from Sychar to Nazareth was not direct but leisurely; and it is remarkably confirmed by John iv. 45, who accounts for the favourable reception of Jesus by saying that they had seen "all the things that He did at Jerusalem at the feast."

16. *And he came to Nazareth*] This is probably the visit related in unchronological order in Matt. xiii. 53—58; Mk. vi. 1—6, since after so violent and decisive a rejection as St Luke narrates, it is unlikely that He should have preached at Nazareth again. If so, we learn from these (1) that His disciples were with Him; (2) that He healed a few of the sick, being prevented from further activity by their unbelief.

as his custom was] This seems to refer to what had been the habit of the life of Jesus while he had lived at Nazareth. Hitherto however He had been, in all probability, a silent worshipper.

into the synagogue] The article shews that the little village only

17 And there was delivered unto him the book of the prophet Esaias. And when he had opened the book, he found the
18 place where it was written, The Spirit of the Lord *is*

possessed a single synagogue. Synagogues had sprung up throughout Judaea since the return from the exile. They were rooms of which the end pointed towards Jerusalem (the *Kibleh*, or consecrated direction, of Jewish worship (Dan. vi. 10), as Mecca is of Mohammedan). The men sat on one side; the veiled women behind a lattice on the other. The chief furniture was the Ark (*tebhah*) of painted wood, generally shrouded by a curtain, and containing the Thorah (Pentateuch), and rolls (*megilloth*) of the Prophets. On one side was a *bema* for the reader and preacher, and there were "chief seats" (Mk. xii. 39) for the Ruler of the Synagogue, and the elders (*zekanim*). The servants of the synagogue were the clerk (*chazzan*), verger (*sheliach*) and deacons (*parnasim*, 'shepherds').

on the sabbath day] Observe the divine sanction thus given to the ordinance of weekly public worship.

stood up for to read] The custom was to read the Scripture standing. There was no recognised or ordained ministry for the synagogues. The functions of Priest and Levites were confined to the Temple, and the various officers of the synagogue were more like our churchwardens. Hence it was the custom of the Ruler or Elders to invite any one to read or preach who was known to them as a distinguished or competent person (Acts xiii. 15).

17. *there was delivered unto him*] Literally, "there was *further* handed to Him." The expression means that after He, or another, had read the *Parashah*, or First Lesson, which was always from the Pentateuch, the clerk handed to him the Roll of Isaiah, which contained the *Haphtarah*, or Second Lesson.

when he had opened the book] If *anaptuxas* is the true reading, it means 'unrolling.' The Thorah, or Law, was written on a parchment between *two* rollers, and was always left unrolled at the column for the day's lesson; but the Megilloth of the Prophets, &c., were on single rollers, and the right place had to be found by the reader (*Maphtir*).

he found] The word *heure* leaves it uncertain whether the 'finding' was what man calls 'accidental,' or whether it was the regular *haphtarah* of the day. It is now the Second Lesson for the great day of Atonement; but according to Zunz (the highest Jewish authority on the subject) the present order of the Lessons in the Synagogue worship belongs to a later period than this.

the place where it was written] Is. lxi. 1, 2. Our Lord, according to the custom of the Synagogue, must have read the passage in Hebrew, and then—either by Himself, or by an interpreter (*Methurgeman*)—it must have been translated to the congregation in Aramaic or Greek, since Hebrew was at this time a dead and learned language. The quotation is here freely taken by the Evangelist from the LXX., possibly from memory, and with reminiscences, intentional or otherwise, of other passages.

upon me, because he hath anointed me to preach the gospel to the poor; he hath sent me to heal the broken-hearted, to preach deliverance to the captives, and recovering of sight to the blind, to set at liberty *them that are* bruised, to preach the accept- 19 able year of the Lord. And he closed the book, and 20 he gave *it* again to the minister, and sat down. And the eyes of all *them that were* in the synagogue were fastened on

18. *he hath anointed me*] Rather, **He anointed** (aorist); the following verb is in the perfect. The word *Mashach* in the Hebrew would recall to the hearers the notion of the Messiah—"il m'a messianisé" (Salvador). "God *anointed* Jesus of Nazareth with the Holy Ghost and with power," Acts x. 38. In illustration of the verse generally, as indicating the work primarily of Isaiah, but in its fullest sense, of Christ, see Matt. xi. 5, v. 3, &c.

the poor] i.e. the poor in spirit (Matt. xi. 28, v. 3), as the Hebrew implies.

to heal the broken-hearted] Omitted in ℵ, B, D, L.

recovering of sight to the blind] Here the LXX. differs from the Hebrew, which has "*opening of prison to the bound.*" Perhaps this is a reminiscence of Is. xlii. 7.

to set at liberty them that are bruised] This also is not in Is. lxi. 1, but is a free reminiscence of the LXX. in lviii. 6. Either the text of the Hebrew was then slightly variant, or the record introduces into the text a reminiscence of the discourse.

19. *the acceptable year*] The primary allusion is to the year of Jubilee, Lev. xxv. 8—10; but this was only a type of the true Jubilee of Christ's kingdom. Many of the Fathers, with most mistaken literalness, inferred from this verse that our Lord's ministry only lasted a year, and the notion acquired more credence from the extraordinary brightness of His first, or Galilaean, year of ministry. This view has been powerfully supported by Mr Browne in his *Ordo Saeclorum*, but is quite untenable (John ii. 13, vi. 4, xi. 55).

20. *he closed the book*] Rather, **rolling up**. Generally the Haphtarah consists of twenty-one verses, and is never less than three; but our Lord stopped short in the second verse, because this furnished sufficient text for His discourse, and because He wished these gracious words to rest last on their ears, rather than the following words, "*the day of vengeance of our God.*"

the minister] The *Chazzan*.

sat down] The ordinary Jewish attitude for the sermon (Matt. xxiii. 2).

fastened on him] A favourite word of St Luke, who uses it eleven times; elsewhere it is only found in 2 Cor. iii. 7, 13. The attitude of Jesus shewed that now for the first time He intended not only to read but to preach.

21 him. And he began to say unto them, This day is this scrip-
22 ture fulfilled in your ears. And all bare him witness, and wondered at the gracious words which proceeded out of his
23 mouth. And they said, Is not this Joseph's son? And he said unto them, Ye will surely say unto me this proverb, Physician, heal thyself: whatsoever we have heard done in Capernaum, do also here in thy country.

21. *he began to say unto them*] i.e. these were the first words of the discourse. It began with the announcement that He was the Messiah in whom the words of the prophet found their fulfilment.

22. *gracious words*] Rather, **words of grace**. The word grace does not here mean mercy or favour (*Gnade*), but beauty and attractiveness (*Anmuth*). This verse and John vii. 46 are the chief proofs that there was in our Lord's utterance an irresistible majesty and sweetness. Comp. Ps. xlv. 2; John i. 14.

And they said, Is not this Joseph's son?] This points to a gradual change in the feeling of the listening Nazarenes. The Jews in their synagogues did not sit in silence, but were accustomed to give full expression to their feelings, and to discuss and make remarks aloud. Jealousy began to work among them, Matt. xiii. 54; John vi. 42. "The village beggarly pride of the Nazarenes cannot at all comprehend the humility of the Great One." Stier.

23. *this proverb*] The Greek word is '*parabolē*,' which is here used for the Hebrew *mashal*, and had a wider meaning than its English equivalent. Thus it is also used for a *proverb* (*Beispiel*), 1 Sam. x. 12, xxiv. 13; Ezek. xii. 22; or a type, Heb. ix. 9, xi. 19. See on viii. 5.

Physician, heal thyself] The same taunt was addressed to our Lord on the Cross. Here it seems to have more than one application,—meaning, 'If you are the Messiah why are you so poor and humble?' or, 'Why do you not do something for us, here in your own home?' (So Theophylact, Euthymius, &c.) It implies radical distrust, like *Hic Rhodos, hic salta*. There seems to be no exact Hebrew equivalent of the proverb, but something like it (a physician who needs healing) is found in Plut. *De Discern. Adul.* 32.

whatsoever we have heard done in Capernaum] St Luke has not before mentioned Capernaum, and this is one of the many indications found in his writings that silence respecting any event is no *proof* that he was unaware of it. Nor has any other Evangelist mentioned any previous miracle at Capernaum, unless we suppose that the healing of the courtier's son (John iv. 46—54) had *preceded* this visit to Nazareth. Jesus had, however, performed the first miracle at Cana, and may well have wrought others during the stay of "not many days" mentioned in John ii. 12. Capernaum was so completely the head-quarters of His ministry as to be known as "His own city." (Matt. iv. 12—16, xi. 23.)

24—30. *Rejection by the Nazarenes.*

And he said, Verily I say unto you, No prophet is accepted 24 in his own country. But I tell you of a truth, many widows 25 were in Israel in the days of Elias, when the heaven was shut up three years and six months, when great famine was throughout all the land; but unto none of them was Elias 26 sent, save unto Sarepta, *a city* of Sidon, unto a woman *that was* a widow. And many lepers were in Israel in the time of 27 Eliseus the prophet; and none of them was cleansed, saving Naaman the Syrian. And all *they* in the synagogue, when 28 they heard these *things*, were filled with wrath, and rose up, 29 and thrust him out of the city, and led him unto the brow of the hill whereon their city was built, that *they* might cast

24—30. REJECTION BY THE NAZARENES.

24. *is accepted in his own country*] St Matthew adds (xiii. 57) "and in his own house," implying that "neither did His brethren believe on Him." This curious psychological fact, which has its analogy in the worldly proverb that 'No man is a hero to his valet,' or, 'Familiarity breeds contempt,' was more than once referred to by our Lord; John iv. 44. ("Vile habetur quod domi est." Sen. *De Benef.* III. 2.)

25. *many widows were in Israel*] So far from trying to flatter them, He tells them that His work is not to be for *their* special benefit or glorification, but that He had now passed far beyond the limitations of earthly relationships.

three years and six months] Such was the Jewish tradition, as we see also in James v. 17 (comp. Dan. xii. 7; Rev. xi. 2, 3, xiii. 5). The book of Kings only *mentions* three years (1 K. xvii. 1, 8, 9, xviii. 1, 2), but in the "many days" it seems to imply more.

26. *save unto Sarepta*] i.e. "but he *was* sent to Sarepta." Zarephath (1 K. xvii. 9) was a Phoenician town near the coast between Tyre and Sidon, now called *Surafend*.

27. *saving Naaman the Syrian*] 2 K. v. 1—14. Thus both Elijah and Elisha had carried God's mercies to Gentiles.

28. *were filled with wrath*] The aorist implies a sudden outburst. Perhaps they were already offended by knowing that Jesus had spent two days at Sychar among the hated Samaritans; and now He whom they wished to treat as "the carpenter" and their equal, was as it were asserting the superior claims of Gentiles and lepers. "Truth embitters those whom it does not enlighten." "The word of God," said Luther, "is a sword, is a war, is a poison, is a scandal, is a stumbling-block, is a ruin"—viz. to those who resist it (Matt. x. 34; 1 Pet. ii. 8).

29. *the brow of the hill whereon their city was built*] The '*whereon*' refers to the hill not to the brow. Nazareth nestles under the southern slopes of the hill. The cliff down which they wished to hurl Him (because this was regarded as a form of 'stoning,' the legal punishment

30 him down headlong. But he passing through the midst of them went *his way*,

31—37. *The Healing of a Demoniac.*

31 and came down to Capernaum, a city of Galilee, and taught

for blasphemy) was certainly not the so-called 'Mount of Precipitation' which is two miles distant, and therefore more than a sabbath day's journey, but one of the rocky escarpments of the hill, and possibly that above the Maronite Church, which is about 40 feet high. This form of punishment is only mentioned in 2 Chr. xxv. 12; but in Phocis it was the punishment for sacrilege. (Philo.)

30. *passing through the midst of them*] This is rather a *mirabile* than a *miraculum*, since no miracle is asserted or necessarily implied. The inherent majesty and dignity of our Lord's calm ascendency, seem to have been sufficient on several occasions to overawe and cow His enemies; John vii. 30, 46, viii. 59, x. 39, 40, xviii. 6 (see Ps. xviii. 29, xxxvii. 33).

went his way] Probably never to return again. Nazareth lies in a secluded valley out of the ordinary route between Gennesareth and Jerusalem. If after thirty sinless years among them they could reject Him, clearly they had not known the day of their visitation. It is the most striking illustration of St John's sad comment, "He came unto His own possessions (τὰ ἴδια) and His own people (οἱ ἴδιοι) received Him not" (John i. 11).

31—37. THE HEALING OF A DEMONIAC.

31. *came down to Capernaum*] St Matthew (iv. 13—16) sees in this the fulfilment of Is. ix. 1, 2, omitting the first part which should be rendered "At the former time he brought contempt on the Land of Zebulun and on the Land of Naphtali, *but in the latter time he brought honour*." It was perhaps on His way to Capernaum that our Lord healed the courtier's son (John iv. 47—54). Capernaum is in all probability Tell Hûm. The name means village (now *Kefr*) of Nahum, and *Tell Hûm* is 'the ruined mound' or 'heap' of (Na)hum. It is now a heap of desolation with little to mark it except the ruins of one white marble synagogue—possibly the very one built by the friendly centurion (vii. 5)—and the widely-scattered *débris* of what perhaps was another. But in our Lord's time it was a bright and populous little town, at the very centre of what has been called "the manufacturing district of Palestine." It lay at the nucleus of roads to Tyre and Sidon, to Damascus, to Sepphoris (the capital of Galilee), and to Jerusalem, and was within easy reach of Peraea and Ituraea. It was in fact on the "*way of the sea*" (Is. ix. 1)—the great caravan road which led to the Mediterranean. It was hence peculiarly fitted to be the centre of a far-reaching ministry of which even Gentiles would hear. These things, as St Paul graphically says, were "not done in a corner," Acts

them on the sabbath days. And they were astonished at 32
his doctrine: for his word was with power.

And in the synagogue there was a man, which had a spirit 33
of an unclean devil, and cried out with a loud voice, saying, 34

xxvi. 26. Besides the memorable events of the day here recorded, it was here that Christ healed the paralytic (v. 18) and the centurion's servant (vii. 2), and called Levi (Matt. ix. 9), rebuked the disciples for their ambition (Mk. ix. 35), and delivered the memorable discourse about the bread of life (John vi.).

a city of Galilee] These little descriptions and explanations shew that St Luke is writing for Gentiles who did not know Palestine. Comp. i. 26, xxi. 37, xxii. 1.

32. *they were astonished*] The word expresses more sudden and vehement astonishment than the more deeply seated 'amaze' of vs. 36.

at his doctrine] Rather, **at His teaching**, referring here to the *manner* He adopted.

his word was with power] St Matthew gives one main secret of their astonishment when he says that "He taught them as one having authority, *and not as the scribes*," vii. 29. The religious teaching of the Scribes in our Lord's day had already begun to be the second-hand repetition of minute precedents supported by endless authorities. ("Rabbi Zeira says on the authority of Rabbi Jose bar Rabbi Chanina, and Rabbi Ba or Rabbi Chija on the authority of Rabbi Jochanan, &c., &c." Schwab, *Jer. Berachôth*, p. 159.) We see the final outcome of this servile secondhandness in the dreary minutiae of the Talmud. But Christ referred to no precedents; quoted no 'authorities;' dealt with fresher and nobler topics than fantastic *hagadoth* ('legends') and weary traditional *halachôth* ('rules'). He spoke straight from the heart to the heart, appealing for confirmation solely to truth and conscience,—the inner witness of the Spirit.

33. *a spirit of an unclean devil*] The word 'unclean' is peculiar to St Luke, who writes for Gentiles. The word for devil is not *diabolos*, which is confined to Satan, or human beings like him (John vi. 70); but *daimonion*, which in Greek was also capable of a good sense. The Jews believed *daimonia* to be the spirits of the wicked (Jos. *B. J.* VII. 6, § 3). Here begins that description of one complete Sabbath-day in the life of Jesus, from morning till night, which is also preserved for us in Matt. viii. 14—17; Mark i. 21—31. It is the best illustration of the life of 'the Good Physician' of which the rarest originality was that "He went about doing good" (Acts x. 38). Into the question of the reality or unreality of 'demoniac possession,' about which theologians have held different opinions, we cannot enter. On the one hand, it is argued that the Jews attributed nearly all diseases, and especially all mental and cerebral diseases, to the immediate action of evil spirits, and that these 'possessions' are ranged with cases of ordinary madness, and that the common belief would lead those thus afflicted to speak as if possessed; on the other hand, the literal interpretation of the

Let *us* alone; what have we to do with thee, *thou* Jesus of Nazareth? art thou come to destroy us? I know thee who
35 thou art, the Holy One of God. And Jesus rebuked him, saying, Hold thy peace, and come out of him. And when the devil had thrown him in the midst, he came out of him,
36 and hurt him not. And they were all amazed, and spake among themselves, saying, What a word *is* this! for with authority and power he commandeth the unclean spirits, and
37 they come out. And the fame of him went out into every place of the country round about.

Gospels points the other way, and in unenlightened ages, as still in dark and heathen countries, the powers of evil seem to have an exceptional range of influence over the mind of man. The student will see the whole question fully and reverently discussed in Jahn, *Archaeologia Biblica*, E. T. pp. 200—216.

34. *Saying, Let us alone*] Omit *saying*, with ℵ, B, L. The word *Ea!* may be not the imperative of *eaō* ('desist!') but a wild cry of horror 'Ha!'

what have we to do with thee] The demon speaks in the plural, merging his individuality in that of all evil powers. (Matt. viii. 29; Mark v. 9.) For the phrase see viii. 28; 2 Sam. xvi. 10, xix. 22; 1 K. xvii. 18; John ii. 4.

to destroy us] "The devils also believe and tremble," James ii. 19.

the Holy One] i. 35; Ps. xvi. 10, "thine Holy One." Dan. ix. 24.

35. *Hold thy peace*] Literally, "*Be muzzled*," as in 1 Cor. ix. 9. See Matt. xxii. 34; Mark i. 25, &c.

had thrown him] St Mark uses the stronger word "tearing him." It was the convulsion which became a spasm of visible deliverance. It is most instructive to contrast the simple sobriety of the narratives of the Evangelists with the credulous absurdities of even so able, polished and cosmopolitan a historian as Josephus, who describes an exorcism wrought in the presence of Vespasian by a certain Eleazar. It was achieved by means of a ring and the 'root of Solomon,' and the demon in proof of his exit was ordered to upset a bason of water! (Jos. *B. J.* vii. 6, § 3; *Antt.* viii. 2, § 5.) As this is the earliest of our Lord's miracles recorded by St Luke, we may notice that the terms used for miracles in the Gospels are *teras* 'prodigy,' and *thaumasion* 'wonderful' (Matt. xxi. 15 only), from the effect on men's minds; *paradoxon* (v. 26 only), from their strangeness; *sēmeia* 'signs,' and *dunameis* 'powers,' from their being indications of God's power; *endoxa* 'glorious deeds' (xiii. 17 only), as shewing His glory; and in St John *erga* 'works,' as the natural actions of One who was divine. See Trench, *On Miracles*, I. 9. "Miracles, it should be observed, are not *contrary to* nature, but *beyond* and *above* it." Mozley.

37. *the fame of him went out*] Rather, **a rumour about Him began to spread.**

38, 39. *The Healing of Simon's Wife's Mother.*

And he arose out of the synagogue, and entered into Simon's house. And Simon's wife's mother was taken with a great fever; and they besought him for her. And he stood over her, and rebuked the fever; and it left her: and immediately she arose and ministered unto them. 38 39

40—44. *Healing the Sick at Evening.*

Now when the sun was setting, all they that had *any* sick 40

38, 39. THE HEALING OF SIMON'S WIFE'S MOTHER.

38. *into Simon's house*] St Mark, nearly connected with St Peter, says more accurately "the house of Simon and Andrew" (i. 29). This is the first mention of Peter in St Luke, but the name was too well known in the Christian Church to need further explanation. Peter and Andrew were of Bethsaida (House of Fish), (John i. 44, xii. 21), a little fishing village, as its name imports, now *Ain et Tabijah* or 'the Spring of the Figtree,' where, alone on the Sea of Galilee, there is a little strip of bright hard sand. St Luke does not mention *this* Bethsaida, though he mentions *another* at the northern end of the Lake (ix. 10). It was so near Capernaum that our Lord may have walked thither, or possibly Simon's mother-in-law may have had a house at Capernaum. It is a remarkable indication of the little cloud of misunderstanding that seems to have risen between Jesus and those of His own house (Matt. xiii. 57; John iv. 44), that though they were then living at Capernaum (Matt. ix. 1, xvii. 24)—having perhaps been driven there by the hostility of the Nazarenes—*their* home was not *His* home.

Simon's wife's mother] "St Peter, the Apostle of Christ, who was himself a married man." Marriage Service. She seems afterwards to have travelled with him (1 Cor. ix. 5). Her (most improbable) traditional name was Concordia or Perpetua (Grabe, *Spicil. Patr.* I. 330).

with a great fever] St Luke, being a physician, uses the technical medical distinction of the ancients, which divided fevers into 'great' and 'little' (Galen). For other medical and psychological touches see v. 12, vi. 6, xxii. 50, 51; Acts iii. 6—8, iv. 22, ix. 33, &c.

they besought him] not, as elsewhere, the imperfect (John iv. 47), but the aorist, implying that they only had to ask Him once. St Mark confirms this when he says (i. 30), "*immediately* they speak to Him about her."

39. *he stood over her*] A graphic touch, found here only. The other Evangelists say that He took her by the hand.

she arose and ministered unto them] Literally, **arising at once she began to wait on them.**

40—44. HEALING THE SICK AT EVENING.

40. *when the sun was setting*] Sunset ended the Sabbath, and thus enabled Jews, without infringing on the many minute '*abhoth*' and

with divers diseases brought them unto him; and he laid
41 *his* hands on every one of them, and healed them. And devils also came out of many, crying out, and saying, Thou art Christ the Son of God. And he rebuking *them* suffered them not to speak: for they knew that he was Christ.
42 And when it was day, he departed and went into a desert place; and the people sought him, and came unto him, and
43 stayed him, that *he* should not depart from them. And he said unto them, I must preach the kingdom of God to other

'*toldoth*'—i.e. primary and subordinate rules of sabbatic strictness—to carry their sick on beds and pallets. (John v. 11, 12; see *Life of Christ*, I. 433.) This twilight scene of Jesus moving about with word and touch of healing among the sick and suffering, the raving and tortured crowd (Matt. iv. 24), is one of the most striking in the Gospels, and St Matthew quotes it as a fulfilment of Is. liii. 4.

41. *crying out*] The word implies the harsh screams of the demoniacs.

Thou art Christ the Son of God] The words "Thou art Christ" should be omitted with ℵ, B, C, D, F, L, &c.

suffered them not to speak] "His hour was not yet come" (John vii. 30), nor in any case would He accept such testimony: so St Paul with the Pythoness at Philippi (Acts xvi. 18).

to speak: for they knew that he was Christ] Rather, **to say that they knew that He was the Christ**, i.e. the Messiah. It was not till after the Crucifixion that 'Christ' became a proper name, and not a title.

42. *when it was day*] St Mark (i. 35) uses the expression "rising up exceedingly early in the morning, while it was yet dark." It was His object to escape into silence, and solitude, and prayer, without being observed by the multitudes.

into a desert place] Densely as the district was populated, such a place might be found in such hill ravines as the Vale of Doves at no great distance.

the people sought him] Rather, **were earnestly seeking for Him**. It is characteristic of the eager impetuosity of St Peter, that (as St Mark tells us, i. 36) he, with his friends, on this occasion (literally) "hunted Him down" (*katedioxan*).

stayed him] Rather, **tried** or *wished* **to detain Him**. It is the *tentative* imperfect.

43. *I must*] "It behoves me"—the 'must' of moral obligation.

preach] Rather, **tell the glad tidings of.** The word is "evangelize," not *kērussō* the word of the next verse.

the kingdom of God] The acceptance of the Faith of Christ, whether in the heart or in the world, was illustrated by Christ in its small beginnings,—the mustard seed (xiii. 19); in its hidden working (xiii. 21); and in its final triumph.

to other cities] Rather, **to the rest of the cities.** In St Mark He says, Let us go elsewhere to the adjoining country villages.

cities also: for therefore am I sent. And he preached in the 44
synagogues of Galilee.

CH. V. 1—11. *The Draught of Fishes. The Calling of four Disciples.*

And it came to pass that, as the people pressed upon him 5
to hear the word of God, he stood by the lake of Gennesa-

44. *he preached*] Rather, **He was preaching,** implying a continued ministry.

of Galilee] Here ℵ, B, C, L and other uncials have the important various reading "of Judaea." If this reading be correct, it is another of the many indications that the Synoptists *assume and imply* that Judaean ministry which St John alone narrates.

CH. V. 1—11. THE DRAUGHT OF FISHES. THE CALLING OF FOUR DISCIPLES.

1. *pressed upon him*] St Mark (as is his wont) uses a stronger word to express the physical inconvenience, and adds that sometimes at any rate, it was with a view to touch Him and be healed (iii. 9, 10).

to hear] The more probable reading is not *tou* but *kai*, 'and listened to.'

the lake of Gennesaret] "The most sacred sheet of water which this earth contains." Stanley. St Luke alone, writing for the Greeks, accurately calls it a lake. The Galilaean and Jewish Evangelists unconsciously follow the Hebrew idiom which applies the name *yam* 'sea,' to every piece of water. Gennesareth is probably a corruption of the old Hebrew name Kinnereth, but the Rabbis derive it from *ganne sarim* 'gardens of princes.' This same inland lake is generally called 'the Sea of Galilee' (Matt. xv. 29, &c.). In the Old Testament it is called "the Sea of Chinneroth" (Josh. xii. 3) from its harplike shape. St John calls it "the Sea of Tiberias;" because by the time he wrote Tiberias, which in our Lord's time had only just been founded by Herod Antipas, had grown into a flourishing town. Gennesareth is a clear sweet lake about five miles long and twelve broad, with the Jordan flowing through it. Its fish produced a valuable revenue to those who lived on its shores. The plain of Gennesareth, which lies 500 feet below the level of the Mediterranean, is now known as *El Ghuweir*, 'the little hollow.' It is so completely a desolation, that the only inhabited places on the western shore of the Lake are the crumbling, dirty earthquake-shaken town of Tiberias and the mud village of *El Mejdel* the ancient Magdala. The burning and enervating heat is no longer tempered by cultivation and by trees. It is still however beautiful in spring, with flowering oleanders, and the soil is fruitful where it is not encumbered with ruins as at *Khan Minyeh* (Tarichaea) and *Tell Hûm* (Capernaum). In our Lord's time it was, as Josephus calls it, "the best part of Galilee" (*B. J.* III. 10, § 7) containing many villages, of which the least had 15000 inhabitants. Josephus becomes quite eloquent over the descriptions of its rich fruits nearly all

² ret, and saw two ships standing by the lake: but the fishermen were gone out of them, and were washing *their* nets.
³ And he entered into one of the ships, which was Simon's, and prayed him that *he* would thrust out a little from the land. And he sat down, and taught the people out of the ship.
⁴ Now when he had left speaking, he said unto Simon, Launch out into the deep, and let down your nets for a
⁵ draught. And Simon answering said unto him, Master, we

the year, its grateful temperature, and its fertilising stream (Jos. *B. J.* III. 10, §§ 7, 8), so that, he says, one might call it 'the ambition of nature.' It belonged to the tribe of Naphtali (Deut. xxxiii. 33) and the Rabbis said that of the "seven seas" of Canaan, it was the only one which God had reserved for Himself. In our Lord's time it was covered with a gay and numerous fleet of 4000 vessels, from ships of war down to fishing boats; now it is often difficult to find a single crazy boat even at Tiberias, and the Arabs fish mainly by throwing poisoned breadcrumbs into the water near the shore. As four great roads communicated with the Lake it became a meeting-place for men of many nations—Jews, Galilaeans, Syrians, Phoenicians, Arabs, Greeks and Romans.

2. *ships*] Rather, **boats** (*ploiaria*).

standing] i.e. lying at anchor.

were washing their nets] If we combine these notices with those in Mark i. 16—20; Matt. iv. 18—22, we must suppose that during a discourse of Jesus the four disciples were fishing with a drawnet (*amphiblestron*) not far from the shore, and within hearing of His voice; and that the rest of the incident (here narrated) took place on the morning after. The disciples had spent the night in fruitless labour, and now Peter and Andrew were washing, and James and John mending, their castingnets (*diktua*), because they felt that it was useless to go on, since night is the best time for fishing.

nets] Here *diktua* or castingnets (from *dikō* I throw, *funda, jaculum*) as in Matt. iv. 20; John xxi. 6. In Matt. iv. 18 we have the *amphiblestron* or drawnet (from *amphi* and *ballo*, I throw around); and in Matt. xiii. 47, *sagēnē*, seine or haulingnet (from *sattō* 'I load').

3. *he sat down*] The ordinary attitude (as we have seen, iv. 20) for a sermon.

4. *when he had left speaking*] The aorist implies that no sooner was His sermon ended than He at once thought, not of His own fatigue, but of His poor disappointed followers.

5. *let down*] Rather, **let ye down**. The first command is in the singular, and is addressed to Peter only as "the *pilot* of the Galilaean Lake."

Master] The word is not *Rabbi* as in the other Evangelists,—a word which Gentiles would not have understood but *Epistata* (in its occasional classic sense of 'teacher') which is peculiar to St Luke v. 5, viii. 24, 45, ix. 33, 49, xvii. 13. These are the only places where it occurs.

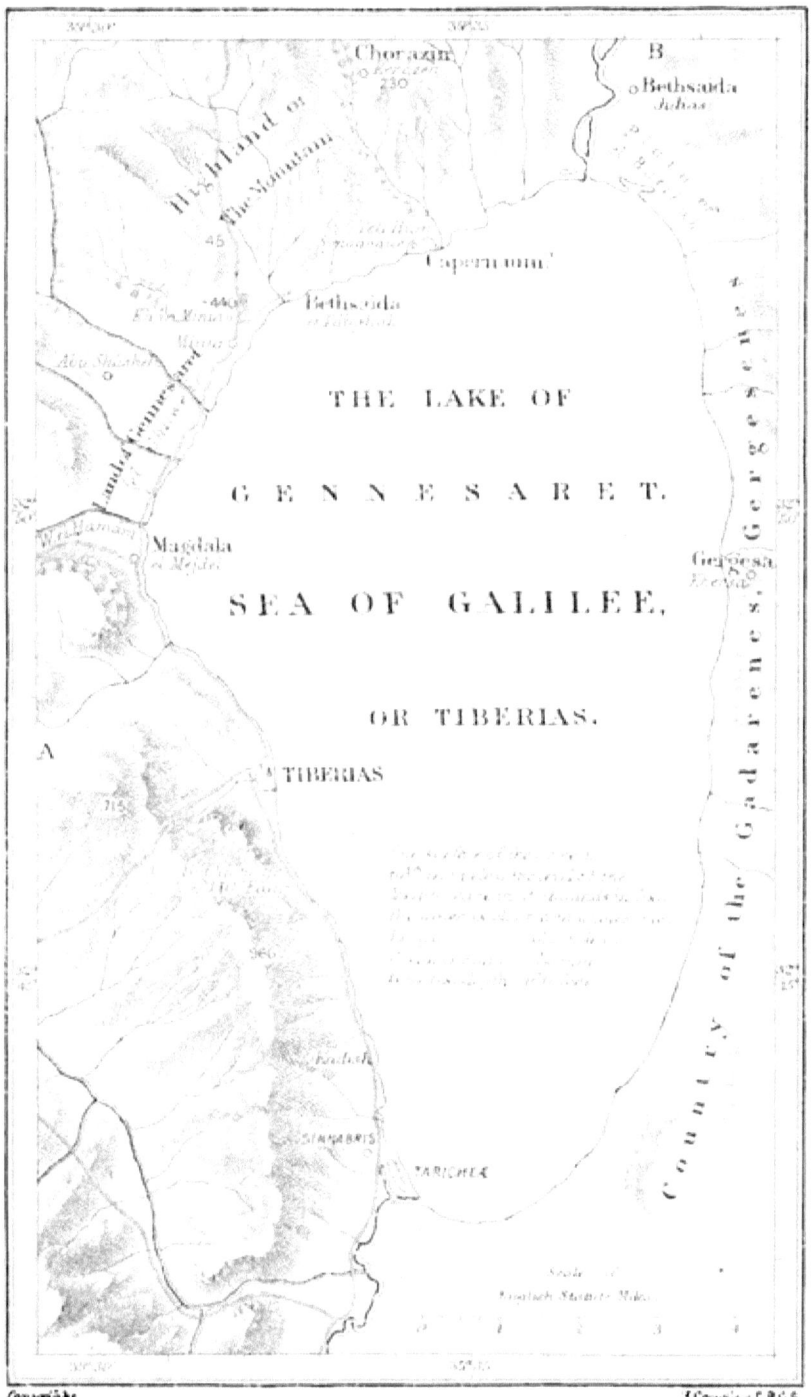

have toiled all the night, and have taken nothing: nevertheless at thy word I will let down the net. And when they 6 had this done, they inclosed a great multitude of fishes: and their net brake. And they beckoned unto *their* partners, 7 which were in the other ship, that *they* should come and help them. And they came, and filled both the ships, so that they began to sink. When Simon Peter saw *it*, he fell 8 down at Jesus' knees, saying, Depart from me; for I am a

6. *a great multitude of fishes*] Of this—as of all miracles—we may say with St Gregory *Dum facit miraculum prodit mysterium*—in other words the miracle was an acted parable, of which the significance is explained in Matt. xiii. 47.

brake] Rather, **were beginning to break** (*dierregnuto*). Contrast this with John xxi. 11, οὐκ ἐσχίσθη. This *breaking* net is explained by St Augustine as the symbol of the Church which now is: he compares the *unrent* net to the Church of the future which shall know no schisms.

7. *they beckoned*] It is one of the inimitable touches of truthfulness in the narrative that the instinct of work prevails at first over the sense that a miraculous power has been exerted.

unto their partners] The word used is *metochois*, meaning fellow-workers.

in the other ship] St Luke uses the Greek word *heteros* for 'another of two,' much more frequently and with stricter accuracy than the other Evangelists.

8. *When Simon Peter saw it*] Apparently it was only when he saw the boats sinking to the gunwale with their load of fish that the tenderness and majesty of the miracle flashed upon his mind.

Depart from me] The words imply *leave my boat* (*exelthe*) and go from me. Here again is the stamp of truthfulness. Any one inventing the scene would have made Peter kneel in thankfulness or adoration, but would have missed the strange psychological truthfulness of the sense of sin painfully educed by the revealed presence of divine holiness. We find the expression of analogous feelings in the case of Manoah (Judg. xiii. 22); the Israelites at Sinai (Ex. xx. 19); the men of Beth-shemesh (1 Sam. vi. 20); David after the death of Uzzah (2 Sam. vi. 9); the lady of Zarephath (1 Kings xvii. 18); Job (Job xlii. 5, 6); and Isaiah (Is. vi. 5). The exclamation of St Peter was wrung from a heart touched with a sense of humility, and his words did not express his thoughts. They were the cry of agonised humility, and only emphasized his own utter unworthiness. They were in reality the reverse of the deliberate and calculated request of the swine-feeding Gadarenes. The dead and profane soul dislikes and tries to get rid of the presence of the Divine. The soul awakened only to conviction of sin is terrified. The soul that has found God is conscious of utter unworthiness, but fear is

₉ sinful man, O Lord. For he was astonished, and all that were with him, at the draught of the fishes which they had ₁₀ taken: and so *was* also James, and John, *the* sons of Zebedee, which were partners with Simon. And Jesus said unto Simon, Fear not; from henceforth thou shalt catch men. ₁₁ And when they had brought *their* ships to land, they forsook all, and followed him.

a sinful man] The Greek has two words for man—*anthropos*, a general term for 'human being' (*homo*); and *anēr* for 'a man' (*vir*). The use of the *latter* here shews that Peter's confession is individual, not general.

O Lord] It must be remembered that this was the second call of Peter and the three Apostles,—the call to Apostleship; they had *already* received a call to *faith*. They had received their *first* call on the banks of Jordan, and had heard the witness of John, and had witnessed the miracle of Cana. They had only returned to their ordinary avocations until the time came for Christ's full and active ministry.

9. *he was astonished*] Rather, **astonishment seized him.**

10. *partners*] Here *koinonoi*, 'associates' in profits, &c.

Fear not] Accordingly, on another occasion, when Peter sees Jesus walking on the sea, so far from crying *Depart from me*, he cries "Lord, if it be Thou, bid me come to Thee on the water" (Matt. xiv. 28); and when he saw the Risen Lord standing in the misty morning on the shore of the Lake "he cast himself into the sea" to come to Him (John xxi. 7).

10. *thou shalt catch*] Literally, 'thou shalt be *catching alive.*' In Jer. xvi. 16 the fishers draw out men to death, and in Amos iv. 2, Hab. i. 14, men are "made as the fishes of the sea" by way of punishment. Here the word seems to imply the contrast between the fish that lay glittering there in *dead* heaps, and men who should be captured not for death (Jas. i. 14), but for life. But Satan too captures men alive (2 Tim. ii. 26, the only other passage where the verb occurs). From this and the parable of the seine or haulingnet (Matt. xiii. 47) came the favorite early Christian symbol of the 'Fish.' "We little fishes," says Tertullian, "after our Fish (ΙΧΘΥΣ, i.e. Ἰησοῦς Χριστὸς Θεοῦ Υἱὸς Σωτήρ) are born in the water (of baptism)." The prophecy was first fulfilled to Peter, when 3000 were converted by his words at the first Pentecost. In a hymn of St Clement of Alexandria we find "O fisher of mortals who are being saved, Enticing pure fish for sweet life from the hostile wave." Thus, He who "spread the fisher's net over the palaces of Tyre and Sidon, gave into the fisher's hand the keys of the kingdom of heaven." "He caught orators by fishermen, and made out of fishermen his orators." We find a similar metaphor used by Socrates, Xen. *Mem.* II. 6, "Try to be good and to catch the good. I will help you, for I know the art of catching men."

11. *they forsook all*] The sacrifice was a willing one, but they were not unconscious of its magnitude; and it was the allusion to it by Peter

12—16. *The Healing of a Leper.*

^{12}And it came to pass, when he was in a certain city, behold a man full of leprosy: who seeing Jesus fell on *his* face, and besought him, saying, Lord, if thou wilt, thou canst make me clean. ^{13}And he put forth *his* hand, and touched

which called forth the memorable promise of the hundredfold (xviii. 28—30; Mk. x. 29, 30). We gather from St Mark that Zebedee (Zabdia) and his two sons had hired servants (i. 20), and therefore they were probably richer than Simon and Andrew, sons of Jona.

12—16. THE HEALING OF A LEPER.

12. *a certain city*] Probably the village of Hattîn, for we learn from St Matthew's definite notice that this incident took place on descending from the Mount of Beatitudes (*Kurn Hattîn*), see Matt. viii. 1—4; Mk. i. 40—45. Hence chronologically the call of Matthew, the choosing of the Twelve, and the Sermon on the Mount probably intervene between this incident and the last.

a man full of leprosy] The hideous and hopeless nature of this disease—which is nothing short of a foul decay, arising from the total corruption of the blood—has been too often described to need further notice. See Lev. xiii., xiv. It was a living death, as indicated by bare head, rent clothes, and covered lip. In the middle ages, a man seized with leprosy was "clothed in a shroud, and the masses of the dead sung over him." In its horrible repulsiveness it is the Gospel type of Sin. The expression "full of" implies the rapid development and horror of the disease; when the man's whole body was *covered* with the whiteness, he was allowed to mingle with others as clean (Lev. xiii. 13).

fell on his face] We get the full picture by combining the three Evangelists. We then see that he came with passionate entreaties, flinging himself on his knees, and worshipping, and finally in his agony prostrating himself on his face.

thou canst make me clean] The faith of this poor leper must have been intense, for hitherto there had been but one instance of a leper cleansed by miracle (iv. 27; 2 K. v.).

13. *and touched him*] This was a distinct violation of the *letter*, but not of course of the *spirit* of the Mosaic law (Lev. xiii. 46; Numb. v. 2). In order to prevent the accidental violation of this law, lepers, until the final stage of the disease, were then as now secluded from all living contact with others, "differing in nothing from a dead man" (Jos. *Ant.* III. 11 § 3), and only appeared in public with the cry *Tamê, Tamê*—'Unclean! Unclean!' But Jesus, "because He is the Lord of the Law, does not obey the Law, but makes the Law" (St Ambrose); or rather, he obeys that divine eternal Law of Compassion, in its sudden impulse ($\sigma\pi\lambda\alpha\gamma\chi\nu\iota\sigma\theta\epsilon$ίς, Mk. i. 40), which is older and grander than the written Law. (So Elijah and Elisha had not scrupled to touch the dead, 1 K. xvii. 21; 2 K. iv. 34.) His touching the leper, yet remaining

8—2

him, saying, I will: be thou clean. And immediately the
14 leprosy departed from him. And he charged him to tell no
man: but go, and shew thyself to the priest, and offer for
thy cleansing, according as Moses commanded, for a testi-

clean, is a type of His taking our humanity upon Him, remaining undefiled.

I will: be thou clean] Two words in the original—"a prompt echo to the ripe faith of the leper"—which are accurately preserved by all three Evangelists. Our Lord's first miracles were done with a glad spontaneity in answer to faith. But when men had ceased to believe in Him, then lack of faith rendered His later miracles more sad and more delayed (Mk. vi. 5; Matt. xiii. 58). We never however hear of a moment's delay in attending to the cry of a leper. When the sinner cries from his heart, "I have sinned against the Lord," the answer comes instantly, "The Lord also hath put away thy sin" (2 Sam. xii. 13).

the leprosy departed] Jesus was not polluted by the touch, but the leper was cleansed. Even so he touched our sinful nature, yet without sin (H. de St Victore).

14. *he charged him to tell no man*] These injunctions to reticence marked especially the early part of the ministry. See iv. 35, v. 14, viii. 56. The reasons were probably (i) personal to the healed sufferer, lest his inward thankfulness should be dissipated by the idle and boastful gossip of curiosity (St Chrys.), but far more (ii) because, as St Matthew expressly tells us, He did not wish His ministry to be accompanied by excitement and tumult, in accordance with the prophecy of Is. xlii. 2 (Matt. xii. 15—50, comp. Phil. ii. 6, 7; Heb. v. 5; John xviii. 36); and (iii) because He came, not merely and not mainly, to be a great Physician and Wonder-worker, but to save men's souls by His Revelation, His Example, and His Death.

It is evident however that there was something very special in this case, for St Mark says (i. 43), "violently enjoining him, immediately He thrust him forth, and said to him, *See that* you say no more to any one" (according to the right reading and translation). Clearly, although the multitudes were following Christ (Matt. viii. 1), He was walking before them, and the miracle had been so sudden and instantaneous (ἰδού... εὐθέως) that they had not observed what had taken place. Probably our Lord desired to avoid the Levitical rites for uncleanness which the unspiritual ceremonialism of the Pharisees might have tried to force upon Him.

On other occasions, when these reasons did not exist, He even enjoined the publication of an act of mercy, viii. 39.

but go, and shew thyself to the priest] We find similar instances of transition from indirect to direct narration, in Acts xxiii. 22; Ps. lxxiv. 16. See my *Brief Greek Syntax*, p. 196. The priest alone could legally *pronounce* him clean.

offer for thy cleansing] The student should read for himself the intensely interesting and symbolic rites commanded by Moses for the

mony unto them. But *so much* the more went there a fame 15
abroad of him: and great multitudes came together to hear,
and to be healed by him of their infirmities. And he with- 16
drew himself into the wilderness, and prayed.

17—26. *The Healing of the Paralytic.*

And it came to pass on a certain day, as he was teaching, 17
that there were Pharisees and doctors of the law sitting *by*,
which were come out of every town of Galilee, and Judea,
and Jerusalem: and the power of the Lord was *present* to

legal pronunciation of a leper clean in Lev. xiv. They occupy fourteen chapters of *Negaim*, one of the treatises of the Mishnah.

according as Moses commanded] A reference to Lev. xiv. 4—10 will shew how heavy an expense the offering entailed.

for a testimony unto them] i.e. that the priests may assure themselves that the miracle is real. In ix. 5; Mk. vi. 11 the words mean 'for a witness *against* them.'

15. *so much the more went there a fame abroad*] It is clear therefore that the leper disobeyed his strict injunction. Such disobedience was natural, and perhaps venial; but certainly not commendable.

great multitudes came together...to be healed] Thus in part defeating our Lord's purpose.

16. *he withdrew himself into the wilderness, and prayed*] Rather, **But He Himself was retiring in the wilderness and praying.** St Mark (i. 45) gives us the clearest view of the fact by telling us that the leper blazoned abroad his cure in every direction, "*so that He was no longer able to enter openly into a city, but was without, in desert spots; and they began to come to Him from all directions.*" We here see that this retirement was a sort of "Levitical quarantine," which however the multitudes disregarded as soon as they discovered where He was.

and prayed] St Luke's is eminently the Gospel of Prayer and Thanksgiving. See on iii. 21.

17—26. THE HEALING OF THE PARALYTIC.

17. *on a certain day*] The vagueness of the phrase shews that no stress is here laid on chronological order. In Matt. ix. 2—8; Mk. ii. 3—12 the scene is in a house in Capernaum, and the time (apparently) after the healing of the Gadarene demoniac on the Eastern side of the Lake, and on the day of Matthew's feast.

as he was teaching] not in a synagogue, but probably in Peter's house. Notice the "He" which is so frequent in St Luke, and marks the later epoch when the title "the Christ" had passed into a name, and when "He" could have but one meaning. See on iv. 15.

Pharisees and doctors of the law] See Excursus on the Jewish Sects.

and Judea and Jerusalem] These had probably come out of simple curiosity to hear and see the great Prophet of Nazareth. They were

18 heal them. And behold, men brought in a bed a man which was taken with a palsy: and they sought *means* to bring
19 him in, and to lay *him* before him. And when they could not find by what *way* they might bring him in because of the multitude, they went upon the housetop, and let him down through the tiling with *his* couch into the midst before
20 Jesus. And when he saw their faith, he said unto him, Man,
21 thy sins are forgiven thee. And the scribes and the Phari-

not the *spies* malignantly sent at the later and sadder epoch of His ministry (Matt. xv. 1; Mk. iii. 2, vii. 1) to dog his footsteps, and lie in wait to catch any word on which they could build an accusation.

to heal them] Some MSS. (ℵ, B, L,) read "*him*." If the reading be correct the verse means "the Power of the Lord (i.e. of the Almighty Jehovah) was with Him to heal."

18. *men*] four bearers, Mk. ii. 3.

taken with a palsy] The word used by Matthew (ix. 1—8) and Mark (ii. 1—12) is "paralytic," but as that is not a classic word, St Luke uses "having been paralysed" (*paralelumenos*).

they sought means to bring him in] St Mark explains that the crowd was so great that they could not even get to the door.

19. *they went upon the housetop*] A very easy thing to do because there was in most houses an outside staircase to the roof, Matt. xxiv. 17. Eastern houses are often only one storey high, and when they are built on rising ground, the roof is often nearly on a level with the street above. Our Lord may have been teaching in the "upper room" of the house, which was usually the largest and quietest. 2 Kings iv. 10; Acts i. 13, ix. 37.

let him down through the tiling] St Mark says they uncovered the roof where he was, and digging it up, let down 'the pallet.' Clearly then two operations seem to have been necessary: (i) to remove the tiles, and (ii) to dig through some mud partition. But the description is too vague to enable us to understand the details. Sceptical writers have raised difficulties about it in order to discredit the whole narrative (comp. Cic. *Phil.* II. 18, "per tegulas demitterere"), but the making of an aperture in the roof is an everyday matter in the East (Thomson, *The Land and the Book*, p. 358), and is here alluded to, not because it was strange, but to illustrate the active, and as it were nobly impatient, faith of the man and the bearers.

with his couch] *klinidion*, 'little bed,' probably a mere mat or mattress. It means the same as St Mark's *krabbaton*, but that being a semi-Latin word (*grabatum*) would be more comprehensible to the Roman readers of St Mark than to the Greek readers of St Luke.

20. *Man*] St Mark has "Son," and St Matthew "Cheer up, son," which were probably the exact words used by Christ.

are forgiven thee] Rather, **have been forgiven thee**, i.e. now and henceforth. In this instance our Lord's power of reading the heart

sees began to reason, saying, Who is this which speaketh blasphemies? Who can forgive sins, but God alone? But when Jesus perceived their thoughts, he answering said unto them, What reason ye in your hearts? Whether is easier, to say, Thy sins be forgiven thee; or to say, Rise up and walk? But that ye may know that the Son of man hath power upon

must have shewn Him that there was a connexion between past sin and present affliction. The Jews held it as an universal rule that suffering was always the immediate consequence of sin. The Book of Job had been directed against that hard, crude, Pharisaic generalisation. Since that time it had been modified by the view that a man might suffer, not for his own sins, but for those of his parents (John ix. 3). These views were all the more dangerous because they were the distortion of half-truths. Our Lord, while he always left the individual conscience to read the connexion between its own sins and its sorrows (John v. 14), distinctly repudiated the universal inference (Luke xiii. 5; John ix. 3).

21. *Who is this*] The word used for 'this person' is contemptuous. St Matthew puts it still more barely, 'This fellow blasphemes,' and to indulge such thoughts and feelings was distinctly "to think evil thoughts."

blasphemies] In classical Greek the word means abuse and injurious talk, but the Jews used it specially of curses against God, or claiming His attributes (Matt. xxvi. 65; John x. 36).

Who can forgive sins, but God alone] The remark in itself was not unnatural, Ps. xxxii. 5; Is. xliii. 25; but they captiously overlooked the possibility of a delegated authority, and the ordinary declaratory idioms of language, which might have shewn them that blasphemy was a thing impossible to Christ, even if they were not yet prepared to admit the Divine Power which He had already exhibited.

22. *when Jesus perceived*] Rather, **Jesus, recognising**.

their thoughts] Rather, **their reasonings**.

23. *Whether is easier, to say*] An impostor might *say* 'thy sins have been forgiven' without any visible sign whether his words had any power or not; no one could by a word make a man 'rise and walk' who had not received power from God. But our Lord had purposely used words which while they brought the *earthly* miracle into less prominence, went to the very root of the evil, and implied a yet loftier prerogative.

24. *the Son of man*] *Ben-Adam* has a *general* sense of any human being (Job xxv. 6, &c.); in a *special* sense in the O. T. it is nearly 90 times applied to Ezekiel, though *never* used by himself *of* himself. In the N. T. it is 80 times used by Christ, but always *by* Himself, except in passages which imply His exaltation (Acts vii. 56; Rev. i. 13—20). The Title, as distinctively *Messianic*, is derived from Dan. vii. 13, and is there *Bar-Enôsh*, a word descriptive of man in his humiliation. The inference seems to be that Christ used it to indicate the truth

earth to forgive sins, (he said unto the sick of the palsy,) I say unto thee, Arise, and take up thy couch, and go into ²⁵ thine house. And immediately he rose up before them, and took up *that* whereon he lay, and departed to his own house, ²⁶ glorifying God. And they were all amazed, and they glorified God, and were filled with fear, saying, We have seen strange *things* to day.

27—39. *The Call and Feast of Levi. On Fasting. The New and the Old.*

²⁷ And after these *things* he went forth, and saw a publican, named Levi, sitting at the receipt of custom: and he said ²⁸ unto him, Follow me. And he left all, rose up, and followed

that "God highly exalted Him" because of his self-humiliation in taking our flesh (Phil. ii. 5—11).

hath power upon earth to forgive sins] and therefore of course, *a fortiori*, hath power in heaven.

I say unto thee] Rather, to keep the emphatic order, **To thee I say.**

25. *took up that whereon he lay*] This circumstance is emphasized in all three narratives to contrast his previous helplessness, "borne of four," with his present activity. He now carried the bed which had carried him, and "the proof of his sickness became the proof of his cure." The labour would have been no more than that of carrying a rug or a cloak, yet it was this which excited the fury of the Pharisees in Jerusalem (John v. 9). It was not *specially* attacked by the simpler and less Pharisaic Pharisees of Galilee.

26. *were filled with fear*] See on vs. 8.

27—39. THE CALL AND FEAST OF LEVI. ON FASTING. THE NEW AND THE OLD.

27. *and saw*] Rather, **He observed.**

named Levi] It may be regarded as certain that Levi is the same person as the Evangelist St Matthew. The name Matthew (probably a corruption of Mattithijah) means, like Nathanael, Theodore, Doritheus, Adeodatus, &c., 'the gift of God,' and it seems to have been the name which he himself adopted after his call (see Matt. ix. 9, x. 3; Mk. ii. 14).

at the receipt of custom] Matthew may have been a tax-gatherer for Herod Antipas—who seems to have been allowed to manage his own taxes—and not for the Romans; but even in that case he would share almost equally with a man like Zacchaeus the odium with which his class was regarded. For the Herods were mere creatures of the Caesars (Jos. *Antt.* XVII. 11 § 6). Probably the 'custom' was connected with the traffic of the Lake, and in the Hebrew Gospel of St Matthew 'publican' is rendered '*Baal abarah*' 'lord of the passage.'

28. *he left all*] It is most probable that St Matthew, like the sons

him. And Levi made him a great feast in his own house: 29
and there was a great company of publicans and of others
that sat down with them. But their scribes and Pharisees 30
murmured against his disciples, saying, Why do ye eat and
drink with publicans and sinners? And Jesus answering 31
said unto them, They that are whole need not a physician;

of Jona and of Zebedee, had known something of our Lord before this
call. If Alphaeus (Matt. x. 3; Mk. ii. 14) be the same as the father of
James the Less, and the same as Clopas (John xix. 25) the husband of
Mary, and if this Mary was the sister of the Virgin, then James and
Matthew were cousins of Jesus. The inferences are uncertain, but
early Christian tradition points in this direction. It was a *rare* but
not unknown custom to call two sisters by the same names.

29. *made him a great feast*] This shews that Matthew had something to sacrifice when he "left all." The word rendered 'feast' literally means 'reception.'

a great company of publicans] Comp. xv. 1. The tax-gatherers in their deep, and not wholly undeserved unpopularity, would be naturally touched by the countenance and kindness of the Sinless One.

sat down] Rather, **were reclining** (at table).

30. *their scribes and Pharisees*] Some MSS. read '*the Pharisees and their scribes*,' i.e. those who were the authorised teachers of the company present. The scribes (*Sopherîm* from *Sepher* 'a book') were a body which had sprung up after the exile, whose function it was to copy and explain the Law. The 'words of the scribes' were the nucleus of the body of tradition known as 'the oral law.' The word was a *general* term, for technically the *Sopherîm* were succeeded by the *Tanaîm* or 'repeaters' from B.C. 300 to A.D. 220, who drew up the *Halachôth* or 'precedents;' and they by the *Amoraim*. The tyranny of pseudo-orthodoxy which they had established, and the insolent terrorism with which it was enforced, were denounced by our Lord (xi. 37—54) in terms of which the burning force can best be understood by seeing from the Talmud how crushing were the 'secular chains' in which they had striven to bind the free conscience of the people—chains which it became His compassion to burst (see Gfrörer, *Jahrh. d. Heils*, I. 140).

murmured against his disciples] They had not yet learnt to break the spell of awe which surrounded the Master, and so they attacked the 'unlearned and ignorant' Apostles. The murmurs must have reached the ears of Jesus after the feast, unless we imagine that some of these dignified teachers, who of course could not sit down at the meal, came and looked on out of curiosity. The house of an Oriental is perfectly open, and any one who likes may enter it.

with publicans and sinners] Rather, "with **the** publicans and sinners." The article is found in nearly all the uncials.

31. *They that are whole*] Our Lord's words had both an obvious and a deeper meaning. As regards the ordinary duties and respectability of life these provincial scribes and Pharisees were really "whole"

32 but they that are sick. I came not to call *the* righteous, but sinners to repentance.

33 And they said unto him, Why do the disciples of John fast often, and make prayers, and likewise the *disciples* of 34 the Pharisees; but thine eat and drink? And he said unto

as compared with the flagrant "sinfulness" of the tax-gatherers and "sinners." In another and even a more dangerous sense they were themselves "sinners" who *fancied* only that they had no need of Jesus (Rev. iii. 17, 18). They did not yet feel their own sickness, and the day had not yet come when they were to be told of it both in parables (xviii. 11—13) and in terms of terrible plainness (Matt. xxiii.), "Difficulter ad sanitatem pervenimus, quia nos aegrotare nescimus." Sen. *Ep.* 50. 4.

32. *I came not to call*] Rather, **I have not come**.

the righteous] This also was true in two senses. Our Lord came to seek and save the lost. He came not to the elder son but to the prodigal; not to the folded flock but to the straying sheep. In a lower and external sense these Pharisees were really, as they called themselves, 'the righteous' (*chasidim*). In another sense they were only self-righteous and self-deceived (xviii. 9). St Matthew tells us that He further rebuked their haughty and pitiless exclusiveness by borrowing one of their own formulae, and bidding them *"go and learn"* the meaning of Hos. vi. 6, "I will have mercy and not sacrifice," i.e. love is better than legal scrupulosity; Matt. ix. 13, xii. 7. The invariable tendency of an easy and pride-stimulating externalism when it is made a substitute for heart-religion is the most callous hypocrisy. The Pharisees were condemned not by Christ only but by their own Pharisaic Talmud, and after B.C. 70 the very name fell into such discredit among the Jews themselves as a synonym for greed and hypocrisy that it became a reproach and was dropped as a title (Jost, *Gesch. d. Juden.* IV. 76; Gfrörer, *Jahrh. d. Heils*, I. 140; Lightfoot, *Hor. Hebr.* on Matt. iii. 7).

33. *And they said*] St Luke here omits the remarkable fact that the disciples of John, who still formed a distinct body, joined the Pharisees in asking this question. It is clear that they were sometimes actuated by a not unnatural human jealousy, from which their great teacher was wholly free (John iii. 26), but which Jesus always treated with the utmost tenderness (vii. 24—28).

the disciples of John fast often] They would naturally adopt the ascetic habits of the Baptist.

and make prayers] Rather, **supplications**. Of course the disciples prayed, but perhaps they did not use so 'much speaking' and connect their *prayers* with fastings. The preservation of these words by St Luke alone, in spite of the emphasis which he lays on prayer, shews his perfect fidelity.

the disciples of the Pharisees] Those who in Jewish writings are so often spoken of as the 'pupils of the wise.' See on xviii. 12, "I

them, Can ye make the children of the bridechamber fast, while the bridegroom is with them? But the days will come, 35 when the bridegroom shall be taken away from them, and then shall they fast in those days. And he spake also a 36 fast twice in the week." Our Lord points out how much self-seeking and hypocrisy were mingled with their fasting, Matt. vi. 16, and the prophets had forcibly taught the utter uselessness of an abstinence dissociated from goodness and charity (Is. lviii. 3—6; Mic. vi. 6—8; Amos v. 21—24).

34. *the children of the bridechamber*] The friends of the bridegroom—the paranymphs—who accompanied him to meet the bride and her maidens; Judg. xiv. 11. The question would be specially forcible to John's disciples who had heard him speak of "the joy of the friend of the bridegroom" (John iii. 29).

fast] St Matthew (ix. 15) uses the word '*mourn*' which makes the antithesis more striking (John xvi. 20).

35. *the days will come*] Rather, **but there will come days.**

when the bridegroom shall be taken away from them] Rather, **and when** (καὶ A, B, D). Comp. John xvi. 16, "A little while and ye shall not see me." The verb used—*aparthê*—occurs nowhere else in the N.T., and clearly hints at a violent end. This is memorable as being the earliest recorded public intimation of His crucifixion, of which a dim hint ("even so shall the Son of man be lifted up") had been given privately to Nicodemus (John iii. 14).

then shall they fast] As we are told that they did, Acts xiii. 2, 3. Observe that is not said, 'then shall ye be able to insist on their fasting.' The Christian fasts would be voluntary, not compulsory; the result of a felt need, not the observance of a rigid command. Our Lord never entered fully into the subject of fasting, and it is clear that throughout the Bible it is never enjoined as a frequent duty, though it is sanctioned and encouraged as an occasional means of grace. In the Law only one day in the year—the Kippur, or Day of Atonement—was appointed as a fast (Lev. xvi. 29; Numb. xxix. 7). After the exile four annual fasts had arisen, but the prophets do not enjoin them (Zech. vii. 1—12, viii. 19), nor did our Lord in any way approve (or apparently practise) the two weekly fasts of the Pharisees (xviii. 12). Probably the reason why fasting has never been commanded as a universal and constant duty is that it acts very differently on different temperaments, and according to the testimony of some who have tried it most seriously, acts in some cases as a powerful stimulus to temptation. It is remarkable that the words "*and fasting*" are probably the interpolations of an ascetic bias in Matt. xvii. 21; Mk. ix. 29; Acts x. 30; 1 Cor. vii. 5, though fasting is implied in Matt. vi. 16. Fasting is not commanded and is not forbidden. The Christian is free (Rom. xiv. 5), but must, while temperate in all things, do exactly that which he finds most conducive to his spiritual and moral welfare. For *now* the bridegroom is not taken from us but is with us (Matt. xxviii. 20; Heb. xiii. 5, 6; John xiv. 16, xvi. 7).

parable unto them; No *man* putteth a piece of a new garment upon an old; if otherwise, *then* both the new maketh a rent, and the piece that was *taken* out of the new agreeth not with the old. And no *man* putteth new wine into old bottles; else the new wine will burst the bottles, and be spilled, and the bottles shall perish. But new wine must be put into new bottles; and both are preserved. No *man* also

36. *a piece of a new garment upon an old*] Rather, **no one rending a patch from a new garment putteth it upon an old garment.** The word σχίσας 'rending' though omitted in our version is found in ℵ, A, B, D, L. Our Lord delighted in using these homely metaphors which brought the truth within the comprehension of his humblest hearers. St Matthew (ix. 16) has 'a patch of unteazled cloth.'

both the new maketh a rent] Rather, with the best uncials, **he will both rend the new.** The inferior readings adopted by the E. V. make us lose sight of the fact that there is a *treble* mischief implied, namely, (1) the rending of the new to patch the old; (2) the incongruity of the mixture; (3) the increase of the rent of the old. The latter is mentioned only by St Matthew, but is implied by the bursten skins of the next similitude. Our Lord is referring to the proposal to enforce the ascetic leanings of the forerunner, and the Pharisaic regulations which had become a parasitic growth on the old dispensation, upon the glad simplicity of the new dispensation. To act thus, was much the same thing as using the Gospel by way of a mere adjunct to—a mere purple patch upon—the old garment of the Law. The teaching of Christ was a new and seamless robe which would only be spoilt by being rent. It was impossible to tear a few doctrines and precepts from Christianity, and use them as ornaments and improvements of Mosaism. If this were attempted (1) the Gospel would be maimed by the rending from its entirety; (2) the *contrast* between the new and the old system would be made more glaring; (3) the decay of the evanescent institutions would only be violently accelerated. Notice how distinctly these comparisons imply the ultimate abrogation of the Law.

agreeth not] Rather, **will not agree** (*sumphonesei*).

37. *new wine into old bottles*] Rather, **wine-skins.** The skins used for holding wine were apt to get seamed and cracked, and old wine-skins would tend to set up the process of fermentation. They could contain the motionless, not expand with the fermenting. To explain this passage, see Excursus III.

38. *new wine...into new bottles*] Rather, **new** (νέος) **wine into fresh** (καινούς) **wine-skins.** The new spirit requires fresh forms for its expression and preservation; the vigour of youth cannot be bound in the swaddling-bands of infancy. It is impossible to be *both* 'under the **Law**' and 'under grace.' The Hebraising Christians against whom St Paul had to wage his lifelong battle—those Judaisers who tried to ruin his work in Galatia, Corinth, and Rome—had precisely failed to grasp the meaning of these truths.

having drunk old *wine* straightway desireth new; for he saith, The old is better.

CH. VI. 1—5. *The Disciples pluck the ears of corn on the Sabbath.* (Matt. xii. 1—8; Mk. ii. 23—28.)

And it came to pass on the second sabbath after the first, 6

39. *having drunk old*] This verse is peculiar to St Luke, and is a characteristic of his fondness for all that is most tender and gracious. It is an expression of considerateness towards the inveterate prejudices engendered by custom and system: a kind allowance for the reluctance of the Pharisees and the disciples of John to abandon the old systems to which they had been accustomed. The spirit for which our Lord here (as it were) offers an apology is the deep-rooted human tendency to prefer old habits to new lights, and stereotyped formulae to fresh truths. It is the unprogressive spirit which relies simply on authority, precedent, and tradition, and says, 'It was good enough for my father, it is good enough for me;' 'It will last my time,' &c. The expression itself seems to have been a Jewish proverb (*Nedarim*, f. 66. 1).

The old is better] Rather, **The old is excellent** (*chrestos* ℵ, B, L, &c.). The reading of the E. V., *chrestoteros*, is inferior, since the man, having declined to taste the new, can institute no comparison between it and the old. The wine which at the beginning has been set forth to him is good (John ii. 10), and he assumes that only 'that which is worse' can follow.

CH. VI. 1—5. THE DISCIPLES PLUCK THE EARS OF CORN ON THE SABBATH. (Matt. xii. 1—8; Mk. ii. 23—28.)

1. *on the second sabbath after the first*] Better, **on the second-first sabbath.** St Luke gives this unique note of time without a word to explain it, and scholars have not—and probably never will—come to an agreement as to its exact meaning. The only analogy to the word is the *deuterodekate* or second tenth in Jerome on Ezekiel xlv. Of the ten or more suggested explanations, omitting those which are wholly arbitrary and impossible, we may mention the following.

α. The first Sabbath of the second month (Wetstein).

β. The first Sabbath after the second day of the Passover (Scaliger, Ewald, De Wette, Neander, Keim, &c.).

γ. The first Sabbath of the second year in the Sabbatic cycle of seven years (Wieseler).

δ. The first Sabbath of the *Ecclesiastical year*. The Jewish year had two beginnings, the civil year began in Tisri (mid-September); the ecclesiastical year in Nisan (mid-March).

The first-first Sabbath *may* therefore have been a name given to the first Sabbath of the civil year in autumn; and second-first to the first Sabbath of the ecclesiastical year in spring (Cappell, Godet).

ε. The Pentecostal Sabbath—the Paschal Sabbath being regarded as the protoproton or *first-first* (Corn. à Lapide).

that he went through the corn fields; and his disciples plucked the ears of corn, and did eat, rubbing *them* in *their* 2 hands. And certain of the Pharisees said unto them, Why

These and similar explanations must be left as unsupported conjectures in the absence of any decisive trace of such Sabbatical nomenclature among the Jews. But we may remark that

(1) The reading itself cannot be regarded as absolutely certain, since it is *omitted* in ℵ, D, L, and in several important versions, including the Syriac and Coptic. Hence of modern editors Tregelles and Meyer omit it; Lachmann and Alford put it in brackets. [Its insertion may then be conceivably accounted for by marginal annotations. Thus if a copyist put 'first' in the margin with the reference to the "*other*" Sabbath of v. 6 it would have been corrected by some succeeding copyist into 'second' with reference to iv. 31; and the two may have been combined in hopeless perplexity. If it be said that this is unlikely, it seems at least equally unlikely that it should either wilfully or accidentally have been omitted if it formed part of the original text. And why should St Luke writing for Gentiles use without explanation a word to them perfectly meaningless and so highly technical that in all the folio volumes of Jewish literature there is not a single trace of it?]

(2) The exact discovery of what the word means is only important as a matter of archaeology. Happily there can be no question as to the time of year at which the incident took place. The narrative seems to imply that the ears which the disciples plucked and rubbed were ears of *wheat* not of *barley*. Now the first ripe sheaf of barley was offered at the Passover (in spring) and the first ripe wheat sheaf at Pentecost (fifty days later). Wheat would ripen earlier in the rich deep hollow of Gennesareth. In any case therefore the time of year was spring or early summer, and the Sabbath (whether the reading be correct or not) was probably some Sabbath in the month Nisan.

he went through the corn fields] Comp. Matt. xii. 1—8; Mk. ii. 23—28. St Mark uses the curious expression that '*He went along through the corn fields*' apparently in a path between two fields—"*and His disciples began to make a way by plucking the corn ears.*" All that we can infer from this is that Jesus was walking apart from His Apostles, and that He did not Himself pluck the corn.

plucked the ears of corn] This shews their hunger and poverty, especially if the corn was barley. They were permitted by the Law to do this—"When thou comest into the standing-corn of thy neighbour, then thou mayest pluck the ears with thine hand," Deut. xxiii. 25. St Matthew in his "*began* to pluck" shews how eagerly and instantly the Pharisees clutched at the chance of finding fault.

2. *certain of the Pharisees*] On the Jewish sects see Excursus VI. As the chronological sequence of the incident is uncertain, these may be some of the spy-Pharisees who as His ministry advanced dogged His steps (Matt. xv. 1; Mk. iii. 22, vii. 1), in the base and demoralising desire to convict Him of heresy or violation of the Law. Perhaps they wished to see whether he would exceed the regulated Sabbath day's

do ye *that* which is not lawful to do on the sabbath days? And Jesus answering them said, Have ye not read so much 3 as this, what David did, when himself was a hungred, and they which were with him; how he went into the house of 4 God, and did take and eat the shewbread, and gave also to

journey of 2000 cubits (Ex. xvi. 29). We have already met with some of the carping criticisms dictated by their secret hate, v. 14, 21, 30.

Why do ye] In St Mark the question is scornfully addressed to Jesus. "See why do *they* do on the sabbath day that which is not lawful?"

that which is not lawful to do] The point was this. Since the Law had said that the Jews were "to do no manner of work" on the Sabbath, the Oral Law had laid down thirty-nine principal prohibitions which were assigned to the authority of the Great Synagogue and which were called *abhôth* 'fathers' or chief rules. From these were deduced a vast multitude of *toldôth* 'descendants' or derivative rules. Now 'reaping' and 'threshing' on the sabbath day were forbidden by the *abhôth*; and by the *toldôth* it was asserted that plucking corn-ears was *a kind of* reaping, and rubbing them *a kind of* threshing. But while they paid servile attention to these trivialities the Pharisees "omitted the weightier matters of the law, judgment, mercy, and faith," Matt. xxii. 23). The vitality of these artificial notions among the Jews is extraordinary. Abarbanel relates that when in 1492 the Jews were expelled from Spain, and were forbidden to enter the city of Fez lest they should cause a famine, they lived on grass; yet even in this state '*religiously avoided the violation of their sabbath by plucking the grass with their hands.*' To avoid this they took the much more laborious method of grovelling on their knees, and cropping it with their teeth!

3. *Have ye not read so much as this*] Rather, **Did ye not even read this?** He answers them in one of their own formulae, but with a touch of irony at their ignorance, which we trace also in the "Did ye never read?" of St Mark;—*never* though ye are Scribes and devote all your time to the Scriptures? Perhaps the reproving question may have derived an additional sting from the fact that the very passage which our Lord quoted (1 Sam. xxi. 1—6) had been read on that Sabbath as the Haphtarah of the day. The service for the day must have been over, because no meal was eaten till then. This fact does not however help us to determine which was the second-first Sabbath, because the present Jewish lectionary is of later date.

and they which were with him] That the day on which this occurred was a Sabbath results from the fact that it was only on the Sabbath that the new shewbread was placed on the table, Lev. xxiv. 8, 9.

4. *did take and eat*] St Mark says that this was "in the days of Abiathar the high priest." The priest who actually *gave* the bread to David was Ahimelech, the father of Abiathar.

the shewbread] Literally, 'loaves of setting forth;' "continual bread," Numb. iv. 7. "Bread of the Face," i.e. set before the Presence

them that were with him; which it is not lawful to eat but
5 for the priests alone? And he said unto them, That the
Son of man is Lord also of the sabbath.

of God, Lev. xxiv. 6, 7. Comp. "Angel of the Face" Lev. xxiv. 6—8; Ex. xxv. 30, xxix. 33. They were twelve unleavened loaves sprinkled with frankincense set on a little golden table.

which it is not lawful to eat but for the priests alone] "It shall be Aaron's and his sons: and they shall eat it in the holy place: for it is most holy unto him," Lev. xxiv. 9. Thus David, their favourite saint and hero, had openly and fearlessly violated the letter of the Law with the full sanction of the High Priest, on the plea of necessity,—in other words because mercy is better than sacrifice; and because the higher law of moral obligation must always supersede the lower law of ceremonial. This was a proof by way of *fact* from the *Kethubim* or sacred books (*Hagiographa*); in St Matthew our Lord adds a still more striking argument by way of *principle* from the Law itself. By its own provisions the Priests in the laborious work of offering sacrifices violated the Sabbath and yet were blameless. Hence the later Jews deduced the remarkable rule that "there is no sabbatism in the Temple," (Numb. xxviii. 9). And Jesus added "But I say to you there is something greater ($\mu\epsilon\hat{\iota}\zeta o\nu$) than the Temple here." The appeal to their own practice is given in xiv. 5.

5. *The Son of man is Lord also of the sabbath*] Rather, 'Lord even of the Sabbath,' though you regard the Sabbath as the most important command of the whole Law. In St Mark we have further, "the Sabbath was made for man, and not man for the Sabbath."

This was one of no less than six great occasions on which the fury of the Pharisees had been excited by the open manner in which our Lord set aside as frivolous and unauthoritative the burdens which the Oral Law had attached to the Sabbath. The other instances are the healing of the cripple at Bethesda (John v. 1—16); the healing of the withered hand (Lk. vi. 1—11); of the blind man at Siloam (John ix. 1—41); of the paralytic woman (Lk. xiii. 14—17); and of the man with the dropsy (Lk. xiv. 1—6). In laying His axe at the root of a proud and ignorant Sabbatarianism, He was laying His axe at the root of *all* that "miserable micrology" which they had been accustomed to take for religious life. They had turned the Sabbath from a holy delight into a revolting bondage. The Apocryphal Gospels are following a true tradition in the prominence which they give to Sabbath healing, as a charge against Him on His trial before the Sanhedrin.

In the famous Cambridge Manuscript (D), the *Codex Bezae*, there is here added the following passage: "*On the same day, seeing one working on the Sabbath, He said to him, O man, if indeed thou knowest what thou doest, thou art blessed: but if thou knowest not, thou art accursed, and a transgressor of the Law.*" This very remarkable addition cannot be accepted as genuine on the authority of a single MS., and can only be regarded as one of the *agrapha dogmata*, or 'unrecorded

6—11. *The Healing of the Man with the Withered Hand.*

And it came to pass also on another sabbath, that he entered into the synagogue and taught: and there was a man whose right hand was withered. And the scribes and Pharisees watched him, whether he would heal on the sabbath day; that they might find an accusation against him. But he knew their thoughts, and said to the man which had the withered hand, Rise up, and stand *forth* in the midst. And he arose and stood *forth*. Then said Jesus unto them, I will ask you one *thing;* Is it lawful on the sabbath days to

traditional sayings' of our Lord. The meaning of the story is that 'if thy work is of faith,—if thou art thoroughly persuaded in thy own mind—thou art acting with true insight; but if thy work is *not* of faith, it is sin.' See Rom. xiv. 22, 23; 1 Cor. viii. 1. What renders the incident improbable is that no Jew would dare openly to violate the Law by *working* on the Sabbath, an act which rendered him legally liable to be stoned. The anecdote, as Grotius thought, may have been written in the margin by some follower of Marcion, who rejected the inspiration of the Old Testament.

6—11. THE HEALING OF THE MAN WITH THE WITHERED HAND.

6. *into the synagogue*] Matt. xii. 9—14; Mk. iii. 1—6. None of the Evangelists enable us to decide on the time or place when the healing occurred.

there was a man whose right hand was withered] Obviously he had come in the hope of being healed; and even this the Pharisees regarded as reprehensible, xiii. 14. The Gospel of the Ebionites adds that he was a stonemason, maimed by an accident, and that he implored Jesus to heal him, that he might not have to beg his bread (Jerome on Matt. xii. 10).

7. *the scribes and Pharisees watched him*] xx. 20. The followers of Shammai, at that epoch the most powerful of the Pharisaic Schools, were so strict about the Sabbath, that they held it a violation of the Law to tend the sick, or even to console them on that day. Hence what the Pharisees were waiting to see was whether He was going to side with them in their Sabbatic views, or with the more lax Sadducees, whom the people detested. If he did the latter, they thought that they could ruin the popularity of the Great Prophet. But in this, as in every other instance, (1) our Lord absolutely refuses to be guided by the popular orthodoxy of the hour, however tyrannous and ostensibly deduced from Scripture; and (2) ignores every consideration of party in order to appeal to *principles*.

8. *their thoughts*] Rather, **their reasonings.**

9. *I will ask you one thing*] Rather, **I further ask you.** Implying that He had already addressed some questions to their consciences on this subject, or perhaps because they had asked Him, 'Is it lawful to heal on the Sabbath?' Matt. xii. 10.

10 do good, or to do evil? to save life, or to destroy *it*? And looking round about upon them all, he said unto the man, Stretch forth thy hand. And he did so: and his hand was
11 restored whole as the other. And they were filled with madness; and communed one with another what they might do to Jesus.

12—19. *The Selection of the Twelve Apostles.*

12 And it came to pass in those days, *that* he went out into a mountain to pray, and continued all night in prayer to

to do good, or to do evil] *He* was intending to work a miracle for good; *they* were secretly plotting to do harm,—their object being, if possible, to put Him to death. They received this question in stolid silence. Mk. iii. 4.

to save life] Rather, a life.

10. *looking round about upon them all*] St Mark adds 'with *anger*, being *grieved* at the callousness (*pōrōsin*, Rom. xi. 25) of their hearts.'

Stretch forth thy hand] Compare 1 K. xiii. 4.

11. *they were filled with madness*] Rather, **unreasonableness**. The word implies *senselessness*, the frenzy of obstinate prejudice. It admirably characterises the state of ignorant hatred which is disturbed in the fixed conviction of its own infallibility. (2 Tim. iii. 9.) The two first Sabbath miracles (iv. 35, 39) had excited no opposition, because none of these religious spies and heresy-hunters (xx. 20) were present.

communed] Rather, **began to commune**. This public miracle and public refutation clinched their hatred against Him (Matt. xii. 14. Comp. John xi. 53).

one with another] And, St Mark adds, with the Herodians. This shews the extremity of their hate, for hitherto the Pharisees had regarded the Herodians as a half-apostate political party, more nearly allied to the Sadducees, and ready with them to sacrifice the true interests of their country and faith. St Matthew (xii. 14) says that they actually "held a council against Him."

what they might do] The form used—what is called the Aeolic aorist—implies extreme perplexity.

12—19. THE SELECTION OF THE TWELVE APOSTLES.

12. *in those days*] wearied with their incessant espionage and opposition. Probably these two last incidents belong to a later period in the ministry, *following* the Sermon on the Mount (as in St Matthew) and the bright acceptable Galilaean year of our Lord's work. In any case we have here, from vi. 12—viii. 56, a splendid cycle of Messianic work in Galilee in the gladdest epoch of Christ's ministry.

into a mountain] Rather, "into **the** mountain," with special reference to the Kurn Hattîn, or Horns of Hattîn, the traditional and almost certainly the actual scene of the Sermon on the Mount.

God. And when it was day, he called unto *him* his disci- 13
ples: and of them he chose twelve, whom also he named
apostles; Simon, (whom he also named Peter,) and Andrew 14

in prayer to God] The expression used is peculiar. It is literally
"in the prayer of God." Hence some have supposed that it should be
rendered "in the Prayer-House of God." The word *proseuchê* meant in
Greek not only 'prayer,' but also '*prayer-house*,' as in the question to
a poor person in Juvenal, "In what *proseucha* am I to look for you?"
The *proseuchae* were merely walled spaces without roof, set apart for
purposes of worship where there was no synagogue, as at Philippi (Acts
xvi. 13). There is however here an insuperable difficulty in thus
understanding the words; for *proseuchae* were generally, if not invariably, in close vicinity to running water (Jos. *Antt.* XIV. 10, § 23),
for purposes of ritual ablution, nor do we ever hear of their being built
on hills. On the other hand, if τὸ ὄρος mean only 'the mountainous
district,' this objection is not fatal. For another instance of a night
spent on a mountain in prayer, see Matt. xiv. 23.

13. *he chose twelve*] doubtless with a reference to the twelve tribes
of Israel.

whom also he named apostles] The word means primarily 'messengers,' as in Phil. ii. 25. It is a translation of the Hebrew *Sheloochim*,
who often acted as emissaries of the Synagogue (comp. Mk. iii. 14, ἵνα
ἀποστέλλῃ αὐτούς). In the other Gospels it only occurs in this sense in
Mk. vi. 30; Matt. x. 2; and only once in the LXX., 1 K. xiv. 6. It
has two usages in the N. T., one general (John xiii. 16; Rom. xvi. 7;
Heb. iii. 1), and one special (1 Cor. ix. 1 and passim). The call of the
Apostles was now necessitated both by the widespread fame of our
Lord, and the deadly animosity already kindled against Him. Their
training soon became the most important part of His work on earth.

14. *Simon*] Lists of the twelve Apostles are given in four passages
of Scripture in the following order:

Matt. x. 2—4.	Mk. iii. 16—19.	Lk. vi. 14—16.	Acts i. 13.
Simon	Simon	Simon	Peter
Andrew	James	Andrew	James
James	John	James	John
John	Andrew	John	Andrew
Philip	Philip	Philip	Philip
Bartholomew	Bartholomew	Bartholomew	Thomas
Thomas	Matthew	Matthew	Bartholomew
Matthew	Thomas	Thomas	Matthew
James of Al- phaeus	James of Al- phaeus	James of Al- phaeus	James of Al- phaeus
Lebbaeus	Thaddaeus	Simon Zelotes	Simon Zelotes
Simon the Ka- nanite	Simon the Ka- nanite	Jude of James	Jude of James
Judas Iscariot	Judas Iscariot	Judas Iscariot	Judas Iscariot

15 his brother, James and John, Philip and Bartholomew, Mat-

In reading these four independent lists several facts are remarkable.

i. Each list falls into three tetrads, and the last two tetrads are arranged in slightly varying pairs. "The Apostolic College was formed of three concentric circles—each less closely intimate with Jesus than the last." Godet.

ii. In each tetrad the names refer to the same persons though the *order* is different.

iii. In each list the *first* of each tetrad is the same—viz. Simon, Philip, and James son of Alphaeus; not as 'supreme among inferior, but as first among equals.'

iv. In each list Simon stands first; and Judas Iscariot last, as the 'son of perdition.'

v. Not only do the Apostles seem to be named in the order of their eminence and nearness to Christ, but the first four seem to stand alone (in the Acts the first four are separated by "and;" the rest are ranged in pairs). The first four were the *eklektōn eklektoteroi*—the chosen of the chosen; the *ecclesiola in ecclesia*. Andrew, who is named last in St Mark and the Acts, though belonging to the inmost band of Apostles (Mk. xiii. 3) and though the earliest of them all (John i. 40), was yet less highly honoured than the other three (who are the θεολογικώτατοι at the healing of Jairus's daughter, Mk. v. 37; at the Transfiguration, Matt. xvii. 1; and in Gethsemane, Matt. xxvi. 37). He seems to have been a link of communication between the first and second tetrads (John xii. 22, vi. 8).

vi. The first five Apostles were of Bethsaida; and all the others seem to have been Galilaeans with the single exception of Judas Iscariot, who belonged to a Jewish town (see vs. 16). The only Greek names are those of Philip and Andrew (see John xii. 21, 22). At this time however many Jews bore Greek names.

vii. In the *second* tetrad it may be regarded as certain that Bartholomew (the son of Tolmai) is the disciple whom St John calls Nathanael. He may possibly have been Philip's brother. St Matthew puts his own name last, and adds the title of reproach *the tax-gatherer*. In the two other Evangelists he precedes St Thomas. The name Thomas merely means 'a twin' (Didymus), and one tradition says that he was a twin-brother of Matthew, and that *his* name too was Jude (Euseb. *H. E.* I. 13).

viii. In the *third* tetrad we find one Apostle with three names. His real name was Jude, but as there was already one Jude among the Apostles, and as it was the commonest of Jewish names, and as there was also a Jude who was one of the 'brethren of the Lord,' he seems to have two surnames—*Lebbaeus*, from *lebh*, 'heart,' and *Thaddaeus* (another form of Theudas, Acts v. 36), from *Thad*, 'bosom'—possibly, as some have conjectured, from the warmth and tenderness of his disposition. (Very few follow Clemens of Alexandria and Ewald in trying to identify Lebbaeus and Levi.) This disciple is called by St Luke (viz. here and in Acts i. 13) "Jude of James," or "James's Jude," and the English Version

thew and Thomas, James the *son* of Alpheus, and Simon supplies the word "brother." There is however no more decisive reason to supply "brother" (which is at any rate a very unusual ellipse) than in the former verse, where James is called "James of Alphaeus" (*Chalpai*, Klôpa, John xix. 25, perhaps also Kleopas (xxiv. 18), since Jews often Graecised the form of their names). This three-named disciple was probably a *son* of James, and therefore a *grandson* of Alphaeus, and a nephew of Matthew and Thomas. James the son of Alphaeus is sometimes called "*the Less;*" but this seems to be a mistaken rendering of ὁ μικρὸς (Mk. xv. 40), which means 'the *short* of stature.' The other James is never called 'the Great.'

ix. Simon Zelotes is called by St Matthew 'the Kananite' (ὁ Κανανίτης), or according to the better readings 'the Kananaean.' The word does not mean "Canaanite," as our Version incorrectly gives it, nor yet 'inhabitant of Kana in Galilee,' but means the same thing as 'the Zealot,' from *Kinedh*, 'zeal.' He had therefore once belonged to the sect of terrible fanatics who thought any deed of violence justifiable for the recovery of national freedom, and had been one of the wild followers of Judas the Gaulonite. (Jos. *B. J.* IV. 3, § 9, and passim.) Their name was derived from 1 Macc. ii. 50, where the dying Mattathias, father of Judas Maccabaeus, says to the Assidaeans (*Chasidim*, i.e. 'all such as were voluntarily devoted to the law') "Be ye *zealous* for the Law, and give your lives for the covenant of your fathers" (comp. 2 Macc. iv. 2). It shews our Lord's divine wisdom and fearless universality of love that he should choose for Apostles two persons who had once been at such deadly opposition as a tax-gatherer and a zealot.

x. For "Judas Iscariot who also betrayed him" St Luke uses the milder description, "*which also was the traitor*," or rather who also became a traitor. Iscariot has nothing to do with *askara*, 'strangulation,' or *sheker*, 'lie,' but is in all probability *Eesh Kerioth*, 'man of Kerioth,' just as Istôbos stands in Josephus (*Antt.* VII. 6, § 1) for 'man of Tôb.' Kerioth (Josh. xv. 25) is perhaps *Kuryetein*, ten miles from Hebron, in the southern border of Judah. If the reading "Iscariot" is right in John vi. 71, xiii. 26 (ℵ, B, C, G, L), as applied also to Simon Zelotes, then, since Judas is called "son of Simon" (John vi. 71), the last pair of Apostles were father and son. If Judas Iscariot had ever shared the wild Messianic patriotism of his father it would partly account for the recoil of disgust and disappointment which helped to ruin his earthly mind when he saw that he had staked all in the cause of one who was rejected and despised.

xi. It is a deeply interesting fact, if it be a fact (and although it cannot be made out with certainty because it depends on data which are conjectural, and on tradition which is liable to error—it is still far from improbable) that so many of the Apostles were related to each other. Simon and Andrew were brothers; James and John were brothers, and, if Salome was a sister of the Virgin (comp. Mk. xv. 40, John xix. 25), they were first cousins of our Lord; Philip and Bartholomew *may have been* brothers; Thomas, Matthew, and James were brothers and first

16 called Zelotes, *and* Judas *the brother* of James, and Judas Iscariot, which also was the traitor.

17 And he came down with them, and stood in the plain,

cousins of our Lord; Lebbaeus, or 'Jude of James,' was His second cousin; Simon Zelotes and Judas Iscariot were father and son. Thus no less than half of the Apostles would have been actually related to our Lord, although His *brethren* did not believe on Him (John vii. 5). The difficulty however of being *sure* of these combinations rises in part from the paucity of Jewish names, and therefore the extreme commonness of Simon, Jude, James, &c.

xii. The separate incidents in which individual Apostles are mentioned are as follows:

Peter: Prominent throughout; xii. 41, xxii. 31; Matt. xvi. 16, xvii. 24, xix. 27, &c.

James,} Both prominent throughout. Boanerges; calling down fire;
John: } petition for precedence, &c.

James was the first Apostolic martyr; John the last survivor (Acts xii. 2; John xxi. 22).

Andrew: the first disciple, John i. 40; with Jesus on Olivet, Mk. xiii. 3.

Philip: "Follow me," John i. 43; his frankness, John vi. 7; the Greeks, id. xii. 22; "shew us the Father," id. xiv. 8.

Bartholomew: "an Israelite indeed," John i. 47; of Cana, John xxi. 2.

Matthew: his call, v. 27, 28.

Thomas: despondent yet faithful, John xi. 16, xiv. 5, xx. 25, xxi. 2.

James son of Alphaeus: no incident.

Jude son of James: his perplexed question, John xiv. 22.

Simon Zelotes: no incident.

Judas Iscariot: the betrayal and ultimate suicide.

15. *called Zelotes*] Rather, **who was called the Zealot**.

16. *which also was the traitor*] Rather, **who also became a traitor**. "Have not I chosen you twelve, and one of you is a devil?" John vi. 70; 1 John ii. 17; typified by Ahithophel, Ps. xli. 9. If it be asked why our Lord chose him, the answer is nowhere given to us, but we may reverently conjecture that Judas Iscariot, like all human beings, had in him germs of good which *might* have ripened into holiness, if he had resisted his besetting sin, and not flung away the battle of his life. It is clear that John (at least) among the Apostles had early found him out (John xii. 6), and that he had received from our Lord more than one solemn warning (xii. 15, xviii. 25, &c.).

17. *And he came down with them, and stood in the plain*] Rather, **And descending with them, He stopped on a level place**. *Topos pedinos* also occurs in Is. xiii. 2, LXX. If it be thus rendered there is no discrepancy between St Matthew, who says that "He went up into the mountain, and when He sat down His disciples approached Him" (Matt. v. 1). I believe that St Luke here meant to give such portions of the Sermon on the Mount as suited his design. Combining the two narratives with what we know of the scene we see that what occurred

and the company of his disciples, and a great multitude of people out of all Judea and Jerusalem, and *from* the sea coast of Tyre and Sidon, which came to hear him, and to be healed of their diseases; and they that were vexed with un- 18 clean spirits: and they were healed. And the whole multi- 19 tude sought to touch him: for there went virtue out of him, and healed *them* all.

20—26. *Beatitudes and Woes.*

And he lifted up his eyes on his disciples, and said, 20 Blessed *be ye* poor: for yours is the kingdom of God.

was as follows. The previous evening Jesus went to one of the peaks of Kurn Hattîn (withdrawing Himself from His disciples, who doubtless bivouacked at no great distance), and spent the night in prayer. In the morning He called His disciples and chose Twelve Apostles. Then going with them to some level spot, either the flat space (called in Greek *plax*) between the two peaks of the hill, or some other spot near at hand, He preached His sermon primarily to His disciples who sat immediately around Him, but also to the multitudes. There is no need to assume two discourses—one esoteric and one exoteric, &c. At the same time there is of course no difficulty in supposing that our Lord may have uttered the same discourse, or parts of the same discourse, more than once, varying it as occasion required.

out of all Judea] St Matthew adds Galilee (which was to a great extent Greek), Decapolis, and Peraea; St Mark also mentions Idumaea. Thus there were Jews, Greeks, Phoenicians, and Arabs among our Lord's hearers.

19. *to touch him*] Compare viii. 44; Matt. xiv. 36; Mk. v. 30.

20—26. BEATITUDES AND WOES.

This section of St Luke, from vi. 20 to ix. 6, resembles in style the great Journey Section, ix. 51—xviii. 34.

20. *Blessed be ye poor*] Rather, **Blessed are the poor.** The *makarioi* is a Hebrew expression (*ashrî*), Ps. i. 1. St Matthew adds "in spirit" (comp. Is. lxvi. 2, "To this man will I look, even to him that is poor and of a contrite spirit, and trembleth at my word"). But (1) St Luke gives the address of Christ to the poor whose very presence shewed that they were *His* poor and had come to seek Him; and (2) the Evangelist seems to have been impressed with the blessings of a faithful and humble poverty in itself (comp. Jas. ii. 5; 1 Cor. i. 26—29), and loves to record those parts of our Lord's teaching which were especially 'the Gospel to the poor' (see i. 53, ii. 7, vi. 20, xii. 15—34, xvi. 9—25). See Introd. p. 27.

"Come ye who find contentment's very core
  In the light store

21   Blessed *are ye* that hunger now: for ye shall be filled.

> And daisied path
> Of poverty,
> And know how more
> A small thing that the righteous hath
> Availeth, than the ungodly's riches great."
>
> Cov. Patmore.

"This is indeed an admirably sweet friendly beginning...for He does not begin like Moses...with command and threatening, but in the friendliest possible way with free, enticing, *alluring* and amiable promises." Luther.

for yours is the kingdom of God] St Matthew uses the expression "the kingdom of the heavens." The main differences between St Matthew's and St Luke's record of the Sermon on the Mount are explained by the different objects and readers of these Gospels; but in both it is the Inaugural Discourse of the Kingdom of Heaven.

(i)   St Matthew writes *for the Jews*, and much that he records has special bearing on the Levitic Law (v. 17—38), which St Luke naturally omits as less intelligible to Gentiles. Other parts here omitted are recorded by St Luke later on (xi. 9—13; Matt. vii. 7—11).

(ii)   St Matthew, presenting Christ as Lawgiver and King, gives the Sermon more in the form of *a Code*. Kurn Hattîn is for him the new and more blessed Sinai; St Luke gives it more in the form of a direct homily ('yours,' &c., not 'theirs,' vi. 20; Matt. v. 3; and compare vi. 46, 47 with Matt. vii. 21, 24).

(iii)   Much of the Sermon in St Matthew is occupied with the *contrast* between the false righteousness—the pretentious orthodoxy and self-satisfied ceremonialism—of the Pharisees, and the true righteousness of the Kingdom which is mercy and love. Hence much of his report is occupied with *Spirituality* as the stamp of true religion, in opposition to formalism, while St Luke deals with Love in the *abstract*.

(iv)   Thus in St Matthew we see mainly the Law of Love as the contrast between the new and the old; in St Luke the Law of Love as the central and fundamental idea of the new.

For a sketch of the Sermon on the Mount, mainly in St Matthew, I may refer to my *Life of Christ*, I. 259—264. The arrangement of the section in St Luke is not obvious. Some see in it the doctrine of happiness; the doctrine of justice; the doctrine of wisdom; or (1) the salutation of love (vi. 20—26); the precepts of love (27—38); the impulsion of love (39—49). These divisions are arbitrary. Godet more successfully arranges it thus: (1) The members of the new society (20—26; Matt. v. 1—12); (2) The fundamental principle of the new society (27—45; Matt. v. 13—vii. 12); (3) The judgment of God on which it rests (46—49; Matt. vii. 13—27):—in other words (1) the appeal; (2) the principles; (3) the sanction.

21.   *Blessed are ye that hunger now*]   Comp. i. 53; Ps. cvii. 9. St Matthew here also brings out more clearly that it is the beatitude of spiritual hunger "after righteousness."

Blessed *are ye* that weep now: for ye shall laugh.

Blessed are ye, when men shall hate you, and when they shall separate you *from their company*, and shall reproach *you*, and cast out your name as evil, for the Son of man's

ye shall laugh] See 2 Cor. vi. 10; Rev. xxi. 4.

22. *hate you...separate you...reproach...cast out your name as evil*] We have here four steps of persecution increasing in virulence: (1) General hatred, (2) Exclusion from the synagogue, a lesser excommunication, viz. the *Nestphah* or exclusion for 30 days, or *Niddout* for 90 days (Gfrörer, *Jahrh. d. Heils*, I. 183; John ix. 34. Hence *aphorismos* means '*excommunication*'), (3) Violent slander, (4) The *Cherem, Shammata*, or greater excommunication,—permanent expulsion from the Synagogue and Temple (John xvi. 2). The Jews pretended that our Lord was thus excommunicated to the blast of 400 ram's horns by Joshua Ben Perachiah (Wagenseil, *Sota*, p. 1057), and was only crucified forty days after because no witness came forward in His favour.

as evil] 'Malefic' or 'execrable superstition' was the favourite description of Christianity among Pagans (Tac. *Ann*. xv. 44; Suet. *Nero*, 16), and Christians were charged with incendiarism, cannibalism, and every infamy. (The student will find such heathen views of Christianity collected in my *Life of St Paul*, Exc. xv. Vol. I.)

for the Son of man's sake] The hatred of men is not in itself a beatitude, because there is a general conscience which condemns certain forms of wickedness, and a man may justly incur universal execration. But the world also hates those who run counter to its pleasures and prejudices, and in that case hatred may be the tribute which vice pays to holiness; 1 Pet. ii. 19, iii. 14. "The world hath hated them, because they are not of the world, even as I am not of the world;" John xvii. 14. Still a man may well tremble when he is enjoying throughout life a beatitude of benediction. And 'the world' by no means excludes the so-called 'religious world,' which has hated with a still fiercer hatred, and exposed to a yet deadlier martyrdom, some of its greatest prophets and teachers. Not a few of the great and holy men enumerated in the next note fell a victim to the fury of priests. Our Lord was handed over to crucifixion by the unanimous hatred of the highest religious authorities of His day.

On the title Son of Man, which occurs in all the four Gospels, see p. 119. In using it Christ "chooses for Himself that title which definitely presents His work in relation to humanity in itself, and not primarily in relation to God or to the chosen people, or even to humanity as fallen." Canon Westcott (on John i. 51) considers that it was not distinctively a Messianic title, and doubts its having been derived from Dan. vii. 13. "The Son of God was made a Son of Man that you who were sons of men might be made sons of God." Aug. *Serm*. 121. As the "Second Adam" Christ is the representative of the race (1 Cor. xv. 45) in its highest ideal;

23 sake. Rejoice ye in that day, and leap *for joy:* for behold, your reward *is* great in heaven: for in the like manner did their fathers unto the prophets.

24 But woe unto you that are rich: for ye have received your consolation.

25 Woe unto you that are full: for ye shall hunger.

Woe unto you that laugh now: for ye shall mourn and weep.

26 Woe unto you, when all men shall speak well of you: for so did their fathers to the false prophets.

as "the Lord from Heaven" He is the Promise of its future exaltation.

23. *Rejoice ye in that day*] See Acts v. 41. "We glory in tribulation;" Rom. v. 3; Jas. i. 2, 3; Col. i. 24; Heb. xi. 26. They accepted with joy that 'ignominy of Christ' which made the very name of 'Christian' a term of execration; 1 Pet. iv. 14, 16.

in the like manner did their fathers unto the prophets] Elijah and his contemporaries, 1 K. xix. 10. Hanani imprisoned by Asa, 2 Chron. xvi. 10. Micaiah imprisoned, 1 K. xxii. 27. Zechariah stoned by Joash, 2 Chr. xxiv. 20, 21. Urijah slain by Jehoiakim, Jer. xxvi. 23. Jeremiah imprisoned, smitten and put in the stocks, Jer. xxxii., xxxviii. Amos slandered, expelled, and perhaps beaten to death (Am. vii.). Isaiah (according to tradition) sawn asunder, Heb. xi. 37, &c. See the same reproach against the Jews in Heb. xi. 36—38; Acts vii. 52; 1 Thess. ii. 14, 15.

24. *But woe*] While sin lasts, there must still be woes over against Beatitudes, as Ebal stands for ever opposite to Gerizim. In St Matthew also we find (Matt. xxiii.) eight woes as well as eight Beatitudes. See too Jer. xvii. 5—8, but there the "cursed" precedes the "blessed."

woe unto you that are rich] The 'woe!' is not necessarily or wholly denunciatory; it is also the cry of compassion, and of course it only applies—not to a Chuzas or a Nicodemus or a Joseph of Arimathaea,—but to those rich who are *not* poor in spirit, but *trust* in riches (Mk. x. 24), or are not rich towards God (xii. 21) and have not got the true riches (xvi. 11; Amos vi. 1; Jas. v. 1). Observe the many parallels between the Epistle of St James and the Sermon on the Mount, Jas. i. 2, 4, 5, 9, 10, ii. 13, 14, 17, 18, iv. 4, 10, 11, v. 2, 10, 12.

ye have received your consolation] Rather, **ye have to the full**, Phil. iv. 18; comp. xvi. 25, "Son, remember that thou in thy lifetime receivedst good things."

25. *you that are full*] "Behold, this was the iniquity of thy sister Sodom, pride, *fulness of bread*," Ezek. xvi. 49.

Woe unto you that laugh now] Compare Eccles. ii. 2, vii. 6; Prov. xiv. 13.

26. *Woe unto you*] Omit *unto you* with ℵ, A, B, E, &c.

when all men shall speak well of you] "Know ye not that the

27—38. *The Laws of Love and Mercy.*

But I say unto you which hear, Love your enemies, do good to them which hate you, bless them that curse you, and pray for them which despitefully use you. *And* unto him that smiteth thee on the *one* cheek offer also the other; 27 28 29

friendship of the world is enmity with God?" Jas. iv. 4. "If ye were of the world, the world would love his own," John xv. 19.

for so did their fathers to the false prophets] "The prophets prophesy falsely...and my people love to have it so," Jer. v. 31. The prophets of Baal and of Asherah, honoured by Jezebel, 1 K. xviii. 19, 22. Zedekiah, son of Chenaanah, supported by Ahab, 1 K. xxii. 11. "Speak unto us smooth things, prophesy deceits," Is. xxx. 10.

27—38. THE LAWS OF LOVE AND MERCY.

[27—30. The *manifestations* of Love. 31. Its formula. 32—35. Its distinctiveness. 35—36. Its model. 37—45. Love as the principle of all judgment. Godet.]

27. *Love your enemies*] This had been distinctly the spirit of the highest part of the Law and the Old Testament. Ex. xxiii. 4, "If thou meet *thine enemy's* ox or ass going astray, thou shalt surely bring it back to him again." Prov. xxv. 21, "If thine enemy be hungry, give him bread to eat." Yet in many passages it had practically been said "to men of old time," at any rate *in some cases*, "thou shalt hate thine enemy," Deut. vii. 2, xxiii. 6; 1 Chr. xx. 3; 2 Sam. xii. 31; Ps. cxxxvii. 8, 9, &c. On these passages the fierce fanaticism of the Pharisaic Jews, after the Exile, had so exclusively fed, that we find the Talmud ringing with precepts of hatred the most bitter against all Gentiles, and the ancients had, not unnaturally, been led to the conclusion that detestation of all but Jews was a part of the Jewish religion ("adversus *omnes alios* hostile odium," Tac. *Hist.* v. 5; Juv. *Sat.* XIV. 103).

do good to them which hate you] See the precept beautifully enforced in Rom. xii. 17, 19—21.

28. *pray for them which despitefully use you*] The Greek word implies the coarsest insults, and is found in 1 Pet. iii. 16. St Luke alone records our Lord's prayer for His murderers, xxiii. 34, from which St Stephen learnt his, Acts vii. 60.

29. *offer also the other*] The general principle "resist not evil" (Matt. v. 39; 1 Cor. vi. 7; 1 Pet. ii. 19—23) impressed for ever on the memory and conscience of mankind by a striking paradox. That it is only meant as a paradox in its *literal* sense is shewn by the fact that our Lord Himself, while most divinely true to its *spirit*, did not act on the letter of it (John xviii. 22, 23). The remark of a good man on reading the Sermon on the Mount, "either this is not true, or we are no Christians," need not be correct of any of us. The precepts are meant, St Augustine said, more "*ad praeparationem cordis quae intus est*" than

and him that taketh away thy cloke forbid not *to take thy*
30 coat also. Give to every man that asketh of thee; and of
31 him that taketh away thy *goods* ask *them* not again. And as
ye would that men should do to you, do ye also to them
32 likewise. For if ye love them which love you, what thank
33 have ye? for sinners also love those that love them. And
if ye do good to them which do good to you, what thank
34 have ye? for sinners also do *even* the same. And if ye lend
to them of whom ye hope to receive, what thank have ye?
for sinners also lend to sinners, to receive as much again.
35 But love ye your enemies, and do good, and lend, hoping
for nothing again; and your reward shall be great, and ye

"*ad opus quod in aperto fit;*" but still, the fewer exceptions we make the better, and the more absolutely we apply *the spirit* of the rules, the fewer difficulties shall we find about the letter.

thy cloke...thy coat] The *himation* was the upper garment, the shawl-like *abba;* the *chitôn* was the tunic. See on iii. 11.

30. *Give to every man that asketh of thee*] Literally, "*be giving,*" implying a *habit*, not an instant act. Here again we have a broad, general principle of unselfishness and liberality safely left to the common sense of mankind, Deut. xv. 7, 8, 9. The *spirit* of our Lord's precept is now best fulfilled by *not* giving to every man that asks, because in the altered circumstances of the age such indiscriminate almsgiving would only be a check to industry, and a premium on imposture, degradation, and vice. By 'giving,' our Lord meant 'conferring a boon;' but mere careless giving now, so far from conferring a boon, perpetuates a curse and inflicts an injury. The *spirit* of the precept is large-handed but *thoughtful* charity. Love must sometimes violate the letter as the only possible way of observing the spirit (Matt. xv. 26, xx. 23).

31. *as ye would that men should do to you*] The golden rule of Christianity of which our Lord said that it was "the Law and the Prophets," Matt. vii. 12. The modern 'Altruism' and '*vivre pour autrui,*' though pompously enunciated as the bases of a new religion, are but a mutilated reproduction of this.

32. *for sinners also love those that love them*] Where St Matthew (v. 46, 47), writing for Jews, uses the term "tax-gatherers" or 'Gentile persons' (*ethnikoi*), St Luke naturally substitutes the nearest equivalents of those words in this connexion, because he is writing for Gentiles. Our Lord meant that our standard must rise above the ordinary dead level of law, habit, custom, which prevail in the world.

34. *to receive as much again*] From this we see that 'interest' and 'usury' are not here contemplated at all.

35. *hoping for nothing again*] See Ps. xv. 5, with the Rabbinic comment that God counts it as universal obedience if any one lends

shall be the children of the Highest: for he is kind unto the unthankful and *to the* evil. Be ye therefore merciful, as 36 your Father also is merciful. Judge not, and ye shall not 37 be judged: condemn not, and ye shall not be condemned: forgive, and ye shall be forgiven: give, and it shall be given 38 unto you; good measure, pressed down, and shaken *together*, and running over, shall *men* give into your bosom. For with the same measure that ye mete withal it shall be measured to you again.

without interest. The words may also mean **despairing in nothing**, or (if μηδέν' be read) **driving no one to despair**.

he is kind unto the unthankful and to the evil] See the exquisite addition in Matt. v. 45.

36. *Be ye therefore merciful*] Rather, **Become**, or **Prove yourselves merciful** (omit οὖν, ℵ, B, D, L).

merciful] St Matthew has "*perfect*," v. 48; but that there is no essential difference between the two Evangelists we may see in such expressions as "the *Father of Mercies*," 2 Cor. i. 3; "The Lord is very pitiful and of tender mercy," James v. 11; "Put on therefore as the elect of God...bowels of mercies, kindness," Col. iii. 12; Is. xxx. 18. "God can only be our ideal in His moral attributes, of which Love is the centre." Van Oosterzee.

"It is an attribute to God Himself,
And earthly power doth then shew *likest God's*
When mercy seasons justice."
SHAKESPEARE.

37. *Judge not*] For comment read Rom. ii. 1—3, xiv. 10, "Why dost thou judge thy brother?...for we shall all stand before the judgment-seat of Christ;" 1 Cor. iv. 3—5, xiii., and the Lord's prayer; James ii. 13, "he shall have judgment without mercy that hath shewed no mercy." Hence a "*righteous* judgment" of others is not forbidden, so long as it be made in a forbearing and tender spirit, John vii. 24.

forgive, and ye shall be forgiven] For comment see the Parable of the Debtors, Matt. xviii. 23—35.

38. *into your bosom*] Pockets were unknown to the ancients. All that was necessary was carried in the fold of the robe (Heb. *Cheyk*, Ps. xxxv. 13, &c.; Lat. *sinus*) or in the girdle.

with the same measure that ye mete] A proverb almost verbally identical with this is found in the Talmud (Duke's *Rabbin. Blumenlese*, p. 162), but it must be remembered that the earliest parts of the Talmud were not committed to writing till more than two centuries after Christ, and long before that time His sayings may have been 'in the air,' i.e. they may have passed unconsciously into the store of the national wisdom even among His enemies.

39—45. *Sincerity. Four Comparisons.*

39 And he spake a parable unto them, Can the blind lead
40 the blind? shall they not both fall into the ditch? The disciple is not above his master: but every one *that is* perfect
41 shall be as his master. And why beholdest thou the mote that is in thy brother's eye, but perceivest not the beam that
42 is in thine own eye? Either how canst thou say to thy brother, Brother, let me pull out the mote that is in thine eye, when thou thyself beholdest not the beam that is in thine own eye? *Thou* hypocrite, cast out first the beam out of thine own eye, and then shalt thou see clearly to pull out
43 the mote that is in thy brother's eye. For a good tree bringeth not forth corrupt fruit; neither doth a corrupt tree
44 bring forth good fruit. For every tree is known by his own fruit. For of thorns *men* do not gather figs, nor of a bram-

39—45. SINCERITY. FOUR COMPARISONS.

39. *Can the blind lead the blind?*] Matt. xv. 14. Prov. xix. 27, "Cease, my son, to hear the instruction that causeth to err." St Paul taunts the Jew with professing to be "a guide of the blind," Rom. ii. 19. St Luke calls this "a parable" in the broader sense (see on iv. 23); and in this Gospel the Sermon thus ends with four vivid 'parables' or similes taken from the sights of daily life—blind leaders of blind; the mote and the beam; good and bad fruit; the two houses.

40. *every one that is perfect shall be as his master*] Rather, **who has been perfected**, 2 Tim. iii. 17. A favourite quotation of St John's, xiii. 16, xv. 20. See Matt. x. 25.

41. *beholdest thou the mote*] The hypocrite *sees* (*blepei*) at the slightest glance the mote in his brother's eye; but not the most careful inspection enables him to *observe* (*katanoein*) the very obvious beam in his own eye. The word *mote* is in the original *karphos*, a stalk or chip, and this is also the idea of *mote*. Thus in Dutch *mot* is *dust of wood*; in Spanish *mota* is a flue on cloth.

the beam] The entire illustration is Jewish, and was used to express impatience of just reproof (*Babha Bathra*, f. 15. 2) so that 'mote' and 'beam' became proverbial for little and great faults. The proverb also implies, 'How can you *see* others' faults properly with a beam in the depth of your eye (ἔκβαλε...ἐκ, Matt. vii. 5)? how dare you condemn when you are so much worse?' Comp. Chaucer (*Reeve's Prologue*),

"He can wel in myn eye see a stalke
But in his owne he can nought seen a balke."

42. *Thou hypocrite*] Rom. ii. 1, "Wherein thou judgest another, thou condemnest thyself." "If we condemn others when we are worse than they, we are like bad trees pretending to bear good fruit." Bengel.

ble bush gather they grapes. A good man out of the good 45
treasure of his heart bringeth forth that which is good; and
an evil man out of the evil treasure of his heart bringeth
forth that which is evil: for of the abundance of the heart
his mouth speaketh.

46—49. *False and true Foundations.*

And why call ye me, Lord, Lord, and do not *the things* 46
which I say? Whosoever cometh to me, and heareth my 47
sayings, and doeth them, I will shew you to whom he is
like: he is like a man which built a house, and digged deep, 48
and laid the foundation on a rock: and when the flood
arose, the stream beat vehemently upon that house, and
could not shake it: for it was founded upon a rock. But 49
he that heareth, and doeth not, is like a man that without a
foundation built a house upon the earth; against which the

44. *do not gather figs*] The simile might have been illustrated by pointing to one of the common Eastern gardens or orchards with its festooning vines and fig-trees just beyond the rough hedges of prickly pear.

45. *of the abundance of the heart his mouth speaketh*] "O generation of vipers, how can ye, being evil, speak good things?" Matt. xii. 34; "the vile person will speak villany," Is. xxxii. 6.

46—49. FALSE AND TRUE FOUNDATIONS.

46. *why call ye me, Lord, Lord*] "If I be a master, where is my fear, saith the Lord of hosts?" Mal. i. 6. Painful comments are supplied by the language of two parables, Matt. xxv. 11, 12; Luke xiii. 25.

47. *and doeth them*] John xiii. 17. "Be ye doers of the word, and not hearers only," James i. 22.

48. *he is like a man which built a house, and digged deep, and laid the foundation on a rock*] The E.V. here loses all the picturesque force of the original. Rather, **he is like a man building a house, who dug, and kept deepening, and laid a foundation on the rock.** The rock is Christ and the teaching of Christ (1 Cor. x. 4). Whether tested by flood, or by fire (1 Cor. iii. 11—15), only the genuine building stands. In another sense, too, "the wicked are overthrown, and are not: but the house of the righteous shall stand," Prov. xii. 7.

the flood] Rather, **an inundation**; the sudden rush of a spait.

for it was founded upon a rock] Rather, **for it had been founded upon the rock.** In some MSS. (ℵ, L) we find, instead of this clause, "*because it was well built.*"

49. *upon the earth*] In St Matthew, more graphically, "*upon the sand;*" e.g. the sand of superficial intellectual acceptance.

stream did beat vehemently, and immediately it fell; and the ruin of that house was great.

CH. VII. 1—10. *Healing of the Centurion's Servant.*

7 Now when he had ended all his sayings in the audience 2 of the people, he entered into Capernaum. And a certain centurion's servant, who was dear unto him, was sick, and 3 ready to die. And when he heard of Jesus, he sent unto him *the* elders of the Jews, beseeching him that he would 4 come and heal his servant. And when they came to Jesus, they besought him instantly, saying, That he was worthy for 5 whom he should do this: for he loveth our nation, and he

it fell] Rather, **it fell in a heap**, reading *sunepesen*.
the ruin] Literally, "*the breach.*"

CH. VII. 1—10. HEALING OF THE CENTURION'S SERVANT.

1. *in the audience*] i.e. in the *hearing*.
he entered into Capernaum] See Matt. viii. 5—13. This was now His temporary home. The incident occurred as He was entering the town.

2. *a certain centurion's servant*] Literally, "*slave.*" The word used by St Matthew (*pais*) might mean son, but is clearly also used for servant (like the Latin *puer*). A centurion is a *captain*; under him is a sergeant (*dekadarch*), and above him a colonel (*chiliarch*), and general (*hegemōn*). Jos. *B. J.* v. 12, § 2. All the centurions in the N.T. are favourably mentioned (xxiii. 47; Acts xxvii. 43).

dear] Rather, **precious.** The love of the captain for his servant was a good example for the Jews themselves, who in the Talmud forbade mourning for slaves.

sick] St Matthew says, "stricken with paralysis, and in terrible pain" (viii. 6). St Luke, as a physician, may have omitted this specification because the description applies rather to *tetanus* than to the strict use of "*paralysis.*"

ready to die] Rather, **was on the point of death.**

3. *when he heard of Jesus*] Rather, **having heard about Jesus.**
he sent unto him the elders] Rather, **elders** (*Zekānim*), with no article. These 'elders' were doubtless some of the ten functionaries, whom the Jews also called *Parnasim*, 'shepherds.' Their functions were not in any respect sacerdotal.

4. *instantly*] i.e. urgently, as in the phrase "continuing *instant* in prayer."

5. *he loveth our nation*] This shews that the centurion was a Gentile,—probably a proselyte of the gate (though the term was invented later), i.e. one of those who embraced Judaism on the whole, but without becoming a 'proselyte of righteousness' by accepting

hath built us a synagogue. Then Jesus went with them. 6
And when he was now not far from the house, the centurion
sent friends to him, saying unto him, Lord, trouble not
thyself: for I am not worthy that thou shouldest enter
under my roof: wherefore neither thought I myself worthy 7

circumcision. It is not impossible that he may have been a Roman, though there is no *direct* proof that Romans ever held such offices under Herod Antipas. More probably he was some Greek or Syrian, holding a commission under the tetrarch.

he hath built us a synagogue] Rather, **our Synagogue he himself built for us.** The expression, "the synagogue," does not necessarily imply that there was only one synagogue in Capernaum, but only that he had built the one from which this deputation came, which was probably the chief synagogue of Capernaum. If Capernaum be Tel Hum (as I became convinced on the spot itself), then the ruins of it shew that it probably possessed two synagogues; and this we should have conjectured beforehand, seeing that Jerusalem is said to have had 400. The walls of one of these, built of white marble, are of the age of the Herods, and stand just above the lake. It may be the very building here referred to. This liberality on the part of the Gentiles was by no means unfrequent. Wealthy Gentile proselytes not seldom sent splendid gifts to the Temple itself. The Ptolemies, Jos. *Antt.* XII. 2, § 5; Sosius, id. XIV. 16, § 4; Fulvia, id. XVIII. 3, § 5, &c. See on xxi. 5.

6. *when he was now not far from the house, the centurion sent friends to him*] Here the narrative of St Luke is much more detailed, and therefore probably more exact, than that of St Matthew, who represents the conversation as taking place between our Lord and the centurion himself. We see from St Luke that he had been prevented from coming in person by deep humility, and the belief that the elders would be more likely to win the boon for him. Meanwhile, he probably stayed by the bedside of his dying slave. St Matthew's narrative is framed on the simple and common principle, *qui facit per alium facit per se.*

Lord] The word in itself may mean no more than "Sir," as in John iv. 19, xii. 21; Acts xvi. 30, &c. It was, in fact, like the Latin *dominus*, an ordinary mode of address to persons whose names were unknown (Sen., *Ep.* 3); but the centurion's entire conduct shews that on his lips the word would have a more exalted significance. In a special sense Κύριος is a name for God (*Adonai*) and Jehovah (1 Thess. v. 2, &c.).

trouble not thyself] The word *skullo* (Matt. ix. 30) would in classical Greek be a slang word. 'Bother not,' or 'worry not thyself.' But in Hellenistic Greek, both slang words (*hupopiazo*, xviii. 5; *katanarkao*, 2 Cor. xii. 13) and purely poetic words (see ii. 35) had become current in ordinary senses.

under my roof] The emphasis is on the *my*, as is shewn by its position in the Greek. "I am not worthy"—*Dicendo se indignum*

to come unto thee: but say in a word, and my servant shall
8 be healed. For I also am a man set under authority, having under me soldiers, and I say unto one, Go, and he goeth; and to another, Come, and he cometh; and to my
9 servant, Do this, and he doeth *it*. When Jesus heard these *things*, he marvelled at him, and turned him *about*, and said unto the people that followed him, I say unto you, I have not
10 found so great faith, no, not in Israel. And they that were sent, returning to the house, found the servant whole that had been sick.

praestitit dignum non in cujus parietes sed in cujus cor Christus intraret. Aug.

7. *say in a word*] The centurion had clearly heard how Jesus, by His mere *fiat*, had healed the son of the 'courtier' at Capernaum (John iv. 46—54). The attempt to make these two miracles identical is to the last degree arbitrary and untenable.

my servant] The centurion here uses the more tender word, *pais*, 'son.'

shall be healed] Perhaps the better reading is *let him be healed*. The faith of the centurion was "an invisible highway for the saving eagles of the great Imperator." Lange.

8. *For I also*] This assigns the reason why he made the request. He was but a subordinate himself, "under authority" of his chiliarch and other officers, and yet he had soldiers under him as well as a servant, who at a word executed his orders. He inferred that Jesus, who had the power of healing at a distance, had at His command thousands of the "Heavenly Army" (ii. 13; Matt. xxvi. 53) who would

"at His bidding speed,
And post o'er land and ocean without rest."

9. *he marvelled at him*] The only other place where the astonishment of Jesus is recorded is astonishment at *unbelief*. Mk. vi. 6.

I have not found so great faith, no, not in Israel] Rather, **Not even in Israel found I so great faith.** These words are preserved with similar exactness in St Matthew. "He had found," says St Augustine, "in the oleaster what He had not found in the olive." Nothing can be more clear than that neither Evangelist had seen the narrative of the other, and, since St Matthew is the less exact, we infer that both Evangelists in this instance drew from some cycle of oral or written apostolic teaching. The words added by St Matthew (viii. 11, 12) are given by St Luke in another connexion (xiii. 28 sq.).

10. *found the servant whole*] Rather, **convalescent**, a medical word which is found also in xv. 27 (and in a metaphorical sense in Tit. i. 13; 1 Tim. i. 10, vi. 3; 2 Tim. i. 13, iv. 3).

that had been sick] These words should probably be omitted.

11—17. *The raising of the Son of the Widow of Nain.*

And it came to pass the *day* after, *that* he went into a 11 city called Nain; and many of his disciples went with him, and much people. Now when he came nigh to the gate of 12 the city, behold, there was a dead man carried out, the only son of his mother, and she was a widow: and much people of the city was with her. And when the Lord saw her, he 13 had compassion on her, and said unto her, Weep not. And 14

11—17. THE RAISING OF THE SON OF THE WIDOW OF NAIN.

11. *the day after*] If the reading τῇ be right we must understand ἡμέρᾳ, 'day.' Some MSS. (A, B, L, &c.) read τῷ, which would give a wider limit of time. St Luke alone, with his characteristic tenderness, preserves for us this narrative.

into a city called Nain] In the tribe of Issachar. The name means 'lovely,' and it deserves the name from its site on the north-west slope of Jebel el Duhy, or Little Hermon, not far from Endor, and full in view of Tabor and the hills of Zebulon. It is twenty-five miles from Capernaum, and our Lord, starting in the cool of the very early morning, as Orientals always do, would reach it before noon. It is now a squalid and wretched village still bearing the name of Nein.

many of his disciples went with him, and much people] More literally, 'there were accompanying Him His disciples, in considerable numbers, and a large multitude.' In this first year of His ministry, before the deadly opposition to Him had gathered head, while as yet the Pharisees and leaders had not come to an open rupture with Him, and He had not sifted His followers by 'hard sayings,' our Lord was usually accompanied by adoring crowds.

12. *came nigh to the gate*] All ordinary Jewish funerals are extramural. Nain is approached by a narrow rocky path, and it must have been at this spot that the two processions met. They were perhaps going to bury the dead youth in one of the rock-hewn sepulchres which are still visible on the hill side.

the only son of his mother] See on viii. 42, ix. 38.

much people of the city] Compare the public sympathy for the family of Bethany (John xi. 19); and on the bitterness of mourning for an only child, see Jer. vi. 26; Zech. xii. 10; Amos viii. 10.

13. *when the Lord saw her*] "The Lord" is far more frequent as a title of Jesus in St Luke (vii. 31, x. 1, xi. 1, xii. 42, xvii. 5, 6, xix. 8, xxii. 61) than in the other Evangelists except St John. The fact is a sign of the spread of Christian faith. Even though St Luke's Gospel may not have been published more than a year or two after St Matthew's, yet St Luke belongs so to speak to a later generation of disciples.

he had compassion on her] Jesus, who was always touched by the sight of human agony (Mk. vii. 34, viii. 12), seems to have felt a peculiar compassion for the anguish of bereavement (John xi. 33—37). The

he came and touched the bier: and they that bare *him* stood still. And he said, Young man, I say unto thee, Arise. ¹⁵ And he that was dead sat up, and began to speak. And he ¹⁶ delivered him to his mother. And there came a fear on all: and they glorified God, saying, That a great prophet is risen ¹⁷ up among us; and, That God hath visited his people. And this rumour of him went forth throughout all Judea, and throughout all the region round about.

18—35. *The Message from the Baptist.*

¹⁸ And the disciples of John shewed him of all these *things*. ¹⁹ And John calling unto *him* two of his disciples sent *them* to Jesus, saying, Art thou he that should come? or look we ²⁰ for another? When the men were come unto him, they

fact that this youth was "the only son of his mother and she a widow" would convey to Jewish notions a deeper sorrow than it even does to ours, for they regarded childlessness as a special calamity, and the loss of offspring as a direct punishment for sin (Jer. vi. 26; Zech. xii. 10; Amos viii. 10).

weep not] Rather, **Be not weeping**, i.e. 'dry thy tears.'

14. *touched the bier*] Rather, 'the coffin.' Here again, as in the case of the leper (v. 12), our Lord sacrificed the mere Levitical ceremonialism, with its rules about uncleanness, to a higher law. Jewish coffins were open, so that the form of the dead was visible.

Arise] Probably the single monosyllable *Kûm!* Compare viii. 54; John xi. 43; Acts ix. 40. How unlike the passionate tentative struggles of Elijah (1 Kings xvii. 21) and Elisha (2 Kings iv. 35)!

16. *a great prophet*] · The expectation of the return of Elijah, Jeremiah, or "one of the Prophets" was at that time widely spread. See on ix. 8, 19.

God hath visited his people] Compare i. 68; John iii. 2.

17. *throughout all Judæa*] The notion that St Luke therefore supposed Nain to be in Judæa is quite groundless. He means that the story of the incident at Nain spread even into Judæa.

18—35. THE MESSAGE FROM THE BAPTIST.

19. *John calling unto him two of his disciples*] The Baptist was now in prison (Matt. xi. 2—6), but was not precluded from intercourse with his friends.

to Jesus] The reading of B and some other Uncials is "to the Lord."

Art thou he that should come? or look we for another?] Rather, **Art thou the coming [Messiah], or are we to expect another?** "The Coming (One)" is a technical Hebrew term for the Messiah (*Habba*). This brief remarkable message is identical with that in St Matthew, except that St Luke uses *allon* ('another') and St Matthew *heteron* ('a second,' or

said, John Baptist hath sent us unto thee, saying, Art thou he that should come? or look we for another? And in 21 that *same* hour he cured many of *their* infirmities and plagues, and of evil spirits; and unto many *that were* blind he gave

'different one'). Probably however there is no significance in this variation, since the accurate classical meaning of *heteros* was partly obliterated. Probably too the messengers spoke in Aramaic. "*The coming*" is clearer in St Matthew, because he has just told us that John heard in prison the works of "*the Christ*," i.e. of the Messiah. Those who are shocked with the notion that the faith of the Baptist should even for a moment have wavered, suppose that (1) St John merely meant to suggest that surely the time had now come for the Messiah *to reveal himself as the Messiah*, and that his question was one rather of 'increasing impatience' than of 'secret unbelief;' or (2) that the message was sent solely to reassure John's own disciples; or (3) that, as St Matthew here uses the phrase "the works *of the Messiah*" and not "of Jesus," the Baptist only meant to ask 'Art thou the *same person* as the Jesus to whom I bore testimony?' These suppositions are excluded, not only by the tenor of the narrative but directly by vs. 23; (Matt. xi. 6). Scripture never presents the saints as ideally faultless, and therefore with holy truthfulness never conceals any sign of their imperfection or weakness. Nothing is more natural than that the Great Baptist—to whom had been granted but a partial revelation—should have felt deep anguish at the calm and noiseless advance of a Kingdom for which, in his theocratic and Messianic hopes, he had imagined a very different proclamation. Doubtless too his faith like that of Elijah (1 K. xix. 4), of Job in his trials (Job iii. 1), and of Jeremiah in prison (Jer. xx. 7), might be for a moment drowned by the tragic briefness, and disastrous eclipse of his own career; and he might hope to alleviate by this message the anguish which he felt when he contrasted the joyous brightness of our Lord's Galilean ministry with the unalleviated gloom of his own fortress-prison among the black rocks at Makor. 'If Jesus be indeed the promised Messiah,' he may have thought, 'why am I, His Forerunner, suffered to languish undelivered,—the victim of a wicked tyrant?' The Baptist was but one of those many glorious saints whose careers God, in His mysterious Providence, has suffered to end in disaster and eclipse that He may shew us how small is the importance which we must attach to the judgment of men, or the rewards of earth. "We fools accounted his life madness, and his end to be without honour: how is he numbered among the children of God, and his lot is among the saints!" Wisd. v. 20. We may be quite sure that "in the fiery furnace God walked with His servant so that his spirit was not harmed, and having thus annealed his nature to the utmost that this earth can do, He took him hastily away and placed him among the glorified in Heaven." Irving.

20. *John Baptist*] Rather, **The Baptist**.

21. *in that same hour*] Omit 'same,' which has no equivalent in the Greek.

plagues] Literally, "*scourges*."

22 sight. Then Jesus answering said unto them, Go *your way*, and tell John what *things* ye have seen and heard; how that the blind see, the lame walk, the lepers are cleansed, the deaf hear, the dead are raised, to the poor the gospel is 23 preached. And blessed is *he*, whosoever shall not be offended 24 in me. And when the messengers of John were departed, he began to speak unto the people concerning John, What went ye out into the wilderness for to see? A reed shaken 25 with the wind? But what went ye out for to see? A man clothed in soft raiment? Behold, they which are gorgeously 26 apparelled, and live delicately, are in kings' courts. But

22. *what things ye have seen*] Our Lord wished His answer to be the announcement of facts not the explanation of difficulties. His enumeration of the miracles involves an obvious reference to Is. xxix. 18, xxxv. 4—6, lx. 1—3 (see iv. 17—19), which would be instantly caught by one so familiar with the language of "the Evangelical Prophet" as the Baptist had shewn himself to be.

to the poor the Gospel is preached] Thus the spiritual miracle is placed as the most convincing climax. The arrogant ignorance and hard theology of the Rabbis treated all the poor as mere peasants and nobodies. The Talmud is full of the two contemptuous names applied to them—'people of the earth' and 'laics;' and one of the charges brought against the Pharisees by our Lord was their attempt to secure the monopoly of knowledge, xi. 52.

23. *shall not be offended*] i.e. caused to stumble. For instances of the stumbling-block which some made for themselves of incidents in our Lord's career, see Matt. xiii. 55—57, xxii. 42; John vi. 60, 66; and compare Is. viii. 14, 15; 1 Cor. i. 23, ii. 14; 1 Pet. ii. 7, 8. The word *skandalon* (Latin *offendiculum*, Hebr. *mokesh* 'snare,' and *mikshol* 'stumbling-block') means anything over which a person falls (e.g. a stone in the road) or on which he treads and is thrown.

24. *when the messengers of John were departed*] We notice here the exquisite tenderness of our Lord. He would not suffer the multitudes who had heard the question of John to cherish one depreciatory thought of the Baptist; and yet he suffers the messengers to depart, lest, while hearing the grand eulogy of their Master, they should be pained by its concluding words. It is natural to suppose that the two disciples carried back to John some private message of peace and consolation.

A reed] John was not like the reeds which they had seen waving in the wind on the banks of Jordan, but rather, as Lange says, 'a cedar half uprooted by the storm.'

25. *A man clothed in soft raiment?*] A contrast to the camel's hair mantle and leathern girdle of the Baptist; Matt. iii. 4.

they which are gorgeously apparelled and live delicately] Rather, **they who are in glorious apparel and luxury.** The Herods were

what went ye out for to see? A prophet? Yea, I say unto you, and much more than a prophet. This is *he*, of whom 27 it is written, Behold, I send my messenger before thy face, which shall prepare thy way before thee. For 28 I say unto you, Among *those that are* born of women there is not a greater prophet than John the Baptist: but he that is least in the kingdom of God is greater than he. And all 29

specially given both to ostentation in dress (Acts xiii. 21) and to luxury, Mk. vi. 21; Jos. *B. J.* I. 20, § 2; *Antt.* XIX. 8, § 2; 18, § 7.

in king's courts] Rather, **in palaces**. Such as the palaces of the Herods which they had seen at Tiberias, Caesarea Philippi, and Jerusalem. We might almost fancy an allusion to Manaen the Essene, who is said in the Talmud to have openly adopted gorgeous robes to shew his allegiance to Herod. To the Herodians generally, and to all whose Judaism was a mere matter of gain and court favour, might have been applied the sneering nickname of the Talmud 'Proselytes of the royal table' (*Gere Shulchan Melachim. Kiddushin*, f. 65. 2; Grätz, III. 308). John had been in palaces, but only to counsel and reprove. Our Lord on the only two occasions on which He entered palaces—on the last day of His life—was mocked by "*bright apparel*" (xxiii. 11), and a purple or scarlet robe (Matt. xxvii. 28).

26. *A prophet?*] "All accounted John as a prophet," xxi. 26.

more than a prophet] Namely, an actual personal herald and forerunner; the Angel or Messenger of Malachi, iii. 1, and so the only Prophet who had himself been announced by Prophecy.

27. *Behold, I send my messenger*] Compare i. 76; Mk. i. 2. In the parallel passage of St Matthew our Lord adds that the Baptist is the promised Elias, Matt. xi. 11, 14, xvii. 10—13; Lk. i. 17 (Mal. iv. 5). The quotation is from Mal. iii. 1, "Behold, I will send My messenger, and he shall prepare the way before *Me*." The words are varied because, in the original, God is speaking in His own person, and here the words are applied to Christ.

28. *there is not a greater than John the Baptist*] "He was the lamp, kindled and burning," John v. 35. 'Major Prophetâ quia finis Prophetarum,' S. Ambr. He closed the former Aeon and announced the new, Matt. xi. 11, 12.

he that is least in the kingdom of God is greater than he] See by way of comment Matt. xiii. 16, 17; Col. i. 25—27, and compare Heb. xi. 13. The simple meaning of these words seems to be that in blessings and privileges, in knowledge, in revealed hope, in conscious admission into fellowship with God, the humblest child of the new kingdom is superior to the greatest prophet of the old; seeing that, as the old legal maxim says, "the least of the greatest is greater than the greatest of the least." The smallest diamond is made of more precious substance than the largest flint. In the old dispensation "the Holy Ghost was not yet given, because that Jesus was not yet glorified," John vii. 39. Of those 'born of women' there was no greater prophet

the people that heard *him*, and the publicans, justified God,
30 being baptized *with* the baptism of John. But the Pharisees and lawyers rejected the counsel of God against themselves, being not baptized of him.

31 And the Lord said, Whereunto then shall I liken the men
32 of this generation? and to what are they like? They are like unto children sitting in the marketplace, and calling one to another, and saying, We have piped unto you, and ye

than John the Baptist, but the members of Christ's Church are "born of water and of the Spirit." This saying of our Lord respecting the privileges of the humblest children of His kingdom has seemed so strange that attempts have been made to give another tone to the meaning by interpreting *"he that is least"* to mean "the younger," and explain it to mean our Lord Himself as "coming after" the Baptist.

29. *justified God*] i.e. they bore witness that God was just; see ver. 35, comp. Ps. li. 4, "that Thou mightest be justified when Thou speakest, and be clear when Thou art judged," and Rom. iii. 26. St Luke has already made prominent mention of the publicans at the baptism of John, iii. 12.

30. *rejected the counsel of God against themselves*] i.e. nullified (Gal. ii. 21; Prov. i. 24) the purpose of God, to their own ruin, or better, 'with reference to themselves.' The "purpose of God" (Acts xx. 27) had been their salvation (1 Tim. ii. 4).

being not baptized of him] They seem to have gone to the ministry of John partly out of curiosity, partly as spies (Matt. iii. 7); and they consistently refused to recognize him as a Prophet, although they were prevented from shewing open hostility by fear of the people (Mk. xi. 32).

31. *And the Lord said*] These words are almost certainly spurious, being omitted by all the best uncials.

Whereunto then shall I liken] Our Lord seems more than once to have used this formula to arrest attention for His parables. Mk. iv. 30.

32. *They are like unto children sitting in the marketplace*] Our Lord constantly drew His deepest instruction from the commonest phenomena of nature, and the everyday incidents of life. Such a method gave far greater force to the delivery of His Gospel *"to the poor,"* and it was wholly unlike the arid, scholastic, technical, and second-hand methods of the Rabbis.

calling one to another, and saying] This interesting comparison was doubtless drawn from the games which Jesus had witnessed, and in which perhaps He as a child had taken part, in Nazareth. Eastern children are fond of playing in groups at games of a very simple kind in the open air. Some have supposed that the game here alluded to was a sort of *guessing game* like that sometimes played by English children, and called 'Dumb Show.' This is not very probable. The

have not danced; we have mourned to you, and ye have not wept. For John the Baptist came neither eating bread 33 nor drinking wine; and ye say, He hath a devil. The Son 34 of man is come eating and drinking; and ye say, Behold a gluttonous man, and a winebibber, a friend of publicans and sinners. But wisdom is justified of all her children. 35

point of the comparison is the peevish sullenness of the group of children who refuse to take part in, or approve of, any game played by their fellows, whether it be the merry acting of a marriage, or the imitated sadness of a funeral. So the men of that generation condemned the Baptist for his asceticism which they attributed to demoniacal possession; and condemned Christ for His genial tenderness by calling Him a man fond of good living. The difficulties and differences of explanation found in this simple parable are only due to a needless literalness. If indeed we take the language quite literally, '*this generation*' is compared with the dancing and mourning *children who complain* of the sullenness of their fellows; and if this be insisted on, the meaning must be that the Jews complained of John for holding aloof from their mirth, and of Jesus for discountenancing their austerities. But it is the children who are looking on who are blamed, not the playing children, as is clearly shewn by the "*and ye say*" of vss. 33, 34. In the explanation here preferred our Lord and the Baptist are *included* in this generation, and the comparison (just as in the Homeric similes) is taken *as a whole* to illustrate the mutual relations between them and their contemporaries. So in Matt. xiii. 24, "The kingdom of heaven is like unto a sower, &c.," where the comparison is more to the *reception of the seed*.

33. *neither eating bread nor drinking wine*] "His meat was locusts and wild honey," Matt. iii. 4. Being a Nazarite he drank no wine, i. 15; see 2 Esdr. ix. 24.

He hath a devil] They sneered at him for a moody or melancholy temperament which they attributed to an evil spirit. This in fact was their coarse way of describing any peculiarity or exaltation which struck them as strange. At a later period they said the same of Christ, John vii. 20, x. 20.

34. *The Son of man is come eating and drinking*] The title explains the reason of our Lord's practice. He came as the Son of man, and therefore He came to shew that the common life of all men could be lived with perfect holiness, and that seclusion and asceticism were not necessary as universal conditions.

Behold a gluttonous man, and a winebibber] These words are too strong. Rather, **an eater, and a drinker of wine.** *Phagos* does not occur in the LXX. or N. T.; *oinopotēs* only in Prov. xxiii. 20.

a friend of publicans and sinners] Thus His divinest mercy was turned into His worst reproach.

35. *But*] Literally, "*And*," but the Greek *kai* often has the force of 'and yet.'

36—39. *Jesus in the House of Simon.*

36 And one of the Pharisees desired him that he would eat with him. And he went into the Pharisee's house, and sat

wisdom] The *personification* of God's wisdom was common in the later Jewish literature, as in the Book of Wisdom. It is also found in the Old Testament (Prov. i. 20, ix., &c.).

is justified of all her children] Rather, **was justified by**, i.e. has from the first been acquitted of all wrong and error, receives the witness of being just, at the hands of all her children. The "children of wisdom" *generally* (Prov. ii. 1, iii. 1, &c.) are those who obey God, and here are those of that generation who accepted the baptism of John and the ministry of Jesus, without making a stumbling-block of their different methods. The Jews, like the petulant children, refused to sympathise either with John or Jesus—the one they condemned for exaggerated strictness, the other for dangerous laxity: yet the Wise,—Wisdom's true children—once for all declare that she is righteous, and free from blame: for they know that wisdom is *polupoikilos*, 'richly-variegated,' 'of many colours,' Eph. iii. 10. The *world's* wisdom was foolishness; those whom the world *called* fools were divinely wise, John iii. 33. Wisdom is thus justified by her children both actively and passively; *they* declare her to be just and holy, and the *world* ultimately sees that her guidance as exemplified by their lives is the best guidance (Wisd. v. 5, 4; Ps. li. 4; Rom. iii. 4). The reading ἔργων 'works' for τέκνων 'children' in ℵ may be derived from the variant reading in Matt. xi. 19.

36—39. Jesus in the House of Simon.

36. *one of the Pharisees*] This exquisite narrative is peculiar to St Luke, and well illustrates that conception of the universality and free gift of grace which predominates in his Gospel as in St Paul. To identify this Simon with Simon the Leper in Mk. xiv. 3 is quite arbitrary. It was one of the commonest Jewish names. There were two Simons among the Twelve, and there are *nine* Simons mentioned in the New Testament alone, and *twenty* in Josephus. There must therefore have been *thousands* of Simons in Palestine, where names were few. The incident itself was one which *might* have happened frequently, being in close accordance with the customs of the time and country. And with the uncritical attempt to identify Simon the Pharisee with Simon the Leper, there also falls to the ground the utterly improbable identification of the woman who was a sinner with Mary of Bethany. The time, the place, the circumstances, the character, the words uttered, and the results of the incident recorded in Matt. xxvi. 7; Mk. xiv. 3; John xii. 3 are all *entirely different*.

that he would eat with him] The invitation was clearly due to a patronising curiosity, if not to a worse and hostile motive. The whole manner of the Pharisee to Jesus was like his invitation, ungracious. But it was part of our Lord's mission freely to accept the proffered hospitality of all, that He might reach every class.

down to meat. And behold, a woman in the city, which 37
was a sinner, when she knew that *Jesus* sat at meat in the
Pharisee's house, brought an alabaster box of ointment, and 38
stood at his feet behind *him* weeping, and began to wash

sat down to meat] Rather, **reclined at table**. The old method of
the Jews had been that of the East in general, to *sit* at table (*anapiptein*,
xi. 37; *anakeisthai*, vii. 37; *anaklinesthai*, xii. 37) generally cross-legged
on the floor, or on divans (Gen. xxvii. 19; 1 Sam. xx. 5, 18; Ps.
cxxviii. 3; Cant. i. 12, &c.). They had borrowed the custom of
reclining on couches (*triclinia*, comp. ἀρχιτρίκλινος, John ii. 8) from
the Persians (Esth. i. 6, vii. 8), the Greeks and Romans, after the Exile
(Tobit ii. 1; 1 Esdr. iv. 10; Judith xii. 15). The influence of the
Greeks had been felt in the nation for three hundred years, and that of
the Romans for nearly a hundred years, since the conquest of Jerusalem
by Pompey, B. C. 63.

37. *a woman in the city*] The harsher reading of A, B, L, is
"who was a sinner in the city." No city is named, but if the Christian
church is right in identifying this woman with Mary Magdalene, we
may assume that the city implied is Magdala, which appears at that
time to have been a flourishing place, though now it is only a mud
village—El Mejdel. It cannot of course be regarded as indisputable
that this woman was the Magdalene, but it is, to say the least, *possible;*
and there is no sufficient reason to disturb the current Christian belief
which has been consecrated in so many glorious works of art. See
further on viii. 2.

which was a sinner] It was the Jewish term for a harlot, and such
had come even to John's baptism, Matt. xxi. 32.

when she knew that Jesus sat at meat] Literally, **getting to know**.
She had not of course received permission to enter, but the prominence
of hospitality as the chief of Eastern virtues led to all houses being left
open, so that during a meal any one who wished could enter and look
on. "To sit down to eat with common people" was one of the six
things which no Rabbi or Pupil of the Wise might do; another was "to
speak with a woman." Our Lord freely did both.

an alabaster box] The word *alabastron* meant originally a vase or
phial of alabaster, such as were used for perfumes and unguents (*unguenta optime servantur in alabastris*, Plin. XIII. 3), but afterwards
came to mean any phial used for a similar purpose (just as our *box*
originally meant a receptacle made of box-wood).

of ointment] This was doubtless one of the implements of her guilty
condition (Prov. vii. 17, Is. iii. 24), and her willingness to sacrifice it
was a sign of her sincere repentance (comp. Cant. iv. 10).

38. *stood at his feet behind him*] This is explained by the arrangement of the *triclinia*, by which the guest reposed on his elbow at the
table, with his unsandalled feet outstretched on the couch. Each guest
left his sandals beside the door on entering. Literally the verse is, "And
standing behind beside His feet weeping, with her tears she began to
bedew His feet, and with the hairs of her head she wiped them off, and

his feet with tears, and did wipe *them* with the hairs of her head, and kissed his feet, and anointed *them* with the ointment. 39 Now when the Pharisee which had bidden him saw *it*, he spake within himself, saying, This *man*, if he were a prophet, would have known who and what manner of 40 woman *this is* that toucheth him: for she is a sinner. And

was eagerly kissing His feet, and anointing them with the perfume." As she bent over His feet her tears began to fall on them, perhaps accidentally at first, and she wiped them off with the long dishevelled hair (1 Cor. xi. 15) which shewed her shame and anguish, and then in her joy and gratitude at finding herself unrepulsed, she poured the unguent over them. The scene and its moral are beautifully expressed in the sonnet of Hartley Coleridge.

> "She sat and wept beside His feet. The weight
> Of sin oppressed her heart; for all the blame
> And the poor malice, of the worldly shame
> To her were past, extinct, and out of date:
> Only the sin remained—the leprous state.
> She would be melted by the heat of love,
> By fires far fiercer than are blown to prove
> And purge the silver ore adulterate.
> She sat and wept, and with her untressed hair
> Still wiped the feet she was so blest to touch;
> And He wiped off the soiling of despair
> From her sweet soul, because she loved so much."

No one but a woman in the very depths of anguish would have violated all custom by appearing in public with uncovered head (1 Cor. xi. 10).

weeping] Doubtless at the contrast of His sinlessness and her own stained life. She could not have done thus to the Pharisee, who would have repelled her with execration as bringing pollution by her touch. The deepest sympathy is caused by the most perfect sinlessness. It is not impossible that on that very day she may have heard the "Come unto me" of Matt. xi. 28.

kissed] The word means 'was earnestly' or 'tenderly kissing,' as in Acts xx. 37.

39. *This man*] The word in the original expresses the supercilious scorn which is discernible throughout in the bearing of the speaker.

who and what manner of woman] 'Who,' because the particular offender was notorious for her beauty and her shame. This rather strengthens the inference that the woman was Mary of Magdala, for the legends of the Jewish Talmud respecting her shew that she was well known.

that toucheth him] Rather, "who is clinging to him." Simon makes a double assumption—first that a prophet would have known the character of the woman, and next that he would certainly have repelled her. The bearing and tone of the Rabbis towards women closely

Jesus answering said unto him, Simon, I have somewhat to say unto thee. And he saith, Master, say *on*. There was a certain creditor which had two debtors: the one ought five hundred pence, and the other fifty. And when they had nothing to pay, he frankly forgave *them* both. Tell me therefore, which of them will love him most? Simon answered and said, I suppose that *he*, to whom he forgave most. And he said unto him, Thou hast rightly judged. And he turned to the woman, and said unto Simon, Seest thou this woman?

resembled that of some mediaeval monks. They said that no one should stand nearer them than four cubits. But Jesus knew more of the woman than Simon did, and was glad that she should shed on His feet the tears of penitence. A great prophet had declared long before that those which say, "Stand by thyself, come not near to me, for I am holier than thou," were "a smoke in my nose." Is. lxv. 5.

40. *answering*] "He heard the Pharisee thinking." S. Aug.

unto thee] The emphasis is on these words, You have been thinking evil of me: I have something to say *to thee*.

Master] Rather, **Teacher**, or **Rabbi**.

41. *a certain creditor*] Rather, **money-lender**.

five hundred pence] A denarius was the day's wages of a labourer and is usually reckoned at $7\frac{1}{2}d.$, but really represents much more. Hence 500 denarii would certainly represent as much as £50 in these days. The frequency of our Lord's illustrations from debtors and creditors shews the disturbed and unprosperous condition of the country under Roman and Herodian oppression.

42. *he frankly forgave them*] In the original, the one word ἐχαρίσατο, 'he remitted,' involving the idea of that free grace and favour (*charis*) on which St Luke, like St Paul, is always glad to dwell. See Rom. iii. 24; Eph. ii. 8, 9, iv. 32.

43. *I suppose*] 'I imagine;' 'I presume.' The original word has a shade of supercilious irony (comp. Acts ii. 15), as though Simon thought the question very trivial, and never dreamt that it could have any bearing on himself.

rightly] There is a touch of gentle sarcasm in the use of this word, which involves Simon's self-condemnation. It is the word so often adopted by Socrates as one of his implements of dialectic irony.

44. *Seest thou this woman*] Rather, **Dost thou mark?** Hitherto the Pharisee, in accordance with his customs and traditions, had hardly deigned to throw upon her one disdainful glance. Now Jesus bids him look full upon her to shew him that she had really done the honours of his house. Her love had more than atoned for his coldness.

We notice in the language here that rhythmic parallelism, which is often traceable in the words of our Lord, at periods of special emotion.

Into *thine* house I entered:
Water upon my feet thou gavest not,

I entered into thine house, thou gavest me no water for my feet: but she hath washed my feet with tears, and wiped
45 *them* with the hairs of her head. Thou gavest me no kiss: but this *woman* since the time I came in hath not ceased to
46 kiss my feet. Mine head with oil thou didst not anoint:
47 but this *woman* hath anointed my feet with ointment. Wherefore I say unto thee, Her sins, which are many, are forgiven;

> But she with her tears bedewed my feet,
> And with her tresses wiped them.
> A kiss thou gavedst me not:
> But she, since I entered, ceased not earnestly kissing my feet.
> My head with oil thou anointedst not,
> But she anointed my feet with perfume.
> Wherefore I say to thee, Her sins, her many sins, have been forgiven, because she loved much.
> But he to whom little is being forgiven loveth little.

"As oft as I think over this event," says Gregory the Great, "I am more disposed to weep over it than to preach upon it."

thou gavest me no water for my feet] Thus Simon had treated his guest with such careless indifference as to have neglected the commonest courtesies and comforts. To sandalled travellers on those burning, rocky, dusty paths, water for the feet was a necessity; John xiii. 4, 5. "*Wash your feet*, and rest yourselves under the tree." Gen. xviii. 4. "Tarry all night, and *wash your feet*," Gen. xix. 2. "He brought them into his house, and they washed their feet," Judg. xix. 21. "If she have washed the saints' feet," 1 Tim. v. 10.

hath washed] Rather, **bedewed** or **wetted**.

with tears] "The most priceless of waters." Bengel. "She poured forth tears, the blood of the heart." S. Aug.

45. *no kiss*] The ordinary salutation of respect in the East, where the first thing when two friends meet and wish to do each other honour is to try to kiss each other's hands. The kiss on the cheek is between equals and also to superiors. Absalom, to gain favour, kissed every man who came near him to do him obeisance; 2 Sam. xv. 5. "The king kissed Barzillai," id. xix. 39. Hence this was a natural signal of recognition for the traitor to give; Matt. xxvi. 49. See Acts xx. 37. Hence the *osculum pacis*, Rom. xvi. 16, &c.

I came in] There is another reading, εἰσῆλθεν, 'she *came* in' (L and some versions), which is probable, for the woman only ascertained that Jesus was at the house after He had entered it.

46. *My head with oil thou didst not anoint*] This would have been an exceptional mark of honour, though not uncommon. "Let thy head lack no ointment," Eccles. ix. 8; Amos vi. 6; Ps. xxiii. 5. Here it is only mentioned to contrast it with the still higher honour of which the sinful woman had thought Him worthy. To anoint the feet was regarded as an extreme luxury (Pliny, *H. N.* XIII. 4), but the love of the sinner thought no honour too great for her Saviour.

for she loved much: but to whom little is forgiven, *the same* loveth little. And he said unto her, Thy sins are forgiven. 48 And they that sat at meat with *him* began to say within 49 themselves, Who is this that forgiveth sins also? And he 50 said to the woman, Thy faith hath saved thee; go in peace.

47. *for she loved much*] Rather, **because**. No doubt, theologically, faith, not love, is the means of pardon (vs. 50); hence, some interpret the '*because*' *a posteriori*, and make it mean 'she is forgiven,' *as you may conclude from the fact* that she loved much. It is more than doubtful whether this was intended. Her love and her forgiveness were mingled with each other in mutual interchange. She loved because she was forgiven; she was forgiven because she loved. Her faith and her love were one; it was "faith working by love" (Gal. v. 6), and the love proved the faith. Spiritual things do not admit of the clear sequences of earthly things. There is with God no before or after, but only an eternal now.

to whom little is forgiven] The life of conventional respectability excludes flagrant and open transgressions; cold selfishness does not take itself to be sinful. Simon *imagined* that he had little to be forgiven, and therefore loved little. Had he been a true saint he would have recognised his debt. The confessions of the holiest are also the most heartrending, because they most fully recognise the true nature of sin. What is wanted to awaken 'much love' is not 'much sin'—for we *all* have that qualification—but deep *sense of sin*. "Ce qui manque au meilleur pour aimer beaucoup, ce n'est pas le péché; c'est *la connaissance du péché*." Godet.

48. *are forgiven*] Rather, **have been forgiven**. The *is forgiven* of the previous verse is in the present, "*is being forgiven*." Both in the Old and New Testaments the readiness of God to forgive the deepest and most numerous sins is dwelt upon (Is. i. 18, lv. 7), and also the *absoluteness* of the forgiveness (Rom. v. 20; 1 John iv. 10, 19). There is an obvious analogy between the little parable of the debtors and that of the uncompassionate servant (Matt. xviii. 23—27).

49. *began to say within themselves*] His words caused a shock of surprised silence which did not as yet dare to vent itself in open murmurs.

50. *he said to the woman*] Our Lord would not on this, as on the previous occasion, rebuke them for their thoughts, because the miracle which He had worked was the purely spiritual one of winning back a guilty soul,—a miracle which they could not comprehend. Further, He compassionately desired to set the woman free from a notice which must now have become deeply painful to her shrinking penitence.

Thy faith hath saved thee] The faith of the recipient was the necessary condition of a miracle, whether physical or spiritual, Mk. v. 34, ix. 23; Matt. ix. 2, xiii. 58, xv. 28; John iv. 50; Acts iii. 16, xiv. 8.

go in peace] Rather, **to** or **into peace**—a translation of the Hebrew

Ch. VIII. 1—3. *The Ministering Women.*

8 And it came to pass afterward, that he went throughout every city and village, preaching and shewing the glad tidings 2 of the kingdom of God: and the twelve *were* with him, and certain women, which had been healed of evil spirits and infirmities, Mary called Magdalene, out of whom went seven

leshalôm, "for peace," 1 Sam. i. 17. "Peace" (*shalom*) was the Hebrew, as '*grace*' (χαίρειν) was the Hellenic salutation. See on ii. 29, and Excursus VII.

Notice that St Luke omits the anointing of Jesus by Mary of Bethany from a deliberate "economy of method," which leads him to exclude all second or similar incidents to those which he has already related. Thus he omits a second feeding of the multitude, and healings of blind, dumb, and demoniac, of which he severally gives a single specimen. The events of Mk. vii. 24—viii. 26 and ix. 12—14 are probably excluded by St Luke on this principle—to avoid repetition. It is a sign of what German writers call his *Sparsamkeit*. Nor must we forget that the records of all the manifold activity which at times left the Lord no leisure even to eat, are confined to a few incidents, and only dwell on the details of a few special days.

Ch. VIII. 1—3. The Ministering Women.

1. *And it came to pass afterward*] The expression marks a new phase, a new departure, in Christ's mode of action. Hitherto He had made Capernaum His head-quarters; regarded it as "His own city," and not gone to any great distance from it. At this period—the exact beginning of which is only vaguely marked—He began a wider range of missions.

shewing the glad tidings] The Baptist had preached 'repentance' as the preparation for the Kingdom: our Lord preached of the Kingdom itself, and this was 'glad tidings,' because the Kingdom of God is "righteousness and peace and joy in the Holy Ghost." Rom. xiv. 17.

2. *certain women*] This most remarkable circumstance is prominently mentioned by St Luke alone, though alluded to in Matt. xxvii. 55, 56; Mark xv. 41. It accords alike with the probability that some of his peculiar sources of information had been derived from women; and with the certainty that he is fond of dwelling on the graciousness and tenderness of Jesus even to a class so much despised and neglected as Eastern women. See Introd. p. 26. At an earlier period (John iv. 27) the disciples had been amazed to see Jesus even talking with a woman.

Mary called Magdalene] i.e. Mary, who to distinguish her from numerous others who bore that very common name (Miriam), was known from her native place as Mary of Magdala. We have already seen that, as far as tradition is concerned, we cannot be *certain* that the Christian world is right in generally identifying her with 'the

devils, and Joanna the wife of Chuza Herod's steward, and 3 Susanna, and many others, which ministered unto him of their substance.

sinner' of the last chapter. Origen rejects the identification; St Ambrose, St Augustine, and St Jerome are doubtful. The identification is first confidently accepted by Gregory the Great (died A.D. 604). There is nothing however to disprove the fact. In the earlier scene her name might well have been suppressed from the spirit of loving and delicate reticence. The locality of the scene, and the stage of the ministry at which she is introduced, agree with the supposition, as well as the intense absorbing affection of one who "loved much."

out of whom went seven devils] St Mark (xvi. 9) uses a similar expression. Some have thought that this excludes the possibility of the life indicated by the words "a sinner in the city." On the contrary it agrees well with it. Early Christian writers see in the "many sins" (vii. 47) a reference which accords with, if it be not the same as, "seven devils," and that this may be the meaning is quite certain from xi. 26. Apart from the general question as to demoniac possession in particular cases, it is quite certain that Jewish colloquial usage adopted the expression to describe many forms of disease (as for instance hydrophobia, epilepsy, &c.), and many forms of sin (as drunkenness, &c.). The Talmudists (as we have seen) have many wild stories to tell of Mary of Magdala, but they agree in describing her as a flagrant sinner rather than as a demoniac.

3. *Joanna*] She is mentioned only in xxiv. 10, but had apparently been healed of some infirmity.

the wife of Chuza Herod's steward] The court of Antipas was well aware of the ministry and claims of Jesus. Not only had John the Baptist been a familiar figure there, but Manaen, Herod's foster-brother, early became a Christian (Acts xiii. 1), and whether Chuzas be the courtier (*basilikos*, E. V. 'nobleman') of John iv. 46 or not, that courtier could only have been in the retinue of Antipas, and must have made known the healing of his son by Jesus. The word *epitropos*, 'administrator,' conveys the impression of a higher rank than steward (*oikonomos*). The Rabbis adopted the word in Hebrew letters, and said that Obadiah was Ahab's *epitropos*. Manaen at Antioch was perhaps the source of St Luke's special knowledge about the Herodian family.

Susanna] The name means 'Lily.'

many others] See Matt. xxvii. 55.

which ministered unto him of their substance] or 'to *them*,' B, D, F, G, H, &c. This notice is deeply interesting as throwing light on the otherwise unsolved problem of the means of livelihood possessed by Jesus and His Apostles. They had a common purse which sufficed not only for their own needs but for those of the poor (John xiii. 29). The Apostles had absolutely forsaken their daily callings, but we may suppose that some of them (like Matthew and the sons of the wealthier

4—15. *The Parable of the Sower.*

4 And when much people were gathered together, and were
5 come to him out of every city, he spake by a parable: A

fisherman Zebedee) had some small resources of their own, and here we see that these women, some of whom (as tradition says of Mary of Magdala) were rich, helped to maintain them. It must also be borne in mind (1) that the needs of an Oriental are very small. A few dates, a little parched corn, a draught of water, a few figs or grapes plucked from the roadside trees, suffice him; and in that climate he can sleep during most of the year in the open air wrapped up in the same outer garment which serves him for the day. Hence the maintenance of a poor man in Palestine is wholly different from the standard of maintenance required in such countries as ours with their many artificial needs. And yet (2) in spite of this our Lord was so poor as to be homeless (ix. 58) and without the means of even paying the small Temple-tribute of a didrachm (about 1s. 6d.), which was demanded from every adult Jew. Matt. xvii. 24; 2 Cor. viii. 9.

4—15. THE PARABLE OF THE SOWER.

4. *when much people were gathered together*] Rather, **were coming together.** Our Lord, though ready at all times to utter the most priceless truths even to one lonely and despised listener, yet wisely apportioned ends to means, and chose the assembling of a large multitude for the occasion of a new departure in His style of teaching.

and were come to him out of every city] Rather, **and (a multitude) of those throughout every city resorting to Him.** A comparison of this Parable and the details respecting its delivery, as preserved in each of the Synoptists (Matt. xiii. 2—13; Mark iv. 1—20), ought alone to be decisive as to the fact that the three Evangelists *did not use each other's narratives*, and did not draw from the same written source such as the supposed Proto-Marcus of German theorists. The oral or written sources which they consulted seem to have been most closely faithful in all essentials, but they differed in minute details and expressions as all narratives do. From St Matthew (xiii. 1) we learn that Jesus had just left "the house," perhaps that of Peter at Capernaum; and therefore the place which He chose for His first Parable was probably the strip of bright hard sand on the shore of the Lake at Bethsaida. Both St Matthew and St Mark tell us that (doubtless, as on other occasions, to avoid the pressure of the crowd) He got on one of the boats by the lake-side and preached from thence.

by a parable] St Luke here only reports the Parable of the Sower and its interpretation. St Mark adds that of the seed growing secretly (Mark iv. 26—29), and that of the grain of mustard seed (30—32; Luke xiii. 18—21). St Matthew (xiii. 24—53) gives his memorable group of seven Parables: the Sower, the Tares, the Mustard Seed, the Leaven, the Hid Treasure, the Pearl, the Drag-net. This is no doubt due to subjective grouping. Our Lord would not bewilder and

sower went out to sow his seed: and as he sowed, some fell by the way side; and it was trodden down, and the fowls of the air devoured it. And some fell upon a rock; and as 6

distract by mere multiplicity of teachings, but taught "as they were able to hear it" (Mark iv. 33). 'Parable' is derived from *paraballo* 'I place beside' in order to compare.

A Parable is a pictorial or narrative exhibition of some spiritual or moral truth, by means of actual and not fanciful elements of comparison. It differs from a *fable* by moving solely within the bounds of the possible and by aiming at the illustration of deeper truths; from a *simile* in its completer and often dramatic development, as also in its object; from an *allegory* in not being *identical with* the truth illustrated. The moral objects which our Lord had in view are explained below (vs. 10), but we may notice here the unapproachable superiority of our Lord's Parables to those of all other teachers. Parables are found scattered throughout the literature of the world. They abound in the poems and sacred books of later religions (Ecclus. i. 25, "Parables of knowledge are in the treasures of wisdom,") and they have been frequently adopted in later days. But "never man spake like this Man," and no Parables have ever touched the heart and conscience of mankind in all ages and countries like those of Christ. "He taught them by Parables under which were hid mysterious senses, which shined through their veil, like a bright sun through an eye closed with a thin eyelid." Jer. Taylor. For Old Testament parables see 2 Sam. xii. 1—7; Eccl. ix. 14—16; Is. xxviii. 23—29. St Luke is especially rich in Parables. The word 'parable' sometimes stands for the Hebrew *mashal* 'a proverb' (iv. 23; 1 Sam. x. 12, xxiv. 13); sometimes for a rhythmic prophecy (Num. xxiii. 7) or dark saying (Ps. lxxviii. 2; Pr. i. 6); and sometimes for a comparison (Mk. xiii. 28).

5. *A sower went out*] Rather, **The sower**; as also **the rock, the thorns**. St Mark (iv. 3) preserves for us the graphic detail that Jesus prefaced this new method of teaching by the one emphatic word "*Hearken!*" as though to prepare them for something unusual and memorable.

some fell by the way side] The nature of the land in the plain of Gennesareth would, as Dean Stanley noticed (*Sin. and Palest.* p. 496), and as many have subsequently remarked, furnish an immediate illustration of the words. In the fields close to the shore may be seen the hard beaten paths into which no seed can penetrate; the flights of innumerable birds ready to peck it up; the rocks thinly covered with soil, and the stony ground; the dense tangled growth of weeds and thistles in neglected corners; and the rich deep loam on which the harvests grew with unwonted luxuriance.

it was trodden down] This touch is found in St Luke only.

6. *upon a rock*] St Matthew and St Mark say "upon stony places," and add its speedy growth, and its withering after sunrise from want of root; St Luke dwells rather on the lack of moisture than on the lack of soil.

soon as it was sprung up, it withered away, because *it* lacked
7 moisture. And some fell among thorns; and the thorns
8 sprang up with *it*, and choked it. And other fell on good
ground, and sprang up, and bare fruit an hundredfold. And
when he said these *things*, he cried, He that hath ears to
hear, let him hear.

9 And his disciples asked him, saying, What might this
10 parable be? And he said, Unto you it is given to know the
mysteries of the kingdom of God: but to others in parables;

7. *thorns*] In rich soils and hot valleys like Gennesareth the growth of weeds and thorns is as rapid and luxuriant as that of good seed. In summer and autumn there are parts of the plain which are quite impervious from the forest of gigantic thistles which covers them—"so tall and so dense that no horse can break through" (Porter, *Palestine*, II. 403). It was natural that this circumstance should suggest several of Christ's illustrations.

8. *bare fruit an hundredfold*] St Luke passes over the 'growing and increasing' of the fruit (Mk. iv. 8) and its various degrees of productiveness—thirty and sixty as well as an hundredfold.

he cried] This word—**spake with a loud voice**—shews, like the "*Hearken!*" in St Mark, the special attention which our Lord called to His new method.

He that hath ears to hear, let him hear] In other words, 'this teaching is worthy the deepest attention of those who have the moral and spiritual capacity to understand it.'

9. *his disciples asked him*] St Mark says "those about Him, with the Twelve;" and that they came to Him afterwards when they found Him alone.

10. *And he said*] This verse is rather an answer to the other question, recorded in St Matthew, "*why* dost thou speak to them in parables?"

it is given] Rather, **it has been given**.

to know the mysteries] i.e. to grasp the revealed secrets, the 'apples of gold' hid in these 'networks of silver.' The proper use of the word 'mystery' is the opposite of its current use. It is now generally used to imply something which we cannot understand; in the New Testament it always means something *once* hidden now revealed, Col. i. 26; 1 Tim. iii. 16; Matt. xi. 25, 26; Rev. xvii. 5, &c. It is derived from μύω, 'I initiate.' "God is a revealer of **secrets**," Dan. ii. 47.

> "What if earth
> Be but the shadow of heaven, and things therein
> Each to the other like, more than on earth is thought?"
> MILTON.

to others] Rather, **to the rest**; "to them that are without," Mk. iv. 11. It has been granted *you* to grasp these mysteries unveiled; to the rest it has been only given to grasp them under the veil of parables.

that seeing they might not see, and hearing they might not understand. Now the parable is this: The seed is the 11 word of God. Those by the way side are they that hear; 12

that seeing they might not see, and hearing they might not understand] These words are difficult, and (without dwelling on the fact that the particle ἵνα loses in later Greek some of its *final* force) must not be pressed with unreasonable and extravagant literalism to mean that the *express object* of teaching by parables was to conceal the message of the kingdom from all but the disciples. This would have been to put the kindled lamp under a couch or a bushel. On the contrary they were addressed to the multitudes, and deeply impressed them, as they have impressed the world in all ages, and have had the effect, not of darkening truth but of bringing it into brighter light. The varying phrase of St Matthew, "*because* seeing they see not, &c.," will help us to understand it. Our Lord *wished* and *meant* the multitudes to hearken and understand, and this method awoke their interest and deepened their attention; but the resultant profit *depended solely on the degree of their faithfulness*. The Parables resembled the Pillar of Fire, which was to others a Pillar of Cloud. If they listened with mere intellectual curiosity or hardened prejudice they would only carry away the parable itself, or some complete misapplication of its least essential details; to get at its real meaning required self-examination and earnest thought. Hence parables had a blinding and hardening effect on the false and the proud and the wilful, just as prophecy had in old days (Is. vi. 9, 10, quoted in this connexion in Matthew xiii. 14, comp. Acts xxviii. 26, 27; Rom. xi. 8). But the Prophecy and the Parable did not *create* the hardness or stolidity, but only educed it when it existed—*as all misused blessings and privileges do*. It was only *unwillingness to see* which was punished by *incapacity of seeing*. The natural punishment of spiritual perversity is spiritual blindness.

Nothing can be better than the profound remark of Lord Bacon, that "a Parable has a double use; it tends to *vail*, and it tends to *illustrate* a truth; in the latter case it seems designed to teach, in the former to conceal."

"Though truths in manhood darkly join,
    Deep seated in our mystic frame,
    We yield all blessing to the name
Of Him who made them current coin.
For Wisdom dealt with mortal powers,
    Where truth in closest words shall fail,
    When truth embodied in a tale
Shall enter in at lowly doors."

11. *The seed is the word of God*] We have the same metaphor in Col. i. 5, 6; 1 Cor. iii. 6; and a *similar* one in Jas. i. 21, "the *engrafted* word;" 2 Esdr. ix. 31, 33, "Behold, I sow my law in you, and it shall bring fruit in you...yet they that received it perished, because they kept not the thing that was sown in them."

then cometh the devil, and taketh away the word out of
13 their hearts, lest they should believe and be saved. They
on the rock *are they*, which, when they hear, receive the
word with joy; and these have no root, which for a while
14 believe, and in time of temptation fall away. And that
which fell among thorns are they, which, when they have
heard, go *forth*, and are choked with cares and riches and

12. *Those by the way side*] These are hearers who are *hardened*—either beaten (i) flat by lifeless familiarity—heartless formalists, Pharisaic theologians, and insincere professors; or (ii) by perversity and indifference, the habit and custom of a worldly and dissolute life. Notice the intensity of thought which identifies the scattered seeds with those in whose hearts they are sown. "The way is the heart beaten and dried by the passage of evil thoughts." H. de S. Victore.

the devil] The Accuser or Slanderer. St Mark has "the wicked one," St Matthew "Satan."

taketh away] "Snatches," Matt. xiii. 19.—It is done in a moment; by a smile at the end of the sermon; by a silly criticism at the Church door; by foolish gossip on the way home. These are "the fowls of the air" whom the Evil One uses in this task.

lest they should believe] Rather, **that they may not believe.** "Therefore we ought to give the more earnest heed to the things which we have heard, lest at any time we should let them slip," or rather "*drift away* from them," Heb. ii. 1.

13. *They on the rock*] Shallow, impulsive listeners, whose enthusiasm is hot and transient as a blaze in the straw.

with joy] "Yet they seek me daily, and *delight* to know my ways," Is. lviii. 2. "Thou art unto them as a very lovely song of one that hath a pleasant voice...for they hear thy words, but they do them not," Ezek. xxxiii. 32. Herod "heard John *gladly*," Mk. vi. 20.

in time of temptation] Temptation in any form of "affliction or persecution" (Matt., Mk.) which tests the moral nature.

fall away] Literally "*stand aloof*," "*apostatise*;" "immediately they are offended," Matt., Mk. See a very striking instance of this in John vi. 66.

14. *that which fell among thorns are they*] Here the grand paradox which identifies the seed with its recipient is very marked. See especially Matt. xiii., where "*he that received the seed* by the way side, &c." should be "*he that was sown* by the way side, &c." The class here described are worldly, ambitious, preoccupied, luxurious listeners who feel the "expulsive power" of earthly careers and pleasures crowding out the growth of the good seed. The former class was more superficially touched; this class have not "broken up their fallow ground," and therefore "sow among thorns."

cares] Catullus talks of 'sowing *thorny* cares in the heart.'

riches] "the *deceitfulness* of riches" (Matt., Mk.).

pleasures of *this* life, and bring no fruit to perfection. But ¹⁵ that on the good ground are they, which in an honest and good heart, having heard the word, keep *it*, and bring forth fruit with patience.

16—18. *How to use the Light.*

No *man*, when he hath lighted a candle, covereth it with ¹⁶ a vessel, or putteth *it* under a bed; but setteth *it* on a candlestick, that they which enter in may see the light. For ¹⁷ nothing is secret, that shall not be made manifest; neither *any thing* hid, that shall not be known and come abroad.

bring no fruit to perfection] Literally, "*do not perfect*" (anything).
15. *keep it*] Comp. xi. 28; John xiv. 21. "Thy word have *I hid in my heart*, that I might not sin against Thee," Ps. cxix. 11. The opposite of the "forgetful hearers," Jas. i. 25. For them the seed does not fall 'on the way.'

bring forth fruit with patience] not as in thorns, not as on the rocky ground. The hundredfold harvest does not come at once, but "first the blade, then the ear, then the full corn in the ear." These words are added by St Luke alone. Patience or persevering consistency is a favourite word with St Paul. It is "strength of mind sustained by good hope...The sum of Christianity." Bengel.

16—18. HOW TO USE THE LIGHT.

16. *a candle*] Rather, **a lamp**.
with a vessel] St Luke uses this word as more intelligible to his Gentile readers than "bushel."
under a bed] Rather, **under a couch**. The ancient Jews had nothing resembling our *bed*. They slept on divans, or on mats laid upon the floor, as is still the case in the East. The best comment on this verse is Matt. v. 14, 16, "Ye are the light of the world....Let your light so shine before men, &c." John the Baptist is compared to 'a lamp kindled and shining,' and here the disciples are compared to it. Christ lighted the flame in their souls to be a beacon to all the world.

setteth it on a candlestick] Rather, **places it on a lamp-stand**.
17. *For nothing is secret*] This verse, like the parallel (which occurs in a different connexion in Matt. x. 26), is usually quoted of the discovery of secret crimes. The truth which would in that case be illustrated is often mentioned *elsewhere* in Scripture (1 Cor. iv. 5), but here in both instances the context shews that the first meaning of Christ was entirely different from this. He is not thinking of the discovery of crimes, but of the right use and further dissemination of divine light. The truths now revealed privately to them, and only dimly shadowed forth to others, should soon be flashed over all the world. Parables first yielded their full significance to the disciples, but found "a springing and germinant fulfilment in every age."

18 Take heed therefore how ye hear: for whosoever hath, to him shall be given; and whosoever hath not, from him shall be taken even *that* which he seemeth to have.

19—21. *Christ's Mother and His Brethren.*

19, 20 Then came to him *his* mother and his brethren, and could not come at him for the press. And it was told him *by certain* which said, Thy mother and thy brethren stand 21 without, desiring to see thee. And he answered and said unto them, My mother and my brethren are these which hear the word of God, and do it.

18. *Take heed therefore how ye hear*] and also "*what* ye hear," Mk. iv. 24.

to him shall be given] Comp. xix. 26. It was evidently a thought to which our Lord recurred, John xv. 2.

that which he seemeth to have] Rather, **that which he thinketh he hath.** This fancied possession is mere self-deception.

19—21. CHRIST'S MOTHER AND HIS BRETHREN.

19. *Then came to him his mother and his brethren*] Our text has the plural; the reading *paregeneto* (*sing.*) would imply that the Virgin took a specially prominent part in the incident. Joseph is never mentioned after the scene in the Temple. This incident can hardly be the same as those in Mk. iii. 31—35; Matt. xii. 46—50, because in both of those cases the context is wholly different. St Luke may however have misplaced this incident, since here, as in the other Evangelists, relatives of Jesus are represented as standing *outside a house* of which the doors were densely thronged; whereas the explanation of the Parable had been given in private. It is here merely said that they wished to see Him; but the fact that they came in a body seems to shew that they desired in some way to direct or control His actions. The fullest account of their motives is found in Mk. iii 21, where we are told that they wished "to seize Him" or "get possession of His person," because they said "He is beside Himself,"—perhaps echoing the feelings which had been encouraged by the Pharisees. We must remember that His brethren "did not believe in Him" (John vii. 5), i.e. their belief in Him was only the belief that he was a Prophet who did not realize *their* Messianic ideal. It needed the Resurrection to convert them.

his brethren] James, Joses, Simon, Judas. Possibly (Matt. xii. 50; Mk. iii. 35) His *sisters* also came.

21. *are these*] The word implies the "looking round at those sitting in a circle about Him" of Mk. iii. 34, and the "stretching forth His hand towards His disciples" of Matt. xii. 49. "Ye are my friends, if ye do whatsoever I command you," John xv. 14 (comp. ii. 49; John ii. 4, xiv. 21; Heb. ii. 11). His earthly relatives needed the lesson that they must recognise in Him a Being who stood far above all relationships

22—25. *Christ stilling the Storm.*

Now it came to pass on a certain day, that he went into 22 a ship with his disciples: and he said unto them, Let us go over unto the other side of the lake. And they launched forth. But as they sailed he fell asleep: and there came 23 down a storm of wind on the lake; and they were filled *with water*, and were in jeopardy. And they came to *him*, 24

"after the flesh" (2 Cor. v. 16). Even disciples must "hate" father and mother *in comparison with* Christ (comp. Deut. xxxiii. 9).

22—25. CHRIST STILLING THE STORM.

22. *Now it came to pass on a certain day*] Rather, **on one of the days.** From Mk. iv. 35; Matt. viii. 18, we should infer that this event took place in the evening on which He began to teach the crowd in parables, and that—attracted by the beauty and novelty of His teaching they lingered round Him till, in utter weariness, He longed to escape to the secluded loneliness of the Eastern shore of the lake. Possibly the interference of His kinsmen may have added the last touch to the fatigue and emotion which imperatively demanded retirement and rest.

into a ship] St Matthew says '*the* boat,' which usually waited on His movements; very probably the one which had belonged to Peter. Before the boat pushed off, we learn that three aspirants for discipleship came to Him, Matt. viii. 19—22 (Lk. ix. 57—62).

unto the other side] The Peraean side of the Lake of Galilee has always been comparatively uninhabited, mainly because the escarpment of barren hills approaches within a quarter of a mile of the shore. Its solitude contrasted all the more with the hum of crowded and busy life on the plain of Gennesareth.

of the lake] See on v. 1.

they launched forth] Such was His weariness and eagerness to get away that they took Him "*as He was*"—without even pausing for any food or refreshment—into the boat, Mk. iv. 36.

23. *he fell asleep*] Rather, **He fell into deep sleep.** The day had been one of incessant toil; and He was resting (as St Mark tells us, reflecting the vivid reminiscence of St Peter) 'in the stern on the steersman's leather cushion,' Mk. iv. 38: contrast with this Jonah i. 5.

there came down a storm of wind] The suddenness and violence of this 'hurricane' is in exact accordance with what we know of the Lake. The winds from the snowy peaks of Hermon rush down the Peraean *wadies* into the burning tropical air of the lake-basin with extraordinary suddenness and impetuosity (Thomson, *Land and Book*, II. 25). The lake may look like a sheet of silver, when in one moment there will be a darkening ripple, and in the next it will be lashed into storm and foam. The outburst of this storm perhaps frightened back the boats which started with Him, Mk. iv. 36.

were filled with water] Rather, **were being filled.** 'The waves were

and awoke him, saying, Master, master, we perish. Then he rose, and rebuked the wind and the raging of the water: 25 and they ceased, and there was a calm. And he said unto them, Where is your faith? And they being afraid wondered, saying one to another, What *manner of man* is this? for he commandeth even the winds and water, and they obey him.

26—39. *The Gergesene Demoniac.*

26 And they arrived at the country of the Gadarenes, which

dashing into the boat, so that it was getting full,' Mk. iv. 37; 'the boat was being hidden under the waves,' Matt. viii. 24. The tossing ship (*Navicella*) has been accepted in all ages as the type of the Church in seasons of peril.

24. *we perish*] Rather, **we are perishing!** "Lord! save! we are perishing," Matt. viii. 25. "Rabbi, carest thou not that we are perishing?" Mk. iv. 38. The peril was evidently most imminent.

Then he rose] Rather, **But He, being roused from sleep.**

rebuked the wind] speaking to the wind and the billows of the water as though they were living powers (Ps. cvi. 9, "He *rebuked* the Red Sea also"), or to the evil powers which may be conceived to wield them to the danger of mankind. St Mark alone preserves the two words uttered "Hush! be stilled!" the first to silence the roar, the second the tumult. St Matthew tells us that He quietly uttered 'Why are ye cowards, ye of little faith?' and *then*, having stilled the tumult of their minds, rose and stilled the tempest.

Where is your faith?] "They had *some* faith, but it was not ready at hand." Bengel.

25. *What manner of man*] Rather, **Who, then.** The *ara* expresses the same surprise and emotion conveyed by the *potapos*, 'what kind of Being,' of St Matthew. Ps. cvii. 23—30.

26—39. THE GERGESENE DEMONIAC.

26. *at the country of the Gadarenes*] In all three narratives, here, Matt. viii. 28—34; Mark v. 1—19, the MSS. vary between Gergesenes, Gadarenes, and Gerasenes, and Tischendorf follows ℵ in reading Gadarenes (by a clerical error Gazarenes) in St Matthew, Gerasenes in St Mark, and Gergesenes here.

i. **Gadara**, of which the large ruins are now seen at *Um Keis*, is three hours' distance from the extreme south end of the Lake, and is separated from the scene of the miracle by the deep precipitous ravine of the Hieromax (Jarmuk). Gadarenes may be the right reading in St Matthew (ℵ, B, C, M, Δ and MSS. mentioned by Origen) but, if so, it only gives the name of the *entire district*. Gadara was essentially a Greek city, and had two amphitheatres, and a literary Greek society, and the worst features of Hellenic life.

is over against Galilee. And when he went forth to land, 27 there met him out of the city a certain man, which had devils long time, and ware no clothes, neither abode in *any* house, but in the tombs. When he saw Jesus, he cried out, 28

ii. Gerasenes may be the right reading in St Mark (א, B, D, &c.). **Gerasa**, now *Djerash*, is fifty miles from the Lake, and almost in Arabia, but it was an important town (Jos. *B. J.* III. 3), and like Gadara may have been used as the name of the *entire district*.

iii. Gergesenes is almost certainly the right reading here (א, L, X). It was the reading which, because of the distance of Gerasa and Gadara, Origen wished to introduce into Matt. viii. 28, being aware that there was a small town called **Gergesa** in the Wady Semakh which was known also to Eusebius and Jerome, and was pointed out as the scene of the miracle. Yet the reading, "Gergesenes" of א, in St Luke, could hardly have been due to the mere conjecture of Origen in the parallel passage of St Matthew, for it is found in other uncials, in most cursives, and in the Coptic, Ethiopic and other versions. Gergesa has however nothing to do with the ancient Girgashites (Deut. vii. 1; Josh. xxiv. 11), who were probably at the West of the Jordan. The question as to the *place intended as the scene of the miracle* (whatever reading be adopted) may be considered as having been settled by Dr Thomson's discovery of ruins named Kerzha (the natural corruption of Gergesa) nearly opposite Capernaum. The name of this little obscure place may well have been given by St Matthew, who knew the locality, and by so accurate an enquirer as St Luke. The reading may have been altered by later copyists who knew the far more celebrated Gadara and Gerasa.

27. *there met him out of the city a certain man*] This rendering contradicts what follows. Rather, **there met him a man of the city.** He had been a native of Gergesa till his madness began. St Matthew (as in the case of Bartimaeus) mentions two demoniacs, but the narrative is only concerned with one. There may of course have been another hovering in the neighbourhood. The variation in St Matthew is at least a valuable proof of the independence of the Evangelists.

which had devils] Rather, **having demons.** The *daimonia* were supposed by the Jews to be not devils (i.e. fallen angels), but the spirits of wicked men who were dead (Jos. *B. J.* VII. 6, § 3). See on iv. 33; viii. 2.

long time, and ware no clothes] Rather (with א, B), *and for a long time wore no cloke.* He *may* have been naked, since the tendency to strip the person of all clothes is common among madmen; here however it only says that he wore no *himation.* He may have had on the *chitôn*, or under-garment. Naked, homicidal maniacs who live in caves and tombs are still to be seen in Palestine. Warburton saw one in a cemetery fighting, amid fierce yells and howlings, with wild dogs for a bone. *Crescent and Cross,* II. 352.

but in the tombs] This was partly a necessity, for in ancient times there were no such things as penitentiaries or asylums, and an uncon-

and fell down before him, and with a loud voice said, What have I to do with thee, Jesus, *thou* Son of God most high? 29 I beseech thee, torment me not. (For he had commanded the unclean spirit to come out of the man. For oftentimes it had caught him: and he was kept bound with chains and in fetters; and he brake the bands, and was driven of the 30 devil into the wilderness.) And Jesus asked him, saying, What is thy name? And he said, Legion: because many 31 devils were entered into him. And they besought him that

trollable maniac, driven from the abodes of men, could find no other shelter. This would aggravate his frenzy, for the loneliness and horror of these dark rocky tombs (traces of which are still to be seen near the ruins of Kherza or the sides of the Wady Semakh) were intensified by the prevalent belief that they were haunted by *shedim*, or 'evil spirits,'— the ghosts of the wicked dead (*Nidda*, f. 17 *a*, &c.). St Mark gives (v. 4) a still more graphic picture of the superhuman strength and violence of this homicidal and ghastly sufferer.

28. *What have I to do with thee*] i.e. Why should'st thou interfere with me? 2 Sam. xvi. 10; xix. 22. See iv. 24. Baur refers to obvious imitations of this narrative in the story of the Lamia expelled by Apollonius of Tyana (Philostr. IV. 25).

Son of God most high] Probably the epithet was customary in exorcisms or attempted exorcisms, and hence we find it used by another demoniac (Acts xvi. 17). Jesus is not so called elsewhere, except in i. 32.

torment me not] "The demons...believe and tremble," Jas. ii. 19. On this conception of torment see Mk. i. 24; Matt. xviii. 34.

29. *he had commanded*] Rather, **He commanded.**

oftentimes] *Pollois chronois* usually means "*for a long time.*"

he was kept bound with chains and in fetters] This rendering misses a curious point in the narrative, preserved by St Luke only,—namely, that "he was bound in chains and fetters, **being under guard.**"

into the wilderness] Rather, **into the deserts,**—regarded as a peculiar haunt of Azazel and other demons. Matt. xii. 43; Tobit viii. 3; see on iv. 1. (There are obvious allusions to the Gospel narrative of this demoniac and the demoniac boy in Lucian, *Philopseudes*, 16.)

30. *What is thy name?*] The question was no doubt asked in mercy. Gently to ask a person's name is often an effectual way to calm the agitations and fix the wavering thoughts of these sufferers.

And he said, Legion] A legion consisted of 6000 soldiers, and this man (who was probably a Jew) would have become familiar with the name since the Roman conquest of Palestine. The ancient Megiddo was now called Legio, still *Ledjûn*. The answer shewed how wildly perturbed was the man's spirit, and how complete was the *duality* of his consciousness. He could not distinguish between himself and the *multitudes* of demons by whom he believed himself to be possessed. His individuality was lost in demoniac hallucinations.

he would not command them to go out into the deep. And ³²
there was there a herd of many swine feeding on the mountain: and they besought him that he would suffer them to
enter into them. And he suffered them. Then went the ³³
devils out of the man, and entered into the swine: and the
herd ran violently down a steep place into the lake, and

31. *they besought*] If *parekalei* be the right reading, it should be rendered "*he* besought Him," for the plural is used in the next verse.

to go out into the deep] The 'abyss' (Hebrew *tehôm*) intended is perhaps the prison of wicked spirits (Rom. x. 7; Jude 6; Rev. xx. 3). St Mark says "that He would not send them out of the country."

32. *a herd of many swine*] St Mark says "about 2000." Of course, if the owners of these swine were Jews, they were living in flagrant violation of the law; but the population of Peraea was largely Greek and Syrian.

that he would suffer them to enter into them] The Jews, as we have already seen, believed that physical and mental evil was wrought by the direct agency of demons, and attributed to demons not only the cases of "possession," but many other classes of illness (melancholia, brain-disease, heart-disease, &c.) which we do not usually regard in this light. They also believed that demons could take possession even of animals, and they attributed to demons the hydrophobia of dogs and the rage of bulls. "Perhaps," says Archbishop Trench (*On the Miracles*, p. 185), "we make to ourselves a difficulty here, too easily assuming that the whole animal world is wholly shut up in itself, and incapable of receiving impressions from that which is above it. The assumption is one unwarranted by deeper investigations, which lead rather to an opposite conclusion—not to the breaking down of the boundaries between the two worlds, but to the shewing in what wonderful ways the lower is receptive of impression from the higher, both for good and for evil." Further than this the incident leads into regions of uncertain speculation, into which it is impossible to enter, and in which none will dogmatize but those who are least wise. Milton seems to find no difficulty in the conception that evil spirits could 'incarnate and imbrute' their essence into a beast: in at the serpent's mouth

> "The devil entered; and his brutal sense
> The heart or head possessing, soon inspired
> With act intelligential." *Par. Lost.*

Comp. Dante, *Inf.* xxv. 136,
> "L'anima, ch' era fiera divenuta
> Si fugge," &c.

33. *down a steep place*] Rather, **down the precipice**. Near Kherza is *the only spot on the entire lake* where a steep slope sweeps down to within a few yards of the sea, into which the herd would certainly have plunged if hurried by any violent impulse down the hill. If it be asked whether this was not a destruction of property, the answer is that the

34 were choked. When they that fed *them* saw what was done, they fled, and went and told *it* in the city and in the country.
35 Then they went out to see what was done; and came to Jesus, and found the man, out of whom the devils were departed, sitting at the feet of Jesus, clothed, and in his right mind: and they were afraid.
36 They also which saw *it* told them by what means he that was possessed of the devils was healed.
37 Then the whole multitude of the country of the Gadarenes round about besought him to depart

compared with the deliverance of a human soul. Our Lord would therefore have had a moral right to act thus even if he had been a mere human Prophet. Besides, to put it on the lowest ground, the freeing of the neighbourhood from the peril and terror of this wild maniac was a greater benefit to the whole city than the loss of this herd. Jesus did not *command* the spirits to go into the swine; if He *permitted* any thing which resulted in their destruction it was to serve higher and more precious ends. "God the Word," says Lord Bacon, "wished to do nothing which breathed not of grace and beneficence;" and after mentioning the stern miracles of Moses, Elijah, Elisha, St Peter and St Paul, he adds, "but Jesus did nothing of this kind...the spirit of Jesus is the spirit of the Dove. He wrought no miracle of judgment, all of beneficence." *Meditt. Sacr.* on Mk. xii. 37. The miracles of Christ were all *redemptive acts* and spiritual lessons.

34. *what was done*] Rather, **what had happened**.

35. *clothed*] Perhaps one of the disciples had thrown a cloke (*himation*) over his nakedness or his rags.

37. *besought him to depart*] The opposite to the request of the Samaritans (John iv. 40). Unlike Peter, they *meant* what they said. Preferring their swine to Christ, they felt that His presence was dangerous to their greed. And our Lord acted on the principle of not casting that which was holy to dogs, nor pearls before men whose moral character tended to become like that of their own swine. At Gadara the worst iniquities were prevalent. It may be that if they had not deliberately begged Christ to leave them they might have been spared the fearful massacre and ruin—fire, and sword, and slavery—which befel them at the hands of the Romans in less than 40 years after this time (Jos. *B. J.* III. 7, § 1, IV. 7, § 4). But

> "We, ignorant of ourselves,
> Beg often our own harms, which the wise powers
> Deny us for our good."

For other instances of prayers fatally granted see Ex. x. 28, 29; Numb. xxii. 20; Ps. lxxviii. 29—31; on the other hand, a refused boon is sometimes a blessing. 2 Cor. xii. 8, 9. The result of their wilful sensuality was that the time never came when

from them; for they were taken with great fear: and he went *up* into the ship, and returned *back again*. Now the 38 man out of whom the devils were departed besought him that *he* might be with him: but Jesus sent him away, saying, Return to thine own house, and shew how great *things* God 39 hath done unto thee. And he went his way, and published throughout the whole city how great *things* Jesus had done unto him.

40. *The waiting Multitude.*

And it came to pass that, when Jesus was returned, the 40 people gladly received him: for they were all waiting for him.

41—56. *The Daughter of Jairus and the Woman with the issue of Blood.*

And behold, there came a man named Jairus, and he 41

> "E'en the witless Gadarene,
> Preferring Christ to swine, shall learn
> That life is sweetest, when 'tis clean."

they were taken] Rather, **they were oppressed.**

39. *shew how great things God hath done unto thee*] This command valuably illustrates one of the *reasons* why our Lord commanded reticence in other instances. To the region of Gadara He did not intend to return, and therefore the proclamation of a miracle would not cause Him to be surrounded by curious crowds.

40. THE WAITING MULTITUDE.

40. *the people gladly received him*] They would see the sail of His boat as it started back from Gergesa, and the storm had probably driven back the other boats. He would naturally sail to Bethsaida or Capernaum. It is impossible here to enter into the uncertain question as to the exact order of events. For all details on that subject I must refer to my *Life of Christ*.

41—56. THE DAUGHTER OF JAIRUS AND THE WOMAN WITH THE ISSUE OF BLOOD.

41. *behold*] St Matthew places this message of Jairus after the farewell feast which he gave to his friends before abandoning for ever his office of tax-gatherer. At that feast arose the question about fasting, and St Matthew (ix. 18) says that Jairus came "while Jesus was yet speaking these things," and in so definite a note of time, on a day to him so memorable, he could hardly be inexact. On the other hand, St Mark

was a ruler of the synagogue: and he fell down at Jesus' feet, and besought him that *he* would come into his house: 42 for he had one only daughter, about twelve years of age, and she lay a dying. (But as he went the people thronged 43 him. And a woman having an issue of blood twelve years, which had spent all *her* living upon physicians, neither 44 could be healed of any, came behind *him*, and touched the border of his garment: and immediately her issue of blood

says, and St Luke implies, that the message reached Jesus as He disembarked on the sea-shore. Hence it has been supposed that Jesus heard the first entreaty from Jairus on the shore when his daughter was dying (vs. 42; Mark v. 23), but instead of going straight to the house of Jairus went first to Matthew's feast; and that Jairus then came to the feast in agony to say that she was just dead (Matt. ix. 18). The very small discrepancies are however quite easily explicable without this conjecture, and it was wholly unlike the method of Jesus to interpose a feast between the request of an agonised father and His act of mercy.

Jairus] Jair, Judg. x. 3.

a ruler of the synagogue] The synagogues had no clergy, but were managed by laymen, at the head of whom was the "ruler," whose title of *Rosh hakkenéseth* was as familiar to the Jews as that of Rabbi. His functions resembled those of a leading elder. The appeal of such a functionary shews the estimation in which our Lord was still held among the Galileans.

that he would come into his house] Jair had not the faith of the heathen centurion.

42. *one only daughter*] St Luke, whose keen sympathies are everywhere observable in his Gospel, mentions the same touching fact in the case of the son of the widow of Nain (vii. 12), and the lunatic boy (ix. 38).

she lay a dying] St Matthew says "*is even now dead.*" Perhaps we catch in these variations an echo of the father's despairing uncertainty.

43. *which had spent all her living*] Literally, 'having *in addition* spent' her whole means of livelihood.

neither could be healed of any] St Luke, perhaps with a fellow-feeling for physicians, does not add the severer comment of St Mark, that the physicians had only made her worse (v. 26). The Talmudic receipts for the cure of this disease were specially futile, such as to set the sufferer in a place where two ways meet, with a cup of wine in her hand, and let some one come behind and frighten her, and say, Arise from thy flux; or "dig seven ditches, burn in them some cuttings of vines not four years old, and let her sit in them in succession, with a cup of wine in her hand, while at each remove some one says to her, Arise from thy flux." (Lightfoot, *Hor. Hebr.* ad loc.)

44. *came behind him, and touched the border of his garment*] Rather,

stanched. And Jesus said, Who touched me? When all 45
denied, Peter and they that were with him said, Master, the
multitude throng thee and press *thee*, and sayest thou, Who
touched me? And Jesus said, Somebody hath touched me: 46
for I perceive that virtue is gone out of me. And when the 47
woman saw that she was not hid, she came trembling, and
falling down before him, she declared unto him before all
the people for what cause she had touched him, and how

approaching from behind touched the tassel of His outer robe.
This is a miracle 'by the way' (*obiter*), but, as Fuller says, "His
obiter is more to the purpose than our *iter*." She sought to steal (as
it were) a miracle of grace, and fancied that Christ's miracles were
a matter of *nature*, not of *will and purpose*. Probably the intense
depression produced by her disease, aggravated by the manner in
which for twelve years every one had kept aloof from her and striven
not to touch her, had quite crushed her spirits. By the Levitic law
she had to be "put apart, and whosoever toucheth her shall be
unclean" (Lev. xv. 19, 25). The word translated "border" (*kraspedon*,
Heb. *tsitsith*) is a tassel at each "wing" or corner of the *tallith*
or mantle (Matt. xiv. 36). The Law (Num. xv. 38—40) required
that it should be bound with a thread (not as in E. V. *ribband*) of blue,
the colour of heaven, and so the type of revelation. The strict Jews
to this day wear these tassels, though they are usually concealed. The
Pharisees, to proclaim their orthodoxy, made them conspicuously large,
Matt. xxiii. 5. One of the four tassels hung over the shoulder at the
back, and this was the one which the woman touched. (For full
particulars of the Rabbinic rules about these tassels see an article by the
present writer, in the *Expositor*, v. 219.) The quasi-sacredness of the
tassels may have fostered her impulse to touch the one that hung in
view.

45. *Peter and they that were with him*] St Mark merely says His
disciples, but the question is in exact accordance with that pre-
sumptuous impetuosity which marked the as yet imperfect stage of
Peter's character.

46. *Somebody hath touched me*] Rather, **Some one touched me.**
"They *press; she* touches." Aug. "Flesh presses; faith touches."
Id. Our Lord's question was meant to reach the woman's heart, comp.
Gen. iii. 9, iv. 9; 2 Kings v. 25.

I perceive that virtue is gone out of me] Literally, "*I recognised power
going forth from me;*" or **perceived that power had gone forth from
me**, if we read *exeleluthuian*. Comp. vi. 19.

47. *she came trembling*] Because by her touch she had communicated to Him Levitical uncleanness; and this by one of the Rabbis
or Pharisees would have been regarded as an intolerable presumption
and wrong. To this day the Jewish Rabbis (or Chakams) in the East
are careful not even to be touched by a woman's dress (Frankl., *Jews
in the East*, II. 81).

⁴⁸ she was healed immediately. And he said unto her, Daughter, be of good comfort: thy faith hath made thee whole;
⁴⁹ go in peace.) While he yet spake, there cometh one from the ruler of the synagogue's *house*, saying to him, Thy daughter
⁵⁰ is dead; trouble not the Master. But when Jesus heard *it*, he answered him, saying, Fear not: believe only, and she
⁵¹ shall be made whole. And when he came into the house, he suffered no *man* to go in, save Peter, and James, and
⁵² John, and the father and the mother of the maiden. And all wept, and bewailed her: but he said, Weep not; she is
⁵³ not dead, but sleepeth. And they laughed him to scorn,

48. *Daughter*] The only recorded occasion on which our Lord used that tender word to a woman.

thy faith hath made thee whole] Literally, "*hath saved thee*." Thy faith —not the superstitious and surreptitious touch of my *tallith's* fringe. Jesus thus compelled her to come forth from her timid enjoyment of a stolen blessing that He might confer on her a deeper and fuller blessing.

go in peace] Literally, *to*, or *for peace*. Tradition says that the name of this woman was Veronica (*Evang. Nicodem.* v. 6), and that it was she who gave to our Lord the famous legendary handkerchief to wipe His face on the way to Calvary. At Paneas (Caesarea Philippi) there was a bronze statue which was supposed to be her votive offering, and to represent this scene (Euseb. *H. E.* VII. 18; Sozomen, *H. E.* V. 21); and on this account Julian the Apostate or Maximin is said to have destroyed it. All this is very improbable. Early Christian writers were too credulous about these statues. Justin Martyr took a statue of the Sabine god *Semo Sancus* for one of Simon Magus.

49. *trouble not the Master*] Literally, "*worry not the Rabbi.*" For the colloquial verb preserved also in St Mark see vii. 6.

50. *when Jesus heard it*] The remark was addressed to Jairus, and St Mark says that Jesus "*overheard* it."

51. *save Peter, and James, and John*] as at the Transfiguration and at Gethsemane, Mark ix. 2, xiv. 33.

52. *bewailed her*] The word means that they were beating their breasts for her (Nahum ii. 7). St Mark gives a graphic picture of the tumult, and loud cries, and wailings (*alalai*, the Egyptian *wilweleh*). Even the poorest were obliged to provide for a funeral two flute-players and one wailing woman. See Eccles. xii. 5; Jer. ix. 17; Amos v. 16; 2 Chron. xxxv. 25. These public mourners were called *sappedans*.

53. *she is not dead, but sleepeth*] To take this literally is to contradict the letter and spirit of the whole narrative. It is true that in "our friend Lazarus sleepeth" the verb used is not *katheudein* but *koimasthai;* but that is in a different writer (John xi. 11), and the

knowing that she was dead. And he put *them* all out, and 54 took her by the hand, and called, saying, Maid, arise. And 55 her spirit came again, and she arose straightway: and he commanded to give her meat. And her parents were asto- 56 nished: but he charged them that they should tell no *man* what was done.

CH. IX. 1—6. *The Mission of the Twelve.*

Then he called his twelve disciples together, and gave 9 them power and authority over all devils, and to cure dis-

word better suits one who had been four days dead. Our Lord's object was to silence this idle uproar.

53. *laughed him to scorn*] Literally, "*were utterly deriding Him.*" 'To laugh to scorn' is used by Shakespeare, e.g.

"Our castle's strength
Will laugh a siege to scorn."
Macbeth, v. 5.

54. *he put them all out*] These words being omitted by ℵ, B, D, L, X, are probably interpolated here, from the other Synoptists. Our Lord could not feel the smallest sympathy for these simulated agonies of people, who (to this day) "weep, howl, beat their breasts, and tear their hair according to contract" (Thomson, *Land and Book*, I. viii.). And further these solemn deeds required calm and faith, Acts ix. 40; 2 Kings iv. 33.

took her by the hand] St Luke preserves this gentle detail, as well as the kind order to give her food. St Mark gives the two Aramaic words which our Lord used, *Talitha cumi!* On these occasions He always used the fewest possible words (vii. 14; John xi. 43).

56. *that they should tell no man*] See on v. 14. And as usual the injunction was probably unheeded. Matt. ix. 26.

CH. IX. 1—6. THE MISSION OF THE TWELVE.

1. *Then he called his twelve disciples together*] This was at the close of the missionary journeys alluded to in Matt. ix. 35; Mk. vi. 6. St Matthew gives a touching reason for the mission of the Twelve. It was because He pitied the multitude, who were like harassed and panting sheep without a shepherd, and like a harvest left unreaped for want of labourers (Matt. ix. 36—38). The Apostles thus became, as their name implied, emissaries (*sheloochîm*), and this was an important step in their training.

and gave them power and authority] Power (*dunamis*) is the *capacity*, and authority (*exousia*), the *right* to act. See x. 19; Rev. xiii. 7.

over all devils] Rather, **over all the demons.**

to cure diseases] The word is not *iasthai*, as in vs. 2, but *therapeuein*, 'to tend;' but there seems to be no essential difference intended, unless

eases. And he sent them to preach the kingdom of God, and to heal the sick. And he said unto them, Take nothing for *your* journey, neither staves, nor scrip, neither bread, neither money; neither have two coats apiece. And whatsoever house ye enter into, there abide, and thence depart. And whosoever will not receive you, when ye go out of that city, shake off the very dust from your feet for a testimony

it points to the curious fact mentioned by St Mark that they anointed the sick with oil (vi. 13; comp. James v. 14).

2. *And he sent them*] Two and two for their mutual comfort. Mk. vi. 7.

3. *And he said unto them*] For a much fuller account of the instructions given to the Twelve see Matt. x. 5—15. Some of these are recorded by St Luke as given also to the Seventy, x. 1—16.

neither staves] Or a *staff* (as ℵ, A, B, and many uncials). The plural may have been frivolously introduced by some copyist who wished to avoid an apparent discrepancy with Mk. vi. 8, "save a staff only." St Matthew also says, "not even a staff." Minute and wholly unimportant as the variation would have been, it may turn on the fact that our Lord told them not specially to *procure* ($\mu\dot{\eta}$ $\kappa\tau\dot{\eta}\sigma\eta\sigma\theta\epsilon$, Matt.) these things for the journey; or on the fact that speaking in Aramaic He used the phrase אם כי (*kee im*), which might be explained "*even if you have a staff* it is unnecessary."

nor scrip] i.e. wallet, a bag carried over the shoulder to contain a few dates or other common necessaries. 1 Sam. xvii. 40.

neither bread] which they usually took with them, vs. 13; Matt. xvi. 7.

neither money] Literally, "*silver*." St Luke uses the word because it was the common metal for coinage among the *Greeks*. St Mark uses "copper," the common *Roman* coinage.

neither have two coats apiece] i.e. do not carry with you a second tunic (*ketoneth*)—which indeed is a rare luxury among poor Orientals. (See on iii. 11.) If they carried a second tunic at all they could only do so conveniently by putting it on (Mk. vi. 9). St Mark adds that they were to wear sandals, and St Matthew that they were *not* to have travelling shoes (*hupodēmata*). The general spirit of the instructions merely is, Go forth in the simplest, humblest manner, with no hindrances to your movements and in perfect faith; and this, as history shews, has always been the method of the most successful missions. At the same time we must remember that the *wants* of the Twelve were very small (see on viii. 3) and were secured by the open hospitality of the East (Thomson, *Land and Book*, p. 346).

4. *whatsoever house ye enter*] After enquiring who were the worthiest people to receive them, Matt. x. 11, comp. infra x. 5—8. This injunction was meant to exclude fastidious and restless changes.

5. *shake off the very dust from your feet*] See Acts xiii. 51, xviii. 6.

against them. And they departed, and went through the 6
towns, preaching the gospel, and healing every where.

7—9. Herod's Alarm.

Now Herod the tetrarch heard of all that was done by 7
him: and he was perplexed, because that it was said of
some, that John was risen from the dead; and of some, that 8
Elias had appeared; and *of* others, that one of the old prophets was risen again. And Herod said, John have I be- 9
headed: but who is this, of whom I hear such *things?* And
he desired to see him.

6. *preaching the gospel*] The word here used is "evangelizing," in vs. 2 it is "to herald."

healing] In the other Evangelists *exorcisms* are prominent. Mk. vi. 13. The special object of the mission of the Twelve is plain from St Matthew. Our Lord had now been preaching for nearly a year in Galilee, and multitudes still thronged to Him. He knew that He would soon be compelled to retire, and He sent the Twelve to give one last opportunity to those who had heard Him.

7—9. Herod's Alarm.

7. *Herod the tetrarch*] Antipas. See iii. 1.

by him] These words are omitted by ℵ, B, C, D, L. The *"all the things that had occurred"* seems to be a special reference to the work of the Twelve which made our Lord's name more widely known.

it was said of some] i. e. by some. To this opinion Herod's guilty conscience made him sometimes incline, Mk. vi. 16. His alarm may have been intensified by the strong condemnation of his subjects, who, long afterwards, looked on his defeat by his injured father-in-law Aretas (Hareth) as a punishment for this crime (Jos. *Antt.* XVIII. 5, §§ 1, 2).

8. *that Elias had appeared*] In accordance with the prophecy of Mal. iv. 5. The verb "appeared" is used instead of 'risen again,' because of Elijah's translation to heaven. The Talmud is full of the expected appearance of Elijah, and of instances in which he shewed himself to eminent Rabbis.

one of the old prophets] Comp. vii. 16; Deut. xviii. 15; Num. xxiv. 17. The Jews thought that Jeremiah or one of the other great prophets (see vs. 19) might rise to herald the Messiah, John i. 21. See 2 Esdras ii. 10, 18, "Tell my people...For thy help will I send my servants Isaiah and Jeremiah;" 1 Macc. xiv. 41, "*Simon* should be high priest...*until there arose a faithful prophet.*" In 2 Macc. ii. 4—8, xv. 13—16, Jeremiah appears in a vision. It was believed that he would reveal the hiding-place of the Ark, Urim, and Sacred Fire.

9. *he desired*] Literally, "*was seeking;*" this agrees with xxiii. 8, "he was desirous to see him of a long season." St Luke may have

10—17. *The Feeding of the Five Thousand.*

10 And the apostles, when they were returned, told him all that they had done. And he took them, and went aside privately into a desert place belonging to the city called

heard particulars about Herod from Chuzas (viii. 3) when he was with St Paul at Caesarea Stratonis, or from Manaen at Antioch (Acts xiii. 1). The curiosity of Herod about Jesus does not seem to have been aroused before this period. A half-alien tyrant such as he was, belonging to a detested house, is often little aware of what is going on among the people; but the mission of the Twelve in all directions, and therefore possibly to Tiberias, produced effects which reached his ears. His wish to see Jesus was not gratified till the day of the crucifixion;—partly because our Lord purposely kept out of his reach, feeling for him a pure contempt ("this fox," xiii. 32), and for this among other reasons never so much as entered the polluted and half-heathen streets of Herod's new town of Tiberias (which partly covered the site of an old cemetery); and partly because, after the news of John's murder, He seems at once to have withdrawn from all permanent work in Gennesareth. During the mission of the Twelve we infer that He made a journey alone to Jerusalem to the unnamed feast of John v. 1, probably the Feast of Purim. During this visit occurred the healing of the cripple at Bethesda.

10—17. THE FEEDING OF THE FIVE THOUSAND.

10. *told him all that they had done*] This brief and meagre record, to which nothing is added by the other Evangelists, contrasts so strongly with the joyous exultation of the Seventy over their success, that we are led to infer that the training of the Twelve was as yet imperfect, and their mission less successful than the subsequent one.

went aside privately] The reasons—beside the natural need of the Twelve and of our Lord for rest—were (1) the incessant interruptions from the multitude, which left them no leisure even to eat (Mk. vi. 31), and (2) (as we see from the context) the news of the murder of John the Baptist and Herod's enquiries about Jesus. Perhaps we may add (3) the desire to keep in retirement the Paschal Feast which He *could* not now keep at Jerusalem. This event constitutes another new departure in the ministry of Christ.

into a desert place belonging to the city called Bethsaida] There are here great variations in the MSS. and the best reading is *to a city called Bethsaida*. The omission may be due to the fact that there was nothing approaching to "a desert place" corresponding to this description near the only Bethsaida which was well known to the copyists, viz. the little fishing suburb of Capernaum on the west of the lake (Bethsaida of Galilee, John xii. 21), Mk. vi. 45. This may also explain the variation of 'village' for 'city.' It is only in recent times that we have been made familiar with the existence of the *other* Bethsaida—Bethsaida Julias (Mk. viii. 22), at the north of the lake, another

Bethsaida. And the people, when they knew *it*, followed 11
him: and he received them, and spake unto them of the
kingdom of God, and healed them that had need of healing.
And *when* the day began to wear away, then came the 12
twelve, and said unto him, Send the multitude away, that
they may go into the towns and country round about, and
lodge, and get victuals: for we are here in a desert place.
But he said unto them, Give ye them to eat. And they said, 13
We have no more but five loaves and two fishes; except we

'House of Fish' which had been recently beautified by Herod Philip
(iii. 1) and named by him after the beautiful but profligate daughter of
Augustus, Jos. *Antt.* XVIII. 2, § 1; *B. J.* II. § 1. The ruins of this
town still exist at Telui (a corruption of Tel *Julias*), and close by it is
the green, narrow, secluded plain of El Batîhah, which exactly meets
the description of the Evangelists. This important discovery, which
explains several serious difficulties of this Gospel, is due to Reland
(*Palaest.* p. 504), and shews us how easily difficulties would be removed
if we knew all the facts.

11. *the people, when they knew it, followed him*] The ensuing
miracle is one of the few narrated by all four Evangelists, Matt. xiv.
13—33; Mk. vi. 30—52; John vi. 1—21, and is most important from
the power displayed, the doctrines symbolized (Christ the bread of life),
and the results to which it led (John vi.). Combining the narratives,
we see that the embarkation of Jesus to sail from Capernaum to the
northern Bethsaida had been noticed by the people, and as it is only a
sail of six miles they went on foot round the head of the lake to find
Him. He had barely time to retire with His disciples to one of
the hills when a crowd assembled on the little plain which was
momentarily swelled by the throngs of pilgrims who paused to see the
Great Prophet on their way to the approaching Passover at Jerusalem
(John vi. 5), which Jesus Himself could not attend without danger,
owing to the outburst caused by the Sabbath healing of the cripple
(John v. 1—16). Towards afternoon He came down the hill to the
multitude to teach them and heal their sick.

12. *to wear away*] Rather, **to decline.**
then came the twelve] They were afraid that when once the brief
twilight was over, the famished multitude might lose their way or come
to harm, and some calamity happen which would give a fresh handle
against Jesus. John alone tells us that He had compassionately suggested the difficulty to Philip, watching with gentle irony the trial of
his faith; and that Philip despairingly said that it would cost more than
200 denarii (as we might say £10) to procure them even a minimum of
food. Philip was "of Bethsaida," but this had nothing to do with
our Lord's speaking to him, for he belonged to the *western* Bethsaida.

13. *We have no more but five loaves and two fishes*] Compare Num.
xi. 22. It was Andrew who first mentioned this fact in a tentative sort

14 should go and buy meat for all this people. For they were about five thousand men. And he said to his disciples,
15 Make them sit down by fifties in a company. And they did
16 so, and made *them* all sit down. Then he took the five loaves and the two fishes, and looking up to heaven, he blessed them, and brake, and gave to the disciples to set
17 before the multitude. And they did eat, and were all filled: and there was taken up of fragments that remained to them twelve baskets.

of way. The little boy (*paidarion*) who carried them seems to have been in attendance on the Apostles; evidently this was the food which they had brought for their own supply, and it proves their simplicity of life, for *barley loaves* (John vi. 9) are the food of the poor (2 K. iv. 42; Judg. vii. 13; Ezek. xiii. 19, iv. 9).

14. *five thousand men*] "Besides women and children," Matt. xiv. 21. These would probably not be numerous, and would not (in accordance with Eastern usage) sit down with the men, but would stand apart.

by fifties in a company] The vivid details of Mark shew the eyewitness of St Peter. He compares them to parterres of flowers (*prasiai prasiai*, 'by garden beds') as they sat on the green grass in their bright Oriental robes of red and blue and yellow. St Luke's word, *klisiai*, means literally *in dining-parties*, from *klisia*, 'a couch.' This systematic arrangement made it easy to tell the number of the multitude.

16. *brake, and gave*] The 'brake' is in the aorist, and the 'gave' in the imperfect, and although it is a useless presumption to enquire into the *mode* of this most remarkable miracle, these two words give us this detail only,—that it took place between the act of breaking and the continuous distribution. But "Falleret momento visum...Est quod non erat; videtur quod non intelligitur" (Hilary). The marvel lay in the Doer, not in the deed. Aug.

17. *of fragments*] Compare 2 K. iv. 43, 44. These were collected by the order of Jesus, who thus strikingly taught that wastefulness even of miraculous plenty is entirely alien to the divine administration.

twelve baskets] *Cophini*, probably wicker-baskets (*salsilloth*, Jer. vi. 9). Every Jew carried such a basket about with him to avoid the chance of his food contracting any Levitical pollution in heathen places (Juv. *Sat.* III. 14, VI. 542). The baskets used at the miracle of the four thousand were large rope-baskets, 'frails' (*spurides*). The accuracy with which each word is reserved by all the narrators for each miracle is remarkable.

At this point there is a considerable gap in the continuity of St Luke's narrative. He omits the amazement of the multitude which made it likely that they would seize Jesus to make Him king; His compelling His reluctant disciples to sail back towards the *other*—the

18—22. *St Peter's Confession. Christ prophesies His Death and Resurrection.*

And it came to pass, as he was alone praying, *his* disci- 18 ples were with him: and he asked them, saying, Whom say the people that I am? They answering said, John the 19 Baptist; but some *say,* Elias; and others *say,* that one of

western—Bethsaida; the gradual dismissal of the multitude; His flight, φεύγει, John vi. 15, ℵ) to the hill top to escape those who still lingered, and to pray alone; the gathering of the storm; the walking on the sea; the failure of Peter's faith; the very memorable discourse at Capernaum, intended to teach what was the *true* bread from heaven, and to dissipate the material expectations of the popular Messianism; the crisis of offence caused by these hard sayings; the dispute with the Pharisees on the question of the Oral Law or Tradition of the Elders; the deepening opposition and the one great day of conflict and rupture with the Pharisees (which St Luke appears to relate out of chronological order in xi.); the flight among the heathen as far as Tyre and Sidon; the incident of the Syrophoenician woman; the feeding of the four thousand; the return to Galilee and demand for a sign; the sailing away, and the warning against the leaven of the Pharisees; and the healing of a blind man at Bethsaida Julias during His second journey northwards. These must be sought for in Matt. xiv.—xvi. 12; Mk. vi. 45—viii. 30; John vi. For my view of them, and their sequence, I may perhaps be allowed to refer the reader to my *Life of Christ,* I. 403—II. 9.

18—22. ST PETER'S CONFESSION. CHRIST PROPHESIES HIS DEATH AND RESURRECTION.

18. *alone*] Rather, **in private**, as the context shews.

the people] Rather, **the multitudes**; those whom Jesus had taught and healed and fed, or those who seem to have been always at no great distance. The two other Evangelists place this memorable scene in the neighbourhood of Caesarea Philippi. His life at this epoch had come to resemble a continuous flight. He did not enter Caesarea Philippi. He always avoided towns (with the single exception of Jerusalem), probably from His love for the sights and sounds of nature, and His dislike for the crowded squalor and worldly absorption of town-communities; and He specially avoided these Hellenic and hybrid cities, with their idolatrous ornaments and corrupted population. This event may well be regarded as the *culminating point* in His ministry. He had now won *the deliberate faith and conviction* of those who had lived in close intercourse with Him, and who, in continuation of His ministry, were to evangelize the world. See Matt. xvi. 13—21; Mk. viii. 27—31.

that I am] "That I, *the Son of man,* am?" Matt. xvi. 13.

19. *John the Baptist*] See on vss. 7—9. The answer of the Apostle shewed the sad truth that Jesus had come to His own possessions and

20 the old prophets is risen again. He said unto them, But whom say ye that I am? Peter answering said, The Christ
21 of God. And he straitly charged them, and commanded
22 *them* to tell no *man* that *thing;* saying, The Son of man must suffer many *things,* and be rejected of the elders and chief priests and scribes, and be slain, and be raised the third day.

His own people received Him not; that the Light had shined in the darkness, and the darkness had not comprehended it. He had not come to *force belief*, but to *win conviction*. He had never even openly proclaimed His Messiahship, but left His works to speak for Him. God's method is not to ensure faith by violence; as the Fathers say "Force is alien to God" ($\beta \iota a\ \dot{\epsilon}\chi\theta\rho\grave{o}v\ \Theta\epsilon\hat{\omega}$).

20. *The Christ of God*] "Thou art the Christ, the Son of the Living God," Matt. xvi. 16. "The Lord's Christ," ii. 26. After the estranging speech at Capernaum our Lord had asked, "Will ye also go away?" and then St Peter's answer had been "we have believed and recognised that thou art *the Holy One of God*," John vi. 69 (א, B, C, D, L, &c.). Nathanael had recognised Him as "the Son of God" and "the King of Israel." Later, Martha confessed Him as "the Christ, the Son of God," John xi. 27. But now for the first time the revealed mystery was openly recognised and confessed. St Luke omits the blessing of St Peter, which whatever may be its exact meaning at any rate can have conferred on him no sort of primacy or superior authority among the Apostles. See xxii. 24—26; Matt. xviii. 1; John xxi. 19—23; Gal. ii. 9, 11, &c.

21. *commanded them to tell no man*] For these perhaps among other reasons:—1. Because His work was not yet finished. 2. Because as yet their faith was very weak and their knowledge very partial. 3. Because they had not yet received the Holy Spirit to give power to their testimony. 4. Because the public proclamation of the truth would have precipitated the workings of God's foreordained plan (*prothesis*, Eph. i. 9, iii. 11).

22. *The Son of man must suffer many things*] It was necessary at once to dissipate the crude Messianic conceptions of earthly splendour and victory in which they had been brought up, and to substitute the truth of a suffering for that of a triumphant Messiah.

be rejected of the elders and chief priests and scribes] i.e. by each of the three great sections which formed the Jewish Sanhedrin; by all who up to that time had been looked upon as religious authorities in the nation.

and be slain] The *mode* of death, and the delivery to the Gentiles, were culminating horrors which He mercifully kept back till the last journey to Jerusalem, Matt. xx. 19. Hitherto He had only spoken of His death in dim and distant intimations, John ii. 19, iii. 14, vi. 51. His revelation of it was *progressive*, as they were able to bear it. Matt. ix. 15, x. 38; John iii. 14; Matt. xvi. 4, 21; xvii. 22, xx. 18, xxvi. 2.

be raised the third day] In vs. 45 St Luke shews us (as events proved)

23—27. *The Cross and the Kingdom.*

²³ And he said to *them* all, If any *man* will come after me, let him deny himself, and take up his cross daily, and follow me. ²⁴ For whosoever will save his life shall lose it: but whosoever will lose his life for my sake, the same shall save it. ²⁵ For what is a man advantaged, if he gain the whole world, and lose himself, or be cast away? ²⁶ For whosoever shall be ashamed of me and of my words, of him shall the Son of man be ashamed, when he shall come in his own glory, and *in his* Father's, and of the holy angels. ²⁷ But I tell you of a truth, there be some standing here, which shall not taste of death, till they see the kingdom of God.

how entirely they failed to attach any distinct meaning to these words, Mark ix. 10.

23—27. THE CROSS AND THE KINGDOM.

23. *And he said to them all*] The word "all" implies the fact mentioned by St Mark (viii. 34), that before continuing His discourse He called up to Him the multitudes who were at a little distance. St Luke here omits the presumption and rebuke of St Peter, which is alone sufficient to dispose of the unworthy theory of some German theologians that he writes with an *animus* against St Peter, or with some desire to disparage his position.

take up his cross] A dim intimation of the still unrevealed imminence of His crucifixion, and a continuance of the lesson that to follow Christ meant not earthly gain but entire self-sacrifice, xiv. 26, 27; Acts xiv. 22.

daily] "For thy sake we are killed all the day long," Rom. viii. 36. "I die daily," 1 Cor. xv. 31.

24. *whosoever will save his life shall lose it*] The words imply *whosoever shall make it his main will to save his life*. See by way of comment the fine fragment (probably) of a very early Christian hymn in 2 Tim. ii. 11, 12, and observe that ψυχή means the natural, animal life of which the main interests are in the earth.

25. *if he gain the whole world*] It was by the constant repetition of this verse that Ignatius Loyola won the life-long devotion of St Francis Xavier.

lose himself, or be cast away] Rather, **destroy himself, and suffer loss**.

26. *whosoever shall be ashamed of me*] Compare xii. 9; 2 Tim. i. 8, 12, ii. 12.

27. *which shall not taste of death*] In the Arabian poem, Antar, Death is represented as slaying men by handing them a cup of poison. This was a common Eastern metaphor.

till they see the kingdom of God] St Mark (ix. 1) adds "coming in power." St Matthew (xvi. 28) says "till they see the Son of man coming

28—36. *The Transfiguration.*

28 And it came to pass about an eight days after these sayings, he took Peter and John and James, and went up into
29 a mountain to pray. And as he prayed, the fashion of his

in His Kingdom." It is clear that the *primary* reference of these words was to the three Apostles who, within a week of that time, were to witness the Transfiguration. So it seems to be understood in 2 Pet. i. 16, and by our Translators, who separate this verse to preface the narrative of the Transfiguration in Mark ix. 1. The significance of the "kingdom" was therefore mainly spiritual, and the verse has an important bearing on the prophecies of the Second Advent (see Matt. xxiv. 14, 15, 30). It was again fulfilled at the Resurrection and Ascension; and in the person of one disciple—St John—it was fulfilled when he lived to witness the close of the Old Dispensation in the destruction of Jerusalem.

28—36. THE TRANSFIGURATION.

28. *about an eight days after*] See Matt. xvii. 1—13; Mark ix. 2—13. This is merely the inclusive reckoning which St Luke saw in his written sources, and means exactly the same thing as "after six days" in Mark ix. 2. (This explains Matt. xxvii. 63.)

he took] The solemnity of this special choice is marked in the other Gospels by the additional word *anapherei*, "He leads them up" (cf. xxiv. 51). Matt. xxvi. 37.

Peter, and John and James] See vi. 14, viii. 51. The object of this occasion was to fill their souls with a vision which should support their faith amid the horrors which they afterwards witnessed.

into a mountain] Rather, **into the mountain**. The others say "into a lofty mountain." There can be little doubt that Mount Hermon (*Jebel esh Sheikh*) is intended, in spite of the persistent, but perfectly baseless tradition which points to Tabor. For (i) Mount Hermon is easily within six days' reach of Caesarea Philippi, and (ii) could alone be called a "lofty mountain" (being 10,000 feet high) or "the mountain," when the last scene had been at Caesarea. Further, (iii) Tabor at that time in all probability was (Jos. *B. J.* I. 8, § 7, *Vit.* 37), as from time immemorial it had been (Josh. xix. 12), an inhabited and fortified place, wholly unsuited for a scene so solemn; and (iv) was moreover in Galilee, which is excluded by Mark ix. 30. "The mountain" is indeed the meaning of the name "Hermon," which being already consecrated by Hebrew poetry (Ps. cxxxiii. 3, and under its old names of Sion and Sirion, or 'breast-plate' Deut. iv. 48, iii. 9; Cant. iv. 8), was well suited for the Transfiguration by its height, seclusion, and snowy splendour.

to pray] The characteristic addition of St Luke. That this awful scene took place *at night*, and therefore that He ascended the mountain in the evening, is clear from vss. 32, 33: comp. vi. 12. It is also implied by the allusions to the scene in 2 Pet. i. 18, 19.

29. *as he prayed*] The enquiry whether this heavenly brightness

countenance was altered, and his raiment *was* white *and* glistering. And behold, there talked with him two men, 30 which were Moses and Elias: who appeared in glory, and 31 spake of his decease which he should accomplish at Jerusalem. But Peter and they that were with him were heavy 32 with sleep: and when they were awake, they saw his glory, and the two men that stood with him. And it came to 33 pass, as they departed from him, Peter said unto Jesus, Master, it is good for us to be here: and let us make three

came from within, or—as when the face of Moses shone—by reflection from communion with God, seems irreverent and idle; but we may say that the two things are practically one.

the fashion of his countenance was altered] "His face did shine as the sun," Matt. xvii. 2. It is interesting to see how St Luke avoids the word "He was *metamorphosed*" which is used by the other Synoptists. He was writing for Greeks, in whose mythology that verb was vulgarised by foolish associations.

white and glistering] Literally, "*lightning forth*," as though from some *inward* radiance. St Matthew compares the whiteness of His robes to the light (xvii. 2), St Mark to the snow (ix. 3), and St Luke in this word to the lightning. See John i. 14; Ps. civ. 2; Hab. iii. 4.

30. *two men, which were Moses and Elias*] The great Lawgiver and the great Prophet, of whom we are told that God buried the one (Deut. xxxiv. 6) and the other had passed to heaven in a chariot of fire (2 Kings ii. 1, 11). The two were the chief representatives of the Old Dispensation. The former had prophesied of Christ (Acts iii. 22; Deut. xviii. 18); of the latter it had been prophesied that he should be His forerunner. "The end of the Law is Christ; Law and Prophecy are from the Word; and things which began from the Word, cease *in* the Word." St Ambrose.

31. *spake of his decease*] The word used is *exodos*, 'departure'—a very unusual word for death, which also occurs in this connexion in 2 Pet. i. 15. The reading *doxan*, 'glory,' though known to St Chrysostom, is only supported by a few cursives. *Exodos* is, as Bengel says, a very weighty word, involving His passion, cross, death, resurrection, and ascension.

32. *were heavy with sleep: and when they were awake*] Rather, **had been heavy with sleep; but on fully awaking**. The word *diagregoresantes* does not here mean 'having kept awake,' but (to give the full force of the compound and aorist) *suddenly starting into full wakefulness*. They started up, wide awake after heavy sleep, in the middle of the vision.

33. *as they departed*] Rather, **were parting**.
it is good for us to be here] The word is not *agathon*, but *kalon*; it is an excellent thing, or 'it is *best*' (cf. Matt. xvii. 4, xxvi. 24).

tabernacles] like the little wattled *booths* (succôth), which the Israelites

tabernacles; one for thee, and one for Moses, and one for
34 Elias: not knowing what he said. While he thus spake,
there came a cloud, and overshadowed them: and they
35 feared as they entered into the cloud. And there came a
voice out of the cloud, saying, This is my beloved Son:
36 hear him. And when the voice was past, Jesus was found
alone. And they kept *it* close, and told no *man* in those
days any of *those things* which they had seen.

37—48. The Demoniac Boy. The Lesson of Meekness.

37 And it came to pass, *that* on the next day, when they
38 were come down from the hill, much people met him. And

made for themselves at the Feast of Tabernacles. The use of *skēnōma* in 2 Pet. i. 13 (Matt. xvii. 4) is another sign that the mind of the writer was full of this scene.

not knowing what he said] Not knowing that the spectacle on Calvary was to be more transcendent and divine than that of Hermon, not knowing that the old was passing away and all things becoming new; not knowing that Jesus was not to die with Moses and Elijah on either side, but between two thieves.

34. *there came a cloud, and overshadowed them*] "A bright cloud," Matt. xvii. 5. Possibly the Sheckinah, or cloud of glory (see on i. 35), which was the symbol of the Divine Presence (Ex. xxxiii. 9; 1 Kings viii. 10). If a mere mountain cloud had been intended, there would have been no reason for their fear.

35. *a voice out of the cloud*] 2 Pet. i. 17, 18. As in two other instances in our Lord's ministry, iii. 22; John xii. 28. The other Synoptists add that at this Voice they fell prostrate, and, on Jesus touching them, suddenly raised their eyes and looked all around them, to find no one there but Jesus.

my beloved Son] Rather, **my chosen Son** (*eklelegmenos*, ℵ, B, L). Cf. Is. xlii. 1.

36. *And they kept it close*] until after the resurrection, in accordance with the express command of Jesus given them as they were descending the hill. Matt. xvii. 9. During the descent there also occurred the conversation about Elijah and John the Baptist. (Matt. xvii. 9—13; Mk. ix. 9—13.)

37—48. THE DEMONIAC BOY. THE LESSON OF MEEKNESS.

37. *on the next day*] Proving that the Transfiguration took place at night: see on vs. 28.

much people met him] St Mark records their "amazement" at seeing Him—perhaps due to some lingering radiance and majesty which clung to Him after the Transfiguration. (Comp. Ex. xxxiv. 30.) They had been surrounding a group of the scribes, who were taunting the disciples with their failure to cure the lunatic boy.

behold, a man of the company cried out, saying, Master, I beseech thee, look upon my son: for he is mine only child. And lo, a spirit taketh him, and he suddenly crieth out; 39 and it teareth him that he foameth again, and bruising him hardly departeth from him. And I besought thy disciples 40 to cast him out; and they could not. And Jesus answering 41 said, O faithless and perverse generation, how long shall I be with you, and suffer you? Bring thy son hither. And 42 as he was yet a coming, the devil threw him down, and tare *him.* And Jesus rebuked the unclean spirit, and healed the child, and delivered him again to his father.

And they were all amazed at the mighty power of God. 43 But while they wondered every one at all *things* which Jesus

38. *of the company*] Rather, **from the crowd.**
Master] Rather, **Teacher** or **Rabbi.**
he is mine only child] See on viii. 42.

39. *a spirit taketh him*] This was the supernatural aspect of his deafness, epilepsy, and madness. St Matthew gives the natural aspect when he says, "he is a lunatic, and sore vexed, &c.," xvii. 15.

40. *and they could not*] Jesus afterwards, at their request, told them the reason of this, which was their deficient faith. Matt. xvii. 19—21.

41. *O faithless and perverse generation*] Doubtless the Spirit of Jesus was wrung by the contrast—so immortally portrayed in the great picture of Raphael—between the peace and glory which He had left on the mountain, and this scene of weak faith, abject misery, and bitter opposition—faltering disciples, degraded sufferers, and wrangling scribes.

how long shall I be with you?] "He was hastening to His Father, yet could not go till He had led His disciples to faith. Their slowness troubled Him." Bengel.

42. *rebuked the unclean spirit*] See the fuller details and the memorable cry of the poor father in Mk. ix. 21—24. The child had been rendered deaf and dumb by his possession; in the last paroxysm he wallowed on the ground foaming, and then lay as dead till Jesus raised him by the hand. Interesting parallels to these strange and horrible paroxysms in a condition which may well be ascribed to demoniac possession may be found in a paper on Demoniacs by Mr Caldwell, *Contemp. Rev.*, Feb., 1876. The boy's 'possession' seems on its natural side to have been the deadliest and intensest form of epileptic lunacy which our Lord had ever healed, and one far beyond the power of the real or pretended Jewish exorcisms. Hence the words of Jesus were peculiarly emphatic, Mk. ix. 25.

43. *mighty power*] Rather, **majesty.** 2 Pet. i. 16.
while they wondered] The power of the last miracle had rekindled some of their Messianic enthusiasm. Jesus had now reached the

44 did, he said unto his disciples, Let these sayings sink down into your ears: for the Son of man shall be delivered into 45 the hands of men. But they understood not this saying, and it was hid from them, that they perceived it not: and they feared to ask him of that saying.

46 Then there arose a reasoning among them, which of them 47 should be greatest. And Jesus, perceiving the thought of 48 their heart, took a child, and set him by him, and said unto them, Whosoever shall receive this child in my name receiveth me: and whosoever shall receive me receiveth him that sent me: for he that is least among you all, the same shall be great.

northern limits of Palestine, and—apparently through bypaths, and with the utmost secresy—was retracing His steps, perhaps along the western bank of the Jordan, to Galilee, Matt. xvii. 22; Mk. ix. 30.

he said unto his disciples] The imperfects in Mk. ix. 31 shew that these warnings of His approaching betrayal, death, and resurrection now formed a constant topic of His teaching.

44. *shall be delivered*] Rather, **is about to be delivered** (i.e. very soon).

45. *they understood not*] This ignorance and incapacity, so humbly avowed, should be contrasted with the boldness and fulness of their subsequent knowledge as one of the strongest proofs of the change wrought in them by the Resurrection and the Descent of the Holy Spirit.

46. *a reasoning*] Rather, **a dispute**.

which of them should be greatest] Their jealous ambition had been kindled partly by false Messianic hopes, partly perhaps by the recent distinction bestowed on Peter, James, and John. Observe how little Christ's words to Peter had been understood to confer on him any special preeminence! This unseemly dispute was again stirred up at the Last Supper, xxii. 24—26.

47. *perceiving the thought of their heart*] He asked the subject of their dispute, and when shame kept them silent, He sat down, and calling a little child, made the Twelve stand around while He taught this solemn lesson.

took a child] This could not have been the future martyr St Ignatius, as legend says (Niceph. II. 3), probably by an erroneous inference from his name of Christophoros or Theophoros, which was derived from his telling Trajan that he carried God in his heart (see *Ep. ad Smyrn.* III. which is of very doubtful genuineness, or Eus. *H. E.* III. 38).

48. *he that is least among you*] Comp. Matt. xxiii. 11, 12. He perhaps added the memorable words about offending His little ones. Matt. xviii. 6—10; Lk. xvii. 2.

shall be great] Rather, **is great** (ℵ, B, C, L, X).

49, 50. *The Tolerance of Jesus.*

And John answered and said, Master, we saw one casting 49 out devils in thy name; and we forbad him, because he followeth not with us. And Jesus said unto him, Forbid *him* 50 not: for he that is not against us is for us.

49, 50. THE TOLERANCE OF JESUS.

49. *And John answered and said*] Mk. ix. 38—41. This sudden question seems to have been suggested by the words *"in my name,"* which Jesus had just used.

casting out devils in thy name] It was common among the Jews to attempt exorcism by many different methods; see on iv. 35, 41; viii. 32. This unknown person—like the sons of Sceva in Acts xix. 13, 14, but evidently in a more faithful spirit—had found that the name of Jesus was more powerful. Specimens of Jewish exorcisms are given in the Jewish *Book of Jubilees*, and in *Shabbath*, 67; *Pesachim*, f. 112 *a, b*; see too Tobit vi. 16, 17; Jos. *B. J.* vii. 6, § 3.

we forbad him] Compare the jealous zeal of Joshua against Eldad and Medad, and the truly noble answer of Moses, Numb. xi. 27—29.

because he followeth not with us] This touch of intolerant zeal is quite in accordance with the natural disposition which shews itself in the incident of vs. 54, and with the story that St John rushed out of a bath in which he saw the heretic Cerinthus. It was this burning temperament that made him a "Son of Thunder."

50. *he that is not against us is for us*] Cf. Phil. i. 18. The complementary but not contradictory truth to this, is "He who is not with me is against me," Matt. xii. 30. Both are true in different circumstances. Neutrality is sometimes as deadly as opposition (Judg. v. 23); it is sometimes as effectual as aid (Sueton., *Jul. Caes.* 75). See Vinet, *La tolérance et l'intolérance de l'Évangile* (*Discours*, p. 268). Renan calls these "two irreconcilable rules of proselytism, and a contradiction evoked by a passionate struggle." Guizot expresses his astonishment at so frivolous a criticism, and calls them two contrasted facts which every one must have noticed in the course of an active life. "Les deux assertions, loin de se contredire, peuvent être également vraies, et Jésus-Christ en les exprimant a parlé en observateur sagace, non en moraliste qui donne les préceptes." *Méditations*, p. 229.

It is a great pity that the chapter does not end at this verse; since it closes another great section in our Lord's ministry—the epoch of opposition and flight. A new phase of the ministry begins at vs. 51.

CHS. IX. 51—XVIII. 31.

This section forms a great episode in St Luke, which may be called the departure for the final conflict, and is identical with the journey (probably to the Feast of the Dedication, John x. 22) which is partially

CH. IX. 51—56. *Rejected by the Samaritans. A lesson of Tolerance.*

51 And it came to pass, when the time was come that he

touched upon in Matt. xviii.—xx. 16 and Mk. x. 1—31. It contains many incidents recorded by this Evangelist alone, and though the recorded identifications of time and place are vague, yet they all point (ix. 51, xiii. 22, xvii. 11, x. 38) to *a slow, solemn, and public progress from Galilee to Jerusalem,* of which the events themselves are often grouped by subjective considerations. So little certain is the *order* of the separate incidents, that one writer (Rev. W. Stewart) has made an ingenious attempt to shew that it is determined by the alphabetic arrangement of the leading Greek verbs (ἀγαπᾶν, x. 25—28, 29—37, 38—42; αἰτεῖν, xi. 1—4, 5, 8, 9—13, &c.). Canon Westcott arranges the order thus: The Rejection of the Jews foreshewn; preparation, ix. 43—xi. 13; Lessons of Warning, xi. 14—xiii. 9; Lessons of Progress, xiii. 10—xiv. 24; Lessons of Discipleship, xiv. 25—xvii. 10; the Coming End, xvii. 10—xviii. 30.

The order of events after 'the Galilaean spring' of our Lord's ministry on the plain of Gennesareth seems to have been this: After the period of flight among the heathen or in countries which were only semi-Jewish, of which almost the sole recorded incident is the healing of the daughter of the Syrophoenician woman (Matt. xv. 21—28). He returned to Peraea and fed the four thousand. He then sailed back to Gennesareth, but left it in deep sorrow on being met by the Pharisees with insolent demands for a sign from heaven. Turning His back once more on Galilee, He again travelled northwards; healed a blind man at Bethsaida Julias; received St Peter's great confession on the way to Caesarea Philippi; was transfigured; healed the demoniac boy; rebuked the ambition of the disciples by the example of the little child; returned for a brief rest in Capernaum, during which occurred the incident of the Temple Tax; then journeyed to the Feast of Tabernacles, during which occurred the incidents so fully narrated by St John (John vii. 1—x. 21). The events and teachings in this great section of St Luke seem to belong mainly, if not entirely, to the two months between the hasty return of Jesus to Galilee and His arrival in Jerusalem, two months afterwards, at the Feast of Dedication;—a period respecting which St Luke must have had access to special sources of information.

For fuller discussion of the question I must refer to my *Life of Christ,* II. 89—150.

CH. IX. 51—56. REJECTED BY THE SAMARITANS. A LESSON OF TOLERANCE.

51. *when the time was come that he should be received up*] Rather, **when the days of His Assumption were drawing to a close** (literally, *were being fulfilled*). St Luke thus clearly marks the arrival of a final stage of our Lord's ministry. "His passion, cross, death, and grave were coming on, but through them all Jesus looked to the goal, and the style

should be received up, he stedfastly set his face to go to Jerusalem, and sent messengers before his face: and they ⁵² went, and entered into a village of the Samaritans, to make ready for him. And they did not receive him, because his ⁵³ face was *as though he* would go to Jerusalem. And when ⁵⁴

of the Evangelist imitates His feelings," Bengel. The word *analēpsis* means the Ascension (in Eccl. Latin *Assumptio*). So ἀνελήφθη of Elijah, 2 K. ii. 11; Mk. xvi. 19.

he] Rather, **He Himself also**.

set his face] Jer. xxi. 10; 2 K. xii. 17 (LXX.), and especially Is. l. 7.

52. *sent messengers*] Some think that they were two of the Seventy disciples; others that they were James and John.

into a village of the Samaritans] On the way to Judaea from Galilee He would doubtless avoid Nazareth, and therefore His road probably lay over Mount Tabor, past Little Hermon (see vii. 11), past Nain, Endor, and Shunem. The first Samaritan village at which He would arrive would be *En Gannim* (Fountain of Gardens), now Jenîn (2 K. ix. 27), a pleasant village at the first pass into the Samaritan hills. The inhabitants are still described as "fanatical, rude, and rebellious" (Thomson, *Land and Book*, II. xxx.). The Samaritans are not mentioned in St Mark, and only once in St Matthew (x. 5).

to make ready for him] As He was now accompanied not only by the Twelve, but by a numerous multitude of followers, His unannounced arrival would have caused embarrassment. But, further than this, He now openly avowed Himself as the Christ.

53. *they did not receive him*] The aorist implies that they at once rejected Him. The Samaritans had shewn themselves heretofore not ill-disposed (John iv. 39), and St Luke himself delights to record favourable notices of them (x. 33, xvii. 18). But (i) there was always a recrudescence of hatred between the Jews and the Samaritans at the recurrence of the annual feasts. (ii) Their national jealousy would not allow them to receive a Messiah whose goal was not Gerizim, but Jerusalem. (iii) They would not sanction the passage of a multitude of Jews through their territory, since the Jews frequently (though not always, Jos. *Antt.* xx. 6, § 1) chose the *other* route on the East of the Jordan.

as though he would go to Jerusalem] This national hatred between Jews and Samaritans (John iv. 9) still continues, and at the present day it is mainly due to the fanaticism of the Jews. In our Lord's day the Jews called the Samaritans 'Cuthites' (2 K. xvii. 24), aliens (xvii. 18), 'that foolish people that dwell in Sichem' (Ecclus. l. 25, 26), and other opprobrious names. They accused them of *continuous* idolatry (2 K. xvii.), and charged them with false fire-signals, and with having polluted the Temple by scattering it with dead men's bones (Jos. *Antt.* xx. 6, § 1, XVIII. 2, § 2; *B. J.* II. 12, § 3). No doubt originally their Monotheism was very hybrid, being mixed up with five heathen religions (2 K. xvii. 33,

his disciples James and John saw *this*, they said, Lord, wilt thou *that* we command fire to come down from heaven, and
55 consume them, even as Elias did? But he turned, and rebuked them, and said, Ye know not what manner of spirit

xix. 37); but they had gradually laid aside idolatry, and it was as much a calumny of the ancient Jews to charge them with the worship of Rachel's amulets (Gen. xxxv. 4) as for modern Jews to call them '*worshippers of the pigeon*' (Frankl. *Jews in the East*, II. 334). But the deadly exacerbation between the two nations, which began after the Exile (Ezr. iv. 1—10; Nehem. iv. 1—16, vi.), had gone on increasing by perpetual collision since the building of the Temple on Gerizim by the renegade priest Manasseh and Sanballat (Neh. xiii. 28; Jos. *Antt.* XI. 7, XII. 5, § 5), which was destroyed by John Hyrcanus B.C. 129.

54. *James and John*] "What wonder that the Sons of Thunder wished to flash lightning?" St Ambrose. But one of these very disciples afterwards went to Samaria on a message of love (Acts viii. 14—25).

fire to come down from heaven] To avenge their helplessness under this gross and open insult of the Messiah. "Christ wrought miracles in every element except fire. Fire is reserved for the consummation of the age." Bengel.

even as Elias did] These words are omitted by ℵ, B, L. But (i) they are singularly appropriate, since the incident referred to also occurred in Samaria (2 K. i. 5—14); and (ii) while it would be difficult to account for their *insertion*, it is quite easy to account for their omission either by an accidental error of the copyists, or on dogmatic grounds, especially from the use made of this passage by the heretic Marcion (Tert. *adv. Marc.* IV. 23) to disparage the Old Testament. (iii) They are found in very ancient MSS., versions, and Fathers. (iv) The words seem to be absolutely required to defend the crude spirit of vengeance, and might have seemed all the more natural to the still half-trained Apostles because they had so recently seen Moses and Elias speaking with Jesus on the Mount of Transfiguration. They needed, as it were, a Scriptural precedent, to conceal from themselves the personal impulse which really actuated them.

55. *Ye know not what manner of spirit ye are of*] The whole of this passage down to "save them" is omitted in ℵ, A, B, C, and other manuscripts; but it is impossible to doubt its genuineness, because it breathes a spirit far purer, loftier, and rarer than is ever discernible in ecclesiastical interpolations. It was omitted on the same grounds as the words in the last verse, because it was regarded as 'dangerous' to the authority of the O.T. It is quite impossible to believe that the narrative abruptly ended with the unexplained "He rebuked them." Ecclesiastical censurers have failed to see that "religionis non est religionem cogere" (Tert. *ad Scap.* 2), and that, as Bp Andrewes says, "The times require sometimes one spirit, sometimes another, Elias' time Elias' spirit." The Apostles learnt these truths better when they had received the Holy Ghost (Rom. xii. 19; Jas. i. 19, 20, iii. 16, 17; John iii. 17,

ye are of. For the Son of man is not come to destroy men's lives, but to save *them*. And they went to another village. 56

57—62. *The Three Aspirants.*

And it came to pass *that*, as they went in the way, a certain *man* said unto him, Lord, I will follow thee whithersoever thou goest. And Jesus said unto him, Foxes have holes, and birds of the air *have* nests; but the Son of man hath not where to lay *his* head. And he said unto another, 57 58 59

xii. 47). They learnt that the spirit of Jesus was the spirit of the dove; and that there is a difference between Carmel and Hermon, between Sinai and Kurn Hattîn. It is possible that the words may be a question—Know ye not that *yours* (emphatically placed last) is the spirit of Elijah, *not* of *Christ*? Our Lord quoted Psalms xxii. and xxxi. on the Cross, and yet prayed for His enemies. Bengel.

56. *For the Son of man is not come*, &c. This clause is omitted by the majority of uncials, and some editors therefore regard it as a repetition of xix. 10 or Matt. xviii. 11. However that may be, we have the same sentiment in John iii. 17, xii. 47; 1 Tim. i. 15. The Sons of Thunder were shewing the spirit of the Talmud (which says, "Let not the Samaritans have part in the Resurrection") rather than that of the Gospel (x. 33, xvii. 18; Acts i. 8).

they went to another village] The word *heteran* (not *allēn*) perhaps implies that it was a *Jewish*, not a Samaritan village. Numb. xx. 21; Matt. ii. 12.

57—62. THE THREE ASPIRANTS.

57. *as they went in the way*] St Matthew (viii. 19—22) places these incidents before the embarkation for Gergesa. Lange's conjecture that the three aspirants were Judas Iscariot, Thomas, and Matthew is singularly baseless.

a certain man] a Scribe (Matt. viii. 19). The dignity of his rank was nothing to Him who had chosen among His Twelve a zealot and a publican.

whithersoever thou goest] There was too little of 'the modesty of fearful duty' in the Scribe's professions.

58. *Jesus said unto him*] "In the man's flaring enthusiasm He saw the smoke of egotistical self-deceit" (Lange), and therefore He coldly checked a proffered devotion which would not have stood the test.

nests] Rather, **habitations, shelters**. Birds do not live in nests. In this verse more than in any other we see the poverty and homelessness of the latter part of the Lord's ministry (2 Cor. viii. 9). Perhaps St Luke placed the incident here as appropriate to the rejection of our Lord's wish to rest for the night at En Gannim. Was this Scribe prepared to follow Jesus for *His own sake* alone?

Follow me. But he said, Lord, suffer me first to go and
60 bury my father. Jesus said unto him, Let the dead bury
their dead: but go thou and preach the kingdom of God.
61 And another also said, Lord, I will follow thee; but let me
first go bid them farewell, which are *at home* in my house.
62 And Jesus said unto him, No *man* having put his hand to the
plough, and looking back, is fit for the kingdom of God.

CH. X. 1—24. *The Mission of the Seventy.*

10 After these *things* the Lord appointed other seventy also,

59. *Lord, suffer me first to go and bury my father*] An ancient, but groundless tradition (Clem. Alex. *Strom.* III. 4, § 25), says that this was Philip. This man was already a disciple (Matt. viii. 21). The request could hardly mean 'let me live at home till my father's death,' which would be too indefinite an offer; nor can it well mean that his father was lying unburied, for in that case the disciple would hardly have been among the crowd. Perhaps it meant 'let me go and give a farewell funeral feast, and put everything in order.' The man was bidden to be Christ's Nazarite (Num. vi. 6, 7).

60. *Let the dead bury their dead*] i.e. let the *spiritually* dead (Eph. ii. 1; John v. 24, 25) bury their physically dead. "Amandus est generator, sed praeponendus est Creator," Aug. The general lesson is that of xiv. 26.

61. *let me first go bid them farewell*] The incident and the allusion closely resemble the call of Elisha (1 K. xix. 20). But the call of Jesus is more pressing and momentous than that of Elijah. "The East is calling thee, thou art looking to the West," Aug. Neither Elijah nor Elisha is an adequate example for the duties of the Kingdom of Heaven, of which the least partaker is, in knowledge and in privileges, greater than they.

62. *No man having put his hand to the plough*] He who would make straight furrows must not look about him (Hesiod, *Works and Days*, II. 60). The light ploughs of the East, easily overturned, require constant attention.

fit] Rather, **well-adapted.** By way of comment see xvii. 32; Ps. lxxviii. 9; Heb. x. 38, 39. The general lesson of the section is, Give yourself wholly to your duty, and count the cost, xiv. 25—33. Christ cannot accept 'a conditional service.' Neither hardship, nor bereavement, nor home ties must delay us from following Him. Is it more than a curious accident that the last four incidents illustrate the peculiarities of the four marked human temperaments—the Choleric (51—56); the Sanguine (57, 58); the Melancholic (59, 60); the Phlegmatic (61, 62)?

CH. X. 1—24. THE MISSION OF THE SEVENTY.

1. *After these things*] i.e. after finally leaving Galilee, and starting on His great Peraean progress.

and sent them two and two before his face into every city and place, whither he himself would come. Therefore said 2 he unto them, The harvest truly *is* great, but the labourers *are* few: pray ye therefore the Lord of the harvest, that he would send forth labourers into his harvest. Go your ways: 3 behold, I send you forth as lambs among wolves. Carry 4 neither purse, nor scrip, nor shoes: and salute no *man* by the way. And into whatsoever house ye enter, first say, 5 Peace *be* to this house. And if the son of peace be 6 there, your peace shall rest upon it: if not, it shall turn

other seventy also] Rather, **also others** (besides the Twelve) **seventy in number**. Some MSS. read seventy-two (B, D, M, &c.). The number had evident reference to the Elders of Moses (Num. xi. 16), where there is the same variation; the Sanhedrin; and the Jewish belief (derived from Gen. x.) as to the number of the nations of the world. The references to Elim with its 12 wells and 70 palm-trees are mere plays of allegoric fancy.

two and two] The same merciful provision that we see in the brother-pairs of the Twelve.

into every city, &c.] Clearly with the same object as in ix. 52. It may have been all the more necessary because hitherto He had worked less in the Transjordanic regions.

2. *The harvest truly is great*] Compare Matt. ix. 37; John iv. 35.

send forth] The word literally means 'drive forth,' and though it has lost its full force implies urgency and haste. See similar uses of the word in John x. 4, Matt. ix. 38, Mk. i. 12.

3. *as lambs*] 'as sheep,' Matt. x. 16 (of the Twelve). The slight variation must not be pressed. The impression meant to be conveyed is merely that of simplicity and defencelessness. A tradition, as old as Clemens Romanus, tells us that St Peter had asked (on the previous occasion), 'But how then if the wolves should tear the lambs?' and that Jesus replied, 'Let not the lambs fear the wolves when the lambs are once dead,' and added the words in Matt. x. 28. There is no reason to doubt this interesting tradition, which may rank as one of the most certain of the 'unwritten sayings' (*agrapha dogmata*) of our Lord.

4. *neither purse*] Compare ix. 1—6, and notes; Matt. x. 1—42. St Luke uses the Greek *balantion*; St Mark the Oriental *zonên* 'girdle.'

salute no man by the way] A common direction in cases of urgency (2 K. iv. 29), and partly explicable by the length and loitering elaborateness of Eastern greetings (Thomson, *Land and Book*, II. xxiv.).

5. *Peace be to this house*] Adopted in our service for the Visitation of the Sick. God's messengers should begin first with prayers for peace, not with objurgations. Bengel.

6. *the son of peace*] Rather, **a son of peace**, i.e. *a man of peaceful heart*. Comp. for the phrase xvi. 8, xx. 36; John xvii. 12; Eph. v. 6, 8.

7 to you again. And in the same house remain, eating and drinking such *things* as they give: for the labourer is
8 worthy of his hire. Go not from house to house. And into whatsoever city ye enter, and they receive you, eat such
9 *things* as are set before you: and heal the sick that are therein, and say unto them, The kingdom of God is come
10 nigh unto you. But into whatsoever city ye enter, and they receive you not, go *your ways* out into the streets of the
11 same, and say, Even the *very* dust of your city, which cleaveth on us, we do wipe off against you: notwithstanding be ye sure of this, that the kingdom of God is come nigh
12 unto you. But I say unto you, that it shall be more tolerable in that day for Sodom, than for that city.
13 Woe unto thee, Chorazin, woe unto thee, Bethsaida: for if the mighty works had been done in Tyre and Sidon, which have been done in you, they had a great while ago repented,
14 sitting in sackcloth and ashes. But it shall be more tolera-

it shall turn to you again] Matt. x. 13. "My prayer returned into mine own bosom," Ps. xxxv. 13.

7. *eating and drinking such things as they give*] As a plain right. 1 Cor. ix. 4, 7—11.

the labourer is worthy of his hire] Referred to by St Paul, 1 Tim. v. 18. Doubtless he may have been aware that our Lord had used it, but the saying was probably proverbial.

9. *The kingdom of God is come nigh unto you*] So that our Lord's last messages resembled His first preaching, Matt. iv. 17.

11. *Even the very dust*] Acts xiii. 49—51, xviii. 5—7.

12. *more tolerable in that day for Sodom*] The great principle which explains these words may be found in xii. 47, 48 (compare Heb. ii. 2, 3, x. 28, 29).

13. *Woe unto thee, Chorazin*] The mention of this town is very interesting because this is the only occasion (Matt. xi. 21) on which the name occurs, and we are thus furnished with a very striking proof of the fragmentariness of the Gospels. The very site of Chorazin was long unknown. It has now been discovered at *Keraseh*, the ruins of an old town on a wady, two miles inland from Tel Hum (Capernaum). At a little distance these ruins look like mere rude heaps of basaltic stones.

Bethsaida] See on ix. 10.

mighty works] Literally, "*powers*."

they had a great while ago repented] like Nineveh (Jon. iii. 5—10), "Surely had I sent thee unto them they would have hearkened unto thee," Ezek. iii. 6; comp. James iv. 17.

ble for Tyre and Sidon at the judgment, than for you. And 15 thou, Capernaum, which art exalted to heaven, shalt be thrust down to hell. He that heareth you heareth me; and 16 he that despiseth you despiseth me; and he that despiseth me despiseth him that sent me.

And the seventy returned *again* with joy, saying, Lord, 17 even the devils are subject unto us through thy name. And 18 he said unto them, I beheld Satan as lightning fall from heaven. Behold, I give unto you power to tread on ser- 19 pents and scorpions, and over all the power of the enemy:

14. *more tolerable...at the judgment*] A very important verse as proving the 'intermediate state' (Hades) of human souls. The guilty inhabitants of these cities had received their temporal punishment (Gen. xix. 24, 25); but the final judgment was yet to come.

15. *And thou, Capernaum*] Christ's "own city."
exalted to heaven] by inestimable spiritual privileges. "Admitted into a holier sanctuary, they were guilty of a deeper sacrilege." A better reading is (for ἡ...ὑψωθεῖσα) μὴ...ὑψωθήσῃ; "Shalt thou be exalted to heaven? Thou shalt be thrust down...!"

shalt be thrust down to hell] Rather, **as far as Hades**. When our Lord uttered this woe these cities on the shores of Gennesareth were bright and populous and prospering; now they are desolate heaps of ruins in a miserable land. The inhabitants who lived thirty years longer may have recalled these woes in the unspeakable horrors of slaughter and conflagration which the Romans then inflicted on them. It is immediately after the celebrated description of the loveliness of the Plain of Gennesareth that Josephus goes on to tell of the shore strewn with wrecks and putrescent bodies, "insomuch that *the misery was not only an object of commiseration to the Jews, but even to those that hated them and had been the authors of that misery*," Jos. *B. J.* III. 10, § 8. For fuller details see my *Life of Christ*, II. 101 sq.

16. *despiseth*] Literally, "setting at nought." For comment on the verse see 1 Thess. iv. 8; Matt. xviii. 5; John xii. 44.

17. *returned again with joy*] The success of their mission is more fully recorded than that of the Twelve.

the devils] Rather, **the demons**. They had been bidden (vs. 9) to "heal the sick;" but these are the only healings that they mention.

are subject] Rather, **are being subjected**.

18. *I beheld Satan as lightning fall from heaven*] Rather, **I was observing Satan as lightning fallen from heaven**, Is. xiv. 9—15. We find similar thoughts in John xvi. 11, xii. 31, "now shall the prince of this world be cast out;" 1 John iii. 8; Heb. ii. 14.

19. *I give*] Read, **I have given**, with ℵ, B, C, L, &c.
power] Rather, **the authority**.
to tread on serpents and scorpions] Compare Mk. xvi. 17, 18. So far as the promise was *literal*, the only fact of the kind referred to in the

20 and nothing shall by any means hurt you. Notwithstanding in this rejoice not, that the spirits are subject unto you; but rather rejoice, because your names are written in heaven.

21 In that hour Jesus rejoiced in spirit, and said, I thank thee, O Father, Lord of heaven and earth, that thou hast hid these *things* from the wise and prudent, and hast revealed them unto babes: even so, Father; for so it seemed

22 good in thy sight. All *things* are delivered to me of my Father: and no *man* knoweth who the Son is, but the

N. T. is Acts xxviii. 3—5. In legend we have the story of St John saved from poison, which is represented in Christian art as a viper escaping from the cup (Jameson, *Sacred and Legendary Art*, I. 159). But it may be doubted whether the meaning was not predominantly spiritual as in Gen. iii. 15; Rom. xvi. 20; Ps. xci. 13; Is. xi. 8.

nothing shall by any means hurt you] Rom. viii. 28, 39.

20. *are written in heaven*] Rather, **have been recorded in the heavens** (reading ἐγγέγραπται). On this 'Book of God,' or 'Book of Life,' see Ex. xxxii. 32; Ps. lxix. 28; Dan. xii. 1; Phil. iv. 3; Heb. xii. 23; Rev. xiii. 8, xx. 12, xxi. 27. It is the opposite to being "written in the earth," Jer. xvii. 13.

21. *rejoiced*] Rather, **exulted**, a much stronger word, and most valuable as recording one element—the element of exultant joy—in the life of our Lord, on which the Evangelists so rarely touch as to have originated the legend, preserved in the spurious letter of P. Lentulus to the Senate, that He wept often, but that no one had ever seen Him smile.

I thank thee, O Father] Literally, "*I make grateful acknowledgment to Thee.*"

from the wise and prudent...unto babes] Here we have the contrast between the 'wisdom of the world,' which is 'foolishness with God,' and the 'foolishness of the world,' which is 'wisdom with God,' on which St Paul also was fond of dwelling, 1 Cor. i. 21, 26; 2 Cor. iv. 3, 4; Rom. i. 22. For similar passages in the Gospels see Matt. xvi. 17, xviii. 3, 4.

unto babes] i.e. to all who have "the young lamb's heart amid the full-grown flocks"—to all innocent childlike souls, such as are often those of the truly wise. Genius itself has been defined as "the heart of childhood taken up and matured into the power of manhood."

22. *All things are delivered to me of my Father*] Rather, **were delivered to me by**, cf. xx. 14. This entire verse is one of those in which the teaching of the Synoptists (Matt. xxviii. 18) comes into nearest resemblance to that of St John, which abounds in such passages (John i. 18, iii. 35, v. 26, 27, vi. 44, 46, xiv. 6—9, xvii. 1, 2; 1 John v. 20). In the same way we find this view assumed in St Paul's earlier Epistles (e.g. 1 Cor. xv. 24, 27), and magnificently developed in the Epistles of the Captivity (Phil. ii. 9; Eph. i. 21, 22).

Father; and who the Father is, but the Son, and *he* to whom the Son will reveal *him*. And he turned him unto *his* disciples, and said privately, Blessed *are* the eyes which see *the things* that ye see: for I tell you, that many prophets and kings have desired to see *those things* which ye see, and have not seen *them;* and to hear *those things* which ye hear, and have not heard *them*.

25—37. *The Parable of the Good Samaritan.*

And behold, a certain lawyer stood up, and tempted him, saying, Master, what shall I do to inherit eternal life? He said unto him, What is written in the law? how readest thou? And he answering said, Thou shalt love the Lord thy God with all thy heart, and with all thy soul, and with all thy strength, and with all thy mind; and thy neighbour as thyself.

23. *Blessed are the eyes*] Comp. Matt. xiii. 16.
24. *prophets and kings*] e.g. Abraham, Gen. xx. 7, xxiii. 6; Jacob, Gen. xlix. 18; Balaam, Num. xxiv. 17; David, 2 Sam. xxiii. 1—5.
and have not seen them] John viii. 56; Eph. iii. 5, 6; Heb. xi. 13.

> "Save that each little voice in turn
> Some glorious truth proclaims;
> *What sages would have died to learn,*
> *Now taught by cottage dames.*"
>
> KEBLE.

25—37. THE PARABLE OF THE GOOD SAMARITAN.

25. *a certain lawyer*] A teacher of the Mosaic Law—differing little from a scribe, as the man is called in Mk. xii. 28. The same person may have had both functions—that of preserving and that of expounding the Law.
tempted him] Literally, "*putting Him fully to the test*" (iv. 12); but the purpose does not seem to have been so deliberately hostile as in xi. 54.
what shall I do to inherit eternal life?] See xviii. 18, and the answer there also given. It is interesting to compare it with the answer given by St Paul *after* the Ascension, Acts xvi. 30, 31.

26. *how readest thou?*] The phrase resembled one in constant use among the Rabbis, and the lawyer deserved to get no other answer because his question was not sincere. The very meaning and mission of his life was to teach this answer.

27. *Thou shalt love the Lord thy God*] This was the summary of the Law in Deut. vi. 5, x. 12; Lev. xix. 18.
and thy neighbour as thyself] Hillel had given this part of the

28 And he said unto him, Thou hast answered right: this
29 do, and thou shalt live. But he, willing to justify him-
30 self, said unto Jesus, And who is my neighbour? And
Jesus answering said, A certain man went down from Jerusalem to Jericho, and fell among thieves, which stripped him of his raiment, and wounded *him*, and departed, leaving
31 *him* half dead. And by chance there came down a certain

answer to an enquirer who similarly came to put him to the test, and as far as it went, it was a right answer (Rom. xiii. 9; Gal. v. 13, 14; Jas. ii. 8); but it became futile if left to stand alone, without the *first* Commandment.

28. *Thou hast answered right*] "If thou doest well, shalt thou not be accepted?" Gen. iv. 7; "which if a man do, he shall live in them," Lev. xviii. 5; Rom. x. 5; but see Gal. iii. 21, 22.

this do] As the passage from Deuteronomy was one of those inscribed in the phylacteries (little leather boxes containing four texts in their compartments), which the scribe wore on his forehead and wrist, it is an ingenious conjecture that our Lord, as He spoke, pointed to one of these.

29. *willing to justify himself*] "before men"—a thing which the Pharisees were ever prone to do, xvi. 15.

who is my neighbour?] He wants his moral duties to be labelled and defined with the Talmudic precision to which ceremonial duties had been reduced.

30. *A certain man*] Clearly, as the tenor of the Parable implies, a Jew.

went down from Jerusalem to Jericho] A rocky, dangerous gorge (Jos. *B. J.* IV. 8, § 3), haunted by marauding Bedawin, and known as 'the bloody way' (*Adommim*, Jerome, *De loc. Hebr.* and on Jer. iii. 2). The "went down" is strictly accurate, for the road descends very rapidly from Jerusalem to the Jordan valley. The distance is about 21 miles. For Jericho, see xix. 1.

thieves] Rather, "*robbers*," "*brigands*." Palestine was notorious for these plundering Arabs. Herod the Great had rendered real service to the country in extirpating them from their haunts, but they constantly sprung up again, and even the Romans could not effectually put them down (Jos. *Antt.* XX. 6, § 1; *B. J.* XI. 12, § 5). On this very road an English baronet—Sir Frederic Henniker—was stripped and murdered by Arab robbers in 1820. "He was probably thinking of the Parable of the Samaritan when the assassin's stroke laid him low," Porter's *Palestine*, I. 151.

wounded him] Rather, **laying blows on him**.

half dead] Some MSS. omit the τυγχάνοντα, 'chancing to be still alive.' So far as the robbers were concerned, it was a mere accident that any life was left in him.

31. *by chance*] Rather, **by coincidence**, i.e. at the same time. The word 'chance' (τύχη) does not occur in Scripture. The nearest approach to it is the participle τυχὸν in 1 Cor. xv. 37 (if τυγχάνοντα be

priest that way: and when he saw him, he passed by on the other side. And likewise a Levite, when he was at the place, came and looked *on him*, and passed by on the other side. But a certain Samaritan, as he journeyed, came where he was: and when he saw him, he had compassion *on him*;

omitted in **vs. 30**). Chance, to the sacred writers, as to the most thoughtful of the Greeks, is 'the daughter of Forethought:' it is "God's unseen Providence, by men nicknamed Chance" (Fuller). "Many good opportunities work under things which seem fortuitous." Bengel.

a certain priest] His official duties at Jerusalem were over, and he was on his way back to his home in the priestly city of Jericho. Perhaps the uselessness of his external service is implied. In superstitious attention to the letter, he was wholly blind to the spirit, Deut. xxii. 1—4. See 1 John iii. 17. He was selfishly afraid of risk, trouble, and ceremonial defilement, and, since no one was there to know of his conduct, he was thus led to neglect the traditional kindness of Jews *towards their own countrymen* (Tac. *Hist.* v. 5, Juv. XIV. 103, 104), as well as the positive rules of the Law (Deut. xxii. 4) and the Prophets (Is. lviii. 7).

that way] Rather, **on that road**. It is emphatically mentioned, because there was *another* road to Jericho which was safer, and therefore more frequently used.

32. *came and looked on him*] This vivid touch shews us the cold curiosity of the Levite, which was even baser than the dainty neglect of the Priest. Perhaps the Priest had been aware that a Levite was behind him, and left the trouble to him: and perhaps the Levite said to himself that *he* need not do what the priest had not thought fit to do. By choosing Gal. iii. 16—23 as the Epistle to be read with this Gospel (13th Sunday after Trinity) the Church indicates her view that this Parable implies the failure of the Jewish Priesthood and Law to pity or remove the misery and sin of man.

33. *a certain Samaritan*] A Samaritan is thus selected for high eulogy—though the Samaritans had so ignominiously rejected Jesus (ix. 53).

as he journeyed] He was not 'coming down' as the Priest and Levite were from the Holy City and the Temple, but from the unauthorised worship of alien Gerizim.

had compassion on him] Thereby shewing himself, in spite of his heresy and ignorance, a better man than the orthodox Priest and Levite; and all the more so because he was an 'alien' (see on xvii. 18), and "the Jews have no dealings with the Samaritans" (John iv. 9), and this very wounded man would, under other circumstances, have shrunk from the touch of the Samaritan as from pollution. Yet this 'Cuthaean' —this 'worshipper of the pigeon'—this man of a race which was accused of misleading the Jews by false fire-signals, and of defiling the Temple with human bones—whose testimony would not have been admitted in a Jewish court of law—with whom no Jew would so much

34 and went to *him*, and bound up his wounds, pouring in oil and wine, and set him on his own beast, and brought him to
35 an inn, and took care of him. And on the morrow when he departed, he took out two pence, and gave *them* to the host, and said unto him, Take care of him; and whatsoever thou
36 spendest more, when I come again, I will repay thee. Which now of these three, thinkest thou, was neighbour unto him
37 that fell among the thieves? And he said, He that shewed mercy on him. Then said Jesus unto him, Go, and do thou likewise.

as eat (Jos. *Antt.* xx. 6, § 1, xviii. 2, § 2; *B. J.* ii. 12, § 3)—shews a spontaneous and perfect pity of which neither Priest nor Levite had been remotely capable. The fact that the Jews had applied to our Lord Himself the opprobrious name of "Samaritan" (John viii. 48) is one of the indications that a deeper meaning lies under the beautiful obvious significance of the Parable.

34. *pouring in oil and wine*] The ordinary remedies of the day. Is. i. 6; Mk. vi. 13; Jas. v. 14. See Excursus VII.

set him on his own beast] The word implies the labour of 'lifting him up,' and then the good Samaritan *walked* by his side.

brought him to an inn] *Pandocheion*. See on ii. 7. There the word is *kataluma*, a mere khan or caravanserai. Perhaps this inn was at Bahurim. In this and the next verse a word or two suffices to shew the Samaritan's sympathy, helpfulness, self-denial, generosity, and perseverance in kindliness.

35. *took out*] Literally, "*throwing out*" of his girdle.

two pence] i.e. two *denarii*; enough to pay for the man for some days. The Parable lends itself to the broader meaning which sees the state of mankind wounded by evil passions and spiritual enemies; left unhelped by systems of sacrifice and ceremonial (Gal. iii. 21); pitied and redeemed by Christ (Is. lxi. 1), and left to be provided for until His return by spiritual ministrations in the Church. But to see in the "two pence" any specific allusion to the Old and New Testaments, or to 'the two sacraments,' is to push to extravagance the elaboration of details.

to the host] The word occurs here only in the N.T., and the fact that in the Talmud the *Greek* word for 'an inn with a host' is adopted, seems to shew that the institution had come in with Greek customs. In earlier and simpler days the open hospitality of the East excluded the necessity for anything but ordinary khans.

37. *He that shewed mercy on him*] Rather, **the pity**. By this poor periphrasis the lawyer avoids the shock to his own prejudices, which would have been involved in the hated word, 'the Samaritan.' "He will not name the Samaritan by name, the haughty hypocrite." Luther.

Go, and do thou likewise] The general lesson is that of the Sermon on the Mount, Matt. v. 44.

38—42. *The Sisters of Bethany.*

38 Now it came to pass, as they went, that he entered into a certain village: and a certain woman named Martha received him into her house. 39 And she had a sister called Mary, which also sat at Jesus' feet, and heard his word. 40 But Martha was cumbered about much serving, and came to *him*, and said, Lord, dost thou not care that my sister hath left me to serve alone? bid her therefore that she help me.

38—42. THE SISTERS OF BETHANY.

38. *into a certain village*] Undoubtedly Bethany, John xi. 1. Both this and the expression "*a certain woman*" are obvious traces of a tendency to reticence about the family of Bethany which we find in the Synoptists (Matt. xxvi. 6; Mk. xiv. 3). It was doubtless due to the danger which the family incurred from their residing in the close vicinity of Jerusalem, and therefore of "the Jews," as St John always calls the Pharisees, Priests, and ruling classes who opposed our Lord. By the time that St John wrote, after the destruction of Jerusalem, all need for such reticence was over. It is mere matter of conjecture whether 'Simon the leper' was the father of the family, or whether Martha was his widow; nor can Lazarus be identified with the gentle and holy Rabbi Eliezer of the Talmud. This narrative clearly belongs to a period just before the winter Feast of Dedication, because Bethany is close to Jerusalem. Its introduction at this point by St Luke (who alone preserves it, see Introd. p. 27) is due to subjective grouping, and probably to the question "what shall I do?" vs. 25.

39. *which also sat at Jesus' feet*] The "also" shews that Mary too, in her way, was no less anxious to give Jesus a fitting reception. Here, in one or two lines, we have a most clear sketch of the contrasted character of the two sisters, far too subtly and indirectly accordant with what we learn of them in St John to be due to anything but the harmony of truth. This is one of the incidents in which the Evangelist shews such consummate psychologic skill and insight that he is enabled by a few touches to set before us the most distinct types of character.

and heard his word] Rather, **was listening to His discourse.**

40. *cumbered about much serving*] The word for "cumbered" literally means 'was being dragged in different directions,' i.e. was *distracted* (1 Cor. vii. 35). She was anxious to give her Lord a most hospitable reception, and was vexed at the contemplative humility which she regarded as slothfulness.

came to him] Rather, **but suddenly coming up** (xx. 1; Acts xxiii. 27). We see in this inimitable touch the little petulant outburst of jealousy in the loving, busy matron, as she hurried in with the words, "Why is Mary sitting there *doing nothing?*"

left me] The Greek word means 'left me alone in the middle of my work' to come and listen to you.

bid her therefore that she help me] We almost seem to hear the

41 And Jesus answered and said unto her, Martha, Martha,
42 thou art careful and troubled about many *things:* but one *thing* is needful: and Mary hath chosen *that* good part, which shall not be taken away from her.

CH. XI. 1—13. *The Lord's Prayer. Persistence in Prayer.*

11 And it came to pass *that,* as he was praying in a certain

undertone of 'It is no use for *me* to tell her.' Doubtless, had she been less 'fretted' (τυρβάζῃ), she would have felt that to leave her alone and withdraw into the background while this eager hospitality was going on was the kindest and most unselfish thing which Mary could do.

41. *Martha, Martha*] The repeated name adds additional tenderness to the rebuke, as in xxii. 31; Acts ix. 4.

thou art careful and troubled about many things] "I would have you without carefulness," 1 Cor. vii. 32; Matt. vi. 25. The words literally mean, 'Thou art anxious and bustling.' Her inward solicitude was shewing itself in outward hastiness.

but one thing is needful] The context should sufficiently have excluded the very bald, commonplace, and unspiritual meaning which has been attached to this verse,—that only *one dish* was *requisite*. Clearly the lesson conveyed is the same as in Matt. vi. 33, xvi. 26, even if our Lord's *first* reference was the lower one. The various readings 'but there is need of few things,' or 'of few things or of one' (ℵ, B, various versions, &c.) seem to have risen from the notion that even for the simplest meal more than one dish would be required. This, however, is not the case in the simple meals of the East.

that good part] Rather, portion (as of a banquet, Gen. xliii. 34, LXX.; John vi. 27) or inheritance, Ps. lxxiii. 26. ἥτις = *quippe quae*. The *nature* of the portion is *such that,* &c.

which shall not be taken away from her] To speak of such theological questions as 'indefectible grace' here, is to use the narrative otherwise than was intended. The general meaning is that of Phil. i. 6; 1 Pet. i. 5. It has been usual with Roman Catholic and other writers to see in Martha the type of the active, and in Mary of the contemplative disposition, and to exalt one above the other. This is not the point of the narrative, for both may and ought to be combined as in St Paul and in St John. The gentle reproof to Martha is aimed *not* at her hospitable activity, but at the 'fret and fuss,' the absence of repose and calm, by which it was accompanied; and above all, at the tendency to reprobate and interfere with excellence of a different kind.

CH. XI. 1—13. THE LORD'S PRAYER. PERSISTENCE IN PRAYER.

1. *And it came to pass that, as he was praying in a certain place*] The better order is 'as he was in a certain place, praying.' The extreme

place, when he ceased, one of his disciples said unto him, Lord, teach us to pray, as John also taught his disciples. And he said unto them, When ye pray, say,

Our Father which art in heaven, Hallowed be thy name.

vagueness of these expressions shews that St Luke did not possess a more definite note of place or of time; but if we carefully compare the parallel passages of Matt. xii. 22—50, xv. 1—20; Mk. iii. 22—35, it becomes probable that this and the next chapter are entirely occupied with the incidents and teachings of one great day of open and decisive rupture with the Pharisees shortly before our Lord ceased to work in Galilee, and that they do not belong to the period of the journey through Peraea. This great day of conflict was marked (1) by the prayer of Jesus and His teaching the disciples what and how to pray; (2) by the healing of the dumb demoniac; (3) by the invitation to the Pharisee's house, the deadly dispute which the Pharisees there originated, and the terrible denunciation consequently evoked; (4) by the sudden gathering of a multitude, and the discourses and incidents of chapter xii. For further details and elucidations I must refer to the *Life of Christ*.

praying] Probably at early dawn, and in the *standing* attitude adopted by Orientals.

as John also taught his disciples] The form of prayer taught by St John has perished. *Terrena caelestibus cedunt*, Tert.; John iii. 30. It was common for Jewish Rabbis to deliver such forms to their disciples, and a comparison of them (e.g. of "the 18 Benedictions") with the Lord's Prayer is deeply instructive.

2. *When ye pray, say, Our Father*] 'The Lord's Prayer' had already been enshrined in the Sermon on the Mount (Matt. vi. 9—13), but it was now more formally delivered as a model. Various parallels for the different petitions of the Lord's Prayer have been adduced from the Talmud, nor would there be anything strange in our Lord thus stamping with His sanction whatever was holiest in the petitions which His countrymen had learnt from the Spirit of God. But note that (1) the parallels are only to *some* of the clauses (e.g. not to the fourth and fifth); (2) they are mostly distant and imperfect; (3) there can be no certainty as to their priority, since even the *earliest* portion of the Talmud (the Mishna) was not committed to writing till the second century after Christ; (4) they are nowhere blended into one incomparable petition. The transcendent beauty and value of the lessons in the Lord's Prayer arise from (i) *the tone of holy confidence*:—it teaches us to approach God as our Father (Rom. viii. 15), in love as well as holy fear; (ii) its absolute unselfishness:—it is offered *in the plural*, not for ourselves only, but for all the brotherhood of man; (iii) *its entire spirituality*:—of its seven petitions, one only is for any earthly boon, and that only for the simplest; (iv) its *brevity* and absence of all vain repetitions (Eccl. v. 2); (v) *its simplicity*, which requires not learning, but only holiness and sincerity for its universal comprehension. For these reasons the Fathers called it 'the Epitome of the Gospel' and 'the pearl of prayers.'

Thy kingdom come. Thy will be done, as in heaven, so in
3 earth. Give us day by day our daily bread. And forgive
4 us our sins; for we also forgive every one *that is* indebted
to us. And lead us not into temptation; but deliver us
from evil.

which art in heaven] Ps. xi. 4. This clause, as well as "Thy will be done, as in heaven, so also upon the earth," and "but deliver us from the evil," are wanting in some MSS., and may be additions from the text of St Matthew. If so, the prayer would stand thus: *O Father! Hallowed be Thy name. Thy kingdom come. Give us day by day our daily bread. And forgive us our sins for we also forgive every one that is indebted to us. And lead us not into temptation.*

Hallowed be thy name] i.e. sanctified, treated as holy. "*Holy, Holy, Holy*" is the worship of the Seraphim (Is. vi. 3). The '*name*' of God is used for all the attributes of His Being.

Thy kingdom come] There seems to have been an early gloss, or reading, "Thy Holy Spirit come upon us, and purify us" (mentioned by St Gregory of Nazianzus).

Thy will be done] This was the one rule of the life of Christ, John v. 30, vi. 38.

as in heaven] "Bless the Lord, ye his angels, that excel in strength, that do his commandments, hearkening unto the voice of his word," Ps. ciii. 20.

3. *Give us day by day our daily bread*] The prayer (i) acknowledges that we are indebted to God for our *simplest* boons; (ii) asks them for *all*; (iii) asks them only day by day; and (iv) asks for no more, Prov. xxx. 8; John vi. 27. St Luke's version brings out the continuity of the gift (Be giving day by day); St Matthew's its immediate need (Give to-day). The word rendered 'daily' is *epiousion*, of which the meaning is much disputed. For a brief discussion of its meaning, see Excursus IV.; but that this prayer is *primarily* a prayer for needful earthly sustenance has been rightly understood by the heart of mankind.

our sins] 'Trespasses' is not in our Bible, but comes, as Dr Plumptre notices, from Tyndale's version. St Matthew uses the word 'debts,' which is *implied* in the following words of St Luke: "For indeed we ourselves *remit* to every one who *oweth* to us." Unforgiving, unforgiven, Matt. xviii. 34, 35; Eph. iv. 32; Col. iii. 13. The absence of any mention here of the Atonement or of Justification is, as Godet observes, a striking proof of the authenticity of the prayer. The variations are, further, a striking proof that the Gospels are entirely independent of each other.

lead us not into temptation] God permits us to be tempted (John xvii. 15; Rev. iii. 10), but we only yield to our temptations when we are "drawn away of our own lust and enticed" (James i. 14). But the temptations which God permits us are only *human* (ἀνθρώπινος), not abnormal or irresistible temptations, and with each temptation He makes also *the way to escape* (καὶ τὴν ἔκβασιν, 1 Cor. x. 13). We pray, therefore, that

And he said unto them, Which of you shall have a friend, 5 and shall go unto him at midnight, and say unto him, Friend, lend me three loaves; for a friend of mine in *his* 6 journey is come to me, and I have nothing to set before him: and he from within shall answer and say, Trouble me 7 not: the door is now shut, and my children are with me in bed; I cannot rise and give thee? I say unto you, Though 8 he will not rise and give him, because *he* is his friend, yet because of his importunity he will rise and give him as many

we may not be tried above what we are able, and this is defined by the following words: Our prayer is, Let not the tempting opportunity meet the too susceptible disposition. If the temptation comes, quench the desire; if the desire, spare us the temptation. See on iv. 2.

but deliver us from evil] Rather, **from the Evil One**. The article, it is true, would not necessitate this translation, but it seems to be rendered probable by the analogy of similar prayers among the Jews. The last three clauses for daily bread, forgiveness, and deliverance, cover the past, present, and future. "All the tones of the human breast which go from earth to heaven, sound here in their key-notes" (Stier). There is no doxology added. Even in St Matthew it is (almost certainly) a liturgical addition, and no real part of the Lord's Prayer.

5. *shall go unto him at midnight*] Orientals often travel at night to avoid the heat. Although idle repetitions in prayer are forbidden, persistency and importunity in prayer—wrestling with God, and not letting Him go until He has blessed us—are here distinctly taught (see xviii. 1—8), as they also were in the acted parable of our Lord's apparent repulse of the Syro-Phoenician woman, Matt. xv. 27, 28.

6. *I have nothing to set before him*] Even the deepest poverty was not held to excuse any lack of the primary Eastern virtue of hospitality. Allegorically we may see here the unsatisfied hunger of the soul, which wakens in the midnight of a sinful life.

7. *Trouble me not*] The answer is rough and discouraging. He does not say 'friend.' His phrase implies irritation. The details are of course not to be pressed. The parable is merely an illustration *à fortiori*.

is now shut] Literally, "*has been already shut*" with the implication 'shut for the night, and I do not mean to open it.'

I cannot] Only a modified form for 'I will not.'

8. *yet because of his importunity*] Literally, "*shamelessness*" (Vulg. *improbitas*), 'impudence,' i.e. unblushing persistence, which is not however *selfish*, but that he may do his duty towards another. Is. lxii. 6, "Ye that make mention of the Lord, keep not silence, and give him no rest, till he establish, &c." Abraham furnishes a grand example of this fearless persistence (Gen. xviii. 23—33). Archbishop Trench quotes the beautiful passage in Dante's *Paradiso:*

> "Regnum caelorum violenzia pate
> Da caldo amore e da viva speranza, &c."

9 as he needeth. And I say unto you, Ask, and it shall be given you; seek, and ye shall find; knock, and it shall be
10 opened unto you. For every one that asketh receiveth; and he that seeketh findeth; and to him that knocketh it shall
11 be opened. *If* a son shall ask bread of any of you that is a father, will he give him a stone? or if *he ask* a fish, will he
12 for a fish give him a serpent? Or if he shall ask an egg, will
13 he offer him a scorpion? If ye then, being evil, know how to give good gifts unto your children: how much more shall *your* heavenly Father give the Holy Spirit to them that ask him?

14—26 *The dumb Devil. Blasphemy of the Pharisees.*

14 And he was casting out a devil, and it was dumb. And it came to pass, when the devil was gone out, the dumb
15 spake; and the people wondered. But some of them said,

he will rise] not merely half raise himself, or get out of bed, as in vs. 7 (*anastas*), but '*thoroughly aroused* and getting up' (*egertheis*).
as many as he needeth] More than the three which he had asked for the bare supply of his wants.

9. *Ask, and it shall be given you*] Matt. vii. 7—11, xxi. 22; Mk. xi. 24; John xvi. 23. Doubtless these teachings were repeated more than once to different listeners. God's *unwillingness* to grant is never more than in semblance, and for our good (Matt. xv. 28; Gen. xxxii. 28).

13. *give the Holy Spirit*] St Matthew has the much more general expression "good things" (vii. 11). The Good Father will give to His children neither what is deadly, nor what is unfit for food.

14—26. THE DUMB DEVIL. BLASPHEMY OF THE PHARISEES.

14. *it was dumb*] i.e., of course, the possession by the spirit caused dumbness in the man. If this incident be the same as in Matt. xii. 22, the wretched sufferer seems to have been both dumb, and blind, and mad.

the people wondered] Exorcisms, and attempted exorcisms (Acts xix. 14), were indeed common among the Jews (see on ix. 49. Gfrörer, *Jahrh. d. Heils*, I. 413), but apparently only in the simplest cases, and *never* when the possession was complicated with blindness and dumbness.

15. *some of them said*] We learn from St Matthew (xii. 24) that this notable suggestion emanated from "the Pharisees" and, as St Mark (iii. 20) adds, from "the scribes *which came from* Jerusalem," i.e. the spies who had been expressly sent down by the ruling hierarchs to dog the footsteps of Jesus, and counteract His influence. The explanation

He casteth out devils through Beelzebub the chief of the devils. And other, tempting *him*, sought of him a sign from heaven. But he, knowing their thoughts, said unto them, Every kingdom divided against itself is brought to desolation; and a house *divided* against a house falleth. If Satan also be divided against himself, how shall his kingdom stand? because ye say that I cast out devils through Beelzebub. And if I by Beelzebub cast out devils, by whom do your sons cast *them* out? therefore shall they be your judges.

was too ingeniously wicked and cleverly plausible to come from the more unsophisticated Pharisees of Galilee.

Beelzebub] The name and reading are involved in obscurity. In 2 Kings i. 3 we are told that Beelzebub was god of Ekron; and the LXX. and Josephus (*Antt.* IX. 2, § 1) understood the name to mean 'lord *of flies*.' He may have been a god worshipped to avert the plagues of flies on the low sea-coast like Zeus *Apomuios* (Averter of flies) and Apollo *Ipuktonos* (Slayer of vermin). But others interpret the name to mean 'lord of dung,' and regard it as one of the insulting nicknames which the Jews from a literal rendering of Ex. xxiii. 13 felt bound to apply to heathen deities. In this place perhaps Beelzebub is the true reading, and that means 'lord of the (celestial) habitation,' i.e. prince of the air, Eph. ii. 3. Possibly the οἰκοδεσπότης of Matt. x. 25 is an allusion to this meaning. In any case the charge was the same as that in the Talmud that Jesus wrought His miracles (which the Jews did not pretend to deny) by *magic*.

16. *tempting him*] i.e. wanting to *try* Him, to put Him to the test. The temptation was precisely analogous to that in the wilderness—a temptation to put forth a self-willed or arbitrary exertion of power for personal ends, see iv. 3, 12.

a sign from heaven] They persuaded the people that His miracles were wrought by unhallowed arts, and that such arts would be impossible in a sign from heaven like the Pillar of Cloud, the Fire of Elijah, &c. But our Lord refused their demand. Miracles were not to be granted to insolent unbelief; nor were they of the nature of mere prodigies. Besides it was His will to win conviction, not to enforce acceptance. This seems therefore to have been the one weapon of attack which the Pharisees found most effective against Him,—the one which most deeply wounded His spirit and finally drove Him away from the plain of Gennesareth (Mk. viii. 11, 12).

17. *their thoughts*] Rather, **their machinations**.

Every kingdom divided against itself, &c.] More briefly and graphically in St Mark "How can Satan cast out Satan?"

and a house divided against a house falleth] The words may also be rendered 'and (in that case) house falleth against house.'

19. *by whom do your sons cast them out?*] The "pupils of the wise" might be called the 'sons of the Pharisees' just as the youths in the

20 But if I with the finger of God cast out devils, no doubt the
21 kingdom of God is come upon you. When a strong *man*
22 armed keepeth his palace, his goods are in peace: but when a stronger than he shall come upon *him*, and overcome him, he taketh *from him* all his armour wherein he trusted, and
23 divideth his spoils. He that is not with me is against me:
24 and he that gathereth not with me scattereth. When the unclean spirit is gone out of a man, he walketh through dry places, seeking rest; and finding none, he saith, I will
25 return unto my house whence I came out. And when he
26 cometh, he findeth *it* swept and garnished. Then goeth he, and taketh to *him* seven other spirits more wicked than himself; and they enter in, and dwell there: and the last *state* of that man is worse than the first.

Prophetic schools were called 'sons of the Prophets.' The reality of the Jewish exorcisms is not here necessarily admitted (Acts xix. 13). It was enough that the admitted pretensions to such powers among the Pharisees justified this incontrovertible *argumentum ad hominem*.

20. *with the finger of God*] "Then the magicians said unto Pharaoh, This is the finger of God," Ex. viii. 19.

is come upon you] The word and tense imply suddenness and surprise.

21. *When a strong man armed keepeth his palace*] The same metaphor is used of the Christian opposing Satan, as here of Satan opposing Christ, Eph. vi. 13. The world is here Satan's palace (John xii. 31, xvi. 11) and men his possessions (2 Tim. ii. 26).

22. *a stronger than he*] Christ, "having spoiled principalities and powers, made a shew of them openly, triumphing over them in His Cross," Col. ii. 15.

his spoils] The spoils which Satan had won from the race of man.—Bengel.

23. *He that is not with me is against me*] Neutrality is sometimes opposition, see on ix. 51 (where we have the complementary truth).

24. *he walketh through dry places*] The unclean spirits were thought to frequent ruins (*Berachôth*, f. 3a) and the waterless desert, Tobit viii. 3; see on iv. 1.

seeking rest] Not to be in possession of some human soul, is (for them) to be in torment.

25. *swept and garnished*] The mischief and danger of the emancipated soul is that it is not occupied by a New Indweller. It has not tested the expulsive power of holy affections. It is 'lying idle' ($\sigma\chi o\lambda\dot{a}\zeta o\nu\tau a$, Matt. xii. 44), i.e. 'to let.'

26. *seven other spirits*] Compare viii. 2, 30. The number is figurative of complete wickedness and (in this case) final possession.

the last state of that man is worse than the first] The most striking comment on the verse is furnished by Heb. vi. 4—6, x. 26—29,

27—32. *The Womanly Exclamation. The Peril of Privileges abused.*

And it came to pass, as he spake these *things*, a certain 27 woman of the company lift up her voice, and said unto him, Blessed *is* the womb that bare thee, and the paps which thou hast sucked. But he said, Yea rather, blessed *are* they 28 that hear the word of God, and keep it.

And when the people were gathered thick together, he 29 began to say, This is an evil generation: they seek a sign; and there shall no sign be given it, but the sign of Jonas the prophet. For as Jonas was a sign unto the Ninevites, so 30 shall also the Son of man be to this generation. *The* queen 31 of the south shall rise up in the judgment with the men of

and especially 2 Pet. ii. 20, 21. "Sin no more," said our Lord to the Impotent Man, "*lest a worse* thing come unto thee," John v. 14. The Parable was an allegory, not only of the awful peril of relapse after partial conversion, but also of the History of the Jews. The demon of idolatry had been expelled by the Exile; 'but had returned in the sevenfold virulence of letter-worship, formalism, exclusiveness, ambition, greed, hypocrisy and hate;' and on the testimony of Josephus himself the Jews of that age were so bad that their destruction seemed an inevitable retribution.

27—32. THE WOMANLY EXCLAMATION. THE PERIL OF PRIVILEGES ABUSED.

27. *Blessed is the womb that bare thee*] See i. 28, 48. "How many women have blessed the Holy Virgin, and desired to be such a mother as she was! What hinders them? Christ has made for us a wide way to this happiness, and not only women, but men may tread it—the way of obedience; this it is which makes such a mother, and not the throes of parturition." St Chrysostom. It is a curious undesigned coincidence that (as we see from Matt. xii. 46) the Virgin had just arrived upon the scene.

28. *Yea rather, blessed are they that hear the word of God, and keep it*] See viii. 21. Our Lord invariably and systematically discouraged all attempt to exalt the merely human relationship or intercourse with Him, and taught that the Presence of His Spirit was to be a nearer and more blessed thing than knowledge of Him "after the flesh" (John xiv. 16; 2 Cor. v. 16).

and keep it] Hearing *without* obedience was more than valueless, Matt. vii. 21, xii. 50; Rom. ii. 13.

29. *were gathered*] Rather, **were densely gathering.**

30. *a sign unto the Ninevites*] Jonah i. 17.

31. *The queen of the south*] The queen of Sheba (1 K. x. 1—13; 2 Chron. ix. 1—12). The visit of this queen of Yemen made a deep

216　　　　　　ST LUKE, XI.　　　　[vv. 32—36.

this generation, and condemn them: for she came from the utmost parts of the earth to hear the wisdom of Solomon; 32 and behold, a greater than Solomon *is* here. *The* men of Nineveh shall rise up in the judgment with this generation, and shall condemn it: for they repented at the preaching of Jonas; and behold, a greater than Jonas *is* here.

33—36. *The Inward Light.*

33 No *man*, when he hath lighted a candle, putteth *it* in a secret place, neither under a bushel, but on a candlestick, 34 that they which come in may see the light. The light of the body is the eye: therefore when thine eye is single, thy whole body also is full of light; but when *thine eye* is evil, 35 thy body also *is* full of darkness. Take heed therefore that 36 the light which is in thee be not darkness. If thy whole

---

impression on Oriental imagination, and is found in the Koran (xxvii., &c.) "dilated with nonsense and encumbered with fables."

to hear the wisdom of Solomon] and also "to prove him with hard questions," 1 Kings x. 1.

a greater] Rather, **something more**.

32. *they repented at the preaching of Jonas*] "The people of Nineveh believed God, and proclaimed a fast, and put on sackcloth, from the greatest of them even to the least of them," Jonah iii. 5.

33—36.　THE INWARD LIGHT.

33. *in a secret place*] Rather, **in a crypt or cellar**.

under a bushel] Rather, 'under **the** bushel'; i.e. the one in use in the house; and similarly 'the candlestick,' or rather, 'lamp-stand.'

that they which come in may see the light] The comparison is the same as in Matt. v. 14, Mk. iv. 21; but the application in the next verse is different. The light is here used for inward enlightenment, not to be seen afar.

34. *The light of the body is the eye*] Rather, **The eye is the candle of the body**, since the word is the same as in the last verse.

therefore when thine eye is single] The eye in this clause is the 'inward eye' of conscience; the 'illuminated eye of the heart,' Eph. i. 17, 18. 'Single,' i.e. unsophisticated; in its normal condition.

when thine eye is evil] The 'evil eye' is especially one of *hate*, Rom. xii. 8; Ecclus. xiv. 8—10. The inward eye should be *spiritual*; when it becomes carnal the man can no longer see that which is only spiritually discerned, and he takes God's wisdom for foolishness, 1 Cor. ii. 14, iii. 18—20.

35. *that the light which is in thee be not darkness*] It becomes so when we are 'wise in our own conceit' (Prov. xvi. 12) which makes us

body therefore *be* full of light, having no part dark, the whole shall be full of light, as when the bright shining of a candle doth give thee light.

37—54. *The Invitation of the Pharisee and the open Rupture.*

And as *he* spake, a certain Pharisee besought him to dine with him: and he went in, and sat down to meat. And when the Pharisee saw *it*, he marvelled that he had not first washed before dinner. And the Lord said unto him, Now

think a way right when it is the way of death (Prov. xvi. 25), and makes us call evil good, and good evil, put darkness for light, and light for darkness, Is. v. 20, 21.

36. *doth give thee light*] The spirit of man is the candle of the Lord. "God will light my candle," Ps. xviii. 28. "Thy word is a lantern unto my feet." In these words we catch an echo of those thoughts on the diffusiveness and divineness of light which are so fully developed in St John's Gospel (viii. 12).

"Wär nicht das Auge sonnenhaft,
Wie könnten wir das Licht erblicken?"
GOETHE.

37—54. THE INVITATION OF THE PHARISEE AND THE OPEN RUPTURE.

37. *besought*] Rather, **asked**.

to dine with him] The meal was not dinner (*deipnon*), but an earlier, lighter, and more informal meal (*ariston*).

he went in, and sat down to meat] The words imply that immediately He entered He sat down to table. The meal was merely some slight refreshment in the middle of the day, and probably our Lord was both suffering from hunger after His long hours of teaching, and was also anxious to save time.

38. *he marvelled that he had not first washed*] Literally, "*bathed*." No washing was necessary to eat a few dates or figs. At the chief meal of the day, where all dipped their hands into a common dish, it was a matter of cleanliness. But the duty of cleanliness had been turned by the Oral Law into a rigorous set of cumbersome and needless ablutions, each performed with certain elaborate methods and gesticulations (Mk. vii. 2, 3) which had nothing to do with religion or even with the Levitical Law, but only with Pharisaic tradition and the Oral Law. In the *Shulchan Aruk*, a book of Jewish Ritual, no less than twenty-six prayers are given with which their washings are accompanied. But all this was not only devoid of divine sanction, but had become superstitious, tyrannous, and futile. The Pharisee 'marvelled' because he and his party tried to enforce the Oral Law on the people as even more sacred than the Written Law. The subject of ablutions was one which

do ye Pharisees make clean the outside of the cup and the platter; but your inward part is full of ravening and wicked-
40 ness. *Ye* fools, did not he that made that *which is* without
41 make that *which is* within also? But rather give alms *of* such *things* as *you* have; and behold, all *things* are clean
42 unto you. But woe unto you, Pharisees! for ye tithe mint

caused several of these disputes with Christ, Matt. xv. 19, 20. The Rabbi Akhibha would have preferred to die of thirst rather than neglect his ablutions, and the Talmud thought that a demon—called Schibta—sat on unwashen hands. Our Lord astonished the conventionalism of these religious teachers and their followers by shewing that what truly defiles a man is that which cometh *from within*—from the heart.

39. *Now do ye Pharisees*] Doubtless other circumstances besides the mere supercilious astonishment of the Pharisee led to the vehement rebuke. The eightfold woe in Matt. xxiii. is fuller than here. Jesus denounces their frivolous scrupulosity (39), combined with gross insincerity (41), their pride (43), and their corruption (44).

make clean the outside of the cup and the platter] Mk. vii. 4, "washing of cups, and pots, brazen vessels, and of tables." On one occasion the Sadducees seeing them busied in washing the great Golden Candelabrum sneeringly observed that they would wash the Sun itself if they could get the opportunity.

your inward part is full of ravening and wickedness] i.e. of *greed*, and of the *depravity* which causes it. A slightly different turn of expression is given in Matt. xxiii. 25, 26. See Excursus VI. on Sects of the Jews; and compare these denunciations with those delivered in the Temple on the last day (Tuesday in Passion Week) of the Lord's public ministry, Matt. xxiii. 25—28. The early Christian heretics reflected the character of these Pharisees in their mixture of elaborate profession with real godlessness, Tit. i. 15, 16.

40. *that which is within also*] See Mk. vii. 18, 19, which contains our Lord's distinctest utterance in abrogation of the Levitic Law—"This He said...*making all meats clean*."

41. *give alms*] See xii. 33, xvi. 14; Matt. vi. 3. Almsgiving is only mentioned as one typical form of Charity, which was in that state of society preeminently necessary. Indeed 'alms' is the same word as *eleemosunē*, which involves the idea of Mercy. The general lesson—that God does *not* care for ceremonies, in themselves, and only cares for them at all when they are accompanied by sincere goodness—is again and again taught in Scripture. 1 Sam. xv. 22; Is. lviii. 6—8; Mic. vi. 8; Dan. iv. 27; Jas. iv. 8.

of such things as you have] Perhaps, "*as for that which is within you, give alms.*" But the entire meaning of the clause is much disputed. Some explain it, Give as alms '*the contents*' of cup and platter, and then they will be *all* clean without washing. 'It is Love which purifies, not lustrations.'

42. *ye tithe mint and rue*] Deut. xiv. 22. In the Talmud there are

and rue and all *manner of* herbs, and pass over judgment and the love of God: these ought *ye* to have done, and not to leave the other undone.

43 Woe unto you, Pharisees! for ye love the uppermost seats in the synagogues, and greetings in the markets.

44 Woe unto you, scribes and Pharisees, hypocrites! for ye are as graves which appear not, and the men that walk over *them* are not aware *of them*.

45 Then answered one of the lawyers, and said unto him, Master, thus saying thou reproachest us also. And he said,

elaborate discussions whether in tithing the seeds of potherbs one ought also to tithe the stalk, &c.

pass over judgment and the love of God] Because the love of God is best shewn by love to men, and the Pharisees were filled with immoral contempt for those whom they regarded as less learned or less attentive to scrupulosities than themselves. The Pharisees still exist as a party among Eastern Jews, and are called *Perushim*. So bad is their character that the bitterest term of reproach in Jerusalem is 'You are a *Porish!*' How little they have changed from their character, as Christ depicted it, may be seen from the testimony of a Jewish writer. "They proudly separate themselves from the rest of their co-religionists......*Fanatical, bigoted, intolerant, quarrelsome, and in truth irreligious*, with them the outward observance of the ceremonial law is everything; the moral law little binding, *morality itself of no importance*" (See Frankl., *Jews in the East*, II. 27).

43. *uppermost seats*] These were places in the synagogue in a conspicuous semicircle facing the congregation, and round the *bema* of the reader, xiv. 7—11; Matt. xxiii. 6.

greetings in the markets] in which they addressed one another by extravagant titles, and required from their followers an exaggerated reverence.

44. *hypocrites*] The first meaning of the word is 'actors.'

as graves which appear not] Any contact with sepulchres involved Levitical uncleanness. Hence graves and tombs were whitewashed that none might touch them unawares. Perhaps our Lord was alluding to Tiberias, which when it was being built was discovered to be partly on the site of an old unsuspected cemetery; so that every true Jew regarded it as pollution to live there, and Herod could only get it inhabited partly by bribes, partly by threats. In St Matthew—several of whose particulars are differently applied—they are called '*whited sepulchres*,' fair outside, polluted within. Here they are *unsuspected graves*.

45. *one of the lawyers*] See on vii. 30, x. 25. This Scribe thought that Jesus could not possibly mean to reflect on the honoured class who copied and expounded the Law.

reproachest] Literally, "*insultest.*" There was a difference between

Woe unto you also, *ye* lawyers! for ye lade men *with* burdens grievous to be borne, and ye yourselves touch not the burdens with one of your fingers.

47 Woe unto you! for ye build the sepulchres of the pro-
48 phets, and your fathers killed them. Truly ye bear witness that ye allow the deeds of your fathers: for they indeed
49 killed them, and ye build their sepulchres. Therefore also said the wisdom of God, I will send them prophets and apostles, and *some* of them they shall slay and persecute:
50 that the blood of all the prophets, which was shed from the foundation of the world, may be required of this generation;
51 from the blood of Abel unto the blood of Zacharias, which

Pharisees and lawyers; the position of the latter involved more culture and distinction. They were the 'divines,' the 'theologians' of that day. Hence the man's reproach. 'Lawyer' and 'Scribe' seem to be more or less convertible terms (vs. 52, 53; Matt. xxiii. 13). Jesus here charges them with tyrannical insincerity (46), persecuting rancour (47—51), and theological arrogance and exclusiveness (52).

46. *burdens grievous to be borne*] These burdens of the Oral Law became yearly more and more grievous, till they were enshrined in the boundless pedantry of ceremonialism which fills the Talmud. But even at this period they were an intolerable yoke (Acts xv. 10), and the lawyers had deserved the Woe pronounced by Isaiah on them "that decree unrighteous decrees, and write grievousness which they have prescribed," Is. x. 1. "Gradus: digito uno attingere, digitis tangere, digito movere, manu tollere, humero imponere. Hoc cogebant populum; illud ipsi refugiebant." Bengel.

47. *your fathers killed them*] This is holy sarcasm. They boasted that they would *not* have done as their fathers had done to the Prophets (Matt. xxiii. 30), yet they rejected John, the greatest of the Prophets, and crucified the Just One, Acts vii. 51, 52.

48. *bear witness...allow*] We find the same two words used of St Paul in Acts vii. 58, viii. 1. Allow means 'approve after trial,' and is derived from *allaudare*. "The Lord *alloweth* the righteous," Ps. xi. 6 (Prayer-Book Version).

49. *the wisdom of God*] There is an allusion to 2 Chr. xxiv. 20—22 (comp. xxxvi. 14—21), but as the exact passage nowhere occurs in the O. T. some suppose that our Lord quotes (1) from a *lost book* called 'The Wisdom of God' (Ewald, Bleek, &c.); or (2) from previous words of His own; or (3) from the Gospel of St Matthew (see Matt. xxiii. 34); or (4) from the Book of Proverbs (i. 20—31). It is a general paraphrase of the *tenor* of several O. T. passages.

some of them they shall slay and persecute] See on vi. 23.

51. *unto the blood of Zacharias*] His murder by Joash is described in 2 Chr. xxiv. 20, 21, and also filled a large place in Jewish

perished between the altar and the temple: verily I say unto you, It shall be required of this generation.

52 Woe unto you, lawyers! for ye have taken away the key of knowledge: ye entered not in yourselves, and them that were entering in ye hindered.

53 And as he said these *things* unto them, the scribes and the Pharisees began to urge *him* vehemently, and to provoke him to speak of many *things:* laying wait for him, and seek- 54 ing to catch something out of his mouth, that they might accuse him.

---

legends. The words "the son of Barachiah," in Matt. xxiii. 35, are probably an erroneous gloss which has crept from the margin into the text. The murdered Zacharias was the son of the High Priest Jehoiada; the Prophet Zechariah was a son of Barachiah, but died, so far as we know, a natural death; and the Zechariah son of Barachiah, who was murdered by the Zealots, did not die till forty years later than this time. The allusions are all the more striking from the direct references to retribution in these two instances, and from the fact that they are drawn from the first and last historical books of the O. T. (Gen. iv. 10; 2 Chr. xxiv. 22).

52. *ye have taken away the key of knowledge*] A key was the regular symbol of the function of a scribe (Matt. xiii. 52, xvi. 19), which was to open the meaning of the Holy Books. The crime charged against them here is their selfish exclusiveness. They declared that only rich and well-born people could be scribes; and while they refused to teach the mass of the people, they at the same time called them 'accursed' for not knowing the law, and spoke about them in terms of the bitterest scorn and detestation. "Ye have caused many to stumble at the law," Mal. ii. 8.

53. *And as he said these things*] Rather (with ℵ, B, C, L), **when He had gone forth from thence.** The Pharisees in their anger followed Him.

to urge him vehemently] It is clear from this and the following verse that the Pharisee's feast had been a base plot to entrap Jesus. None of His disciples seem to have been with Him, nor any of the people; and after these stern rebukes the Pharisees surrounded Him in a most threatening and irritating manner, in "a scene of violence perhaps unique in the Life of Jesus.

to provoke him to speak of many things] Perhaps "to cross-question Him," or **to catch words from His mouth about very many things.** The *classical* sense of the verb *apostomatizein* is 'to dictate.'

54. *to catch*] Literally, "*to hunt.*" They were members of a body of a sort of 'commission of enquiry' which had been sent from Jerusalem for this express purpose, Mk. xii. 13.

CH. XII. 1—12. *The Duty of bold Sincerity and Trust in God.*

12 In the mean time, when there were gathered together an innumerable multitude of people, insomuch that *they* trode one upon another, he began to say unto his disciples first *of all*, Beware ye of the leaven of the Pharisees, which is 2 hypocrisy. For there is nothing covered, that shall not be 3 revealed; neither hid, that shall not be known. Therefore whatsoever ye have spoken in darkness shall be heard in the light; and *that* which ye have spoken in the ear in 4 closets shall be proclaimed upon the housetops. And I say

CH. XII. 1—12. THE DUTY OF BOLD SINCERITY AND TRUST IN GOD.

1. *when there were gathered together an innumerable multitude of people*] Rather, **when the myriads of the multitude had suddenly assembled.** It is evident that the noise of this disgraceful attack on our Lord had been heard. This scene was as it were the watershed of our Lord's ministry in Galilee. At this period He had excited intense opposition among the religious authorities, but was still beloved and revered by the people. They therefore flocked together for His protection, and their arrival hushed the unseemly and hostile vehemence of the Pharisees.

they trode one upon another] Literally, "*trod one another down.*"

he began to say] The words seem to imply a specially solemn and important discourse.

unto his disciples first of all, Beware] Rather, **to His disciples, Beware first of all of**, &c.

the leaven of the Pharisees] See for comment Matt. xvi. 12; Mark viii. 15.

2. *For there is nothing covered, that shall not be revealed*] Rather, **But** (unless with ℵ we omit the δὲ altogether). This whole discourse, in its vividness and compression, and the apparent abruptness of some of its causal connexions, indicates the tumult of emotion through which our Lord had been passing in the last trying scene. The line of thought is—'Hypocrisy aims at *concealment;* but, &c.' Hypocrisy is not only sinful but *useless.*

covered—revealed] Literally, "*veiled over—unveiled.*" You will be made *responsible* for any part of my teaching which you conceal or keep back.

3. *whatsoever ye have spoken in darkness*] The *application* of the similar language in Matt. x. 26, Mark iv. 22, is different. See viii. 17.

in closets] Literally, "*in the treasuries* or *storehouses,*" i.e. in closed, secret places.

unto you my friends, Be not afraid of them that kill the body, and after that have no more that *they* can do. But I 5 will *fore*warn you whom you shall fear: Fear him, which after *he* hath killed hath power to cast into hell; yea, I say

upon the housetops] i.e. in the most public places of resort, so as to be heard in the streets below.

4. *my friends*] John xv. 14, 15, "Henceforth I call you not servants but *friends*." The term comes the more naturally and pathetically because Jesus had just been in the thick of enemies.

Be not afraid of] μὴ φοβηθῆτε ἀπό, i.e. afraid of anything which can come *from* them. This construction is only found in the LXX. and N.T., and is a Hebraism (v. Schleusner s. v.). For similar thoughts see Jer. i. 8; Is. li. 12, 13.

after that have no more that they can do] The same truth was an encouragement to the partially illuminated fortitude of Stoicism. Hence it constantly occurs in the Manual of Epictetus.

5. *Fear him, which after he hath killed*] Many commentators have understood this expression of the Devil, and one of the Fathers goes so far as to say that it is the only passage in the Bible in which we cannot be certain whether God or Satan is intended. There can, however, be no doubt that the reference is to God. If "fear" ever meant 'be on your guard against,' the other view might be tenable, but there is no instance of such a meaning, and we are bidden to defy and resist the Devil, but *never* to fear him; nor are we ever told that *he* has any power to cast into Gehenna.

to cast into hell] Rather, **into Gehenna**. It is a deep misfortune that our English Version has made no consistent difference of rendering between 'the place of the dead,' 'the intermediate state between death and resurrection' (*Hades, Sheol*), and Gehenna, which is sometimes metaphorically used (as here) for a place of *punishment* after death. Gehenna was a purely Hebrew word, and corresponded primarily to purely Hebrew conceptions. Our Lord (if He spoke Greek) did not attempt to represent it by any analogous, but imperfectly equivalent, Greek term like Tartarus (see 2 Pet. ii. 4), and certainly the Apostles and Evangelists did not. They simply *transliterated* the Hebrew term (גֵי הִנֹּם, *Gê Hinnom*, Valley of Hinnom) into Greek letters. It is surely a plain positive duty to follow so clear an example, and not to render Gehenna by English terms which *cannot* connote *exactly* the same conceptions. The Valley of Hinnom, or of the Sons of Hinnom (Josh. xv. 8, xviii. 16; 2 K. xxiii. 10; Jer. vii. 31), was a pleasant valley outside Jerusalem, which had first been rendered infamous by Moloch worship; then defiled by Josiah with corpses; and lastly kept from putrefaction by large fires to consume the corpses and prevent pestilence. Milton describes it with his usual learned accuracy:

"First Moloch, horrid king, besmeared with blood
 Of human sacrifice, and parents' tears;
 Though for the noise of drums and timbrels loud

6 unto you, Fear him. Are not five sparrows sold for two far-
7 things, and not one of them is forgotten before God? But
even the *very* hairs of your head are all numbered. Fear
not therefore: ye are of more value than many sparrows.
8 Also I say unto you, Whosoever shall confess me before
men, him shall the Son of man also confess before the
9 angels of God: but he that denieth me before men shall be
10 denied before the angels of God. And whosoever shall
speak a word against the Son of man, it shall be forgiven
him: but unto him that blasphemeth against the Holy
11 Ghost it shall not be forgiven. And when they bring you

> Their children's cries unheard that passed through fire
> To his grim idol......
>   and made his grove
> The pleasant Valley of Hinnom, Tophet thence
> And black Gehenna called, the type of Hell."
>   *Par. Lost,* I. 392.

Tophet is derived from the word *Toph* 'a drum' (compare τύπτω, *dub, thump,* &c.).

6. *Are not five sparrows sold for two farthings*] St Matthew says '*two* sparrows for *one* farthing.' The little birds were sold in the markets strung together, or on skewers. The varying expressions of St Matthew and St Luke lead us to the interesting fact that if five were bought *one was thrown in,* which still more forcibly proves how insignificant was the value of the sparrows; yet even that unvalued odd one was not "forgotten before God." The word for "farthings" is *assaria;* St Mark uses κοδράντης (*quadrans*), xii. 42.

7. *even the very hairs of your head*] See xxi. 18; Acts xxvii. 34; and in the O. T. 1 Sam. xiv. 45; 1 K. i. 52.

8. *before the angels of God*] Compare ix. 26. "Before my Father which is in heaven," Matt. x. 32.

10. *it shall be forgiven him*] Thus our Lord prayed even for His murderers. This large rich promise is even further amplified in Matt. xii. 31. It is the sign of a dispensation different from that of Moses, Lev. xxiv. 16.

unto him that blasphemeth against the Holy Ghost] The other passages in which mention is made of this awful 'unpardonable sin' and of the "blasphemy against the Holy Ghost" are Matt. xii. 31, 32; Mark iii. 29, 30; 1 John v. 16. The latter sin is expressly declared to be closely connected with the attributing of Christ's miracles to Beelzebul. On the exact nature of the 'unpardonable sin' theologians have speculated in vain, and all that we can see is that it must be the most flagrant degree of sin against the fullest light and knowledge.

it shall not be forgiven] St Matthew adds "neither in this age (or 'this dispensation'), nor in the age to come (the 'future dispensation,' i.e. the dispensation of the Messianic kingdom)." The two terms 'this

unto the synagogues, and *unto* magistrates, and powers, take ye no thought how or what *thing* ye shall answer, or what ye shall say: for the Holy Ghost shall teach you in 12 the same hour what ye ought to say.

13—21. *Egotism rebuked. The Rich Fool.*

And one of the company said unto him, Master, speak to 13 my brother, that *he* divide the inheritance with me. And 14 he said unto him, Man, who made me a judge or a divider over you? And he said unto them, Take heed, and beware 15 of covetousness: for a man's life consisteth not in the

aeon' and 'the future aeon' are of *constant* occurrence in Rabbinic literature. The passage—if it means more than 'in either dispensation'—proves, as St Augustine says, that some would be forgiven if not in this life yet in the next (*De Civ. Dei*, XXI. 24).

11. *unto the synagogues, and unto magistrates, and powers*] The 'synagogues' were the small Jewish tribunals of synagogue officials in every town, which had the power of inflicting scourging for minor religious offences. 'Magistrates' and 'powers' would be the superior authorities Jewish or Gentile.

take ye no thought] Rather, **be not anxiously careful.**

how or what thing] i.e. about either the manner and line, or the phraseology of your defence.

12. *the Holy Ghost shall teach you*] A similar promise had been given to Moses, Ex. iv. 12—15; see xxi. 15. For fulfilments of the promise, see Acts vi. 8, 10 (St Stephen); 2 Tim. iv. 17 (St Paul), &c.

13—21. EGOTISM REBUKED. THE RICH FOOL.

13. *Master, speak to my brother*] This was the most foolish and unwarrantable interpellation ever made to our Lord. The few words at once reveal to us an egotist incapable of caring for anything but his own selfishness.

that he divide the inheritance with me] Deut. xxi. 15—17.

14. *Man*] The word is sternly repressive. Comp. Rom. ii. 1.

who made me a judge] "My kingdom is not of this world," John xviii. 36.

or a divider] i.e. umpire, arbitrator. There is an evident allusion to Ex. ii. 14.

15. *beware of covetousness*] The better reading is "of all covetousness," i.e. not only beware of avarice, but also of selfish possession. Both the O. and N. T. abound with repetitions of this warning. Balaam, Achan, Gehazi are awful examples of this sin in the O. T.; Judas Iscariot, the Pharisees and Ananias in the New. See 1 Tim. vi. 10—17.

a man's life consisteth not] i.e. a man's *true* life—his *zoē*: his earthly natural life—his *bios*, is supported by what he *has*, but his *zoē* is what

16 abundance of the *things* which he possesseth. And he spake a parable unto them, saying, The ground of a certain rich
17 man brought forth plentifully: and he thought within himself, saying, What shall I do, because I have no room where
18 to bestow my fruits? And he said, This will I do: I will pull down my barns, and build greater; and there will I
19 bestow all my fruits and my goods. And I will say to my soul, Soul, thou hast much goods laid up for many years;

he *is*. Such phrases as that a man 'is *worth*' so many thousands a year, revealing the current of worldly thought, shew how much this warning is needed. The order of words in this paragraph is curious. It is literally, "*For not in any man's abundance is his life* (derived) *from his possessions*," or (as De Wette takes it) "is his life *a part of* his possessions." The English Version well represents the sense. Comp. Sen. *ad Helv*. IX. 9, "Corporis exigua desideria sunt.... Quicquid extra concupiscitur, vitiis non usibus laboratur."

16. *The ground*] Rather, **The estate**. In this parable (peculiar to St Luke) our Lord evidently referred mentally to the story of Nabal, whose name means 'Fool' or 'Churl' (1 Sam. xxv.). Observe that his riches, like those of Nabal, were acquired, not by fraud or oppression, but in the most innocent way. His crime was his greedy and callous selfishness. He cared not for generous use, but for self-admiring acquisition. Being "a fool" his "prosperity destroyed him." Prov. i. 32.

17. *What shall I do*] "He that loveth silver shall not be satisfied with silver, nor he that loveth abundance with increase," Eccl. v. 10.

my fruits] So "*my* barns," "*my* fruits and *my* goods," and "*my* soul." This touch is evidently intended and is most vividly natural. So Nabal says, "Shall I then take *my* bread, and *my* water, and *my* flesh that I have killed for *my* shearers," &c., 1 Sam. xxv. 11. So

"'Their child.' '*Our* child!' '*Our* heiress!' '*Ours!*' for still
Like echoes from beyond a hollow, came
Her sicklier iteration." *Aylmer's Field*.

18. *my barns*] Rather, **storehouses** (*apothēkas*—not only for corn). He never thought of the admonition of the Son of Sirach, "Shut up *alms* in thy storehouses," Ecclus. xxix. 12.

my fruits] Not the same word as before. Rather, **my produce**.

my goods] Such 'good things' as he was alone capable of recognising, xvi. 25. And "*all my goods*," with no mention of the poor.

19. *I will say to my soul, Soul*] "What folly! Had thy soul been a sty, what else couldst thou have promised to it? Art thou so bestial, so ignorant of the soul's goods, that thou pledgest it the foods of the flesh? And dost thou convey to thy *soul*, the things which the draught receiveth?" St Basil.

for many years] "Boast not thyself of to morrow," Prov. xxvii. 1.

take thine ease, eat, drink, *and* be merry. But God said 20 unto him, *Thou* fool, this night thy soul shall be required of thee: then whose shall *those things* be, which thou hast provided? So *is* he that layeth up treasure for himself, and is 21 not rich towards God.

22—53. *Lessons of Trustfulness* (22—32), *Almsgiving* (33, 34), *and Faithful Watchfulness* (35—48). *The searching Effect of Christ's Work* (49—53).

And he said unto his disciples, Therefore I say unto you, 22 Take no thought for your life, what ye shall eat; neither

take thine ease, eat, drink, and be merry] More energetically in the four words of the original, **rest, eat, drink, enjoy.** His motive is the same as that of the selfish and cynical Epicureans, who say, "Let us eat and drink;" but the reason he assigns is different. They snatch pleasure, "for to morrow we die" (1 Cor. xv. 32); he because he hopes to be "happy" for "many years." For similar warnings see Jas. iv. 13—17, v. 1—3; Eccl. xi. 9.

20. *Thou fool*] Literally, "*Senseless!*" 1 Cor. xv. 36.

this night] Compare the death of Nabal, 1 Sam. xxv. 36.

thy soul shall be required of thee] Rather, **they demand thy soul of thee.** Who are 'they'? Some say God (Job xxvii. 8), or His death-angels (Job xxxiii. 22), or robbers whom they suppose to attack the rich man on the night that his wealth has flowed in. There is however no *definite* pronoun, the phrase is impersonal, as often in Hebrew.

then whose shall those things be] "He heapeth up riches and knoweth not who shall gather them," Ps. xxxix. 6, xlix. 16, 17; comp. lii. 7 and James iv. 13—15. St James seems to have been deeply impressed with this teaching.

21. *is not rich towards God*] Rather, **if he is not.** We are often taught elsewhere in Scripture in what way we can be rich toward God. Matt. vi. 19—21; 1 Tim. vi. 17—19; Jas. ii. 5. There is a close parallel to this passage in Ecclus. xi. 18, 19, "There is that waxeth rich by his wariness and pinching, and this is the portion of his reward. Likewise he saith, I have found rest, and now will eat continually of my goods, and yet he knoweth not what time shall come upon him, and that he must leave those things to others, and die." This would seem to shew that our Lord was not unfamiliar with some of the Apocryphal writings.

22—53. LESSONS OF TRUSTFULNESS (22—32), ALMSGIVING (33, 34), AND FAITHFUL WATCHFULNESS (35—48). THE SEARCHING EFFECT OF CHRIST'S WORK (49—53).

22. *Take no thought*] This rendering is *now* unfortunate, since it might be abused to encourage an *immoral* carelessness (1 Tim. v. 8).

23 for the body, what ye shall put on. The life is more than
24 meat, and the body *is more* than raiment. Consider the
ravens: for they neither sow nor reap; which neither have
storehouse nor barn; and God feedeth them: how much
25 more are ye better than the fowls? And which of you with
26 taking thought can add to his stature one cubit? If ye then
be not able *to do that thing which is* least, why take ye
27 thought for the rest? Consider the lilies how they grow:
they toil not, they spin not; and yet I say unto you, *that*
Solomon in all his glory was not arrayed like one of these.
28 If then God so clothe the grass, which is to day in the field,
and to morrow is cast into the oven; how much more *will*
29 *he clothe* you, O ye of little faith? And seek not ye what ye
shall eat, or what ye shall drink, neither be ye of doubtful
30 mind. For all these *things* do the nations of the world seek
after: and your Father knoweth that ye have need of these
31 *things*. But rather seek ye the kingdom of God; and all
32 these *things* shall be added unto you. Fear not, little flock;

But in the 17th century *thought* was used for *care* (1 Sam. ix. 5). See *The Bible Word-Book*, s.v. Rather, **Be not anxious about.** "Cast thy *burden* upon the Lord and He shall sustain thee," Ps. lv. 22; 1 Pet. v. 7.

23. *The life is more than meat*, &c.] and the spirit is more than either the body, or the natural life.

24. *the ravens*] More specific, and therefore more poetic, than "the fowls" in St Matthew. Perhaps there is a reference to Job xxxviii. 41; Ps. cxlv. 15.

25. *to his stature*] Some would here render the word ἡλικία, 'age' (comp. Ps. xxxix. 5); but 'stature' is probably right.

27. *the lilies*] The term is perfectly general. The scarlet anemones (*anemone coronaria*), or the 'Hulêh lilies' growing around may have given point to the lesson. (Thomson, *Land and Book*, p. 256.)

Solomon in all his glory] 1 K. iii. 13, x. 1—29, and for a splendid description of his progresses in the royal chariot Cant. iii. 6—11.

28. *the grass...in the field*] The common Scripture symbol for evanescence, Is. xl. 6; 1 Pet. i. 24; Jas. i. 10, 11.

is cast into the oven] In the absence of wood this is the usual method of heating ovens in the East.

29. *neither be ye of doubtful mind*] Literally, "Do not toss about like boats in the offing,"—a metaphor for *suspense*. Cicero says, "So I am in suspense (μετέωρος) and entangled in great perplexities." *Ad Att.* XV. 14.

30. *the nations of the world*] But you have not the same excuse that the heathen have for over-anxiety about transient needs.

for it is your Father's good pleasure to give you the kingdom. Sell that ye have, and give alms; provide yourselves 33 bags which wax not old, a treasure in the heavens that faileth not, where no thief approacheth, neither moth corrupteth. For where your treasure is, there will your heart be also. 34

Let your loins be girded about, and *your* lights burning; 35 and ye yourselves like unto men that wait for their lord, 36 when he will return from the wedding; that when *he* cometh and knocketh, they may open unto him immediately. Blessed 37 *are* those servants, whom the lord when he cometh shall find watching: verily I say unto you, that he shall gird himself, and make them to sit down to meat, and will come forth and serve them. And if he shall come in the second watch, 38 or come in the third watch, and find *them* so, blessed are

---

32. *little flock*] The address was primarily to disciples, vs. 1. For the metaphor, see Ps. xxiii. 1; Is. xl. 11; Matt. xxvi. 31; John x. 12—16.

the kingdom] How much more shall He give you *bread*.

33. *Sell that ye have*] This command was taken very literally by the early Church, Acts ii. 44, 45. Comp. xvi. 9; Matt. xix. 21.

35. *Let your loins be girded*] Without which active service is impossible in the loose flowing dress of the East (Ex. xii. 11; 1 K. xviii. 46); and spiritually, for the Christian amid worldly entanglements, 1 Pet. i. 13; Eph. vi. 14.

your lights burning] The germ of the Parable of the Ten Virgins, Matt. xxv. 1.

36. *when he will return from the wedding*] The word here used (*pote analusei*) is very rare, occurring only in Phil. i. 23; 2 Tim. iv. 6. Here there is a variation from the commoner metaphor of *going to* the wedding feast.

37. *he shall gird himself, and make them to sit down to meat*] Doubtless some of the Apostles must have recalled these words when Jesus washed their feet. To Roman readers the words would recall the customs of their Saturnalia when slaves were waited on by their masters.

38. *come in the second watch, or come in the third watch*] It is not clear, nor very important, whether St Luke here alludes to the *three* watches of the Jews and Greeks (Lam. ii. 19; Judg. vii. 19; Ex. xiv. 24) or to the *four* of the Romans (Jerome, Ep. CXL.). But it *is* very important to observe that often as our Lord bade His disciples to *be ready* for His return, He as often indicates that His return might be long delayed, Matt. xxv. 5—19. He always implied that He should come suddenly (xxi. 34—36; 1 Thess. v. 2—6; Rev. iii. 3) but not necessarily soon, vs. 46; 2 Pet. iii. 8, 9. "The *Parousia* does not come so quickly as impatience, nor yet so late as carelessness, supposes." Van Oosterzee.

39 those servants. And this know, that if the goodman of the house had known what hour the thief would come, he would have watched, and not have suffered his house to be broken 40 through. Be ye therefore ready also: for the Son of man cometh at an hour when ye think not.

41 Then Peter said unto him, Lord, speakest thou this para-42 ble unto us, or even to all? And the Lord said,

Who then is *that* faithful and wise steward, whom *his* lord shall make ruler over his household, to give *them their* por-43 tion of meat in due season? Blessed *is* that servant, whom 44 his lord when he cometh shall find so doing. Of a truth I say unto you, that he will make him ruler over all that he 45 hath. But and if that servant say in his heart, My lord delayeth his coming; and shall begin to beat the menservants and maidens, and to eat and drink, and to be 46 drunken; the lord of that servant will come in a day when he looketh not for *him*, and at an hour when he is not ware, and will cut him in sunder, and will appoint *him* his por-

39. *this know*] Rather, **this ye know**.
the goodman of the house] An archaic expression for the master of the house, the *paterfamilias*. It is said to be a corruption of the Saxon *gumman* 'a man,' *good wife* being formed from it by false analogy.
to be broken through] Literally, "*to be dug through*," the houses being often of mud.

41. *Then Peter said unto him*] Peter's intercourse with his Lord seems to have been peculiarly frank and fearless, in accordance with his character. In the immaturity of the disciples we may suppose that the blessing on the faithful servants mainly prompted his question. But if so the lesson of our Lord was by no means lost on him, 1 Pet. v. 3, and passim.

42. *Who then is that faithful and wise steward*] Our Lord, in the deeply instructive method which He often adopted, did not answer the question, but taught the only lesson which was needful for the questioner. St Paul perhaps refers to these words of Christ in 1 Cor. iv. 1, 2.
their portion of meat in due season] "Take heed therefore unto yourselves, and to all the flock over which the Holy Ghost hath made you overseers, *to feed the church of God*," Acts xx. 28.

44. *ruler over all that he hath*] See xxii. 29, 30.

45. *say in his heart, My lord delayeth his coming*] Eccl. viii. 11. It was not long before the temptation to use this language arose with fatal results, 2 Pet. iii. 8, 9.

46. *will cut him in sunder*] This was literally a punishment prevalent among some ancient nations, 2 Sam. xii. 31; 1 Chr. xx. 3; Dan. ii. 5; Herod. VII. 39. Comp. Hebr. xi. 37 (the legendary martyrdom of Isaiah)

tion with the unbelievers. And that servant, which knew his lord's will, and prepared not *himself*, neither did according to his will, shall be beaten with many *stripes*. But he that knew not, and did commit *things* worthy of stripes, shall be beaten with few *stripes*. For unto whomsoever much is given, of him shall be much required: and to whom *men* have committed much, of him they will ask the more.

I am come to send fire on the earth; and what will I, if it be already kindled? But I have a baptism to be baptized *with;* and how am I straitened till it be accomplished!

and Susannah 55—59. Hence Bengel says "Qui cor *divisum* habet, *dividetur*." But because of the following clause, which evidently refers to a *living* person, it is thought that *dichotomesei* must here be used in the sense of "shall *scourge*" (compare the next verse), although there is no other instance of such a sense.

with the unbelievers] Rather, **with the faithless.** (See vs. 42, and Matt. xxiv. 51.)

47. *shall be beaten with many stripes*] Exceptional privileges if rejected involve exceptional guilt and punishment, x. 13; Jas. iv. 17; 2 Pet. ii. 21.

48. *that knew not*] i.e. that knew not fully (Jon. iv. 11; 1 Tim. i. 13), for there is no such thing as absolute moral ignorance (Rom. i. 20, ii. 14, 15).

shall be beaten with few stripes] A most important passage as alone clearly stating that punishment shall be only proportional to sin, and that there shall be a righteous relation between the amount of the two. They who knew not will not of course be punished for any *involuntary* ignorance, but only for actual misdoing.

49. *I am come to send fire on the earth*] St John had preached "He shall baptize you with the Holy Ghost and with fire" and that "He should burn up the chaff with unquenchable fire." The metaphor is probably to be taken in all its meanings; fire as a spiritual baptism; the refining fire to purge gold from dross, and burn up the chaff of all evil in every imperfect character; and the fire of retributive justice. There is a remarkable 'unwritten saying' of Christ, "*He who is near me is near the fire*," which is preserved in Ignatius, Origen, and Didymus.

what will I, if it be already kindled?] Rather, **how I would that it had been already kindled!** (as in Ecclus. xxiii. 14). It may also be punctuated 'what will I? O that it were already kindled!' For the fire is salutary as well as retributive; it warms and purifies as well as consumes.

50. *a baptism to be baptized with*] Matt. xx. 22.

how am I straitened] i.e. How heavy is the burden that rests upon me; how vast are the obstacles through which I have to press onwards. It is the same spirit that spoke in "What thou doest, *do quickly*." The word is found in 2 Cor. v. 14; Phil. i. 23.

51 Suppose ye that I am come to give peace on earth? I tell
52 you, Nay; but rather division: for from henceforth there
shall be five in one house divided, three against two, and
53 two against three. The father shall be divided against the
son, and the son against the father; the mother
against the daughter, and the daughter against the
mother; the mother in law against her daughter in law,
and the daughter in law against her mother in
law.

54—59. *The Signs of the Times, and resultant Duty.*

54 And he said also to the people, When ye see a cloud rise
out of the west, straightway ye say, There cometh a shower;
55 and so it is. And when *ye see* the south wind blow, ye say,
56 There will be heat; and it cometh to pass. *Ye* hypocrites,

till it be accomplished] John xix. 28, 30.
51. *Suppose ye*] as they were far too much inclined to suppose, xix. 11.
that I am come to give peace on earth] It is only in His *ultimate* kingdom that Christ will be fully the Prince of Peace, as was understood even by Simeon, ii. 34, 35; see too John ix. 39.
Nay; but rather division] "I came not to send peace *but a sword*," Matt. x. 34. "Near me, near the sword" (unwritten saying of Christ). "There was a *division* among the people because of him," John vii. 43.
53. *The father shall be divided against the son*] The verse seems to be a distinct allusion to Mic. vii. 6. There is in the Greek a delicate change of phrase which can hardly be reproduced in English. It is 'father *against son*' (ἐφ' υἱῷ), where the preposition takes *the dative;* but in 'mother-in-law against her daughter-in-law' (ἐπὶ τὴν νύμφην αὐτῆς) the preposition takes the *accusative*;—perhaps to indicate the difference in the relationships, the one natural, the other legal.

54—59. THE SIGNS OF THE TIMES, AND RESULTANT DUTY.

54. *to the people*] Rather, **to the multitudes,** whom He now addresses, having finished the lessons which were most necessary for His timid and discouraged disciples.
a cloud] Rather, **the cloud,** comp. Matt. xvi. 2, 3.
rise out of the west] In Hebrew the same word is used for 'west' and 'sea.' A cloud rising from the Mediterranean indicated heavy rain, 1 K. xviii. 44, 45.
55. *heat*] Rather, **a Simoom** or scorching wind, because 'the South wind' in Palestine would blow from the desert.
56. *Ye hypocrites*] The insincerity consisted in the fact that though the signs of the Kingdom were equally plain they *would* not see them, and pretended not to see them. The Prophets had long ago pointed

ye can discern the face of the sky and of the earth; but how *is it that* ye do not discern this time? *Yea*, and why even of yourselves judge ye not what *is* right? When thou goest with thine adversary to the magistrate, *as thou art* in the way, give diligence that *thou* mayest be delivered from him; lest he hale thee to the judge, and the judge deliver thee to the officer, and the officer cast thee into prison. I tell thee, thou shalt not depart thence, till thou hast paid the very last mite.

them out. Among them were, miracles (Is. xxxv. 4—6); the political condition (Gen. xlix. 10); the preaching of the Baptist (Matt. iii.).

discern] Rather, **test** or **prove**.

57. *even of yourselves*] i.e. without the necessity for *my* thus pointing out to you facts which are so plain.

what is right!] what is your duty to do under circumstances so imminent.

58. *When thou goest*] Rather, **For as thou goest**. Our translators omitted the "for" probably because they could not see the connexion. It seems however to be this. 'For *this* is your clear duty,—to reconcile yourselves with God, as you would with one whom you had alienated, before the otherwise inevitable consequences ensue.'

with thine adversary] This is a parable. If you had wronged a man it would be obviously wise to avert the consequences of your wrongdoing before it became too late. Even so must you act towards God. To press the *details* is obviously false theology. "Theologia parabolica non est argumentativa." Here again St Matthew quotes the parable in a slightly different connexion (v. 25, 26) to teach that love and forgiveness to man are an indispensable condition of forgiveness from God.

give diligence] A curious Latinism, *da operam*.

to the officer] i.e. the jailor, literally the *exactor* (πράκτορι). "God is here shadowed forth as at once the adversary, the judge, and the officer; the first by His holiness, the second by His justice, the third by His power." Godet.

59. *till thou hast paid the very last mite*] Mite is *lepton* (*minutum*), the smallest of all coins, Mk. xii. 42. If it be asked, 'can this ever be paid?' the answer of course is, as far as *the parable* is concerned, 'it depends entirely on whether the debt be great or small.' As far as the *application* of the parable is concerned, the answer lies out of the contemplated horizon of the illustration, nor is there any formal answer to it. But if it be asserted that *no* man's debt to God, which he has incurred by his sins, however 'common to man,' can ever be paid by him, we are at least permitted to find hope in the thought that Christ has paid our debt for us (Matt. xx. 28; 1 Tim. ii. 6). The *general* lesson is that of which Scripture is full, "Seek ye the Lord while He may be found," Is. lv. 6; Ps. xxxii. 6; Heb. iv. 7.

CH. XIII. 1—9. *Accidents and Judgments. The Barren Fig-Tree.*

13 There were present at that season some that told him of the Galileans, whose blood Pilate had mingled with their 2 sacrifices. And Jesus answering said unto them, Suppose ye that these Galileans were sinners above all the Galileans,

CH. XIII. 1—9. ACCIDENTS AND JUDGMENTS. THE BARREN FIG-TREE.

1. *There were present at that season*] Rather, **There arrived at that very season.** The curious phrase seems to imply that they had come on purpose to announce this catastrophe. Hence some have supposed that they wished to kindle in the mind of Jesus as a Galilaean (xxiii. 5) a spirit of Messianic retribution (Jos. *Antt.* XVII. 9, § 3). But Christ's answer proves rather that they were connecting the sad death of these Galilaeans with their *imaginary crimes*. They were not calling His attention to them as *martyrs*, but as supposed victims of divine anger. Their report indicates a sort of pleasure in recounting the misfortunes of others (ἐπιχαιρεκακία).

of the Galileans] who regularly attended the Jewish feasts at Jerusalem, John iv. 45.

whose blood Pilate had mingled with their sacrifices] Probably at some Passover outbreak, on which the Roman soldiers had hurried down from Fort Antonia. This incident, which was peculiarly horrible to Jewish imaginations, often occurred during the turbulent administration of Pilate and the Romans; see on xxiii. 1; Acts xxi. 34. At one Passover, "during the sacrifices," 3000 Jews had been massacred "like victims," and "the Temple courts filled with dead bodies" (Jos. *Antt.* XVII. 9, § 3); and at another Passover, no less than 20000 (id. XX. 5, § 3; see also *B. J.* II. 5, V. 1). Early in his administration Pilate had sent disguised soldiers with daggers among the crowd (id. XVIII. 3, § 1; *B. J.* II. 9, § 4). The special incidents here alluded to were far too common to be specially recorded by Josephus; but in the fact that the victims in this instance were Galilaeans, we may perhaps see a reason for the "enmity" between Pilate and Herod Antipas (xxiii. 12).

2. *were sinners above all the Galileans*] The 'were' is literally, 'became,' i.e. 'stamped themselves as,' 'proved themselves to be.' We trace a similar mistaken 'supposition' in the question of the disciples about the blind man (John ix. 2). It was indeed deeply engrained in the Jewish mind, although the Book of Job had been expressly levelled at the uncharitable error of assuming that individual misfortune could *only* be the consequence of individual crime. Such is *sometimes* the case (Gen. xlii. 21; Judg. i. 7), but although all human sorrow has its ultimate cause in human sin, it is wrong to assume in *individual cases* the connexion of calamity with crime.

because they suffered such *things?* I tell you, Nay: but, except ye repent, ye shall all likewise perish. Or those eighteen, upon whom the tower in Siloam fell, and slew them, think ye that they were sinners above all men that dwelt in Jerusalem? I tell you, Nay: but except ye repent, ye shall all likewise perish. He spake also this parable; A certain *man* had a fig tree planted in his vineyard; and he came and sought fruit thereon, and found none. Then said he unto the dresser of his vineyard, Behold, *these* three

suffered such things] Rather, **have suffered these things.**

3. *except ye repent, ye shall all likewise perish*] The first meaning of the words was doubtless prophetic. As a matter of historic fact, the Jewish nation did not repent, and myriads of them in the siege of Jerusalem perished by a doom closely analogous to that of these unhappy Galilaeans (see Jos. *B. J.* V. 1, 3, 7, 11, 12, and especially 13; VI. passim, VII. 3). And since all life and all history are governed by the same divine laws, the warning is applicable to men and to nations at all periods.

4. *those eighteen, upon whom the tower in Siloam fell*] It is an ingenious, but of course uncertain conjecture of Ewald, that the death of these workmen was connected with the notion of retribution because they were engaged in building part of the aqueduct to the Pool of Siloam, for the construction of which Pilate had seized some of the sacred Corban-money (Mk. vii. 11; Jos. *B. J.* II. 9, § 4).

Siloam] The pool (John ix. 7; Is. viii. 6), near the village of *Silwân*, at the entrance of the Tyropoeon valley, which runs into the valley of Jehoshaphat between Sion and Moriah.

that they were sinners] Rather, **that they themselves were debtors.**

5. *ye shall all likewise perish*] The readings of the word 'likewise' vary between '*homoiōs*' and '*hōsautōs*;' but no distinct difference of meaning between the two words can be established, unless the latter be rather stronger, '*in the very same way.*' Here again the actual incidents of the siege of Jerusalem—the deaths of many under the falling ruins of the city (Jos. *B. J.* VI. 9, VII. 1)—are the directest comment on our Lord's words which yet bear the wider significance of the warning in Rom. ii. 1—11.

6. *a fig tree planted in his vineyard*] The corners of vineyards were often utilised in this way, as they still are (Tristram, *Nat. Hist. Bib.* p. 352). Here the Jewish nation is compared to the fig-tree (Hos. ix. 10; Jer. xxiv. 3), as in the *acted* parable of the Barren Fig-tree (Matt. xxi. 19); more often Israel is compared to the Vine or the Vineyard (Ps. lxxx. 8—11; Is. v. 2).

7. *unto the dresser of his vineyard*] It seems clear that in the truth which the parable shadows forth, Christ corresponds to the vine-dresser, and Jehovah to the owner (Is. v. 7). Some however prefer to see in the vine-dresser the Holy Spirit as Intercessor.

years I come seeking fruit on this fig tree, and find none: 8 cut it down; why cumbereth it the ground? And he answering said unto him, Lord, let it alone this year also, till 9 I shall dig about it, and dung *it*: and if it bear fruit, *well*: and if not, *then* after that thou shalt cut it down.

10—17. *The Sabbatical Hypocrite and the Suffering Woman.*

10 And he was teaching in one of the synagogues on the 11 sabbath. And behold, there was a woman which had a spirit of infirmity eighteen years, and was bowed together, and 12 could in no wise lift up *herself*. And when Jesus saw her, he called *her* to *him*, and said unto her, Woman, thou art 13 loosed from thy infirmity. And he laid *his* hands on her:

Behold, these three years] Many suppose an allusion to the length up to this time of our Lord's ministry. Others explain it of the periods of the Judges, Kings, and High Priests. It is very doubtful how far these lesser details—which are essential to the colouring of the parable—are intended to be pressed.

cut it down] *at once*—as the tense implies (Matt. iii. 10; John xv. 2). It was fulfilled in the rejection of Israel (Rom. xi. 22).

why cumbereth it the ground?] Rather, **why doth it also sterilise the ground?** i.e. it is *not only* useless, but positively mischievous by preventing other growth.

8. *Lord*] Rather, **Sir**, as far as the parable is concerned.

this year also] "The Lord...is longsuffering to usward, not willing that any should perish, but that all should come to repentance," 2 Pet. iii. 9. In "this year also" it is better to see generally the respite of forty years between the crucifixion and the destruction of Jerusalem, than merely the yet remaining period of our Lord's ministry. God never strikes without warning, because He desires to save.

9. *if it bear fruit, well*] The '*well*' is not in the original, the idiom being a common but striking *aposiopesis:* i.e. the conclusion of the sentence is left to the speaker's imagination. The phrase implies, If, as is at least possible, it bears fruit; but if not, as thou supposest, then, &c.

10—17. THE SABBATICAL HYPOCRITE AND THE SUFFERING WOMAN.

10. *in one of the synagogues*] The mention of synagogue-teaching becomes much rarer at this later stage of Christ's ministry. It is most probable that from some at least of the synagogues of Galilee he was excluded by the 'lesser excommunication.' See John xvi. 2.

11. *a spirit of infirmity*] Her curvature is thus directly attributed to Satanic agency. Job ii. 6, 7; Acts x. 38.

12. *thou art loosed*] Here, as elsewhere, the delicacy and force of

and immediately she was made straight, and glorified God. And the ruler of the synagogue answered with indignation, 14 because that Jesus had healed on the sabbath day, and said unto the people, There are six days in which *men* ought to work: in them therefore come and be healed, and not on the sabbath day. The Lord then answered him, and said, 15 *Thou* hypocrite, doth not each one of you on the sabbath loose his ox or *his* ass from the stall, and lead *him* away to watering? And ought not this *woman*, being a daughter of 16

the Greek tense implying the *immediateness* and the *permanence* of the cure can only be expressed in English by a periphrasis.

14. *ruler of the synagogue*] See viii. 41.

with indignation] The same strong word—implying a *personal* resentment—is used in Matt. xx. 24, xxvi. 8.

on the sabbath day] See on vi. 2.

in which men ought to work] Ex. xx. 9.

in them therefore come and be healed] As though the reception of divine grace were Sabbath-breaking toil! Few remarks of the opponents of our Lord were so transparently illogical and hypocritical as this. It was meanly indirect because it was *aimed at* Jesus, though the man is too much in awe to address it to Him, and the implied notion that *it was a crime to allow oneself to be healed* on the Sabbath day springs from an abyss of Pharisaic falsity which could hardly have been conceived. It was the underhand ignorance and insolence, as well as the gross insincerity of the remark, which called forth a reproof exceptionally severe.

15. *Thou hypocrite*] Rather (with the best uncials), **Hypocrites!** (א, A, B), classing the man with the whole sect to which he belonged, and whose shibboleths he used. They were hypocrites (i.e. they were acting a part) because they were disguising secret enmity under a pretence of sabbatical zeal.

on the sabbath loose his ox] Our Lord varied from time to time the arguments with which He abolished the fanatical formalism of the Pharisees respecting the Sabbath. Sometimes He appealed to His own inherent authority (John v. 17—47); sometimes to Scripture precedents (vi. 3—5); or to common sense and eternal principles (vi. 9). Here, as in xiv. 5, He uses an *argumentum ad hominem*, refuting their traditional rules by the selfish insincerity with which they applied them. They allowed men to unloose and lead to water their *cattle* on the sabbath, and thus to break their own Sabbatic rules to save themselves the trouble of providing water overnight, or, at the best, to abridge a few hours' thirst; was then this suffering *woman* not to be *touched*, not to be *spoken to*, to end 18 years of suffering?

16. *ought not*] Our Saviour gives him back his own word "*ought;*"— but the man's *ought* had been one of ceremonial obligation, and the *ought* of Jesus was founded on the divine necessity of love.

Abraham, whom Satan hath bound, lo *these* eighteen years, be loosed from this bond on the sabbath day? And when he had said these *things*, all his adversaries were ashamed: and all the people rejoiced for all the glorious *things* that were done by him.

18—21. *The Mustard Seed and the Leaven.*

Then said he, Unto what is the kingdom of God like? and whereunto shall I resemble it? It is like a grain of mustard seed, which a man took, and cast into his garden; and it grew, and waxed a great tree; and the fowls of the air lodged in the branches of it. And again he said, Whereunto shall I liken the kingdom of God? It is like leaven, which a woman took and hid in three measures of meal, till the whole was leavened.

being a daughter of Abraham] See xix. 9.
whom Satan hath bound] Compare 2 Cor. xii. 7.
17. *when he had said these things*] Rather, **while He was saying these things**.
were ashamed] See Is. xlv. 16 (LXX.).

18—21. THE MUSTARD SEED AND THE LEAVEN.

18. *Unto what is the kingdom of God like?*] For this solemn introduction see Is. xl. 18.

19. *waxed a great tree*] Omit *great* with ℵ, B, D, L, &c. The points of comparison are the sudden, secret growth, and the immense development of the kingdom of God. The mustard seed was colloquially spoken of by the Jews as 'the smallest of all seeds,' and it grew into a herbaceous plant, as tall as a horse and his rider (Thomson, *Land and Book*).

the fowls of the air lodged in the branches of it] The substantive corresponding to the verb '*lodged*' is found in ix. 58 ('nests,' rather **shelters**). Finches, and other small birds, throng the mustard beds to live on the seed (Tristram, *Nat. Hist. Bib.* 473).

21. *It is like leaven*] Except in this parable, *leaven* in Scripture (being connected with corruption and fermentation) is used as the type of sin. See xii. 1; Ex. xii. 1, 15—20; 1 Cor. v. 6—8; Gal. v. 9. Here, however, the only point considered is its rapid, and unseen, and effectual working.

in three measures of meal] The verisimilitude, simplicity, and vividness of the parables arise from the natural and specific details introduced into them. To press these into separate lessons only leads to arbitrary exegesis and false theology. Probably the 'three measures' are only mentioned because they are the ordinary amount which a

22—30. *The Narrow Door.*

And he went through the cities and villages, teaching, and journeying towards Jerusalem. Then said one unto him, Lord, are there few that be saved? And he said unto them, Strive to enter in at the strait gate: for many, I say unto

22

23

24

woman would leaven at one time. If any one likes to improve the detail by applying it to (1) body, soul, and spirit (1 Thess. v. 23); or (2) to Jews, Samaritans, and Galilaeans; or (3) to the three sons of Noah (!), as representing Semites, Aryans, and Allophylians,—it should be understood that these are pious applications, and interesting plays of fancy, not comments on our Lord's words.

till the whole was leavened] The whole heart of each man (2 Cor. x. 5), and the whole world (xxiv. 47).

22—30. THE NARROW DOOR.

22. *he went through the cities and villages*] Some see in this the starting-point of a separate journey. The expression is too vague on which to build. It may imply a fresh progress after some brief period of rest.

23. *are there few that be saved?*] The question may naturally have arisen from the last teachings respecting the small beginnings of the Kingdom of God. There is nothing to shew whether it was suggested by speculative curiosity, or by despondent pity. But without directly rebuking such questions, our Lord, as in other instances, strove to place the questioners in a wiser frame of mind (Deut. xxix. 29). The answer is a direct discouragement to all pitiless, and especially to all self-righteous, eschatologists. It is a solemn assertion of the necessity for earnest, personal endeavour. Thus to all idle attempts to define the certainties of the future, our Lord says, Consider the question with reference to *yourself*, not with reference to *others*. Look at it in the spirit of the publican, not in the spirit of the Pharisee. The wisdom and necessity of the answer may be seen from 2 Esdras viii., where the question is discussed, and where it is *assumed* that few only will be saved, "The most High hath made this world for many, but the world to come for few" (viii. 1). "There are many more of them which perish than of them which shall be saved; like as a wave is greater than a drop" (ix. 15, 16). "Let the multitude perish then" (id. 22). Part, at least, of the Book of Esdras is probably post-Christian.

that be saved] Literally, "*who are being saved*," i.e. who are in the way of salvation. The same word occurs in Acts ii. 47, and is the opposite to *apollumenoi*, 'those that are perishing,' 1 Cor. i. 18; 2 Cor. ii. 15.

24. *Strive*] The word implies the strong efforts of a contest. 1 Tim. vi. 12.

at the strait gate] Rather, **through the narrow door**; reading *thuras* (א, B, D, L) for *pules*. Matt. vii. 13.

25 you, will seek to enter in, and shall not be able. When once the master of the house is risen up, and hath shut to the door, and ye begin to stand without, and to knock at the door, saying, Lord, Lord, open unto us; and he shall answer 26 and say unto you, I know you not whence you are: then shall ye begin to say, We have eaten and drunk in thy presence, 27 and thou hast taught in our streets. But he shall say, I tell you, I know you not whence you are; depart from me, all 28 *ye* workers of iniquity. There shall be weeping and gnashing of teeth, when ye shall see Abraham, and Isaac, and Jacob, and all the prophets, in the kingdom of God, and 29 you yourselves thrust out. And they shall come from the east, and *from* the west, and from the north, and *from* the south, 30 and shall sit down in the kingdom of God. And behold,

will seek to enter in, and shall not be able] because they only *seek*, and do not *strive;* they wish for heaven, but will not abandon earth. Sometimes also because they seek too late (Prov. i. 28, 29; Is. i. 15; John vii. 34; Heb. xii. 17), but mainly because they seek to enter through other ways by which there is no entrance, since Christ is the only door (John x. 7, xiv. 6).

25. *to stand without, and to knock at the door*] Matt. xxv. 10. That the first application of the warning was to Jews who relied on their privileges appears from the fact that the excluded class are not poor sinners, but self-righteous Pharisees who claim entrance as their right.

Lord, Lord, open unto us] Matt. vii. 22, 23.

26. *then shall ye begin to say*] All excuse shall be cut short at once, iii. 8.

thou hast taught in our streets] Here again (see xiii. 28) we see how our Lord discouraged all notions of any privilege derived from fleshly privileges, or even proximity to Himself. Rom. ii. 17—20.

27. *I know you not......depart from me, all ye workers of iniquity*] 2 Tim. ii. 19, "The foundation of God standeth sure, having this seal, The Lord knoweth them that are His. And, Let every one that nameth the name of Christ depart from iniquity."

28. *weeping and gnashing of teeth*] The signs respectively of anguish and of rage (Acts vii. 54).

Abraham, and Isaac, and Jacob] Marcion, always anxious to disown the Old Testament, altered this into "all the just."

29. *they shall come from the east, and from the west*] There is an obvious reference to Is. xlix. 12, xlv. 6. Nothing more furiously excited the envy of the Jews than the free admission of the Gentiles to those privileges of the Kingdom of Heaven (Eph. iii. 6) which they rejected. Rom. xi. 1—36; Acts xiii. 44—52.

shall sit down] Rather, **shall recline at banquet**, xi. 37, xiv. 8, &c.; Mark vi. 39.

there are last which shall be first, and there are first which shall be last.

31—35. *A Message to Herod Antipas.*

The same day there came certain *of the* Pharisees, saying unto him, Get *thee* out, and depart hence: for Herod will kill thee. And he said unto them, Go ye, and tell that fox, 31 32

30. *And behold*] The phrase sometimes implies 'strange as you may think it.' It occurs 23 times in St Matthew, 16 in St Luke; but not in St Mark.

there are last which shall be first] Our Lord used this proverbial expression more than once. Matt. xix. 30. It had, besides its universal truthfulness, a special bearing on His own time. "The *publicans and the harlots* go into the Kingdom of God before you," Matt. xxi. 31. "The *Gentiles*, which followed not after righteousness, have attained to righteousness," Rom. ix. 30.

> "There above (on earth)
> How many hold themselves for mighty kings,
> Who here like swine shall wallow in the mire,
> Leaving behind them horrible dispraise."
> DANTE, *Inferno*.

31—35. A MESSAGE TO HEROD ANTIPAS.

31. *The same day*] Or, *In that very hour* (א, A, D, L, &c.).

Get thee out, and depart hence] These Pharisees were as eager as the Gadarenes to get rid of Jesus; but whether this was their sole motive or whether they further wished to separate Him from the multitudes who as yet protected His life, and to put Him in the power of the Sadducean hierarchy, is not clear. That any solicitude for His safety was purely hypocritical appears in the tone of our Lord's answer, which is yet far more merciful than that in which the prophet Amos had answered a similar message from an analogous quarter. Amos vii. 12—17.

for Herod will kill thee] Rather, **wills to kill thee**. The assertion was probably quite untrue. Herod had not even wished to kill John, but had done so with great reluctance, and had been deeply troubled in conscience ever since. He did indeed wish to *see* Christ, but it was with the very different desire of "seeing some miracle done by Him" (xxiii. 8).

32. *that fox*] Rather, **this she-fox**, as though Christ saw him actually present, or identified *his* fox-like nature with that which the Pharisees were now displaying. The fact that the word is feminine may be only due to its being *generic*. The fox was among the ancients, as well as among the moderns, the type of knavish craftiness and covert attack. This is the only word of unmitigated *contempt* (as distinguished from rebuke and scorn) recorded among the utterances of Christ, and it was

Behold, I cast out devils, and I do cures to day and to
33 morrow, and the third *day* I shall be perfected. Nevertheless I must walk to day, and to morrow, and the *day* following: for it cannot be that a prophet perish out of Jeru-
34 salem. O Jerusalem, Jerusalem, which killest the prophets, and stonest them that are sent unto thee; how often would I have gathered thy children together, as a hen *doth gather*

more than justified by the mingled tyranny and timidity, insolence and baseness of Herod Antipas—a half-Samaritan, half-Idumaean tetrarch, who, professing Judaism, lived in heathen practices, and governed by the grace of Caesar and the help of alien mercenaries; who had murdered the greatest of the Prophets to gratify a dancing wanton; and who was living at that moment in an adultery doubly-incestuous with a woman of whom he had treacherously robbed his brother while he was his guest.

to day and to morrow] It is probable that these expressions are general (as in Hos. vi. 2). They mean 'I shall stay in Herod's dominions with perfect security for a brief while longer till my work is done.' It must be remembered that Peraea was in the tetrarchate of Herod, so that this incident may have occurred during the slow and solemn progress towards Jerusalem.

the third day I shall be perfected] The word *teleioumai* has been variously rendered and explained. Bleek makes it mean 'I shall end' (my work in Galilee); Godet, '*I am being perfected*,' in the sense of 'I shall arrive at the destined end of my work;' Resch, '*I complete my work*' by one crowning miracle (John xi. 40—44). This solemn meaning best accords with other usages of the word, e.g. in the cry from the Cross *tetelestai*, 'It is finished' (John xix. 30). See too Heb. v. 9, xi. 40. *Teleiosis* became an ecclesiastical term for 'martyrdom.'

33. *I must walk*] Rather, **I must journey**; the same word as in vs. 31, "depart." It seems to imply, 'I will not leave Herod's dominion, but I shall journey on at my own leisure through them.'

it cannot be] i.e. there is a moral unfitness in the murder of a Prophet anywhere but in Jerusalem. The words are those of terrible irony; and yet, even amid the irony, the voice of the Speaker seemed to break with tears as He uttered the tender appeal of the next verse.

34. *O Jerusalem, Jerusalem*] The words were perhaps spoken again in the Great Denunciation of the Tuesday in Passion Week, Matt. xxiii. 37.

which killest the prophets] "It was full of judgment; righteousness lodged in it; but now *murderers*" (Is. i. 21). See xi. 47, xx. 14; Matt. xxiii. 34; 2 Esdr. i. 32, "I sent unto you my servants the prophets whom ye have taken and slain, and torn their bodies in pieces, whose blood I will require of your hands, saith the Lord."

how often] This, like other passages in the Synoptists, *implies* more frequent visits to Jerusalem than they actually record.

as a hen doth gather her brood under her wings] A metaphor still

her brood under *her* wings, and ye would not? Behold, your house is left unto you desolate: and verily I say unto you, Ye shall not see me, until *the time* come when ye shall say, Blessed *is* he that cometh in the name of the Lord.

CH. XIV. *The various Discourses of Jesus at a Banquet. "The Son of Man eating and drinking."*

1—6. *Sabbath healing of a Man with the Dropsy.*

And it came to pass, as he went into the house of one of 14

more tender and appealing than that of the eagle which "stirreth up her nest, fluttereth over her young, spreadeth abroad her wings, taketh them, beareth them on her wings" of Deut. xxxii. 11, 12.

ye would not] In contrast with the "would I" of vs. 34; it indicates "the sad privilege which man possesses of resisting the most serious influences of grace."

35. *Behold, your house is left unto you desolate*] The authenticity of the word 'desolate' is very doubtful, as it is omitted in ℵ, A, B, K, L, &c. The words therefore mean 'The Shechinah has vanished from you now (Ezek. x. 19, xi. 23). The house is now *yours*, not God's; and because yours therefore a cave of brigands.' If the word 'desolate' be genuine, it may allude to Dan. ix. 27 and "the desolating wing of abomination," as well as to other prophecies, Lev. xxvi. 31; Mic. iii. 12; Is. v. 5, 6. There is a remarkable parallel in 2 Esdras i. 30—33, "I gathered you together as a hen gathereth her chickens under her wings: but now, what shall I do unto you? I will cast you out from my face. ...Thus saith the Almighty Lord, your house is desolate, I will cast you out as the wind doth stubble."

Ye shall not see me] "Their senses are still blinded. The veil of the Talmud that hangs over their eyes is twice as heavy as the veil of Moses." Van Oosterzee.

until the time come when ye shall say] It is a most frivolous interpretation of these words to make them merely refer to the Hosannas of Palm Sunday (xix. 38) as though they meant, 'I shall not visit Jerusalem till the day of my humble triumph.' They clearly refer to the future and final penitence of Israel. The 'perfecting' of Jesus would be His death, and then once again He would return as "the Coming One." Hos. iii. 4, 5; Ps. cxviii. 26. Here, as in so many other stern passages of Scripture, in the Valley of Achor is opened a door of Hope, for the phrase implies 'till the time comes as come it will' (Zech. xii.; Rom. xi.).

CH. XIV. THE VARIOUS DISCOURSES OF JESUS AT A BANQUET. "THE SON OF MAN EATING AND DRINKING."

1—6. SABBATH HEALING OF A MAN WITH THE DROPSY.

1. *of one of the chief Pharisees*] Rather, **of the Rulers of the**

the chief Pharisees to eat bread on the sabbath day, that ²they watched him. And behold, there was a certain man ³before him, which had the dropsy. And Jesus answering

Pharisees. The rendering of our version gives the general sense but is inadmissible. It is perhaps due to the translators being aware that the Pharisees had (strictly speaking) no Rulers. There were no grades of distinction between Pharisees *as such*. But obviously the expression would be popularly used of a Pharisee who was an eminent Rabbi like Hillel or Shammai, or of one who was also a Sanhedrist.

to eat bread on the sabbath day] Sabbath entertainments of a luxurious and joyous character were the rule among the Jews, and were even regarded as a religious duty (Nehem. viii. 9—12). All the food was however cooked on the previous day (Ex. xvi. 23). That our Lord accepted the invitation, though He was well aware of the implacable hostility of the Pharisaic party towards Him, was due to His gracious spirit of forgiving friendliness; and to this we owe the beautiful picture of His discourse and bearing throughout the feast which this chapter preserves for us. Every incident and remark of the banquet was turned to good. We have first the scene in the house (1—6); then the manœuvres to secure precedence at the meal (7—11); then the lesson to the host about the choice of guests (12—14); then the Parable of the King's Feast suggested by the vapid exclamation of one of the company (15—24).

that they watched him] More emphatically in the original '*and they themselves were carefully watching Him*,' comp. vi. 7. The invitation in fact even more than those in vii. 36, xi. 37 was a mere plot;—part of that elaborate espionage, and malignant heresy-hunting (xi. 53, 54; xx. 20; Mk. xii. 13), which is the mark of a decadent religion, and which the Pharisees performed with exemplary diligence. The Pharisees regarded it as their great object in life to exalt their sacred books; had they never read so much as this? "the wicked *watcheth* the righteous and seeketh occasion to slay him," Ps. xxxvii. 32; "all that *watch for iniquity* are cut off, that *make a man an offender for a word, and lay a snare for him that reproveth in the gate*," Is. xxix. 20, 21.

2. *And behold, there was a certain man before him, which had the dropsy*] The verse represents with inimitable vividness the flash of recognition with which the Lord at once grasped the whole meaning of the scene. The dropsical man was not one of the guests; he stood *as though by accident* in the promiscuous throng which may always enter an Oriental house during a meal. But his presence was no accident. The dropsy is an unsightly, and was regarded as an incurable, disease. The Pharisaic plot had therefore been concocted with that complex astuteness which marks in other instances (xx. 19—38; John viii. 5) also the deadliness of their purpose. They argued (i) that He could not ignore the presence of a man conspicuously placed in front of Him; (ii) that perhaps He might fail in the cure of a disease exceptionally inveterate; (iii) that if He *did* heal the man on the Sabbath day there would be room for another charge before the synagogue or the

spake unto the lawyers and Pharisees, saying, Is it lawful to
heal on the sabbath day? And they held their peace. And 4
he took *him*, and healed him, and let *him* go; and answered 5
them, saying, Which of you shall have an ass or an ox fallen
into a pit, and will not straightway pull him out on the

Sanhedrin. One element which kindled our Lord's indignation against
the Pharisees for these crafty schemes was the way in which they made
a mere tool of human misery and human shame.

3. *answering spake unto the lawyers and Pharisees*] See on v. 22.
He took the initiative, and answered their unspoken thoughts.

Is it lawful to heal on the sabbath day?] We have already seen
(vi. 1—11, xiii. 11—17; comp. John v. 11, ix. 14), that these Sabbath
disputes lay at the very centre of the Pharisaic hatred to him, because
around the ordinance of the Sabbath they had concentrated the worst
puerilities and formalisms of the Oral Law; and because the Sabbath
had sunk from a religious ordinance into a national institution, the badge
of their exclusiveness and pride. But this perfectly simple and transparent question at once defeated their views. If they said 'It is not
lawful' they exposed themselves before the people to those varied and
overwhelming refutations which they had already undergone (see on
xiii. 15). If they said 'It is lawful' then *cecidit quaestio*, and their plot
had come to nothing.

4. *they held their peace*] It was the silence of a splenetic pride and
obstinacy which while *secretly* convinced determined to remain unconvinced. But such silence was His complete public justification.
If the contemplated miracle was unlawful why did not they—the great
religious authorities of Judaism—forbid it?

he took him] Rather, **taking hold of him**, i.e. laying his hand upon
him.

5. *an ass or an ox*] The unquestionable reading if we are to follow
the MSS. is 'a *son* or an ox.' The strangeness of the collocation (which
however may be taken to imply 'a son—nay even an ox') has led to
the conjectural emendation of *huios* into *oïs* 'a sheep' (whence the reading
probaton 'a sheep' in D) or *onos* 'an ass' which was suggested by
Deut. xxii. 4. When however it is a question between two readings
it is an almost invariable rule that *the more difficult* is to be preferred
as the more likely to have been tampered with. Further (i) Scripture
never has "ass and ox" but always "ox and ass;" and (ii) "son" is
a probable allusion to Ex. xxiii. 12, "thine ox and thine ass and the
son of thine handmaid shall rest on the sabbath," and (iii) the collocation
'son and ox' is actually found in some Rabbinic parallels. If it be
said that 'a son falling into a well' is an unusual incident, the answer
seems to be that it *may* be an allusion to the man's disease (dropsy = the
watery disease); also that pits and wells are so common and often so
unprotected in Palestine that the incident must have been less rare
than it is among us.

straightway pull him out] although the Sabbath labour thus involved
would be considerable. And why would they do this? because they

6 sabbath day? And they could not answer him again to these *things*.

7—11. *Humility; a Lesson for the Guests.*

7 And he put forth a parable to those which were bidden, when he marked how they chose out the chief rooms; say-
8 ing unto them, When thou art bidden of any *man* to a wed-

had been taught, and in their better mind distinctly felt, that mercy was above the ceremonial law (Deut. xxii. 4). An instance which had happened not *many* years before shews how completely they were blinding and stultifying their own better instincts in their Sabbath quibblings against our Lord. When Hillel—then a poor porter—had been found half-frozen under masses of snow in the window of the lecture-room of Shemaiah and Abtalion where he had hidden himself to profit by their wisdom because he had been unable to earn the small fee for entrance, they had rubbed and resuscitated him *though it was the Sabbath day*, and had said that he was one for whose sake it was well worth while to break the Sabbath.

6. *they could not answer him again to these things*] A fact which never makes any difference to the convictions of ignorant hatred and superstitious narrowness.

7—11. Humility; a Lesson for the Guests.

7. *he put forth a parable*] See on iv. 23.
to those which were bidden] to the invited guests, as distinguished from the onlookers.
they chose out] Rather, **they were picking out for themselves**. The selfish struggle for precedence as they were taking their places—a small ambition so universal that it even affected the Apostles (Mk. ix. 34)—gave Him the opportunity for a lesson of Humility.
the chief rooms] i.e. the chief places at table. These at each of the various *triclinia* would be those numbered 2, 5, and 8. The host usually sat at 9.

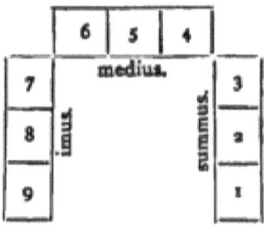

8. *to a wedding*] The term is used generally for any great feast; but perhaps our Lord here adopted it to make His lesson less immediately personal.

ding, sit not down in the highest room; lest a more honourable *man* than thou be bidden of him; and he that bade thee and him come and say to thee, Give this *man* place; and thou begin with shame to take the lowest room. But when thou art bidden, go and sit down in the lowest room; that when he that bade thee cometh, he may say unto thee, Friend, go up higher: then shalt thou have worship in the presence of them that sit at meat with thee. For whosoever exalteth himself shall be abased; and he that humbleth himself shall be exalted.

12—14. *Whom to invite; a Lesson to the Host.*

Then said he also to him that bade him, When thou makest a dinner or a supper, call not thy friends, nor thy

a more honourable man than thou] Phil. ii. 3, "in lowliness of mind let each esteem other better than themselves."

9. *thou begin with shame to take the lowest room*] If, by the time that the guests are seated, it be found that some one has thrust himself into too high a position for his rank, when he is removed he will find all the other good places occupied. There is an obvious reference to Prov. xxv. 6, 7. How much the lesson was needed to check the arrogant pretensions of the Jewish theologians, is shewn again and again in the Talmud, where they assert no reward to be too good or too exalted for their merits. Thus at a banquet of King Alexander Jannaeus, the Rabbi Simeon Ben Shetach, in spite of the presence of some great Persian Satraps, had thrust himself at table between the King and Queen, and when rebuked for his intrusion, quoted in his defence Ecclus. xv. 5, "Exalt wisdom, and she...shall make thee sit among princes."

10. *then shalt thou have worship*] Rather, **glory**. It need, however, hardly be said that nothing is farther from our Lord's intentions than to teach mere calculating worldly politeness. From the simple facts of life that an intrusive person renders himself liable to just rebuffs, he draws the great spiritual lesson so much needed by the haughty religious professors by whom He was surrounded, that

"Humble we must be if to heaven we go;
High is the roof there, but the door is low."

11. *whosoever exalteth himself shall be abased*] Rather, **humbled**. See on i. 52, xiii. 30, and Matt. xxiii. 12. A similar lesson is prominent in the Book of Proverbs (xv. 33, xvi. 18, 19, xxix. 23), and is strongly enforced by St Peter (1 Pet. v. 5).

12—14. WHOM TO INVITE; A LESSON TO THE HOST.

12. *call not thy friends, nor thy brethren*] In this, as many of our Lord's utterances, we must take into account (1) the idioms of Oriental

brethren, neither thy kinsmen, nor *thy* rich neighbours; lest they also bid thee again, and a recompence be made thee. 13 But when thou makest a feast, call the poor, the maimed, 14 the lame, the blind: and thou shalt be blessed; for they cannot recompense thee: for thou shalt be recompensed at the resurrection of the just.

15—24. *The Refused Banquet; a Lesson to a Guest.*

15 And when one of them that sat at meat with *him* heard these *things*, he said unto him, Blessed *is he* that shall eat 16 bread in the kingdom of God. Then said he unto him, A

speech; (2) the rules of common sense, which teach us to distinguish between the letter and the spirit. It is obvious that our Lord did not mean to *forbid* the common hospitalities between kinsmen and equals, but only, as the context shews, (1) to discourage a mere *interested* hospitality intended to secure a return; and (2) to assert that unselfish generosity is superior to the common civilities of friendliness. The "*not*" therefore means, as often elsewhere in Scripture, "not only, but also,' or "not so much...as," as in Prov. viii. 10; John vi. 27; 1 Cor. i. 17, xv. 10; 1 Tim. ii. 9, &c. In other words, "not" sometimes denies "not absolutely but conditionally (Gal. v. 21) and comparatively (1 Cor. i. 17)." See Matt. ix. 13; Jer. vii. 22; Joel ii. 13; Heb. viii. 11.

and a recompence be made thee] In a similar case Martial says, "You are asking for *gifts*, Sextus, not for *friends*." There is a remarkable parallel in Plato's *Phaedrus*.

13. *call the poor*] Matt. xxv. 35. The duty is recognised in another form by Nehemiah. "Eat the fat, and drink the sweet, and send portions unto them for whom nothing is prepared," Nehem. viii. 10.

14. *at the resurrection of the just*] The same duty is enforced with the same motive by St Paul, 1 Tim. vi. 17—19. By the phrase "*the resurrection of the just*," our Lord possibly referred to the twofold resurrection, xx. 35; 1 Cor. xv. 23; 1 Thess. iv. 16, &c. But the allusion may be more general, Acts xxiv. 15.

15—24. THE REFUSED BANQUET; A LESSON TO A GUEST.

15. *when one of them that sat at meat with him heard these things*] He may have wanted to diminish the force of the rebukes implied in the previous lessons by a vapid general remark. At any rate, he seems to have assumed that *he* would be one of those who would sit at the heavenly feast which should inaugurate the new aeon, and from which, like all Jews, he held it to be almost inconceivable that any circumcised son of Abraham should be excluded. Hence the warning involved in this parable which was meant to prove how small was the real anxiety to accept the divine invitation.

shall eat bread in the kingdom of God] Almost the same words occur in Rev. xix. 9. The Jews connected the advent of the Messianic

certain man made a great supper, and bade many: and sent 17 his servant at supper time to say to them that were bidden, Come; for all *things* are now ready. And they all with one 18 *consent* began to make excuse. The first said unto him, I have bought a piece of ground, and I must needs go and see it: I pray thee have me excused. And another said, I 19 have bought five yoke of oxen, and I go to prove them: I pray thee have me excused. And another said, I have 20 married a wife, and therefore I cannot come. So that ser- 21

Kingdom with banquets of food more delicious than manna, the flesh of Leviathan, and the bird Bar Juchne.

16. *A certain man made a great supper*] The difference between this parable and that of the King's Supper will be clear to any one who will read it side by side with Matt. xxii. 1—10. He who gives the invitation is God. Ps. xxv. 6.

and bade many] The breadth and ultimate universality of the Gospel message. But as yet the "many," are the Jews, who (in the first appliention) are indicated by those who refuse.

17. *sent his servant at supper time*] This is still a custom in the East, Prov. ix. 1—5; Thomson, *Land and Book*, I. ch. ix. The message of the servant corresponds to the ministry of John the Baptist and of Jesus Himself.

Come; for all things are now ready] "Repent ye; for the kingdom of heaven is at hand," x. 1, 9; Matt. iii. 1, 2.

18. *with one consent*] i.e. *apo mias gnomēs;* or 'with one voice,' if we understand *phonēs*.

to make excuse] The Greek word is the exact equivalent of our '*to beg off*.' The same fact is indicated in John i. 11, v. 40, and in the "ye would not" of xiii. 34; and the *reason* is the antipathy of the natural or carnal man (ὁ ψυχικὸς) to God, John xv. 24.

have me excused] The original is *consider me as having been excused*. The very form of the expression involves the consciousness that his excuse of necessity (ἀνάγκην ἔχω) was *merely* an excuse. There is, too, an emphasis on the *me*—"excusatum *me* habeas"—it may be the duty of others to go; *I* am an exception.

19. *I go to prove them*] The second has not even the decency to plead any *necessity*. He merely says 'I am going to test my oxen,' and implies ' my will is sufficient reason.'

20. *I cannot come*] The 'I cannot,' as in xi. 7, is only an euphemism for 'I will not.' He thinks his reason so strong that there can be no question about it. He relies doubtless on the principle of the exemption from war, granted to newly-married bridegrooms in Deut. xxiv. 5. Perhaps St Paul is alluding to this parable in 1 Cor. vii. 29—33, "The time is short: it remaineth, that both they that have wives be as though they had none;...and they that buy, as though they possessed not; and they that use this world, as not using it to the full." Thus the three hindrances

vant came, and shewed his lord these *things*. Then the master of the house being angry said to his servant, Go out quickly into the streets and lanes of the city, and bring in hither the poor, and the maimed, and the halt, and the 22 blind. And the servant said, Lord, it is done as thou hast 23 commanded, and yet there is room. And the lord said unto the servant, Go out into the *high*ways and hedges, and 24 compel *them* to come in, that my house may be filled. For

are possessions, wealth, pleasures. But, as Bengel says, neither the field (Matt. xiii. 44), nor the plowing (ix. 62), nor the wedding (2 Cor. xi. 2) need have been any real hindrance. The 'sacred hate' of vs. 26 would have cured all these excuses.

21. *that servant came, and shewed his lord these things*] We have here a shadow of the complaints and lamentations of our Lord over the stiffnecked obstinacy of the Jews in rejecting Him.

Then the master of the house being angry]

"God, when He's angry here with any one
His wrath is free from perturbation;
And when we think His looks are sour and grim
The alteration is in us, not Him."

HERRICK.

the streets and lanes of the city] This corresponds to the call of the publicans, sinners, and harlots—the lost sheep of the House of Israel, iv. 18; Mk. xii. 37; Matt. xxi. 32; James ii. 5.

22. *and yet there is room*] 'Grace, no less than Nature, abhors a vacuum.' Bengel.

23. *into the highways and hedges*] i.e. *outside* the city; intimating the ultimate call of the Gentiles.

compel them to come in] By such moral suasion as that described in 2 Tim. iv. 2. The compulsion wanted is that used by Paul the Apostle, not by Saul the Inquisitor. The abuse of the word "Compel" in the cause of intolerance is one of the many instances which prove the deadliness of that mechanical letter-worship which attributes infallibility not only to Scripture, but even to its own ignorant misinterpretations. The compulsion is merciful, not sanguinary; it is a compulsion to inward acceptance, not to outward conformity; it is employed to overcome the humble despair of the penitent, not the proud resistance of the heretic. Otherwise it would have been applied, not to the poor suffering outcasts, but to the haughty and privileged persons who had refused the first invitation. Yet even Augustine shews some tendency to this immoral perversion of the words in his "*Foris inveniatur necessitas, nascitur intus voluntas.*" Others apply it to threats of eternal punishment, and a ministry which dwells on lessons of wrath.

24. *For I say unto you*] Since the '*you*' is plural this verse is probably the language of our Lord, indirectly assuming that His hearers would see the bearing of this parable.

I say unto you, That none of those men which were bidden shall taste of my supper.

25—35. *Lessons of Whole-heartedness, and of Counting the Cost; the Tower-builder; the warring King; the savourless Salt.*

And there went great multitudes with him: and he turned, 25 and said unto them, If any *man* come to me, and hate not 26 his father, and mother, and wife, and children, and brethren, and sisters, yea, and his own life also, he cannot be

none of those men which were bidden shall taste of my supper] It must be remembered that Jesus had now been distinctly and deliberately rejected at Nazareth (iv. 29) and Jerusalem (John viii. 59); in Judaea, Samaria (ix. 53), Galilee (x. 13), and Peraea (viii. 37). "Seeing ye put it from you, and judge yourselves unworthy of everlasting life, lo, we turn to the Gentiles," Acts xiii. 46; Heb. xii. 25; Matt. xxi. 43, xxii. 8.

25—35. LESSONS OF WHOLE-HEARTEDNESS, AND OF COUNTING THE COST; THE TOWER-BUILDER; THE WARRING KING; THE SAVOURLESS SALT.

25. *And there went great multitudes with him*] This is evidently a scene of the journey, when multitudes of the Galilaean pilgrims were accompanying Him on their way to one of the great Jewish feasts. The warning might have prevented them from following Him now, and shouting 'Crucify Him' afterwards.

26. *and hate not his father and mother*] It is not so much the true explanation to say that *hate* here means *love less* (Gen. xxix. 31), as to say that when our nearest and dearest relationships prove to be positive obstacles in coming to Christ, then all natural affections must be flung aside; comp. Deut. xiii. 6—9, xxi. 19—21, xxxiii. 8, 9. A reference to Matt. x. 37 will shew that 'hate' means *hate by comparison*. Our Lord purposely stated great principles in their boldest and even most paradoxical form by which He alone has succeeded in impressing them for ever *as principles* on the hearts of His disciples. The 'love of love' involves a necessity for the possible 'hate of hate,' as even worldly poets have understood.

"Va, je t'aimais trop pour ne pas te haïr."
"I could not love thee, dear, so much
Loved I not honour *more*."
                                        LOVELACE.

yea, and his own life also] This further explains the meaning of the word 'hate.' The *psuchē* 'soul' or 'animal life' is the seat of the passions and temptations which naturally alienate the spirit from Christ. These must be hated, mortified, crucified if they cannot be controlled; and life itself must be cheerfully sacrificed, Rev. xii. 11; Acts xx. 24.

27 my disciple. And whosoever doth not bear his cross, and
28 come after me, cannot be my disciple. For which of you, intending to build a tower, sitteth not down first, and counteth the cost, whether he have sufficient to finish it?
29 Lest haply, after he hath laid the foundation, and is not
30 able to finish *it*, all that behold *it* begin to mock him, saying,
31 This man began to build, and was not able to finish. Or what king, going to make war against another king, sitteth not down first, and consulteth whether he be able with ten thousand to meet him that cometh against him with twenty
32 thousand? Or else, while the other is yet a great way off, he sendeth an ambassage, and desireth conditions of peace.

"Il faut vivre dans ce monde," says St Francis de Sales, "comme si nous avions l'esprit au ciel, et le corps au tombeau."

27. *doth not bear his cross*] Not only must self be mortified, but even the worst sufferings endured, 1 Thess. iii. 4, 5. The allusion to the cross must still have been mysterious to the hearers (Matt. x. 38), the more so since they were dreaming of Messianic triumphs and festivities.

28. *intending to build a tower*] This and the next similitude are meant, like the previous teachings, to warn the expectant multitudes that to follow Christ in the true sense might be a far more serious matter than they imagined. They are significant lessons on the duty of deliberate choice which will not shrink from the ultimate consequences—the duty of counting the cost (see Matt. xx. 22). Thus they involve that lesson of "patient continuance in well-doing," which is so often inculcated in the New Testament.

29. *all that behold it begin to mock him*] Very possibly this might have actually happened in some well-known instance, since the Herodian family had a passion for great buildings and probably found many imitators. First failure, then shame awaits renegade professions and extinguished enthusiasms.

31. *what king, going to make war against another king*] Rather, **to meet another king in battle.** There may be an historical allusion here to the disturbed relations between Herod Antipas and his injured father-in-law Hareth, king of Arabia, which (after this time) ended in the total defeat of the former (Jos. *Antt.* XVIII. 5, § 3).

32. *desireth conditions of peace*] This is sufficient to overthrow the interpretation which sees Man and Satan in the warring kings. Another view is that it implies the hostility of man to God, and the urgent need of being reconciled to Him (e.g. Bengel says on the word 'king,' "Christiana militia regale quiddam"). *That* however is never a calculated hostility which deliberately sits down and expects to win the victory; otherwise it would be a good inference that "a Christian's weakness is his strength." It is a mistake, and one which often leads to

So likewise, whosoever *he be* of you that forsaketh not all 33 that he hath, he cannot be my disciple. Salt *is* good: but 34 if the salt have lost his savour, wherewith shall it be seasoned? It is neither fit for the land, nor yet for the dung- 35 hill; *but men* cast it out. He that hath ears to hear, let him hear.

CH. XV. *Parables for Publicans and Sinners. The Love and free Forgiveness of God.*

1—10. *The Lost Sheep.*

Then drew near unto him all the publicans and sinners 15

serious errors, to press unduly the details of parables; as when for instance some would see in the 10,000 soldiers a reference to the Ten Commandments. The general lesson is—Do not undertake what you have neither the strength nor will to achieve, nor that in which you are not prepared, if need be, to sacrifice life itself.

33. *forsaketh not all that he hath*] i.e. every affection, gift or possession that interferes with true discipleship. We must be ready 'to count all things but loss for Christ,' Phil. iii. 7, 8.

34. *Salt is good*] The true reading is *Salt therefore is good*, connecting this verse with what has gone before. This similitude was thrice used by Christ with different applications. "Ye are the salt of the earth," Matt. v. 13. "Have salt in yourselves," Mk. ix. 50. Here the salt is the inward energy of holiness and devotion, and in the fate of salt which has lost its savour we see the peril which ensues from *neglect* of the previous lessons.

35. *men cast it out*] There is nothing stronger than salt which can restore to it its lost pungency. Hence, if it have been spoilt by rain or exposure, it is only fit to be used for paths. The peril of backsliding, the worthlessness of the state produced by apostasy, is represented in St John (xv. 6) by the cutting off and burning of the dead and withered branch. The main lesson of these three similitudes is expressed with its full force in Heb. vi. 4—12, x. 26—39; and the importance of it is emphasized by the proverbial expression, "He that hath ears to hear," &c. (Matt. xi. 15; Deut. xxix. 4; Is. vi. 9, 10).

CH. XV. PARABLES FOR PUBLICANS AND SINNERS. THE LOVE AND FREE FORGIVENESS OF GOD.

1—10. THE LOST SHEEP.

1. *Then drew near unto him*] Rather, **And there were drawing near to Him all the tax-gatherers and the sinners to listen to Him.** St Chrysostom says that their very life was legalised sin and specious greed. On the publicans, see iii. 12, v. 27. 'The sinners' mean in general the degraded and outcast classes. See Introd. and Wordsworth, ad loc.

² for to hear him. And the Pharisees and scribes murmured, saying, This *man* receiveth sinners, and eateth with them. ³ And he spake this parable unto them, saying, What man of ⁴ you, having an hundred sheep, if he lose one of them, doth not leave the ninety and nine in the wilderness, and go after ⁵ that which is lost, until he find it? And when he hath ⁶ found *it*, he layeth *it* on his shoulders, rejoicing. And when he cometh home, he calleth together *his* friends and neighbours, saying unto them, Rejoice with me; for I have found

2. *the Pharisees and scribes*] See Excursus VI.

murmured] Rather, **were loudly murmuring** (xix. 7; Josh. ix. 18). "With arid heart they blame the very Fount of Mercy," Gregory the Great. In all ages it had been their sin that they 'sought not the lost.' Ezek. xxxiv. 4.

and eateth with them] Even their *touch* was regarded as unclean by the Pharisees. But our Lord, who read the heart, knew that the religious professors were often the worse sinners before God, and He associated with sinners that He might save them. "Ideo secutus est... usque ad mensam, ubi maxime peccatur." Bengel. It is this yearning of redemptive love which finds its richest illustration in these three parables. They contain the very essence of the Glad Tidings, and two of them are peculiar to St Luke.

3. *he spake this parable*] Matt. xviii. 12—14. In these three parables we have pictures of the *bewildered* sinner (3—7); the *unconscious* sinner (8—10); the *voluntary* sinner (11—32).

4. *an hundred sheep*] And yet out of this large flock the good shepherd grieves for *one* which strays. There is an Arab saying that God has divided pity into a hundred parts, and kept ninety-nine for Himself.

in the wilderness] i. e. the *Midbar*, or pastures; see ii. 8. The sheep are left of course under minor shepherds, not uncared for. Some see in the Lost Sheep the whole human race, and in the ninety-nine the Angels: as though mankind were but a hundredth part of God's flock.

until he find it] Strange that utterances so gracious as this should be utterly passed over, when so many darker details are rigidly pressed!

5. *he layeth it on his shoulders, rejoicing*] Literally, "*his own shoulders.*" All anger against the folly of the wanderer is swallowed up in love, and joy at its recovery. "He bare our sins in His own body," 1 Pet. ii. 24. We have the same metaphor in the Psalm of the shepherd king (Ps. cxix. 176; comp. Is. liii. 6; John x. 11), and in the letter of the Apostle, to whom had been addressed the words, "Feed my sheep," 1 Pet. ii. 25. This verse supplied a favourite subject for the simple and joyous art of the catacombs. Tert. *De Pudic.* 7. See Lundy, *Monumental Christianity*, pp. 150 sqq.

6. *calleth together his friends and neighbours*] See on xiv. 12.

my sheep which was lost. I say unto you, that likewise joy 7 shall be in heaven over one sinner that repenteth, *more* than over ninety and nine just *persons* which need no repentance.

Either what woman having ten pieces of silver, if she 8 lose one piece, doth not light a candle, and sweep the house, and seek diligently till she find *it?* And when she 9 hath found *it*, she calleth *her* friends and *her* neighbours together, saying, Rejoice with me; for I have found the

Rejoice with me] "For the *joy* set before Him, He endured the cross," Heb. xii. 2; comp. Is. liii. 11.

7. *I say unto you*] *I*—who know (John i. 51).

in heaven] See vs. 10; Matt. xviii. 13.

just persons, which need no repentance] See v. 32. The 'Pharisees and scribes' in an external sense were 'just persons,' for *as a class* their lives were regular, though we learn from Josephus and the Talmud that many individuals among them were guilty of flagrant sins. But that our Lord uses the description with a holy irony is clear from the parable of the Pharisee and the publican (see xviii. 9). They trusted in themselves that they were righteous, and despised others. They *did need* repentance (carebant), but did not *want* it (non egebant). It was a fixed notion of the Jews that God had "*not appointed repentance to the just*, and to Abraham, and Isaac, and Jacob, *which have not sinned against thee*" (Prayer of Manasses).

8. *having ten pieces of silver*] Ten drachmas. This parable is peculiar to St Luke. The Greek drachma (about 10*d*.) corresponds to the Latin denarius. Each represented a day's wages, and may be roughly rendered shilling. Tob. v. 14; Thuc. III. 17; Tac. *Ann.* I. 17. These small silver coins were worn by women as a sort of ornamental fringe round the forehead (the *semedi*). The loss might therefore seem less trying than that of a sheep, but (1) in this case it is a *tenth* (not a *hundredth*) part of what the woman possesses; and (2) the coin has on it the image and superscription of a king (Gen. i. 27; Matt. xxii. 20). "We are God's drachma"—"I feel more strongly every day that everything is vanity; I cannot leave my soul in this heap of mud." Lacordaire (Chocarne, p. 42, E. Tr.).

light a candle, and sweep the house, and seek diligently] We should notice the thorough and deliberate method of the search. Some see in the woman a picture of the Church, and give a separate meaning to each particular; but "if we should attribute to every single word a deeper significance than appears, we should not seldom incur the danger of bringing much into Scripture which is not at all contained in it." Zimmermann.

till she find it] If it be admissible to build theological conclusions on the incidental expressions of parables, there should be, in these words, a deep source of hope.

piece which I had lost. Likewise, I say unto you, there is joy in the presence of the angels of God over one sinner that repenteth.

11—32. *The Son lost and found.*

And he said, A certain man had two sons: and the younger of them said to *his* father, Father, give me the portion of goods that falleth to *me*. And he divided unto them *his* living. And not many days after the younger son

9. *I have found the piece which I had lost*] She does not say 'my piece.' If the woman be intended to represent the Church, the loss of the 'piece' entrusted to her may be in part, at least, her own fault.

10. *joy in the presence of the angels of God*] The same as the 'joy in heaven' of vs. 7; the Te Deums of heaven over the victories of grace.

over one sinner that repenteth] "I have no pleasure in the death of the wicked; but that the wicked turn from his way and live." Ezek. xxxiii. 11.

11—32. THE SON LOST AND FOUND.

11. *had two sons*] The primary applications of this divine parable,—which is peculiar to St Luke, and would alone have added inestimable value to his Gospel—are (1) to the Pharisees and the 'sinners'—i.e. to the professedly religious, and the openly irreligious classes; and (2) to the Jews and Gentiles. This latter application however only lies indirectly in the parable, and it is doubtful whether it would have occurred consciously to those who heard it. This is the *Evangelium in Evangelio*. How much it soars above the conceptions of Christians, even after hundreds of years of Christianity, is shewn by the 'elder-brotherly spirit' which has so often been manifested (e.g. by Tertullian and all like him) in narrowing its interpretation.

12. *the portion of goods that falleth to me*] This would be one third (Deut. xxi. 17). The granting of this portion corresponds to the natural gifts and blessings which God bestows on all alike, together with the light of conscience, and the rich elements of natural religion. Here we have the history of a sinful soul. Its sin (12, 13); its misery (14—16); its penitence (17—20); its forgiveness (20—24).

he divided unto them his living] See vi. 35. "The Lord is good *to all*," Ps. cxlv. 9. "God is no respecter of persons," Acts x. 34. "He maketh His sun to rise on the evil, and on the good, and sendeth rain on the just and on the unjust," Matt. v. 45.

> "God answers sharp and sudden on some prayers;
> And flings the thing we have asked for in our face,
> A gauntlet—with a gift in it."
> E. B. BROWNING.

13. *not many days after*] This shadows forth the *rapidity* (1) of national, and (2) of individual degeneracy. "In some children," says

gathered all together, and took his journey into a far country, and there wasted his substance with riotous living. And when he had spent all, there arose a mighty famine in 14 that land; and he began to be in want. And he went and 15

Sir Thomas Elyot in *The Governour*, "nature is more prone to vice than to vertue, and in the tender wittes be sparkes of voluptuositie, whiche norished by any occasion or objecte, encrease oftentymes into so terrible a fire, that therwithall vertue and reason is consumed." The first sign of going wrong is a yearning for spurious liberty.

took his journey into a far country] The Gentiles soon became 'afar off' from God (Acts ii. 39; Eph. ii. 17), "aliens from the commonwealth of Israel, and strangers from the covenants of promise, having no hope, and without God in the world."—So too the individual soul, in its temptations and its guiltiness, ever tries in vain to *escape* from God (Ps. cxxxix. 7—10) into the 'far country' of sin, which involves *forgetfulness* of Him. Jer. *Ep.* 146. Thus the younger son becomes "Lord of himself, that heritage of woe."

with riotous living] Literally, "*living ruinously*"—*asōtōs*. The adverb occurs here only, and is derived from *a* 'not,' and σώζω 'I save.' The substantive occurs in 1 Pet. iv. 4; Eph. v. 18. Aristotle defines *asotia* as a mixture of intemperance and prodigality. For the *historical* fact indicated, see Rom. i. 19—32. The *individual* fact needs, alas! no illustration. One phrase—two words—is enough. Our loving Saviour does not dwell upon, or darken the details, of our sinfulness.

14. *And when he had spent all*] Historically,

"On that hard Roman world, disgust
 And secret loathing fell;
Deep weariness and sated lust
 Made human life a hell."
                                            M. ARNOLD.

Individually, "The limits are narrow within which, by wasting his capital, a man obtains a supply of pocket-money." G. Macdonald.

there arose a mighty famine in that land] God has given him his heart's desire and sent leanness withal into his bones. The worst famine of all is "not a famine of bread or a thirst of water, but of hearing the words of the Lord" (Amos viii. 11); and in such a famine even "the fair virgins and young men faint for thirst" (id. vs. 13). "They have forsaken me the fountain of living waters, and hewed them out cisterns; broken cisterns, that can hold no water," Jer. ii. 13.

he began to be in want] The whole heathen world at this time was saying, "Who will shew us any good?" Weariness, despair, and suicide were universal. Individually this is the retributive anguish of those who have wasted the gifts of life.

"My days are in the yellow leaf,
 The flowers and fruits of love are gone,
The worm, the anguish, and the grief
 Are mine alone.

joined himself to a citizen of that country; and he sent him
into his fields to feed swine. And he would fain have filled
his belly with the husks that the swine did eat: and no *man*
gave unto him. And when he came to himself, he said,

> The fire that on my bosom preys
> Is lone as some volcanic isle;
> No torch is kindled at its blaze—
> A funeral pile."
>
> BYRON.

15. *joined himself to a citizen of that country*] Rather, **one of the citizens.** Even in its worst and most willing exile the soul cannot cease to be by right a citizen of God's kingdom—a fellow-citizen with the saints, Eph. ii. 19. Its true citizenship (πολίτευμα) is still in heaven (Phil. iii. 20). By 'the citizen of the far country' is indicated either men hopelessly corrupt and worldly; or perhaps the powers of evil. We observe that in this far-off land, the Prodigal, with all his banquets and his lavishness, has not gained a single *friend*. Sin never forms a real bond of pity and sympathy. The cry of tempters and accomplices ever is, "What is that to us? see *thou* to *that*."

he sent him] 'Freedom' from righteousness is *slavery* to sin.

to feed swine] The intensity of this climax could only be duly felt by Jews, who had such a loathing and abhorrence for swine that they would not even *name* them, but spoke of a pig as *dabhar acheer*, 'the other thing.'

16. *he would fain*] Literally, "*he was longing.*"

filled his belly with] The plain expression—purposely adopted to add the last touch to the youth's degradation—gave offence to some copyists, who substituted for it the verb 'to be fed.' The reading adopted in our text is, however, certainly the true one, and perhaps implies that from such food nothing could be hoped for but to allay the pangs of famine. He only hopes to 'fill his belly,' not to sate his hunger. Even the world's utmost gorgeousness and most unchecked sensuality could not avail to raise the soul of men or of nations out of utter misery.

the husks that the swine did eat] Literally, "*the carob-pods of which the swine were eating.*" The word rendered 'husks' means 'little horns,' i.e. the long, coarse, sweetish, bean-shaped pods of the carob tree (*ceratonia siliqua*, St John's bread tree), which were only used by the poorest of the population. Some (incorrectly) give the same meaning to the ἀκρίδες ('locusts') which formed the food of St John the Baptist.

and no man gave unto him] No one 'was giving,' or 'chose to give' him either the husks or anything else. Satan has no desire for, and no interest in, even the smallest alleviation of the anguish and degradation of his victims. Even the vile earthly gifts, and base sensual pleasures, are withheld or become impossible. "Who *follows* pleasure, pleasure slays."

17. *And when he came to himself*] His previous state was that of

How many hired *servants* of my father's have bread enough and to spare, and I perish with hunger? I will arise and go to my father, and will say unto him, Father, I have sinned against heaven, and before thee, and am no more worthy to be called thy son: make me as one of thy hired *servants*. And he arose, and came to his father. But when he was yet a great way off, his father saw him, and had compassion, and ran, and fell on his neck, and kissed him. And the son said unto him, Father, I have sinned against

his false self—a brief delusion and madness—'the old man with his affections and lusts.' Now he was once more beginning to be "in his right mind." "The heart of the sons of men is full of evil, and madness is in their heart while they live," Eccl. ix. 3.

How many hired servants of my father's] The hired servants correspond to any beings who stand in a lower or more distant relation to God, yet for whom His love provides.

18. *I will arise and go to my father*] The youth in the parable had loved his father, and would not doubt about his father's love; and in the region which the parable shadows forth, the mercy of God to the returning penitent has always been abundantly promised. Is. lv. 7; Jer. iii. 12; Hos. xiv. 1, 2, &c.; and throughout the whole New Testament.

Father, I have sinned] "Repentance is the younger brother of innocence itself." Fuller, *Holy War*.

20. *And he arose and came to his father*] A mere flash of remorse is not enough; a journey must be taken: the back must be at once and finally turned on the far land; and all the shame of abandoned duties and forsaken friends be faced. "The course to the unific rectitude of a manly life" always appears to the sinner to be, and sometimes really is, "in the face of a scorching past and a dark future."

But when he was yet a great way off] "Now in Christ Jesus ye who sometimes were far off, are made nigh by the blood of Christ." Eph. ii. 13.

had compassion, and ran, and fell on his neck] On this full, frank, absolute forgiveness, see Ps. ciii. 8—10, 12. On the tender Fatherly love of God see Is. xlix. 15; Matt. vii. 11, &c.

and kissed him] Literally, "*kissed him warmly or closely,*" Gen. xxxiii. 4.

21. *And the son said unto him, Father, I have sinned*] Rather, I **sinned**. Like a true penitent he grieves not for what he has *lost*, but for what he has *done*. Here again the language of David furnishes the truest and most touching comment, "I acknowledged my sin unto Thee, and mine iniquity have I not hid. I said, I will confess my transgressions unto the Lord, and thou forgavest the iniquity of my sin," Ps. xxxii. 5. "There is forgiveness with Thee, that Thou mayest be feared," Ps. cxxx. 4. The Prodigal's penitence is not mere remorse or sorrow for punishment.

sinned against heaven] This includes and surpasses all the other guilt,

heaven, and in thy sight, and am no more worthy to be
22 called thy son. But the father said to his servants, Bring
forth the best robe, and put *it* on him; and put a ring on
23 his hand, and shoes on *his* feet: and bring hither the fatted
24 calf, and kill *it*; and let us eat, and be merry: for this my
son was dead, and is alive again; he was lost, and is found.
25 And they began to be merry. Now his elder son was in

which is the reason why David, though he had sinned so deeply against
man, says "against Thee, Thee only have I sinned, and done this evil
in Thy sight," Ps. li. 4.

22. *But the father said to his servants*] It is as though he had
purposely cut short the humble self-reproaching words of shame which
would have entreated him to make his lost son like one of his hired
servants. "While they are yet speaking, I will hear," Is. lxv. 24.

Bring forth] The true reading is probably 'Bring forth *quickly*'
ℵ, B, L, &c.

the best robe] The *talar* or *stolē podērēs*, xx. 46; John xix. 23; Is. lxi.
10; Rev. iii. 18. Compare the remarkable scene of taking away the
filthy rags from the High Priest Joshua, and clothing him with change
of raiment, in Zech. iii. 1—10. It is literally 'the *first* robe' and some
have explained it of the robe he *used* to wear at home—the former robe.

shoes on his feet] Another sign that he is to be regarded as a son,
and not as a mere sandalled or unsandalled slave (see on x. 4). Some
have given special and separate significance to the best robe, as corresponding to the 'wedding garment,' the robe of Christ's righteousness
(Phil. iii. 9); and have identified the seal-ring with Baptism (Eph.
i. 13, 14); and the shoes with the preparation of the Gospel of peace
(Eph. vi. 15; Zech. x. 12); and in the next verse have seen in the
'fatted calf' an allusion to the Sacrifice of Christ, or the Eucharist.
Such applications are pious and instructive afterthoughts, though the
latter is as old as Irenaeus; but it is doubtful whether the elaboration
of them does not weaken the impressive grandeur and unity of the
parable, as revealing the love of God even to His erring children. We
must not confuse *Parable* with *Allegory*. The one dominant meaning
of the parable is that God loved us even while we were dead in sins,
Eph. ii. 1, 5.

kill it] Rather, **sacrifice it** (comp. Herod. I. 118 where there is a
sacrifice and supper for a son's safety). Hence perhaps one reason for
assigning to St Luke the Cherubic symbol of the calf (Introd. p. 13).

24. *was dead, and is alive again*] The metaphor of 'death' to express the condition of impenitent sin is universal in the Bible. "Thou
hast a name that thou livest and art dead," Rev. iii. 1. "Awake thou
that sleepest, and arise from the dead," Eph. v. 14. "You hath He
quickened who were dead in trespasses and sins," Eph. ii. 1. "Yield
yourselves unto God *as those that are alive from the dead*," Rom. vi. 13.

was lost] This poor youth had been in the exact Roman sense *per-
ditus*—a 'lost,' an 'abandoned' character.

the field: and as he came and drew nigh to the house, he heard musick and dancing. And he called one of the ser- 26 vants, and asked what these *things* meant. And he said 27 unto him, Thy brother is come; and thy father hath killed the fatted calf, because he hath received him *safe and* sound. And he was angry, and would not go in: therefore 28 came his father out and intreated him. And he answering 29 said to *his* father, Lo, these many years do I serve thee, neither transgressed I at any time thy commandment: and

25. *Now his elder son was in the field*] Many have felt a wish that the parable had ended with the moving and exquisite scene called up by the last words; or have regarded the remaining verses as practically a *separate* parable. Such a judgment—not to speak of its presumption—shews a narrow spirit. We must not forget that the Jews, however guilty, were God's children no less than the Gentiles, and Pharisees no less than publicans from the moment that Pharisees had learnt that *they too* had need of repentance. The elder son is still a son, nor are his faults intrinsically more heinous,—though more perilous because more likely to lead to self-deception—than those of the younger. Self-righteousness is sin as well as unrighteousness, and may be even a worse sin, Matt. xxi. 31, 32; but God has provided for both sins a full Sacrifice and a free forgiveness.

musick and dancing] Literally, "*a symphony and chorus.*"

28. *he was angry*] The feelings of the Jews towards the Gentiles (1 Thess. ii. 14—16) when they were embracing the offers of the Gospel —("The Jews...were filled with envy and spake against those things which were spoken by Paul, contradicting and blaspheming," Acts xiii. 45)—and the feelings of the Pharisees towards our Lord, when He ate with publicans and sinners, are the earliest historical illustrations of this phase of the parable. It illustrates feelings which refer more directly to such historical phenomena; the earlier part is of more universal application. Yet envy and lovelessness are too marked characteristics of modern religionism to render the warning needless.

would not go in] "*Foris* stat Israel," sed "*Foris stat* non *excluditur.*" Ambrose.

therefore came his father out and intreated him] "How often would I have gathered thy children together...but ye would not," xiii. 34; see Acts xvii. 5, 13, xxii. 21, xxviii. 27. The yearning chapters addressed to the obstinacy of Israel by St Paul (Rom. x. xi.) furnish another illustration of this picture.

29. *do I serve thee*] Rather, **I am thy slave.** He does not say 'Father:' and evidently regards the yoke not as perfect freedom but as distasteful bondage. The slave is ever dissatisfied; and this son worked in the spirit of a 'hired-servant.'

neither transgressed I at any time thy commandment] This is the very spirit of the Pharisee and the Rabbi, xviii. 11, 12. "All these things

yet thou never gavest me a kid, that I might make merry
30 with my friends: but as soon as this thy son was come,
which hath devoured thy living with harlots, thou hast
31 killed for him the fatted calf. And he said unto him, Son,
32 thou art ever with me, and all that I have is thine. It was
meet that *we* should make merry, and be glad: for this thy

have I kept from my youth up." Such self-satisfaction can only spring from an ignorance of the breadth and spirituality of God's commandments. The respectable Jews, sunk in the complacency of formalism and letter-worshipping orthodoxy, had lost all conception that they were, at the best, but unprofitable servants. Like this elder son they "went about to establish their own righteousness" (Rom. ix. 14); and though they kept many formal commandments they 'transgressed' the love of God (xi. 42). Observe that while the younger son confesses with no excuse, the elder son boasts with no confession. This at once proves his hollowness, for the confessions of the holiest are ever the most bitter. The *antitheses* in the verse are striking, 'You never gave me a *kid*, much less *sacrificed* a *fatted calf*;—not even for my *friends*, much less for *harlots*.'

thou never gavest me a kid] The reward of a life near his father's presence, and in the safety of the old home, was nothing to him. He is like the rescued Israelites still yearning for the flesh-pots of Egypt.

30. *this thy son...which hath devoured thy living with harlots*] Every syllable breathes rancour. He disowns all brotherhood; and says 'came' not '*returned*,' and tries to wake his father's anger by saying '*thy* living,' and malignantly represents the conduct of his erring brother in the blackest light.

31. *Son*] Rather, **Child.**

thou art ever with me, and all that I have is thine] Literally, "*all mine are thine.*" "Who are Israelites; to whom pertaineth the adoption, and the glory, and the Shechinah, and the covenants, and the giving of the Law, and the service of God, and the promises; whose are the fathers, and of whom after the flesh Christ came who is God over all, blessed for ever," Rom. ix. 4, 5. Religionists of the Elder-brother type cannot realize the truth that *they* are not impoverished by the extension to others of God's riches (Matt. xx. 14). Let us hope that after this appeal the elder son also went in.

32. *It was meet that we should make merry, and be glad*] "They glorified God...saying, Then hath God also to the Gentiles granted repentance unto life," Acts xi. 18. It would be impossible to mark more emphatically God's displeasure at the narrow, exclusive, denunciatory spirit which would claim for ourselves only, or our party, or our Church, a monopoly of heaven. The hard dogmatism and speculative theories of a self-asserting Theology "vanish like oppressive nightmares before this single parable in which Jesus reveals the heavenly secrets of human redemption, not according to a mystical or criminal theory of punishment, but anthropologically, psychologi-

brother was dead, and is alive again; and was lost, and is found.

Сн. XVI. 1—13. *The Unjust Steward.*

And he said also unto his disciples, There was a certain 1 rich man, which had a steward; and the same was accused unto him that he had wasted his goods. And he called 2 him, and said unto him, How *is* it *that* I hear this of thee? give an account of thy stewardship; for thou mayest be no longer steward. Then the steward said within himself, 3 What shall I do? for my lord taketh away from me the stewardship: I cannot dig; to beg I am ashamed. I am 4

cally, and theologically to every pure eye that looks into the perfect law of liberty." Von Ammon, *Leb. Jesu*, III. 50.

this thy brother] For he *is* thy brother, and I thy Father, though thou wouldest refuse this name to him, and didst not address that title to me.

Сн. XVI. 1—13. THE UNJUST STEWARD.

1. *And he said also unto his disciples*] In interpreting the two following parables it is specially necessary to bear in mind the *tertium comparationis*, i.e. the one special point which our Lord had in view. To press each detail into a separate dogmatic truth is a course which has led to flagrant errors in theology and even in morals.

a certain rich man, which had a steward] The rich man and the steward are both men of the world. It is only in one general aspect that they correspond to God and to ourselves as His stewards (Tit. i. 7) who are 'required to be faithful,' 1 Cor. iv. 1—5. No parable has been more diversely and multitudinously explained than this. For instance in the steward some have seen the Pharisees, or the publicans, or Judas Iscariot, or Christ, or Satan, &c. To enter into and refute these explanations would take up much space and would be quite fruitless. We *cannot* be wrong if we seize as the main lesson of the parable the one which Christ Himself attached to it (8—12), namely, the use of earthly gifts of wealth and opportunity for heavenly and not for earthly aims.

was accused] In Classic Greek the word means 'was slandered.' Here it has the more general sense, but perhaps involves the notion of a secret accusation.

that he had wasted] i.e., had squandered upon himself.

2. *give an account*] Rather, render the account.

thou mayest be no longer steward] Rather, thou canst not be any longer steward.

3. *I cannot dig*] Rather, to dig I am not strong enough.

to beg I am ashamed] Ecclus. xl. 28, "better die than beg."

resolved what to do, that, when I am put out of the stewardship, they may receive me into their houses. So he called every one of his lord's debtors unto *him*, and said unto the first, How much owest thou unto my lord? And he said, An hundred measures of oil. And he said unto him, Take thy bill, and sit down quickly, and write fifty. Then said he to another, And how much owest thou? And he said, An hundred measures of wheat. And he said unto him, Take thy bill, and write fourscore. And the lord commended the unjust steward, because he had done

4. *I am resolved what to do*] The original graphically represents the sudden flash of discovery 'I have it! I know now what to do.'

into their houses] Literally, "*into their own houses*." I will confer on them such a boon that they will not leave me houseless. This eating the bread of dependence, which was all the steward hoped to gain after his life of dishonesty, was after all a miserable prospect, Ecclus. xxix. 22—28. If different parts of the parable shadow forth different truths, we may notice that the steward has not *enriched* himself; what he has had he has spent. So at death, when we have to render the account of our stewardship to God, we cannot take with us one grain of earthly riches.

5. *So he called every one of his lord's debtors unto him*] In the East rents are paid in kind, and a responsible steward, if left quite uncontrolled, has the amplest opportunity to defraud his lord, because the produce necessarily varies from year to year. The unjust steward would naturally receive from the tenants much more than he acknowledged in his accounts.

6. *measures*] The Hebrew *bath* and the Greek *metretes;* rather less than, but roughly corresponding to, the *firkin* = 9 gallons. This remission would represent a large sum of money.

Take thy bill] Rather, **Receive thy bill**. The steward hands the bill back to the tenant to be altered.

write fifty] Since Hebrew numerals were *letters*, and since Hebrew letters differed very slightly from each other, a very slight forgery would represent a large difference.

7. *measures of wheat*] Not the same word as before, but *cors*. The *cor* is believed to be about an English 'quarter,' i.e. 8 bushels, but from Jos. *Antt.* xv. 9, § 92, it seems to have been nearly 12 bushels. The steward knows what he is about, and makes his remissions according to the probabilities of the case and the temperament of the debtor.

8. *the lord commended the unjust steward, because he had done wisely*] The lord is of course only the landlord of the parable. The word *phronimōs* does not mean 'wisely' (a word which is used in a higher sense), but *prudently*. The tricky cleverness, by which the steward had endeavoured at once to escape detection, and to secure friends who would help him in his need, was exactly what an Oriental landlord would *admire as clever*, even though he saw through it. And the last act of the steward had been so far honest that for the first time

wisely: for the children of this world are in their generation wiser than the children of light. And I say unto you, 9 Make to yourselves friends of the mammon of unrighteousness; that, when ye fail, they may receive you into everlasting habitations. He that is faithful in *that which is* 10

he charged to the debtors the correct amount, while he doubtless represented the diminution as due to his kindly influence with his lord. The lesson to us is *analogous* skill and prudence, but spiritually employed. This is the sole point which the parable is meant to illustrate. The childish criticism of the Emperor Julian that it taught cheating(!) is refuted by the intention of parables to teach lessons of heavenly wisdom by even the 'imperfections' of earth. There is then no greater difficulty in the Parable of the Unjust Steward than in that of the Unjust Judge, or the Importunate Friend. The fraud of this "steward of injustice" is neither excused nor palliated; the lesson is drawn from his worldly prudence in supplying himself with friends for the day of need,—which *we* are to do by wise and holy use of earthly gifts.

in their generation wiser than the children of light] Rather, **the sons of this age are more prudent than the sons of the light towards** or **as regards their own generation**; i.e. they make better use of their earthly opportunities for their own lifetime than the sons of the light (John xii. 36; Eph. v. 8; 1 Thess. v. 5) do for *their* lifetime; or even than the sons of light do of their heavenly opportunities for eternity. The zeal and alacrity of the "devil's martyrs" may be imitated even by God's servants.

9. *Make to yourselves friends of the mammon of unrighteousness*] The Greek may mean either *Make the unrighteous mammon your friend;* or *make yourselves friends by your use of the unrighteous mammon.* There is no proof that Mammon is the Hebrew equivalent to Plutus, the Greek god of wealth (Matt. vi. 24). Mammon simply means wealth and is called 'unrighteous' by metonymy (i.e. the ethical character of the use is represented as cleaving to the thing itself) because the abuse of riches is more common than their right use (1 Tim. vi. 10). It is not therefore necessary to give to the word 'unrighteous' the sense of 'false' or 'unreal,' though sometimes in the LXX. it has almost that meaning. We turn mammon into a friend, and make ourselves friends by its means, when we use riches not as our own to squander, but as God's to employ in deeds of usefulness and mercy.

when ye fail] i.e. when ye die; but some good MSS. read "when *it* (mammon) fails," which the true riches never do (xii. 33).

they may receive you] The '*they*' are either the poor who have been made friends by the right use of wealth; or the word is impersonal, as in xii. 11, 20, xxiii. 31. The latter sense seems to be the best, for it is only by a very secondary and subordinate analogy that those whom we aid by a right use of riches can be said ('by their prayers on earth, or their testimony in heaven') to 'receive' us.

into everlasting habitations] Rather, **into the eternal tents**, John

least is faithful also in much: and he that is unjust in the
11 least is unjust also in much. If therefore ye have not been
faithful in the unrighteous mammon, who will commit to
12 your trust the true *riches?* And if ye have not been faithful
in that which is another *man's*, who shall give you that
13 which is your own? No servant can serve two masters: for
either he will hate the one, and love the other; or else he
will hold to the one, and despise the other. Ye cannot
serve God and mammon.

14—31. *Dives and Lazarus,—a Parable to the Covetous, preceded by Rebukes to the Pharisees.*

14 And the Pharisees also, who were covetous, heard all
15 these *things:* and they derided him. And he said unto

xiv. 2. "And give these the everlasting tabernacles which I had prepared for them," 2 Esdr. ii. 11. (Comp. 2 Cor. v. 1; Is. xxxiii. 20, and see p. 384). The general duty inculcated is that of "laying up treasure in heaven" (Matt. vi. 20; comp. 1 Tim. vi. 17—19). There is no Ebionite reprobation of riches *as* riches here; only a warning not to trust in them. (Mk. x. 24.)

10. *faithful in that which is least*] Comp. xix. 17. The most which we can have in this world is 'least' compared to the smallest gift of heaven.

11. *the true riches*] Literally, "*that which is true*," i.e. real and not evanescent. Earthly riches are neither true, nor ours.

12. *that which is another man's*] The lesson of the verse is that nothing which we possess on earth is our own; it is entrusted to us for temporary use (1 Chron. xxix. 14), which shall be rewarded by real and eternal possessions (1 Pet. i. 4). "Vitaque *mancipio* nulli datur, omnibus *usu*," Lucr. III. 985.

13. *No servant can serve two masters*] God requires a whole heart and an undivided service. "If I yet pleased men, I should not be the servant of Christ," Gal. i. 10. "Whosoever...will be the friend of the world is the enemy of God," Jas. iv. 4. "Covetousness...is *idolatry*," Col. iii. 5.

14—31. DIVES AND LAZARUS,—A PARABLE TO THE COVETOUS, PRECEDED BY REBUKES TO THE PHARISEES.

14. *who were covetous*] Rather, **lovers of money,** 2 Tim. iii. 2. The charge is amply borne out by the references in the Talmud to the rapacity shewn by the Rabbis and Priests of the period. See Matt. xxiii. 13.

they derided him] The word is one expressive of the strongest and most open insolence, xxiii. 35. There is a weaker form of the word in Gal. vi. 7. Here the jeering was doubtless aimed by these haughty and respected plutocrats at the deep poverty of Jesus and His humble followers. It marks however the phase of daring opposition which was

them, Ye are they which justify yourselves before men; but God knoweth your hearts: for that which is highly esteemed amongst men is abomination in the sight of God. The law ¹⁶ and the prophets *were* until John: since that time the kingdom of God is preached, and every *man* presseth into it. And it is easier for heaven and earth to pass, than one tittle ¹⁷ of the law to fail. Whosoever putteth away his wife, and ¹⁸

not kindled till the close of His ministry. They thought it most ridiculous to suppose that riches hindered religion—for were not they rich and religious?

15. *Ye are they which justify yourselves before men*] vii. 39, xv. 29; Matt. xxiii. 25, &c.

God knoweth your hearts] Hence God is called "a heart-knower" in Acts xv. 8; and "in thy sight shall no man living be justified," Ps. cxliii. 2. There is perhaps a reference to 1 Sam. xvi. 7; 1 Chron. xxviii. 9.

highly esteemed] Rather, lofty.

abomination] Their 'derision' might terribly rebound on themselves. Ps. ii. 4.

16. *The law and the prophets were until John*] This is one of our Lord's clearest intimations that the aeon of the Law and the Prophets was now merging into a new dispensation, since they were only "a shadow of things to come," Col. ii. 17.

every man presseth into it] The word implies 'is making *forcible* entrance into it,' Matt. xi. 12, 13. The allusion is to the eagerness with which the message of the kingdom was accepted by the publicans and the people generally, vii. 20; John xii. 19. The other rendering, 'every man useth violence against it,' does not agree so well with the parallel passage in St Matthew.

17. *than one tittle of the law*] The word for 'tittle' is *keraia*, the tip or horn of a letter, such as that which distinguishes ב from כ or ח from ה. Thus the Jews said that the letter Yod prostrated itself before God, because Solomon had taken it from the law (in the word *Nashim*) by marrying many wives and God made this same answer to them. Similarly they said that when God took the Yod (the "jot" of Matt. v. 18) from the name Sara*i*, He divided it between Sara*h* and Abra*h*am, since Yod = 10, and H = 5.

to fail] Rather, to fall. See Matt. v. 18. The law did not fall to the ground; its abrogation was only its absolute fulfilment in all its eternal principles. The best comment on the verse is Matt. v. 27—48. The bearing of these remarks on the previous ones seems to be that our Lord charges the Pharisees with hypocrisy and men-pleasing, because while they professed the most scrupulous reverence to the Law, they lived in absolute violation of its *spirit*, which was alone valuable in God's sight.

18. *Whosoever putteth away his wife*] At first sight this verse (which also occurs with an important limitation in Matt. v. 32) appears

marrieth another, committeth adultery: and whosoever marrieth her that is put away from *her* husband committeth adultery.

19, 20 There was a certain rich man, which was clothed in purple and fine linen, and fared sumptuously every day: and there

so loosely connected with the former as to lead the Dutch theologian Van der Palm to suppose that St Luke was merely utilising a spare fragment on the page by inserting isolated words of Christ. But compressed as the discourse is, we see that this verse illustrates, no less than the others, the spirit of the Pharisees. They professed to reverence the Law and the Prophets, yet divorce (so alien to the primitive institution of marriage) was so shamefully lax among them that great Rabbis in the Talmud practically abolished *all* the sacredness of marriage in direct contradiction to Mal. ii. 15, 16. Even Hillel said a man might divorce his wife if she over-salted his soup. They made the whole discussion turn, not on eternal truths, but on a mere narrow verbal disquisition about the meaning of two words *ervath dabhar*, 'some uncleanness' (lit. 'matter of nakedness'), in Deut. xxiv. 1, 2. Not only Hillel, but even the son of Sirach (Ecclus. xxv. 26) and Josephus (*Antt.* IV. 8, § 23), interpreted this to mean 'for any or every cause.' (Matt. xix. 3—12; Mark x. 2—12.) Besides this shameful laxity the Pharisees had never had the courage to denounce the adulterous marriage and disgraceful divorce of which Herod Antipas had been guilty.

19. *There was a certain rich man*] He is left nameless, perhaps to imply that *his* name was not "written in heaven" (x. 20). Legend gives him the name *Nimeusis*. Dives is simply the Latin for 'a rich man.' Our Lord in the parable continues the subject of his discourse against the Pharisees, by shewing that wealth and respectability are very differently estimated on earth and in the world beyond. The parable illustrates each step of the previous discourse:—Dives regards all he has as his very own; uses it selfishly, which even Moses and the Prophets might have taught him not to do; and however lofty in his own eyes is an abomination before God.

in purple and fine linen] The two words express extreme luxury. Robes dyed in the blood of the *murex purpurarius* were very costly and were only worn by the greatest men—

"Over his lucent arms
A military vest of purple flowed
Livelier than Melibaean or the grain
Of Sarra (Tyre) worn by kings and heroes old
In time of truce."

Byssus is the fine linen of Egypt (Gen. xli. 42; Esth. viii. 15; Prov. xxxi. 22; Ezek. xxvii. 7; Rev. xviii. 12), a robe of which was worth twice its own weight in gold.

and fared sumptuously every day] Literally, "*making merry* (xii. 19) *every day, splendidly*," Luther, *lebte herrlich und in Freuden*. It

was a certain beggar named Lazarus, which was laid at his gate, full of sores, and desiring to be fed with the crumbs 21 which fell from the rich *man's* table: moreover the dogs came and licked his sores. And it came to pass that the 22 beggar died, and was carried by the angels into Abraham's bosom: the rich *man* also died, and was buried; and in hell 23

indicates a life of banquets. The description generally might well apply to Herod Antipas, vii. 25; Mark vi. 14, 21.

20. *named Lazarus*] Lazarus is not from *lo ezer*, 'no help,' i.e. 'forsaken,' but from *El' ezer*, 'helped of God,' *Gotthilf*. It is contracted from the commoner Eleazar. This is the only parable in which a proper name occurs; and the only miracles of which the recipients are named are Mary Magdalene, Jairus, Malchus, and Bartimaeus. Whether in the name there be some allusive contrast to the young and perhaps wealthy Lazarus, brother of Martha and Mary, as Prof. Plumptre has conjectured, is uncertain. From this parable come the words—lazaretto, lazzarini, a lazar, &c.

at his gate] Not a mere *pulé* but a *pulōn*—a stately portal.

21. *with the crumbs*] The same word as in Matt. xv. 27. It is not said that such fragments were refused him.

the dogs] The only dogs in the East are the wild and neglected Pariah dogs, which run about masterless and are the common scavengers.

came and licked his sores] The incident is only added to give in one touch the abjectness of his misery, and therefore to enhance the rich man's neglect. The fault of Dives was callous selfishness.

22. *into Abraham's bosom*] Comp. xiii. 28. This expression is used as a picture for the banquet of Paradise (comp. Numb. xi. 12; John i. 18, xiii. 23, and Josephus, *De Maccab.* 13).

the rich man also died] "They spend their days in wealth, and in a moment go down to the grave," Job xxi. 13.

and was buried] Nothing is said of the pauper-funeral of Lazarus. In one touch our Lord shews how little splendid obsequies can avail to alter the judgment of heaven.

"One second, and the angels alter that."

23. *in hell*] Rather, **in Hades**. Hades, which is represented as containing both Paradise and Gehenna, and is merely the Greek equivalent of the Hebrew *Sheol*, 'the grave,' is *the intermediate condition of the dead between death and the final judgment*. The scene on earth is contrasted with the reversed conditions of the other world. The entire scenery and phraseology are Jewish, and are borrowed from those which were current among the Rabbis of Christ's day. Beyond the awful truth that death brings no necessary forgiveness, and therefore that the retribution must continue beyond the grave, we are not warranted in pressing the details of the imagery which was used as part of the vivid picture. And since the scene is in Hades, we cannot draw from it any safe inferences as to the *final* condition of the lost. The state of Dives may be, as

he lift up his eyes, being in torments, and seeth Abraham
24 afar off, and Lazarus in his bosom. And he cried and said, Father Abraham, have mercy on me, and send Lazarus, that he may dip the tip of his finger in water, and cool my
25 tongue; for I am tormented in this flame. But Abraham said, Son, remember that thou in thy lifetime receivedst thy good *things*, and likewise Lazarus evil *things:* but now he is
26 comforted, and thou art tormented. And besides all this, between us and you there is a great gulf fixed: so that they

Tertullian says, a *praelibatio sententiae*, but it is not as yet the absolute sentence.

24. *I am tormented*] Rather, **I am suffering pain.** The verb is not *basanizomai* but *odunōmai*, as in ii. 48, where it is rendered 'sorrowing.'

in this flame] Perhaps meant to indicate the agony of remorseful memories. In Hades no

> "Lethe the river of oblivion rolls:
> Her watery labyrinth, whereof who drinks
> Forthwith his former state and being forgets,
> Forgets both joy and grief, pleasure and pain."

As for the material flame and the burning tongue, "we may," says Archbishop Trench, "safely say that the form in which the sense of pain, with the desire after alleviation, embodies itself, is figurative." Even the fierce and gloomy Tertullian says that how to understand what is meant by these details "is scarcely perhaps discovered by those who enquire with gentleness, but by contentious controversialists never."

25. *Son*] Rather, **Child.** Even in the punishment of Hades he is addressed by a word of tenderness (xv. 31, xix. 9).

receivedst] Rather, **receivedst to the full.**

thy good things...evil things] The 'good things' of Dives were such as he had accounted to be absolutely his own, and to be really good (Matt. vi. 2); the 'evil things' of Lazarus were not 'his,' but part of God's merciful discipline to him, Rev. vii. 14. The parable gives no ground for the interpretation that the temporal felicity of Dives was a reward for any good things he had done, or the misery of Lazarus a punishment for his temporal sins.

but now] Add '*here,*' with the best MSS.

thou art tormented] 'Pained,' as before. The parable is practically an expansion of the beatitudes and woes of vi. 22—25.

26. *there is a great gulf fixed*] *Change of place* is not a possible way of producing *change of soul*. Dives while he still had the heart of Dives would have been in agony even in Abraham's bosom. But 1 Pet. iii. 19, 20 throws a gleam of hope athwart this gulf. It *may* be (for we can pretend to no certainty) no longer impassable, since Christ died and went to preach to spirits in prison. With this "great

which would pass from hence to you cannot; neither can they pass to us, that *would come* from thence. Then he said, I pray thee therefore, father, that thou wouldest send him to my father's house: for I have five brethren; that he may testify unto them, lest they also come into this place of torment. Abraham saith unto him, They have Moses and the prophets; let them hear them. And he said, Nay, father Abraham: but if one went unto them from the dead, they will repent. And he said unto him, If they hear not Moses and the prophets, neither will they be persuaded, though one rose from the dead.

CH. XVII. 1—4. *The Peril of causing Men to Stumble.*

Then said he unto the disciples, It is impossible but that offences will come: but woe *unto him*, through whom

gulf" compare the interesting passage of Plato on the vain attempts of great criminals to climb out of their prisons. *Rep.* x. 14.

27. *that thou wouldest send him to my father's house*] It is difficult not to see in this request the dawn of a less selfish spirit in the rich man's heart.

28. *I have five brethren*] If there be any special meaning in this detail, the clue to it is now lost. Some have seen in it a reference to the five sons of the High Priest Annas, all of whom succeeded to the Priesthood,—Eleazar, Jonathan, Theophilus, Matthias, and the younger Annas, besides his son-in-law Caiaphas. But this seems to be very unlikely. An allusion to Antipas and his brethren is less improbable, but our Lord would hardly have admitted into a parable an oblique personal reflexion.

29. *They have Moses and the prophets*] See John i. 45, v. 39, 46.

31. *neither will they be persuaded, though one rose from the dead*] "We are saved by faithful hearing, not by apparitions," Bengel. This was most remarkably exemplified in the results which followed the raising of another Lazarus (John xii. 10) and the resurrection of our Lord Himself (Matt. xxviii. 11—13). Observe that the reply of Abraham ('be persuaded,' 'arose, 'from among' [ἐκ not ἀπό] the dead) is much stronger than the words used by Dives. "A far mightier miracle ...would be ineffectual for producing a far slighter effect," Trench.

CH. XVII. 1—4. THE PERIL OF CAUSING MEN TO STUMBLE.

1. *It is impossible*] i.e. in the present condition of the world it is morally impossible.

offences] See on vii. 23. While the world remains what it is, some will always set snares and stumblingblocks in the path of their brethren, and some will always fall over them, and some will make them for themselves (1 Cor. xi. 19; 1 Pet. ii. 8).

they come. It were better for him that a millstone were hanged about his neck, and he cast into the sea, than that he should offend one of these little ones. Take heed to yourselves: If thy brother trespass against thee, rebuke him; and if he repent, forgive him. And if he trespass against thee seven times in a day, and seven times in a day turn again to thee, saying, I repent; thou shalt forgive him.

5—10. *The Power of Faith. The Insufficiency of Works.*

5 And the apostles said unto the Lord, Increase our faith.

woe unto him, through whom they come] No moral necessity, no predestined certainty, removes the responsibility for individual guilt.

2. *It were better for him,* &c.] The literal rendering of the verse is "It is for his advantage if a millstone *is hanging* round his neck, and *he has been flung* into the sea, rather than that, &c." In other words, the fate of a man who is lying drowned at the bottom of the sea is better than if his continuance in life would have led to causing "one of these little ones" to stumble. The general thought is like that of Queen Blanche, who used to say of her son St Louis when he was a boy, that *she would rather see him dead at her feet* than know that he had fallen into a deadly sin.

a millstone] The true reading here is *lithos mulikos*, not *mulos onikos*, a millstone so large as to require an ass to work it. This is introduced from Matt. xviii. 6.

one of these little ones] St Mark adds "that believe in me" (ix. 42). The reference is not to children, or the young, though of course the warning applies no less to their case; but primarily to publicans and weak believers. Christ calls even the Apostles 'children,' John xiii. 33 (cf. 1 John ii. 12, 13).

3. *Take heed to yourselves*] The following lesson of forgiveness is added because the hard repellent spirit of aggressive Pharisaism and spiritual pride was of all others the most likely to cause offences. It broke up the bruised reed, and stamped on the smoking flax.

If thy brother trespass against thee] Rather, **If he sin**, omitting "*against thee.*" Comp. Matt. xviii. 15—17, 21, 22.

rebuke him...forgive him] The former duty had been fully recognised in the old dispensation (Lev. xix. 17; Prov. xvii. 10); the latter far more distinctly and emphatically in the new (Matt. xviii. 15). The former is only intended as a help to the latter, 1 Thess. v. 14.

4. *seven times in a day*] A purely general expression, which as little involves the quantitative limitation of forgiveness upon repentance as the "seventy times seven" of Matt. xviii. 22. Some of the Rabbis had limited the duty of forgiveness to a thrice-repeated offence; but

> "Who with repentance is not satisfied,
> Is not of heaven or earth."

And the Lord said, If ye had faith as a grain of mustard 6
seed, ye might say unto this sycamine tree, Be thou plucked
up by the root, and be thou planted in the sea; and it
should obey you. But which of you, having a servant plow- 7
ing or feeding cattle, will say *unto him* by and by, when he
is come from the field, Go and sit down to meat? and will 8

5—10. THE POWER OF FAITH. THE INSUFFICIENCY OF WORKS.

5. *the apostles said unto the Lord*] The high title given, and the spontaneous united request, shew how deeply they had felt the previous lessons.

Increase our faith] Literally "*Add to us faith*," without which we can never fulfil these great moral requirements.

6. *as a grain of mustard seed*] "which is the least of all seeds," Matt. xiii. 32.

unto this sycamine tree] The 'this' is interesting because it shews that our Lord was teaching in the open air, and pointed to the tree as He spoke. The sycamine (Hebr. *shikmah*, 1 Chr. xxvii. 28) seems to be a generic name for various kinds of mulberries (e.g. the *Morus alba* and *nigra*), which were freely cultivated in the East. The black mulberry is still called *sycamenea* in Greece (see xix. 4). In Matt. xvii. 20 we have a similar passage with the variation of "this mountain," which our Lord doubtless spoke pointing to Mount Hermon. The Jews gave to a great Rabbi the title of 'uprooter of mountains,' in the sense of 'remover of difficulties;' and our Lord here most appropriately expresses the truth that Faith can remove all difficulties and obstacles, Mk. ix. 23, xi. 23. Perhaps the warning never to be spiritually elated springs from the magnificence of this promise.

Be thou plucked up by the root] Literally, "*Be instantly uprooted;*" and yet it is a tree with very deep roots. See p. 384.

7. *having a servant plowing*] The Parable of the Ploughing Slave is simply an illustration from daily life. The slave is working in the fields, at ploughing or pasturing, and when he comes back the master orders him to prepare his dinner, nor does he give him any special daily thanks for his ordinary daily duties, even if they be duly performed. So even the best of us do not do more than our commonest and barest duty, even if we attain to that. Perhaps the "which *of you*," as addressed to the poor Apostles, may be surprising; but the sons of Zebedee at least had once had hired servants, Mk. i. 20.

feeding cattle] Rather, **tending sheep**. So that here we have two great branches of pastoral work.

will say unto him by and by, when he is come from the field, Go and sit down to meat] 'By and by' is an old English phrase for 'immediately,' and the verse should be punctuated 'will say to him, when he enters from the field, Come forward immediately, and recline at table.' There is none of the harshness which some have imagined. The master merely says, Get me my dinner, and then take your own.

not *rather* say unto him, Make ready wherewith I may sup, and gird thyself, and serve me, till I have eaten and drunk-
9 en; and afterward thou shalt eat and drink? Doth he thank that servant because he did the *things* that were commanded
10 him? I trow not. So likewise ye, when ye shall have done all those *things* which are commanded you, say, We are unprofitable servants: we have done *that* which was our duty to do.

11—19. *The Cleansed Ten; the Thankless Nine.*

11 And it came to pass, as he went to Jerusalem, that he

9. *Doth he thank that servant...?*] i.e. does he feel or express any *special gratitude* to him (ἔχει χάριν). As a matter of fact, men are not in the habit of acknowledging the daily services of their dependents. Our Lord draws from this common circumstance of life a rebuke of the spirit which would spin out to eternity a selfish desire for personal rewards (Matt. xix. 27, xx. 21).

I trow not] The words are probably genuine, though omitted in ℵ, B, L, &c. There is a touch of irony in them, and doubtless they express a passing shade of disapproval at the thanklessness and discourtesy with which dependents are too often treated. The other side of the picture—God's approval of our efforts—is given in xii. 37; Rev. iii. 20.

10. *when ye shall have done all*] and this can never be, Ps. cxliii. 2. Even if it could "non est *beneficium* sed *officium* facere quod debetis," Sen. *Controv.*

We are unprofitable servants] The same word for unprofitable occurs in Matt. xxv. 30; Rom. iii. 12. This verse, like many others (Is. lxiv. 6; Rom. iii. 27), cuts at the root of the whole Romish notion as to the possibility of 'works of supererogation,' see Article XIV. "Servi inutiles sunt, insufficientes quia nemo tantum timet, tantum diligit Deum, tantum credit Deo quantum oportuit," Augsb. Conf. "We sleep half our lives; we give God a tenth of our time; and yet we think that with our good works we can merit Heaven. What have I been doing to day? I have talked for two hours. I have been at meals three hours. I have been idle four hours. Ah! enter not into judgment with thy servant, O Lord!" Luther. Yet in a lower sense—though 'insufficient,' though 'unmeritorious'—it is possible for us to be 'good and faithful servants,' Matt. xxv. 21, 23.

11—19. THE CLEANSED TEN; THE THANKLESS NINE.

11. *as he went to Jerusalem*] Rather, **as they were on their way**. The most natural place chronologically, for this incident would have been after ix. 56. St Luke places it here to contrast man's thanklessness to God with the sort of claim to thanks *from* God which is asserted by spiritual pride.

passed through the midst of Samaria and Galilee. And as 12 he entered into a certain village, there met him ten men *that were* lepers, which stood afar off: and they lifted up 13 *their* voices, and said, Jesus, Master, have mercy on us. And when he saw *them*, he said unto them, Go shew your- 14 selves unto the priests. And it came to pass *that*, as they went, they were cleansed. And one of them, when he saw 15 that he was healed, turned back, and with a loud voice glorified God, and fell down on *his* face at his feet, giving him 16 thanks: and he was a Samaritan. And Jesus answering 17 said, Were there not ten cleansed? but where *are* the nine?

he passed through the midst of Samaria and Galilee] The most natural meaning of these words is that our Lord, when rejected at the frontier village of En Gannim (see on ix. 52, 56), altered His route, and determined to pass towards Jerusalem through Peraea. In order to reach Peraea He would have to pass down the Wady of Bethshean, —which lies between the borders of Galilee and Samaria,—and there to cross the bridge over Jordan.

12. *ten men that were lepers*] So in 2 K. vii. 3 we find *four* lepers together. The one Samaritan would not have been allowed to associate with the nine Jews had not leprosy obliterated religious distinctions, as it still sadly does in the leper-houses (Biut el Masakin, 'Abodes of the Unfortunate') at Jerusalem, where alone Jews and Mahometans will live together.

which stood afar off] as the Law required, Lev. xiii. 45, 46. See on v. 12. Usually they stood at the roadside, as they still do, clamorously demanding alms, but they had heard the fame of Jesus, and asked from Him a vaster benefit.

14. *when he saw them*] Jesus always listened *instantly* to the appeal of the leper, whose disease was the type of that worse moral leprosy which He specially came to cleanse. See on v. 13.

he said] Apparently he called out this answer to them while they were *still* at the required legal distance of 100 paces.

unto the priests] See on v. 14.

15. *one of them, when he saw that he was healed, turned back*] The healing took place when they had shewn, by starting on their way to fulfil the command of Jesus, that they had faith. The Samaritan was on his way to his own priests at Gerizim.

with a loud voice] Some see in this an implied contrast to the harsh, husky voice of his leprous condition; but this is unlikely.

16. *he was a Samaritan*] See on x. 33.

17. *Were there not ten cleansed? but where are the nine?*] Literally, "*Were not the ten cleansed? but the nine—where?*" What worse leprosy of superstition, ignorance, eager selfishness, or more glaring ingratitude had kept back the others? We do not know.

18 There are not found that returned to give glory to God,
19 save this stranger. And he said unto him, Arise, go *thy way:* thy faith hath made thee whole.

20—37. The 'When?' and 'Where?' of the Kingdom of God.

20 And when he was demanded of the Pharisees, when the kingdom of God should come, he answered them and said,
21 The kingdom of God cometh not with observation: neither shall they say, Lo here: or, lo there: for behold, the king-
22 dom of God is within you. And he said unto the disciples,

18. *There are not found*] Ingratitude is one of the most universal and deeply seated of human vices, and our Lord was perfectly familiar with it. But in this instance He was moved by the depth of this thanklessness in so many recipients of so blessed a favour. Hence His sorrowful amazement. He felt as if all His benefits "were falling into a deep silent grave."

> "Blow, blow, thou winter wind;
> Thou art not so unkind
> As man's ingratitude."

save this stranger] Rather, **alien**, 2 K. xvii. 24. See on x. 33. Josephus says that the Samaritans eagerly called themselves ἀλλοεθνεῖς when they wanted to disclaim a consanguinity which might be perilous (*Antt.* IX. 14, § 3, XI. 8, § 6): but it is almost impossible to suppose that Samaria was swept clean of *every* inhabitant, and the ethnographical and other affinities of the Samaritans to the Jews seem to shew *some* mixture of blood, which they themselves claimed at other times (Jos. *Antt.* XI. 8, § 6; John iv. 12).

19. *hath made thee whole*] Rather, **hath saved thee**.

20—37. THE 'WHEN?' AND 'WHERE?' OF THE KINGDOM OF GOD.

20. *And when he was demanded of the Pharisees*] Literally, "*But being further questioned by the Pharisees.*"

should come] Literally, "*is coming.*" They seem to have asked with impatient irony, 'When is all this preparation and preaching to end, and the New Kingdom to begin?'

with observation] i.e. by narrow, curious watching. See xiv. 1. He implies that their entire *point of view* is mistaken; they were peering about for great external signs, and overlooking the slow and spiritual processes which were at work before their eyes.

21. *for behold, the kingdom of God is within you*] *intra vos est*, Vulg. As far as the Greek is concerned, this rendering of *entos* is defensible (comp. Matt. xxiii. 26), and the spiritual truth expressed by such a rendering— which implies that "the Kingdom of God is...righteousness and peace,

The days will come, when ye shall desire to see one of the days of the Son of man, and ye shall not see *it*. And they 23 shall say to you, See here; or, see there: go not after *them*, nor follow *them*. For as the lightning, that lighteneth out 24 of the one *part* under heaven, shineth unto the other *part* under heaven; so shall also the Son of man be in his day. But first must he suffer many *things*, and be rejected of this 25 generation. And as it was in the days of Noe, so shall it 26 be also in the days of the Son of man. They did eat, they 27 drank, they married *wives*, they were given in marriage, until the day that Noe entered into the ark, and the flood came, and destroyed *them* all. Likewise also as it was in 28

and joy in the Holy Ghost" (Rom. xiv. 17)—is most important. See Deut. xxx. 14. So that Meyer is hardly justified in saying that the conception of the Kingdom of God as an ethical condition of the soul is modern not historico-biblical. But *entos humōn* may also undoubtedly mean *among you* (marg.), 'in the midst of your ranks,' as in Xen. *Anab.* I. 10, § 3; and this rendering is more in accordance (i) with the *context*—as to the sudden coming of the Son of Man; and (ii) with the *fact*,—for it certainly could not be said that the Kingdom of God was in the hearts of the Pharisees. The meaning then is the same as in John i. 26; Matt. xii. 28. But in either case our Lord implied that His Kingdom had *already* come while they were straining their eyes forward in curious observation, vii. 16, xi. 20.

22. *The days will come, when ye shall desire*, &c.] Compare Matt. ix. 15, "The days will come, when the bridegroom shall be taken from them, and then shall they fast, in those days." See, too, John xii. 35, xiii. 33, xvii. 12. They were looking *forwards* with no realization of that rich *present* blessedness for which they would one day yearn. Rev. vi. 10.

23. *See here; or, see there*] A vivid description of the perpetual Messianic excitements, which finally ceased in the days of Barcochba and the Rabbi Akibba. We find a similar warning in xxi. 8. See Jos. *Antt.* xx. 8; *B. J.* II. 13, VI. 5; Tac. *Hist.* v. 13. With the whole passage compare Matt. xxiv. 23—41.

24. *as the lightning, that lighteneth*] bright, swift, sudden, universal, irresistible.

25. *But first must he suffer many things*] It was essential to our Lord's training of the Twelve at this period of His ministry, that He should again and again—as in solemn *refrain* to all His teaching—warn them of this coming end. See xviii. 31.

26. *as it was in the days of Noe*] as described in Gen. vii. 11—23. The Second Advent should flame upon a sensual and unexpectant world.

27. *They did eat, they drank*] Rather, **They were eating, they were drinking**—retaining the imperfects of the original.

the days of Lot; they did eat, they drank, they bought, they ²⁹ sold, they planted, they builded; but the *same* day that Lot went out of Sodom it rained fire and brimstone from heaven, ³⁰ and destroyed *them* all. Even thus shall it be in the day ³¹ when the Son of man is revealed. In that day, he which shall be upon the housetop, and his stuff in the house, let him not come down to take it away: and he that is in the ³² field, let him likewise not return back. Remember Lot's ³³ wife. Whosoever shall seek to save his life shall lose it; ³⁴ and whosoever shall lose *his life* shall preserve it. I tell you, in that night there shall be two *men* in one bed; the ³⁵ one shall be taken, and the other shall be left. Two *women* shall be grinding together; the one shall be taken, and the ³⁶ other left. Two *men* shall be in the field; the one shall be

28. *in the days of Lot*] See Gen. xix. 15—25; Jude 7; Ezek. xvi. 46—56; Am. iv. 11; Is. xiii. 19.

30. *Even thus shall it be*] St Paul, no less than St Luke, had caught the echo of these solemn warnings. 2 Thess. i. 6—10.

31. *upon the housetop*] the common Oriental place for cool and quiet resort. See on xii. 3, v. 19.

his stuff] i. e. his furniture or goods:

"Therefore away to get our stuff aboard."
SHAKSP. *Com. of Errors.*

let him not come down to take it away] let him escape at once by the outer steps, Matt. xxiv. 16—18. It is clear that in these warnings, as in Matt. xxiv., our Lord has distinctly in view the Destruction of Jerusalem, and the awful troubles and judgments which it brought, as being the first fulfilment of the Prophecy of His Advent.

32. *Remember Lot's wife*] Gen. xix. 26; Wisd. x. 7, "and a standing pillar of salt is a monument of an unbelieving soul." The warning is the same as in ix. 62. Turn no regretful gaze on a guilty and forsaken world.

33. *Whosoever shall seek to save his life*] See the same utterance, with slight verbal alterations, in ix. 24; John xii. 25. St Paul's high confidence as to the issue of his own apparently ruined and defeated life, furnishes us with a beautiful comment, 2 Tim. iv. 6—8. For 'to save' (*sosai*) some MSS. read to 'make his own,' 'to purchase' (*peripoiesasthai*).

34. *two men in one bed*] Not necessarily men; but human beings, e.g. man and wife. The numerals are of course masculine, because the man might be either the one 'taken' or the one 'left.'

35. *grinding together*] as to this day in the use of the common handmills of the East.

36. *Two men shall be in the field*] This verse is of more than

taken, and the other left. And they answered and said unto him, Where, Lord? And he said unto them, Wheresoever the body *is*, thither will the eagles be gathered together.

CH. XVIII. 1—8. *The Duty of Urgent Prayer. The Unjust Judge.*

And he spake a parable unto them *to this end*, that *men* ought always to pray, and not to faint; saying, There was in a

doubtful authenticity in this place, being omitted by nearly all the important MSS. It is probably interpolated from Matt. xxiv. 40.

37. *Where, Lord?*] This question also our Lord declines to answer. The Coming of God's Kingdom is not to be limited either by chronological or by geographical conditions.

Wheresoever the body is] Rather, *the carcass*, although here the specific word for carcass (*ptoma*) is not used as in Matt. xxiv. 28.

thither will the eagles be gathered together] Rather, **the vultures**. The same generic word is indeed used for both genera of birds, but the eagle does not feed on carcasses. Some commentators both ancient and modern have interpreted 'the body' to mean Christ, and 'the eagles' His gathering Saints. Scriptural usage seems to make such an interpretation impossible, especially as there is probably a direct allusion to Job xxxix. 30, "Her young ones also suck up blood: *and where the slain are, there is she.*" See too Hab. i. 8; Hos. viii. 1; Rev. xix. 17—21. Sometimes a reference is supposed to the eagle-standards of Rome. (Comp. Deut. xxviii. 49—52; John xi. 48.) This is very possible especially as the Jews were very familiar with the Roman eagle, and so strongly detested it that the mere erection of the symbol in Jerusalem was sufficient to lash them into insurrection (Jos. *Antt.* XVII. 6, § 3). But the proverb has a far wider significance, and is illustrated by the rush of avenging forces whenever the life of a nation has fallen into dissolution and decay. See the vision of the eagle in 2 Esdras xi. 45, "And therefore appear no more, O eagle, nor thy horrible wings, nor thy wicked feathers, nor thy malicious heads, nor thy hurtful claws, nor all thy vain body."

CH. XVIII. 1—8. THE DUTY OF URGENT PRAYER. THE UNJUST JUDGE.

1. *that men ought always to pray*] Rather, **that they ought always to pray**, since the true reading adds αὐτούς. It is only here and in vs. 9 that the explanation or point of a parable is given before the parable itself. Both parables are peculiar to St Luke. The duty inculcated is rather *urgent* prayer (as in xi. 5—13) than that spirit of unflagging prayer which is elsewhere enforced, xxi. 36; 1 Thess. v. 17; Eph. vi. 18. "Prayer is the *soul's sincere desire*
  Uttered, or *unexpressed*."

and not to faint] The word used is a late word meaning *to give in* through cowardice, or *give up* from faint-heartedness. It is a Pauline word, 2 Cor. iv. 1, 16; Gal. vi. 9.

a city a judge, which feared not God, neither regarded man: and there was a widow in that city; and she came unto him, saying, Avenge me of mine adversary. And he would not for a while: but afterward he said within himself, Though I fear not God, nor regard man; yet because this widow troubleth me, I will avenge her, lest by her continual coming she weary me. And the Lord said, Hear what the

2. *a judge*] Rather, **a certain judge**. The little story is not improbably taken from life, and doubtless the inferior judges under such a sovereignty as that of the Herods might afford many instances of carelessness and venality.

which feared not God, neither regarded man] The description of a character perfectly abandoned. He is living in violation of both of the two great commandments; in contradiction to the spirit of both Tables of the Decalogue. His conduct is the reverse of the noble advice of Jehoshaphat to his judges, 2 Chr. xix. 6, 7; (2 Cor. viii. 21).

a widow] See Ex. xxii. 22; Deut. x. 18; Is. i. 17, 23; Mal. iii. 5; 2 Sam. xiv. 2, 5. The necessity for *special* justice and kindness to them rose from the fact that in the East they were of all classes the most defenceless and oppressed. Hence the prominent place which they occupy in the arrangements of the early Church (Acts vi. 1, ix. 41; 1 Tim. v. 3, &c.).

3. *she came unto him*] Rather, **she kept coming to him**. The widow woman is a representative alike of the Christian Church and of the Christian soul.

Avenge me of mine adversary] Rather, **Do me justice**. The word 'avenge' is a little too strong. The technical term *ekdikeson* implies 'settle my case (so as to free me) from my adversary.' The same word is found in Rom. xii. 19; Rev. vi. 10. There is again a curious parallel in Ecclus. xxxv. 14—17, "He will not despise...the widow when she poureth out her complaint. Do not the tears run down the widow's cheeks? and is not her cry against him that causeth them to fall?...The prayer of the humble pierceth the clouds, and...he will not depart till the Most High shall behold to judge righteously and *execute judgment*."

4. *he said within himself*] The shamelessness with which he acknowledges his own sin renders it still more aggravated.

Though I fear not God, nor regard man] 'The creed of a powerful atheist.' Bengel.

5. *troubleth me*] Rather, **gives me trouble**.

lest by her continual coming] Literally, "*coming to the end*," "*coming for ever*"—another colloquialism.

she weary me] The original has the curious word *hupōpiazē*; literally, "*should blacken me under the eyes*." Some have supposed that he is afraid lest the widow should be driven by desperation to make an assault on him (*ne sugillet me*, Vulg.; ne *obtundat* me, Beza); but undoubtedly the word is a colloquialism (Ar. *Pax*, 519) retained in Hellenistic Greek, and found also in St Paul in 1 Cor. ix. 27, where

unjust judge saith. And shall not God avenge his own 7 elect, which cry day and night unto him, though he bear long with them? I tell you that he will avenge them 8 speedily. Nevertheless when the Son of man cometh, shall he find faith on the earth?

9—14. *The Duty of Humble Prayer. The Pharisee and the Tax-gatherer.*

And he spake this parable unto certain which trusted in 9

it is rendered, "I *keep under* my body." It is like the English colloquialism "to *plague* a person." Comp. Matt. xv. 23.

6. *the unjust judge*] Literally, "*the judge of injustice.*" Cp. xvi. 8.

7. *And shall not God*] The argument is simply *a fortiori*. Even an unjust and abandoned judge grants a just petition at last out of base motives when it is often urged, to a defenceless person for whom he cares nothing; how much more shall a just and merciful God hear the cry and avenge the cause of those whom He loves?

avenge his own elect, which cry day and night unto him] The best comment is furnished by Rev. vi. 9—11. But the 'avenging' is rather the 'vindication,' i.e. the deliverance from the oppressor.

which cry] Literally, shout. It is "strong crying," comp. Jas. v. 4, 'the *shouts* of the reapers of your fields.'

though he bear long with them] Literally, "*though being longsuffering in their case.*" Here the longsuffering of God is shewn not to His elect (though they too need and receive it, 2 Pet. iii. 9), but to their enemies. See Ecclus. xxxv. 17, 18—another close parallel, probably an interpolated plagiarism from this Gospel. The elect are far more eager not only for deliverance, but even for vengeance, than God is. They shew too much of the spirit which God reproves in Jonah. But God knows man's weakness and "therefore is He patient with them and poureth His mercy upon them." Ecclus. xviii. 11. But the best supported reading is καὶ μακροθυμεῖ ἐπ' αὐτοῖς. This would denote that the longsuffering is shewn toward the elect. He *is* pitiful to them, in the midst of their impatience.

8. *he will avenge them*] Is. lxiii. 4; Ps. ix. 12, "When He maketh inquisition for blood, He remembereth them, He forgetteth not the cry of the humble." "Yet a little while," Heb. x. 37; 2 Pet. iii. 8, 9. The best comment on the Parable and our Lord's explanation of it may be found in His own Discourses, John xiv., xv.

speedily] in reality (2 Pet. iii. 8) though not in semblance.

shall he find faith on the earth?] Rather, **shall He find this faith on the earth?** So St Peter tells of scoffers in the last days who shall say "Where is the promise of His coming?" 2 Pet. iii. 3, 4; and before that day "the love of many shall wax cold," Matt. xxiv. 12; 2 Thess. ii. 3. Even the faith of God's elect will in the last days be sorely tried (Matt. xxiv. 22).

themselves that they were righteous, and despised other: 10 Two men went up into the temple to pray; the one a Pharisee, and the other a publican. The Pharisee stood and prayed thus with himself, God, I thank thee, that I am not

9—14. THE DUTY OF HUMBLE PRAYER. THE PHARISEE AND THE TAX-GATHERER.

9. *which trusted in themselves that they were righteous*] See xvi. 15; Phil. iii. 4; 2 Cor. i. 9. The Jewish words '*Jashar*,' 'the upright man,' and '*Tsaddik*,' 'just,' expressed their highest moral ideal; but they made their uprightness and justice consist so much in attention to the ceremonial minutiae of the Levitic Law, and rigid externalism so engrossed their thoughts, that they had lost sight of those loftier and truer ideals of charity which the Prophets had continually set before them. This fetish-worship of the letter, this scrupulosity about trifles, tended only to self-confidence and pride. It had long been denounced in Scripture. "There is a generation that are pure in their own eyes, and yet is not washed from their filthiness," Prov. xxx. 12; "which say, *Stand by thyself, come not near to me; for I am holier than thou*. These are a smoke in my nose, a fire that burneth all the day," Is. lxv. 5. This is the sort of 'faith' which the Son of Man shall find on the earth, —men's faith in themselves!

and despised other] Rather, **the rest**. The word 'despise' means 'treat as nothing,' 'regard as mere cyphers,' Rom. xiv. 3, 10. The Rabbis invented the most highflown designations for each other, such as 'Light of Israel,' 'Uprooter of Mountains,' 'The Glory of the Law,' 'The Holy,' &c.; but they described the vast mass of their fellow-countrymen as "accursed" for not knowing the law (John vii. 49), and spoke of them as '*empty cisterns*,' '*people of the earth*,' &c. See on v. 32, vii. 34, &c. This Pharisee regards with perfect self-complacency the assumed ruin and degradation of *all the rest of mankind*. In one sense the Parable represents the mutual relations of Jew and Gentile.

10. *went up into the temple*] The Temple stood on Mount Moriah, and was always called the 'Hill of the House' (*Har ha-Beit*).

to pray] The Temple had long become naturally, and most fitly, a "House of Prayer" (xix. 46), though this was not its main original function.

11. *stood and prayed thus with himself*] Standing was the ordinary Jewish attitude of prayer (1 K. viii. 22; Mk. xi. 25), but the word *statheis* (which is not used of the Tax-gatherer) seems to imply that he stood by himself to avoid the contaminating contact of the 'people of the earth,' and posed himself in a conspicuous attitude (Matt. vi. 5), as well as 'prayed with himself' as the words are perhaps rightly rendered. He was "a *separatist* in spirit as in name," Trench. (Pharisee from *Pharash* ' to separate.')

God, I thank thee] Rather, **O God**. His prayer is no prayer at all; not even a thanksgiving, only a boast. See the strong denunciation of such insolent self-sufficiency in Rev. iii. 17, 18.

as other men *are*, extortioners, unjust, adulterers, or even as this publican. I fast twice in the week, I give tithes of all 12

as other men] Rather, **as the rest of mankind.**

extortioners, unjust, adulterers] Could he, in any real sense, have made out even this claim to be free from glaring crimes? His class at any rate are charged by Christ with being " full of extortion " (Matt. xxiii. 25); and they were unjust, seeing that they 'omitted judgment' (id. 23). They are not indeed charged by Jesus with adultery either in the metaphorical or literal sense, but they are spoken of as being prominent members of an adulterous generation, and on several occasions our Lord sternly rebuked their shameful laxity in the matter of divorce (Matt. xix. 3—9). And not only does Josephus charge them with this crime also, but their Talmud, with perfect self-complacency, shews how the flagrant immorality of even their most eminent Rabbis found a way to shelter itself, with barefaced and cynical casuistry, under legal forms. See John viii. 1—11, and Lightfoot, *Hor. Hebr.* ad loc.; *Life of Christ*, II. 152. It appears from the tract *Sotah* in the Mishnah, that the ordeal of the 'water of jealousy' had been abolished by Jochanan Ben Zakkai, the greatest Rabbi of this age, because the crime had grown so common.

or even as this publican] He thus makes the Publican a foil to his own virtues. "This," says St Augustine, "is no longer to *exult*, but to *insult*."

12. *I fast twice in the week*] This practice had no divine sanction. The Law appointed only a single fast-day in the year, the Day of Atonement (Lev. xvi. 29). By the time of Zechariah there seem to have been *four* yearly fasts (Zech. viii. 19). The bi-weekly fast of the Pharisees was a mere burden imposed by the oral Law. The days chosen were Thursday and Monday, because on those days Moses was believed to have ascended and descended from Sinai, *Babha Kama*, f. 82, 1. The man boasts of his empty ceremonialism.

I give tithes of all that I possess] Rather, **of all that I acquire**. As though he were another Jacob! (Gen. xxviii. 22; comp. Tob. i. 7, 8). Here too he exceeds the Written Law, which only commanded tithes of corn, wine, oil, and cattle (Deut. xiv. 22, 23), and not of mint, anise, and cummin (Matt. xxiii. 23). The fact that he does not say a word about his sins shews how low was his standard. "He that covereth his sins shall not prosper," Prov. xxviii. 13. He was clothed with phylacteries and fringes, not with humility, 1 Pet. v. 5. A Talmudic treatise, the *Berachôth* (Schwab, p. 336), furnishes us with a close analogy to the prayer of the Pharisee in that of Rabbi Nechounia Ben Hakana, who on leaving his school used to say, 'I thank thee, O Eternal, my God, for having given me part with those who attend this school instead of running through the shops. I rise early like them, but it is to study the Law, not for futile ends. I take trouble as they do, but I shall be rewarded, and they will not; we run alike, but I for the future life, while they will only arrive at the pit of destruction.'

that I possess. And the publican, standing afar off, would not lift up so much as *his* eyes unto heaven, but smote upon his breast, saying, God be merciful to me a sinner. I tell you, this man went down to his house justified *rather* than the other: for every one that exalteth himself shall be abased; and he that humbleth himself shall be exalted.

13. *standing afar off*] The word for standing is not *statheis* as in the case of the Pharisee, but merely *hestōs*. It is not certain whether the "afar off" means 'afar off from the Pharisee,' or (as is more probable) afar off from the Holy Place to which the Pharisee would thrust himself, as of right, into closest proximity.

would not lift up so much as his eyes] The Jew usually stood with arms outspread, the palms turned upwards, as though to receive the gifts of heaven, and the eyes raised. "Unto Thee lift I up mine eyes," Ps. cxxiii. 1, 2; but on the other hand, "Mine iniquities have taken such hold upon me that I am not able to look up," Ps. xl. 12; "O my God, I am ashamed and blush to lift up my face to thee, my God: for our iniquities are increased over our head, and our trespass is grown up unto the heavens," Ezra ix. 6.

smote upon his breast] For this custom of expressing grief, see xxiii. 48; Nahum ii. 7; Jer. xxxi. 19. "Pectus, conscientiae sedem," Bengel.

God be merciful to me a sinner] Rather, **O God, be merciful to me the sinner**. The word for 'be merciful' means 'be propitiated' as in Heb. ii. 17. He speaks of himself as the chief of sinners, 1 Tim. i. 15.

14. *went down to his house justified rather than the other*] Of the Pharisee it might be said, "His soul which is lifted up is not upright in him;" but of the Tax-gatherer, "the just shall live by his faith," Hab. ii. 4. But the day had not yet come in which the words 'be merciful' (*hilaskou*), and 'justified' (*dedikaiōmenos*), possessed the deep full meaning which they were soon to acquire (Heb. ii. 17; Rom. iii. 20). The phrase was not unknown to the Talmud, which says that while the Temple stood, when every Israelite had offered sacrifice, 'his sin was pardoned and he departed justified.' The reading of our Greek text ἢ ἐκεῖνος is untenable, though it correctly gives the meaning. The best supported reading is ἢ γὰρ ἐκεῖνος, but it seems to have originated by mistake from παρ' ἐκεῖνον. Abp Trench quotes Crashaw's striking epigram:

> "Two went to pray: or rather say
> One went to brag, the other to pray;
> One stands up close, and treads on high,
> Where th' other dares not send his eye.
> One nearer to the altar trod,
> The other to the altar's God."

every one that exalteth himself] See xiv. 11. In this Parable, as in that of the Prodigal son, we have the contrast between unrighteousness and self-righteousness.

15—17. *Jesus and the Children. A Lesson of Humility.*

15 And they brought unto him also infants, that he would touch them: but when *his* disciples saw *it*, they rebuked them. 16 But Jesus called them unto *him*, and said, Suffer little children to come unto me, and forbid them not: for of such is the kingdom of God. 17 Verily I say unto you, Whosoever shall not receive the kingdom of God as a little child shall in no wise enter therein.

18—30. *The Great Refusal. The Young Ruler who loved Riches more than Christ.*

18 And a certain ruler asked him, saying, Good Master, what

15—17. JESUS AND THE CHILDREN. A LESSON OF HUMILITY.

15. *they brought unto him also infants*] Rather, **their babes**. It seems to have been a custom of Jewish mothers to carry their babes to eminent Rabbis for their blessing; naturally therefore these mothers would bring their children and babes to Jesus. See Matt. xix. 13—15; Mk. x. 13.

16. *called them*] St Mark adds that Jesus was much displeased with the officious interference of the disciples who so little understood His tenderness.

Suffer little children] Rather, **the little children**.

for of such is the kingdom of God] Because children are meek, humble, trustful, guileless, unsophisticated, pure. It was a lesson which Jesus often taught, Matt. v. 3, xi. 25, xvii. 10, 14; 1 Cor. xiv. 20; 1 Pet. ii. 1, 2.

receive the kingdom of God as a little child] See Matt. xi. 25. Hence the Psalmist says, "My soul is even as a weaned child," Ps. cxxxi. 2. Tradition (erroneously) supposed that St Ignatius was one of these children.

18—30. THE GREAT REFUSAL. THE YOUNG RULER WHO LOVED RICHES MORE THAN CHRIST.

18. *a certain ruler*] St Matthew (xix. 20) only calls him "a young man." He was probably the young and wealthy ruler of a synagogue. The touch added by St Mark (x. 17), that he suddenly ran up and fell on his knees before Him, seems to imply that he was eager to catch the opportunity of speaking to Jesus before He started on a journey, probably the journey from the Peraean Bethany, beyond Jordan (John x. 41, 42), to the Bethany near Jerusalem, to raise Lazarus.

Good Master] This title was an impropriety, almost an impertinence; for the title 'good' was never addressed to Rabbis by their

19 shall I do to inherit eternal life? And Jesus said unto him, Why callest thou me good? none *is* good, save one, *that is*,
20 God. Thou knowest the commandments, Do not commit adultery, Do not kill, Do not steal, Do not bear false witness, Honour thy father and thy mother.
21 And he said, All these have I kept from my youth up. Now
22 when Jesus heard these *things*, he said unto him, Yet lackest

pupils. Therefore to address Jesus thus was to assume a tone almost of patronage. Moreover, as the young Ruler did not look on Jesus as divine, it was to assume a false standpoint altogether.

what shall I do to inherit eternal life?] In St Matthew the question runs, 'what *good* thing shall I do?' Here, again, the young ruler betrays a false standpoint, as though 'eternal life' were to be won by quantitative works, or by some single act of goodness,—by *doing* and not by *being*. It was indeed the fundamental error of his whole class. Rom. ix. 32.

19. *Why callest thou me good?*] According to St Matthew the question also ran, 'Why askest thou me about the good?' The emphasis is not on the *me* (for the form used in the original is the enclitic με not ἐμέ) but on *good*. Why do you give me this strange title which from *your* point of view is unwarrantable? Comp. Plato *Phaed.* 27, "to be a good man is impossible...God alone could have this honour."

none is good, save one, that is, God] 1 John iii. 5.

20. *Thou knowest the commandments*] St Matthew says that our Lord first answered, 'Keep the commandments,' and when the young man asked, '*What kind* of commandments?' expecting probably some recondite points of casuistry—minute rules (*Halachôth*) out of the oral Law—our Lord to his surprise mentions the broadest and most obvious commandments of the Decalogue.

Do not kill, &c.] Our Lord seems purposely to have mentioned only the plainest commandments of the Second Table, to shew the young man that he had fallen short *even of these* in their true interpretation; much more of that love to God which is the epitome of the first Table. Thus does Christ 'send the *proud* to the Law, and invite the *humble* to the Gospel.'

21. *All these have I kept*] There seems to have been an accent of extreme surprise in his reply. 'You bid me not be a thief, adulterer, murderer! For whom do you take me? I am no criminal. *These* I kept since I was a child.' And then he added, 'what lack I yet?' (Matt. xix. 20).—Here, again, the Gospel is true to the letter in its picture of a Pharisaic Rabbi. Thus the Talmud describes one of the classes of Pharisees as the tell-me-something-more-to-do-and-I-will-do-it Pharisee; and when R. Chaninah was dying he said to the Angel of Death, "Go and fetch me the Book of the Law, and see whether there is anything in it which I have not kept."

22. *when Jesus heard these things*] St Mark says that 'looking on him, he loved him,' or rather, 'was pleased with him.' Some have

thou one *thing*: sell all that thou hast, and distribute unto the poor, and thou shalt have treasure in heaven: and come, follow me. And when he heard this, he was very sorrowful: 23 for he was very rich. And when Jesus saw that he was very 24 sorrowful, he said, How hardly shall they that have riches enter into the kingdom of God! For it is easier for a camel 25

rendered the words 'He kissed him,' since Rabbis in token of approval sometimes kissed a good scholar on the head; this, however, would require not ἠγάπησεν, but ἐφίλησεν. There was something gracious and sincere in the youth's eagerness, and therefore Jesus gave him that test of something more high and heroical in religion which he seemed to desire, but to which he failed to rise.

Yet lackest thou one thing] This command to sell all and give to the poor was *special*, not general. The youth had asked for some great thing to do, and Jesus, by thus revealing to him his own self-deception, shews him that in spite of his spiritual pride and profession of magnanimity he is but trying to serve two masters. The disciples had already accepted the test, xii. 33, xvi. 9. To the world in general the command is not to sell all, but 'not to trust in uncertain riches, but to be rich in good works, ready to distribute, willing to communicate,' 1 Tim. vi. 17—19.

23. *he was very sorrowful*] St Matthew says, 'he went away grieving;' St Mark adds that 'his brow grew gloomy and cloudy at the command' (στυγνάσας ἐπὶ τῷ λόγῳ). And thus at the time he made, through cowardice or meanness of mind, what Dante (*Inf.* X. 27) calls '*il gran rifiuto*,' 'the great refusal,' and the poet sees his shade among the whirling throng of the useless and the facing-both-ways on the confines of the Inferno. Nothing, however, forbids us to hope that the words of Jesus who 'loved him' sank into his soul, and brought him to a humbler and holier frame of mind. But meanwhile he lost for his earthly dross that eternal blessedness of self-sacrifice which Christ had offered him. The day came when Saul of Tarsus was like this youth 'touching the righteousness which is in the law blameless;' but *he* had grace to count all things but loss for Christ. Phil. iii. 6—9.

24. *saw that he was very sorrowful*] Several good uncials read merely 'when Jesus saw him.'

shall they that have riches] Rather, **do they**. The striking reading of some MSS. (א, B, &c.) in Mk. x. 24, is that Christ, seeing the pained astonishment of the disciples, said, "Children! how hard it is to enter into the kingdom of God"—hard for all; above all, hard for the rich. Other MSS. have "for those *that trust in* riches" (comp. Prov. xi. 28)—but that would be a truism; and, indeed, *while* they trust in riches, it would be not only *hard*, but impossible. The point that Jesus wished to teach was that riches are always a temptation and a snare. 1 Tim. vi. 9, 10. Let us not forget that Judas heard these words only a few days or weeks before he sold his Lord. It was almost a proverb among the ancients that "the very rich are not good." Stobaeus, XCIII. 27.

to go through a needle's eye, than for a rich *man* to enter
26 into the kingdom of God. And they that heard *it* said,
27 Who then can be saved? And he said, The *things which are* unpossible with men are possible with God.
28 Then Peter said, Lo, we have left all, and followed thee.
29 And he said unto them, Verily I say unto you, There is no *man* that hath left house, or parents, or brethren, or wife,
30 or children, for the kingdom of God's sake, who shall not receive manifold more in this *present* time, and in the world to come life everlasting.

25. *for a camel to go through a needle's eye*] To soften the apparent harshness of this expression, some have conjectured *Kamilon*, 'a rope;' and some have explained 'the needle's eye' of the small side gate for passengers (at the side of the large city gates), through which a camel might press its way, *if it were first unladen*. But (i) the conjecture *Kamilon* is wholly without authority. (ii) The name of 'the needle's eye' applied to small gates is probably a modern one which has actually originated from an attempt to soften this verse:—at any rate there is no ancient trace of it. (iii) The Rabbinic parallels are decisive to prove that *a camel* is meant because the Babylonian Jews using the same proverb substitute 'an elephant' for 'a camel.' (iv) It is the *object* of the proverb to express *human impossibility*. In the *human* sphere—apart from the special grace of God—it would be certain that those who *have* riches would be led to *trust* in them, and so would fail to enter into the kingdom of God, which requires absolute humility, ungrudging liberality, and constant self-denial.

26. *Who then can be saved?*] Here once more we catch the echo of the sighing despair caused in the minds of the still immature Apostles by some of our Lord's harder sayings.

27. *are possible with God*] See on i. 37. "There is nothing too hard for thee," Jer. xxxii. 17; comp. Job xlii. 2; Zech. viii. 6.

28. *Then Peter said*] The feeling which dictated his remark is uncertain; perhaps it was a passing touch of self-congratulation; perhaps a plea for pity in the hard task of salvation.

we have left all] Rather, **we left all**, alluding to a particular crisis, v. 11.

29. *There is no man that hath left house*] Compare the sacrifice and reward of the sons of Levi, Deut. xxxiii. 8—11.

for the kingdom of God's sake] Unless the motive be pure, the sacrifice is unavailing.

30. *manifold more*] St Matthew and St Mark say 'a hundredfold,' and St Matthew adds that in the Palingenesia—the New Birthday of the World, the Restoration of all things—they shall sit on twelve thrones, judging the twelve tribes of Israel. St Luke naturally omits the more purely Hebraic conceptions. St Mark adds the two striking

31—34. *Jesus prophesies that He should be crucified.*

Then he took unto *him* the twelve, and said unto them, 31 Behold, we go up to Jerusalem, and all *things* that are written by the prophets concerning the Son of man shall be accomplished. For he shall be delivered unto the Gentiles, 32

words, "*with persecutions.*" Of course, the promise of "the hundredfold" is neither literal nor quantitative, but qualitative and spiritual.

in this present time] *Kairō*—not only in this present aeon, but at this very season.

31—34. JESUS PROPHESIES THAT HE SHOULD BE CRUCIFIED.

Between these verses and the last should probably be inserted the journey from the Peraean Bethany to the Judaean Bethany, and the Raising of Lazarus (John xi. 1—46). This signal miracle was omitted by the Synoptists for the same reasons as those which led them to a marked reticence about the family of Lazarus (see on x. 38 and my *Life of Christ*, II. 173). This miracle led to a meeting of the Sanhedrin, at which it was decided—mainly on the authority of Caiaphas—that Jesus must be put to death though not during the ensuing Passover,—with such precautions as were possible. The terrible decision became known. Indeed, it led to attempts to murder Lazarus and seize Jesus, which compelled Him to retire secretly to the obscure village of Ephraim (John xi. 54)— probably Et-Taiyibeh, not far from Bethel (Beitin), and about 20 miles from Jerusalem. Here our Lord spent, in undisturbed and unrecorded calm, the last few weeks of His life, occupied in training the Apostles who were to convert the world. Towards the close of the time He would see, from the hill of Ephraim, the crowds of Galilaean pilgrims streaming down the Jordan valley to keep the Passover at Jerusalem; and, secure under their protection till His brief days of destined work were done, He left His place of retreat to join their caravans for His last solemn progress to Jerusalem.

31. *Then he took unto him the twelve*] apart, and on the road, as we learn from Matt. xx. 17. St Mark, with one of his graphic touches of detail, describes Jesus walking before them, and (as we infer from the expression of the Evangelist) in such awful majesty of sorrow that those nearest Him were filled with deep amazement, and those who were following at a greater distance felt a hush of fear (Mark x. 32). Then it was that He beckoned them to Him, and revealed the crowning circumstances of horror respecting His death.

all things that are written by the prophets concerning the Son of man shall be accomplished] Rather, **all the things that have been written through the prophets for the Son of Man shall be accomplished**; or, perhaps, *shall be accomplished to the Son of Man.*

32. *unto the Gentiles*] This was the third, and by far the clearest and most circumstantial prophecy respecting His death. Hitherto, except for scattered hints which they could not understand (ix. 22, 45), the Apostles might have supposed that Jesus would be put to death by

and shall be mocked, and spitefully entreated, and spitted
33 on: and they shall scourge *him*, and put him to death: and
34 the third day he shall rise again. And they understood none
of these *things*: and this saying was hid from them, neither
knew they the *things* which were spoken.

35—43. *Bartimaeus healed at Jericho.*

35 And it came to pass, *that* as he was come nigh unto
Jericho, a certain blind man sat by the way side begging:

the Jewish authorities. Now He tells them that He shall be delivered *to the Gentiles*, which involved the fact that He should be crucified, as indeed now for the first time He plainly told them (Matt. xx. 19). It was necessary thus to check all blind material Messianic hopes, the ineradicable prevalence of which was proved immediately afterwards by the ambitious request of Salome and her sons (Mark x. 35—45; Matt. xx. 20—28). But while the magnificent promises which they had just heard, and the magnificent miracle which they would immediately witness, together with the shouting multitudes who would soon be attending our Lord, made it necessary thus to extinguish all *worldly* hopes in their minds, yet to prevent them from being crushed with sorrow, He now adds, without any ambiguity, the prophecy of His resurrection on the third day.

34. *they understood none of these things*] as had been the case before, ix. 43—45; and St Mark tells us (ix. 32) that 'they were afraid to ask Him.' It was only at a later period that the full significance of all these words dawned on them (John xii. 16). We must learn, as Pascal says, to *love* divine truths before we can understand them. The Apostles *refused to admit* the plain meaning of these clear statements (Matt. xvi. 22).

35—43. BARTIMAEUS HEALED AT JERICHO.

35. *as he was come nigh unto Jericho*] This would be a week before our Lord's death—on the evening of Thursday, Nisan 7, or the morning of Friday, Nisan 8. St Mark (x. 46) and St Matthew (xx. 29) say that this miracle took place as He was leaving Jericho. With simple and truthful writers like the Evangelists, we may feel sure that some good reason underlies the obvious apparent discrepancy which would however in any case be unimportant. Possibly it may arise from the two Jerichos—the old town on the ancient site, and the new semi-Herodian town which had sprung up at a little distance from it. And, as Chrysostom says, such discrepancies have their own value as a marked proof of the mutual independence of the Evangelists.

a certain blind man] St Matthew (xx. 30), as in the case of the Gadarene demoniac, mentions *two* blind men; and in any case a blind man would hardly have been sitting quite alone. The name of Bartimaeus is only preserved by St Mark.

and hearing the multitude pass by, he asked what it meant. And they told him, that Jesus of Nazareth passeth by. And he cried, saying, Jesus, *thou* Son of David, have mercy on me. And they which went before rebuked him, that he should hold his peace: but he cried *so* much the more, Thou Son of David, have mercy on me. And Jesus stood, and commanded him to be brought unto him: and when he was come near, he asked him, saying, What wilt thou *that* I shall do unto thee? And he said, Lord, that I may receive my sight. And Jesus said unto him, Receive thy sight: thy faith hath saved thee. And immediately he received his sight, and followed him, glorifying God: and all the people, when they saw *it*, gave praise unto God.

CH. XIX. 1—10. *Zacchaeus the Tax-gatherer.*

And *Jesus* entered and passed through Jericho. And be-

38. *Jesus, thou Son of David*] The use of this Messianic title implies a strong faith in Bartimaeus.
have mercy on me] "The Kyrie Eleison of the soul which precedes its Hosanna." Van Oosterzee.
39. *rebuked him, that he should hold his peace*] Compare xviii. 15; Matt. xix. 13.
40. *and when he was come near*] The narrative of St Mark, which is evidently derived from an immediate eye-witness, describes Bartimaeus as 'springing to his feet and flinging away his outer robe,' when he was told that Jesus had called him.
41. *Lord*] In St Mark the title given is *Rabboni*, the highest form of the title Rabbi.
42. *thy faith hath saved thee*] The brief sentences of the narrative have been beautifully woven by Mr Longfellow into his little poem of Blind Bartimaeus:

"Those mighty voices three
Ἰησοῦ ἐλέησόν με.
Θάρσει, ἔγειρε, φωνεῖ σε.
Ἡ πίστις σου σέσωκέ σε."

43. *followed him, glorifying God*] The time for any reticence respecting miracles was long past. St Luke is specially fond of recording doxologies. See v. 26, vii. 16, xiii. 17, xvii. 15, xxiii. 47.

CH. XIX. 1—10. ZACCHAEUS THE TAX-GATHERER.

1. *entered and passed through*] Literally, "*having entered Jericho was passing through it.*"
Jericho] Jericho (the City of Palm trees, Deut. xxxiv. 3; Judg. i. 16) is about 6 miles from the Jordan, and 15 from Jerusalem. It was

hold, *there was* a man named Zaccheus, which was *the* chief
3 among the publicans, and he was rich. And he sought to see
Jesus who he was; and could not for the press, because he
4 was little of stature. And he ran before, and climbed up
into a sycomore tree to see him: for he was to pass that *way*.
5 And when Jesus came to the place, he looked up, and
saw him, and said unto him, Zaccheus, make haste, and
6 come down; for to day I must abide at thy house. And he
made haste, and came down, and received him joyfully.
7 And when they saw *it*, they all murmured, saying, That he

from a point opposite to it that Moses had viewed Canaan, Deut. xxxiv. 1. When taken by Joshua the site had been cursed (Josh. vi. 26): but, in the reign of Ahab, Hiel of Bethel defied and underwent the curse (1 Kings xvi. 34). In later times Jericho became a great and wealthy town, being fertilised by its abundant spring (2 K. ii. 21) and enriched by its palms and balsams, Jos. *Antt.* IV. 6; *B. J.* IV. 8; Ecclus. xxiv. 14, "I was exalted like a palm tree in Engaddi and *like a rose plant in Jericho.*" The plant however usually called the rose of Jericho is the *Anastatica Hierochuntia* of Linnaeus. A mediaeval Itinerary says that the site—on which now stands the miserable and degraded village of Riha—was 'most rich in flowers and odoriferous shrubs.'

2. *behold*] The style of this chapter shews that St Luke is using a document of Aramaic origin.

a man named Zaccheus] *Zakkai* means 'pure.' Ezr. ii. 9; Nehem. vii. 14; Jos. *Vit.* 46. There is a Zakkai in the Talmud, father of the famous Rabbi Jochanan, and he also lived at Jericho.

the chief among the publicans] Rather, *a chief tax-gatherer*. He may even have risen as some Jews did, from the subordinate rank of the *portitores* to that of *publicanus* (Jos. *B. J.* II. 14, § 9). Priests (see on x. 31) and publicans—the latter employed to regulate the balsam-duties, and the exports and imports between the domains of the Romans and of Antipas—were the chief classes at Jericho (Jos. *Antt.* XIV. 4, § 1, XV. 4, § 2; Justin *Hist.* VI. 3).

3. *he sought to see Jesus*] Doubtless his riches increased the odium of his position, and being accustomed to contempt and hatred, he wished to see One who was not only a great prophet, but also kind to tax-gatherers and sinners.

4. *into a sycomore tree*] Not the same as the *sycamine* (*mulberry*) of xvii. 6, or with our *sycamore* (or pseudo-platanus) but the Egyptian fig, of which the low spreading branches are very easy to climb.

5. *Zaccheus, make haste*] Zacchaeus was so prominent a person in Jericho that we can see no difficulty in his being known to Jesus by name.

6. *joyfully*] This public honour done by the Messiah to one so despised by all classes of his countrymen, ennobled him with a new feeling of happiness and self-respect.

was gone to be guest with a man *that is* a sinner. And Zac- 8
cheus stood, and said unto the Lord; Behold, Lord, the
half of my goods I give to the poor; and if I have taken
any *thing* from any *man* by false accusation, I restore *him*
fourfold. And Jesus said unto him, This day is salvation 9
come to this house, forsomuch as he also is a son of Abraham. For the Son of man is come to seek and to save that 10
which was lost.

11—27. *The Parable of the Pounds.*

And as they heard these *things*, he added and spake a 11
parable, because he was nigh to Jerusalem, and *because* they
thought that the kingdom of God should immediately ap-

---

7. *they all murmured*] Rather, **they all began to murmur aloud.**
The '*all*' is very significant as shewing how deep-seated was the national feeling which, because it was unworthy, our Lord at the very zenith of His earthly popularity thus unflinchingly braved. Many of them may not have heard His previous vindication of His object (Matt. ix. 11—13).

to be guest] Literally, "*to put up*" as though at a guest-chamber (*kataluma*), ii. 7; Mk. xiv. 14.

8. *stood*] The word means 'taking his position' in sight of all the crowd; see xviii. 11.

unto the Lord] Not to the crowd who had nothing but contempt and hatred for him, but to Him who loved the nobler self which He saw in him, and of whose notice he desired to be more worthy.

the half of my goods] A vast sacrifice for one whose very position shewed that he had not been indifferent to wealth.

I give] i.e. I now propose to give; a *purpose* not a *past habit*.

by false accusation] On the word *esukophantēsa*, see iii. 14.

fourfold] far more therefore than was required by the Mosaic Law, which only demanded the restitution of a *fifth part* beyond the principal, Num. v. 7. The words neither deny nor affirm that any part of his wealth had been thus dishonestly gained.

9. *a son of Abraham*] Used here in the high spiritual sense (Rom. iv. 11, 12, 16; Gal. iii. 7) though also true (as the name shews) in the literal sense. See i. 55, iii. 8.

10. *that which was lost*] See xv. 1—32; Matt. xviii. 11; 1 Tim. i. 15; Ezek. xxxiv. 11—16.

11—27. THE PARABLE OF THE POUNDS.

11. *because he was nigh to Jerusalem*] Probably therefore the parable was spoken on the journey.

should immediately appear] Literally, "*be manifested to view.*" The disciples had the same excited anticipation after the Resurrection, Acts

294 ST LUKE, XIX. [vv. 12—14.

12 pear. He said therefore, A certain nobleman went into a far country to receive for himself a kingdom, and to return.
13 And he called his ten servants, and delivered them ten
14 pounds, and said unto them, Occupy till I come. But his citizens hated him, and sent a message after him, saying,

i. 6, 7. Our Lord was always careful to lead them away from false material hopes. The lessons of the parable are patient waiting and active work.

12. *A certain nobleman*, &c.] This would seem a most unintelligible incident if we did not know what suggested it. The Evangelists throw no gleam of light upon it, and the fact that we can from contemporary secular history not only explain it, but even trace (without the slightest aid from any of the Gospels) the exact circumstances *which suggested it at this very place and time*, is one of the many invaluable independent circumstances which enable us to prove from history the absolute truthfulness of these records. Two 'nobles'—Herod the Great and his son Archelaus—had actually gone from Jericho to a far country, even to Rome, for the express purpose of 'receiving a kingdom' from the all-powerful Caesar (Jos. *Antt.* XIV. 14, XVII. 9, § 4: comp. 1 Macc. viii. 13), and the same thing was subsequently done by Antipas (id. *Antt.* XVIII. 5, § 1). It is deeply interesting to see how Jesus thus utilises any incident—social or political—as a vehicle for spiritual instruction. Probably if we knew the events of His day more minutely, we should see the origin of many others of the parables. The facts here alluded to would naturally be brought both to His mind, and to those of the Galilaeans, by the sight of the magnificent palace at Jericho which Archelaus had rebuilt. (Jos. *Antt.* XVII. 13, § 1.) How little the incidental machinery of parables should be theologically pressed, we may see from the fact that here our Lord takes the movements and the actions of a cruel and bad prince like Archelaus, to shadow forth certain truths of His own ministry (compare the Parables of the Unjust Steward and the Unjust Judge).

13. *his ten servants*] Rather, **ten servants of his own**; for such a noble would count his servants by hundreds.

ten pounds] The *mina* was 100 drachmas (xv. 8), and was worth £3. 6s. 8d. in nominal value. The word is a corruption of the Hebrew *maneh*. (2 Chr. ix. 16.) A comparison of this parable with that of the *Talents* (Matt. xxv. 14—30) will shew the wide diversities between the two. Archelaus did actually leave money in the charge of some of his servants, especially entrusting Philippus to look after his pecuniary interests in his absence.

Occupy] Rather, **Trade**, *negotiamini*. Ps. cvii. 23, "that...*occupy their business* in great waters" (Prayer-Book). For the command see 1 Pet. iv. 10.

till I come] Another reading (ἐν ᾧ, א, A, B, D, &c.) would mean 'while I am on my journey,' but would involve a very dubious sense of *erchomai*.

We will not have this *man* to reign over us. And it came 15
to pass, that when he was returned, having received the
kingdom, then he commanded these servants to be called
unto him, to whom he had given the money, that he might
know how much every *man* had gained by trading. Then 16
came the first, saying, Lord, thy pound hath gained ten
pounds. And he said unto him, Well, *thou* good servant: 17
because thou hast been faithful in a very little, have thou
authority over ten cities. And the second came, saying, 18
Lord, thy pound hath gained five pounds. And he said 19
likewise to him, Be thou also over five cities. And another 20
came, saying, Lord, behold, *here is* thy pound, which I have
kept laid up in a napkin: for I feared thee, because thou 21
art an austere man: thou takest up that thou layedst not
down, and reapest that thou didst not sow. And he saith 22

14. *hated him*] And this was not strange, seeing that the very beginning of his reign had been signalised by a hideous massacre of his subjects. (Jos. *Antt.* XVII. 9, § 3.)

and sent a message after him] Rather, **an embassy to follow him** (xiv. 32). Here again the incident would be entirely obscure, if we did not know from Josephus that the Jews *did* send an embassy of 50 to Augustus—who were met on their arrival at Rome by 8000 Jews—to recount the cruelties of Archelaus, and plead for deliverance from him and the Herods generally. (Jos. *Antt.* XVII. 11, § 1, &c.) Although not immediately successful, the embassy was one of the circumstances which led to his ultimate deposition.

this man] The 'this' is supremely contemptuous. For the fact shadowed forth see John xv. 18, xix. 14, 15, 21.

15. *having received the kingdom*] Not however the coveted title of king, which was refused him.

had gained by trading] *diepragmateusato*, a compound form of the *pragmateuesthai* in vs. 13. The calling of the servants corresponds to the "Give an account of thy stewardship" of xvi. 2.

16. *thy pound hath gained*] Literally, "*earned in addition.*" As though there were no merit of his own in the matter.

17. *in a very little*] See xii. 48, xvi. 10.

have thou authority over ten cities] Another strange touch explained by the history of the times. Archelaus had actually assigned the government of cities to his adherents who had proved faithful, and this was not an uncommon plan among the Herodian princes. "We shall also reign with Him," 2 Tim. ii. 12.

21. *I feared thee*] A sure sign that he did not love him, 1 John iv. 18.

takest up that thou layedst not down] A typical description of injustice forbidden alike by Jewish and Greek laws (Jos. *c. Ap.* II. 130).

unto him, Out of thine own mouth will I judge thee, *thou wicked servant.* Thou knewest that I was an austere man, taking up that I laid not down, and reaping that I did not sow: wherefore then gavest not thou my money into the bank, that at my coming I might have required *mine own* with usury? And he said unto them that stood by, Take from him the pound, and give *it* to him that hath ten pounds. (And they said unto him, Lord, he hath ten pounds.) For I say unto you, That unto every one which hath shall be given; and from him that hath not, even that he hath shall be taken away from him. But those mine enemies, which would not that I should reign over them, bring hither, and slay *them* before me.

And when he had thus spoken, he went before, ascending up to Jerusalem.

22. *Out of thine own mouth*] "A powerful instance of the *argumentum ex concessis*." Lange.

23. *into the bank*] Rather, **into a bank**. The Greek word for 'bank' is *trapeza* ('a table'); hence a banker is *trapezites*. This touch contains the germ of the unrecorded saying (*agraphon dogma*) of our Lord, which is one of the most certainly genuine of those which are preserved by tradition—"Shew yourselves approved money-changers" (γίνεσθε τραπεζῖται δόκιμοι).

I might have required mine own with usury] Rather, **I might have exacted it with interest** (on *epraxa*, see iii. 13).

24. *Take from him the pound*] Here our Lord leaves the historical groundwork. Compare Matt. xxi. 43, "The kingdom of God shall be taken from you, and given to a nation bringing forth the fruits thereof." viii. 18.

25. *they said unto him*] Perhaps the officials round the king; but as this verse is purely parenthetical, it may not impossibly be an interpellation of the crowd, expressive of their vivid interest in the narrative.

26. *even that he hath*] Comp. viii. 18, "even that which he *seemeth to have*."

27. *mine enemies*] They had once been 'citizens,' vs. 14.

slay them before me] Archelaus had similarly put some of his political opponents to death. This, too, corresponds to ulterior truths—the ruin and massacre of the unbelieving Jews. Comp. 1 Cor. xv. 25.

28. *he went before*] Literally, "*he began to journey in front of them;*" as though, for the delivery of the parable, He had paused to let the crowd gather round Him.

ascending] The road from Jericho to Jerusalem is a continual ascent. See x. 30, 31.

29—40. *The Triumphal Entry into Jerusalem.*

²⁹ And it came to pass, when he was come nigh to Bethphage and Bethany, at the mount called *the mount* of Olives, he sent two of his disciples, ³⁰ saying, Go ye into the village over against *you;* in the which at your entering ye shall find a colt tied, whereon yet never man sat: loose him, and bring *him hither.* ³¹ And if any *man* ask you, Why do ye loose *him?* thus shall ye say unto him, Because the Lord hath need of him. ³² And they that were sent went their way, and found even as he had said unto them. ³³ And as they were loosing the colt, the owners thereof said unto them, Why loose ye the colt? ³⁴ And they said, The Lord hath need of him. ³⁵ And they brought him to Jesus: and they cast their garments upon the colt, and they set Jesus

29—40. THE TRIUMPHAL ENTRY INTO JERUSALEM.

29. *Bethphage*] The site is not identified, but it seems to have been regarded as a suburb of Jerusalem. The name means *House of* (*unripe*) *Figs*.

and Bethany] Perhaps the *House of Dates*, but this is very uncertain. The mention of Bethany *after* Bethphage is surprising. Here, however, St Luke omits the supper in the house of 'Simon the leper' (Matt. xxvi. 6—13; Mk. xiv. 3—9; John xii. 1—19) and the anointing of Jesus by Mary of Bethany. Jesus arrived at Bethany before sunset on Friday, Nisan 8 (March 31, A. D. 30), and therefore before the Sabbath began. Here the throng of Galilaean pilgrims would leave Him to go to their friends in Jerusalem, or to make booths for themselves in the valley of the Kidron and on the slopes of Olivet. The Sabbath was spent in quiet. The supper was in the evening, otherwise the Jews could not have come from Jerusalem, as the distance exceeded a Sabbath day's journey. It was on the next morning (Palm Sunday) that our Lord started for Jerusalem. His stay at Bethany may have been due to friendship, or may have been dictated by prudence. It was the brooding over the imagined loss of the value of the precious ointment —an assault of Satan at the weakest point—which first drove Judas to his secret interview with the Sadducean priests.

two of his disciples] The minute touch of description in Mk. xi. 4 has led to the conjecture that Peter was one of these two.

30. *a colt tied*] St Luke is here less circumstantial than the other Evangelists, and does not refer to the prophecy of Zech. ix. 9.

whereon yet never man sat] and therefore adapted for a sacred use. See Num. xix. 2; Deut. xxi. 3; 1 Sam. vi. 7.

35. *cast their garments upon the colt*] to do Jesus royal honour. Comp. 2 K. ix. 13.

they set Jesus thereon] It is clear that He rode upon the unused foal, which was probably led by the bridle, while it is possible that the

thereon. And as he went, they spread their clothes in the way. And when he was come nigh, *even* now at the descent of the mount of Olives, the whole multitude of the disciples began to rejoice and praise God with a loud voice for all the mighty works that they had seen; saying, Blessed *be* the King that cometh in the name of the Lord: peace in heaven, and glory in the highest. And some of the Pharisees from among the multitude said unto him, Master, rebuke thy disciples. And he answered and said unto them, I tell you that, if these should hold their peace, the stones would immediately cry out.

mother went by its side. St Matthew, however, alone (apparently) mentions two animals (xxi. 2, 7), and possibly this may have been due to some confusion arising out of the Hebrew parallelism (Zech. ix. 9, "riding upon an ass, *even* upon a colt, son of she-asses") in the translation into Greek from an Aramaic document. The ass in the East is not a despised animal (Gen. xlix. 14, xxii. 3; Judg. v. 10), and it is only because it was despised by Gentiles that Josephus substitutes for it 'horse' or 'beast of burden,' and the Seventy (LXX.) soften it down into 'foal,' &c. The Gentile world abounded in sneers against this narrative, and had all sorts of absurd stories about the Jews and the ass, or ass's head, which they were supposed to worship (Jos. *c. Ap.* II. 10; Tac. *Hist.* v. 3. 4). The Christians were also called ass-worshippers (Tert. *Apol.* 16; Minuc. Fel. *Oct.* 9), and this calumny is alluded to in one of the hideously blasphemous wall caricatures (*Graffiti*). (See however King's *Gnostics*, p. 90; Lundy, *Monumental Christianity*, p. 60.)

36. *spread their clothes in the way*] as well as leaves of trees and branches of the palms, which they tore off and kept strewing as they went along (Matt. xxi. 8), as in the reception of Mordecai (Targum on *Esther* x. 15) and of the Maccabees (2 Macc. x. 7). The very same mode of shewing honour was adopted when Mr Farran, the consul at Damascus, visited Jerusalem in 1834, at a time of great distress.

37. *even now at the descent of the mount of Olives*] at the spot where the main road from Bethany sweeps round the shoulder of the hill, and the city first bursts full on the view. At this point the palm-bearing procession from the city seems to have met the rejoicing crowd of the Galilaean pilgrims who had started with Jesus from Bethany.

38. *Blessed be the King*] The various cries recorded by the three Evangelists all come from the Great Hallel (Pss. cxiii.—cxviii). St John alone (xii. 17 reading ὅτι) points out that the Messianic enthusiasm had been mainly kindled by the raising of Lazarus.

39. *Master, rebuke thy disciples*] St Matthew puts into the mouth of "the Chief Priests and scribes" the ruder interpellation, "Hearest thou what these say?"

40. *the stones would immediately cry out*] There seems to be an allusion to the passage "For the stone shall cry out of the wall," which

41—44. *Jesus weeping over Jerusalem.*

And when he was come near, he beheld the city, and 41 wept over it, saying, If thou hadst known, even thou, at 42 least in this thy day, the *things* which belong unto thy peace! but now they are hid from thine eyes. For the days 43 shall come upon thee, that thine enemies shall cast a trench about thee, and compass thee round, and keep thee in on every side, and shall lay thee even with the ground, and thy 44

occurs amid denunciations of destruction on covetousness and cruelty in Hab. ii. 11.

41—44. JESUS WEEPING OVER JERUSALEM.

41. *he beheld the city*] The Temple was at that time magnificent with gilding and white marble, which flashed resplendently in the spring sunlight (Jos. *B. J.* v. 5, § 6), and the city was very unlike the crumbling and squalid city of to-day. But that "mass of gold and snow" woke no pride in the Saviour's heart. Few scenes are more striking than this burst of anguish in the very midst of the exulting procession.

wept over it] Not merely *edakrusen* 'shed silent tears' as at the grave of Lazarus (John xi. 35) but *eklausen* 'wept aloud;' and that although not all the agonies and insults of four days later could wring from Him one tear or sigh.

42. *at least in this thy day*] Is. lv. 6; 2 Cor. vi. 2.

which belong unto thy peace] Perhaps with a *paronomasia* on the name of *Salem* or 'Peace,' and on the *sound* though not the derivation of Jerusalem (*Yeroo Shalom* 'they shall see peace,' comp. Ps. cxxii. 6, 7). Such plays on words often spring from deep emotion. (See my *Chapters on Language*, pp. 269—276.) Is. xlviii. 18, "O that thou hadst hearkened to my commandments! then had *thy peace* been as a river."

43. *the days*] often used of troublous times, like the Latin *tempora*.

shall cast a trench about thee] Rather, **shall surround thee with a palisade**, Is. xxix. 3, 4, xxxvii. 33, LXX. Literally fulfilled forty years afterwards at the siege of Jerusalem, when Titus surrounded the city first with a palisaded mound (*vallum* and *agger*), and then with a wall of masonry.

keep thee in on every side] The blockade established was so terribly rigid that myriads of the Jews perished of starvation.

44. *shall lay thee even with the ground*] Titus, if we may trust Josephus, accomplished this prophecy wholly against his will, being driven to the utter subversion and destruction of the city, by the desperate obstinacy of the Jews. Sulpicius Severus (*Hist.* II.), who is supposed to be here incorporating a fragment of Tacitus, says, "alii et *Titus ipse* evertendum templum in primis censebant quo plenius Judaeorum *et Christianorum* religio tolleretur." Josephus says that it was so frightfully desolated by the siege, that any Jew coming suddenly upon it would have asked what place it was (Jos. *B. J.* VI. 1, § 1). It was again laid waste in the rebellion under Barcochba.

children within thee: and they shall not leave in thee one stone upon another; because thou knewest not the time of thy visitation.

45, 46. *Final Cleansing of the Temple.*

45, 46 And he went into the temple, and began to cast out them that sold therein, and *them that* bought; saying unto them, It is written, My house is the house of prayer: but ye have made it a den of thieves.

47, 48. *Eagerness of the People to hear.*

47, 48 And he taught daily in the temple. But the chief priests and the scribes and the chief of the people sought to destroy him, and could not find what they might do: for all the people were very attentive to hear him.

and thy children within thee] The siege began at the Passover, and hence it is said that nearly 3,000,000 Jews were crowded into the city.

shall not leave in thee one stone upon another] The subsequent attempt of the Jews to rebuild the Temple was frustrated by the outburst of subterranean fires. See Gibbon, ch. xxiii. II. 309 (ed. Milman). Comp. Mic. iii. 12.

of thy visitation] See Is. xxix. 2—4; Hos. x. 14, 15. For the word 'visitation' see 1 Pet. ii. 12; Ecclus. xviii. 20. The 'visitation' which they had neglected was one of mercy, i. 68.

45, 46. FINAL CLEANSING OF THE TEMPLE.

45. *he went into the temple*] The procession of Galilaean pilgrims would leave Jesus at the foot of Mount Moriah—(the 'Mountain of the House,' Is. ii. 2), beyond which none might advance with dusty feet or stained by travel. Jesus would enter by the Shushan gate.

began to cast out, &c.] As He had also done at the *beginning* of His ministry, John ii. 15. The needs of the pilgrims—the money which had to be changed—the purchase of cattle for sacrifice, &c.—had made the cloisters, precincts, and even the outer court of the Temple a scene of noisy and greedy barter, as the nave of St Paul's used to be a few generations ago. For further details, see Matt. xxi. 12, 13; Mk. xi. 15—17.

46. *My house is the house of prayer*] Is. lvi. 7. See on i. 10, xviii. 10.

a den of thieves] Rather, **a brigands' cave.** Our Lord had seen many of these brigands' caves on the steep rocky sides of the Wady Hamâm and elsewhere. Comp. Jer. vii. 11, "Is this house which is called by my name become a den of robbers in your eyes?" It became still more a murderers' cave when the *sicarii* made its pavement swim with blood (Jos. *B. J.* IV. 3, §§ 7, 10).

47, 48. EAGERNESS OF THE PEOPLE TO HEAR.

48. *were very attentive to hear him*] Literally, "*were hanging from him*," i.e. hung on His lips; "*pendebat ab ore,*" Verg. *Aen.* IV. 79.

CH. XX. 1—8. *Sudden Question of the Priests and Scribes.*

And it came to pass, *that* on one of those days, as he 20 taught the people in the temple, and preached the gospel, the chief priests and the scribes came upon *him* with the

> "On thee the loyal-hearted *hung*."
> TENNYSON.

"Hanged on him, as the bee doth on the flower, the babe on the breast, the little bird on the bill of her dam. Christ drew the people after Him by the golden chain of His heavenly eloquence." J. Trapp.

CH. XX. 1—8. SUDDEN QUESTION OF THE PRIESTS AND SCRIBES.

1. *on one of those days*] 'Those' is omitted in ℵ, B, D, L, Q. By careful comparison of the Evangelists we find that after the Triumphal Entry into Jerusalem on Palm Sunday, our Lord was received in the Temple by the children—probably those engaged in the Choral Service of the Temple—with shouts of Hosanna, which again called forth the embittered rebuke of the priests. These rebukes He silenced by a reference to Ps. viii. 2. Then came the message brought to Him by Andrew and Philip from the Greek enquirers (supposed by some to have been sent by Abgarus V., King of Edessa), and the Voice from Heaven. After this he retired privately from the Temple, and bivouacked (ηὐλίσθη) for the night on the Mount of Olives (John xii. 20—5; Matt. xxi. 17). Next morning—Monday in Passion Week—occurred the incident of the Fruitless Figtree (Matt. xxi. 18, 19), and it was after this that our Lord entered the Temple. This Monday in Passion week may be called a Day of Parables, since on it were uttered the Parables of the Two Sons (Matt. xxi. 28—32); the Rebellious Husbandmen (9—16); the Rejected Cornerstone (17, 18); and the Marriage of the King's Son (Matt. xxii. 1—14).

preached the gospel] *euangelizomenou*, iii. 18, iv. 43, &c. This beautiful word is almost confined to St Luke, who uses it twenty-five times, and St Paul, who uses it twenty times.

the chief priests and the scribes] The chief priests were the heads of the twenty-four courses. It was probably the humble triumph of Palm Sunday, and the intense excitement produced in the city (ἐσείσθη) by the arrival of Jesus (Matt. xxi. 10), which first awoke the active jealousy of the chief priests of Jerusalem, who were wealthy Sadducees in alliance with the Herodians, and who had hitherto despised Jesus as only a 'Prophet of Nazareth.' From this period of the narrative, the hostility of the Pharisees, as such, is much less marked. Indeed they would have sympathised with the cleansing of the Temple, which involved a terrible reflexion on the greed and neglect of the hierarchic party.

came upon him] The word implies a sudden and hostile demonstration (Acts xxiii. 27, iv. 1, vi. 12). They thus surrounded Him while He was walking in the Temple (Mark xi. 27).

elders, and spake unto him, saying, Tell us, by what authority doest thou these *things ?* or who is he that gave thee this authority? And he answered and said unto them, I will also ask you one thing; and answer me: The baptism of John, was it from heaven, or of men? And they reasoned with themselves, saying, If we shall say, From heaven; he will say, Why then believed ye him not? But *and* if we say, Of men; all the people will stone us: for they be persuaded that John was a prophet. And they answered, that *they* could not tell whence *it was*. And Jesus said unto

with the elders] There were probably three great sections of the Sanhedrin: 1, Priests; 2, Scribes and Rabbis (Sopherîm, Tanaîm, &c.); and 3, Levites. Derenbourg, *Pal.* ch. vi.

2. *by what authority*] Rather, **by what kind of authority**. The implication is 'you are only called a Rabbi by courtesy;' you are not a 'pupil of the wise;' you are not a priest, or a scribe, or a political functionary. Yet you usurp functions which rather belong to Caiaphas, or the President of the Sanhedrin, or the Romans, or Herod. If you act as a Prophet *shew us a sign.* Practically it was the old taunt by which he had been grieved in Galilee (Matt. xii. 39, xvi. 4).

who is he that gave thee this authority?] Every recognised Rabbi had received his diploma; every Priest his ordination.

3. *I will also ask you one thing*] Rather, **a question**. The divine *readiness* and (if we may be allowed the expression) *presence of mind* of Jesus was most conspicuously shewn on this perilous day and the next day.

and answer me] We see from St Mark (xi. 30) that this emphatic expression came *after* His question—as though to hasten their delay, and break up a whispered colloquy of perplexity.

4. *was it from heaven, or of men?*] Rather, **from men**. This was equivalent to the question—with which surely the teachers of Israel should *at once* have been provided with an answer—was the Baptist a prophet or a seducer? If they could not answer this question they were obviously *incompetent to decide* as to the authority by which He worked.

5. *they reasoned with themselves*] They went aside to discuss together what answer they should give. This deliberation rendered their confession of ignorance more glaring and more fatal to their claims.

Why then believed ye him not?] See vii. 30. It never occurred to them to speak with the courage of their convictions.

6. *all the people will stone us*] The word is a strong compound—*katalithasei*—used here only—'will stone us to death.' Herod had been daunted by the same dread, Matt. xiv. 5; Jos. *Antt.* XVIII. 5, § 2. It illustrates the furious bursts of fanaticism to which the Jews were liable (John viii. 59, x. 31, &c.).

persuaded] Rather, **firmly convinced**. The tense implies an unalterable conclusion.

them, Neither tell I you by what authority I do these things.

9—19. *The Parable of the Labourers in the Vineyard.*

Then began he to speak to the people this parable; A certain man planted a vineyard, and let it forth to husbandmen, and went into a far country for a long time. And at the season he sent a servant to the husbandmen, that they should give him of the fruit of the vineyard: but the husbandmen beat him, and sent *him* away empty. And again he sent another servant: and they beat him also, and en-

7. *they could not tell*] Rather, **did not know.** A wise answer in cases of real uncertainty, as the Hebrew proverb taught—"*Learn to say I do not know;*" but a base answer when they *had* an opinion but did not dare to avow it; and doubly base in the matter of a question on which it was their plain duty to have arrived at a judgment. To be reduced to this ignominious necessity of confessing ignorance (though "*we know*" was one of their favourite phrases, John ix. 24, &c.) was a public humiliation which they had brought upon themselves.

8. *Neither tell I you*] If they were incompetent to decide as to the authority of the Prophet who had saluted Jesus as the Messiah, they were obviously incompetent to decide as to *His* authority.

9—19. THE PARABLE OF THE LABOURERS IN THE VINEYARD.

9. *to the people*] but still in the hearing of the priests and scribes who had only withdrawn a little into the background (vs. 19; Matt. xxi. 32, 45). St Luke here omits the Parable of the Two Sons (Matt. xxi. 28—32), in which, as in this Parable, the hidden meaning—applicable in the first instance to Pharisees and the people, and in the second to Jews and Gentiles—was hardly veiled.

a vineyard] As in Is. v. 1—7; Ps. lxxx.; Ezek. xv. 1—6; Jer. ii. 21. St Luke omits the special isolation, &c. of the vineyard. Vines, grapes, and vineleaves were symbols of Palestine, on the coins of the Maccabees.

to husbandmen] namely, (1) the Jewish nation; (2) their rulers and teachers.

for a long time] The nearly two thousand years of Jewish History. Comp. Matt. xxv. 19. In this long time they learnt to say "the Lord hath forsaken the earth," Ezek. viii. 12; Ps. x. 5.

10. *he sent a servant*] The various 'servants' are the Judges, the better Priests, and the Prophets.

that they should give him of the fruit] The payment is in *kind*, on the *métayer* system.

11. *And again he sent another*] Jer. xliv. 4. Literally, "*And he added to send another*"—a Hebraism, xix. 11; Acts xii. 3; Gen. iv. 2.

¹² treated *him* shamefully, and sent *him* away empty. And again he sent a third: and they wounded him also, and cast ¹³ *him* out. Then said the lord of the vineyard, What shall I do? I will send my beloved son: it may be they will ¹⁴ reverence *him* when they see him. But when the husbandmen saw him, they reasoned among themselves, saying, This is the heir: come, let us kill him, that the inheritance may ¹⁵ be ours. So they cast him out of the vineyard, and killed *him*. What therefore shall the lord of the vineyard do unto ¹⁶ them? He shall come and destroy these husbandmen, and shall give the vineyard to others. And when they heard *it*, ¹⁷ they said, God forbid. And he beheld them, and said,

entreated him shamefully] There is a gradation in their impious audacity. In St Matthew (xxi. 35) it is (1) beat, (2) killed, (3) stoned. In St Mark (xii. 3—5) it is (1) beat, and sent away empty; (2) wounded in the head, and insulted; (3) killed. And when more servants are sent they beat some and kill some.

12. *cast him out*] On this treatment of God's messengers see on xiii. 33, 34 and Neh. ix. 26; 1 K. xxii. 24—27; 2 Chr. xxiv. 19—22; Acts vii. 52; 1 Thess. ii. 15; Heb. xi. 36, 37, where the same charge is reiterated.

13. *What shall I do?*] Gen. i. 26, vi. 7.

I will send my beloved son] who "took on Him the form of a servant." Our Lord's teaching respecting His own divine dignity advanced in distinctness as the end was approaching.

it may be] Literally, "*perhaps*." It occurs here alone in the N. T. and once only in the LXX., 1 Sam. xxv. 21 (Heb. אך, E. V. 'surely'). This 'perhaps' belongs of course only to the parable, but it (i) indicates their free will, and (ii) enhances their awful crime to represent it as having seemed all but inconceivable.

when they see him] Omitted in א, B, C, D, L, Q.

14. *that the inheritance may be ours*] "His Son, whom he hath appointed heir of all things," Heb. i. 2. Comp. John xi. 47—53. "They killed that they might possess, and because they killed they lost." Aug.

15. *cast him out of the vineyard*] This may involve an allusion to Christ suffering "without the gate," Heb. xiii. 12, 13; John xix. 17. The prophecy was meant if possible at the last hour to prevent the guilt of its own fulfilment (2 K. viii. 12, 13).

16. *He shall come and destroy*] In Matt. xxi. 41 this is the answer of the people themselves to our Lord's question.

shall give the vineyard to others] "Lo, we turn to the Gentiles," Acts xiii. 46.

God forbid] Literally, "*Might it not be!*" Heb. *Chalîlah*. In this utterance we hear the groan of the Jewish people when the truth that they

What is this then that is written, The stone which the builders rejected, the same is become the head of the corner? Whosoever shall fall upon that stone 18 shall be broken; but on whomsoever it shall fall, it will grind him to powder. And the chief priests and the scribes 19 the same hour sought to lay hands on him; and they feared the people: for they perceived that he had spoken this parable against them.

20—26. *Question about the Tribute Money.*

And they watched *him*, and sent forth spies, which *should* 20

were indeed to be rejected burst upon them. It woke an echo even in the heart of the Apostle of the Gentiles. For the Hebrew expression *Chalilah* see Gen. xliv. 7, 17; Josh. xxii. 29. It occurs ten times in the Epistle to the Romans alone. See *Life of St Paul*, II. 206. It is the opposite of Amen, but occurs here alone in the Gospels.

17. *he beheld them*] Rather, **looking fixedly on them**, to add solemnity to His reference to their own Scriptures.

that is written] He here refers them to the very Psalm from which the Hosanna of the multitude had been taken.

The stone which the builders rejected] This is a quotation from Ps. cxviii. 22, comp. Is. xxviii. 16. The stone is regarded both as a foundation-stone, and a stone at the angle of the building, binding the two walls together. These words made a deep impression on St Peter (1 Pet. ii. 7, 8).

18. *shall fall upon that stone*] as the Jews did from the first, 1 Cor. i. 23. See Is. viii. 14, 15.

shall be broken] Literally, "*shall be sorely bruised.*"

it shall fall] as it did on the finally impenitent Jews after Christ's Ascension.

it will grind him to powder] Literally, "*it shall winnow him*" (Jer. xxxi. 10), with obvious reference to the great Image which 'the stone cut without hands' smote and broke to pieces, so that its fragments became "like the chaff of the summer threshingfloor, and the wind carried them away," Dan. ii. 35.

19. *against them*] This decidedly shews the *primary* sense of the Parable. As yet they hardly realized its wider significance. So when the priests and rulers saw that Jeremiah spoke against them, "Come," said they, "and let us devise devices against Jeremiah...come, and let us smite him with the tongue," Jer. xviii. 18.

After this parable our Lord added the Parable of the Marriage of the King's Son. Thus in three continuous Parables He convicted the Priests and Scribes (1) of false professions; (2) of cruel faithlessness; (3) of blind presumption. This with their public humiliation about John's baptism made them thirst for speedy vengeance.

feign themselves just *men*, that they might take hold of his words, that *so they* might deliver him unto the power and authority of the governor. And they asked him, saying, Master, we know that thou sayest and teachest rightly, neither acceptest thou the person *of any*, but teachest the way

20—26. QUESTION ABOUT THE TRIBUTE MONEY.

20. *And they watched him*] For the word used see vi. 7, xiv. 1, xvii. 20. The incident now related took place on the Tuesday in Passion-week—the Day of Temptations, or insidious questions—the last and greatest day of the public ministry of Jesus. On the previous evening He had again retired to the Mount of Olives, and in the morning the disciples remarked that the Fig-tree had withered. He had scarcely arrived in the Temple when the plot of the Jewish rulers on the previous evening began to be carried out.

spies] Literally, "*liers in wait*" (*enkathetous*, Josh. viii. 14; Job xxxi. 9).

just men] Rather, **righteous**; ingenuous and scrupulous 'disciples of the wise,' honestly seeking for instruction. They pretend to be strict legalists who revive the scruples of Judas the Gaulonite.

they] i.e. the priests.

take hold of his words] Comp. Ecclus. viii. 11, "Rise not up in anger at the presence of an injurious person, *lest he lie in wait to entrap thee in thy words.*" The words might be rendered '*take hold of Him by His speech.*'

unto the power and authority of the governor] Rather, **to the** (Roman) **magistracy and to the jurisdiction of the procurator.** Comp. xii. 11. They had not the power or the courage to put Christ to death themselves. We see from Matt. xxii. 15; Mark xii. 16 that this plot sprang from an unholy alliance of Pharisees with Herodians—i.e. of scrupulosity with indifferentism—of devotees with sycophants;—not the first or last instance of the ill-omened conjunction of Priests and Statesmen—

> "Statesmen bloodstained and Priests idolatrous
> With dark lies maddening the blind multitude—"

who mutually hate each other, but unite in common hatred "to crush a reformer whose zeal might be inimical to both." (Neander.)

21. *Master, we know*, &c.] There is something in this fawning malice, and treacherous flattery, almost as repulsive as the kiss of Judas.

neither acceptest thou the person of any] Gal. ii. 6. The word for 'person' is *prosopon*, 'a mask;' it is as though they would imply that Jesus was not only an Impartial Judge, too true for sycophancy, but also *too keen-sighted to be deceived by hypocrisy*. And the one blighting word 'Ye hypocrites!' shewed them that their words were truer than they had intended. From the phrase *lambaneis prosopon* are formed the words *prosopolemptes* and *prosopolempsia*; see Eph. vi. 9; Col. iii. 25; Acts x. 34, &c. It is a Hebrew phrase, Lev. xix. 15; Mal. i. 8.

of God truly: is it lawful for us to give tribute unto Cesar, 22
or no? But he perceived their craftiness, and said unto 23
them, Why tempt ye me? Shew me a penny. Whose 24
image and superscription hath it? They answered and said,
Cesar's. And he said unto them, Render therefore unto 25
Cesar the *things* which be Cesar's, and unto God the *things*
which be God's. And they could not take hold of his words 26
before the people: and they marvelled at his answer, and
held their peace.

22. *is it lawful for us to give tribute unto Cesar, or no?*] The question was devised with so superlative a craft that it seemed impossible for our Lord to escape. If He said 'It is lawful,' the *Pharisees* hoped at once to undermine His popularity with the multitude. If He said 'It is not lawful' (Deut. xvii. 15), the *Herodians* could at once hand Him over, as a traitor, to the secular power. For '*tribute*' each Evangelist uses a different word—*epikephalaion*, 'poll-tax' (Mark in D); the Latin *kenson* 'census' (Matt.); and the classical *phoron* here and xxiii. 2. It was a capitation-tax, the legality of which was indignantly disputed by scrupulous legalists.

craftiness] *panourgian*, a classical word only found in St Paul and St Luke, 2 Cor. iv. 2, xi. 3, &c.

23. *Why tempt ye me*, &c.] Our Lord saw at once that it was a cunning test-question meant only to entrap Him. Not for a moment did these fawning spies deceive him though

> "Neither man nor angel can discern
> Hypocrisy, the only evil that walks
> Invisible, except to God alone."

These Pharisees were illustrating the truth that "no form of self-deceit is more hateful than that which veils spite and falsehood under the guise of frankness, and behind the profession of religion."

24. *Shew me a penny*] A denarius. See on vii. 41. We see from Mk. xii. 15, 16 that they were obliged to borrow the heathen coin from one of the tables of the money-changers. They would only carry Jewish money in their own girdles.

Whose image and superscription hath it?] On one side would be the once beautiful but now depraved features of Tiberius; the title *Pontifex Maximus* was probably inscribed on the obverse.

25. *unto Cesar the things which be Cesar's*] St Paul very clearly enforces the same duty in Rom. xiii. 6, 7. The 'tribute' in Matt. xvii. 24 was quite different; it was the Temple didrachma.

and unto God the things which be God's] To Caesar you owe what he demands of *his own* coinage; to the Temple the tribute which you *can* only pay in the shekel of the sanctuary; to God you owe *yourselves*. Pay to Caesar the coins which bear his stamp, to God the duties of your own souls which bear *His* image.

26. *they marvelled at his answer*] Comp. ii. 47. They thought that

27—40. *Discomfiture of the Sadducees.*

27, 28 Then came to *him* certain of the Sadducees, which deny that there is any resurrection; and they asked him, saying, Master, Moses wrote unto us, If any *man*'s brother die, having a wife, and he die without children, that

escape was impossible for Him; and yet He instantly shatters their deeply-laid plot to pieces by shewing that they—Pharisees and Herodians alike—*had absolutely decided the question already* (according to their own rule "He whose coin is current is king of the land"), so that there is no need for Him to give any opinion whatever about it. The point was this,—their national acceptance of Caesar's coinage was an unanswerable admission of Caesar's right. Tribute to them was no longer a cheerful offering, but a legal due; not a voluntary gift, but a political necessity. The very word He used was decisive. They had asked "Is it lawful to *give* (*dounai*)?" He answers, 'Give back' (*apodote*). By using these coins they all alike admitted that 'they had no king but Caesar.' The Christians understood the principle perfectly (1 Pet. ii. 13, 14) as the ancient Jews had done (Jer. xxvii. 4—8). Yet these hypocrites dared to shout three days afterwards that Jesus 'had forbidden to give tribute to Caesar!'

27—40. Discomfiture of the Sadducees.

27. *certain of the Sadducees*] Matt. iii. 7. On the Sadducees see the Excursus on Jewish Sects. They were undeterred by the discomfiture of the Pharisees and Herodians, and perhaps their plot had been so arranged as coincidently to humiliate our Lord, if they could, by a difficult question, and so to shake His credit with the people. Some have supposed that the memorable incident of the Woman taken in Adultery (John viii. 1—11) also took place on this day; in which case there would have been three temptations of Christ, one *political*, one *doctrinal*, and one *speculative*. But that incident rose spontaneously, whereas these had been pre-arranged.

which deny that there is any resurrection] Jos. *Antt.* XVIII. 1, § 4; *B. J.* II. 8, § 14. They refused to see any proof of it in the Books of Moses; and to the Prophets and the other books (the *Ketubhim* or Hagiographa) they only attached a subordinate importance. Their question was inspired less by deadly hatred than by supercilious scorn. Wealthy and powerful, they only professed to despise Jesus, up to this time, as a 'Prophet of Nazareth,' though now they became His *main* murderers. They are not so much as mentioned by St John, and very slightly by St Mark and St Luke, nor did Christ utter against them the same denunciations as against the Pharisees, who were His daily opponents. All the leading families of high priests at this period were Sadducees, and—except where it comes into *direct collision* with religion—Epicurean worldliness is more tolerant than interested fanaticism.

28. *Moses wrote unto us*] The law of levirate marriage. Deut. xxiii. 4. See on iii. 23.

his brother should take *his* wife, and raise up seed unto his brother. There were therefore seven brethren: and the first took a wife, and died without children. And the second took her to wife, and he died childless. And the third took her; and in like manner the seven also: and they left no children, and died. Last of all the woman died also. Therefore in the resurrection whose wife of them is she? for seven had her to wife. And Jesus answering said unto them, The children of this world marry, and are given in marriage: but they which shall be accounted worthy to obtain that world, and the resurrection from the dead, neither marry, nor are given in marriage: neither can they die

29. *There were therefore seven brethren*] In Matt. xxii. 25 it runs "there were *with us*," as though they were alluding to an actual case.

30. *And the second took her*] This question about the husband of the "Sevenfold widow" was one of the materialistic objections to the Resurrection, which as an insipid 'difficulty' had often been discussed in Jewish schools. It was excessively commonplace, and even if Jesus had given the answer which contented the most eminent Rabbis of the Pharisaic schools—that the woman would be the wife of the *first* husband—it is hard to see what triumph these shallow Epicureans (as the Talmud calls them) would have gained by their question.

33. *whose wife?*] The forcible order of B, L is "*the woman, therefore, in the resurrection, whose wife does she become of the seven?*"
for seven] Rather, **for the seven.**

34. *The children of this world*] i.e. all who live in the present dispensation. Here, as often elsewhere, the word rendered 'world' is *aeon*, which properly means 'age.' It is not the *kosmos* or material Universe, but the Universe regarded subjectively, i.e. the Time-world.

35. *accounted worthy*] Comp. xxi. 36; Rev. iii. 4; 2 Thess. i. 5. *Sane magna dignatio.* Bengel.
to obtain that world] i.e. the genuine inheritors of the future aeon beyond the grave, xiv. 14; Phil. iii. 11. The answer of Jesus is not only full of tolerant condescension, but also of a divine wisdom which at once dwarfs into insignificance the most vaunted insight of the Rabbinic Hillels and Shammais. It is further most important, as being one of the very few passages which give us a clear glimpse into the actual conditions of future blessedness. These Sadducees erred because, in their ignorance of the Scriptures and the power of God (Mark xii. 24), they were imagining a kingdom which could be inherited by "flesh and blood."

36. *neither can they die any more*] Rather, **for neither,** &c. There is no marriage and no more birth. "There shall be no more death," Rev. xxi. 4. "The dead shall be raised *incorruptible*," 1 Cor. xv. 52.

any more: for they are equal unto *the* angels; and are the
37 children of God, being the children of the resurrection. Now
that the dead are raised, even Moses shewed at the bush,
when he calleth the Lord the God of Abraham, and
38 the God of Isaac, and the God of Jacob. For he is
not a God of the dead, but of the living: for all live unto
him.

39 Then certain of the scribes answering said, Master, thou

equal unto the angels] Like the angels in being immortal, but superior to them in privileges (Heb. i. 4; ii. 5—8). "When He shall appear, we shall be *like Him*; for we shall see Him as He is," 1 John iii. 2. In this one word our Lord refutes the Sadducean denial of the existence of angels, Acts xxiii. 8; and incidentally those *material* notions of future bliss (xiv. 15) which all the Jews held.

the children of God, being the children of the resurrection] "*I* am the resurrection, and the life," John xi. 25.

37. *are raised*] Literally, "*are being raised*"—the present of eternal certainty.

even Moses] The argument is *à fortiori*, as though our Lord would say, "the Prophets prove it abundantly, but I will not quote them since you attach higher importance to the Law. You quote Moses to throw doubt on the Resurrection; but *even Moses*, &c."

shewed] Rather, **disclosed**, or *revealed*.

at the bush] Rather, **in the Bush**, i.e. in that section of Exodus (Ex. iii.) which they called by that name, just as they called 2 Sam. i. 'the Bow' and Ezek. i. 'the Chariot.' Comp. "in Elias," Rom. xi. 2 (*marg.*).

38. *he is not a God of the dead, but of the living*] Rather, **of dead beings, but of living beings**. The Pharisees had endeavoured to draw proofs of immortality from the Law, i.e. from Numb. xv. 31. In later times they borrowed this proof from Christ,—lighting their torches at the sun though they hated its beams. But they had, up to this time, offered no proof so deep and true as this. The argument is that God would never have called Himself "the God of Abraham, of Isaac, and of Jacob," if these Patriarchs, after brief and sad lives, had become mere heaps of crumbling dust. Would He have given confidence by calling Himself the God of dust and ashes? So Josephus (?) says, 4 *Macc.* xvi. 24, "they who die for God's sake, live unto God as Abraham, Isaac, and Jacob, and all the Patriarchs." Acts xvii. 28.

for all live unto him] Rom. xiv. 8, 9. Our Lord added, "Ye therefore do greatly err." But how incomparably less severe is the condemnation of religious and intellectual error, than the burning rebuke against Pharisaic lovelessness!

39. *Then certain of the scribes*] Even the Pharisees could not fail to see the luminous wisdom and spiritual depth of our Lord's reply, and while *all* of them would rejoice at this unanswerable confutation of their hereditary opponents, some of them would have the candour to express

hast well said. And after that they durst not ask him any 40 question at all.

41—47. *The Scribes, Sadducees, and Pharisees reduced to a Confession of Ignorance.*

And he said unto them, How say they that Christ is 41 David's son? And David himself saith in the book of 42 Psalms, The LORD said to my Lord, Sit thou on my right hand, till I make thine enemies thy foot- 43 stool. David therefore calleth him Lord, how is he then 44 his son?

their approval. Truth will always offend some, but others will value it. After this grateful acknowledgment, however, one of them could not refrain from gratifying the insatiable spirit of casuistry by asking Christ 'which is the great commandment of the Law?' (Matt. xxii. 34—40; Mk. xii. 28—34.) This incident is omitted by St Luke, because he has given similar ones before.

40. *they durst not ask him any question*] The total collapse of their stratagems enhanced our Lord's peril, by shewing how impossible it was for these rich and learned "pupils of the wise" to pose themselves as superiors to Christ in wisdom and knowledge. Assumed contempt was deepened into real hatred, and all the more after the next incident.

41—47. THE SCRIBES, SADDUCEES, AND PHARISEES REDUCED TO A CONFESSION OF IGNORANCE.

41. *How say they that Christ is David's son?*] Rather, **the Christ.** See John vii. 42; Ps. cxxxii. 11; Jer. xxiii. 5; Mic. v. 2.

42. *in the book of Psalms*] Ps. cx. 1. The Jews universally regarded it as a Messianic Psalm, and in vs. 3 the LXX. renders, "From the womb, *before the morning star*, did I beget thee."

The LORD said to my Lord] In the Hebrew it is "Jehovah said to my Lord (*Adonai*)."

Sit thou on my right hand] Comp. Matt. xxvi. 64.

43. *till I make thine enemies thy footstool*] "He must reign till He hath put all enemies under His feet," 1 Cor. xv. 25.

44. *how is he then his son?*] To a Jew it was inconceivable that a father, or ancestor, should call his son "Lord." The only possible solution—that the Messiah was only "made of the seed of David *after the flesh*" (Rom. i. 3) was one which they had never chosen to accept. They, like the Ebionites, expected for their Messiah a mere 'beloved man.' And thus, for the second time on this day, they had drawn on their own heads, by their hypocritic craft, the humiliating necessity of publicly confessing their ignorance respecting matters of primary importance before the people, whose absolute reverence they claimed. They 'did not know' whether the Baptist was an Impostor or a Prophet; they 'could not answer a word' to a most obvious question as to the

45 Then in the audience of all the people he said unto his
46 disciples, Beware of the scribes, which desire to walk in long robes, and love greetings in the markets, and the highest seats in the synagogues, and the chief rooms at feasts;
47 which devour widows' houses, and for a shew make long prayers: the same shall receive greater damnation.

CH. XXI. 1—4. *The Widow's Mite.*

21 And he looked up, and saw the rich *men* casting their

Messianic hope which they put forward as the very centre of their religion! Comp. xiv. 6.

45. *in the audience of all the people*] Rather, **while all the people were listening.** Here followed the final rupture of Jesus with the authorities—political, social, and religious—of His nation. They had now made their own condemnation inevitable, and had justly provoked that great Denunciation on which (as less intelligible to Gentiles) St Luke here only touches. But he has given it in part before (xi. 39—52) in his account of the hostile banquet at the house of a Pharisee. In St Matthew it occupies, with its rhythmic grandeur and awfully solemn condemnation, the whole of the twenty-third chapter.

46. *to walk in long robes*] with special conspicuousness of fringes, Numb. xv. 38—40. "The supreme tribunal," said R. Nachman, "will duly punish *hypocrites who wrap their talliths round them* to appear, what they are not, true Pharisees."

greetings in the markets] See on xi. 43: *Videri quam esse* was their secret rule.

47. *which devour widows' houses*] Josephus expressly tells us that the Pharisees had large female followings, and an absolute sway in the Gynaekonitis or women's apartments, Jos. *Antt.* XVIII. 2, § 4.

for a shew] Rather, **in pretence.** Their hypocrisy was so notorious that even the Talmud records the warning given by Alexander Jannaeus to his wife on his deathbed against *painted* Pharisees. And in their seven classes of Pharisees the Talmudic writers place "*Shechemites*"— Pharisees from self-interest; *Stumblers*—so mock-humble that they will not raise their feet from the ground; *Bleeders*—so mock-modest, that because they will not raise their eyes, they run against walls, &c. Thus the Jewish writers themselves depict the Pharisees as the Tartuffes of antiquity.

long prayers] Such as the twenty-six forms of prayer at ablution; the Eighteen Benedictions (Shemoneh Esreh), &c.

damnation] Rather, **judgment.** The word is not even *katakrima*, or 'condemnation.' Their 'judgment' shall be more severe than that of those who practised *none* of these religious ordinances. It should be "more tolerable for Tyre and Sidon at the judgment" than for these, x. 14.

CH. XXI. 1—4. THE WIDOW'S MITE.

1. *he looked up*] The expression seems to shew that He was sitting

gifts into the treasury. And he saw also a certain poor 2
widow casting in thither two mites. And he said, Of a 3
truth I say unto you, that this poor widow hath cast in more
than *they* all: for all these have of their abundance cast in 4
unto the offerings of God: but she of her penury hath cast
in all the living that she had.

5—7. *The Doom of the Temple, and the Question about the End.*

And as some spake of the temple, how it was adorned 5
with downcast eyes, saddened, perhaps, in His human spirit and
agitated by the great Denunciation; but this last little incident is 'like
a rose amid a field of thistles,'—an act genuinely beautiful in the desert
of 'official devotion.'

the rich men] More literally, "*He saw those who were casting their
gifts into the treasury—rich men.*" St Mark tells us that the gifts were
large (Mk. xii. 41).

into the treasury] See John viii. 20. This was in the Court of the
Women. The High Priest Jehoiada had put a chest for this purpose
at the entrance of the House, 2 K. xii. 9; see Neh. x. 38; Jos. *B. J.*
VI. 5; *Antt.* XIX. 6, § 1, and 2 Macc. iii. 6—12. It contained the Corban,
Matt. xxvii. 6. But in our Lord's day there were thirteen chests called
Shopheroth, from their trumpet-shaped openings, adorned with various
inscriptions. These rich men do not seem to have been observing the
injunctions both sacred and Talmudic to give secretly, Matt. vi. 4, 18.

2. *also*] If the *kai* be genuine, it should perhaps follow the *tina*—
"some one—even a widow."

two mites] "which make a farthing," Mk. xii. 42. The *lepton* or
prutah was the smallest of coins, and the Rabbis did not allow any one
to give less than two.

3. *more than they all*] because "one coin out of a little is better
than a treasure out of much, and it is not considered how much is
given, but how much remains behind." S. Ambrose. See 2 Cor. viii.
12. In the Talmud a High Priest is similarly taught by a vision not to
despise a poor woman's offering of meal. The true estimate of human
actions, as Godet well observes, is according to their *quality*, not
according to their *quantity*.

4. *of their abundance*] Rather, **out of their overplus.** The essence
of charity is self-denial. But in these days most people give '*mites*' out
of their vast superfluity,—which is no charity at all; and they talk of
these offerings as '*mites*,' as though that word excused and even
consecrated an offering miserably inadequate.

5—7. THE DOOM OF THE TEMPLE, AND THE QUESTION ABOUT
THE END.

5. *as some spake*] We learn from the other Evangelists that those

6 with goodly stones and gifts, he said, *As for* these *things* which ye behold, the days will come, in the which there shall not be left one stone upon another, that shall not be 7 thrown down. And they asked him, saying, Master, but when shall these *things* be? and what sign *will there be* when these *things* shall come to pass?

8—27. *Signs of the End.*

8 And he said, Take heed that ye be not deceived: for

who spoke were the Apostles, and that the question was asked as Jesus sat on the Mount of Olives opposite to the Temple, perhaps gazing on it as it shone in the last rays of sunset.

with goodly stones] bevelled blocks of stone, of which some are described as having been forty cubits long and ten high; double cloisters; monolithic columns; alternate slabs of red and white marble, &c. See Jos. *B. J.* v. 5 and *Bab. Succa*, f. 51, 1.

and gifts] Rather, **sacred offerings** (Ps. lxii.), such as the golden chain of Agrippa; gifts of Ptolemy Philadelphus, Augustus, Helen of Adiabene, and crowns, shields, goblets, &c.; the golden vine with its vast clusters given by Herod. (Jos. *B. J.* v. 5, § 4. See 2 Macc. v. 16; and Jos. *Antt.* XIII. 3, XV. 11, § 3.) Hence Tacitus calls it "a temple of immense opulence," *Hist.* v. 8.

6. *As for these things which ye behold*] Rather, **these things which ye are gazing on** (it is what is called the 'pendent nominative').

there shall not be left one stone upon another] See on xix. 44 and the remarkable passage in 2 Esdras x. 54, "in the place where the Highest beginneth to shew *His* city, there can no man's building be able to stand." This was fulfilled in spite of the strong wish of Titus to spare the Temple, Jos. *B. J.* VI. 4, § 5; but see on xix. 44. He was himself so amazed at the massive substructures that he could only see in his conquest the hand of God (id. VI. 9, § 1). This prophecy was in reality that "Let us depart hence" which Josephus (*B. J.* VI. 5, § 3) and Tacitus (*Hist.* V. 13) tell us was uttered by a mysterious Voice before the destruction of Jerusalem.

7. *they asked him*] The questioners were Peter and James and John and Andrew, Mark xiii. 3.

when...and what sign] Our Lord leaves the former question unanswered (see on xvii. 20) and only deals with the latter. This was His gentle method of discouraging irrelevant or inadmissible questions (comp. xiii. 23, 24).

8—27. SIGNS OF THE END.

8. *Take heed that ye be not deceived*] A danger incurred even by the elect. Matt. xxiv. 24. The moral key-notes of this great Discourse of the Last Things (Eschatology) are Beware! Watch! Endure! Pray!

many shall come in my name, saying, I am *Christ;* and the time draweth near: go ye not therefore after them. But when ye shall hear of wars and commotions, be not terrified: for these *things* must first come to pass; but the end is not by and by.

Then said he unto them, Nation shall rise against nation, and kingdom against kingdom: and great earthquakes shall

for many shall come in my name] "Even now are there many antichrists," 1 John ii. 18.

the time draweth near] Rather, **the crisis has approached.**

9. *wars and commotions*] The best comment on the *primary* fulfilment of this Discourse is the *Jewish War* of Josephus, and the Annals and History of Tacitus (*Ann.* XII. 38, XV. 22, XVI. 13), whose narrative is full of earthquakes, wars, crimes, violences and pollutions, and who describes the period which he is narrating as one which was "rich in calamities, horrible with battles, rent with seditions, savage even in peace itself." The main difficulties of our Lord's Prophecy vanish when we bear in mind (i) that Prophecy is like a landscape in which time and space are subordinated to eternal relations, and in which events look like hills seen chain behind chain which to the distant spectator appear as one; and (ii) that in the necessarily condensed and varying reports of the Evangelists, sometimes the *primary* fulfilment (which is shewn most decisively and irrefragably by vs. 32 to be the Fall of Jerusalem), sometimes the *ultimate* fulfilment is predominant. The Fall of Jerusalem was the Close of that Aeon and a symbol of the Final End (*telos*). This appears most clearly in the report of St Luke.

commotions] *akatastasias*, conditions of instability and rottenness, the opposite to *peace.* 1 Cor. xiv. 33; Jas. iii. 16. Such commotions were the massacre of 20,000 Jews in their fight with the Gentiles at Caesarea; the assassinations or suicides of Nero, Galba, Otho, and Vitellius; the civil wars, &c.

be not terrified] The Greek word is the exact equivalent of our English word 'be not *scared*,' xxiv. 37; 1 Pet. iii. 6; Prov. iii. 25.

but the end is not by and by] Rather, **but not immediately is the end.** For 'by and by' see xvii. 7; Matt. xiii. 21; Mk. vi. 25. The words are most important as a warning against the same eschatological excitement which St Paul discourages in 2 Thess. ("The end is *not yet*," Matt. xxiv. 6; Mk. xiii. 7.) The things which 'must first come to pass' before the *final* end were (1) physical disturbances—which so often synchronise with historic crises, as Niebuhr has observed; (2) persecutions; (3) apostasy; (4) wide evangelisation; (5) universal troubles of war, &c. They were the "beginning of birth-throes" (Matt. xxiv. 8); what the Jews called the "birth-pangs of the Messiah."

11. *earthquakes*] Tac. *Hist.* I. 2. For such physical portents at great crises see Thuc. I. 23; Tac. *Ann.* XII. 43, 64, *Hist.* I. 56; Liv. XLIII. 13, &c.

be in divers places, and famines, and pestilences; and fearful sights and great signs shall there be from heaven. But before all these, they shall lay their hands on you, and persecute *you*, delivering *you* up to *the* synagogues, and into prisons, being brought before kings and rulers for my name's sake. And it shall turn to you for a testimony. Settle *it* therefore in your hearts, not to meditate before *what ye* shall answer: for I will give you a mouth and wisdom, which all your adversaries shall not be able to gainsay nor resist. And

famines] Acts xi. 28. The original gives the common *paronomasia* (play on words) *limoi kai loimoi*.

pestilences] Josephus (*B. J.* VI. 9, § 3) mentions both pestilence and famine as the immediate preludes of the storming of Jerusalem. They were due, like the plague at Athens, to the vast masses of people—Passover pilgrims—who were at the time crowded in the city.

fearful sights] See Wisdom xvii. 1—22. The word *phobetra*, 'terrors,' occurs here alone. Among these would be the "Abomination of Desolation," or "desolating wing of Abomination," which seems best to correspond with the foul and murderous orgies of the Zealots which drove all worshippers in horror from the Temple (Jos. *B. J.* IV. 3, § 7, V. 6, § 1, &c.). Such too would be the rumour of monstrous births (id. VI. 5, § 3); the cry 'woe, woe' for seven and a half years of the peasant Jesus, son of Hanan; the voice and sound of departing guardian-angels (Tac. *Hist.* v. 13), and the sudden opening of the vast brazen Temple-gate which required twenty men to move it (Jos. ib.).

signs...from heaven] Josephus mentions a sword-shaped comet. Both Tacitus and Josephus mention the portent that

" Fierce fiery warriors fought upon the clouds,
   In rank, and squadron, and right form of war;"

and Tacitus tells us how the blind multitude of Jews interpreted these signs in their own favour (*Hist.* V. 13).

12. *they shall lay their hands on you*, &c.] The best comment on the whole verse is found in Acts iv. 3, v. 17—41, vi. 11—13, xii. 2, xvi. 19—39, xxv. 23; 2 Tim. iv. 16, 17. Comp. John xv. 20, xvi. 2, 3.

13. *for a testimony*] See Mark xiii. 9. "In nothing terrified by your adversaries, which is to them *an evident token of perdition*, but *to you of salvation*," Phil. i. 28. "A manifest token of the righteous judgment of God," 2 Thess. i. 5.

14. *not to meditate before*] xii. 11; Matt. x. 19, 20. The meaning is that they were neither to *be anxious about* the form of their Apologia, not to make it skilfully elaborate.

15. *I will give you a mouth*] as in Ex. iv. 11, 12; Jer. i. 9; Is. vi. 6. God, as Milton says, 'sendeth forth His cherubim with the hallowed fire of His altar to touch the lips of whom He will.'

shall not be able to gainsay] See Acts iv. 14, vi. 10.

ye shall be betrayed both by parents, and brethren, and kinsfolks, and friends; and *some* of you shall they cause to be put to death. And ye shall be hated of all *men* for my name's sake. But there shall not a hair of your head perish. In your patience possess ye your souls.

And when ye shall see Jerusalem compassed with armies, then know that the desolation thereof is nigh. Then let them which are in Judea flee to the mountains; and let them which are in the midst of it depart out; and let not them that are in the countries enter thereinto. For these

16. *ye shall be betrayed*] In consequence of the disunions prophesied in i. 34, xii. 53; Matt. x. 21.

some of you] of the four to whom He was immediately speaking, perhaps all, and certainly two were martyred.

17. *hated of all men*] ii. 34, vi. 22; John xvii. 14; 1 Pet. iv. 14, 16. "As concerning this sect we know that everywhere it is spoken against," Acts xxviii. 22. "We have found this man a pestilent fellow, and a mover of sedition, and a ringleader of the sect of the Nazarenes," id. xxiv. 5. "They speak against you as evil doers," 1 Pet. ii. 12. "Reproached for the name of Christ," id. iv. 14. "A malefic, an excessive, execrable superstition" (Tac., Plin., Suet.). 'Away with the godless!' 'The Christians to the lions!'

18. *not a hair of your head*] for they are "all numbered," Matt. x. 30. The previous verse (16) is of course sufficient to shew that the meaning is *spiritual* here, not literal as in Acts xxvii. 34.

shall...perish] i.e. not without the special Providence of God, nor without reward, nor before the due time. Bengel.

19. *In your patience possess ye your souls*] Rather, with the better reading, **By your patience ye shall gain your souls** *or* **lives**. Mk. xiii. 13. The need of patience and endurance to the end is very prominently inculcated in the N. T., Rom. v. 3; 2 Thess. vii. 4; Heb. x. 36; Jas. i. 4, &c. Endurance, not violence, is the Christian's protection, and shall save the soul, and the *true* life, even if it loses all else.

20. *Jerusalem compassed with armies*] See on xix. 43, and Jos. *B. J.* v. 2, § 6, 12. Some regard this as the "abomination that maketh desolate."

21. *them which are in Judea*] This expression again most clearly proves what was the *near horizon* of this Prophecy.

flee to the mountains] The Christians, in consequence of "a certain oracular utterance" (Euseb. *H. E.* III. 5), or an angel-warning (Epiphan. *Haer.* I. 123), but more probably in consequence of *this* warning, fled, before the siege, *out of Judaea*, to the little Peraean town of Pella, among the Transjordanic hills.

in the midst of it] Rather, **her**, i.e. Jerusalem.

in the countries] Rather, **in the fields**.

be *the* days of vengeance, that all *things* which are written may be fulfilled. But woe unto them that are with child, and to them that give suck, in those days, for there shall be great distress in the land, and wrath upon this people. And they shall fall by the edge of the sword, and shall be led away captive into all nations: and Jerusalem shall be trodden down of the Gentiles, until the times of the Gentiles be fulfilled. And there shall be signs in the sun, and in the moon, and in the stars; and upon the earth distress of

22. *the days of vengeance*] See Dan. ix. 26, 27. Josephus again and again calls attention to the abnormal wickedness of the Jews as the cause of the divine retribution which overtook them. In his *Wars of the Jews* he declares that no generation and no city was "so plunged in misery since the foundation of the world." *B. J.* v. 10, § 5.

all things which are written] See xix. 42; Is. xxix. 2—4; Hos. x. 14, 15; Deut. xxviii. 49—57; 1 K. ix. 6—9; Ps. lxxix. 1—13; Mic. iii. 8—12.

23. *woe unto them that are with child*] The 'woe' is only an expression of pity for them because their flight would be retarded or rendered impossible.

great distress...and wrath] 1 Thess. ii. 16, "Wrath is come upon them to the uttermost." Josephus says that, when there were no more to plunder or slay, after "incredible slaughter and miseries," Titus ordered the city to be razed so completely as to look like a spot which had been never inhabited. *B. J.* VI. 10, VII. 1.

24. *fall by the edge of the sword*] Literally, "*mouth of the sword.*" Gen. xxxiv. 26. 1,100,000 Jews are said to have perished in the war and siege. "It seems as though the whole race had appointed a rendezvous for extermination." Renan.

led away captive into all nations] Josephus speaks of 97,000 Jews sent to various provinces and to the Egyptian mines. *B. J.* VI. 9.

shall be trodden down of the Gentiles] So that the very thing happened which the Maccabees had tried to avert by their fortifications (1 Macc. iv. 60). All sorts of Gentiles—Romans, Saracens, Persians, Franks, Norsemen, Turks—have 'trodden down' Jerusalem since then. The *estai patoumenē* of the original implies a more permanent result than the simple future. Comp. Rev. xi. 2.

until the times of the Gentiles be fulfilled] By the times—'seasons' or 'opportunities' of the Gentiles—is meant the period allotted for their full evangelisation. Rom. xi. 25, "Blindness in part is happened to Israel, *until the fulness of the Gentiles* be come in."

25. *signs in the sun, and in the moon, and in the stars*] The articles should be omitted. These signs are mainly metaphorical—the eclipse of nations and the downfall of potentates—though there may be literal fulfilments also. The language is that of the ancient prophets, Amos viii. 9; Joel ii. 30, 31; Ezek. xxxii. 7, 8, as in Rev. vi. 12—14.

nations, with perplexity; the sea and the waves roaring; men's hearts failing them for fear, and *for* looking after 26 those *things* which are coming on the earth: for the powers of heaven shall be shaken. And then shall they see the Son of 27 man coming in a cloud with power and great glory.

28. *Hope for the Faithful.*

And when these *things* begin to come to pass, *then* look 28 up, and lift up your heads; for your redemption draweth nigh.

29—36 *Parable of the Fig-tree. Duty of Watchfulness.*

And he spake to them a parable; Behold the fig tree, and 29 all the trees; when they now shoot forth, ye see and know 30 of your own selves that summer is now nigh at hand. So 31 likewise ye, when ye see these *things* come to pass, know ye that the kingdom of God is nigh at hand. Verily I say 32 unto you, This generation shall not pass away, till all be ful-

---

distress of nations] *Synochē*, xii. 50 and 2 Cor. ii. 4.

the sea and the waves roaring] The true reading is probably ἤχους, and the translation, "*in perplexity at the roar of the sea and surge.*" Comp. Ps. xlvi. 4. "*In that day they shall roar against them like the roaring of the sea,*" Is. v. 30. The raging sea is the sea of nations, Jude 13; Rev. xvii. 15.

26. *men's hearts failing them*] Literally, "*men fainting.*"

on the earth] Literally, "*on the habitable world.*"

the powers of heaven] i.e. the "bright dynasts" (Aesch. *Ag.* 6)—the Hosts of the Heavens.

27. *coming in a cloud*] Metaphorically in great world crises (Matt. xvi. 17, 28); *actually* at the Last Coming. Acts i. 11; Matt. xxvi. 64; Rev. xiv. 14.

28. HOPE FOR THE FAITHFUL.

28. *look up*] The 'earnest expectation' (*apokaradokia*—'watching with outstretched neck') of the creature, Rom. viii. 19, 23. This verb *anakuptein* only occurs in xiii. 11. Comp. Matt. xxiv. 31.

29—36. PARABLE OF THE FIG-TREE. DUTY OF WATCHFULNESS.

29. *and all the trees*] This is added by St Luke only. The fig-tree would be specially significant to Jewish readers.

32. *This generation shall not pass away, till all be fulfilled*] This

33 filled. Heaven and earth shall pass away: but my words shall not pass away.

34 And take heed to yourselves, lest at any time your hearts be overcharged with surfeiting, and drunkenness, and cares
35 of *this* life, and *so* that day come upon you unawares. For as a snare shall it come on all them that dwell on the face
36 of the whole earth. Watch ye therefore, and pray always, that ye may be accounted worthy to escape all these *things* that shall come to pass, and to stand before the Son of man.

verse has a nearer and a farther meaning. That very generation would not have passed when, 40 years later, the Jewish nation was crushed, and the Mosaic dispensation rendered impossible. But *genea* also means race, and the Jewish race shall last till the end of all things.

33. *Heaven and earth shall pass away*] 2 Pet. iii. 7; Is. li. 6; Ps. cii. 26.

but my words shall not pass away] Rather, **my sayings**, my utterances. Is. xl. 8.

34. *surfeiting*] The headache after drunkenness.—Lat. *crapula*.

drunkenness] Comp. Rom. xiii. 13. Hence the exhortation "be sober," *nēpsate*, 1 Pet. iv. 7; 1 Thess. v. 6.

cares of this life] Comp. Matt. xiii. 22. The surfeit of *yesterday*; drunkenness of *to-day*; cares for *to-morrow* (Van Oosterzee).

35. *as a snare*] Eccles. ix. 12 "as the fishes that are taken in an evil net, and as the birds that are caught in the snare, so are the sons of men snared in an evil time." There is the same metaphor in Is. xxiv. 17. The common metaphor is "*as a thief*," 1 Thess. vi. 3; Rev. iii. 3, xvi. 15; but St Paul uses this metaphor also, Rom. xi. 9; 1 Tim. iii. 7.

them that dwell] Literally, "*them that sit*." A Hebraism (Gen. xix. 30, &c.), but perhaps with the collateral notion of 'sitting at ease,' Jer. viii 14, xxv. 29 (LXX.). 'Face of the earth' is also a Hebraism, 2 Sam. xviii. 8.

36. *pray always*] xviii. 1; Eph. vi. 18. Render, **watch ye at all times, making supplication.**

accounted worthy] See on xx. 35. Another reading is "*ye may prevail*" (*katischusēte*).

to stand before the Son of man] "The ungodly shall not stand in the judgment," Ps. i. 5. "Who shall stand when He appeareth." Mal. iii. 2.

the Son of man] See on v. 24, ix. 58. On this day our Lord also uttered the Parables of the Ten Virgins and of the Talents, and other warnings, Matt. xxv. On this occasion too (as Van Oosterzee conjectures) our Lord may have used His *agraphon dogma* "in that wherein I shall find you, in that will I judge you," Just. Mart. *Dial.* XLVII.

37, 38. *How Jesus spent the last Public Days of His Ministry.*

And in the day time he was teaching in the temple; and at night he went out, and abode in the mount that is called *the mount* of Olives. And all the people came early in the morning to him in the temple, for to hear him.

CH. XXII. 1, 2. *Approach of the Passover. The Purpose of the Priests.*

Now the feast of unleavened bread drew nigh, which is called the Passover. And the chief priests and scribes

37, 38. HOW JESUS SPENT THE LAST PUBLIC DAYS OF HIS MINISTRY.

37. *in the day time*] Rather, **during the days**. The notice is retrospective, applying to Palm Sunday, and the Monday and Tuesday in Passion Week. After Tuesday evening He never entered the Temple again. Wednesday and Thursday were spent in absolute and unrecorded retirement, perhaps with His disciples in the house at Bethany, until Thursday evening when He went into Jerusalem again for the Last Supper.

at night] Rather, **during the nights**.

and abode] Literally, "*used to bivouac;*" it is very probable that He slept in the open air with His disciples, as is very common with Orientals. He would be safe on the slopes of Olivet, among the booths of the Galilaean pilgrims; see xxii. 39; John xviii. 1, 2.

in the mount] Literally, "*into;*" i.e. he went to, and stayed upon.

38. *came early in the morning*] The verb, which does not occur elsewhere in the N.T., means '*resorted to Him at early dawn,*' Jer. xxix. 19, 'rising up early' (LXX.).

in the temple] Comp. xix. 47; Acts v. 21. They came for the last time on Tuesday morning. On the Thursday morning, Nisan 13, our Lord woke never to sleep on earth again.

A few cursive MSS. here add the "Gospel for Penitents," John vii. 53—viii. 11.

CH. XXII. 1, 2. APPROACH OF THE PASSOVER. THE PURPOSE OF THE PRIESTS.

In this narrative of the Last Supper, Passion, Trial, and Crucifixion the chief points peculiar to St Luke are in xxii. 8, 15, 24, 28—30, 43, 44, 61, xxiii. 2, 5—16, 27—31, 34, 39—43, 46, 51.

1. *drew nigh*] Rather, **was drawing near**.

which is called the Passover] This little explanation shews most clearly that St Luke is writing mainly for Gentiles. *Strictly* speaking the Passover was *not* co-extensive with the Feast of Unleavened Bread, as

sought how they might kill him; for they feared the people.

3—6. *The Traitor and the Priests.*

3 Then entered Satan into Judas surnamed Iscariot, being

is clearly stated in Numb. xxviii. 16, 17, "In the *fourteenth* day of the first month is the *passover*...and in the *fifteenth* is the feast" (Lev. xxiii. 5, 6). Passover is the translation of the Hebrew *Pesach*; of this the Greek *pascha* is a transliteration with a sort of alliterative allusion to the Greek *pascho*, I suffer. See on the Passover Ex. xii. 11—20. The Jews of later ages had gradually assumed that a wide difference was intended between the "Egyptian passover" and the "permanent passover."

2. *the chief priests and scribes*] Their humiliation and defeat before the people—the immense and divine superiority of the wisdom of Jesus so publicly displayed—had at last aroused them into irreconcilable hostility. It is very noticeable that the Pharisees, as a distinct party, now vanish entirely into the background. They are scarcely mentioned again except in Matt. xxvii. 62.

sought] Rather, *were seeking*. The word involves a continuous effort, and probably includes the memorable meeting in the Palace of Caiaphas, which is traditionally placed on the 'Hill of Evil Counsel,' but was probably close to the Temple precincts. They seem to have come on that occasion, in consequence of the advice of Caiaphas, to three conclusions. (1) To put Jesus to death; (2) to do it as secretly as possible; and (3) not to do it during the Feast, so as to avoid the chance of tumults on the part of the Galilaean pilgrims. If this meeting was on Tuesday evening, at the very time that they were deciding *not* to kill Jesus (Ps. ii. 2) for more than eight days—and it was unusual to put to death during the Passover, Acts xii. 4—He, seated on the slopes of Olivet, was telling His disciples that before the Passover He should be slain, Matt. xxvi. 1—5.

3—6. THE TRAITOR AND THE PRIESTS.

3. *Then entered Satan into Judas*] No other expression seems adequately to explain his wickedness. It began in avarice, disappointment, and jealousy; and, when he had long weakened his soul by indulgence in these dark, besetting sins, the imaginary loss of the "300 pence" of which he would have had the disposal (John xii. 4, 5; Mk. xiv. 10),—the now undisguised announcement of our Lord that He should be not only rejected, but *crucified* (Matt. xx. 19)—the consequent shattering of all Messianic hopes—the growing sense that he was becoming distasteful to his Master and his fellows—the open rebuke which he had drawn on his own head by his hypocritic greed at Bethany (John xii. 6)—the rumoured hostility of all the most venerated authorities of the nation—all these formed the climax of his temptations:—and then, at last, the tempting opportunity met the susceptible disposition. "Instead of dominion—service; instead of power—per-

of the number of the twelve. And he went his way, and communed with the chief priests and captains, how he might betray him unto them. And they were glad, and covenanted to give him money. And he promised, and sought opportunity to betray him unto them in the absence of the multitude.

secution; instead of honour—shame; this was all that was left of his hopes and prospects once so brilliant." His crime was but the epitome of months—perhaps years—of secret faithlessness. "Dicitur Satan in reprobos intrare, cum reverso Dei metu, extincta rationis luce, pudore etiam excusso, sensus omnes occupat." Calvin.

Iscariot] See on vi. 16.

4. *he went his way*] We infer from the combined accounts that he met the priests on two occasions, on one of which the bargain was proposed, and on the other concluded.

communed] Spoke with.

captains] Literally, "*generals*." The *Levitic* captains of the Temple who kept order during the Feasts. There was strictly only one who bore the title of "the general of the Temple"—"man of the mountain of the House" (see Neh. ii. 8, vii. 2; Jer. xx. 1; 2 Macc. iii. 4); but he had guards under him (Jos. *B. J.* VI. 5, § 3), and the name might be applied to the whole body. One of the bitter complaints against the High Priests of the day was that they made their own sons "generals of the Temple." St Luke was aware that the *special* title applied only to one person, as appears from Acts iv. 1.

how he might betray him] Rather, **give Him up**. The word used is not *prodō*, but the milder *paradō*.

5. *they were glad*] This spontaneous offer—and that too from one of Christ's immediate followers—seemed to solve all their difficulties.

covenanted] Or, 'agreed;' in St Mark, '*promised*.' In Matt. xxvi. 15 it is said that they 'paid' or 'weighed' him the money, with a reference to Zech. xi. 12, 13 (LXX.). This was perhaps done at a second meeting when the actual plan was ripened.

to give him money] The proposal came from the wretched man himself (Matt. xxvi. 15). The paltry sum given (which is mentioned by St Matthew only)—30 shekels, about £3. 16*s*., the price given for the meanest slave—shews that this sum was either regarded as *earnest-money*, or more probably that the Priests felt themselves quite able to carry out their plot, though less conveniently, without any aid from Judas. On one side of these shekels would be stamped the olive-branch, the emblem of peace; on the obverse the censer, the type of prayer, with the inscription, "Jerusalem the Holy"!

6. *sought opportunity*] Doubtless he was baffled at first by the entire and unexpected seclusion which Jesus observed on the Wednesday and Thursday.

in the absence of the multitude] Rather, **without a mob**; *drep* is poetic, and only occurs here and in vs. 35.

7—13. *Preparation for the Passover.*

⁷ Then came the day of unleavened bread, when the passover must be killed. ⁸ And he sent Peter and John, saying, Go and prepare us the passover, that we may eat. ⁹ And they said unto him, Where wilt thou *that* we prepare? ¹⁰ And he said unto them, Behold, when ye are entered into the city, there shall a man meet you, bearing a pitcher of water; follow him into the house where he entereth in. ¹¹ And ye shall say unto the goodman of the house, The Master saith unto thee, Where is the guestchamber, where I shall eat the passover with my disciples? ¹² And he shall shew you a large

7—13. PREPARATION FOR THE PASSOVER.

7. *Then came the day of unleavened bread*] All leaven was most carefully and scrupulously put away on the afternoon of Thursday, Nisan 13.

when the passover must be killed] Rather, **be sacrificed**. On the difficult question whether the Last Supper was the actual Paschal meal, or an *anticipatory* Passover, see the Excursus.

8. *he sent Peter and John*] Apparently our Lord, now withdrawn from His active work, said nothing about the Passover till the disciples questioned Him as to His wishes. The old law that the Paschal Lamb must be chosen ten days beforehand had long fallen into desuetude. Its observance would have been impossible for the myriads of pilgrims who came from all parts of the world.

10. *a man...bearing a pitcher of water*] A very unusual sight in the East, where the water is drawn by women. He must probably have been the slave of one who was an open or secret disciple; unless we have here a reference to the Jewish custom of the master of a house himself drawing the water with which the unleavened bread was kneaded on Nisan 13. If so the "man bearing a pitcher of water" may have even been the Evangelist St Mark, in the house of whose mother, and probably in the very upper room where the Last Supper was held, the disciples used at first to meet (Acts xii. 12). The mysteriousness of the sign was perhaps intended to baffle, as long as was needful, the machinations of Judas.

11. *goodman*] See on xii. 39.

guestchamber] *Kataluma*, rendered "*inn*" in ii. 7.

the passover] Although reasons will be given in Excursus V. for the view that this was not the *actual* Passover, it is clear that our Lord designedly spoke of it as *His* Passover, and gave it a paschal character. It is *possible* that Jewish customs unknown to us made it allowable for individuals on special occasions to anticipate the regular passover.

upper room furnished: there make ready. And they went, 13
and found as he had said unto them; and they made ready
the passover.

14—38. *The last Supper.*

And when the hour was come, he sat down, and the 14
twelve apostles with him. And he said unto them, With 15
desire I have desired to eat this passover with you before
I suffer: for I say unto you, I will not any more eat thereof, 16
until it be fulfilled in the kingdom of God. And he took 17
the cup, and gave thanks, and said, Take this, and divide

12. *upper room*] The usual place of resort for large gatherings in a Jewish house; probably the very room which also witnessed the appearance of the Risen Christ to the Twelve, and the Descent of the Holy Ghost at Pentecost.

furnished] with divans, cushions, &c. Ezek. xxiii. 41 (LXX.); Acts ix. 34 (Greek).

14—38. THE LAST SUPPER.

14. *when the hour was come*] If the meal was intended to be directly Paschal, this would be "between the two evenings" (Ex. xii. 6); a phrase interpreted by the Jews to mean between three and six, and by the Samaritans to mean between twilight and sunset. Probably Jesus and His disciples, anxious to avoid dangerous notice, would set forth towards dusk.

he sat down] Rather, **reclined**. The custom of eating the Passover standing had long been abandoned.

15. *With desire I have desired*] i.e. I earnestly desired. A Hebraism. Matt. xiii. 14, &c.

to eat this passover] The expression may perhaps point to the fact that *this* was not the actual Jewish Paschal meal, but one which was intended to supersede it by a Passover of far more divine significance.

16. *I will not any more eat thereof*] The true reading probably is, **I will not eat it.** The 'not any more' however is a correct gloss.

until it be fulfilled in the kingdom of God] i.e. until the true Passover has been offered by my death, and so the new kingdom established.

17. *he took the cup, and gave thanks*] Literally, "*and after receiving the cup, and giving thanks.*" From *eucharistein* comes our word *Eucharist.*

The main customs of the Jewish Passover are as follows:—(1) Each drinks a cup of wine—'the cup of consecration'—over which the master of the house pronounces a blessing. (2) Hands are washed, and a table carried in, on which are placed bitter herbs, cakes of unleavened bread, the *Charoseth* (a dish made of dates, raisins, and vinegar), the paschal lamb, and the flesh of the *Chagigah* or feast-offering. (3) The father

18 it among yourselves: for I say unto you, I will not drink of the fruit of the vine, until the kingdom of God shall come.

19 And he took bread, and gave thanks, and brake *it*, and gave unto them, saying, This is my body which is given for

20 you: this do in remembrance of me. Likewise also the cup after supper, saying, This cup *is* the new testament in my blood, which is shed for you.

dips a morsel of unleavened bread and bitter herbs, about the size of an olive, in the *Charoseth*, eats it with a benediction, and distributes a similar 'sop' to all present. (4) A second cup of wine is poured out, and the youngest present asks the meaning of the service, to which the father replies. (5) The first part of the Hallel (Ps. cvii.—cxiv.) is sung. (6) Grace is said, and a benediction again pronounced; after which the father distributes bitter herbs and unleavened bread dipped in the *Charoseth*. (7) The Paschal lamb is eaten, and a third cup of wine handed round. (8) After another thanksgiving, a fourth cup—the cup of joy—is drunk. (9) The rest of the Hallel (Ps. cxv.—cxviii.) is sung.

The cup mentioned in this verse has been supposed to be the *third* cup of wine in the Jewish ceremonial; and the actual chalice of the Eucharist (the "cup of blessing," 1 Cor. x. 16, *Cos ha-Berâchah*) is identified with the *fourth* cup. We also see in the Last Supper the benediction, and possibly the Hallel (Matt. xxvi. 30). But (1) the identifications are somewhat precarious. (2) There is no certainty that the "*Sacrificial Passover*" thus observed by the Jews was identical in ceremonial with the "*Memorial Passover*" which now alone they are able to observe.

18. *of the fruit of the vine*] This is perhaps a reference to the Jewish benediction pronounced over the first cup, 'Blessed be Thou, O Lord our God, who hast created the fruit of the vine.'

19. *he took bread*] The account in St Luke closely agrees with that given by St Paul (1 Cor. xi. 23—26), which he 'received from the Lord.'

This is my body] Comp. "I am the door," John x. 7. "That rock was Christ," 1 Cor. x. 4. "The bread which we break, is it not the communion of the body of Christ?" 1 Cor. x. 16. All the fierce theological debates between Roman Catholics, Lutherans, Zuinglians, Calvinists, &c. might have been avoided if men had borne in mind the warning of Jesus, "It is the spirit that quickeneth; the flesh profiteth nothing: the words that I speak unto you, they are spirit, and they are life," John vi. 63.

in remembrance of me] The emphasis is on the latter words. The Christian Passover was no more to be in remembrance of the deliverance from Egypt, but of that far greater deliverance wrought by Christ.

20. *the new testament*] Hence the name of the New Testament. The word *Diathēkē* (Heb. *Berîth*) means both a will, and an agreement

But behold, the hand of him that betrayeth me *is* with 21
me on the table. And truly the Son of man goeth, as it was 22
determined: but woe unto that man by whom he is betrayed.
And they began to inquire among themselves, which of them 23
it was that should do this *thing*.

And there was also a strife among them, which of them 24
should be accounted the greatest. And he said unto them, 25
The kings of the Gentiles exercise lordship over them; and
they that exercise authority upon them are called benefactors. But ye *shall* not *be* so: but he that is greatest among 26

or covenant, see Jer. xxxi. 31. "It contains all the *absolute* elements of the one, with the *conditional* elements of the other. Hence the New Testament (*kainē Diathēkē*) is the revelation of a new relation on God's part with the conditions necessary to its realisation on man's part." Fairbairn.

in my blood] i.e. ratified by my blood shed for you. The best comment is Heb. ix. 15, 18—22; 1 Cor. xi. 25. The other Synoptists have "my blood of the New Testament."

21. *the hand of him that betrayeth me*] For fuller details of this last awful warning to Judas, and of the intimation of the person intended to His nearest disciples, see Matt. xxvi. 21—25; Mk. xiv. 18—21; John xiii. 21—26. Whether Judas actually partook of the Holy Communion has always been uncertain. Bengel quotes the language of St Ambrose to Theodosius, "Will you hold forth those hands still dripping with the blood of unjust slaughter, and with them take the most holy body of the Lord?"

22. *as it was determined*] "being delivered by the determinate counsel and foreknowledge of God," Acts ii. 23, iv. 27, 28. "The Lamb *slain from the foundation of the world*," Rev. xiii. 8. The type of Judas was Ahithophel, Ps. xli. 9.

23. *to inquire among themselves*] The pathetic details are given by St John. It is characteristic of their noble, simple, loving natures that they seem to have had no suspicions of Judas.

24. *And there was also a strife*] *Philoneikia*, 'an ambitious contention,' occurs here only. It is probable that this dispute arose while they were taking their places at the couches (*triclinia*), and may possibly have been occasioned by some claim made by Judas for official precedence. He seems to have reclined on the left of our Lord, and John on the right, while Peter seems to have been at the top of the next mat or couch, at the left of Judas, across and behind whom he stretched forward to whisper his question to St John (John xiii. 23, 24). For previous instances of this worldly ambition see ix. 46—48; Matt. xx. 20—24.

25. *exercise lordship*] Peter learnt this lesson well. 1 Pet. v. 3.
are called benefactors] *Euergetai*—a name often inscribed on coins. How worthless and hollow the title was the disciples knew from the

you, let him be as the younger; and he that is chief, as he
27 that doth serve. For whether *is* greater, he that sitteth at
meat, or he that serveth? *is* not he that sitteth at meat?
28 but I am among you as he that serveth. Ye are they which
29 have continued with me in my temptations. And I appoint
unto you a kingdom, as my Father hath appointed unto me;
30 that ye may eat and drink at my table in my kingdom, and
sit on thrones judging the twelve tribes of Israel.
31   And the Lord said, Simon, Simon, behold, Satan hath
32 desired *to have* you, that *he* may sift *you* as wheat: but I
have prayed for thee, that thy faith fail not: and when thou
33 art converted, strengthen thy brethren. And he said unto

instances of Ptolemy Euergetes and other Syrian tyrants. Onias had
been more deserving of the name, 2 Macc. iv. 2.

   26. *let him be*] Rather, **let him become**,—let him shew himself to
be in *reality*.
   the younger] who in Eastern families often fulfils menial duties. Acts
v. 6.
   27. *I am among you as he that serveth*] The true Euergetes is the
humble brother, not the subtle tyrant. See Matt. xx. 28. "Took upon
him the form of a servant," Phil. ii. 7. St Luke here omits the beautiful acted parable of the Lord washing the disciples' feet (John xiii. 1—
20), as also the words to Judas, and his going forth into the night.
   28. *in my temptations*] See on iv. 13.
   29. *I appoint unto you a kingdom*] See xii. 32. "If we suffer
we shall also reign with Him," 2 Tim. ii. 12. *Diatithemai* is 'I appoint by way of bequest,' Ps. lxxxi. 4 (LXX.).
   30. *sit on thrones*] Our Lord here perhaps designedly omitted the
word "twelve," Matt. xix. 28 (Rev. iii. 21).
   judging] "The saints shall judge the world," 1 Cor. vi. 2. But the
clause is omitted in some MSS.
   31. *Simon, Simon*] The repetition of the name gave combined
solemnity and tenderness to the appeal (x. 41).
   Satan hath desired to have you] Rather, **Satan demanded you** (plur.),
or 'gained you by asking.' "Not content with Judas," vs. 3. Bengel.
   that he may sift you] The word *siniasai*, from *sinion*, a sieve,
occurs here only. Satan, too, has his winnowing fan, that he may get
his chaff. Judas has been already winnowed away from the Apostolic
band, and now Satan demands Peter (comp. Job i. 9). The warning
left a deep impression on Peter's mind. 1 Pet. v. 8, 9. For the
metaphor see Amos ix. 9, 10.
   32. *I have prayed for thee*] Rather, **I made supplication concerning
thee**, shewing that Peter, the most confident, was at that moment
the most imperilled, though Jesus had prayed for them all (John xvii.
9, 11).
   that thy faith fail not] The word means 'fail not *utterly*, or *finally*.'

him, Lord, I am ready to go with thee, both into prison, and to death. And he said, I tell thee, Peter, *the* cock shall 34 not crow this day, before that thou shalt thrice deny that *thou* knowest me. And he said unto them, When I sent 35 you without purse, and scrip, and shoes, lacked ye any thing? And they said, Nothing. Then said he unto them, 36 But now, he that hath a purse, let him take *it*, and likewise *his* scrip: and he that hath no sword, let him sell his garment, and buy one. For I say unto you, that this that is 37 written must yet be accomplished in me, And he was reckoned among the transgressors: for the *things*

when thou art converted, strengthen thy brethren] Comp. Ps. li. 13. So, after the Resurrection, Jesus said to him, "Feed my sheep" (John xxi. 17). The very word for 'strengthen' sank into his heart, and is repeated in his Epistle, 1 Pet. v. 10. 'Converted' has not here its *technical* meaning—but 'when thou hast turned again.' It means more, however, than merely *vicissim*, 'in turn.' Comp. 1 Pet. ii. 25; 2 Pet. ii. 21, 22; Matt. xiii. 15, &c.

33. *I am ready to go with thee, both into prison, and to death*] Rather, even into prison, even into death, and the order and emphasis should be, 'Lord, *with Thee* I am ready,' &c. This 'flaring enthusiasm' is always to be suspected of weakness. Prov. xxviii. 26; 1 Cor. x. 12.

34. *Peter*] The only occasion on which Jesus is recorded to have used to him the name He gave. It is used to remind him of his *strength* as well as his weakness.

the cock shall not crow this day] It was, perhaps, already past midnight. St Mark says more exactly (xiv. 30) 'shall not crow *twice*.' But St Luke's expression merely means, 'that part of the dawn which is called the cock-crow (*alektorophōnia, gallicinium*) shall not be over before, &c.'

35. *without purse*, &c.] See ix. 3, x. 4.

36. *But now*] This was an intimation of their totally changed relation to the world. There was no spontaneous hospitality, no peaceful acceptance, no honoured security, to be looked for now.

he that hath no sword, let him sell his garment, and buy one] Rather, **he that hath not** (either purse or scrip to buy a sword with), **let him**, &c. Of course the expression was not meant to be taken with unintelligent literalness. It was in accordance with that kind metaphorical method of expression which our blessed Lord adopted that His words might never be forgotten. It was to warn them of days of hatred and opposition in which *self-defence* might become a daily necessity, though not aggression. To infer that the latter is implied has been one of the fatal errors which arise from attributing infallibility to wrong inferences from a superstitious letter-worship.

37. *he was reckoned among the transgressors*] A quotation from Is.

38 concerning me have an end. And they said, Lord, behold, here *are* two swords. And he said unto them, It is enough.

39—46. *The Agony in the Garden.*

39 And he came out, and went, as he was wont, to the
40 mount of Olives; and his disciples also followed him. And

liii. 12. Hence clearly the sword could not be for *His* defence, as they carelessly assumed.

for] Rather, **for indeed**.

have an end] The end (*telos*) was drawing near; it would come on the following day (*Tetelestai*, John xix. 30).

38. *here are two swords*] It was a last instance of the stolid literalism by which they had so often vexed our Lord (Matt. xvi. 6—12). As though He could have been thinking of two miserable swords, such as poor Galilaean pilgrims took to defend themselves from wild beasts or robbers; and as though two would be of any use against a world in arms! It is strange that St Chrysostom should suppose 'knives' to be intended. This was the verse quoted by Boniface VIII., in his famous Bull *Unam sanctam*, to prove his possession of both secular and spiritual power!

And he said unto them, It is enough] Not of course meaning that two swords were enough, but sadly declining to enter into the matter any further, and leaving them to meditate on His words. The formula was one sometimes used to waive a subject; comp. 1 Macc. ii. 33. See p. 384. "It is a sigh of the God-man over all violent measures meant to further His cause."

39—46. THE AGONY IN THE GARDEN.

39. *And he came out*] St Luke here omits all the touching incidents which St John alone records—the discourses so "rarely mixed of sadness and joys, and studded with mysteries as with emeralds;" Peter's question, "Lord, whither goest thou?"; the melancholy remark of Thomas about the way; Philip's "Lord, shew us the Father;" the perplexed enquiry of Judas Lebbaeus; the rising from the Table; the Parable of the Vine and the Branches, perhaps suggested by the trellised vine under which they passed out into the moonlight; and the great High Priest's prayer.

to the mount of Olives] down the valley over the brook, or, rather, dry wady of the Kedron, and then up the green slope beyond it to the garden or small farm ($\chi\omega\rho\iota o\nu$) of Gethsemane, "the oil press," which is about half a mile from the city. Probably (John xviii. 2) it belonged to a disciple; possibly to St Mark. Judas knew the spot, and had ascertained that Jesus was going there. He had gone out to get the band necessary for His arrest.

followed him] The walk would be under the full Paschal moon amid the deep hush that falls over an Oriental city at night. The only recorded

when he was at the place, he said unto them, Pray that ye
enter not into temptation. And he was withdrawn from 41
them about a stone's cast, and kneeled down, and prayed,
saying, Father, if thou be willing, remove this cup from me: 42
nevertheless not my will, but thine, be done. And there 43
appeared an angel unto him from heaven, strengthening
him. And being in an agony he prayed more earnestly: 44
and his sweat was as it were great drops of blood falling

incident of the walk is one more warning to the disciples, and specially to St Peter. Matt. xxvi. 32—35.

40. *he said unto them*] First He left eight of them to sleep under the trees while He withdrew with Peter and James and John, whom He told to watch and pray.

41. *he was withdrawn*] Literally, "*He was taken away*," or 'He tore Himself away' (comp. xxi. 1), shewing the reluctance with which He parted from this support of loving sympathy under the imperious necessity of passing through His darkest hour alone. Perhaps He withdrew deeper into the shadow of the ancient olive-trees. (In estimating the force of such words as *ekballo*, *apospao*, &c., it should however be borne in mind that in Hellenistic Greek their old classical force was weakened by colloquialism. See 2 Macc. xii. 10.)

and kneeled down] "and fell on His face," Matt. xxvi. 39.

42. *if thou be willing*] The principle of His whole life of suffering obedience, John v. 30, vi. 38.

this cup] Matt. xx. 22; comp. Ezek. xxii. 31; Ps. lxxv. 8. This prayer is an instance of the "strong crying and tears," amid which He "learned obedience by the things which He suffered," Heb. v. 7, 8.

43. *there appeared an angel*] As after His temptation, Matt. iv. 11. This and the next verse are not of absolutely certain authenticity, since they are omitted in A, B, and by the first corrector of ℵ; and Jerome and Hilary say that they were omitted in "very many" Greek and Latin MSS. Their omission may have been due to mistaken reverence; or their insertion may have been made by the Evangelist himself in a later recension.

44. *being in an agony*] The word which occurs here only in the N.T.—though we often have the verb *agonizomai*—means intense struggle and pressure of spirit, which the other Evangelists also describe in the strong words *ademonein* (Matt. xxvi. 37) and *ekthambeisthai* (Mk. xiv. 33). It was an awful anguish of His natural life, and here alone (Matt. xxvi. 38; John xii. 27) does He use the word $\psi\nu\chi\eta$ of Himself. It was not of course a mere shrinking from death and pain, which even the meanest natures can overcome, but the mysterious burden of the world's guilt (2 Cor. v. 21)—the shrinking of a sinless being from the depths of Satanic hate and horror through which He was to pass. As Luther says 'our hard impure flesh' can hardly comprehend the sensitiveness of a fresh unstained soul coming in contact with horrible antagonism.

as it were great drops of blood] Such a thing as a 'bloody sweat'

45 down to the ground. And when he rose up from prayer, and was come to his disciples, he found them sleeping for
46 sorrow, and said unto them, Why sleep ye? rise and pray, lest ye enter into temptation.

47—53. The Traitor's Kiss. The Arrest. Malchus.

47 And while he yet spake, behold a multitude, and he that was called Judas, one of the twelve, went before them, and
48 drew near unto Jesus to kiss him. But Jesus said unto him,

seems not to be wholly unknown (Arist. *Hist. Anim.* III. 19) under abnormal pathological circumstances. The blood of Abel 'cried from the ground;' but this blood 'spake better things than the blood of Abel' (Gen. iv. 10; Heb. xii. 24). St Luke does not however use the term 'bloody sweat,' but says that the dense sweat of agony fell from him "*like* blood gouts"—which may mean as drops of blood do from a wound.

45. *sleeping for sorrow*] Ps. lxix. 20. The last two words give rather the cause than the excuse. They are analogous to "the spirit indeed is willing, but the flesh is weak" of Matt. xxvi. 41. St Luke here abbreviates the fuller records given in Matt. xxvi.; Mk. xiv., from which we find that Jesus *thrice* came to His Apostles, and thrice found them sleeping (see Is. lxiii. 3),—each momentary pause of prayer marking a fresh step in His victorious submission. This was the Temptation of Jesus by every element of anguish, as He had been tempted in the wilderness by every element of desire.

46. *Why sleep ye?*] "Simon, sleepest thou? Were ye so unable to watch with me a single hour?" Matt. xxvi. 40; Mk. xiv. 37. The *second* time He does not seem to have spoken to them. The third time He knew that it was too late. The object of their watching had now ceased, for He heard the tramp of men in the distance, and saw the glare of their torches; and therefore it was with a tender irony that He said, 'Sleep on now and take your rest' (as far as any help which you can render to Me is concerned), but 'Rise, let us be going,' for now sleep will be alike impossible to us all.

47—53. THE TRAITOR'S KISS. THE ARREST. MALCHUS.

47. *behold a multitude*] Composed of Levitical guards under their 'general;' a Roman chiliarch ('tribune'), with some soldiers, part of a maniple or cohort (σπεῖρα) from the Fort of Antonia (John xviii. 12); and some priests and elders.

one of the twelve] It seems as if in narrating the scene the Evangelists unconsciously add the circumstance which to their mind branded the deed with its worst horror. For the terror which seized the multitude, the precipitate entrance of Judas into the garden, and our Lord's first words to him, see John xviii. 3—9.

Judas, betrayest thou the Son of man with a kiss? When they which were about him saw what would follow, they said unto him, Lord, shall we smite with the sword? And one of them smote the servant of the high priest, and cut off his right ear. And Jesus answered and said, Suffer ye thus far. And he touched his ear, and healed him. Then Jesus said unto the chief priests, and captains of the temple, and the elders, which were come to him, Be ye come out, as against a thief, with swords and staves? When I was daily with you

48. *with a kiss*] He exclaimed 'Rabbi, Rabbi, hail' ('Peace to thee, Rabbi'), Mk. xiv. 45; but received no 'Peace to thee' in reply. Overacting his part, he not only kissed His Lord (*ephilesen*), but kissed Him fervently (*katephilesen, deosculatus est*).

49. *they*] Specially Peter, but the Synoptists suppress his name from obviously prudential reasons which no longer existed when St John wrote.

Lord, shall we smite with the sword?] Since it was illegal to carry swords on a feast-day, we have here another sign that the Last Supper had not been the Passover. The bringing of the sword was part of the misconception which Jesus had not cared further to remove at the supper; and if Judas had pressed into the enclosure they may have been entirely unaware as yet of the number of the captors. Future years would teach them that Christ's cause is served by dying, not by killing. The full reply of our Lord on this incident must be found by combining Matt. xxvi. 53, John xviii. 10, 11.

50. *the servant of the high priest*] Malchus.

right ear] A specific touch not found in the other Evangelists. All three use the diminutive—if the readings can be relied on. (ὠτίον, Matt. xxvi. 51; ὠτάριον, Mk. xiv. 47; ὠτίον, John xviii. 10. In this passage we have both οὖς and ὠτίον.) No stress can be laid on this. Languages in their later stage often adopt diminutives to avoid the trouble of genders. See my *Language and Languages*, p. 319.

51. *Suffer ye thus far*] Probably addressed to the captors, and meaning *Excuse thus much resistance;* or 'Allow me liberty thus far'—free my arms a moment that I may heal this wounded man. These snatches of dialogue—often of uncertain interpretation from their fragmentary character (e.g. Mk. ix. 23; Matt. xxvi. 50; John viii. 25), are inimitable marks of genuineness. It was probably during this pause that 'all His disciples'—even Peter, even John—'forsook Him and fled.'

52. *unto the chief priests...which were come to him*] The expression shews that these venerable persons had kept safely in the background till all possible danger was over. It is evident that the whole band dreaded some exertion of miraculous power.

as against a thief] Rather, a **brigand** or **robber**. Am I one of the *Sicarii*, or bandits? It is a reproach to them for their cowardice and secrecy. 'If I had really done wrong, how is it that you did not arrest me in the Temple?'

in the temple, ye stretched forth no hands against me: but this is your hour, and the power of darkness.

54—62. *Peter's Denial.*

54 Then took they him, and led *him*, and brought him into 55 the high priest's house. And Peter followed afar off. And

---

53. *this is your hour, and the power of darkness*] A reproach to them for their base, illegal, midnight secrecy. St Luke omits the incident of the young man with the *sindôn* cast round his naked body, Mk. xiv. 51, 52.

the power of darkness] Rather, **the authority** (*exousia*). The power is not independent, but delegated or permitted, since the Death of Christ is part of a divine plan (John xviii. 4, xix. 11, &c.).

54—62. PETER'S DENIAL.

54. *Then took they him*] Rather, **seizing Him**.

and led him] with His hands bound, probably behind His back, John xviii. 12.

into the high priest's house] The actual High Priest was Joseph Caiaphas (another form of Kephas), son-in-law of Annas (see on iii. 2). The trial of our Lord by the Jews was in three phases—(1) before Annas (John xviii. 12—18); (2) before Caiaphas (here and Matt. xxvi. 59—68; Mk. xiv. 55—65); (3) before the entire Sanhedrin at dawn (vs. 66; Matt. xxvii. 1; Mk. xv. 1). Each trial might be regarded as supremely important. Annas, or Hanan son of Seth, was the most influential of the ex-High Priests, and may, as Sagan (Deputy) or Nasi (President), have virtually wielded the sacerdotal power. The result therefore of a trial before him would involve a fatal *praejudicium*, since the utmost reverence was paid to his age, wealth, power, and shrewdness.—The second trial was before the most important committee of the Sanhedrin, which might in one sense be called 'the whole Sanhedrin' (Mk. xiv. 55), and though it could have no legal validity, being held at night, it served as a sort of *anakrisis* or preliminary enquiry, which left the final decision only formal.—The third trial was held at dawn before the entire Sanhedrin, and passed the final decree of condemnation against Jesus for blasphemy, which had been already pre-determined. The enmity of the priests may have partly arisen (as I have given reasons for believing in the *Life of Christ*, II. 334) from the fact that the cleansing of the Temple involved an interference with their illicit gains. After the first trial—at which Jesus was first smitten— He was sent bound to Caiaphas, who perhaps lived in the same house. These three Jewish trials were illegal in almost every particular. The Sanhedrin was generally a merciful and cautious tribunal, but was now a mere dependent body entirely under the influence of the Sadducees, who were the most ruthless of Jewish sects.

Peter followed afar off] "to see the end," Matt. xxvi. 58. It was a

when they had kindled a fire in the midst of the hall, and were set down together, Peter sat down among them. But ⁵⁶ a certain maid beheld him as he sat by the fire, and earnestly looked upon him, and said, This *man* was also with him. And he denied him, saying, Woman, I know him not. ⁵⁷ And after a little while another saw him, and said, Thou art ⁵⁸

most unwise exposure of himself to temptation. His admission into the courtyard of the High Priest's house was due to the influence of John, who was known to the High Priest, and spoke to the portress (John xviii. 15, 16).

55. *they had kindled a fire*] The spring nights at Jerusalem, which is 2610 feet above the level of the sea, are often cold.

in the midst of the hall] Rather, of **the court**.

sat down among them] i.e. among the servants of the High Priest—sat in the middle (*mesos*) of a group composed of the very men who had just been engaged more or less directly in the arrest of His Lord. It was like the impetuosity of his character, but most unwise for one of his temperament. St John says (xviii. 18) that 'he stood,' and perhaps we have here a touch of restlessness.

a certain maid] Apparently the portress (John xviii. 17) who had been meanwhile relieved, and who, after a fixed gaze, recognised Peter as the man whom she had admitted. She therefore exclaimed, "This fellow *too* (as well as John) was with Him." The reports of the Evangelists differ, but each faithfully preserves the *kai*.

a certain maid beheld him] The accounts of these denials by the Evangelists are (as St Augustine says of their narratives generally) "various, but not contrary." They are capable of perfectly easy and perfectly natural reconcilement, and are a valuable proof of independence.

56. *by the fire*] Rather, **to the light**, i.e. with the light of the brazier shining full on him.

earnestly looked upon him] See iv. 20.

57. *Woman, I know him not*] "nor do I understand what you mean," Mk. xiv. 68. The 'Woman!' should come last. Peter—who has been described as '*homalōs anomalon*' or 'consistently inconsistent'—shewed just the same kind of weakness many years later. Gal. ii. 12, 13.

58. *after a little while*] The trial before the Sacerdotal Committee naturally took some time, and they were awaiting the result.

another saw him] After his first denial "before them all" (Matt. xxvi. 70) he probably hoped to shake off this dangerous curiosity; and, perhaps as his guilt was brought more home to him by the first crowing of the cock (Mk. xiv. 68), he stole back out of the light of the brazier where he had been sitting with the servants, to the gate or vestibule (*pulona*, Matt. xxvi. 71, *proaulion*, Mk. xiv. 68). Of this second denial St John says, "*they* said to him" (xviii. 25); and as the portress was sure to have gossipped about him to the girl who relieved her at her post, the

59 also of them. And Peter said, Man, I am not. And about the space of one hour after another confidently affirmed, saying, Of a truth this *fellow* also was with him: for he is a Galilean.
60 And Peter said, Man, I know not what thou sayest. And
61 immediately, while he yet spake, the cock crew. And the Lord turned, and looked upon Peter. And Peter remembered the word of the Lord, how he had said unto him,

second denial was due to his being pointed out by the second maid to the group of idlers who were hanging about the door, one of whom was prominent in pressing the charge against him. Matt. xxvi. 71 (Ἄλλη); Mk. xiv. 69 (ἡ παιδίσκη); John xviii. 25 (εἶπον); here ἕτερος. What discrepancy then worth speaking of is there here? Doubtless the second and third charges became more and more general as the news spread among the group. It is much more important to notice the moral law of "linked lies" by which 'once denied' always has a tendency to become 'thrice denied.' "Whom," asks St Augustine, "have you ever seen contented with a *single* sin?"

Man] A mode of displeased address. xii. 14.

59. *about the space of one hour after*] To St Peter it must have been one of the most terrible hours of his life.

another] Here again the main charge was prominently made by *one* —a kinsman of Malchus, who had seen Peter in the garden, and was known to St John from his acquaintance with the High Priest's household (John xviii. 26, συγγενής); but others came up (προσελθόντες οἱ ἑστῶτες, Matt. xxvi. 73; οἱ παρεστῶτες, Mk. xiv. 70), and joined in it, and this is implied by St Mark's "kept saying to Peter" (ἔλεγον).

for he is a Galilean] This they could at once tell by the misplaced gutturals of the provincial dialect which 'bewrayed him' (i.e. pointed him out).

60. *Man, I know not what thou sayest*] St Luke drops a veil over the 'cursing and swearing' which accompanied this last denial (Matt. xxvi. 74).

the cock crew] Rather, **a cock**. It crew for the second time. Minute critics have imagined that they found a 'difficulty' here because the Talmud says that cocks and hens, from their scratching in the dung, were regarded as unclean. But as to this the Talmud contradicts itself, since it often alludes to cocks and hens at Jerusalem (e.g. *Berachôth*, p. 27, 1). Moreover the cock might have belonged to the Roman soldiers in Fort Antonia.

61. *the Lord turned, and looked upon Peter*] St Luke alone preserves this most touching incident. Jesus must have looked on His erring Apostle either from the chamber in which He was being tried, if it was one of those chambers with open front (called in the East *muck 'ad*); or else at the moment when the trial was over, and He was being led across the courtyard amid the coarse insults of the servants. If so the moment would have been one of awful pathos to the unhappy Apostle.

Before *the* cock crow, thou shalt deny me thrice. And Peter 62 went out, and wept bitterly.

63—65. *The First Derision.*

And the men that held Jesus mocked him, and smote 63 him. And when they had blindfolded him, they stroke him 64 on the face, and asked him, saying, Prophesy, who is it that smote thee? And many other *things* blasphemously spake 65 they against him.

62. *went out*] into the night, but "to meet the morning dawn."
and wept] Not only *edakruse*, 'shed tears,' but *eklause*, 'wept aloud;' and, as St Mark says (xiv. 72), *eklaie*, 'he *continued* weeping.' It was more than a mere burst of tears.
bitterly] St Mark says *epibalōn*, which *may* mean, 'when he thought thereon,' or 'flinging his mantle over his head.'

63—65. THE FIRST DERISION.

Hanan had simply tried to entangle Jesus by insidious questions.
The course of the trial before Caiaphas was different. The Priests on that occasion "sought false witness," but their false witnesses contradicted each other in their attempt to prove that He had threatened to destroy the Temple. Since Jesus still kept silence, Caiaphas rose, walked into the midst of the hall, and adjured Jesus by the Living God to say whether He was "the Christ, the Son of God." So adjured, Christ answered in the affirmative, and then Caiaphas, rending his robes, appealed to the assembly, who, most illegally setting aside the need of any further witnesses, shouted aloud that He was 'A man of Death' (*Ish maveth*), i.e. deserving of capital punishment. From this moment He would be regarded by the dependents of the Priests as a condemned criminal.

63. *smote him*] No less than five forms of beating are referred to by the Evangelists in describing this pathetic scene—*derontes* here (a general term); *etupton*, 'they kept smiting;' *paisas* in the next verse, implying violence; *ekolaphisan*, 'slapped with the open palm,' Matt. xxvi. 67; *errapisan*, 'smote with sticks' (id.); and *rapismasin eballon*, Mk. xiv. 65. See the prophecy of Is. l. 6. The Priests of that day, and their pampered followers, were too much addicted to these brutalities (Acts xxi. 32, xxiii. 2), as we learn also from the Talmud.

64. *blindfolded him*] Probably by throwing an *abba* over his head and face. Mk. xiv. 65. The Talmud says that the False Messiah, Bar Cochba, was similarly insulted.

65. *blasphemously*] This term now bears a different meaning. Here it merely means '*reviling Him.*'

66—71. *The third Jewish Trial.*

66 And as soon as it was day, the elders of the people and the chief priests and the scribes came together, and led 67 him into their council, saying, Art thou the Christ? tell us. And he said unto them, If I tell you, you will not believe: 68 and if I also ask *you*, you will not answer me, nor let *me* 69 go. Hereafter shall the Son of man sit on the right hand 70 of the power of God. Then said they all, Art thou then the Son of God? And he said unto them, Ye say that

66—71. THE THIRD JEWISH TRIAL.

66. *as soon as it was day*] The Oral Law decided that the Sanhedrin could only meet by daylight.

elders of the people] Literally, "*the presbytery* of the people," as in Acts xxii. 5.

elders...chief priests...scribes] See Mk. xv. 1. The three constituent parts of the Sanhedrin, 1 Macc. xiv. 28. The Sanhedrin was the successor of the Great Synagogue, which ended with Simon the Just. *Where* they met is uncertain. It was either in the Paved Hall, or 'Hall of Squares' (*Lischath haggazzith*); or in the *Beth Midrash* (Temple Synagogue), a chamber which abutted on the "middle wall of partition" (*Chêl*), or in the *Chanujoth* 'shops' or 'booths' founded by the house of Hanan to sell doves, &c. for the temple.

their council] *Synedrion*, from which the word Sanhedrin (mistakenly spelt *Sanhedrim*) is derived. The word is first found on the occasion when they summoned before them Hyrcanus II., son of Alexander Jannaeus. It gloried in being a mild tribunal, but was now an extremely degenerate body, and unworthy of its earlier traditions (Jos. *Antt.* XIII. 10, § 6; *B. J.* II. 8, § 14). The Jewish authorities had lost the power of inflicting death; they could only pass sentence of excommunication, and hand over to the secular arm.

67. *Art thou the Christ?*] The object of the Sanhedrin was somewhat different from that of the Priests in the house of Caiaphas. They had only succeeded in establishing (by a most illegal personal appeal) a charge of constructive blasphemy. But 'blasphemy' was not a charge on which a Roman could pronounce capital sentence. Hence, in order to get Christ crucified, they needed a charge of *treason*, which might be constructed out of His claim to be the Messiah.

ye will not believe] As they had shewn already. John viii. 59, x. 31.

68. *if I also ask you, you will not answer*] This is our Lord's protest against the illegal violence of the whole proceedings.

69. *Hereafter shall the Son of man sit*] Rather, **But from henceforth** (comp. i. 48, v. 10) **shall the Son of man be seated at.** Our Lord seems at last to have broken His silence in these words, in order to end a miserable and useless scene. The words would at once recall Dan. vii. 13, 14; see John i. 51.

I am. And they said, What need we any further witness? 71 for we ourselves have heard of his own mouth.

CH. XXIII. 1—4. *First phase of the Trial before Pilate.*

And the whole multitude of them arose, and led him 23 unto Pilate. And they began to accuse him, saying, We 2

70. *Ye say that I am*] A Hebrew formula (*antî amarta*). "Your words verify themselves." See some striking remarks in De Quincey, *Works*, III. 304. But the formula like "Thou sayest" in John xviii. 37 seems also to have been meant to waive further discussion. See p. 385.

What need we any further witness?] Caiaphas had made the same appeal to the audience at the night trial. Van Oosterzee mentions that at the trial of the Reformer Farel, the Genevan Priests addressed him in these very words, and he replied, "Speak the words of God, and not those of Caiaphas."—This trial was followed by the *second* derision, in which it almost seems as if the Sanhedrists themselves took part. Matt. xxvi. 67. St Luke here omits the remorse and horrible end of Judas, on which he touches in Acts i. 18.

CH. XXIII. **1—4.** FIRST PHASE OF THE TRIAL BEFORE PILATE.

1. *the whole multitude*] Rather, **the whole number** (*plethos*, not *ochlos*).

unto Pilate] The fact that our Lord "suffered under Pontius Pilate" is also mentioned by Tacitus (*Ann.* XV. 44). Pontius Pilatus was a Roman Knight, who (A.D. 26) had been appointed, through the influence of Sejanus, sixth Procurator of Judaea. His very first act—the bringing of the silver eagles and other insignia of the Legions from Caesarea to Jerusalem—a step which he was obliged to retract—had caused fierce exasperation between him and the Jews. This had been increased by his application of money from the Corban or Sacred Treasury to the secular purpose of bringing water to Jerusalem from the Pools of Solomon (see xiii. 4). In consequence of this quarrel Pilate sent his soldiers among the mob with concealed daggers—(a fatal precedent for the *Sicarii*)—and there had been a great massacre. A third tumult had been caused by his placing gilt votive shields dedicated to the Emperor Tiberius, in his residence at Jerusalem. The Jews regarded these as idolatrous, and he had been obliged by the Emperor's orders to remove them. He had also had deadly quarrels with the Samaritans, whom he had attacked on Mount Gerizim in a movement stirred up by a Messianic impostor; and with the Galilaeans "whose blood he had mingled with their sacrifices" (xiii. 1). He reflected the hatred felt towards the Jews by his patron Sejanus, and had earned the character which Philo gives him of being a savage, inflexible, and arbitrary ruler. The Procurator, when at Jerusalem for the great Festivals, seems to have occupied an old palace of Herod's, known in consequence as Herod's Praetorium (Philo, *Leg. ad Caium*, p. 1034).

found this *fellow* perverting the nation, and forbidding to give tribute to Cesar, saying that he himself is Christ a 3 King. And Pilate asked him, saying, Art thou the King of the Jews? And he answered him and said, Thou sayest *it.* 4 Then said Pilate to the chief priests and *to* the people, I find no fault in this man.

It was a building of peculiar splendour, and our Lord was conducted to it from the Hall of Meeting, across the bridge which spanned the Valley of Tyropoeon. It is however *possible* that Pilate may have occupied a part of Fort Antonia, and it has been supposed that this view receives some confirmation from the discovery by Capt. Warren of a subterranean chamber with a pillar in it, which is believed to be not later than the age of the Herods, and is on the suggested site of Antonia. Mr Fergusson (*Temples of the Jews*, p. 176) inclines to the view that this newly-discovered chamber may have been the very scene of our Lord's flagellation. Our Lord was bound (Matt. xxvii. 2) in sign that He was now a condemned criminal. This narrative of the Trial should be compared throughout with John xviii., xix.

2. *We found*] A word intended to excite prejudice.

perverting the nation] The technical Jewish name for an offender of this sort was *Mesith*, 'seducer' or 'impostor,' Acts xiii. 8—10. This was their *first* head of indictment, and had the advantage of being perfectly vague.

forbidding to give tribute to Cesar] This was a complete falsehood; but a *political* accusation was necessary for their purpose, since a heathen would not have listened to any religious accusation. The mixture of religion with politics is always perilous to truth and sincerity. This was their *second* charge.

that he himself is Christ a King] The word 'King' is an explanation to bring the case under the head of treason. Yet they must have been well aware that this charge was all the more false in spirit from being true in the letter;—for Christ had always refused and prevented every effort to make Him a temporal king (John vi. 15). This was their *third* charge.

3. *Art thou the King of the Jews?*] St Luke narrates the trial very briefly. The Jewish priests had expected that on their authority Pilate would at once order Him to execution; but, on the contrary, he meant first to hear the case, and asked them what accusation they brought, refusing to accept their bare assertion that He was "a malefactor." Pilate only attends to the *third* charge, and asks Christ this question on the Roman principle that it was always desirable to secure the confession of the accused. We see from St John (xviii. 33) that Jesus had been led *into* the Praetorium while His accusers stayed without; that He had not heard their accusations (id. vs. 34), and that Pilate was now questioning Him at *a private examination.*

Thou sayest it] For a fuller account of the scene read John xviii. 33—38. It is alluded to in 1 Tim. vi. 13.

5—24. *The Trial before Herod. Further endeavours of Pilate to procure His acquittal. The Choice of Barabbas. The condemnation to the Cross.*

And they were the more fierce, saying, He stirreth up ⁵ the people, teaching throughout all Jewry, beginning from Galilee to this place. When Pilate heard of Galilee, he ⁶ asked whether the man were a Galilean. And as soon as ⁷ he knew that he belonged unto Herod's jurisdiction, he sent him to Herod, who himself also was at Jerusalem

4. *I find no fault in this man*] This conclusion, which sounds so abrupt in St Luke, was the result of the conversation with Pilate in which Jesus had said "My Kingdom is not of this world." It had convinced Pilate of His innocence, and he expressed his conviction in this unhesitating acquittal. The word for 'fault' (*aition*) occurs in Acts xix. 40.

5—24. THE TRIAL BEFORE HEROD. FURTHER ENDEAVOURS OF PILATE TO PROCURE HIS ACQUITTAL. THE CHOICE OF BARABBAS. THE CONDEMNATION TO THE CROSS.

5. *And they were the more fierce*] Rather, **But they were more urgent.** This and similar expressions hardly convey to us the terrible violence and excitement of an Oriental mob.

Jewry] Rather, **Judaea** (comp. Dan. v. 13). These words furnish one of the traces in the Synoptists of the Judaean ministry which they imply, but do not narrate. Comp. "throughout the whole of Judaea," Acts x. 37.

beginning from Galilee] See iv. 14. This is probably mentioned to prejudice Pilate all the more against Him, as he had a quarrel with the Galilaeans, but *dum rem amplificant, Pilato dant rimam.* Bengel.

7. *he sent him to Herod*] The word used is technical—*anepempsen*, the Lat. *remisit*—and means the remission of a question to a higher court (Acts xxv. 1; comp. Philem. 11; Jos. *B. J.* II. 20, § 5). St Luke alone preserves this interesting incident. He seems to have had special information about Herod's court. Pilate's object may have been (1) to get rid of the responsibility—or at least to divide it—by ascertaining Herod's opinion; (2) to do a cheap act of courtesy which might soothe the irritation which Herod, as well as the Jews, felt against him. Vespasian paid a similar compliment to Agrippa. Jos. *B. J.* III. 10, § 10.

who himself also was at Jerusalem] "*also*," i.e. as well as Pilate. Herod lived at Tiberias, and Pilate at Caesarea. During the immense assemblages of the Jewish feasts the two rulers had come to Jerusalem, Pilate to maintain order, Herod to gain popularity among his subjects by a decent semblance of conformity to the national religion. At Jerusalem Herod occupied the old palace of the Asmonaean princes (Jos. *B. J.* II. 16; *Antt.* XX. 8, § 11).

8 at that time. And when Herod saw Jesus, he was exceeding glad: for he was desirous to see him of a long *season*, because *he* had heard many *things* of him; and
9 he hoped to have seen some miracle done by him. Then he questioned *with* him in many words; but he answered
10 him nothing. And the chief priests and scribes stood and
11 vehemently accused him. And Herod with his men of war set him at nought, and mocked *him*, and arrayed him in
12 a gorgeous robe, and sent him again to Pilate. And the same day Pilate and Herod were made friends together: for before they were at enmity between themselves.

at that time] Rather, **in those days** (of the Feast).

8. *many things*] These words should be omitted (א, B, D, K, L, M).

and he hoped to have seen some miracle done by him] ix. 7—9. Herod seems to have deteriorated. He had encouraged the visits of the Baptist on less frivolous grounds than these. It must have been a deep aggravation of Christ's sufferings to be led bound, amid coarse attendants, through the densely crowded streets.

9. *he answered him nothing*] Is. liii. 7. A murderer of the Prophets, who was living in open and flagrant incest, and who had no higher motive than mean curiosity, deserved no answer. Our Lord used of Antipas the only purely contemptuous word which He is ever recorded to have uttered (xiii. 32).

10. *and vehemently accused him*] They were now bent on securing their purpose, and perhaps feared that Herod's well-known weakness and superstition might rob them of their prey;—especially as he was much less afraid of them than Pilate was, having strong influence in Rome.

11. *with his men of war*] Literally, "*with his armies*," i.e. with his soldiers.

set him at nought] treating Him not as a *criminal*, but only as a person worthy of contempt. "He is despised and rejected of men;" "he was despised and we esteemed him not," Is. liii. 3.

in a gorgeous robe] Literally, "*bright raiment*," Acts x. 30. Probably a *white* festal garment.

sent him again] anepempsen as before—*remisit in forum apprehensionis*. This involved a *second* distinct acquittal of our Lord from every political charge brought against Him. Had He in any way been guilty of either (1) perverting the people, (2) forbidding to pay tribute, or (3) claiming to be a king, it would have been Herod's duty, and still more his interest, to punish Him. His dismissal of the case was a deliberate avowal of His innocence.

12. *were made friends together*] Rather, **became friends with one another**. Ps. ii. 1—3.

they were at enmity] perhaps in consequence of the incident mentioned

And Pilate, when he had called together the chief priests and the rulers and the people, said unto them, Ye have brought this man unto me, as one that perverteth the people: and behold, I, having examined *him* before you, have found no fault in this man *touching those things* whereof ye accuse him: no, nor yet Herod: for I sent you to him; and lo, nothing worthy of death is done unto him. I will therefore chastise him, and release *him*. (For of necessity he must

in xiii. 1. This is the first type of Judaism and Heathenism leagued together to crush Christianity.

13. *called together the chief priests*] This was a formal speech from a *bema*—perhaps the throne of Archelaus—set on the tessellated pavement called by the Jews *Gabbatha* (John xix. 13). Now was the golden opportunity which Pilate should have seized in order to do what he knew to be *right;* and he was really anxious to do it because the meek Majesty of the Lord had made a deep impression upon him, and because even while seated on the *bema*, he was shaken by a presentiment of warning conveyed to him by the dream of his wife (Matt. xxvii. 19). But men live under the coercion of their own past acts, and Pilate by his cruelty and greed had so bitterly offended the inhabitants of every province of Judaea that he dared not do anything more to provoke the accusation which he knew to be hanging over his head (comp. Jos. *Antt.* XVIII. 3, § 2. *B. J.* II. 9, § 4).

14. *have found no fault in this man*] Thus Pilate's word (*heuron*) is a direct contradiction of that of the High Priest's (*heuromen*, vs. 2). The *I* is emphatic; you bring a charge, *I* after a public examination find it to be baseless.

15. *for I sent you to him*] Or *for he sent Him back to us*, (ℵ, B, K, L, M).

is done unto him] Rather, **hath been done by Him.**

16. *I will therefore chastise him*] This was the point at which Pilate began to yield to the fatal vacillation which soon passed into guilt and made it afterwards impossible for him to escape. He had just declared the prisoner *absolutely innocent*. To subject Him, therefore, to the horrible punishment of scourging merely to gratify the pride of the Jews, and to humble Him in their eyes (Deut. xxv. 3), was an act of disgraceful illegality, which he must have felt to be most unworthy of the high Roman sense of 'Justice.' The guilty dread which made Pilate a weak man is well illustrated by what Philo says of him (*Leg. ad Caium*, 38). But he was the unconscious fulfiller of prophecy (Is. liii. 5). The restless eagerness of his various attempts to secure the acquittal of Jesus is brought out most forcibly by St John.

17. *For of necessity*, &c.] Rather, **But.** The whole verse, however, is of dubious genuineness, and may have come from a marginal gloss. It is omitted in A, B, K, L. In D it is placed after vs. 19. The Gospels are our sole authority for this concession, which is, however, entirely in accordance with Roman policy.

18 release one unto them at the feast.) And they cried out all at once, saying, Away with this *man*, and release unto us
19 Barabbas: (who for a certain sedition made in the city, and
20 *for* murder, was cast into prison.) Pilate therefore, willing
21 to release Jesus, spake again to *them*. But they cried, saying,
22 Crucify *him*, crucify him. And he said unto them the third time, Why, what evil hath he done? I have found no cause

18. *all at once*] If we read *plethei* for *pamplethei*, the meaning will be that 'they (the priests) called aloud *to the* multitude,' as in Matt. xxvii. 20. The choice of Barabbas by the mob was not spontaneous; it was instigated by these priestly murderers. The guilt of the Crucifixion rests *mainly* with the Priests, because it was mainly due to their personal influence (Mk. xv. 11).

release unto us Barabbas] This was the last drop in the cup of Jewish iniquity. Rom. xi. 30—33.

Barabbas] Rather, Bar-Abbas, 'Son of a (distinguished) father,' or Bar-Rabbas, 'Son of a great Rabbi.' Origen had the reading, 'Jesus Bar-Abbas,' in Matt. xxvii. 17, and as Jesus was a common name, and Bar-Abbas is only a patronymic, the reading is not impossible. At this stage of the trial, Barabbas may have been led out, and the choice offered them between 'Jesus Bar-Abbas and Jesus which is called Christ' as they stood on the pavement side by side.

19. *who*] The word implies 'a man of such a kind, that, &c.'

and for murder] "Ye denied the Holy One and the Just, and desired *a murderer* to be granted unto you," Acts iii. 14. Nothing is known of Bar-Abbas, but it has been conjectured from his name that he or his father belonged to the order of the Sanhedrists, who therefore desired his release. If he had been a follower of Judas of Galilee, or engaged in the riot against Pilate about his use of the *Corban*, he would enlist the sympathies of the people also.

20. *spake again to them*] Rather, **called unto them again**. He did not make them a second speech, but simply called out again his question as to their choice.

21. *they cried*] The word implies a continuous cry of increasing vehemence. The *vox populi* was in this instance *vox Diaboli*.

Crucify him, crucify him] This wild and terrible outcry was provoked by Pilate's unjust question to them how he should deal with Jesus. After this it was quite vain to say, "Why, what evil hath he done?" Yet even in yielding he cannot refrain from irritating them with the expression, "your king." It was something more than a mere taunt. It was due to a flash of genuine conviction that the Prisoner before him was greater and nobler than the greatest and noblest Jew he had ever seen.

22. *the third time*] We can only obtain from all the four Evangelists, and especially from St John, a full conception of the earnestness with which Pilate strove to escape from the necessity of what he felt to be

of death in him: I will therefore chastise him, and let *him* go. And they were instant with loud voices, requiring that he might be crucified. And the voices of them and of the chief priests prevailed. And Pilate gave sentence that it should be as they required. And he released unto them him that for sedition and murder was cast into prison, whom they had desired; but he delivered Jesus to their will.

a needless crime. If he was not, as Tertullian says, "*jam pro conscientia sua Christianus,*" he was evidently deeply impressed; and the impossibility of doing right must have come upon him as a terrible Nemesis for his past sins. It is very noteworthy that he took step after step to secure the acquittal of Jesus. 1. He emphatically and publicly announced His perfect innocence. 2. He sent Him to Herod. 3. He made an offer to release Him as a boon. 4. He tried to make scourging take the place of crucifixion. 5. He appealed to compassion. St John shews still more clearly how in successive stages of the trial he sets aside, i. the vague general charge of being "an evil doer" (xviii. 30); ii. of being in any seditious sense "a king" (xviii. 39); iii. of any guilt in His religious claims (xix. 12). He only yields at last through fear (xix. 12), which makes him release a man guilty of *the very crime* for which he delivers Jesus to a slave's death. The fact that Pilate's patron Sejanus had probably by this time fallen, and that Tiberius was executing all connected with him, may have enhanced Pilate's fears. He knew that an accusation of High Treason (under the *Lex Majestatis*) was generally fatal (Tac. *Ann.* III. 38. Suet. *Tib.* 58). All this, with other phases of these last scenes, will be found fully brought out in my *Life of Christ*, II. pp. 360—391.

23. *the voices of them and of the chief priests prevailed*] St Luke here omits the flagellation (Matt. xxvii. 26); the derision and mock homage of the soldiery—the scarlet sagum and crown of thorns; the awful scene of the Ecce Homo; the fresh terror of Pilate on hearing that He called Himself "the Son of God," and the deepening of that terror by the final questioning in the Praetorium; the "Behold your King!"; the introduction of the name of Caesar into the shouts of the multitude; Pilate's washing his hands; the last awful shout "His blood be on us and on our children;" and the clothing of Jesus again in His own garments. (See Matt. xxvii.; Mk. xv.; John xviii., xix.) To suppose that there was a *second* scourging after the sentence is a mistake. Matt. xxvii. 26 is retrospective.

24. *gave sentence*] *Epekrine* (only found in 2 Macc. iv. 47), not 'followed their praejudicium,' but *gave final sentence*. The two technical formulae for the sentence of death would be—to the Prisoner 'Ibis ad crucem' ('Thou shalt go to the Cross'); to the attendant soldier, 'I miles, expedi crucem' ('Go soldier, get ready the Cross').

whom they had desired] Rather, **whom they were demanding**. Comp. Acts xiii. 18.

26—32. *Simon the Cyrenian. The Daughters of Jerusalem.*

26 And as they led him away, they laid hold upon one Simon, a Cyrenian, coming out of the country, and on him 27 they laid the cross, that *he* might bear *it* after Jesus. And there followed him a great company of people, and of 28 women, which also bewailed and lamented him. But Jesus

26—32. SIMON THE CYRENIAN. THE DAUGHTERS OF JERUSALEM.

26. *Simon, a Cyrenian*] There was a large colony of Jews in the powerful African city of Cyrene, and the Cyrenians had a synagogue at Jerusalem (Acts ii. 10, vi. 9, xi. 20). Simon may have come to keep the feast. St Mark calls him "the father of Alexander and Rufus," *possibly* the Christians mentioned in Acts xix. 33; Rom. xvi. 13.

coming out of the country] Not necessarily from labouring in the fields: still the notice accords with the many other incidental signs that this was not the Feast-Day, but the day preceding it. See Excursus V. The Apocryphal 'Acts of Pilate' says that the soldiers met Simon at the city gate (John xix. 17). There is no historical authority for the identification of the *Via Dolorosa* or for the 'Stations' of the *Via Crucis*. The latter are said to have originated among the Franciscans.

on him they laid the cross] Probably because our Lord, enfeebled by the terrible scourging and by the long hours of sleepless agitation, was too feeble to bear it. This seems to be specially implied by Mk. xv. 21. It is not certain whether they made Simon carry the entire cross or merely part of the burden. (Comp. Gen. xxii. 6; Is. ix. 6.) The Cross was not carried in the manner with which pictures have made us familiar, but either in two separate pieces—the body of the cross (*staticulum*) and its transom (*antenna*); or by tying these two pieces together in the shape of a V (*furca*). The Cross was certainly not the *crux decussata* (X) or St Andrew's Cross; nor the *crux commissa* (T St Anthony's Cross); but the ordinary Roman Cross († *crux immissa*. See Matt. xxvii. 37). The Hebrew word for Cross is the letter Thau (Ezek. ix. 4), which gave abundant opportunities for the allegorising tendency of the Fathers. On the body of the Cross was certainly a projecting piece of wood ($\pi\hat{\eta}\gamma\mu\alpha$, *sedile*) to support the sufferer, but there was no *suppedaneum* or rest for the feet; and from xxiv. 39 it seems certain that one nail (if not two) was driven through the feet. Nothing could exceed the agony caused by this "most cruel and horrible punishment" as even the ancients unanimously call it.

that he might bear it after Jesus] Hence various Gnostic sects (e.g. the Basilidians) devised the fable that Simon was executed by mistake for Jesus, a fable which, through Apocryphal legends, has found its way into the Koran (Koran, Suras 3, 4). St Matthew (xxvii. 32) and St Mark use the technical word ἠγγάρευσαν, 'impressed for service.' Perhaps the Jews had received a hint that Simon was a disciple.

27. *of women*] Some of them may have come to offer the ano-

turning unto them, said, Daughters of Jerusalem, weep not for me, but weep for yourselves, and for your children. For 29 behold, the days are coming, in the which they shall say, Blessed *are* the barren, and the wombs that never bare, and the paps which never gave suck. Then shall they be- 30 gin to say to the mountains, Fall on us; and to the hills, Cover us. For if they do these *things* in a green 31 tree, what shall be done in the dry? And there were also 32 two other, malefactors, led with him to be put to death.

dynes which were supposed to be demanded by the Rabbinic interpretation of Prov. xxxi. 6. This is the only other recorded incident of the procession to Calvary, and it is mentioned by St Luke alone. It is a sad fact that no man—not even His Apostles—seems to have come forward to support these His last hours.

bewailed] Rather, **were beating their breasts for Him**. Comp. viii. 52, xviii. 13.

28. *turning unto them said*] The only recorded words between His condemnation and crucifixion. Pity wrung from Him the utterance which anguish and violence had failed to extort.

Daughters of Jerusalem] The wailing women were *not* therefore His former Galilaean followers, viii. 2, 3.

for yourselves] Some of them at least would survive till the terrible days of the Siege.

and for your children] Comp. Matt. xxvii. 25, "His blood be on us and on our children."

29. *Blessed are the barren*] Comp. xi. 27; Hos. ix. 12—16. The words received their most painful illustration in the incident of the Siege, which had long been foretold in prophecy (Deut. xxviii. 53—57; Jer. xix. 9), that women were driven even to kill and eat their own children: Jos. *B. J.* v. 10, vi. 3. The 'Blessed' shewed an awful reversal of the proper blessedness of motherhood.

30. *to the mountains, Fall on us*] Comp. Hos. x. 8. Hundreds of the Jews at the end of the siege hid themselves in subterranean recesses, and no less than 2000 were killed by being buried under the ruins of these hiding-places (Jos. *B. J.* vi. 9, § 4). We cannot fail to see in these events something of what St John calls "the wrath of the Lamb," Rev. vi. 16. Even a terror is entreated as a relief from yet more horrible calamities.

31. *For if they do these things in a green tree, what shall be done in the dry?*] Rather, **what must happen in the dry?** The meaning of this proverb is not clear, and hence it early received the most absurd explanations. It can however only mean either (1) 'If they act thus cruelly and shamefully while the tree of their natural life is still green, what horrors of crime shall mark the period of its blighting?'—in which case it receives direct illustration from Ezek. xx. 47; comp. xxi. 3, 4; or (2) 'If they act thus to Me the Innocent and the Holy, what shall be the fate of these, the guilty and false?'—in which case it expresses the

33—38. *The Crucifixion and Mockery. The Title.*

33 And when they were come to the place, which is called Calvary, there they crucified him, and the malefactors, one
34 on the right hand, and the other on the left. Then said Jesus, Father, forgive them; for they know not what they

same thought as 1 Pet. iv. 17, 18. (See Prov. xi. 31; Ezek. xx. 47, xxi. 4; Matt. iii. 10, and p. 385.) For the historic fulfilment in the horrors of a massacre so great as to weary the very soldiers, see Jos. *B. J.* VI. 44.

32. *two other*] Perhaps followers of the released Barabbas. They were not 'thieves,' but 'robbers' or 'brigands,' and this name was not undeservedly given to some of the wild bands which refused Roman authority. See Is. liii. 9.

malefactors] *Kakourgoi*. The same English word is used in John xviii. 30, where it is literally "*doing evil*."

33—38. THE CRUCIFIXION AND MOCKERY. THE TITLE.

33. *the place, which is called Calvary*] It is nowhere in Scripture called 'a hill,' and it was certainly not in any sense a steep or lofty hill. The only grounds for speaking of it as a hill are (1) tradition; and (2) the name. Calvary is the Latin form of Golgotha, and means 'a skull' (as the same Greek word *kranion* is rendered in Matt. xxvii. 33). Like the French *Chaumont*, this name might describe a low rounded hill. Ewald identifies it with Gareb (Jer. xxxi. 39), and Kraft accordingly derives Golgotha from גל, 'hill,' and גוית, 'death.' The name has led to the legend about Adam's skull lying at the foot of the Cross, which is so often introduced into pictures.

34. *Father, forgive them*] Is. liii. 12, "He bare the sins of many, and made intercession for the transgressors." These words were probably uttered at the terrible moment when the Sufferer was outstretched upon the Cross and the nails were being driven through the palms of the hands. They are certainly genuine, though strangely omitted by B, D. We must surely suppose that the prayer was uttered not only for the Roman soldiers, who were the mere instruments of the executors, but for all His enemies. It was in accordance with His own teaching (Matt. v. 44), and His children have learnt it from Him (Acts vii. 59, 60; Euseb. *H.E.* II. 29). They were the first of the seven words from the Cross, of which three (vs. 34, 43, 46) are recorded by St Luke only, and three (John xix. 27, 28, 30) by St John only. The last cry also began with the word "Father." The seven words are

Luke xxiii. 34. The Prayer for the Murderers.
Luke xxiii. 43. The Promise to the Penitent.
John xix. 26. The provision for the Mother.
Matt. xxvii. 46; Mk. xv. 34. Eli, Eli, lama sabachthani?
John xix. 28. The sole expression of human agony.
John xix. 30. "It is finished."
Luke xxiii. 46. "Father, into Thy hands I commend My spirit."

Thus they refer to His enemies, to penitents, to His mother and disciple,

vv. 35—38.]   ST LUKE, XXIII.   349

do. And they parted his raiment, and cast lots. And the 35
people stood beholding. And the rulers also with them derided *him*, saying, He saved others; let him save himself, if
he be Christ, the chosen of God. And the soldiers also 36
mocked him, coming to *him*, and offering him vinegar, and 37
saying, If thou be the King of the Jews, save thyself. And 38

to the agony of His soul, to the anguish of His body, to His work, and to His Heavenly Father. St Luke here omits our Lord's refusal of the *sopor*—the medicated draught, or myrrh-mingled wine (Mk. xv. 23; Matt. xxvii. 34), which, if it would have deadened His pains, would also have beclouded His faculties.

forgive them] *aphes*; Christ died "for the remission (*aphesin*) of sins," Matt. xxvi. 28.

they know not what they do] Rather, **are doing**. "Through ignorance ye did it," Acts iii. 17; 1 Cor. ii. 8. "Judaei clamant Crucifige; Christus clamat Ignosce. Magna illorum iniquitas sed major tua, O Domine, pietas." St Bernard.

they parted his raiment] For the fuller details see John xix. 23, 24.

35. *beholding*] The word implies that they gazed as at a solemn spectacle, Ps. xxii. 17; Zech. xii. 10. They seem as a body to have been far less active in insult than the others.

with them] These words are omitted in ℵ, B, C, D, L, &c.

derided] The same strong word which is used in xvi. 14; 1 Esdr. i. 51.

He saved others] They said this in the same spirit as the Nazarenes, iv. 23.

if he be Christ, the chosen of God] Literally, "if *this* man (contemptuously) be the Christ of God, the chosen." For other insults see Matt. xxvii. 40—43; Mk. xv. 29—32. Observe how the universal derision of what appeared to be such abject failure and humiliation enhances our estimate of the faith of the dying robber.

36. *the soldiers also mocked him*] A quaternion of soldiers (John xix. 53) with a centurion. Similarly Tacitus says of the Christian martyrs who perished in the Neronian persecution, "*pereuntibus addita ludibria*" (*Ann.* XV. 44).

offering him vinegar] It was their duty to watch Him (Matt. xxvii. 36), for sufferers sometimes lingered alive upon the cross for days. It is hardly to be wondered at if, with such a vile example before them as the derision by the Priests and Elders, these provincial or Roman soldiers —men of the lowest class, and "cruel by their wars, to blood inured"— beguiled the tedious hours by the mockery of the Innocent. By the word "mocked" seems to be meant that they lifted up to His lips the vessels containing their ordinary drink—sour wine (*posca*, John xix. 29. Comp. Num. vi. 3; Ruth ii. 14)—and then snatched them away. Probably a large earthen jar of *posca* for the use of these soldiers lay near the foot of the Cross (Ps. lxix. 21; John xix. 29). All these insults took place during the earlier part of the Crucifixion, and before the awful darkness came on.

37. *If thou be the King of the Jews*] as the title over Thy Cross asserts.

a superscription also was written over him in letters of Greek, and Latin, and Hebrew, THIS IS THE KING OF THE JEWS.

The soldiers would delight in these taunts, because, like the ancients generally, they detested all Jews. Tumults of the most violent kind often arose from the brutal insolence of hatred which they shewed to the conquered nation.

38. *a superscription*] A *titulus* written in black letters on a board smeared with white *gypsum*, and therefore very conspicuous. To put such a board over the head of a crucified person was the ordinary custom. The jeers of the soldiers were aimed at the Jews in general quite as much as at the Divine Sufferer; and these jeers probably first opened the eyes of the priests to the way in which Pilate had managed to insult them.

in letters of Greek, and Latin, and Hebrew] This is omitted in א, B, L, and some ancient versions, though the fact is undoubted from John xix. 20. Thus the three great languages of the ancient world—the languages of Culture, of Empire, and of Religion—bore involuntary witness to Christ.

This is the King of the Jews] The superscription is given differently by each Evangelist. St Luke perhaps gives the peculiarly scornful Latin form. "*Rex Judaeorum hic est.*" The other Evangelists give

This is Jesus the King of the Jews. Matt. xxvii. 37.
The King of the Jews. Mk. xv. 26.
Jesus of Nazareth the King of the Jews. John xix. 19.

Although no serious and sensible writer would dream of talking about 'a discrepancy' here, it is very probable that the differences arise from the different forms assumed by the Title in the three languages. We may then assume that the Title over the Cross was as follows:

ישו הנצרי מלך היהודים	John.
Ὁ βασιλεὺς τῶν Ἰουδαίων	Mark.
Rex Judaeorum hic est.	Luke.

It will be seen that St Matthew's is an *accurate combination of the three*, not *one of which was an accusation*.

It was only while the Priests were deriding Christ that it began to dawn on them that Pilate, even in angrily yielding to their violent persistence, had avenged himself in a way which they could not resent, by a deadly insult against them and their nation. *This* was their King, and *this* was how they had treated Him. Thus our Lord reigned even on His Cross, according to the curious old reading of Ps. xcvi. 10, ἐβασίλευσεν ἀπὸ τοῦ ξύλου (LXX.), Regnavit a ligno. (See *Life of Christ*, I. 12, *n.*) For the attempt of the Priests to get the superscription altered

39—43. *The Penitent Robber.*

And one of the malefactors which were hanged railed on him, saying, If thou be Christ, save thyself and us. But the other answering rebuked him, saying, Dost not thou fear God, seeing thou art in the same condemnation? And we

see John xix. 21, 22. In refusing it Pilate shewed the insolent obstinacy which Philo attributes to him. The actual title was a glorious testimony to Jesus and an awful reproach to the Jews. Ps. ii. 6. Thus His Cross becomes, as St Ambrose says, His trophy; the gibbet of the Malefactor becomes the *feretrum*—the spoil-bearing sign of triumph—of the Victor. See this alluded to in Col. ii. 14, 15. (*Life of St Paul*, II. 461.)

39—43. THE PENITENT ROBBER.

39. *one of the malefactors*] In St Matthew and St Mark we are told that *both* the robbers "reviled" Him. Here then we might suppose that there was an irreconcilable discrepancy. But though the Evangelists sometimes seem to be on the very verge of mutual contradiction, no single instance of a positive contradiction can be adduced from their independent pages. The reason of this is partly that they wrote the simple truth, and partly that they wrote under divine guidance. The explanation of the apparent contradiction lies in the Greek words used. The two first Synoptists tell us that both the robbers during an early part of the hours of crucifixion *reproached* Jesus (ὠνείδιζον), but we learn from St Luke that only one of them used injurious and insulting language to Him (ἐβλασφήμει). If they were followers of Barabbas or Judas of Galilee they would recognise no Messiahship but that of the sword, and they might, in their very despair and agony, join in the reproaches levelled *by all classes alike* at One who might seem to them to have thrown away a great opportunity. It was quite common for men on the cross to talk to the multitude, and even to make harangues (for instances see my *Life of Christ*, II. 409, *n.*); but Jesus, amid this universal roar of execration or reproach from mob, priests, soldiers, and even these wretched fellow-sufferers, hung on the Cross in meek and awful silence.

If thou be Christ] or, **Art thou not the Christ?** ℵ, B, C, L.

40. *But the other*] The 'bonus latro,' or 'Penitent Robber,' is called by various traditional names, and in the Arabic 'Gospel of the Infancy' (an Apocryphal book) he is called Titus and Dysmas in *Ev. Nicodem.* x., and a story is told that he had saved the Virgin and her Child from his comrades during their flight into Egypt. There are robber caves in the Valley of Doves which leads from Gennesareth to Kurn Hattin (see on vi. 12), and he may have been among the crowds who hung on the lips of Jesus in former days. "Doubtless the Cross aided his penitence. On the *soft* couch conversion is rare." Bengel.

Dost not thou fear God] Rather, **Dost not thou even fear God?**

indeed justly; for we receive the due reward of our deeds:
42 but this *man* hath done nothing amiss. And he said unto Jesus, Lord, remember me when thou comest into thy king-
43 dom. And Jesus said unto him, Verily I say unto thee, To day shalt thou be with me in paradise.

44—49. *Darkness. The Veil of the Temple rent. The End. Remorse of the Spectators.*

44 And it was about the sixth hour, and there was a darkness

41. *we receive the due reward of our deeds*] Literally, "*we receive back things worthy of the crimes we did.*"

hath done nothing amiss] Literally, "*did nothing out of place*" (like our "out of the way," i.e. nothing unusual or wrong). The word *prasso* in both clauses implies grave actions (see vs. 51), and this testimony implies *entire* innocence. It is the broadest possible acquittal. The word *atopos* occurs in 2 Thess. iii. 2.

42. *Jesus, Lord*] Rather, **Oh, Jesus**; the "Lord" is omitted in ℵ, B, C, L. He may well have been encouraged by having heard the prayer of Jesus for His murderers, vs. 34. "*Oravit misericordia ut oraret miseria.*" Aug.

Lord, remember me] A truly humble prayer for a far-off remembrance. He calls *Him* Lord whom the very Apostles had left, and recognises Him as a King who even when dead could benefit the dead. Even Apostles might have learnt from him. (Bengel.)

into thy kingdom] Rather, **in thy kingdom**. We must not lose sight of the faith which can alone have dictated this intense appeal to One who hung mute upon the Cross amid universal derision.

43. *To day*] An unexpected boon,—for the crucified often lingered in agony for more than two days.

To day shalt thou be with me in paradise] *Paradeisos* is derived from the Persian word *Pardes*, meaning a king's garden or pleasaunce. Here it is 'a garden' in which are more blessed trees than those in the garden of Golgotha. (Bengel.) It is used (1) for the garden of Eden (Gen. ii. 8, &c.); and (2) for that region of Hades (*Sheol*) in which the spirits of the blest await the general Resurrection, Acts ii. 31; 1 Cor. xv. 55; Rev. ii. 7. The Sapphic verse on the tomb of the great Copernicus alludes to the prayer of the Penitent Robber:

> "Non parem Paulo veniam requiro
> Gratiam Petri neque posco, sed quam
> In crucis ligno dederis latroni
> Sedulus oro."

44—49. DARKNESS. THE VEIL OF THE TEMPLE RENT. THE END. REMORSE OF THE SPECTATORS.

44. *it was about the sixth hour*] i.e. mid-day. This seems at first sight to contradict John xix. 14, but there is fair ground to conjecture that 'sixth' (which would be written ς´) was an early misreading for 'third' (written Γ´). For other proposed solutions of the discrepancy see *Life*

over all the earth until the ninth hour. And the sun was 45 darkened, and the vail of the temple was rent in the midst. And when Jesus had cried with a loud voice, he said, 46 Father, into thy hands I commend my spirit: and having said thus, he gave up the ghost.

of Christ, II. 385. The solution which asserts that St John used a different way of reckoning time is very precarious. St Luke omits the presence of the Virgin and the two other Marys and Salome at the Cross, and the words "Woman, behold thy son," "Behold thy mother." During the three hours' darkness no incident is recorded, but we trace a deepening sense of remorse and horror in the crowd. The fact that the sun was thus "turned into darkness" was, at last, that 'sign from heaven' for which the Pharisees had mockingly asked.

over all the earth] Rather, **over all the land**. There is no reason to believe that the darkness was over all the world. The Fathers (Origen, *c. Cels.* II. 33, 59, and Jerome, *Chron.*) indeed appeal to two heathen historians—Phlegon and Thallus—for a confirmation of it, but the testimony is too vague to be relied on either as to time or circumstance. They both speak of *an eclipse*.

45. *And the sun was darkened*] Instead of these words some MSS. (א, B, C, &c.) read "*the sun eclipsing*," or "*failing*." The reading seems only to be an attempt, and that a very unsuccessful one, to account for the darkness. That it could not have been due to an eclipse is certain, for the Paschal moon was at the full.

the vail of the temple was rent in the midst] The veil intended must be what was called the *Parocheth*, or *inner veil*, which hung between the Holy Place and the Holy of Holies. It was very heavy, and splendid with embroidery. It is alluded to in Heb. vi. 19, ix. 3, x. 19, 20. The obvious significance of the portent was the departure of the Shechinah or Presence of God from His now-deserted Temple. This particular event is (naturally) not mentioned by the Jews, but we may have a reference to it in the various omens of coming wrath which they say occurred "forty years" before the destruction of the Temple, and in which Jochanan Ben Zakkai saw the fulfilment of Zech. xi. 1. For a fuller account of these events see Matt. xxvii. 51—53; Mk. xv. 33. Jerome on Matt. xxvii. 51 says that a great lintel over the gate of the Temple fell and was shattered.

46. *And when Jesus had cried with a loud voice, he said*] Rather, **And, crying with a loud voice, Jesus said**. St Luke here omits the *Eli, Eli, lama sabachthani*, and the effect of that cry on the multitude (Matt. xxvii. 46—50); the "I thirst," which was the sole word of physical suffering wrung from Him in all His agonies; and the one word (*Tetelestai*) in which He expressed the sense that His work was finished.

Father, into thy hands I commend my spirit] A reference to Ps. xxxi. 5; comp. Acts vii. 59; 1 Pet. ii. 23. These words have been among the dying utterances of St Polycarp, St Augustine, St Bernard, John Huss, Jerome of Prague, Luther, Melancthon and Columbus.

he gave up the ghost] None of the Evangelists use the word "He

47 Now when the centurion saw what was done, he glorified
48 God, saying, Certainly this was a righteous man. And all
the people that came together to that sight, beholding the
things which were done, smote their breasts, and returned.
49 And all his acquaintance, and the women that followed him
from Galilee, stood afar off, beholding these *things*.

50—54. *Joseph of Arimathaea. The taking down from the Cross. The Entombment.*

50 And behold, *there was* a man named Joseph, a counsel-

died" (*ethanen*), but *exepneusen* (literally, 'He breathed forth,' here and Mk. xv. 37), and 'He sent forth' or 'gave up His spirit' (*apheken, paredōken to pneuma*, Matt. xxvii. 50; John xix. 30); probably because they wish to indicate the truth stated in John x. 18, that He gave up His life "because He willed, when He willed, how He willed." Aug. Comp. Eph. v. 2; Gal. ii. 20.

47. *the centurion*] who commanded the quaternion of soldiers. It is remarkable that St Luke gives us several instances of 'good centurions,' vii. 2, xxiii. 47; Acts x. 1, xxii. 26, xxvii. 43.

saw what was done] See Mk. xv. 39; Matt. xxvii. 54.

he glorified God] A notice characteristic of St Luke (ii. 20, v. 25, vii. 16, xiii. 13, xvii. 15, xviii. 43).

this was a righteous man] This remark might have been drawn forth by the silent majesty and holiness of the Sufferer. After the earthquake he may have added, "Truly this man was a Son of God" (Matt. xxvii. 54). The latter phrase sounds at first incongruous on the lips of a heathen, though 'Son of God' is found as a title of Augustus in some inscriptions. But the centurion had twice heard our Lord pray to 'His FATHER' (vss. 34, 46), and even Pilate had been overpowered by the awful dread lest He should be something more than man (John xix. 7—9).

48. *all the people*] Rather, **all the crowds.**

smote their breasts, and returned] Rather, **returned, smiting their breasts.** It must be remembered that the People had not acted spontaneously in this matter, but had been goaded on by the Priests.

49. *And all his acquaintance*] Rather, **But.** Peculiar to St Luke. Comp. ii. 44.

stood afar off, beholding these things] The word used is not *theorountes*, as in vs. 35. There is, perhaps, in the "afar off," a sad allusion to Ps. xxxviii. 11, "My lovers and my friends stand aloof from my sore; and my kinsmen *stand afar off*." St Luke omits the breaking of the legs of the robbers, and the piercing of the side of Jesus by the soldiers, which are narrated in John xix. 31—37.

ler; *and he was* a good man, and a just: (the same had not 51 consented to the counsel and deed of them;) *he was* of Arimathea, a city of the Jews: who also himself waited for the kingdom of God. This *man* went unto Pilate, and begged 52 the body of Jesus. And he took it down, and wrapped it in 53

50—54. JOSEPH OF ARIMATHAEA. THE TAKING DOWN FROM THE CROSS. THE ENTOMBMENT.

50. *a counsellor*] i.e. a member of the Sanhedrin, and therefore (as one of the 70 most distinguished members of the ruling classes) a person of great distinction. St Mark (xv. 43) calls him 'an honourable councillor.' Godet somewhat fancifully sees in St Mark's description of him the Roman ideal; as in St Luke's 'good and just,' the Greek ideal (καλὸς κἀγαθός); and in St Matthew's 'a *rich* man,' the Jewish ideal.

a good man, and a just] The first word describes his moral character, the latter his strict religious life as an orthodox Jew. Rom. v. 7.

51. *the same had not consented to the counsel and deed of them*] It is remarkable that Joseph is the only Sanhedrist of whom this exception is recorded. We cannot, however, doubt that it was true of Nicodemus also, since he was "*the* teacher of Israel" (John iii. 10), which may possibly mean the third officer of the Synagogue, who was known by the name of the *Chakam* or 'Wise Man.' The word 'deed' might almost be rendered 'crime.'

Arimathea] The name is a modification of the later Hebrew *Ramtha*, 'a hill,' and is the same name as Ramah, Ramathaim, &c. Hence the town of Joseph has been variously identified with Ramleh in Dan, Ramathaim in Ephraim (1 Sam. i. 1), and Ramah in Benjamin (Matt. ii. 18).

also] i.e. as well as Christ's open followers. The same word is preserved in Matt. xxvii. 57, "who *also* himself was a disciple," though as St John (xix. 38) adds, "secretly for fear of the Jews."

waited for the kingdom of God] See ii. 25, and p. 382.

52. *went unto Pilate, and begged the body of Jesus*] This was a bold, and might even have proved to be a perilous request. Hence the 'boldly' (*tolmēsas*) of Mk. xv. 43. Pilate seems to have granted the boon without a bribe because the Jewish care for burial was well known (Matt. xiv. 12; Acts viii. 2; Jos. *B. J.* IV. 5, § 2), and was indeed a part of their Law (Deut. xxi. 23). For the surprise of Pilate at the rapid death of Jesus, and his enquiry about it from the centurion, and other details, see Mk. xv. 44.

53. *wrapped it in linen*] in a *sindōn*, or piece of fine white linen. Comp. Mk. xiv. 51. Two other words, *othonia* (John xix. 40) and *soudarion* (John xx. 7), are used of the various cerements of Jesus. That Joseph bought this *sindōn*, apparently on this day (Mk. xv. 46), is one of the many incidental signs furnished even by the Synoptists that the true Passover did not begin till the *evening* of the Friday on which our Lord was crucified. On the part taken by Nicodemus in the En-

linen, and laid it in a sepulchre *that was* hewn in stone,
54 wherein never man before was laid. And *that* day was the
preparation, and the sabbath drew on.
55 And the women also, which came with him from Galilee,
followed after, and beheld the sepulchre, and how his body
56 was laid. And they returned, and prepared spices and ointments; and rested the sabbath day according to the com-

tombment, and the spices which he brought, see John xix. 39, 40. Both Joseph and Nicodemus in acting thus not only shewed great courage, but also great self-sacrifice; for the touching of a corpse made them ceremonially unclean, and thus prevented them from any share in the Paschal Feast.

in a sepulchre that was hewn in stone] This rock-hewn tomb (Matt., Mk., comp. Is. xxii. 16) was in a garden (comp. Jos. *Antt.* IX. 10, § 4; X. 3, § 2) adjoining the scene of the crucifixion, if not an actual part of it. John xix. 41. "He made His grave with the rich," Is. liii. 9. The mouth of these rocky tombs was closed with a large stone, called by the Jews *Gôlal*, which could only be rolled there by the labour of several men (John xi. 39).

54. *the preparation*] This word *paraskeuē* became the ordinary Greek word for Friday, because on Friday the Jews diligently prepared for the Sabbath, which began at sunset. The afternoon is called *prosabbaton* in Mk. xv. 42. Jos. *Antt.* XVI. 6. We are told that Shammai, the almost contemporary founder of the most rigid school of legalists, used to spend the whole week in meditating how he could best observe the Sabbath.

drew on] Literally, "began to *dawn*." This expression is used, although the Sabbath began at *sunset* (Mk. xv. 42), because the whole period of darkness was regarded as anticipatory of the dawn. Hence the Jews sometimes called the evening of Friday '*the daybreak*.' When St John (xix. 31) calls the coming Sabbath "a high day," the expression seems clearly to imply that it was *both* the Sabbath and the day of the Passover.

55. *the women also*] The two other Synoptists mention specially Mary of Magdala and Mary the mother of James and Joses.

followed after] Literally, "*following closely*."

56. *they returned*] As the sunset was now rapidly approaching, they must have hurried home to complete their preparations before the Sabbath began.

prepared spices and ointments] The spices are dry, the 'perfumes' liquid. They wished to complete the imperfect embalming of the body which Joseph and Nicodemus had hastily begun. Comp. 2 Chr. xvi. 14. They had to purchase the spices (Mk. xvi. 1). St Matthew alone relates the circumstances under which the Jews obtained leave to place a watch over the sepulchre, and to seal the stone, xxvii. 62—66.

and rested] This clause is closely connected with the next chapter,

mandment. Now upon the first *day* of the week, very early **24** in the morning, they came unto the sepulchre, bringing the spices which they had prepared, and certain *others* with them.

2—12. *Vision of Angels to the Women. Peter visits the Tomb.*

And they found the stone rolled away from the sepul- 2 chre. And they entered in, and found not the body of 3

"And during the Sabbath day they rested...but on the first day of the week, &c."
 CH. XXIV. **1.** *Now*] Rather, **But.**
very early in the morning] Literally, **at deep dawn,** i.e. at the earliest morning twilight, 'while it was yet dark' (John xx. 1), though the sun began to rise before they reached the tomb (Mk. xvi. 2). St John mentions only Mary of Magdala (xx. 1); St Matthew adds Mary, mother of James (xxviii. 1); St Mark adds Salome (xvi. 1); and St Luke Joanna, vs. 10. They may have gone singly or in small groups, the Marys being separate from the others. There is no discrepancy in the different narratives, although, as we might have expected, they are fragmentary and seem to reflect the varied and tumultuous emotions of those who were the first to see the Lord. The Easter music, as Lange says, is not 'a monotonous chorale' but an impassioned fugue.
and certain others with them] These words are probably spurious, not being in א, B, C, L.

2—12. VISION OF ANGELS TO THE WOMEN. PETER VISITS THE TOMB.

2. *they found the stone rolled away*] On their way they had considered how they should get over this difficulty, since the stone was "very great" (Mk. xvi. 3). From St Mark's expression, "looking up," we infer that the tomb was slightly elevated; and from St John's "lifted" ($\eta\rho\mu\acute{e}\nu o\nu$) that the first aperture of the tomb was horizontal. St Matthew also tells us of the Angel and the Earthquake (xxviii. 2—4).

3. *found not the body*] Even advanced sceptics admit this circumstance as *indisputable*, nor has one of them been able to invent the most remotely plausible explanation of the fact by natural causes. For the white-robed angel or angels in the tomb, see Mark xvi. 5; John xx. 11, 12. On the mention, omission, and numbers of these angels Van Oosterzee quotes a very striking remark from Lessing. "Cold discrepancy-mongers, do ye not then see that the Evangelists do not count the angels?...There were not only two angels, there were millions of them. They appeared not always one and the same, not always the same two; sometimes this one appeared, sometimes that; sometimes on this place, sometimes on that; sometimes alone, sometimes in company; sometimes they said this, sometimes they said that."

the Lord Jesus. And it came to pass, as they were *much* perplexed thereabout, behold, two men stood by them in shining garments: and as they were afraid, and bowed down *their* faces to the earth, they said unto them, Why seek ye the living among the dead? He is not here, but is risen: remember how he spake unto you when he was yet in Galilee, saying, The Son of man must be delivered into the hands of sinful men, and be crucified, and the third day rise again. And they remembered his words, and returned from the sepulchre, and told all these *things* unto the eleven, and *to* all the rest. It was Mary Magdalene, and Joanna, and Mary *the mother* of James, and other *women that were* with them, which told these *things* unto the apostles. And their words seemed to them as idle tales, and they believed them not. Then arose Peter, and ran unto the sepulchre; and stooping down, he beheld the linen clothes laid by them-

of the Lord Jesus] These words are omitted in D. The combination 'Lord Jesus' would however naturally begin at this point, as it is common in the Acts and Epistles, where 'Lord Jesus Christ' occurs about 40 times, though not found in the Gospels.

4. *much perplexed*] The word means 'utterly at a loss.'

in shining garments] Literally, "*flashing as with lightning*," which recalls the expression of Matt. xxviii. 3; comp. ix. 29.

5. *Why seek ye the living among the dead?*] Comp. Acts i. 11. The expression "*the living*" is probably used on the lips of the angels with something of its true mystic depth. John i. 4, v. 26, xi. 25, xx. 31.

6. *when he was yet in Galilee*] Matt. xvii. 22, 23.

9. *returned from the sepulchre*] Comp. Matt. xxviii. 8. From John xx. 2 we infer that Mary of Magdala had, in the first instance, run from the sepulchre to tell Peter and John of the removal of the stone, and had therefore not seen the first vision of angels. The apparent contradiction in Mk. xvi. 8 obviously means that they 'said not one word on the subject to any one' *except* the Apostles to whom they were expressly told to announce it (Matt. xxviii. 7).

10. *and other women*] See viii. 2, 3.

11. *as idle tales*] The strong word used (*lēros*) implies mere nonsensical talk.

believed them not] The imperfect shews *persistent* incredulity; 'they *disbelieved* them.'

12. *Then arose Peter*] For the fuller details see John xx. 2—9. It should be simply '*but Peter arose.*' The 'but' implies his readiness to believe. The presence of John, though omitted here, is implied in vs. 24. The verse is probably genuine, though omitted in D.

the linen clothes] *Othonia*, a very general term, and perhaps including

selves, and departed, wondering in himself at that which was come to pass.

13—35. *The Disciples at Emmaus.*

And behold, two of them went *that* same day to a village 13 called Emmaus, which was from Jerusalem *about* threescore furlongs. And they talked together of all these *things* which 14 had happened. And it came to pass, that while they com- 15

---

the linen bands in which the Body had been swathed in spices. Comp. John xx. 6, 7.

laid by themselves] Important as incidentally refuting the story disseminated by the Jews (Matt. xxviii. 11—15). Such a stealing of the body was on every ground impossible under the conditions, and *had* it been even possible could only have been a hurried and perilous work. Yet this absurd Jewish fiction was repeated and amplified twelve centuries later in the blasphemous *Toldoth Jeshu.*

departed, wondering in himself] Rather, **departed to his own house, wondering** (comp. John xx. 10). The surprise, the alarm, the perplexed incredulity of the Disciples, admitted by all the Evangelists alike, add force to those evidences which so absolutely convinced them of the miracle which they had never contemplated. The stunning blow of the Crucifixion had made them forget the prophecies of Jesus, which even at the time they had been unable to receive with any comprehension or conviction. (See ix. 43—45; John ii. 18—22, vi. 61—64, x. 17, 18, xiii. 31; Matt. xii. 38—42, xvi. 13—27, xvii. 1—9; Mk. x. 32—34, &c.)

13—35. THE DISCIPLES AT EMMAUS.

13. *two of them*] It is expressly implied in vs. 33 that they were not Apostles. One was Cleopas (an abbreviation of Cleopatros), of whom we know nothing, for the *name* is not the same as Clopas (=Alphaeus or Chalpai, John xix. 25), though they *may* have been the same person (see on vi. 15). The other is unknown, and unconjecturable. There is no shadow of probability that it was St Luke himself (Theophylact). This exquisite narrative is given by St Luke alone, though *mentioned* in Mk. xvi. 12, 13.

went] Rather, **were going.**

a village called Emmaus, which was from Jerusalem about threescore furlongs] Omit "*about*," which has nothing to sanction it in the text. The distance (6½ miles) shews that Emmaus could not have been the Emmaus of 1 Macc. iii. 40, ix. 50, &c. (Amwâs or Nicopolis), which is 176 furlongs (22 miles) from Jerusalem, Jos. *B. J.* II. 20, § 4, or the Galilaean Emmaus or "Hot Springs" (Jos. *B. J.* IV. 1, § 3, VII. 6, § 6). It may be the Emmaus of Jos. *B. J.* VII. 6, § 6 (*Kulonieh* Succah, IV. 5), which according to one reading was 60 furlongs from Jerusalem. Had the Emmaus been 160 furlongs distant (as in the reading of א, I, K, N, &c.) they could not have returned the same evening to Jerusalem.

muned *together* and reasoned, Jesus himself drew near, and
16 went with them. But their eyes were holden that *they*
17 should not know him. And he said unto them, What *manner of* communications *are* these that ye have one to another, as
18 ye walk, and are sad? And the one *of them*, whose name *was* Cleopas, answering said unto him, Art thou only a stranger in Jerusalem, and hast not known the *things* which are
19 come to pass there in these days? And he said unto them, What *things?* And they said unto him, Concerning Jesus of Nazareth, which was a prophet mighty in deed and word
20 before God and all the people: and how the chief priests and our rulers delivered him to be condemned to death,
21 and have crucified him. But we trusted that it had been he which should have redeemed Israel: and beside all this,

15. *Jesus himself drew near*] A beautiful illustration of the promise in Matt. xviii. 20.

16. *that they should not know him*] Rather, **recognise Him.** There are two other instances of the same remarkable fact. Mary of Magdala did not recognise Him (John xx. 14), nor the disciples on the Lake (John xxi. 4). The same thing is evidently implied in vs. 37 and in Matt. xxviii. 17; and it exactly accords with the clear indications that the Resurrection Body of our Lord was a Glorified Body of which the conditions transcended those of ordinary mortality. It is emphasized in Mk. xvi. 12, where we are told that He was manifested in a different form from that which He had worn before.

17. *that ye have one to another*] Literally, "*cast to and fro.*"

and are sad] The true reading seems to be **and they stood still** (*estathesan*, ℵ, A, B, and some ancient versions; *estesan*, L), **looking sad.** They stopped short, displeased at the unwelcome, and possibly perilous, intrusion of a stranger into their conversation.

18. *whose name was Cleopas*] See on vs. 13. The mention of so entirely obscure a name alone proves that the story is not an invention. *Pii non sua sed aliorum causa memorantur.* Bengel.

Art thou only a stranger in Jerusalem] Rather, **Dost thou live alone as a stranger in Jerusalem**; art thou some lonely sojourner in Jerusalem, come from a distance?

19. *a prophet, mighty in deed and word*] See a remarkable parallel to this description in Acts ii. 22.

21. *we trusted*] This would imply that now their hope was dimmed, if not quenched. This perhaps led to the reading '*we trust*' (*elpizomen* for *ēlpizomen*) in ℵ and some inferior MSS., which Alford calls a "*correction for decorum.*"

which should have redeemed Israel] The *form* of the expected redemption is explained in Acts i. 6.

to day is the third day since these *things* were done. Yea, and certain women *also* of our company made us astonished, which were early at the sepulchre; and when they found not his body, they came, saying, that *they* had also seen a vision of angels, which said that he was alive. And certain of them which were with us went to the sepulchre, and found *it* even so as the women had said: but him they saw not. Then he said unto them, O fools, and slow of heart to believe all that the prophets have spoken: ought not Christ to have suffered these *things*, and to enter into his glory? And beginning at Moses and all the prophets, he

to day is the third day] The words might be literally rendered 'He is leading this third day.' The expression seems to imply, 'if there had been any hope it would have been confirmed before now.'

23. *which said*] Rather, **which say**. This mention of a sort of double hearsay ('women *saying*—of angels who *say*') shews the extreme hesitation which appears throughout the narrative.

24. *but him they saw not*] This phrase most naturally and tenderly expresses their incredulity and sorrow. It also shews how impossible is the sceptical theory that the Disciples were misled by hallucinations. "*Les hallucinés*," says Bersier, "*parlent en hallucinés*;" but against any blind enthusiasms we see that the Apostles and Disciples were most suspiciously on their guard. They accepted nothing short of most rigid proof.

25. *O fools*] The expression is much too strong. It is not the word *aphrones* (see xi. 40), but *anoetoi*, 'foolish,' 'unintelligent.' (Gal. iii. 1.)

26. *ought not Christ to have suffered*] Rather, **the Christ**. It was a divine necessity (*ouchi edei?*), Matt. xxvi. 54; John xii. 24, 32, xi. 49—52; Acts xvii. 3; 1 Pet. i. 10, 11. Thus St Luke mainly dwells on the Resurrection as a spiritual necessity; St Mark as a great fact; St Matthew as a glorious and majestic manifestation; and St John in its effects on the minds of the members of the Church. (Westcott.)

27. *beginning at Moses*] The promise to Eve (Gen. iii. 15); the promise to Abraham (Gen. xxii. 18); the Paschal Lamb (Ex. xii.); the Scapegoat (Lev. xvi. 1—34); the brazen serpent (Numb. xxi. 9); the greater Prophet (Deut. xviii. 15); and the star and sceptre (Numb. xxiv. 17); the smitten rock (Num. xx. 11; 1 Cor. x. 4), &c.

and all the prophets] Immanuel, Is. vii. 14. "Unto us a Child is born, &c." Is. ix. 6, 7. The Good Shepherd, Is. xl. 10, 11. The Meek Sufferer, Is. l. 6. He who bore our griefs, Is. liii. 4, 5. The Branch, Jer. xxiii. 5, xxxiii. 14, 15. The heir of David, Ezek. xxxiv. 23. The Ruler from Bethlehem, Mic. v. 2. The Branch, Zech. vi. 12. The lowly King, Zech. ix. 9. The pierced Victim, Zech. xii. 10. The smitten Shepherd, Zech. xiii. 7. The Messenger of the Covenant, Mal. iii. 1. The Sun of Righteousness, Mal. iv. 2; and many other passages. Dr Davison, in his admirable and standard book on Pro-

expounded unto them in all the scriptures the *things* con-
28 cerning himself. And they drew nigh unto the village, whither they went: and he made as though *he* would have gone
29 further. But they constrained him, saying, Abide with us: for it is towards evening, and the day is far spent. And he
30 went in to tarry with them. And it came to pass, as he sat at meat with them, he took bread, and blessed *it*, and
31 brake, and gave to them. And their eyes were opened, and
32 they knew him; and he vanished out of their sight. And they said one to another, Did not our heart burn within us, while he talked with us by the way, and while he opened to us the
33 scriptures? And they rose up the same hour, and returned to Jerusalem, and found the eleven gathered together, and

phecy, pp. 266—287, shews that there is not one of the Prophets without some distinct reference to Christ except Nahum, Jonah (who was himself a type and Prophetic Sign), and Habakkuk, who however uses the memorable words quoted in Rom. i. 17. The expression is important, as shewing the prevalently Messianic character of the Old Testament; for of course we cannot suppose that our Lord went through each prophet separately, but only that He pointed out "the *tenor* of the Old Testament in its ethical and symbolical character."

in all the scriptures] fragmentarily (*polumerōs*) and multifariously (*polutropōs*), Heb. i. 1, e.g. in the Psalms passim, and in the types of Joshua, &c.

28. *he made as though he would have gone further*] Rather, **would go**. It is of course implied that He would have gone further, but for the strong pressure of their entreaty. Comp. Mk. vi. 48. We learn from these passages how needful it is to win Christ's Presence by praying for it.

29. *Abide with us*] It is this beautiful verse which has furnished the idea of Lyte's dying hymn, 'Abide with me, fast falls the eventide.'

he went in to tarry with them] Comp. Heb. xiii. 2, "thereby some have entertained angels unawares."

30. *he took bread, and blessed it, and brake, and gave to them*] Rather, **the bread**. Comp. xxii. 19. Our Lord seems, by a kind of natural authority, to have assumed the position of host; which shews that they were at an inn.

31. *he vanished*] See on vs. 16.

32. *Did not our heart burn*] Rather, **Was not our heart burning?**

while he talked with us] Rather, **to us**. "Never man spake like this man," John vii. 46.

33. *and returned to Jerusalem*] "They fear no longer the night journey from which they had dissuaded their unknown companion." Bengel.

them that were with them, saying, The Lord is risen indeed, ³⁴ and hath appeared to Simon. And they told what *things* ³⁵ *were done* in the way, and how he was known of them in breaking of bread.

36—49. *Appearance of Jesus to the Apostles.*

And as they thus spake, Jesus himself stood in the midst ³⁶

34. *hath appeared to Simon*] The same appearance, to Simon alone, is mentioned in 1 Cor. xv. 5, but there is not even a tradition as to the details. (The passage in 1 Cor. xv. 4—8 is the earliest written allusion to the facts of the Resurrection.)

35. *in breaking of bread*] Rather, **in the breaking of the bread**. The alteration is important as giving to the act a sacramental character. It has been objected that Cleopas and his companion, not being Apostles, had not been present at the institution of the Lord's Supper; but this was by no means the *only* occasion on which Christ had solemnly broken bread and blessed it (see ix. 16). St Mark adds that some of the disciples received even this narrative with distrust (xvi. 13), which once more proves that, so far from being heated enthusiasts ready to accept any hallucination, they shewed on the contrary a most cautious reluctance in accepting even the most circumstantial evidence.

The young reader will be glad to see a part of the beautiful passage of Cowper on this scene:

"It happen'd on a solemn eventide
Soon after He who was our surety died,
Two bosom friends, each pensively inclined,
The scene of all those sorrows left behind,
Sought their own village, busied as they went
In musings worthy of this great event.
They spake of Him they loved, of Him whose life,
Though blameless, had incurred perpetual strife.
* * * *
Ere yet they brought their journey to an end
A stranger joined them, courteous as a friend,
And asked them with a kind engaging air
What their affliction was, and begged a share.
* * * *
He blessed the bread, but vanished at the word,
And left them both exclaiming, 'Twas the Lord!
Did not our hearts feel all He deigned to say,
Did not they burn within us by the way?"

Conversation.

36—49. APPEARANCE OF JESUS TO THE APOSTLES.

36. *stood in the midst of them*] The words imply a sudden appearance. The Eleven, with the exception of Thomas the Twin, were sitting

37 of them, and saith unto them, Peace *be* unto you. But they were terrified and affrighted, and supposed that *they* had
38 seen a spirit. And he said unto them, Why are ye troubled?
39 and why do thoughts arise in your hearts? Behold my hands and my feet, that it is I myself: handle me, and see; for a spirit hath not flesh and bones, as ye see me have.
40 And when he had thus spoken, he shewed them *his* hands
41 and *his* feet. And while they yet believed not for joy, and
42 wondered, he said unto them, Have ye here any meat? And they gave him a piece of a broiled fish, and of a honey-

at supper with the doors closed through their fear of the Jews (John xx. 19). This is one of the most remarkable appearances of the Risen Christ. His intercourse with them on this occasion consisted of a greeting (36); a reproach and consolation (38; Mk. xvi. 14); a demonstration of the reality of His person (39—43; John xx. 20); an opening of their understandings (44—46); an appointment of the Apostles to the ministries of remission and witness (47, 48; John xix. 21, 23); a promise of the Spirit, for the fulfilment of which they were to wait in Jerusalem (49). At the close of this great scene He once more pronounced the benediction of Peace, and breathed on them with the words 'Receive the Holy Spirit' (John xx. 22). It is doubtless the extreme fulness with which St Luke has narrated this appearance which led him in accordance with his economy of method to omit some of the other appearances.

37. *terrified*] Literally, "*scared.*"

that they had seen a spirit] Rather, **that they were gazing on a spirit.** See on vs. 16.

38. *thoughts*] Rather, **reasonings.**

39. *handle me, and see*] *Psēlaphēsate*; "which we have looked upon and *our hands have handled* (*epsēlaphēsan*) of the Word of Life," 1 John i. 1; comp. John xx. 20, 27. For other uses of the word see Acts xvii. 27; Heb. xii. 18.

hath not flesh and bones] "I am not a bodiless spirit" are words attributed to Him in Ignatius (*ad Smyrn.* 3). Clemens of Alexandria has preserved a curious, but utterly baseless, legend, that St John, touching the body, found that his hands passed through it. From the omission of "blood" with "flesh and bones" very precarious inferences have been drawn.

40. *and his feet*] which must therefore have been *pierced*, and not merely *tied* to the Cross.

41. *believed not for joy*] One of the psychological touches of which St Luke is fond, and profoundly true to nature (comp. Liv. XXXIX. 49).

any meat] Rather, **anything to eat**; see on iii. 11, viii. 55.

42. *a piece of a broiled fish*] A meal of fish at Jerusalem might surprise us, if we did not learn from the Talmud that it was regularly supplied from the inexhaustible stores of the Lake of Gennesareth (*Life of Christ,* I. 142).

comb. And he took *it*, and did eat before them. And he said unto them, These *are* the words which I spake unto you, while I was yet with you, that all *things* must be fulfilled, which were written in the law of Moses, and *in* the prophets, and *in* the psalms, concerning me. Then opened he their understanding, that *they* might understand the scriptures, and said unto them, Thus it is written, and thus it behoved Christ to suffer, and to rise from the dead the third day: and that repentance and remission of sins should be preached in his name among all nations, beginning at Jeru-

and of a honeycomb] Omitted in ℵ, A, B, D, L, &c.

43. *and did eat before them*] This was one of the 'infallible proofs' appealed to in Acts i. 3; comp. John xxi. 12, 13; "who did eat and drink with Him after He rose from the dead," Acts x. 41. Jerome (*adv. Pelag.* II.) mentions a strange addition in some MSS., viz. that the disciples said that 'the wickedness and incredulity of the age is a substance which does not permit the true virtue of God to be apprehended through impure spirits; therefore even now reveal Thy justice.' A few MSS. and versions here add, 'and gave them the remains.'

44. *These are the words*] i.e. this is the meaning of the words.

which I spake unto you] xviii. 31; Matt. xvi. 21.

while I was yet with you] Important as shewing that the forty days between the Resurrection and the Ascension were not *intended* to be a continuous sojourn with the Disciples, or an integral portion of the Lord's human life.

which were written] See on vss. 26, 27.

the law...the prophets...the psalms] This corresponds with the (possibly later) Jewish division of the Old Testament into the Pentateuch, Prophets, and Ketubhim (Hagiographa).

45. *opened he their understanding*] Spiritual things can only be spiritually discerned, 1 Cor. ii. 10—13. On this most important truth see Matt. xi. 27, xiii. 11, xvi. 17; John xvi. 13; Acts xvi. 14. "Open thou mine eyes, that I may behold wondrous things out of thy law," Ps. cxix. 18.

that they might understand the scriptures] Hence the power with which they—till this time so dull and slow of heart—henceforth explained them, Acts i. 16, 20, ii. 16, 25, &c.

46. *and thus it behoved Christ to suffer*] Read, *thus it is written that the Christ should suffer*, ℵ, B, C, D, L.

47. *remission of sins*] See on i. 77. "Your sins are forgiven you for His name's sake," and 1 John ii. 12.

among all nations] See Gen. xii. 3, "all families of the earth." Ps. xxii. 27, "all kindreds of the nations." Is. xlix. 6, "a light to the Gentiles," &c. See on ii. 32.

beginning at Jerusalem] "For out of Zion shall go forth the law, and the word of the Lord from Jerusalem," Is. ii. 3; Mic. iv. 2.

⁴⁸ salem. And ye are witnesses of these *things*. And behold,
⁴⁹ I send the promise of my Father upon you: but tarry ye in the city of Jerusalem, until ye be endued with power from on high.

50—53. *The Ascension.*

50 And he led them out as far as to Bethany, and he lift up

48. *ye are witnesses*] John xv. 27. How prominent in the minds of the Apostles was this ministry of *witness* may be seen from Acts i. 8, ii. 32, iii. 15, iv. 33, v. 30—32, &c.

49. *the promise of my Father*] both in the Prophecies of the Old Testament (Is. xliv. 3; Ezek. xxxvi. 26; Joel ii. 28) and by His own mouth (John xiv. 16, 17, 20, xv. 26, xvi. 7). Comp. Acts i. 4, 5, 8. It is difficult not to see in this expression a distinct *allusion* to the discourses which are *recorded* by St John alone.

until ye be endued] Rather, **until ye put on the garment of**. For the metaphor see Rom. xiii. 14; Eph. iv. 24, &c. We are unclothed till we receive heavenly gifts. "They had been washed (John xv. 3), now the clothing is promised." Bengel.

There are ten recorded appearances of the Risen Christ (including that at the Ascension), of which St Luke only narrates three (the 4th, 5th, and 10th), though he alludes to others (e.g. the 3rd). They are

1. To Mary of Magdala. John xx. 11—17 ('*Noli me tangere*'); Mk. xvi. 9.
2. To other women, who adore Him. Matt. xxviii. 9, 10.
3. To Peter. Luke xxiv. 34; 1 Cor. xv. 5.
4. To the Disciples on the way to Emmaus. Luke xxiv. 13—35; Mk. xvi. 12, 13.
5. To ten Apostles and others. Luke xxiv. 36—49; John xx. 19—23; Mk. xvi. 14.
6. To the Eleven Apostles. The incredulity of Thomas removed. John xx. 26—29.
7. To seven Apostles at the Lake of Galilee. John xxi. 1—24.
8. To five hundred on a hill of Galilee. Matt. xxviii. 16—20; Mk. xvi. 15—18; 1 Cor. xv. 6.
9. To James, the Lord's brother. 1 Cor. xv. 7.
10. Before the Ascension. Luke xxiv. 50, 51; Acts i. 6—9.

Since more Appearances of the Risen Christ than those here narrated were well known to St Paul (1 Cor. xv. 5—7), it may be regarded as certain that they were known also to St Luke. If he here omits them it must be borne in mind (i) that neither he nor any of the Evangelists profess to furnish a complete narrative; (2) that St Luke especially shews a certain 'economy' (as has been already pointed out) in only narrating *typical* incidents; (iii) that he is here hastening to the close of his Gospel; and (iv) that he has other particulars to add in the Acts of the Apostles.

his hands, and blessed them. And it came to pass, while he ⁵¹ blessed them, he was parted from them, and carried up into heaven. And they worshipped him, and returned to Jeru- ⁵² salem with great joy: and were continually in the temple, ⁵³ praising and blessing God. Amen.

50—53. THE ASCENSION.

50. *he led them out*] Not of course at the conclusion of the last scene, but at the end of the forty days, Acts i. 3.

as far as to Bethany] Rather, **as far as towards Bethany** (*pros*, ℵ, B, C, D, &c.). The traditional scene of the Ascension is the central summit of the Mount of Olives (*Jebel et-Tur*); but it is far more probable that it took place in one of the secluded uplands which lie about the village. See a beautiful passage in Dean Stanley's *Sinai and Palestine*, ch. iii.

51. *he was parted from them*] "A cloud received Him out of their sight," Acts i. 9. The original however conveys a clearer impression. *He stood apart from them* (aorist) *and was gradually borne into heaven*. The latter words are not found in ℵ, D.

carried up into heaven] See Eph. iv. 8. The withdrawal of His Bodily Presence preceded His Spiritual Omnipresence. The omission of the Ascension by St Matthew and St John would be more remarkable if it was not assumed by them both (John iii. 13, vi. 62, xx. 17; Matt. xxiv. 30).

52. *returned to Jerusalem*] For fuller details see Acts i. 3—12.

with great joy] as Jesus had promised (John xvi. 20, 22). It is remarkable that they shewed great joy now that they were losing for ever the earthly presence of their Lord. It shews their faith in the promise that His spiritual presence should be even nearer and more precious (John xiv. 28, xvi. 7).

53. *continually in the temple*] This expression is one of the links between the Gospel and the Acts (see Acts ii. 46, iii. 1, &c.).

praising and blessing God] Acts ii. 46, v. 42. 'Praise is the fruit of joy.' A characteristic close in accordance with the usual spirit of St Luke. See Introd. p. 24, and ii. 20, v. 25, vii. 16, xiii. 13, xvii. 15, xviii. 43, xxiii. 47.

Amen] Probably a liturgical addition, as it is omitted in ℵ, C, D, L, &c. "The Ascension," says Godet, "realises in the person of the Risen Son of Man the design of God towards Humanity." That divinely-foreordained purpose (*prothesis*) was to make of sanctified believers a Family of God's children like His only Son. Rom. viii. 28, 29; Eph. ii. 6; Heb. ii. 10. The work of Christ is continued by the Church, enlightened by the Spirit of God at Pentecost, and awaiting its perfection at the Second Advent. "Since then salvation involves these three things—Grace, Holiness, Glory, each Gospel, especially that of St Luke, requires, as its second volume, the Acts; as its third, the Revelation of St John."

EXCURSUS I.

ON THE MEANING OF ἐν τοῖς τοῦ πατρός μου IN LK. II. 49 (THE FIRST RECORDED WORDS OF JESUS).

In my *Life of Christ* (I. 78) I deliberately adopted the rendering of the English Version, but my view of the meaning has since been changed by a monograph kindly sent me by the Rev. Dr Field of Norwich, from which I here borrow some illustrations.

It might seem that the words lose something of their force and beauty by the adoption of the rendering "*in my Father's house;*" but we must remember (1) that they are the words of a young and guileless Boy who was "subject unto his parents;" (2) that they must be interpreted with reference to their *context*. Joseph and his mother might have known that He would be "about *His Father's business*" without knowing *where He was*. The answer had reference to His mother's gentle reproach about their agonising search for Him. His answer is "Why this search? might you not have conjectured that I was *in my Father's House?*" The other meaning would therefore be less appropriate. It is also less supported. We have no *exact* instance of ἐν τοῖς τινος εἶναι meaning "to be about a person's business," though we have something like it, e.g. 1 Tim. iv. 15 ἐν τούτοις ἴσθι, and the Latin "*totus in illis.*" This idiom seems however to imply an absolute *absorption* which is not here intended. If the word ὅλος had been added the sense and the idiom would indeed have been clear, and there would have been a distant analogy to the phrase employed in the story that when the young Alexander talked with the Persian Ambassadors he did not ask about the Golden Vine, the king's dress, &c. but "was entirely occupied with the most important matters of the government" (ὅλος ἐν τοῖς κυριωτάτοις ἦν τῆς ἡγεμονίας), so that the strangers were amazed (ἐκτεπλῆχθαι), Plut. II. 342. But had our Lord meant to say 'Know ye not that I must be *absorbed in my Father's work?*' He would have expressed His meaning less ambiguously, and if He spoke in Aramaic those who recorded the sentence in Greek would hardly have left the meaning doubtful.—On the other hand "in my Father's House" is the ordinary and natural meaning of the words.—*Oikēmasi* or *dōmasi* might be understood, but in fact the article alone—*ta*, 'the things or belongings of'—was colloquially used in this sense; e.g. ᾆ τὰ Λύκωνος (Theocr. II. 76), 'where Lycon's *house* is;' εἰς τὰ τοῦ ἀδελφοῦ, 'into my brother's' (Lysias *c. Eratosth.* p. 195), ἐν τοῖς τοῦ δεσπότου ἑαυτοῦ εἶναι αὐτὸν ἀνάγκη (Chrysost. *Hom.* LII. *in Gen.*), 'wherever he may chance to go he must be in his Master's house.' Esther vii. 9, ἐν τοῖς Ἀμὰν, 'in Haman's house;' (LXX.) Job xviii. 20, ἐν τοῖς αὐτοῦ ἥσονται ἕτεροι, 'others shall live *in his house.*' See too Gen. xli. 51, LXX. In this interpretation the Vulgate, Arabic, Ethiopic, and Peshito Syriac concur, as do Origen, Theophylact, Euthymius, Epiphanius, and Theodoret.

But it may be asked 'may we not admit both meanings, one as primary and one as secondary?' This is the view adopted by Alford and others; but I agree with Dr Field in the remark that "it is certain that only one of the meanings was in the mind of the artless Child from whose lips they fell, and that *that* meaning" (so far as the mere significance of the words was concerned) "was rightly apprehended by those who heard them."

EXCURSUS II.

THE DOUBLE GENEALOGIES OF CHRIST AS THE SON OF DAVID.

The general facts are these:

(i) The genealogy of our Lord in St Matthew *descends from Abraham* to Jesus, in accordance with his object in writing mainly for the Jews.

The genealogy in St Luke *ascends from Jesus to Adam*, and to God, in accordance with his object in writing for the world in general. He spans the generations of mankind from the first Adam to the Second Adam, who was the Lord from heaven (1 Cor. xv. 20, 45, 47).

(ii) The generations are introduced in St Matthew by the word "*begat;*" in St Luke by the genitive with the ellipse of "son." Thus in St Matthew we have

> Abraham begat Isaac,
> And Isaac begat Jacob, &c.;

but in St Luke

    Being the son (as was reputed) of Joseph,
               (The son) of Eli
                     of Matthat, &c.

(iii) St Matthew says that	St Luke (merely reversing the
David begat Solomon	order) traces the line through
Rehoboam	David
Abijah	Nathan
Asa	Mattathah
Jehoshaphat	Menna
Jehoram [Ahaziah, Joash, Amaziah omitted]	Meleah
Uzziah	Eliakim
Jotham	Jonan
Ahaz	Joseph
Hezekiah	Judas
Manasseh	Symeon
Amos	Levi
Josiah	Matthat
Jeconiah and his brethren	Jorim
Shealtiel	Eliezer
Zerubbabel	Jesus
	Er
	Elmadam
	Kosam
	Adaiah
	Melchi
	Neriah
	Shealtiel (in 1 Chr. iii. 19 we find Pedaiah, who was perhaps the actual father; Shealtiel may have *adopted* his nephew[1]).
	Zerubbabel]

Thus St Luke gives 21 names between David and Zerubbabel where St Matthew only gives 15, and all the names except that of Shealtiel (Salathiel) are different.

[1] Some authorities maintain that Zerubbabel was the *grandson* of Shealtiel, and that we have six sons of Shealtiel in 1 Chron. iii. 18.

EXCURSUS II. 371

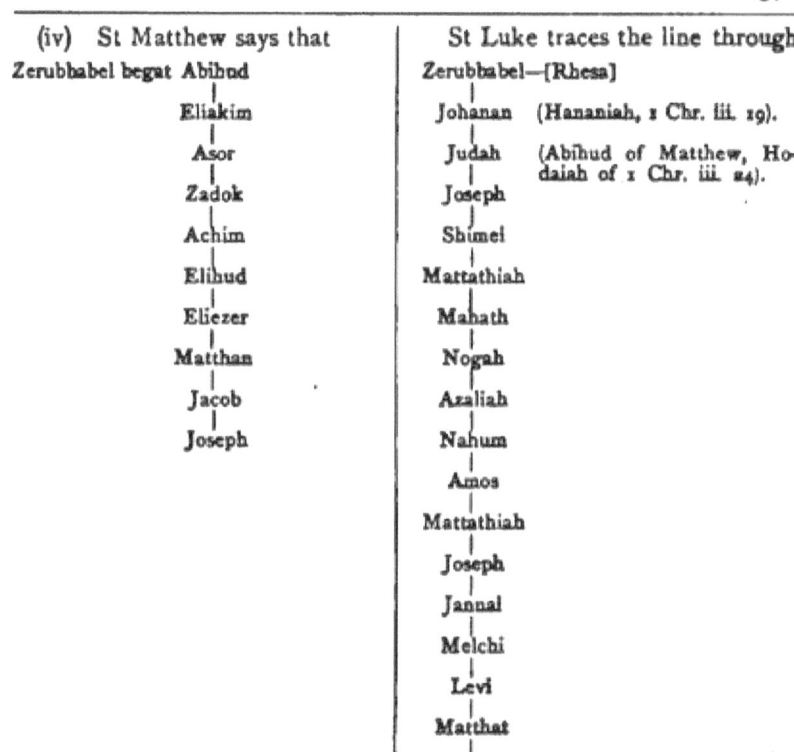

Thus it will be seen that St Luke gives 17 generations between Zerubbabel and Joseph, where St Matthew only gives 9, and all the names are different.

The two main difficulties then which we have to meet are
(α) The difference in the number of the generations;
(β) The difficulties in the dissimilarity of the names.

(α) The difficulty as to *the number of the generations* is not serious, because (1) it is a matter of daily experience that the number of generations in one line often increases far more rapidly than that in another; but also because (2) St Matthew has arranged his genealogies in an arbitrary numerical division of tesseradecads (for the manner in which these tesseradecads are arranged the student must refer to commentaries on St Matthew), and because nothing was more common among the Jews than the adoption of this symmetrical method, at which they arrived by the free omission of generations, provided that the *fact* of the succession remained undoubted. Thus in 2 Chron. xxii. 9 "son" stands for "grandson," and Ezra (in Ezra vii. 1—5) omits no less than seven steps in his own pedigree, and among them his own father,—which steps are preserved in 1 Chron. vi. 3—15.

EXCURSUS II.

(β) The difficulty as to *the dissimilarity of names* will of course only affect the two steps of the genealogies at which they *begin* to diverge, before they again coalesce in the names of Shealtiel and of Joseph.

One of the commonest ways of meeting the difficulty has been to suppose that St Luke is giving the genealogy not of Joseph but of Mary—the genealogy of Christ by *actual birth*, not by legal claim.

This solution (first suggested by Annius of Viterbo at the close of the 15th century), though still adopted by some learned men, must be rejected, (1) because there is no trace that the Jews recognised the genealogies of women as constituting a legal right for their sons; and (2) because it would do the strongest violence to the language of St Luke to make it mean 'Being, as was reputed, the son of Joseph [*but really the son of Mary, who was the daughter*] of Eli, &c.'

We must therefore regard it as certain that both genealogies are genealogies of Joseph adduced to prove that *in the eye of the Jewish law* Jesus was of the House of David. The question is *not* what we should have expected about the matter, but what is actually the case.

A. First then, how can Joseph be called in St Matthew the son of Jacob, in St Luke the son of Eli?

(a) An ancient explanation was that Matthan, a descendant of David in the line of Solomon (as given by St Matthew) was the husband of a woman named **Estha**, and became the father of Jacob; on his death his widow Estha married Melchi, a descendant of David in the line of Nathan (as given by St Luke), and had a son named Eli. Eli, it is said, died childless, and Jacob, his half-brother, in accordance with the law of levirate[1] marriages (Deut. xxv. 5, 6; Matt. xxii. 23—27), took his widow to wife, and became the father of Joseph. Thus

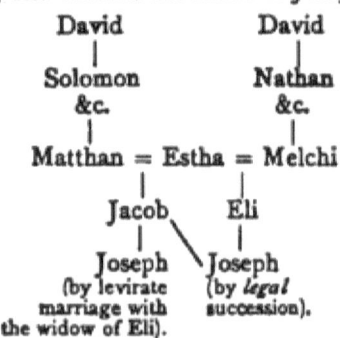

St Luke might naturally give the latter genealogy because it would be the one recognised by Romans, with whom the notion of *legal* as distinguished from natural sonship was peculiarly strong. This solution derives very great authority from the fact that it is preserved for us by Eusebius (*H. E.* 1. 7) from a letter of Julius Africanus, a Christian writer who lived in Palestine in the third century, and who *professed to derive it from private memoranda preserved by* 'the Desposyni' *or kindred of the Lord.*

---

[1] So called from the Latin word *levir*, 'a brother-in-law.'

(β) But the difficulty about this view—not to mention the strange omission of Levi and Matthat, which may be possibly due to some transposition—is that St Matthew's genealogy will then be *partly legal* (as in calling Shealtiel the *son* of Jeconiah) and *partly natural* (in calling Joseph the son of Jacob). But perhaps (since Jul. Africanus does not vouch for *the exact details*) there was so far a confusion that it was *Jacob* who was childless, and *Eli* who became by a levirate marriage the father of Joseph. If this be so, then St Matthew's is *throughout* the legal, and St Luke's throughout the *natural* genealogy. Even without the supposition of a levirate marriage, if Jacob were childless then Joseph, the son of his younger brother Eli, would become heir to his claims. The tradition mentioned may *point in the direction of the true solution* even if the details are inexact.

(γ) We may here add that though the Virgin's genealogy is not given (οὐκ ἐγενεαλογήθη ἡ παρθένος, S. Chrys.), yet her Davidic descent is assumed by the sacred writers (Lk. i. 32; Acts ii. 30, xiii. 23; Rom. i. 3, &c.), and was in all probability involved in that of her husband. *How* this was we cannot say with certainty, but if we accept the tradition which has just been mentioned it is not impossible that Mary may have been a *daughter* of Eli (as is stated in an obscure Jewish legend, Lightfoot, *Hor. Hebr.* ad loc.) *or* of Jacob, and may have married her cousin Joseph *jure agnationis*. At any rate we have decisive and independent proof that *the Davidic descent of our Lord was recognised by the Jews*. They never attempted to avert the jealousy of the Romans about the royal descent of the Desposyni (Euseb. *H. E.* i. 7), and Rabbi Ulla (circ. 210) says that "Jesus was exceptionally treated because *of royal descent*" (T. B. *Sanhedr.* 43 a, Amsterdam ed., see Derenbourg, *Palest.* p. 349. But it is possible that the words mean 'influential with the (Roman) government').

B. We have now to explain why St Matthew says that Shealtiel (Salathiel) was *the son of Jeconiah*, while St Luke says that he was *the son of Neriah*.

The old suggestion that the Zerubbabel and Shealtiel of St Luke are *different persons* from those of St Matthew may be set aside at once. But the true answer seems to be that Jehoiachin (Jeconiah) was either actually **childless**, as was so emphatically prophesied by Jerem. xxii. 24—30, or that, at any rate, his children (if he ever had any, as seems possible from vs. 28; 1 Chr. iii. 17—19; and Jos. *Antt.* x. 11, § 2) died childless in Babylon. It is true that the word rendered 'childless' (עֲרִירִי) *may* mean 'forlorn' or 'naked;' but the other is the more natural meaning of the word, and so it was understood by the Jews, who however supposed that, after a long captivity, he repented and the curse was removed. Setting aside this mere conjecture, it seems probable that Jeconiah was, or became, absolutely childless, and that therefore in the 37th year of his captivity he adopted a son to preserve his race from extinction. His choice however was limited. Daniel and others of the seed royal were eunuchs in the palace of the King of Babylon (Dan. i. 3; 2 Kings xx. 16), and Ishmael and others were excluded by their murder of Gedaliah; to say nothing of the fact that the royal line had been remorselessly mown down by Jehu and by Athaliah. He therefore adopted the seven sons of Neri, the twentieth from David in the line of Nathan. We seem to have an actual intimation of this in Zech. xii. 12, where "*the family of Nathan apart*" is commemorated *as well as* "the family of David apart" because of the splendid Messianic prerogative which they thus obtained. And this is remarkably confirmed by Rabbi Shimeon Ben Jochai in the *Zohar*, where he speaks of Nathan, the son of David, as the father of Messiah *the Comforter* (because Menachem, 'comforter,' stands numerically for 138, which is the numerical value of the letters of *Tsemach*, 'the Branch'). Hence too Hephzibah, the wife of Nathan, is called the mother of the Messiah. (See Schöttgen, *Hor. Hebr.* on i. 31.)

The failure of the Messianic promise in the *direct* natural line of Solomon is no difficulty in the way of this hypothesis, since while the promise to David was *absolute* (2 Sam. vii. 12) that to Solomon was *conditional* (1 Kings ix. 4, 5).

If these very simple and probable hypotheses be accepted no difficulty remains; and this at least is certain—that no error can be demonstrated. *A single adoption, and a single levirate marriage*, account for the apparent discrepancies. St Matthew gives the *legal* descent through a line of Kings descended from Solomon—the *jus successionis*; St Luke the natural descent—the *jus sanguinis*. St Matthew's is a royal, St Luke's a natural pedigree. It is a confirmation of this view that in Joseph's *private* and *real* genealogy we find the names Joseph and Nathan recurring (with slight modifications like Matthat, &c.) no less than seven times. That there must be some solution of this kind is indeed self-evident, for if the desire had been to *invent* a genealogy no one would have neglected a genealogy deduced through a line of Kings.

C. i. We need only further notice that in vs. 27 the true translation probably is "*the son of the Rhesa* Zerubbabel." Rhesa is not a proper name, but a Chaldee title meaning 'Prince.' Thus the head of the Captivity is always known by Jewish writers as the *Resh Galootha*.

ii. In vs. 32 we have only three generations—Boaz, Obed, Jesse—between Salmon and David; a decisive proof that the common chronology is wrong in supposing that more than four hundred years elapsed between the conquest of Canaan and David.

iii. In vs. 24 the Matthat is perhaps identical with the Matthan of Matt. i. 15; if so the line recorded by St Matthew may have failed at Eliezer, and Matthan, the lineal descendant of a younger branch, would then be his heir.

iv. In vs. 36 the *Cainan* (who must be distinguished from the Cainan of vs. 37) is possibly introduced by mistake. The name, though found in this place of the genealogy in the LXX., is not found in any Hebrew MS. of the O. T., nor in the Samaritan, Chaldee, and Syriac versions (Gen. xi. 12; 1 Chr. i. 24). It is omitted in the Codex Bezae (D), and there is some evidence that it was unknown to Irenaeus.

v. The difference between the two genealogies thus given without a word of explanation constitutes a strong probability that neither Evangelist had seen the work of the other.

The conclusions arrived at as *probable* may be thus summarized.

David's line through Solomon failed in Jeconiah, who therefore adopted Shealtiel, the descendant of David's line through Nathan.

(Shealtiel being also childless adopted Zerubbabel, son of his brother Pedaiah, 1 Chr. iii. 17—19.)

Zerubbabel's grandson, Abihud (Matt.), Judah (Lk.), or Hodaiah (1 Chr.)—for the three names are only modifications of one another—had two sons, Eliakim (Matt.) and Joseph (Lk.).

Eliakim's line failed in Eliezer; and thus Matthan or Matthat became his legal heir.

This Matthan had two sons, Jacob the father of Mary, and Eli the father of Joseph; and Jacob having no son adopted Joseph his heir and nephew.

It is true that these suggestions are not capable of rigid demonstration, but (α) they are entirely in accordance with Jewish customs; (β) there are independent reasons which shew that they are probable; (γ) no other hypotheses are adequate to account for the early existence of a double genealogy in Christian circles.

EXCURSUS III.

ON PUTTING NEW (νέον) WINE INTO FRESH (καινούς) BOTTLES.

It is usually considered a sufficient explanation of this passage to say that the 'bottles' of the ancients were skins, and not bottles of glass; and that whereas fermenting wine would burst old, worn, and sun-cracked skins, it would only distend new skins.

It is exceedingly doubtful whether such an explanation is tenable.

a. It is quite true that the 'bottles' of the East were skins, as the Greek word *askos* implies[1]. They are still made in the East exactly as they used to be made thousands of years ago, by skinning an animal from the neck, cutting off the head and legs, and drawing off the skin without making a slit in the belly. The legs and neck are then tightly tied and sewn up, and the skin with the hair on it is steeped in tannin and pitched at the sutures (Tristram, *Nat. Hist. Bib.*, p. 92).

β. It is also quite true that 'wine' must here mean the juice of the grape which has not yet fermented, '**must**,' as this explanation implies. For '*still wine*'—wine *after* fermentation—may be put in any bottles whether old or new. It has no tendency to burst the bottles that contain it.

γ. But unfermented wine *which was intended to ferment* certainly could not be kept in any kind of leather bottle whether old or new. The fermentation would split open the sutures of the leather, however new the bottle was.

---

[1] The root is *sk*, found also in *skin*.

δ. It seems, therefore, to be a very probable conclusion that our Lord is not thinking at all of fermented, intoxicating wine, but of '*must*'—the liquid which the Greeks called ἀεὶ γλεῦκος—tuns of which are kept for years in France, and in the East; which (as is here stated) improves by age; which is a rich and refreshing, but non-intoxicating beverage; and which might be kept with perfect safety in *new leather bottles*.

ε. Why, then, would it be unsafe to put the *must* in old bottles?

Because if the old bottles had contained 'wine' in the ordinary sense—i.e. the fermented juice of the grape—or other materials, "minute portions of albuminoid matter would be left adhering to the skin, and receive yeast germs from the air, and keep them in readiness to set up fermentation in the new unfermented contents of the skin......As soon as the unfermented grape-juice was introduced, the yeast germs would begin to grow in the sugar and to develop carbonic dioxide. If the must contained one-fifth sugar it would develop 47 times its volume of gas, and produce an enormous pressure which no bottle, new or old, could withstand."

Unless, therefore, some other explanation can be produced, it is at least possible—if not most probable—that our Lord, in speaking of 'wine,' here means *must*.

Thus much is at any rate certain:—the conditions of our Lord's comparison are not fulfilled either by fermented wine, or by grape-juice intended for fermentation. Fermented wine could be kept as well in old bottles as in new; and grape-juice intended to ferment would burst far stronger receptacles than the newest leathern bottle. See Job xxxii. 19. "The rending force of the pent-up gas would burst even the strongest iron-bound cask." When fermentation is intended, it goes on in the wine-vat.

Columella, an almost contemporary Latin writer, describing the then common process of preserving grape-juice in the form of unfermented *must*, lays the same stress on its being put *into a new amphora*.

EXCURSUS IV.

On the Meaning of *EPIOUSION* in Lk. xi. 3.

After the very learned and elaborate examination to which the word has been subjected by Bishop Lightfoot, *On Revision* 195—234, and Dr McClellan, *New Testament* 632—647, it will be sufficient here to touch on their conclusions.

This word was so rare that even learned Greek Fathers like Origen considered that it had been invented by the Evangelists and were uncertain as to its meaning. It is even still a dispute whether it has a *temporal* or a *qualitative* meaning, i.e. whether it means

i. *bread for the day*, in one of the subordinate senses of α. *continual* or β. *future*:—or

ii. *for our subsistence*, whether a. *physical*, or β. *spiritual*:—
or again (giving to *epi* the sense of 'upon,' i.e. 'in addition to') whether it meant

iii. *beyond other substances*, implying either a. '*supersubstantial*,' i.e. preeminent, or β. *consubstantial*.

The meanings suggested under iii. may be at once dismissed as the mere artificial 'afterthoughts of theology.'

The decision depends partly on the etymology. It has been thought that the word may be derived from *epi* and *ienai*, or from *epi* and *ousia*.

It seems however an insuperable objection to the latter etymology that it has the form *epiousios* not *epousios*, and with the etymology fall the meanings suggested under ii., i.e. bread for our *physical*, or *spiritual*, subsistence.

If then the word be derived from *epi* and *ienai* it comes either from (*ho*) *epiōn* (*chronos*) or (*he*) *epiousa* (*hemera*). In either case it would mean 'bread for the coming day,' i.e. for to-morrow, or for to-day; and Bishop Lightfoot brings some evidence to shew that this was the sense accepted by the Church till the more mystical sense was supported by Origen. He sums up his essay by the words "Thus the familiar rendering 'daily' which has prevailed uninterruptedly in the Western Church from the beginning is a fairly adequate representation of the original; nor indeed does the English language furnish any one word which would answer the purpose so well" (p. 234). On the other hand Dr McClellan, as the result of another exhaustive criticism, decides on the meaning "*proper to the future world*," and would render it "*needful*," an interpretation which he argues that "etymology, original tradition, sense and context unite in establishing" (p. 646). He would therefore take it in the sense of "Give us day by day *our bread of Life Eternal*."

May we not however suppose that our Lord mentally referred to Prov. xxx. 8, "Feed me with food convenient for me," LXX. σύνταξον δέ μοι τὰ δέοντα καὶ τὰ αὐτάρκη? If so the simpler and more obvious meaning is to be preferred.

But I may observe in conclusion that *practically* the difference is nothing: for—in uttering the prayer—whichever sense the Christian may attach to the *adjective* he will certainly include the spiritual sense in using the word "bread" (John vi. 51).

EXCURSUS V. ON XXII. 7.

WAS THE LAST SUPPER AN ACTUAL PASSOVER?

The question whether, before the institution of the Lord's Supper, our Lord and His Disciples ate the usual Jewish Passover—in other words, whether in the year of the Crucifixion the ordinary Jewish passover

(Nisan 15) began on the evening of Thursday or on the evening of Friday—is a question which has been ably and voluminously debated, and respecting which eminent authorities have come to opposite conclusions.

From the Synoptists alone we should no doubt *infer* that the ordinary Paschal Feast was eaten by our Lord and His Disciples, as by all the Jews, on the evening of Thursday (Matt. xxvi. 2, 17, 18, 19; Mk. xiv. 14—16; Luke xxii. 7, 11—13, 15).

On the other hand, St John uses language which seems quite as distinctly to imply that the Passover was *not* eaten till the next day (xiii. 1, "*before* the Feast of the Passover;" 29, "those things that we have need of *against* the feast;" xviii. 28, "they themselves went not into the judgment-hall lest they should be defiled; but *that they might eat the passover*"). He also calls the Sabbath (Saturday) a high day (a name given by the Jews to the *first* and *last* days of the octave of a feast) apparently because it was both a Sabbath and the first day of the Passover; and says (xix. 14) that Friday was "the preparation of the Passover." Here the word used is *Paraskeuē* (as in Luke xxiii. 54). Now this word may no doubt merely mean 'Friday,' since every Friday was a preparation for the Sabbath; but it seems very difficult to believe that the expression means 'Passover Friday.'

Now since the language of St John seems to be perfectly explicit, and since it is impossible to explain away his expressions by any natural process—though no doubt they *can* be explained away by a certain amount of learned ingenuity—it seems more simple to accept his express statement, and to interpret thereby the less definite language of the Synoptists.

We may set aside many current explanations of the difficulty, such as that—

α. Two different days may have been observed in consequence of different astronomical calculations about the day.

or β. Some laxity as to the day may have been introduced by different explanations of "between the two evenings."

or γ. The Jews in their hatred put off their Passover till the next evening.

or δ. St John, by "eating the Passover," may have meant no more than eating the *Chagigah* or festive meal.

or ε. The supper described by St John is not the same as that described by the Synoptists.

or ζ. The Last Supper was an ordinary Passover, only it was eaten *by anticipation*.

Setting aside these and many other untenable views, it seems probable that the Last Supper was *not* the ordinary Jewish Paschal meal, but was eaten the evening before the ordinary Jewish Passover; and that the language of the Synoptists is perfectly consistent and explicable on the view that our Lord gave to His last Supper *a Paschal character* ("to eat *this* Passover," or "*this* as a Passover," Lk. xxii. 15), and spoke of it to His disciples as *their* Passover. Hence had arisen in the

Church the view that it actually was the Paschal meal—which St John silently corrects. The spread of this impression in the Church would be hastened by the fact that in any case Thursday was, in one sense, 'the first day of unleavened bread,' since on that day all leaven was carefully searched for that it might be removed.

When we adopt this conclusion—that the Last-Supper was not the Paschal Feast itself, but intended to supersede and abrogate it—it is supported by a multitude of facts and allusions in the Synoptists themselves; e.g. i. The occupations of the Friday on which Jesus was crucified shew *no sign whatever* of its having been a very solemn festival. The Jews kept their chief festival days with a scrupulosity almost as great as that with which they kept their Sabbaths. Yet on this Friday working, buying, selling, holding trials, executing criminals, bearing burdens, &c. is going on as usual. Everything tends to shew that the day was a common Friday, and that the Passover only began at sunset.

ii. The Sanhedrin had distinctly said that it would be both dangerous and impolitic to put Christ to death on the Feast day (Mk. xiv. 2, and comp. Acts xii. 4).

iii. Not a word is said in any of the Evangelists about the Lamb—the most important and essential element of the Paschal meal; nor of the unleavened bread at the Supper; nor of the bitter herbs; nor of the sauce *Charoseth;* nor of the account given by the Chief Person present of the Institution of the Passover, &c.

Further than this, many arguments tend to shew that this Last Supper was not a Paschal meal; e.g.:

α. Early Christian tradition—apparently down to the time of Chrysostom—distinguished between the Last Supper and the Passover. Hence the Eastern Church always uses *leavened* bread at the Eucharist, as did the Western Church down to the 9th century.

β. Jewish tradition—with no object in view—fixes the Death of Christ on the afternoon *before* the Passover (*Erebh Pesach*).

γ. The language of St Paul (1 Cor. v. 7, xi. 23) seems to imply that the Lord's Supper was not the Passover, but a Feast destined to supersede it.

δ. If our Lord had eaten an actual Paschal meal the very evening before His death, the Jews might fairly have argued that He was not Himself the Paschal Lamb; whereas

ε. There was a peculiar symbolic fitness in the fact that He—the True Lamb—was offered at the very time when the Lamb which was but a type was being sacrificed.

For these and other reasons—more fully developed in the *Life of Christ*, pp. 471—483—I still hold that the Last Supper was not the actual Jewish Passover, but a *quasi*-Passover, *a new and Christian Passover*.

EXCURSUS VI.

ON SECTS OF THE JEWS.

In the time of our Lord the main Jewish sects were—the ESSENES, the SADDUCEES, and the PHARISEES.

The Herodians, mentioned in Mk. iii. 6, xii. 13; Matt. xxii. 16, were not so much a religious sect as a political party which accepted the rule of the Herods. *Politically* they were descended from the old Grecising apostates, for whom Jason proposed the title of Antiochians (2 Macc. iv. 9). They may be most briefly described as the *anti-national* party, who wished the Jews to forget as much as possible their customs and aspirations, adopt cordial relations with Rome, and accept 'Greek fashions and heathenish manners,' 2 Macc. iv. 13, 14. They seem to have been Sadducees in religion, and were closely connected with the powerful families which Herod the Great had introduced from Babylon and Egypt, and who at this time monopolised the High Priesthood among themselves. The Talmud connects them with the *Boethusim*, so called from Simon son of Boethus, whose daughter (named Mariamne) Herod the Great married. They had gone so far at one time as to attempt to represent Herod the Great to the Jews as the promised Messiah! (Tert. *Praesc.* 45).

The ESSENES are not mentioned in the Gospels, nor is there any indication that Jesus ever came into contact with them. They were a small, exclusive, ascetic, isolated community, with whose discouragement of marriage, and withdrawal from all the active duties of life, our Lord could have had no sympathy. Their importance as a sect belongs to a somewhat later period of the Gospel History.

The SADDUCEES were the priestly-aristocratic party, who were in close alliance with the ruling powers. The name is probably derived from *Tsedakah* 'righteousness,' and was originally meant to distinguish them from the *Separatist* or Pharisaic party, which in their opinion was too narrow and exclusive. The names, like all party names, soon acquired an insulting force, and may be roughly illustrated by saying that the Sadducees were regarded as Rationalists and the Pharisees as Ritualists. In the time of our Lord the Sadducees had much political power, derived from their wealth, their offices, and their political connexions, but they had no popular following. Their grasping and avaricious spirit made them hateful to the people, and this hatred was specially felt towards their chief representatives—the family of Annas.

They rightly refused to recognise the extravagant importance attached by the Pharisees to the Oral Law; and they seem to have unduly depreciated the authority of the Hagiographa and the Prophets in comparison with that of Moses. It was this which led to their scepticism about the immortality of the soul and the existence of angels and spirits. Their worldliness and want of moral earnestness made them less useful than they might otherwise have been in counteracting the hypocritic externalism and frivolous scrupulosity of the Pharisees.

EXCURSUS VI.

The name PHARISEES seems to have been derived from *Perishoot*, 'separation.' They were the national party, and were politically descended from the *Chasidim*, mentioned in 1 Macc. ii. 42, vii. 13. No doubt many good and faithful men, like Nicodemus and Joseph of Arimathaea, existed in their body, but Jewish writers themselves admit, and the Talmud amply and in many passages confirms, the terrible charges brought against them by our Lord in His Great Denunciation (Matt. xxiii.; see notes on Luke xi. 42—54). Those charges were mainly against their greed, ambition, tyranny, and sacrifice of things essential to unimportant minutiae,—in one word, their arbitrary and excessive ceremonialism, which had led them to sacrifice the spirit and even the letter of the Mosaic Law to their own Oral Law or Tradition of the Fathers. "Long prayers, and devouring of widows' houses; flaming proselytism and subsequent moral neglect; rigorous stickling for the letter, boundless levity as to the spirit; high-sounding words as to the sanctity of oaths, and cunning reservations of casuistry; fidelity in trifles, gross neglect of essential principles; the mask of godliness without the reality; petty orthodoxy and artificial morals—such was Pharisaism." "It was," says Canon Mozley, "an active religion founded upon egotism" —religion allied with the pride of life in its most childish and empty forms. It was a "false goodness"—and therefore "an *unrepentant* type of evil." "The Pharisaic conscience was a *tame* conscience—with a potent sway over mint, anise, and cumin, but no power over the heart." And therefore the Pharisees were "the only *class* which Jesus cared publicly to expose." See 'Sermon on the Pharisees' in Mozley's *Univ. Sermons*, pp. 28—51.

Josephus (*Antt.* XVIII. 1, §§ 3, 4, XIII. 5, § 9, *B. J.* II. 8, § 14) gives some notices of these sects, but his account of them can by no means be exclusively trusted.

EXCURSUS VII.

ILLUSTRATIONS OF ST LUKE DERIVED FROM THE TALMUD.

A few only of the following illustrations—which will I think be found both curious and important—may be found in Schöttgen's *Horae Hebraicae*. The majority of them are entirely new, and I have chiefly derived them from the yet unpublished Talmudic collections of Mr P. J. Hershon.

I. 21. *Marvelled that he tarried so long in the Temple.*

The Jews believed that catastrophes sometimes occurred, not only (as in the case of Heliodorus, 2 Macc. iii. 24) for intrusion into the Temple, but for any *irregularity* in it. See the story of the death of a (Saducean) High Priest in *Yoma*, f. 19 *b*. Comp. Lev. xvi. 13, "that he die not."

II. 25. *Waiting for the consolation of Israel.*
II. 38. *That looked for redemption.*

"Ravah said, When a man is brought up for judgment (after death) he is asked...*Hast thou been waiting for salvation?*" (i.e. looking for the advent of the Messiah). *Shabbath*, f. 31 *a*.

II. 41. *His parents went to Jerusalem every year at the feast of the Passover.*

In *Mechilta* f. 17 *b* the *wife* of Jonah is commended for going to the yearly feasts.

II. 46. *Both hearing them and asking them questions.*

I have shewn that this was entirely in accordance with Jewish custom: besides the self-attested instance of the young Josephus we find that "when Rabbi Shimon Ben Gamaliel and Rabbi Jehoshua Ben Korcha were seated in the debating room upon divans Rabbi Elazer Ben Rabbi Shimon and Rabbi [i.e. Judah the Holy] *sat before them on the ground* asking questions and *starting objections.* The other Rabbis exclaimed 'We drink of their water' (i.e. of their wisdom) 'and they sit upon the ground!' Seats were therefore brought in, and the two children were seated upon them." *Babha Metsia*, f. 84 *b*.

VI. 35. *Lend, hoping for nothing again.*

From Ps. xv. 5 the Rabbis said that he who lent his money without usury was regarded as having kept the whole law. *Shemoth Rabba*, f. 130, 3.

VII. 50. *Go in peace.*

Lit. '*into* peace' (εἰς εἰρήνην), comp. ii. 29, "Now lettest thou thy servant depart in peace" (ἐν εἰρήνῃ).

"Rabh Laive Bar Chaitha said, In taking leave of a dying man one should say 'Go in peace' (*beshalôm*), and not 'into peace' (*leshalôm*), for God said to Abraham 'Thou shalt go to thy fathers *in peace*.' Otherwise one should not say 'Go in peace' but '*unto* peace;' for David said to Absalom 'Go *in peace*' (2 Sam. xv. 9), and he went and was hanged; but Jethro said to Moses (Ex. iv. 18) 'Go *unto peace*,' and he went and prophesied." *Moed Katon*, f. 29, 1. The same rule is given with the same reasons in *Berachoth*, f. 64 *a*.

X. 31. *He passed by on the other side.*

In *Midrash Koheleth*, f. 91 *b*, a beautiful story is told of the blessing earned by Abba Techama for carrying a sick man into a town, and going back (in spite of the Sabbath) to fetch his bundle. See Schöttgen, *Hor. Hebr.* ad loc.

X. 34. *Pouring in oil and wine.*

Speaking of circumcision, and the method adopted to heal the wound, we find the rule "*If there is no mixed oil and wine ready* each may be added separately" (*Shabbath*, f. 133 *a*).

As an additional instance of the extreme Sabbath scrupulosity among the Jews we may add the rest of the passage: "*No dressing is to be prepared for it on the Sabbath*, but a rag may be put on" (see John vii. 22). "If the latter is not ready on the spot it may be fetched from other premises *wrapped on the finger*." The latter rule is given *to avoid the appearance of breaking the Sabbath by carrying the rag*.

x. 42. *The good part.*

No doubt the use of the word μερὶς is a reference to the feast which Martha was preparing. The phrase and the metaphor are found in Hebrew literature. See Schöttgen ad loc.

XII. 19. *Soul...take thine ease, eat, drink, and be merry.*

So in *Taanith*, f. 11 *a*, "When the people is in trouble let no man say, I will go home, and eat, and drink, and peace be to thee, O my soul."

XII. 53. *The daughter in law against her mother in law.*

"In the generation when the Son of David will come daughters will stand up against their mothers, daughters in law against their mothers in law." *Sanhedrin*, f. 97, 1.

XIII. 14. *In them therefore come and be healed, and not on the Sabbath day.*

Thus we are told that thorough bathing was permitted on the Sabbath *except* in the *Mediterranean, and the Dead Sea*, because the waters of these seas were supposed to possess medicinal properties, and healing is not allowed on the Sabbath day. *Shabbath*, f. 109 *a*.

XIII. 23. *Are there few that be saved?*

Some of the Rabbis answered this question in the affirmative, and Rabbi Shimeon Ben Jochai was so satisfied about his own righteousness as to say that if only two were saved, he and his son would be those two. *Succa*, f. 45 *b*.

XIV. 8—11. *On taking the lowest place.*

"Ben Azai said, Descend from thy place, and sit down two or three degrees lower. Let them rather bid thee go up higher than come down lower; as it is said, 'For better it is that it should be said unto thee, Come up hither, than that thou shouldest be put lower in the presence of the prince whom thine eyes have seen,' Prov. xxv. 7." *Abhoth of Rabbi Nathan*, 2.

XIV. 11. *Whosoever exalteth himself shall be abased.*

"Greatness flees from him who strives for it, but it follows him who flees from it," *Erubhin*, f. 13 *b*. "Whoever abases himself, the

Holy One, blessed be He, exalts him, and whoever exalts himself, the Holy One, blessed be He, abases him." Id. ib.

The latter coincidence compels the belief either that our Lord was here (as elsewhere) using a current Jewish proverb, or that the Talmudic writer, consciously or unconsciously, borrows from Him.

XV. 7. *Who need no repentance.*

The Jews distinguished between two classes of good men; those who, like David, had repented after sin; and the 'perfect just.' *Succa*, f. 45 b.

XVI. 8. *The children of this world* (or '*age*').

'The children of this age' are opposed to 'the children of the age to come,' who in *Berachoth*, f. 4 b, are defined to be "those who to their evening prayers add prayers about (Israel's) redemption."

XVI. 9. *Into everlasting habitations* ('*into the eternal tents*').

"When the wicked are burnt up, God makes a tent in which He hides the just, Ps. xxvii. 5." *Siphra*, f. 187.

XVI. 22. *Was carried by the angels into Abraham's bosom.*

"'This day,' said Rabbi [Judah the Holy], 'he sits in the bosom of Abraham,' i. e. he died." *Kiddushin*, f. 72 b.

XVII. 6. *Be thou plucked up by the root.*

In the famous story of Babha Metsia, f. 59 b, Rabbi Eliezer is said to have given this among other miraculous proofs that his rule (*halacha*) was right.

XXI. 5. *How it was adorned with goodly stones and gifts.*

"It is said, Whoever has not seen Herod's temple, has never seen a beautiful structure in his life. How did he build it? Ravah replied, With white and green marble, so that it appeared in the distance like the waves of the sea." *Babha Bathra*, f. 3 b.

XXI. 7. *When shall these things be?*

"Rabbis Jochanan and Elazer both said, The present generation (i. e. after the destruction of Jerusalem), whose iniquities are hidden, have not been informed of the time of their restoration.' *Yoma*, f. 19, 2.

XXII. 38. *It is enough.*

Schöttgen compares this with the very frequent Rabbinic phrase דייך, used generally with a shade of indignation to stop useless remarks.

XXII. 70. *Art thou the Son of God? And he said unto them, Ye say that I am.*

In the description of the death of Rabbi (Judah Hakkodesh, or the Holy, the compiler of the Mishna), we are told that Bar Cappara was commissioned by the other Rabbis to see whether he was dead or alive. He returned with his robe rent behind, and said, "The angels are victorious, and the holy ark is taken away." "*Is Rabbi dead?*" asked they. "*You have said it*," he answered. *Kethubhoth*, f. 103 *b*.

XXIII. 31. *For if they do these things in a green tree, what shall be done in the dry?*

Although this exact proverb does not occur (apparently) in Jewish literature, there are others exceedingly like it, e.g. "Rabbi Ashi asked Bar Kippok what mourning he made on the death of Ravina. He replied, 'If the flame has fallen among the cedars, what chance is there for the hyssop on the wall? If Leviathan is drawn up with a hook, what hope is there for little fish? If the net is thrown in flooding streams, what chance is there for stagnant pools?'" *Moed Katon*, f. 25 *b*. Comp. Jer. xii. 5.

The proverb adduced by Schöttgen on 1 Cor. xv. 33, 'Two dry logs and one green one; the dry burn up the green,' seems to have no connexion with it.

INDEX I.

Abia, course of, 45
Abila, its position, 81; capital of Abilene, 81
Abilene, Lysanias tetrarch of, 81
Abraham's seed, Jews supposed privileges of, 85
Ahithophel, a type of Judas Iscariot, 327
almsgiving, 218
angel, appearance of, to Zacharias, 47
angels, ministry of, dwelt on by St Luke, 46; visit to shepherds, 67; at the sepulchre, 358
Anna, the prophetess, 74
Annas, some account of, 82
annunciation of the birth of St John the Baptist, 44; of the birth of Jesus, 51
Apocryphal Gospels, account of annunciation in, 53; on the questioning of the doctors by Christ, 77
Apostles, selection of, 131—134; lists of, 131; some account of, 132—134; mission of, 179; instructions to, 180; return of, after mission, 182; lesson to, on meekness, 192; strife among, at the Last Supper, 327
Archelaus, 294, 296
Arnold quoted, 257
ascension of our Lord, 367
Aser, the tribe of, 74
Ave Maria, 51

baptism, symbol of John the Baptist's, 83; by the Spirit, 90; by fire, 90; reasons for our Lord's, 92
Barabbas, his crime, 344
Bartimæus, healing of blind, 291
beatitudes, 135—137
Beelzebub, 213
Benedictus, the, 59, 60
Bethany, meaning of, 297; the sisters of, 207; the ascension near, 367
Bethlehem, inn at, 66; meaning of, 65
Bethphage, its probable situation, 297
Bethsaida, western, 182; eastern = Bethsaida-Julias, 182
blasphemy against the Holy Ghost, 224
blind leaders of the blind, 142
brethren of our Lord, 168

Browning, quoted 256
Byron, quoted 257

Caiaphas, son-in-law of Annas, 82
Calvary, our Lord's crucifixion on, 348
Capernaum, first mention of, by St Luke, 104; some account of, 106; Christ's woe uttered on, 201
census of Caesar Augustus, 62, 63
centurion, healing of servant of, 144—146; probably a proselyte, 144
chief priests, seek to slay our Lord, 322; clamour for His crucifixion, 345
childlessness, how regarded by Jews, 148
children brought to our Lord, 285
Chorazin, 200
church, woman in parable of ten pieces of silver likened to, 255, 256
circumcision, of St John the Baptist, 57; of Jesus, 70
Codex Bezae, a reading of, 128
Coleridge quoted on the Nativity, 68, 69
colt, 297
confession of St Peter, 185
corn, plucking ears of, 125
Cowper quoted, on the walk to Emmaus, 363
cross, taking up of, daily, 187; form of our Lord's, 346; our Lord's borne by Simon of Cyrene, 346
Cyrenius, 64

darkness, the, at the Crucifixion, 352
demoniac, healing of, 108; Gergesene, healing of, 171; boy, healing of, 191
demons, Jews' belief in power of, 173
denials, the three, of our Lord by St Peter, 335, 336
devil, the temptation of Christ by the, 95—100; power delivered to, 98; a dumb, cast out, 212
disciples at Emmaus, 359—363
Dives and Lazarus, parable of, 268
divorce, laxity of the law of, among the Jews, 268
dogs of the East, 269

INDEX. 387

door, the narrow, 239
dropsy, healing of man with, 244

el Ghôr, wilderness of, 82
Elias, resemblance between St John and, 48
Elisabeth visited by Mary, 53, 54
Emmaus, two disciples at, 359
epiousion, 376, 377
Essenes, 380
evangelists, compared to four cherubim in Ezekiel's vision, 13; silence on the childhood of Jesus, 76
eye, the evil, 216

faith of centurion, 146
fasting, Jewish rules concerning, 283
fig-tree, parable of, 235
five thousand, feeding of, 184
foundations, false and true, 143
fox, likeness of Herod Antipas to a, 241
funeral at Nain, 147

Gabriel, appearance to Zacharias, 48; appearance to Mary, 51
Gadara, situation of, 170
Gadarenes, rejection of our Lord by, 174
Galileans, outbreak of Romans on, 234
Galilee, situation of, 51; its extent, 80; sea of, 111
genealogy of our Lord, 93; Excursus on 369—375
Gennesaret, lake of, 111; storm on, 169
Gerasa, situation of, 171
Gergesene demoniac, healing of, 170—174
gospels, table of peculiarities and coincidences, 8; written in Hellenistic Greek, 10; compared to river of Eden, 12; prophetic picture of, in Ezekiel's vision of the four cherubim, 13; summary of differences of, 17
graves, Pharisees likened to, 219

head, custom of anointing, 158
Hermon, probable scene of the transfiguration, 188
Herod Antipas, parents of, 80; his banishment, 80; his dominions, 80; imprisons John the Baptist, 91; his alarm at the progress of Christ's ministry, 181; is likened by our Lord to a fox, 241; our Lord before, 342
Herodians, some account of, 380
Herod Philip, parents of, 80; marriage with Salome, 80; extent of his tetrarchate, 81
Herods, genealogy of the, 39
Herod the Great, kingdom of, 44
Herrick quoted, 250
high priests, order of, 82
Hillel, 246; on divorce, 268
Hinnom, valley of, 223; infamy of, 223

Holy Ghost, the descent of, at our Lord's baptism, 92; blasphemy against, 224
horn of salvation, 59
house built upon a rock, 143

incense, offering of, 46
Ituraea, Herod Philip tetrarch of, 80; position of, 81
Ituraeans, 81

Jairus, daughter of, restored to life, 179
James, St, call of, 114; presence at the raising of Jairus' daughter, 178; at the transfiguration, 188; rebuked by our Lord, 196
Jericho, road to, 204; blind Bartimæus healed at, 290; some account of, 291
Jerusalem, Christ's lament over, 242; our Lord's triumphal entry into, 297; fall of, foretold by our Lord, 299, 317; time of the siege of, 300; desolation of, 317
JESUS
(i) *Nativity and Manifestation*
annunciation of His birth, 52; day of birth uncertain, 65; His birth, 66; His circumcision, 70; presentation in the temple, 70; return to Nazareth, 75; goes up to the passover, 76; tarries behind in the temple, 77; returns with His parents, 78; is baptized by John, 92; tempted of the devil, 94—100
(ii) *Ministry in Galilee*
preaches at Nazareth, 101; is rejected, 105; heals a demoniac at Capernaum, 108; heals Simon's wife's mother, 109; and the sick at evening, 110; calls four disciples, 114; heals a leper, 116; heals a paralytic, 117; reproves Pharisees, 127; heals the man with a withered hand, 129; heals the centurion's servant, 144—146; raises the widow's son at Nain, 147; receives John the Baptist's disciples, 148; eats in the house of Simon the Pharisee, 154; His feet anointed by Mary Magdalene, 156; stills the storm, 169; heals the Gergesene demoniac, 170—174; heals the woman with an issue of blood, 178; restores the daughter of Jairus to life, 179; sends forth the twelve, 179; feeds the five thousand, 184; prophesies His death and resurrection, 185; heals demoniac boy, 191; teaches His apostles meekness, 192; tolerance, 193
(iii) *Ministry after leaving Galilee*
is rejected by the Samaritans, 194; sends forth the seventy, 199; is entertained by the sisters at Bethany, 207; teaches His disciples to pray, 210; casts out a dumb devil, 211; rebukes the blasphemous Pharisees,

213, 214; rebukes egotism, 225; teaches trustfulness, 227; almsgiving, 228; and watchfulness, 229; heals woman on sabbath, 236; rebuked by ruler of synagogue, 237; is entertained by a Pharisee, 243; heals a man with the dropsy, 244; teaches humility, 246; and that the poor are to be invited to feasts, 247; teaches whole-heartedness, 251; rebukes the covetous Pharisees, 266; shews the peril of those through whom offences come, 271; the power of faith, 273; and insufficiency of works, 274; heals the ten lepers, 275; tells of the kingdom of God, 276; and His own coming, 278; blesses little children, 285; puts the young ruler to test, 286; reveals the danger of riches, 287

(iv) *Last Journey to Jerusalem and Passion*

predicts His crucifixion, 289; heals blind Bartimæus, 291; his triumphal entry into Jerusalem, 297; weeps over Jerusalem, and foretells its destruction, 299; questions the priests and scribes, 302; replies to the Pharisees respecting tribute money, 307; to the Sadducees respecting resurrection, 308, 309, 310; reduces the scribes, Pharisees, and Sadducees to a confession of ignorance, 311, 312; predicts destruction of the temple, 314; the end of the world, 315; and the desolation of Jerusalem, 317; sends St Peter and St John to prepare the passover, 324; institutes the Holy Eucharist, 326; foretells Peter's denial of Him, 329; His agony in the garden, 331; prayer, 331; finds His disciples asleep and reproaches them, 332; is denied by St Peter, 335; mocked by the Jews, 337; is tried before the Sanhedrin, 338; and before Pilate 339; sent to Herod, 341; sentenced by Pilate, 345; is led to Calvary, 346; and crucified, 348; His superscription, 350; forgives the penitent robber, 352; dies, 353; is buried, 356

(v) *Victory over the Grave and Ascension*

His resurrection, 358; and walk to Emmaus, 360; His appearance to the apostles, 363—366; His ascension, 367

Jews, hatred between Samaritans and, 195; self-satisfaction of, compared to elder son in parable of the prodigal, 262; parable against self-righteous, 281; sects of, 380, 381

Joanna ministers to our Lord, 161

John, St, call of, 114; presence at the raising of Jairus' daughter, 178; at the transfiguration, 188; rebuked by our Lord, 196; sent to prepare the passover, 324

John's, St, gospel, time of composition, 9; difference between this and the synoptic gospels, 10, 11; distinctive peculiarities of, 16, 17; records preserved in, 181

John, St, the Baptist, annunciation of his birth, 44; is to be a Nazarite, 47; his office foretold, 48; his resemblance to Elias, 48; his birth and circumcision, 57; his preaching and baptism, 83; answers to the multitude, 86—89; announces the Messiah, 89; imprisoned by Herod Antipas, 91; sends to Jesus from prison, 148; account of, by Jesus, 151

Joseph of Arimathæa, begs the body of Jesus, 355; his new tomb, 356

Joseph, the husband of the Blessed Virgin, his lineage, 51; journeys to Bethlehem, 65

Judas Iscariot, call of, 133; conspires with the chief priests, 323; his betrayal of our Lord, 332

judge, parable of the unjust, 279

judgment of others, 141

Keble quoted, 69, 203

kingdom of God, coming of, 276; to be received as a little child, 285

knowledge of salvation, 60

labourers in the vineyard, parable of, 303, 304

lawyers rebuked by our Lord, 220; difference between Pharisees and, 220

Lazarus, parable of Dives and, 268

lepers, healing of the ten, 275; the thankless nine, 275

leprosy, some account of, 115

Levi, identity of, with St Matthew, 120

liberality, principle of, 140

light, the inward, 216

livelihood, means of, possessed by Jesus and the twelve, 161

Lord's prayer, the, 209; explanation of, 210, 211

Lot's wife, held up as a warning, 278

love, laws of, 139

Lovelace quoted, 251

Luke, St, mention of his name in Scripture, 18; nationality, 19; early connection with St Paul, 19; his stay at Philippi, 19; journey to Rome with St Paul, 20; traditions as to his death, 20; his profession, 21

Luke's, St, gospel; time of composition, 9; distinctive peculiarities of, 16; a void in continuity of, 184;

(i) authenticity of, 22, 23;

(ii) characteristics of, 23—30; hymnology, 23—24; thanksgiving, 24; prayer, 24; good tidings, 25; of infancy, 26; to the world, 26; of womanhood, 26; of the poor and despised, 27; of the outcast, 28; of tolerance, 28; miracles peculiar to, 29; parables peculiar to, 29;
(iii) analysis of, 30—36;
(iv) illustrations derived from the Talmud, 381—385
Lysanias, tetrarch of Abilene, 81; not mentioned in history, 81

Magnificat, the, compared with Judith's Song and that of Hannah, 55
Malchus, the ear of, cut off by St Peter, 333; healed by our Lord, 333
malefactors, the two, 347, 351
Makor, fortress of, 91
Mark's, St, Gospel, resemblance with that of St Luke, 8, 9; time of composition, 9; written on the testimony of St Peter, 10; distinctive peculiarities of, 15, 16
marriage, question of the Sadducees concerning, 308
Martha, entertains our Lord, 207; is reproved by Him, 208
Mary Magdalene, identity of, with the woman at Simon's house, 155, 161; anoints our Lord's feet, 156; her sins are forgiven, 159; ministers to our Lord, 161; at sepulchre, 358
Mary, mother of James, at sepulchre, 358
Mary, sister of Lazarus, chooses the better part, 208
Mary, St, the Virgin, her early residence at Nazareth, 51; visited by Gabriel, 51; her ready faith, 52; visits Elizabeth, 53, 54; returns to her home, 57; purification of, 71
Matthew, St, call of, identity with Levi, 120; feast at the house of, 121
Matthew's, St, Gospel, time of composition, 9; distinctive peculiarities of, 14, 15
mercy, laws of, 141
Milton, quoted on "Angels of the Presence," 49; the Nativity, 68; the Circumcision, 70; the Holy Spirit, 92, 95; evil spirits, 173; Moloch worship, 223
miracles, peculiar to St Luke, 29; words used to express, in the Gospels, 108
mission of Apostles, 179; object of, 181
mustard-seed, parable of, 238

Naaman the Syrian, 105
Nain, raising of widow's son of, 147; situation of, 147
nature of Christ, declaration of by the Church, 75

Nazareth, fitness for early abode of Jesus, 78; its situation and beauty, 79; synagogue of, 102
Nazarite, St John the Baptist a, 47
Nunc Dimittis, 71

Olives, Mount of, our Lord's abode in, 321
oral law, instances of, set aside by Christ, 128

parables peculiar to St Luke, 29; of the new and the old, 124; houses built on good and bad foundations, 143; the children in the market-place, 152; the creditor and two debtors, 157; the sower, 162; the candle, 167; the good Samaritan, 204; the rich fool, 226; servants waiting for their lord, 229; faithful steward, 230; the barren fig-tree, 235; the grain of mustard-seed and leaven, 238; the wedding supper, 246; the great supper, 249; the lost sheep, 254; the piece of silver, 255; the prodigal son, 256; the unjust steward, 263; Dives and Lazarus, 268; the ploughing slave, 273; the unjust judge, 279; the Pharisee and the publican, 282; the pounds, 294; the labourers in the vineyard, 303, 304; the fig-tree, 319
paralytic, healing of, 118
Passover, the first attended by our Lord, 76; our Lord's preparation for, 324; customs of, as practised by the Jews, 325, 326; "was the last supper an actual ?" 377—379
people, eagerness of, to hear Jesus, 300
Peter, St, first mention of by St Luke, 109; his wife's mother is healed, 109; call of, 114; presence at raising of Jairus' daughter, 178; his confession, 185; at the Transfiguration, 188; sent to prepare the passover, 324; his denials foretold, 329; his fall, 335; at sepulchre, 358
Pharisees, righteousness of, 122; reject the counsel of God, 152; blasphemy of, 213; our Lord rebukes hypocrisy of, 218, 219; modern existence of, 219; the leaven of, 222; rebukes to the covetous, 267; Excursus on, 381
Philippi, St Luke's stay at, 19
Pilate, predecessors and successors of, 89; some account of, 339; our Lord's first appearance before, 340; His second appearance before, 343; the efforts of, to secure our Lord's acquittal, 345; gives the irrevocable sentence, 345
pinnacle of temple, 99
prayer in temple, 46; our Lord's, 209; persistence in, 211; duty of urgent, 279; of humble, 284; of publican, 284; posture of the Jews at, 284; of our Lord for His murderers, 348

INDEX.

prayers of our Lord mentioned by St Luke, 92
preaching of John the Baptist, 86, 87
presentation in temple, 71
priests, courses of, 44, 45; their sudden question, 301
prison of John the Baptist, 91
privileges, peril of, abused, 213
procurator, title of Pilate, 80
prodigal son, parable of, 256; applications of, 256; explanations of, 256—263
prophecy of John the Baptist, 84, 85; general meaning of, 84
pounds, parable of the, 294; its lesson, 294
poverty of Christ, 197
publicans, their question to John the Baptist, 88; the office of, 88, 292; dislike of by Jews, 88
punishment, proportional to sin, 231
purification, offerings at, 71

Quarantania, Mount, 95

reed, likeness of John the Baptist to a, 150
reign of Christ for ever, 52
relation of apostles to our Lord, 134
rents, mode of payment of, in the East, 264
resurrection of the widow's son at Nain, 147; of Jairus' daughter, 179; Christ foretells his, 186, and answers the Sadducees respecting, 309, 310; of our Lord, 358; appearances of our Lord after, 360, 363
riches, danger of, 287
righteousness of Pharisees, 122
ruler, question of the young, 285

sabbath, plucking of corn on, 127; miracles wrought on, 129, 236, 244; argument against Jewish formalism of, 237, 245; Jewish entertainments on, 244
Sadducees, attempt to ensnare our Lord, 308, 309; Excursus on, 380
salt, the savourless, 253
Samaritan, Parable of Good, 204; healing of the, leper, 275
Samaritans, reject Christ, 195; hatred between Jews and, 195
Sanhedrin, 338; our Lord before the, 338
Sarepta, 105
Satan tempts our Lord, 94—100; compared to a strong man, 214; entered into Judas, 322
scribes, teaching of, compared with Christ's, 107; some account of, 121
sepulchre, visit of women to, 357; stone of, 357
sermon on the Mount, differences between St Matthew and St Luke's record of, 136
seventy, Mission of the, 198; instructions of our Lord to, 199
Shakespeare quoted, on temptation, 96; on the devil's use of Scripture, 99; on mercy, 141; on ingratitude, 276
Sheba, the queen of, 215
Shechinah, 67, 190
sheep, parable of the lost, 254
signs of the times, 232; duty resultant from, 232; of the End, 314, 319
silence of healed leper enjoined, reasons for, 116
Siloam, Pool of, 235; tower of, 235
Simeon, 71; his song, 72; called Theodokos, 72; prophesies of Jesus, 73
Simon of Cyrene, bears the cross, 346
Simon Peter, see Peter
Simon the Pharisee entertains our Lord, 154
Simon Zelotes, 133
slave, parable of the ploughing, 273
soldiers, their question to John the Baptist, 88; special temptations of, 89; mockery of, at crucifixion, 349
Son of God, 53
Son of Man, meaning and use of the title, 119, 137; the coming of, 277, 278, 319
sower, parable of the, 162; its explanation, 165
sparrows, 224
steward, parable of the unjust, 263; main lesson of, 264, 265
superscription, on the Cross, 350
supper, the last, celebration of, 325; our Lord's preparations for, 324; "was the, an actual Passover?" 377—379
Susanna, ministers to our Lord, 161
synagogue, officers of, 102; Christ reads in, 102; ruler of, 176
synoptic Gospels, 8; difference between them and that of St John, 10, 11; theory of resemblances to each other, 11, 12
swine, devils enter into, 173

table, Jews' method of sitting at, 155
Talmud, illustrations of St Luke derived from, 381—385
Tel Hum, ruins of synagogue at, 145
temple, presentation of Jesus in the, 71; final cleansing of the, by Jesus, 300; Christ prophesies destruction of, 314; stones and gifts of, 314; veil of, rent in twain, 353
temptation, the, of Christ, 95; supposed scene of, 95; how to be viewed, 96; order of, in St Matthew, 98
tetrarch, use of term in New Testament, 80
Theophilus, dedication of St Luke's works to, 21, 43

INDEX. 391

Tiberius Caesar, 80, 307
tolerance, lesson of, by our Saviour, 193
tombs, demoniac among the, 171
Trachonitis, a country of robbers, 81; its position, 81
transfiguration, the, 188; probable scene of, 188; circumstances attending, 189; time of, 190
treasure-chests in the temple, 313
trials of our Lord, the three, by the Jews, 334
tribute to Caesar, Christ questioned respecting, 307: Christ falsely accused of forbidding, 340

uncial manuscripts, table of, 37

veil of temple rent in twain at the Crucifixion, 353
vision of Ezekiel, 12

washing, custom of, among Jews, 217

widow, the importunate, 280; the offering of the, 313
wine, new, into fresh bottles, 124, 375, 376
woes, 138
woman with issue of blood healed by our Lord, 178; with spirit of infirmity healed by our Lord, 236
women, minister to our Lord, 160; follow our Lord to Calvary, 346; at Crucifixion, 354; go to the sepulchre, 357
words of our Lord, the first recorded, 368, 369
Wordsworth (Bp) on comparison of the Gospels to the Four Cherubim of Ezekiel's vision, 13
world, gain of, and loss of soul, 187; end of, foretold, 315

Zacchaeus, the tax-gatherer, 292
Zacharias, the blood of, 220
Zacharias, vision of, 46; is struck dumb, 50; recovers his speech, 57
zealots, some account of, 133
Zebedee, social position of, 115

INDEX II.

WORDS AND PHRASES EXPLAINED.

Abhôth, 127
Abila, 81
acceptable year, 103
accused, 263
after three days, 77
alabaster, 155
alms, 218
altar of incense, 47
apostles, 131
ass or an ox, 245
assaria, 224
attentive to hear him, 300
avenge, 280
babes, 202
Barabbas, 344
baskets, 184
beam, 142
bed, 167
Beelzebub, 213
Bethany, 297
Bethlehem, 65
Bethphage, 297
Bethsaida, 109
best robe, 260
blasphemy, 119
border of His garment, 177
bosom, 141
Calvary, 348
came upon them, 67
camel, 288
captains, 323
centurion, 144

chaff, 90
chance, 204
chief rooms, 246
Christ, 68
closets, 222
commandments, 45
compel, 250
couch, 118
covered, 222
cross, 346
decree, 62
denarius, 157, 206
depart from me, 113
divider, 225
drachma, 255
eagles gathered together, 279
Elizabeth, 45
En Gannim, 195
epiousion, 376, 377
everlasting habitations, 265
faint, 279
fan, 90
farthing, 224
fastings, 74
five hundred pence, 157
Gehenna, 223
generation of vipers, 84
Gennesareth, 111
glory of the Lord, 67
goodman, 230
goodwill toward men, 69
gospel, 7

INDEX.

guest, to be, 293
guest-chamber, 324
Hades, 269
hate, 251
highly favoured, 51
hold thy peace, 108
housetop, 118, 278
husks, 258
hypocrites, 219
importunity, 211
increased, 79
in order, 43
inn, 66
instantly, 144
Iscariot, 133
Jericho, 291
Jesus, 52
John, 47
key of knowledge, 221
kiss, 158
latchet, 89
Lazarus, 269
legion, 172
leprosy, 115
lilies, 228
linen, 355
loins girded, 229
Lord, 68, 145
Lord's Christ, 72, 186
mammon of unrighteousness, 265
man's life, 225
manger, 66
master, 112
Matthew, 120
measures, 264
measures of wheat, 264
meat, 86
millstone, 272
mite, 233, 313
most excellent, 43
mote, 142
mystery, 164
Nazareth, 51, 65
needle's eye, 288
nets, 112
Nunc Dimittis, 72
ordinances, 45
parable, 163
paradise, 352
passover, 322
perfected, 242
Phanuel, 74
phylacteries, 204

pondered, 70
proselyte, 144
proseuchae, 131
publicans, 88
purification, 70
purple and fine linen, 268
rejoiced, 202
riotous living, 257
Salem, 299
Satan, 95
Saviour, 67
scribe, 121
scrip, 180
servant, 144, 146
shewbread, 127
sixth hour, 352
stature, 79
stone, 96
stood, 293
stuff, 278
superscription, 350
surfeiting, 320
Susanna, 161
swaddling-clothes, 66
sword, 73
sycamine tree, 273
sycomore tree, 292
synagogue, 102, 225
synoptists, 8
tabernacle, 189
ten pieces of silver, 255
ten pounds, 294
tetrarch, 80
Theodokos, 72
Theophilus, 43
thieves, 204
tiling, 118
tittle, 267
Toldôth, 127
Tophet, 224
Trachonitis, 81
tribute money, 307
twelve years old, 76
two coats, 86, 140, 188
unloose, 90
uppermost seats, 219
weary me, 280
wept over it, 299
wisely, 264
write fifty, 264
writing table, 58
Zacchaeus, 292
Zacharias, 44

CAMBRIDGE: PRINTED BY C. J. CLAY, M.A. AND SONS, AT THE UNIVERSITY PRESS.

CAMBRIDGE UNIVERSITY PRESS.

THE PITT PRESS SERIES.

*** *Many of the books in this list can be had in two volumes, Text and Notes separately.*

I. GREEK.

Aristophanes. Aves—Plutus—Ranae. By W. C. GREEN, M.A., late Assistant Master at Rugby School. *3s. 6d.* each.
Aristotle. Outlines of the Philosophy of. By EDWIN WALLACE, M.A., LL.D. Third Edition, Enlarged. *4s. 6d.*
Euripides. Heracleidae. By E. A. BECK, M.A. *3s. 6d.*
——— **Hercules Furens.** By A. GRAY, M.A., and J. T. HUTCHINSON, M.A. New Edit. *2s.*
——— **Hippolytus.** By W. S. HADLEY, M.A. *2s.*
——— **Iphigeneia in Aulis.** By C. E. S. HEADLAM, M.A. *2s. 6d.*
Herodotus, Book V. By E. S. SHUCKBURGH, M.A. *3s.*
——— **Book VI.** By the same Editor. *4s.*
——— **Books VIII., IX.** By the same Editor. *4s.* each.
——— **Book VIII. Ch. 1—90. Book IX. Ch. 1—89.** By the same Editor. *3s. 6d.* each.
Homer. Odyssey, Books IX., X. By G. M. EDWARDS, M.A. *2s. 6d.* each. **Book XXI.** By the same Editor. *2s.*
——— **Iliad. Book VI.** By the same Editor. *2s.*
——— ——— **Book XXII.** By the same Editor. *2s.*
——— ——— **Book XXIII.** By the same Editor. *2s.*
Lucian. Somnium Charon Piscator et De Luctu. By W. E. HEITLAND, M.A., Fellow of St John's College, Cambridge. *3s. 6d.*
——— **Menippus and Timon.** By E. C. MACKIE, M.A. *3s. 6d.*
Platonis Apologia Socratis. By J. ADAM, M.A. *3s. 6d.*
——— **Crito.** By the same Editor. *2s. 6d.*
——— **Euthyphro.** By the same Editor. *2s. 6d.*
Plutarch. Lives of the Gracchi. By Rev. H. A. HOLDEN, M.A., LL.D. *6s.*
——— **Life of Nicias.** By the same Editor. *5s.*
——— **Life of Sulla.** By the same Editor. *6s.*
——— **Life of Timoleon.** By the same Editor. *6s.*
Sophocles. Oedipus Tyrannus. School Edition. By R. C. JEBB, Litt.D., LL.D. *4s. 6d.*
Thucydides. Book VII. By H. A. HOLDEN, M.A., LL.D. *5s.*
Xenophon. Agesilaus. By H. HAILSTONE, M.A. *2s. 6d.*
——— **Anabasis.** By A. PRETOR, M.A. Two vols. *7s. 6d.*
——— **Books I. III. IV. and V.** By the same. *2s.* each.
——— **Books II. VI. and VII.** By the same. *2s. 6d.* each.
Xenophon. Cyropaedeia. Books I. II. By Rev. H. A. HOLDEN, M.A., LL.D. 2 vols. *6s.*
——— ——— **Books III. IV. and V.** By the same Editor. *5s.*
——— ——— **Books VI. VII. VIII.** By the same Editor. *5s.*

II. LATIN.

Beda's Ecclesiastical History, Books III., IV. By J. E. B. MAYOR, M.A., and J. R. LUMBY, D.D. Revised Edition. 7s. 6d.

────── **Books I. II.** *[In the Press.*

Caesar. De Bello Gallico, Comment. I. By A. G. PESKETT, M.A., Fellow of Magdalene College, Cambridge. 1s. 6d. COMMENT. II. III. 2s. COMMENT. I. II. III. 3s. COMMENT. IV. and V. 1s. 6d. COMMENT. VII. 2s. COMMENT. VI. and COMMENT. VIII. 1s. 6d. each.

────── **De Bello Civili, Comment. I.** By the same Editor. 3s.

Cicero. De Amicitia.—De Senectute. By J. S. REID, Litt.D., Fellow of Gonville and Caius College. 3s. 6d. each.

────── **In Gaium Verrem Actio Prima.** By H. COWIE, M.A. 1s. 6d.

────── **In Q. Caecilium Divinatio et in C. Verrem Actio.** By W. E. HEITLAND, M.A., and H. COWIE, M.A. 3s.

────── **Philippica Secunda.** By A. G. PESKETT, M.A. 3s. 6d.

────── **Oratio pro Archia Poeta.** By J. S. REID, Litt.D. 2s.

────── **Pro L. Cornelio Balbo Oratio.** By the same. 1s. 6d.

────── **Oratio pro Tito Annio Milone.** By JOHN SMYTH PURTON, B.D. 2s. 6d.

────── **Oratio pro L. Murena.** By W. E. HEITLAND, M.A. 3s.

────── **Pro Cn. Plancio Oratio,** by H. A. HOLDEN, LL.D. 4s. 6d.

────── **Pro P. Cornelio Sulla.** By J. S. REID, Litt.D. 3s. 6d.

────── **Somnium Scipionis.** By W. D. PEARMAN, M.A. 2s.

Horace. Epistles, Book I. By E. S. SHUCKBURGH, M.A., late Fellow of Emmanuel College. 2s. 6d.

Livy. Book IV. By H. M. STEPHENSON, M.A. 2s. 6d.

────── **Book V.** By L. WHIBLEY, M.A. 2s. 6d.

────── **Book IX.** By H. M. STEPHENSON, M.A. 2s. 6d.

────── **Book XXI.** By M. S. DIMSDALE, M.A. 2s. 6d.

────── **Book XXII.** By the same Editor. 2s. 6d.

────── **Book XXVII.** By Rev. H. M. STEPHENSON, M.A. 2s. 6d.

Lucan. Pharsaliae Liber Primus. By W. E. HEITLAND, M.A., and C. E. HASKINS, M.A. 1s. 6d.

Lucretius, Book V. By J. D. DUFF, M.A. 2s.

Ovidii Nasonis Fastorum Liber VI. By A. SIDGWICK, M.A., Tutor of Corpus Christi College, Oxford. 1s. 6d.

Quintus Curtius. A Portion of the History (Alexander in India). By W. E. HEITLAND, M.A., and T. E. RAVEN, B.A. With Two Maps. 3s. 6d.

Vergili Maronis Aeneidos Libri I.—XII. By A. SIDGWICK, M.A. 1s. 6d. each.

────── **Bucolica.** By the same Editor. 1s. 6d.

────── **Georgicon Libri I. II.** By the same Editor. 2s.

────── ────── **Libri III. IV.** By the same Editor. 2s.

────── **The Complete Works.** By the same Editor. Two vols. Vol. I. containing the Introduction and Text. 3s. 6d. Vol. II. The Notes. 4s. 6d.

III. FRENCH.

Corneille. La Suite du Menteur. A Comedy in Five Acts. By the late G. MASSON, B.A. 2s.

De Bonnechose. Lazare Hoche. By C. COLBECK, M.A. Revised Edition. Four Maps. 2s.

D'Harleville. Le Vieux Célibataire. By G. MASSON, B.A. 2s.

De Lamartine. Jeanne D'Arc. By Rev. A. C. CLAPIN, M.A. New edition revised, by A. R. ROPES, M.A. 1s. 6d.

De Vigny. La Canne de Jonc. By H. W. EVE, M.A. 1s. 6d.

Erckmann-Chatrian. La Guerre. By Rev. A. C. CLAPIN, M.A. 3s.

La Baronne de Staël-Holstein. Le Directoire. (Considérations sur la Révolution Française. Troisième et quatrième parties.) Revised and enlarged. By G. MASSON, B.A., and G. W. PROTHERO, M.A. 2s.

—— —— **Dix Années d'Exil. Livre II. Chapitres 1—8.** By the same Editors. New Edition, enlarged. 2s.

Lemercier. Fredegonde et Brunehaut. A Tragedy in Five Acts. By GUSTAVE MASSON, B.A. 2s.

Molière. Le Bourgeois Gentilhomme, Comédie-Ballet en Cinq Actes. (1670.) By Rev. A. C. CLAPIN, M.A. Revised Edition. 1s. 6d.

—— **L'École des Femmes.** By G. SAINTSBURY, M.A. 2s. 6d.

—— **Les Précieuses Ridicules.** By E. G. W. BRAUNHOLTZ, M.A., Ph.D. 2s. **Abridged Edition.** 1s.

Piron. La Métromanie. A Comedy. By G. MASSON, B.A. 2s.

Racine. Les Plaideurs. By E. G. W. BRAUNHOLTZ, M.A. 2s.

—— —— **Abridged Edition.** 1s.

Sainte-Beuve. M. Daru (Causeries du Lundi, Vol. IX.). By G. MASSON, B.A. 2s.

Saintine. Picciola. By Rev. A. C. CLAPIN, M.A. 2s.

Scribe and Legouvé. Bataille de Dames. By Rev. H. A. BULL, M.A. 2s.

Scribe. Le Verre d'Eau. By C. COLBECK, M.A. 2s.

Sédaine. Le Philosophe sans le savoir. By Rev. H. A. BULL, M.A. 2s.

Thierry. Lettres sur l'histoire de France (XIII.—XXIV.). By G. MASSON, B.A., and G. W. PROTHERO, M.A. 2s. 6d.

—— **Récits des Temps Mérovingiens I—III.** By GUSTAVE MASSON, B.A. Univ. Gallic., and A. R. ROPES, M.A. With Map. 3s.

Villemain. Lascaris ou Les Grecs du XVe Siècle, Nouvelle Historique. By G. MASSON, B.A. 2s.

Voltaire. Histoire du Siècle de Louis XIV. Chaps. I.—XIII. By G. MASSON, B.A. and G. W. PROTHERO, M.A. 2s. 6d. PART II. CHAPS. XIV.—XXIV. 2s. 6d. PART III. CHAPS. XXV. to end. 2s. 6d.

Xavier de Maistre. La Jeune Sibérienne. Le Lépreux de la Cité D'Aoste. By G. MASSON, B.A. 1s. 6d.

London: Cambridge Warehouse, Ave Maria Lane.

IV. GERMAN.

Ballads on German History. By W. WAGNER, Ph.D. 2s.
Benedix. Doctor Wespe. Lustspiel in fünf Aufzügen. By KARL HERMANN BREUL, M.A., Ph.D. 3s.
Freytag. Der Staat Friedrichs des Grossen. By WILHELM WAGNER, Ph.D. 2s.
German Dactylic Poetry. By WILHELM WAGNER, Ph.D. 3s.
Goethe's Knabenjahre. (1749—1761.) By W. WAGNER, Ph.D. New edition revised and enlarged, by J. W. CARTMELL, M.A. 2s.
—— **Hermann und Dorothea.** By WILHELM WAGNER, Ph.D. New edition revised, by J. W. CARTMELL, M.A. 3s. 6d.
Gutzkow. Zopf und Schwert. Lustspiel in fünf Aufzügen. By H. J. WOLSTENHOLME, B.A. (Lond.) 3s. 6d.
Hauff. Das Bild des Kaisers. By KARL HERMANN BREUL, M.A., Ph.D., University Lecturer in German. 3s.
—— **Das Wirthshaus im Spessart.** By A. SCHLOTTMANN, Ph.D. 3s. 6d.
—— **Die Karavane.** By A. SCHLOTTMANN, Ph.D. 3s.
Immermann. Der Oberhof. A Tale of Westphalian Life, by WILHELM WAGNER, Ph.D. 3s.
Kohlrausch. Das Jahr 1813. By WILHELM WAGNER, Ph.D. 2s.
Lessing and Gellert. Selected Fables. By KARL HERMANN BREUL, M.A., Ph.D. 3s.
Mendelssohn's Letters. Selections from. By J. SIME, M.A. 3s.
Raumer. Der erste Kreuzzug (1095—1099). By WILHELM WAGNER, Ph.D. 2s.
Riehl. Culturgeschichtliche Novellen. By H. J. WOLSTENHOLME, B.A. (Lond.) 3s. 6d.
Schiller. Wilhelm Tell. By KARL HERMANN BREUL, M.A., Ph.D. 2s. 6d. **Abridged Edition.** 1s. 6d.
Uhland. Ernst, Herzog von Schwaben. By H. J. WOLSTENHOLME, B.A. 3s. 6d.

V. ENGLISH.

Ancient Philosophy from Thales to Cicero, A Sketch of. By JOSEPH B. MAYOR, M.A. 3s. 6d.
An Apologie for Poetrie by Sir PHILIP SIDNEY. By E. S. SHUCKBURGH, M.A. The Text is a revision of that of the first edition of 1595. 3s.
Bacon's History of the Reign of King Henry VII. By the Rev. Professor LUMBY, D.D. 3s.
Cowley's Essays. By the Rev. Professor LUMBY, D.D. 4s.
Discourse of the Commonwealf of thys Realme of Englande. First printed in 1581, and commonly attributed to W. S. Edited from the MSS. by ELIZABETH LAMOND. [*In the Press.*
Milton's Comus and Arcades. By A. W. VERITY, M.A., sometime Scholar of Trinity College. 3s.
Milton's Ode on the Morning of Christ's Nativity, L'Allegro, Il Penseroso and Lycidas. By the same Editor. 2s. 6d.
Milton's Samson Agonistes. By the same Editor. 2s. 6d.
Milton's Paradise Lost. Books XI. XII. By the same Editor. [*In the Press.*

London: Cambridge Warehouse, Ave Maria Lane.

More's History of King Richard III. By J. RAWSON LUMBY, D.D. 3s. 6d.
More's Utopia. By Rev. Prof. LUMBY, D.D. 3s. 6d.
The Two Noble Kinsmen. By the Rev. Professor SKEAT, Litt. D. 3s. 6d.

VI. EDUCATIONAL SCIENCE.

Comenius, John Amos, Bishop of the Moravians. His Life and Educational Works, by S. S. LAURIE, A.M., F.R.S.E. 3s. 6d.
Education, Three Lectures on the Practice of. I. On Marking, by H. W. EVE, M.A. II. On Stimulus, by A. SIDGWICK, M.A. III. On the Teaching of Latin Verse Composition, by E. A. ABBOTT, D.D. 2s.
Stimulus. A Lecture delivered for the Teachers' Training Syndicate, May, 1882, by A. SIDGWICK, M.A. 1s.
Locke on Education. By the Rev. R. H. QUICK, M.A. 3s. 6d.
Milton's Tractate on Education. A facsimile reprint from the Edition of 1673. By O. BROWNING, M.A. 2s.
Modern Languages, Lectures on the Teaching of. By C. COLBECK, M.A. 2s.
Teacher, General Aims of the, and Form Management. Two Lectures delivered in the University of Cambridge in the Lent Term, 1883, by F. W. FARRAR, D.D., and R. B. POOLE, B.D. 1s. 6d.
Teaching, Theory and Practice of. By the Rev. E. THRING, M.A., late Head Master of Uppingham School. New Edition. 4s. 6d.

British India, a Short History of. By E. S. CARLOS, M.A., late Head Master of Exeter Grammar School. 1s.
Geography, Elementary Commercial. A Sketch of the Commodities and the Countries of the World. By H. R. MILL, D.Sc., F.R.S.E. 1s.
Geography, an Atlas of Commercial. (A Companion to the above.) By J. G. BARTHOLOMEW, F.R.G.S. With an Introduction by HUGH ROBERT MILL, D.Sc. 3s.

VII. MATHEMATICS.

Arithmetic for Schools. By C. SMITH, M.A., Master of Sidney Sussex College, Cambridge. 3s. 6d.
Elementary Algebra (with Answers to the Examples). By W. W. ROUSE BALL, M.A. 4s. 6d.
Euclid's Elements of Geometry. Books I. and II. By H. M. TAYLOR, M.A. 1s. 6d. **Books III. and IV.** By the same Editor. 1s. 6d.
—— —— Books I.—IV., in one Volume. 3s.
Solutions to the Exercises in Euclid, Books I—IV. By W. W. TAYLOR, M.A. [*In the Press.*
Elements of Statics and Dynamics. By S. L. LONEY, M.A. 7s. 6d.
   Part I. Elements of Statics. 4s. 6d.
   Part II. Elements of Dynamics. 3s. 6d.
An Elementary Treatise on Plane Trigonometry for the use of Schools. By E. W. HOBSON, M.A, and C. M. JESSOP, M.A. [*In the Press.*

Other Volumes are in preparation.

London: Cambridge Warehouse, Ave Maria Lane.

The Cambridge Bible for Schools and Colleges.

GENERAL EDITOR: J. J. S. PEROWNE, D.D.,
BISHOP OF WORCESTER.

"*It is difficult to commend too highly this excellent series.*—Guardian.

"*The modesty of the general title of this series has, we believe, led many to misunderstand its character and underrate its value. The books are well suited for study in the upper forms of our best schools, but not the less are they adapted to the wants of all Bible students who are not specialists. We doubt, indeed, whether any of the numerous popular commentaries recently issued in this country will be found more serviceable for general use.*"—Academy.

Now Ready. Cloth, Extra Fcap. 8vo. With Maps.

Book of Joshua. By Rev. G. F. MACLEAR, D.D. 2s. 6d.
Book of Judges. By Rev. J. J. LIAS, M.A. 3s. 6d.
First Book of Samuel. By Rev. Prof. KIRKPATRICK, B.D. 3s. 6d.
Second Book of Samuel. By the same Editor. 3s. 6d.
First Book of Kings. By Rev. Prof. LUMBY, D.D. 3s. 6d.
Second Book of Kings. By Rev. Prof. LUMBY, D.D. 3s. 6d.
Book of Job. By Rev. A. B. DAVIDSON, D.D. 5s.
Book of Psalms. Book I. By Prof. KIRKPATRICK, B.D. 3s. 6d.
Book of Ecclesiastes. By Very Rev. E. H. PLUMPTRE, D.D. 5s.
Book of Jeremiah. By Rev. A. W. STREANE, B.D. 4s. 6d.
Book of Hosea. By Rev. T. K. CHEYNE, M.A., D.D. 3s.
Books of Obadiah & Jonah. By Archdeacon PEROWNE. 2s. 6d.
Book of Micah. By Rev. T. K. CHEYNE, M.A., D.D. 1s. 6d.
Haggai, Zechariah & Malachi. By Arch. PEROWNE. 3s. 6d.
Book of Malachi. By Archdeacon PEROWNE. 1s.
Gospel according to St Matthew. By Rev. A. CARR, M.A. 2s. 6d.
Gospel according to St Mark. By Rev. G. F. MACLEAR, D.D. 2s. 6d.
Gospel according to St Luke. By Arch. FARRAR, D.D. 4s. 6d.
Gospel according to St John. By Rev. A. PLUMMER, D.D. 4s. 6d.
Acts of the Apostles. By Rev. Prof. LUMBY, D.D. 4s. 6d.
Epistle to the Romans. By Rev. H. C. G. MOULE, M.A. 3s. 6d.
First Corinthians. By Rev. J. J. LIAS, M.A. With Map. 2s.
Second Corinthians. By Rev. J. J. LIAS, M.A. With Map. 2s.

Epistle to the Galatians. By Rev. E. H. PEROWNE, D.D. 1s. 6d.
Epistle to the Ephesians. By Rev. H. C. G. MOULE, M.A. 2s. 6d.
Epistle to the Philippians. By the same Editor. 2s. 6d.
Epistles to the Thessalonians. By Rev. G. G. FINDLAY, B.A. 2s.
Epistle to the Hebrews. By Arch. FARRAR, D.D. 3s. 6d.
General Epistle of St James. By Very Rev. E. H. PLUMPTRE, D.D. 1s. 6d.
Epistles of St Peter and St Jude. By Very Rev. E. H. PLUMPTRE, D.D. 2s. 6d.
Epistles of St John. By Rev. A. PLUMMER, M.A., D.D. 3s. 6d.
Book of Revelation. By Rev. W. H. SIMCOX, M.A. 3s.

Preparing.

Book of Genesis. By the BISHOP OF WORCESTER.
Books of Exodus, Numbers and Deuteronomy. By Rev. C. D. GINSBURG, LL.D.
Books of Ezra and Nehemiah. By Rev. Prof. RYLE, M.A.
Book of Isaiah. By Prof. W. ROBERTSON SMITH, M.A.
Book of Ezekiel. By Rev. A. B. DAVIDSON, D.D.
Epistles to the Colossians and Philemon. By Rev. H. C. G. MOULE, M.A.
Epistles to Timothy & Titus. By Rev. A. E. HUMPHREYS, M.A.

The Smaller Cambridge Bible for Schools.

"*We can cordially recommend this series of text-books.*"—Church Review.

"*The notes elucidate every possible difficulty with scholarly brevity and clearness, and a perfect knowledge of the subject.*"—Saturday Review.

"*Accurate scholarship is obviously a characteristic of their productions, and the work of simplification and condensation appears to have been judiciously and skilfully performed.*"—Guardian.

Now ready. Price 1s. each Volume, with Map.

Book of Joshua. By J. S. BLACK, M.A.
First and Second Books of Samuel. By Rev. Prof. KIRKPATRICK, B.D.
First and Second Books of Kings. By Rev. Prof. LUMBY, D.D.
Gospel according to St Matthew. By Rev. A. CARR, M.A.
Gospel according to St Mark. By Rev. G. F. MACLEAR, D.D.
Gospel according to St Luke. By Archdeacon FARRAR, D.D.
Gospel according to St John. By Rev. A. PLUMMER, D.D.
Acts of the Apostles. By Rev. Prof. LUMBY, D.D.

London: Cambridge Warehouse, Ave Maria Lane.

The Cambridge Greek Testament for Schools and Colleges,

with a Revised Text, based on the most recent critical authorities, and English Notes, prepared under the direction of the

GENERAL EDITOR, J. J. S. PEROWNE, D.D.,
BISHOP OF WORCESTER.

Gospel according to St Matthew. By Rev. A. CARR, M.A. With 4 Maps. 4s. 6d.

Gospel according to St Mark. By Rev. G. F. MACLEAR, D.D. With 3 Maps. 4s. 6d.

Gospel according to St Luke. By Archdeacon FARRAR. With 4 Maps. 6s.

Gospel according to St John. By Rev. A. PLUMMER, D.D. With 4 Maps. 6s.

Acts of the Apostles. By Rev. Professor LUMBY, D.D. With 4 Maps. 6s.

First Epistle to the Corinthians. By Rev. J. J. LIAS, M.A. 3s.

Second Epistle to the Corinthians. By Rev. J. J. LIAS, M.A. [*In the Press.*]

Epistle to the Hebrews. By Archdeacon FARRAR, D.D. 3s. 6d.

Epistles of St John. By Rev. A. PLUMMER, M.A., D.D. 4s.

London: C. J. CLAY AND SONS,
CAMBRIDGE WAREHOUSE, AVE MARIA LANE.
Glasgow: 263, ARGYLE STREET.
Cambridge: DEIGHTON, BELL AND CO.
Leipzig: F. A. BROCKHAUS.
New York: MACMILLAN AND CO.

THE CAMBRIDGE BIBLE FOR SCHOOLS AND COLLEGES.

General Editor, J. J. S. Perowne,
Bishop of Worcester.

Opinions of the Press.

"*It is difficult to commend too highly this excellent series.*"—Guardian.

"*The modesty of the general title of this series has, we believe, led many to misunderstand its character and underrate its value. The books are well suited for study in the upper forms of our best schools, but not the less are they adapted to the wants of all Bible students who are not specialists. We doubt, indeed, whether any of the numerous popular commentaries recently issued in this country will be found more serviceable for general use.*"—Academy.

"*One of the most popular and useful literary enterprises of the nineteenth century.*"—Baptist Magazine.

"*Of great value. The whole series of comments for schools is highly esteemed by students capable of forming a judgment. The books are scholarly without being pretentious: and information is so given as to be easily understood.*"—Sword and Trowel.

"*The notes possess a rare advantage of being scholarly, and at the same time within the comprehension of the average reader. For the Sunday-School Teacher we do not know of a more valuable work.*"—Sunday-School Chronicle.

The Book of Judges. J. J. Lias, M.A. "His introduction is clear and concise, full of the information which young students require."—*Baptist Magazine.*

II. Samuel. A. F. Kirkpatrick, M.A. "Small as this work is in mere dimensions, it is every way the best on its subject and for its purpose that we know of. The opening sections at once prove the thorough competence of the writer for dealing with questions of criticism in an earnest, faithful and devout spirit; and the appendices discuss a few special difficulties with a full knowledge of the data, and a judicial reserve, which contrast most favourably with the superficial dogmatism which has too often made the exegesis of the Old Testament a field for the play of unlimited paradox and the ostentation of personal infallibility. The notes are always clear and suggestive; never trifling or irrelevant; and they everywhere demonstrate the great difference in value between the work of a commentator who is also a Hebraist, and that of one who has to depend for his Hebrew upon secondhand sources."—*Academy.*

I. Kings and Ephesians. "With great heartiness we commend these most valuable little commentaries. We had rather purchase these than nine out of ten of the big blown up expositions. Quality is far better than quantity, and we have it here."—*Sword and Trowel.*

II. Kings. "The Introduction is scholarly and wholly admirable, the notes must be of incalculable value to students."—*Glasgow Herald.*

"It would be difficult to find a commentary better suited for general

The Book of Job. "Able and scholarly as the Introduction is, it is far surpassed by the detailed exegesis of the book. In this Dr DAVIDSON's strength is at its greatest. His linguistic knowledge, his artistic habit, his scientific insight, and his literary power have full scope when he comes to exegesis...."—*The Spectator.*

"In the course of a long introduction, Dr DAVIDSON has presented us with a very able and very interesting criticism of this wonderful book. Its contents, the nature of its composition, its idea and purpose, its integrity, and its age are all exhaustively treated of....We have not space to examine fully the text and notes before us, but we can, and do heartily, recommend the book, not only for the upper forms in schools, but to Bible students and teachers generally. As we wrote of a previous volume in the same series, this one leaves nothing to be desired. The notes are full and suggestive, without being too long, and, in itself, the introduction forms a valuable addition to modern Bible literature."—*The Educational Times.*

"Already we have frequently called attention to this exceedingly valuable work as its volumes have successively appeared. But we have never done so with greater pleasure, very seldom with so great pleasure, as we now refer to the last published volume, that on the **Book of Job**, by Dr DAVIDSON, of Edinburgh....We cordially commend the volume to all our readers. The least instructed will understand and enjoy it; and mature scholars will learn from it."—*Methodist Recorder.*

Psalms. Book I. "His commentary upon the books of Samuel was good, but this is incomparably better, shewing traces of much more work and of greater independence of scholarship and judgment....As a whole it is admirable, and we are hardly going too far in saying that it is one of the very ablest of all the volumes that have yet appeared in the 'Cambridge Bible for Schools'."—*Record.*

"Another volume of this excellent Bible, in which the student may rely on meeting with the latest scholarship. The introduction is admirable. We know of nothing in so concise a form better adapted for Sunday-School Teachers."—*Sunday-School Chronicle.*

"It is full of instruction and interest, bringing within easy reach of the English reader the results of the latest scholarship bearing upon the study of this ever new book of the Bible. The Introduction of eighty pages is a repertory of information, not drily but interestingly given."—*Methodist Recorder.*

"For a masterly summary of all that is known and much that is hazarded about the history and authorship of this book of religious lyrics we can point to that with which Mr KIRKPATRICK prefaces his new volume. From a perusal of this summary the student will be unimpressionable indeed if he rise not convinced of the vitality imparted to the Psalter by a systematic study of its literary character and historical allusions....In conclusion, we may say that for a work which is handy, and withal complete, we know none better than this volume; and we await with considerable interest the next instalment."—*Education.*

"It seems in every way a most valuable little book, containing a mass of information, well-assorted, and well-digested, and will be useful not only to students preparing for examinations, but to many who want a handy volume of explanation to much that is difficult in the Psalter. ......We owe a great debt of gratitude to Professor Kirkpatrick for his scholarly and interesting volume."—*Church Times.*

"In this volume thoughtful exegesis founded on nice critical scholarship and due regard for the opinions of various writers, combine, under the influence of a devout spirit, to render this commentary a source of much valuable assistance. The notes are 'though deep yet clear,' for they seem to put in a concentrated form the very pith and marrow of all the best that has been hitherto said on the subject, with striking freedom from anything like pressure of personal views. Throughout the work care and pains are as conspicuous as scholarship."—*Literary Churchman.*

Job—Hosea. "It is difficult to commend too highly this excellent series, the volumes of which are now becoming numerous. The two books before us, small as they are in size, comprise almost everything that the young student can reasonably expect to find in the way of helps towards such general knowledge of their subjects as may be gained without an attempt to grapple with the Hebrew; and even the learned scholar can hardly read without interest and benefit the very able introductory matter which both these commentators have prefixed to their volumes. It is not too much to say that these works have brought within the reach of the ordinary reader resources which were until lately quite unknown for understanding some of the most difficult and obscure portions of Old Testament literature."—*Guardian.*

Ecclesiastes; or, the Preacher.—"Of the Notes, it is sufficient to say that they are in every respect worthy of Dr PLUMPTRE's high reputation as a scholar and a critic, being at once learned, sensible, and practical....Commentaries are seldom attractive reading. This little volume is a notable exception."—*The Scotsman.*

Jeremiah, by A. W. STREANE. "The arrangement of the book is well treated on pp. xxx., 396, and the question of Baruch's relations with its composition on pp. xxvii., xxxiv., 317. The illustrations from English literature, history, monuments, works on botany, topography, etc., are good and plentiful, as indeed they are in other volumes of this series."—*Church Quarterly Review.*

Malachi. "Archdeacon Perowne has already edited Jonah and Zechariah for this series. Malachi presents comparatively few difficulties and the Editor's treatment leaves nothing to be desired. His introduction is clear and scholarly and his commentary sufficient. We may instance the notes on ii. 15 and iv. 2 as examples of careful arrangement, clear exposition and graceful expression."—*Academy.*

"**The Gospel according to St Matthew**, by the Rev. A. CARR. The introduction is able, scholarly, and eminently practical, as it bears on the authorship and contents of the Gospel, and the original form in which it is supposed to have been written. It is well illustrated by two excellent maps of the Holy Land and of the Sea of Galilee."—*English Churchman.*

"**St Mark**, with Notes by the Rev. G. F. MACLEAR, D.D. Into this small volume Dr Maclear, besides a clear and able Introduction to the Gospel, and the text of St Mark, has compressed many hundreds of valuable and helpful notes. In short, he has given us a capital manual of the kind required—containing all that is needed to illustrate the text, i.e. all that can be drawn from the history, geography, customs, and manners of the time. But as a handbook, giving in a clear and succinct form the information which a lad requires in order to stand an examination in the Gospel, it is admirable......I can very heartily commend it, not only to the senior boys and girls in our High Schools, but also to Sunday-school teachers, who may get from it the very kind of knowledge they often find it hardest to get."—*Expositor.*

"With the help of a book like this, an intelligent teacher may make 'Divinity' as interesting a lesson as any in the school course. The notes are of a kind that will be, for the most part, intelligible to boys of the lower forms of our public schools; but they may be read with greater profit by the fifth and sixth, in conjunction with the original text."—*The Academy.*

"**St Luke.** Canon FARRAR has supplied students of the Gospel with an admirable manual in this volume. It has all that copious variety of illustration, ingenuity of suggestion, and general soundness of interpretation which readers are accustomed to expect from the learned and eloquent editor. Anyone who has been accustomed to associate the idea of 'dryness' with a commentary, should go to Canon Farrar's **St Luke** for a more correct impression. He will find that a commentary may be made interesting in the highest degree, and that without losing anything of its solid value....But, so to speak, it is *too good* for some of the readers for whom it is intended."—*The Spectator.*

The Gospel according to St John. "The notes are extremely scholarly and valuable, and in most cases exhaustive, bringing to the elucidation of the text all that is best in commentaries, ancient and modern."—*The English Churchman and Clerical Journal.*

"(1) **The Acts of the Apostles.** By J. RAWSON LUMBY, D.D. (2) **The Second Epistle of the Corinthians**, edited by Professor LIAS. The introduction is pithy, and contains a mass of carefully-selected information on the authorship of the Acts, its designs, and its sources. ......The Second Epistle of the Corinthians is a manual beyond all praise, for the excellence of its pithy and pointed annotations, its analysis of the contents, and the fulness and value of its introduction."—*Examiner.*

"The Rev. H. C. G. MOULE, M.A., has made a valuable addition to THE CAMBRIDGE BIBLE FOR SCHOOLS in his brief commentary on the **Epistle to the Romans.** The 'Notes' are very good, and lean, as the notes of a School Bible should, to the most commonly accepted and orthodox view of the inspired author's meaning; while the Introduction, and especially the Sketch of the Life of St Paul, is a model of condensation. It is as lively and pleasant to read as if two or three facts had not been crowded into well-nigh every sentence."—*Expositor.*

"**The Epistle to the Romans.** It is seldom we have met with a work so remarkable for the compression and condensation of all that is valuable in the smallest possible space as in the volume before us. Within its limited pages we have 'a sketch of the Life of St Paul,' we have further a critical account of the date of the Epistle to the Romans, of its language, and of its genuineness. The notes are numerous, full of matter, to the point, and leave no real difficulty or obscurity unexplained."—*The Examiner.*

The First Epistle to the Corinthians. Edited by Professor LIAS. Every fresh instalment of this annotated edition of the Bible for Schools confirms the favourable opinion we formed of its value from the examination of its first number. The origin and plan of the Epistle are discussed with its character and genuineness."—*The Nonconformist.*

Galatians. "Dr PEROWNE deals throughout in a very thorough manner with every real difficulty in the text, and in this respect he has faithfully followed the noble example set him in the exegetical masterpiece, his indebtedness to which he frankly acknowledges."—*Modern Church.*

"The introductory matter is very full and informing, whilst the Notes are admirable. They combine the scholarly and the practical in an unusual degree....It is not the young students in 'schools and colleges' alone who will find this Commentary helpful on every page."—*Record.*

"This little work, like all of the series, is a scholarly production; but we can also unreservedly recommend it from a doctrinal standpoint; Dr E. H. PEROWNE is one who has grasped the distinctive teaching of the Epistle, and expounds it with clearness and definiteness. In an appendix, he ably maintains the correctness of the A. V. as against the R. V. in the translation of II. 16, a point of no small importance."—*English Churchman.*

The Epistle to the Ephesians. By Rev. H. C. G. MOULE, M.A. "It seems to us the model of a School and College Commentary—comprehensive, but not cumbersome; scholarly, but not pedantic."—*Baptist Magazine.*

The Epistle to the Philippians. "There are few series more valued by theological students than 'The Cambridge Bible for Schools and Colleges,' and there will be no number of it more esteemed than that by Mr H. C. G. MOULE on the *Epistle to the Philippians.*"—*Record.*

Thessalonians. "It will stand the severest scrutiny, for no volume in this admirable series exhibits more careful work, and Mr FINDLAY is a true expositor, who keeps in mind what he is expounding, and for whom he is expounding it."—*Expository Times.*

"Mr FINDLAY maintains the high level of the series to which he has become contributor. Some parts of his introduction to the Epistles to the Thessalonians could scarcely be bettered. The account of Thessalonica, the description of the style and character of the Epistles, and the analysis of them are excellent in style and scholarly care. The notes are possibly too voluminous; but there is so much matter in them, and the matter is arranged and handled so ably, that we are ready to forgive their fulness....Mr FINDLAY'S commentary is a valuable addition to what has been written on the letters to the Thessalonian Church."—*Academy.*

"Of all the volumes of this most excellent series, none is better done, and few are so well done as this small volume....From beginning to end the volume is marked by accurate grammatical scholarship, delicate appreciation of the apostle's meaning, thorough investigation of all matters open to doubt, extensive reading, and deep sympathy with the spiritual aim of these epistles. It is, on the whole, the best commentary on the Thessalonians which has yet appeared, and its small price puts it within reach of all. We heartily recommend it."—*Methodist Recorder.*

"Mr FINDLAY has fulfilled in this volume a task which Dr Moulton was compelled to decline, though he has rendered valuable aid in its preparation. The commentary is in its own way a model—clear, forceful, scholarly—such as young students will welcome as a really useful guide, and old ones will acknowledge as giving in brief space the substance of all that they knew."—*Baptist Magazine.*

Hebrews. "Like his (Canon Farrar's) commentary on Luke it possesses all the best characteristics of his writing. It is a work not only of an accomplished scholar, but of a skilled teacher."—*Baptist Magazine.*

The Epistles of St John. By the Rev. A. PLUMMER, M.A., D.D. "This forms an admirable companion to the 'Commentary on the Gospel according to St John,' which was reviewed in *The Churchman* as soon as it appeared. Dr Plummer has some of the highest qualifications for such a task; and these two volumes, their size being considered, will bear comparison with the best Commentaries of the time."—*The Churchman.*

Revelation. "This volume contains evidence of much careful labour. It is a scholarly production, as might be expected from the pen of the late Mr W. H. SIMCOX.…The notes throw light upon many passages of this difficult book, and are extremely suggestive. It is an advantage that they sometimes set before the student various interpretations without exactly guiding him to a choice."—*Guardian.*

"Mr SIMCOX has treated his very difficult subject with that conscious care, grasp, and lucidity which characterises everything he wrote."—*Modern Church.*

The Smaller Cambridge Bible for Schools.

"*We can only repeat what we have already said of this admirable series, containing, as it does, the scholarship of the larger work. For scholars in our elder classes, and for those preparing for Scripture examinations, no better commentaries can be put into their hands.*"—Sunday-School Chronicle.

"*Despite their small size, these volumes give the substance of the admirable pieces of work on which they are founded. We can only hope that in many schools the class-teaching will proceed on the lines these commentators suggest.*"—Record.

"*We should be glad to hear that this series has been introduced into many of our Sunday-Schools, for which it is so admirably adapted.*"—Christian Leader.

University Press are rendering great services both to teachers and to scholars by the publication of such a valuable series of books, in which slipshod work could not have a place."—Literary World.

"For the student of the sacred oracles who utilizes hours of travel or moments of waiting in the perusal of the Bible there is nothing so handy, and, at the same time, so satisfying as these little books..... Nor let anyone suppose that, because these are school-books, therefore they are beneath the adult reader. They contain the very ripest results of the best Biblical scholarship, and that in the very simplest form."—Christian Leader.

"Altogether one of the most perfect examples of a Shilling New Testament commentary which even this age of cheapness is likely to produce."—Bookseller.

Samuel I. and II. "Professor KIRKPATRICK'S two tiny volumes on the First and Second Books of Samuel are quite model school-books; the notes elucidate every possible difficulty with scholarly brevity and clearness and a perfect knowledge of the subject."—*Saturday Review.*

"They consist of an introduction full of matter, clearly and succinctly given, and of notes which appear to us to be admirable, at once full and brief."—*Church Times.*

Kings I. "We can cordially recommend this little book. The Introduction discusses the question of authorship and date in a plain but scholarly fashion, while the footnotes throughout are brief, pointed, and helpful."—*Review of Reviews.*

Matthew. "The notes are terse, clear, and helpful, and teachers and students cannot fail to find the volume of great service."—*Publishers' Circular.*

Mark. Luke. "We have received the volumes of St Mark and St Luke in this series....The two volumes seem, on the whole, well adapted for school use, are well and carefully printed, and have maps and good, though necessarily brief, introductions. There is little doubt that this series will be found as popular and useful as the well-known larger series, of which they are abbreviated editions."—*Guardian.*

Luke. "We cannot too highly commend this handy little book to all teachers."—*Wesleyan Methodist Sunday-School Record.*

John. "We have been especially interested in Mr PLUMMER'S treatment of the Gospel which has been entrusted to his charge. He is concise, comprehensive, interesting, and simple. Young students of this inimitable book, as well as elder students, even ministers and teachers, may use it with advantage as a very serviceable handbook."—*Literary World.*

John. "A model of condensation, losing nothing of its clearness and force from its condensation into a small compass. Many who have long since completed their college curriculum will find it an invaluable handbook."—*Methodist Times.*

Acts. "The notes are very brief, but exceedingly comprehensive, comprising as much detail in the way of explanation as would be needed by young students of the Scriptures preparing for examination. We again give the opinion that this series furnishes as much real help as would usually satisfy students for the Christian ministry, or even ministers themselves."—*Literary World.*

THE CAMBRIDGE GREEK TESTAMENT
FOR SCHOOLS AND COLLEGES

with a Revised Text, based on the most recent critical authorities, and English Notes, prepared under the direction of the General Editor,

THE BISHOP OF WORCESTER.

"*Has achieved an excellence which puts it above criticism.*"—Expositor.

St Matthew. "Copious illustrations, gathered from a great variety of sources, make his notes a very valuable aid to the student. They are indeed remarkably interesting, while all explanations on meanings, applications, and the like are distinguished by their lucidity and good sense."—*Pall Mall Gazette.*

St Mark. "Dr MACLEAR'S introduction contains all that is known of St Mark's life; an account of the circumstances in which the Gospel was composed, with an estimate of the influence of St Peter's teaching upon St Mark; an excellent sketch of the special characteristics of this Gospel; an analysis, and a chapter on the text of the New Testament generally."—*Saturday Review.*

St Luke. "Of this second series we have a new volume by Archdeacon FARRAR on *St Luke*, completing the four Gospels.... It gives us in clear and beautiful language the best results of modern scholarship. We have a most attractive *Introduction*. Then follows a sort of composite Greek text, representing fairly and in very beautiful type the consensus of modern textual critics. At the beginning of the exposition of each chapter of the Gospel are a few short critical notes giving the manuscript evidence for such various readings as seem to deserve mention. The expository notes are short, but clear and helpful. For young students and those who are not disposed to buy or to study the much more costly work of Godet, this seems to us to be the best book on the Greek Text of the Third Gospel."—*Methodist Recorder.*

St John. "We take this opportunity of recommending to ministers on probation, the very excellent volume of the same series on this part of the New Testament. We hope that most or all of our young ministers will prefer to study the volume in the *Cambridge Greek Testament for Schools.*"—*Methodist Recorder.*

The Acts of the Apostles. "Professor LUMBY has performed his laborious task well, and supplied us with a commentary the fulness and freshness of which Bible students will not be slow to appreciate. The volume is enriched with the usual copious indexes and four coloured maps."—*Glasgow Herald.*

I. Corinthians. "Mr LIAS is no novice in New Testament exposition, and the present series of essays and notes is an able and helpful addition to the existing books."—*Guardian.*

The Epistles of St John. "In the very useful and well annotated series of the Cambridge Greek Testament the volume on the Epistles of St John must hold a high position... The notes are brief, well informed and intelligent."—*Scotsman.*

www.ingramcontent.com/pod-product-compliance
Lightning Source LLC
Chambersburg PA
CBHW050849300426
44111CB00010B/1186